SOUTHERN LITERARY STUDIES
Fred Hobson, Editor

WAKEFUL ANGUISH

A Literary Biography of William Humphrey

ASHBY BLAND CROWDER

LOUISIANA STATE UNIVERSITY PRESS
BATON ROUGE

Copyright © 2004 by Louisiana State University Press
All rights reserved
Manufactured in the United States of America
First printing
13   12   11   10   09   08   07   06   05   04
5   4   3   2   1

DESIGNER: AMANDA McDONALD SCALLAN
TYPEFACE: MINION
TYPESETTER: COGHILL COMPOSITION CO., INC.
PRINTER AND BINDER: THOMSON-SHORE, INC.

Library of Congress Cataloging-in-Publication Data

Crowder, A. B.
    Wakeful anguish : a literary biography of William Humphrey / Ashby
Bland Crowder.
       p.   cm. — (Southern literary studies)
Includes bibliographical references and index.
    ISBN 0-8071-2887-2 (alk. paper)
    1. Humphrey, William.   2. Authors, American—Homes and
haunts—Texas—Red River County.   3. Authors, American—20th
century—Biography.   4. Red River County (Tex.)—In literature.   5. Red
River County (Tex.)—Biography.   I. Title.   II. Series.
    PS3558.U448Z64   2003
    813'.54—dc22
                                                2003018755

To Lynn
With love and gratitude

For shade to shade will come too drowsily,
And drown the wakeful anguish of the soul.

—Keats, "Ode on Melancholy"

CONTENTS

CONTENTS

Illustrations

Following page 156

William Humphrey at age twelve
Clarence Humphrey
Confederate memorial in the town square of Clarksville
Red River County Courthouse
Former Episcopal church in Clarksville
Humphrey and Harry Grabstald
Jean Lambert
Humphrey in New York, ca. 1960
Dorothy Humphrey in the 1960s
William and Dorothy Humphrey, Andrews Wanning, and Ted and Renée Weiss
Humphrey in 1980
Humphrey in the 1990s

ACKNOWLEDGMENTS

Many friends and strangers have assisted me in this project. I must emphasize the contributions of Michael Bright, Park Honan, Toru Sasaki, George Roupe, David Teague, and my wife Lynn—for these six have lent their insightful minds and perfect taste in prose to my enterprise. Fred Hobson, the general editor of the series to which this book belongs, has provided much-appreciated advice on the organization of this book. I must also single out Harry Grabstald, M.D., Humphrey's oldest friend, who sent me a large box of early letters and then flew to Little Rock in order to spend two days telling me about William Humphrey's early adult life. And I must acknowledge Jean Lambert, who as his death was obviously approaching, escorted me from Paris to his country house in Souvigny, where he provided me with a wealth of materials about Humphrey. Hendrix College has generously supported my research in England, France, New Jersey, New York, and Texas; and the Hendrix-Murphy Foundation has provided me with a computer to write this book on. Members of Humphrey's immediate family—Dorothy Humphrey and her daughter Antonia Weidenbacher—have kindly provided a wealth of manuscripts and photographs and have generously given their time for interviews and telephone conversations. Theodore and Renée Weiss fed me, told me all they knew of the Humphreys, made available all of the letters that they had saved over the years, and provided a comfortable bed at the end of the day. Finally, Bill Humphrey himself over the years contributed to this book, even before either of us knew that I was writing it.

Others have provided invaluable help as well: access to manuscripts, entry through doors that might have remained closed, information about Humphrey's life, bed and board, a sympathetic ear and good advice, suggestions, encouragement, or companionship in work. To tell the story of their generosity and kindness would be to write another book; therefore I list in alphabetical order their names: Pierre Affre, Beth Alvarez, Helen Bard, Stan Bardwell, M.D., Saul Bellow, John Berkey, Margaret Berkey, Steve Bodio, Kay Bost, Michael Bott, Isabelle Bowden, Charles Chappell, Alvord Clements, Stevie Clements, George Core, Hope Coulter, Ashby Crowder III, Geoffrey Crowder, Bernard R. Crystal, Mark

Daims, Barbara Dupee, John Easterly, Don Emery, Bob Fisher, Pat Fox, Howard Frisch, Jeannine Haboyan, Jason Hall, Fred Harris, Cathy Henderson, Earl Humphrey, Dean Humphreys, Elizabeth Inglis, Margaret Johnson, Don Kay, Amy Ketchum, DebbieLee Landi, Cory Ledoux, Hermione Lee, James W. Lee, Barbara Lindsley, the Reverend James Elliott Lindsley, Nick Lyons, Hilary Masters, Lori McCullough, Sheila Miller, Frank Murphy, Jean Nunn, Suzanne Paris, Lelian Phan, Sharron Eve Sarthou, Grace Schulman, Michael Slater, Ken Story, William Styron, Sally Thomas, Sara Thomas, Barbara Tonne, Arturo Vivante, Esther Wanning, Rufus Wanning, Gavin Watson, Joan Williams, Howard Woolmer, Betty Wright, Brooks Wright, Sherman Yellen, and Nanci Young.

Abbreviations

AF	Humphrey, William. Autobiographical fragment (1992) among papers at Humphrey residence, Hudson, N.Y.
Almon	Almon, Bert. *William Humphrey: Destroyer of Myths.* Denton, Tex.: University of North Texas Press, 1998.
Au Int.	Humphrey, William. Interview by author. Hudson, N.Y., 5 August 1995.
CS	*The Collected Stories of William Humphrey.* New York: Delacorte Press/Seymour Lawrence, 1985.
C&W	Chatto & Windus Archive. University of Reading, England.
Dunwell Int.	Humphrey, William. Interview by Virginia Dunwell. Hudson, N.Y., 1984.
Dupee Coll.	F. W. Dupee Collection. Manuscript and Rare Book Library, Columbia University. New York.
FOFH	Humphrey, William. *Farther Off from Heaven.* New York: Knopf, 1977.
Gallimard	William Humphrey Papers. Editions Gallimard, Paris.
HF	Humphrey, William. *Hostages to Fortune.* New York: Delacorte Press/Seymour Lawrence, 1984.
HFH	Humphrey, William. *Home from the Hill.* New York: Knopf, 1958.
HG Letters	Letters from the Humphreys to Harry Grabstald, New York.
KAP Coll.	Katherine Anne Porter Collection. Special Collections, Hornbake Library, University of Maryland at College Park.
Knopf Coll.	Alfred A. Knopf Collection. Harry Ransom Humanities Research Center, University of Texas at Austin.
Lambert Coll.	Journal of Jean Lambert (manuscript) and letters from the Humphreys to Lambert, Souvigny-en-Sologne, Lamotte-Beuvron, France.
Lawrence Coll.	Seymour Lawrence Collection. John Davis Williams Library, University of Mississippi, Oxford.
LH	Humphrey, William. *The Last Husband and Other Stories.* 1953. Reprint, New York: Books for Libraries Press, 1970.

Lyons Coll.	Humphrey, William. Letters. Nick Lyons Collection, DeGolyer Library, Southern Methodist University, Dallas.
Notes	Humphrey, William. "Notes on the Orestia." Harry Ransom Humanities Research Center, University of Texas at Austin.
NRP	Humphrey, William. *No Resting Place.* New York: Delacorte Press/Seymour Lawrence, 1989.
O	Humphrey, William. *The Ordways.* New York: Knopf, 1965.
OS	Humphrey, William. *Open Season.* New York: Delta/Seymour Lawrence, 1989.
PF	Humphrey, William. *Proud Flesh.* New York: Knopf, 1973.
SS	Humphrey, William. *September Song.* Boston: Houghton Mifflin/Seymour Lawrence, 1992.
TP	Humphrey, William. *A Time and a Place.* New York: Knopf, 1968.
Weiss Coll.	Humphrey, William. Letters. Theodore and Renée Weiss Collection, Princeton University Library, Princeton, N.J.
WH Coll., UT	William Humphrey Collection. Harry Ransom Humanities Research Center, University of Texas at Austin.
WH res.	Letters and manuscripts from the Humphrey residence, Hudson, N.Y.
Williams Coll.	Annie Laurie Williams Collection. Manuscript and Rare Book Library, Columbia University, New York.
Woolf Coll.	Humphrey, William. Letters. Leonard Woolf Collection, University of Sussex Library, Brighton, England.
WST	Crowder, Ashby Bland. *Writing in the Southern Tradition: Interviews with Five Contemporary Authors.* Amsterdam and Atlanta: Rodopi, 1990.

Citations of and quotations from the Bible refer to the King James Version.

Citations of and quotations from Shakespeare refer to *The Riverside Shakespeare,* ed. G. B. Evans et al. (Boston: Houghton Mifflin, 1974).

WAKEFUL ANGUISH

INTRODUCTION

> He gave himself a hundred pseudonyms, less to hide behind than to feel
> himself live in several versions.
>
> —VALÉRY, *Variety: Second Series*

I N HIS *Sports Illustrated* essay "Birds of a Feather," William Humphrey rather
archly describes himself in this way: "Like the woodcock, I too am an odd
bird; I know I am, and I would change if I could, because being odd is
uncomfortable. . . . My brain, I often think, must surely be upside down, so out
of step with the world am I. Like the woodcock, I'm a loner. I don't sleep well of
nights, either. It's true, I'm bigger than my little mate, but not by much. I don't
migrate from south to north annually, but did it once, performed my courtship
rites, and settled in the nest."[1]

Thus William Humphrey describes three essential features of his nature: his
oddness, his particular brand of humor, and his isolation from society. His deep
feeling that he is a "loner" has its origin in his father's death when Bill was thirteen years old. He was awakened in the middle of the night to an anguish that
remained with him all of his days—and nights. That wakeful anguish sharpened
his literary vision and gave him the subject for much of his fiction.

Humphrey writes about pain. That he does it in prose of great beauty does
not mute the impact. Robert Penn Warren has said that the main reason we read
literature is that "it gives us an image of the human soul confronting its fate."[2]
The fate that Humphrey's characters face over and over is that they must live
with great loss. In one way or another, they lose someone or something that
they valued greatly—a father, a son, a brother, a wife, a friend, God, confidence,
integrity, authenticity, freedom, respect, home. Whatever the loss, "the grieving
heart grieves all alone, in unbridgeable isolation," a fact of life that Humphrey
learned early on when at thirteen he watched his father die (*FOFH*, 153). Indeed,
the separation of father and son is the most common loss in Humphrey's writing,
being a prominent feature of "The Shell," *Home from the Hill, The Ordways, Hostages to Fortune,* and *No Resting Place.* He relives repeatedly the great loss of his
life—the death of his father—through the losses of his characters.

---

1. Reprinted in *OS*, 291.

2. Robert Penn Warren, "The Use of the Past," in *New and Selected Essays* (New York: Random
House, 1989), 46.

Like William Styron, who has an equally melancholy perspective and probably for the same reason (Styron was also an only child who witnessed the death
of a parent when he was thirteen), Humphrey grasps the small things of this
world with an intense perception. With big delights forever out of reach, he holds
fast to the small pleasures and real and solid things of his fictional world. As
Hardy created Wessex and as Faulkner created Yoknapatawpha County, so Humphrey created a Red River County of the imagination. He does not give the
county a fictional name and sometimes calls Clarksville (the county seat) by its
real name, although in various stories he does assign made-up names: Columbia,
New Jerusalem, and Blossom Prairie. The courthouse clock that Humphrey remembered from his first thirteen years of life chimes throughout his Clarksville
novels, the nickelodeon in the Greek's confectionery on the town square plays a
happy tune as counterpoint to repeated sad losses, the mourning dove croons its
inconsolable lament, and the hot tamale shucks (evidence of the popular business of Finus Goodman, Humphrey's black childhood friend) are strewn through
the gutters of his fictional Clarksville world. Humphrey depicts the place with
uncommon fidelity. When his uncle Bernard Varley asserted that pine trees did
not grow deep in Sulphur Bottom, as Humphrey says they do in *Home from the
Hill,* a local game warden verified that Humphrey, though absent from the area
for many years when he wrote the novel, had "placed them exactly." He also
attends to the voices, manners, customs, clothes, and attitudes of the people, capturing them like a folklorist.[3]

Humphrey was not immune to literary influence. He betrays unmistakable
resemblances to Faulkner that go beyond references to statues of Confederate
infantrymen in the town squares and hunting episodes. For example, one particular feature of Faulkner's style that Humphrey sometimes employs is the sentence that revises itself in order to establish a more definite premeditation to a
character's utterance or action, such as: "'And did you climb that tree like I told
you?' said his father, with a look in his eye which said he knew the answer, had
known it when he first made the suggestion" (*HFH,* 93). Humphrey acknowledges kinship to Faulkner: "I was born about two hundred miles from William
Faulkner, and [he] was born the year my father was. But by the time I came on
the scene, nothing had changed in that particular [area]. . . . I consider myself a
contemporary of . . . Faulkner because I grew up in the very same way. . . . It
would be very odd indeed if some of my writing didn't sound like some of his,
wouldn't it?" (*WST,* 10).[4]

3. James W. Lee, *William Humphrey,* Southwest Writers Series, no. 7 (Austin, Tex.: Steck-
Vaughn, 1967), 10.
4. Clarksville is actually closer to four hundred miles west of Oxford.

The most significant literary influence on Humphrey, however, was a fellow Texan, Katherine Anne Porter. When he began writing seriously, he kept four of Porter's stories on his writing table—"Old Mortality," "Noon Wine," "The Cracked Looking Glass," and "The Old Order." These stories served as a successful Texan's inspiration for an aspirant writer more than they did as models, for there is a precious delicacy and lightness in Porter's style, which is unlike the strong expression of harsh realities that characterizes Humphrey's writing. There is, nonetheless, a similarity in the regional expressions that both use.

Despite his widely acknowledged virtues as a writer, however, Humphrey has failed to achieve the fame that many lesser writers have won for themselves. His books, with the exception of *Proud Flesh*, have been praised unstintingly by their reviewers, sometimes by very fine fellow novelists (Reynolds Price, for example), and some have made the best-seller lists. They have been translated into French, German, Italian, Dutch, Swedish, Danish, Norwegian, Czech, and Hungarian. Yet his books have gone out of print periodically. As the twenty-first century begins, only the first three are in print: *The Last Husband and Other Stories, Home from the Hill,* and *The Ordways.* There are several reasons for this development. An obvious one is that, unlike Truman Capote and Norman Mailer—to name the most shameless self-promoters—Humphrey refused to seek celebrity. He only once made a book tour, which he limited to Texas, and never played the literary personality on a television or radio talk show. As close as he ever came to doing a publicity stunt was allowing the Today show to film him fly-fishing on the opening day of trout season in 1979. And in 1988 he discussed the custom of graveyard cleaning—a significant cultural practice in several of his works—on a Memorial Day broadcast of National Public Radio. Sometimes he refused to cooperate with those who wished to recognize his accomplishments. He did not acknowledge Mark Morrow's request for permission to photograph and interview him for *Images of the Southern Writer,*[5] and he never filled out questionnaires sent to him by the editors of biographical publications.

Scholarly criticism has remained somewhat standoffish to Humphrey's work. Part of the reason is that academics themselves are not immune to the cult of personality. But primarily, I believe, critics find that Humphrey's most significant fiction evokes emotional experiences on the verge of what most people can endure. His tragic novels explore the outer limits of human suffering; they are the kinds of books that Kafka said we ought to read:

5. Mark Morrow, *Images of the Southern Writer* (Athens: University of Georgia Press, 1985); Morrow to William Humphrey, 27 January 1981, WH Coll., UT.

3

> I think we ought to read only the kind of books that wound and stab us.
> If the book we're reading doesn't wake us up with a blow on the head,
> what are we reading it for? So that it will make us happy? . . . Good Lord,
> we would be happy precisely if we had no books, and the kind of books
> that make us happy are the kind we could write ourselves if we had to. But
> we need the books that affect us like a disaster, that grieve us deeply, like
> the death of someone we loved more than ourselves, like being banished
> into forests far from everyone, like a suicide. A book must be the axe for
> the frozen sea inside us.[6]

Humphrey's novels are to some people what *King Lear* was to Dr. Johnson: too
painful to reread, an act that of course is necessary for a proper critical consideration.

Humphrey's work has been ill served by the academic criticism it has thus far
received. Some is uninformed and superficial. I include myself in this indictment,
for before reading all of his works and before considering them properly, I advocated the view that *Home from the Hill* "express[es] the concept that Allen Tate
writes about in 'Ode to the Confederate Dead': a glorious insanity is a serious
rebuke to a paltry present."[7] To make such a statement is to place Humphrey in
the long line of southern writers described by Elizabeth Bowen. The work of such
a writer

> takes its character from his own strongly personal and often also inherited
> sense of life. His loyalties are involuntary and inborn—not like the intellectual's, of his choice or seeking—and are the more powerful for that.
> Psychologically if not actually he is a regionalist, in his work relying not
> only for subject but for atmosphere, texture, colour, and flavour upon the
> particular enclave which has given him birth. In return for the inspiration
> he owes pieties; his ancestor-worship—however much this may be diluted
> by irony—is fundamental.[8]

Gary Davenport, after quoting this passage from Bowen, asserted that such "a
sense of owed pieties, of ancestor-worship, is at the center of Humphrey's [fic-

6. Franz Kafka to Oscar Pollack, 27 January 1904, *Letters to Friends, Family, and Editors,* trans.
Richard and Clara Winston (New York: Schocken Books, 1977), 16.

7. Ashby Bland Crowder, "History, Family, and William Humphrey," *Southern Review* 24, no. 4
(Autumn 1988): 825.

8. Elizabeth Bowen, *Seven Winters: Memories of a Dublin Childhood and Afterthoughts: Pieces on
Writing* (New York: Alfred A. Knopf, 1962), 67.

tion]."[9] It would not be surprising to find that Humphrey, growing up under the shadow of Clarksville's Confederate memorial, had aligned himself with what Tate has identified as "the pervasive Southern subject of our time": the cult of memory that sees the "image of the past in the present."[10] Irving Howe has said that the South's "regional memory [is] the main shaper of its life," explaining: "because it had so little else to give its people the South nurtured in them a generous and often obsessive sense of the past."[11]

The South's defeat in the Civil War, the loss of a way of life and its replacement by a new order that could not hold a candle to the former, was the beginning point for many southern writers. They felt that the past must not be forgotten, must at least be held on to in imagination, where it can inform the lives of southern people and their literature. Andrew Lytle expresses this view: "If we dismiss the past as dead and not as a country of the living which our eyes are unable to see, as we cannot see a foreign country but know it is there, then we are likely to become servile," by which he means we would be living with "a lesser sense of ourselves, lacking that fuller knowledge which only the living past can give."[12] In *I'll Take My Stand,* Tate argued that the South must "take hold" of its tradition "by violence."[13]

One might expect Humphrey to agree with Lytle and Tate. He experienced as a child the urge to possess again what seems gone forever. The house he was born in (torn down, he thought, shortly after his birth) assumed in his mind the exaggerated importance of something lost and irretrievable, and yet "for that very reason is something one cannot give up hope of finding" (*FOFH,* 38). His longing for a house became for him "a longing for a state of being which the house had come to symbolize for [him]"—a period of profound and happy innocence (*FOFH,* 39). He used to dream that his dead father had returned. The longing for the lost, then, is an emotion that Humphrey is familiar with, and it is an emotional condition that permeates his fiction.

At the same time, Humphrey's wistfulness is limited to his personal experience. Though susceptible to a cultural dream of the past, he refuses to participate. John Grammar, who has written the best essay to date on Humphrey's fiction, argues that "Humphrey gives us a present from which the past is utterly and

---

9. Gary Davenport, "The Desertion of William Humphrey's Circus Animals," *Southern Review* 23, no. 2 (April 1987): 494.

10. Allen Tate, *Memoirs and Opinions, 1926–1974* (Chicago: Swallow Press, 1975), 148.

11. Irving Howe, *William Faulkner: A Critical Study,* 2nd ed. (New York: Vintage, 1962), 23.

12. Andrew Lytle, *A Wake for the Living: A Family Chronicle* (New York: Crown, 1972), 4.

13. Twelve Southerners, *I'll Take My Stand: The South and the Agrarian Tradition* (1930; reprint, Baton Rouge: Louisiana State University Press, 1977), 174.

painfully absent."[14] He is a southern writer who refuses to engage in what Lewis P. Simpson has termed "delusionary remembrance."[15] Quite simply, he rejects the entire southern cult of memory. That rejection is what sets his fiction apart from the fiction of many of his southern contemporaries; according to Grammar, early in his career Humphrey "began creating a distinctly new literary response to the South, one that resembles (and often anticipates) the work of Percy and O'Connor more than it harks back to that of Faulkner and the Agrarians" (5–6). He writes in the southern tradition but with a cold eye to its transgressions and illusions. He is, thereby, its most intimate, penetrating, and sometimes harsh observer, lashing himself to the mast, one sometimes feels, in order that he might avoid the old seduction and move ahead. To make a closer literary analogy, Humphrey's fictional world resembles what is left when the curtain falls in a Tennessee Williams play. His fiction is the bare light that exposes Blanche DuBois's paper-lamp illusions in *A Streetcar Named Desire*.

In that play Williams presents a lost southern past that deserves to be lost because it is corrupt at the core, and efforts to preserve it or revive it are fantastical, impossible. Much of Humphrey's fiction enacts the same theme. Whatever gross reality has been born in the ruin of the South must be faced and lived in. Humphrey's fiction takes a position very much like that of the son in Flannery O'Connor's "Everything That Rises Must Converge." Julian insists that his mother face the fact that "the old world is gone. The old manners are obsolete and your graciousness is not worth a damn"—and then he adds: "You needn't act as if the world had come to an end, . . . because it hasn't. From now on you've got to live in a new world and face a few realities for a change. Buck up."[16] Humphrey's work, like O'Connor's, is a link between the generation of Faulkner, whose characters struggle to find meaning in their collective past, and the generation of Bobbie Ann Mason, whose characters are absorbed in television culture and can visit Shiloh without awareness that anything of importance ever happened there.

In his early adulthood, Humphrey determined to leave the South to avoid being mired in its past, and so he migrated—like the woodcock that he associated himself with—to New York State. This geographical distance from his native land has perhaps helped his writing to embody its hard critical position. And Hum-

---

14. John M. Grammer, "Where the South Draws Up to a Stop: The Fiction of William Humphrey," *Mississippi Quarterly*, 44 (Winter 1990/91): 8.

15. Lewis P. Simpson, *The Fable of the Southern Writer* (Baton Rouge: Louisiana State University Press, 1994), 77.

16. Flannery O'Connor, *Everything That Rises Must Converge* (1965; reprint, New York: Farrar, Straus and Giroux, 1972), 21, 22.

phrey has in fact since the beginning of his career set stories in the Northeast; half of those in *The Last Husband* take place in the North, and two of his last three books, *Hostages to Fortune* and *September Song,* are set almost entirely in the Northeast.

Humphrey's favorite author, Thomas Hardy, once remarked that "Literature is the written expression of revolt against accepted things."[17] Humphrey readily asserted: "I am a destroyer of myths. My whole work has shown the danger and falseness of myths . . .—[especially] the myth of the South" (Notes, 38). The discussions that follow in most of these chapters will demonstrate that Humphrey has taken pains to show that living in the southern past is not to live at all. It is not just the myth of the South that Humphrey takes aim at, for he exposes the inefficacy of "the myth of the hunter," "the myth of the West," "the myth of the Outlaw," "the myth of Oil," "the myth of Texas," and others. In November 1965 he remarked that

> I have attacked these in everything I have written. Yet I am called a creature of myths! Those who criticize my writing say that I live in the past. My writing has concerned itself with the past because I am concerned to show how deadening the past can be upon the present—how falsification, romanticization of the past—can be deadly. . . . I try so hard to write clearly, and I am completely misunderstood. . . . Either nobody sees what I am getting at, or else nobody cares. But I think it's an important thing to do. And I shall certainly go on doing it. I don't know of a more important thing to do than to try to show the truth[:] the dangers of romanticizing and sentimentalizing, the danger of making myths. (Notes, 38–41)

Humphrey's fiction accomplishes what he means to accomplish. In short stories and in *Home from the Hill, The Ordways,* and *Proud Flesh,* he demonstrates that the past is past and is significant only in the kind of present and future that it gives way to. The tradition-obsessed hunter cannot hunt until he leaps from past attachments to the present ("The Shell"); oil, believed to be an antidote to the troubles of the Great Depression, brings its own troubles and heartache ("A Job of the Plains"); the "poreboy" gangster myth proves disastrous for those lured by it ("The Ballad of Jesse Neighbours"); the myth of the West turns into a joke *(The Ordways);* and the mythic heroes of Texas are exposed as shams *(No Resting Place).*

Even as Humphrey's male characters work free of stifling tradition, they take

17. Martin Seymour-Smith, *Hardy* (New York: St. Martin's Press, 1994), 233.

their place in a line of characters in American fiction that begins with Natty Bumppo. In *The Pathfinder,* when the hero of the Leatherstocking Tales fails to win the love of Mabel Dunham and is forced to remain faithful in the end to his "other mistress, the forest"—this is Humphrey's expression in *Ah, Wilderness!: The Frontier in American Literature* (1977)—we have the type for Theron Hunnicutt *(Home from the Hill)* who loses the love of Libby Halstead as he disappears into the deep woods of Sulphur Bottom. The character of Theron is also related to Ike McCaslin, and the meaning of the killing of the wild boar in *Home from the Hill* is little different from that of the killing of the bear in *Go Down, Moses.* Some of Humphrey's other protagonists take their places alongside the emotional cripples of Hemingway. Ben Curtis, carefully seeking his emotional balance in an old fishing stream, performs a ritualistic reenactment of the patterns of Nick Adams and Jake Barnes retreating from the traumata of their lives into woods and streams.

It is fitting, then, that Humphrey's style reflects at times the Spartan style of Hemingway, at other times the cadenced lyricism of Faulkner. What else can be said of Humphrey's style and technique? Humphrey read widely in American, British, and Continental literature, partly by virtue of his years as an academic at Bard, Washington and Lee, MIT, Princeton, and Smith; and he appropriated the techniques of conveying emotion through image and action from Flaubert, Hardy, and Hemingway, to name here just his main sources. Sometimes the technique of a predecessor is so transformed and the dramatic situation different enough that one feels reluctant to assert so whispered an influence. In other instances, Humphrey's technique is sufficiently close to his source that he crosses over to the ambit of literary allusion.

Humphrey also retells ancient stories, as in "A Job of the Plains," "The Last of the Caddoes," and *Proud Flesh*; the tale of long suffering from the Book of Job and the story of the Aeschylean and Sophoclean Orestes and Electra find themselves rediscovered for a modern generation. Ghosts from Hardy's *Jude the Obscure* hover about in *Home from the Hill:* Theron is to Jude as Libby is to Sue, and Fred Shumway is to Phillotson as Opal is to Arabella; as we read of the disappointments of Humphrey's characters, we know that literature is a sacred repetition: in the flesh of the moment the ancient stories are immortal, like a wave interminably flowing, as Wallace Stevens might remind us. At other times, Humphrey's allusions are just a phrase—but a phrase calculated to remind us that an emotion or an epiphany or a sad death is not an isolated event but has a literary antecedent. Many authors are bid to join the solemn procession of allusion in Humphrey's fictions, among them Joyce, Warren, Dickens, T. S. Eliot, Hardy, Cather, Katherine Anne Porter, Valéry, Thomas Moore, Wyatt, Spenser, Shakespeare, Milton, Emily Brontë, Bryant, Wordsworth, Keats, Poe, Housman, Robinson, Yeats, Frost, and Cole Porter.

Humphrey lived to write and wrote out of his life, the manifold allusions notwithstanding. Because his life and his fiction are so entangled, I have reckoned that the best way to approach his fiction is through his biography. The first chapter sets the context out of which Humphrey emerged as a writer. I then discuss his novels and collections of short stories chronologically, devoting a chapter to each. I consider each work as a product of Humphrey's life—his experience as he wrote it as well as the experience that he drew upon—and then the work's themes, methods, accomplishments, and failures. I include the critical reception and his response to it.

The act of writing was for Humphrey, as his friend the poet and critic Theodore Weiss put it, always "reeling and writhing." His letters and manuscripts indicate that he belongs to the Flaubertian school of composition, achieving style only by severe discipline—"by atrocious labour, a fanatic and dedicated stubbornness." He almost always wrote in the third person; in this way he could exercise his writerly skill and doggedness in shaping the narrative artfully and formulating classically pure sentences or acutely perceptive and reflective figures. Thus through structure Humphrey created in *Home from the Hill*, for example, an engaging tension between what we know will happen and what we fervently hope can be avoided, and his similes and metaphors beget a sense of a solid world—so that we feel the "bone-warming sun," see the "brown hillsides sprinkled with white sheep like mushrooms," and hear "that faint scratchy voice . . . like a worn-out phonograph record."[18] With his craftsmanship and high purpose all too evident, Humphrey is the opposite of the most popular Texas writer today, Larry McMurtry, who tells a good story but without art and clearly without care of construction.

My literary criticism is conducted in a radical manner—in the sense that it begins where the activity of criticism originated, in the margins of books as a response to and commentary on what is going on in them, formally, thematically, and linguistically. I go beyond this only by integrating biographical information. In 1982, I became acquainted with Humphrey, and we began to talk on the telephone about once a month, more often in the final years of his life. Knowing him has clarified much in his fiction for me, and that is why I have taken a biographical approach in this book.

18. Theodore and Renée Weiss to William and Dorothy Humphrey, 16 February 1963, Weiss Coll.; James Wood, "Half-Against Flaubert," *New Republic*, 18 January 1999, 37; *OS*, 344, 335; *PF*, 112.

1

FROM RED RIVER COUNTY TO NEW YORK CITY

> Every writer compensates himself as best he can
> for some wrong done him by fate.
> —VALÉRY, *Variety: Second Series*

CLARKSVILLE, TEXAS, William Humphrey's birthplace, is more truly a town of the Old South than of the West. Founded in 1835, it grew up in the slave-owning, cotton-growing part of Red River County in East Texas, a county settled mainly by immigrants from the deep southern states of Georgia, Alabama, and Mississippi. These founders and their descendants supplied ten companies to the Confederate army during the Civil War. A Confederate monument—a foot soldier with bedroll on his back—is the centerpiece of the town square. In the 1920s of William Humphrey's boyhood, Clarksville had a population of nearly three thousand, about a third of whom were of American Indian origin. It still had a livery stable, a blacksmith shop, and two Confederate veterans (*FOFH*, 4, 50). In Humphrey's boyhood days the town bustled with activity, especially in August and September when the farmers from all over the county brought their long-staple cotton in to have it ginned, compressed, stored, and then shipped out by rail. The delicious aroma from the cottonseed mill on the northern edge spread all over town. The cafés were open sometimes around the clock, the gins ran all night, and in the afternoons a local band played in the square. There were times when "you couldn't even walk around the square it was so crowded," remembered Gavin Watson, one of Humphrey's childhood acquaintances.[1]

William Joseph Humphrey (Billy Joe Humphreys) was born on 18 June 1924 at about 3:00 A.M. in a small house without running water or electricity on a nameless dirt lane behind the cemetery in Clarksville. He was the only child of Clarence and Nell (née Varley) Humphreys (Nell quickly dropped the *s* in a vain attempt to disguise the connection between their own family and the rest of her husband's family). Born with his right foot turned up against his shin, Billy's earliest consciousness, it might seem, told him that life plays dirty tricks, though

---

1. *Red River Recollections* (Clarksville, Tex.: Red River County Historical Society, 1986), 5; *Fourteenth Census of the United States*, vol. 3 (Washington: Government Printing Office, 1922), 1018; Gavin Watson, interview by author, tape recording, Clarksville, Tex., 17 July 1997.

in fact he recalled nothing of his first three years. He found out later that his deformed condition had put a pall on the lively, devil-may-care life that his parents had been leading. Nell cried for six months over her crippled baby, the country wisdom being that Billy's deformity was because she had slept on her side instead of on her back during pregnancy. Nell sought the best medical treatment available for him, finding a doctor in Dallas who corrected his foot with a graduated series of braces. By age three Billy could walk, and he never limped. In fact, he had no inkling of having been born a cripple until he was nine years old: his mother told him only to explain her hysterical reaction to his spraining his right ankle; when she saw the swollen ankle, she thought the correction to his foot had suddenly failed (*FOFH*, 45, 164–65, 208–12).

Although Billy's birth was the beginning of trouble between his parents, the rift became more evident when in 1930 he started school. He met boys from the best families in Clarksville; his manners—taught him by his mother—and his natural outgoingness made him acceptable everywhere. His teacher at Clarksville Grammar School was Miss Ruth Marable, daughter of the prominent townsman and model for the dinner guest in "Quail for Mr. Forester," an early story. Billy did exceptionally well in school and was double-promoted from the low first to the high second grade. Nell, who had had only two years of schooling, her husband only three, began to imagine that through education and the right connections her son could advance in life, and she meant to give him every chance. She sent him to the Episcopal Church because it was socially the most prestigious one. But she knew that the wild life that she and Clarence had been leading would undermine his chances. An ingrained outsider, part Indian but more "pore-white," a rebel and a loner, Clarence saw no value in Nell's aspirations for their son; he wished his son well, but he was not going to let that concern change his habits. Nell undertook to reform her husband: she wanted him to quit drinking, fighting, and keeping disreputable company. Her scolding and nagging, however, drove him to intensify his wild behavior. Disapproved of at home, Clarence resorted to other women. When his father came home late, Billy buried his head under his pillow to block the angry voices of his parents. The arguing eventually gave way to physical fighting, making Billy feel that he had failed in the one thing that he had been born for—to make his parents happy and to keep them together (*FOFH*, 160, 166–67, 218).

The material living conditions of the family were uncertain and variable. In the memoir of his childhood, *Farther Off from Heaven*, Humphrey himself says that during the Great Depression, when people who did not own houses could not even afford to rent them, landlords in Clarksville allowed people to occupy them rent free if they would keep the houses up. His mother Nell had the reputation for keeping house so well that the family was forever being offered a better house by Clarksville landlords (*FOFH*, 19–20). Gavin Watson, who in childhood lived at one time within a hundred feet of Billy's family, remembers it differently: the Humphreys moved frequently because Clarence Humphrey never paid the rent: "they moved about every two months. The first month, he wouldn't pay his rent; the second month they kicked him out." Although Humphrey says his family moved only fifteen times in five years, the frequency was sufficient to confuse the boy about just where he lived. Once he came home from school, poured a glass of milk, and peeled a banana before he heard a woman not his mother say, "Billy? Is that you? But you don't live here any more, hon'. Did you forget? You all moved out today and we moved in here. You live out on Third Street now" (*FOFH*, 19–20). One of the benefits of moving frequently was that Billy had the opportunity of walking to school by so many different routes that he came to know the town's streets better than any of its other inhabitants. Watson says Billy "grew up in every neighborhood in Clarksville."[2]

A disadvantage of moving frequently, however, was that it undermined his mother's desire that he maintain friendship with the children of the best families; as it turned out, he never had consistent friends, and this situation, coupled with his father's reputation for drinking, brawling, and fornicating, eventually made him a boy that respectable children were advised to avoid. People who knew him then report that he did not continue to be outgoing. James Lee remarks that classmates remember him "as a quiet, somewhat withdrawn child," and Watson said that by the time he knew Billy "he was about as loner as you get—not necessarily by choice. The type of family he was raised in" stood in the way of his making firm friendships.[3]

Nonetheless, Billy thought of himself as a lucky boy. His death certificate, which he treasured as a talisman for years, was proof that he led a charmed life. Billy was thought to have drowned at Crystal Lake when he was seven years old. The same doctor who had nearly killed him the year before with an overdose of ether while drunkenly extracting his tonsils had pronounced him drowned and, being the county coroner, had filled out his death certificate. Providentially, Billy's cousin Ramsay Floyd grabbed the supposedly dead Billy by the heels and shook him back to life (*FOFH*, 220–27).

Clarence Humphrey had escaped from horribly abusive sharecropper parents and had started a car repair garage in Clarksville with another man who saw the

2. Watson, interview.

3. James W. Lee, *William Humphrey*, Southwest Writers Series, no. 7 (Austin: Steck-Vaughn, 1967), 1; Watson, interview.

coming of the age of the automobile. Barton and Humphrey's Garage turned out to be fairly successful, since cars were just then becoming common, and Clarence was a good mechanic. He taught himself to be a body man when cars were becoming more numerous and faster and as accidents thereby increased. Humphrey says his father did not allow him to hang around his shop, but a childhood friend recalls Billy "as a tiny, tow-headed, barefoot lad," getting grease smudges on his feet at his father's garage.[4]

The 1930s drought affected the life of the Humphreys profoundly. Fissures opened in the earth during the first year of the drought and widened and deepened as it continued in the next: "The earth looked like a jig-saw puzzle that had been put together and then jarred apart," Billy recalls. "One had to learn to walk on the detached pieces of earth as on stones in a creek. Once that summer, playing in my own back yard, I fell into a crack so deep I had to yell for my mother to come from the house and pull me out" (FOFH, 171). The population of Clarksville dropped by about five hundred as many left for California, and for those remaining the drought meant that neither the cotton farmers nor their suppliers could pay for car repairs.[5] Clarence's customers owed him $10,000 in never-to-be-paid bills during these years. Hard times like these encouraged Clarence to drink more than usual, drive his car faster out of frustration, and incur Nell's disapproval, which led to his staying away from home. He took to carrying a pistol, which alarmed Nell; she feared how he might use it in the sullen, resentful mood that had become customary. Still, he kept his family fed, not with butcher's meat—a rarity at the Humphrey house—but by exercising his skill with a shotgun. The habit of watching for bird shot in his meat became ingrained in Billy (OS, 278). Nell did her part as well, intensifying her summer canning, buying all that she could from local farmers all summer long as crops became ripe. In the autumn, some of the farmers who owed Clarence for car repairs paid him in black walnuts, pecans, fresh pork, country-cured hams, and sorghum. The family would need nothing to get through the winter (FOFH, 205–7).

Billy's father was an accomplished hunter, and he taught his son the ways of the woods, evidence of which appears throughout the fiction that he would go on to write. When Billy was only four, his father bought him a .22-caliber rifle and taught him to shoot, and when he was eleven, a four-shot bolt-action .410 shotgun. Billy at first was no Natty Bumppo and stepped on almost every twig that his father had carefully avoided, but gradually he learned to be a woodsman,

4. Paul Rosenfield to William Humphrey, 17 April 1979, in WH Coll., UT.

5. Fifteenth Census of the United States, vol. 1 (Washington: Government Printing Office, 1931), 1087.

and though father and son did not talk a great deal, Billy became a devoted son, remarking: "My oneness with him gave me some of his sense of oneness with that world" (*FOFH*, 178, 112). Father and son hunted together in Sulphur Bottom, the hunting preserve of Captain Wade Hunnicutt in *Home from the Hill.* There were days when they brought home fifty ducks (the limit was twenty-five; Billy would get one, his father forty-nine, making the bag for both).[6] One of Humphrey's most vivid memories is of his father "stepping on the tail of a squirrel and peeling it out of its skin" (*FOFH*, 108).

Until the summer of 1933 the only book that Billy had read other than schoolbooks was *The Arabian Nights,* a Christmas gift when he was six. If not hunting with his father, he was playing outside. He came in to eat and sleep. On 4 July 1933, his life took a turn. He was "it" in a game of tag, and while chasing Sarah Goltz, a girl he had recently fallen in love with, he slipped and fell on a wooden stake hidden in the grass, slicing off his right kneecap. (When he registered for the draft in June 1942, he listed "large scar on right knee" as his one physical characteristic that would aid in identification.) Being confined to bed for the rest of the summer of 1933 provided a hidden benefit: a neighbor boy named James Storey, three years older than Billy, brought into his life something that would eventually mean more to him than anything else: books. James brought the first in the series of Tom Swift books, promising to bring the next one as soon as Billy was ready for it. That summer, too, Billy listened from his bed to his mother singing as she did housework—plaintive country ballads about the cruelty and loneliness of the world, about the disappointments of life that could always be counted on, about the fleeting nature of fortune's smile and the unreliability of friends. These songs that mourn all the losses of life she sang in a voice "pitched to a near-sob and frequently breaking into one" (*FOFH*, 196–200, 203–4). These themes and tones soaked into Billy's consciousness, later coming out reworked in his writing. At the time, though, those sad songs cheered him up, for he still knew that he was lucky: he was bedridden only for a summer, not like Cleo Kelty, a neighbor girl, for whom TB of the spine meant that she would never walk—and he still treasured his death certificate and what it meant to him (*FOFH*, 205).

Nell had filled so many Mason jars that Clarence had to store them on makeshift shelves at his shop. In the autumn after Billy had relearned how to walk after almost three months in bed, he was eating black walnuts in the shop storeroom, cracking them open with a hammer. His response to blasting his thumb was to sling the offending hammer around in anger and pain—breaking nearly every jar of his mother's canning (*FOFH*, 207–8). The horror at what he had

6. William Humphrey to Nick Lyons, 28 October 1970, Lyons Coll.

done, the sudden destruction of winter's security, undermined his confidence in the future. To this distressing event was added yet another. His family's house on Third Street burned to the ground. All of his keepsakes, including his death certificate, were turned to ashes—a sign, it seemed to him, that his charmed existence was at an end. And so it would be in the coming years (*FOFH*, 194).

But before shattering misfortune struck, life seemed headed for the better. Though the Depression continued, prospects improved in Red River County when the long drought broke: the dust storms had blown themselves out, and by the summer of 1937 the prairies surrounding Clarksville were once again whitening with cotton. Just as things in general were looking up, the great grief of Humphrey's life occurred: the death of his father at age thirty-eight, fatally injured in a car wreck on the Fourth of July, 1937. Watson remembers that when oil was first discovered in Texas, Clarence was working on the rigs being drilled near Kilgore. Watson's recollection of the accident is colored by Clarence's reputation: "he was coming back off of the night shift and just ran off the road, probably drinking. Another word is that he had been visiting a woman of the night, which he occasionally did" and so was not coming straight home from work. According to Dean Humphreys, Clarence's nephew, he was racing home with an irate husband from Bogata, Texas, on his tail; apparently he had caught Clarence in bed with his wife. The accident occurred on a twenty-mile-per-hour curve just outside of Clarksville. Clarence tried to take it at sixty.[7] As Humphrey says, "he was the sort about whom stories circulated" (*FOFH*, 121). Whatever the circumstances, the death of his father was the central event of Humphrey's life, a fact made clear in the remarkable memoir of his childhood, *Farther Off from Heaven*, which takes its title from Thomas Hood's "I Remember":

> I remember, I remember,
> The fir trees dark and high;
> I used to think their slender tops
> Were close against the sky:
> It was a childish ignorance,
> But now 'tis little joy
> To know I'm farther off from heav'n
> Than when I was a boy.

The narrative of *Farther Off from Heaven* begins when thirteen-year-old Billy learns of his father's fatal accident. It was a middle-of-the-night horror from

7. Watson interview; Dean Humphreys, telephone conversation with author, 1 August 2001.

which Billy never recovered: "What I saw stretched on the tabletop looked like a scarecrow thrown there. Its clothes, a suit of coveralls exactly like my own, were dyed with blood, stained with motor oil, ripped and slashed, and the entire body so swollen it seemed to have been stuffed into them. The legs and arms were splayed, twisted, limp. The chest on one side was crushed, forcing out the other side. It looked as if it had been hanged, trampled, like the defiled effigy of a man" (*FOFH*, 8). Billy was used to seeing his father's face black with the grease of his trade, but now it was bruised black and caked with blood. He looked so much unlike himself that Billy had to try hard to reassemble his features from memory. His right eye was missing, and his forehead was caved in on one side, bulging on the other. The nose was split open and the teeth mauled. As the ambulance whisked his father to the nearest hospital, in Paris, thirty-one miles away, Billy listened to his father's groans and gurgled breathing and the wail of the siren above his head, and he sought to fix in his mind a map of Clarksville, to assemble the images and memories of his lost childhood, not knowing then that these would provide the settings and circumstances of much of the fiction that he would one day write (see *FOFH*, 8–9, 14).

Billy knew now that life would be "a succession of severances," and so he longed to give his father up, since he must, to "detach him from me and begin the process of transformation in my mind that his body must now undergo in the earth. I must relegate him to a life of mine now lost and irrecoverable, for only after I had done so would the wound of his death begin to scar over" (*FOFH*, 229, 233). Yet for his dead father he never shed a tear. Never purging his grief, he felt the loss all his life, reviving his relationship with his father in the disguise of the fathers and sons of his fiction and suffering severance over and over.

On the Sunday of his father's death, Billy was scheduled to be confirmed by the Right Reverend Harry T. Moore, Episcopal Bishop of the Diocese of Dallas, but the ceremony had already been postponed owing to the holiday. The postponement turned out to be an eternal one, for Humphrey never again attended a religious service—not even his father's funeral. Billy rejected religion as emotionally inadmissible: he would have nothing to do with a heavenly father who would take his earthly father when he himself was only thirteen years old.

The next severance for Billy would be from Clarksville. He felt that he could have grown straight in the native soil enriched by the fallen older tree, but, destitute after paying for her husband's funeral, Nell had to leave Clarksville because cooking and housekeeping were the only skills she possessed, and it was unthinkable for a white woman in 1937 to hire out in one of these capacities (AF). Billy and his mother left Clarksville for Dallas on the afternoon of the day Clarence was buried. The spindly boy pulled up his taproot and transplanted himself to poor city soil. He was sure that he would not thrive. Though Billy did survive Dallas, where his mother found work to support them, he was never again light-hearted, observing in his memoir: "Aeneas, when he was driven from his home town, went carrying his father on his back. So did I, so do we all, whether bodily or in memory, and the burden is as heavy either way" (*FOFH*, 187–88, 193). Thereafter Humphrey developed a basic sadness, an affinity for gloom, and an incapacity for balanced, wholesome-minded living: "The fact was," he wrote, "I had now advanced to that chapter in the textbook of life which teaches that plea-sure is nothing but a short holiday from pain" (*FOFH*, 195–96). This Thomas Hardy–like view of life Humphrey was to cultivate as the muse for his fiction; his was an *esthétique du mal*. He created out of his expulsion from a relatively happy Clarksville childhood fictional worlds of his own people who must learn to suffer and find a way to endure.

Billy and his mother lived for a time with Nell's sister Gertrude Ridgeway, and Nell had an eleven-dollar-a-week job as a stock clerk at the Sears, Roebuck mail-order warehouse; she was fitted out in roller skates to boost efficiency, a detail from real life that Humphrey was later to draw upon in one of his last stories, "Portrait of the Artist as an Old Man." In just four months' time Nell married Andy Fleming, whom she had known for only two weeks, and with him operated a blue-plate-special diner on Jackson Street in the garment district.[8] Humphrey blamed himself for his mother's overhasty remarriage: "The man had picked her up while she was waiting for a streetcar. She married him to support me. I knew that without being told," Humphrey wrote in 1992 (AF).

During his first year in Dallas, Billy attended Adamson High School, but then he transferred to Bryant Technical High School, where most of the students learned a trade; college preparatory courses, especially in the humanities, were few. Latin was offered, however, and Billy studied it with enthusiasm. Further-more, the desire to paint had come upon him suddenly: "I had seen a man paint-ing a picture of calla lilies in a park in Dallas, and, for reasons unknown to me, I was taken like Paul Cézanne" (Au Int.). Billy then bought an anatomy book for art students and copied drawings out of it. On the strength of these drawings he won a scholarship to the Dallas Institute of Fine Arts, which he attended along with high school for the next three years (Dunwell Int.).

The summer of 1938, his second in Dallas, saw Billy take a step beyond the mere pleasure of reading that James Storey had introduced him to: he discovered great literature. Walking down Elm Street, he stopped at Gene Wagner's Book

8. Don Emery to author, 15 February 2000.

Shop; the sidewalk shelves contained some books going for five cents apiece. He picked up *Don Quixote* and noted that the preface identified it as one of the world's great books. He took it home and was captivated. Having found great pleasure from his nickel investment in great literature, he was back the next week asking the clerk for another book as good as the last. This clerk, who would be his guide through the summer's reading, was Jack Boss, who was the age Humphrey's father would have been—thirty-nine. Friendless, lonely, and feeling very much the loss of his father, Billy found that Boss, an insurance man from Ohio who worked in the shop on Saturdays because he liked books, filled the emptiness in his life. A rather cool man, he was never demonstrative, but he was very kind to Billy. He lent him books by E. M. Forster, Virginia Woolf, and James Joyce out of the bookshop and out of his own collection. Boss also encouraged Billy in his artistic studies, before the summer was over taking him to the Cokesbury Bookstore and buying him three Phaeton Books on Art—on Cézanne, Gauguin, and Renoir. Those books cost Boss fifteen dollars, a good week's wages in 1938. The father of four little girls, Boss treated Billy Humphrey as his only son.

Although Billy was very fond of Boss, the boy would never allow anyone to supplant his father in his affections: "I wanted no one to remind me of his loss; I wanted no one to touch me to tears," Humphrey later wrote (AF). One of their bonds was that both were socialists. That Humphrey's real father was a socialist—"I think my father was a socialist," he said, "although if you had told him that, he would have knocked you into the middle of next week"—brought him emotionally closer to Boss, and the two formed a little secret cell of the only two socialists in Dallas, Humphrey liked to think (Au Int.). Boss was free of racial prejudice, and in emulation of him Billy molted those inherited views that he had fledged out with (AF).

Billy, his mother, and his stepfather lived in the Oak Cliff section of Dallas at 911 South Waverly Drive. His mother would telephone him from the diner to wake him for school, and he would take a long streetcar ride to Tech High—time for him to read those books that Boss continued to lend him. After school Billy would walk four miles downtown to the diner, stopping off to see Boss at his insurance office if he needed another book. At the diner he sat in one of the booths memorizing Latin to the tune of the customers' favorite on the jukebox, Ernest Tubbs's "I'm Walking the Floor over You." When the diner closed, Billy ate with his parents, who, exhausted, went to bed as soon as they got home. It was then that Billy climbed up to his "studio" and painted until late in the night. The woman who owned a local art supply store saved scraps of canvas, brushes with loose ferrules, and tubes of paint with missing caps for him (AF).

Humphrey was graduated from high school in February 1941 and wanted then to attend the Art Institute of Chicago, reasoning that a school as good as that could make of him the artist he longed to be. The feasible alternative to this grand scheme was the one Humphrey followed: he enrolled in Southern Methodist University, where, as the descendant of a Confederate veteran, he was eligible for a scholarship. He matriculated in mid-academic-year 1941 at age sixteen (five feet one and 101 pounds), among the youngest students ever to be admitted to SMU. He quickly found a friend in Harry Grabstald, born in Hope, Arkansas, the son of immigrant Polish Jews, who was, like Humphrey, a premedical student. Although Humphrey transferred the next academic year to the University of Texas at Austin in order to get away from home (tuition was then free to citizens of the state), he and Grabstald would remain friends for the rest of their lives.

On the second day of the semester at UT news spread across the campus that three young instructors in the English department had been fired because they included a book by John Dos Passos, a leftist, on their freshman class reading lists. The left-leaning Humphrey immediately joined the swelling student protest. He had a talk with a young English professor by the name of Harry Ransom, himself a native of Clarksville who would later become president of the University of Texas. From Ransom, Humphrey learned that the political climate in Texas was polluted by the influence of its powerful congressman Martin Dies, who headed the special House committee that eventually became the House Un-American Activities Committee.[9] Realizing that he had more to protest than faculty firings, Humphrey took a giant step to the left, deciding that militant communism was a surer means of achieving social justice than socialism. He joined the Young Communist League at a time when he felt so threatened by the anticommunist forces in Texas that he entertained the paranoid delusion that his political actions were punishable by death in the electric chair. In the face of this assumed threat, the young Humphrey and his comrades were to organize and agitate. They were not discouraged by setbacks to the cause. In recalling that period, Humphrey said, "False hopes had been raised by swelling unemployment, lengthening soup lines, banks closing, the prospect of the petit bourgeoisie closing ranks with the working class. The New Deal had put a Band-Aid on all this. But we were in the third period of capitalist decline; the seismometer of Dialectal Materialism was monitoring the coming quake. Meanwhile Roosevelt was no more than the boy with his finger in the dike." In 1992 Humphrey wrote, "Had I been caught my youth might have gotten me a commutation, but knowing what I know now about the cause I believed in and the risk I took for it, I

9. See A. R. Ogden, *The Dies Committee: A Study of the Special House Committee for the Investigation of Un-American Activities, 1938–1944* (Washington: Catholic University Press, 1945).

could cry" (AF). When Humphrey returned to Dallas, Boss was appalled that his protégé had become a communist and set about to penetrate his innocence. Humphrey's faith in the movement was soon shattered.

In 1942, when Bill was eighteen, Nell divorced her second husband. She had fallen in love with one of her customers, a soldier by the name of Butch Troughton who was stationed at the Army recruiting office. Humphrey was, in his own dry words, "not invited to share her new home," so he returned to SMU for his junior year, living in a furnished garret at 3609 McFarlin, near the campus, although he often spent nights in the Grabstald house on Wendelkin Street. He supported himself with a part-time job as clerk of the court of University Park, a Dallas suburb. During the preceding year he had grown six inches and gained twenty-four pounds (according to his Selective Service card). To the unsettling event of his mother's divorce was added an event more unsettling: Jack Boss fell dead on the street of heart failure at the age of forty-two.[10] Many years later, in remembrance of this man's importance to his life, Humphrey dedicated *No Resting Place* "To the memory of Mr. Jack Boss, who shaped my life."

Humphrey had not painted for a year, feeling that his talent was insufficient; when he volunteered for the navy and was rejected because he was color-blind, he knew he had to abandon the idea of being a painter. Therefore when his mother and her second husband broke up house, Bill took his five-year accumulation of paintings and drawings to the backyard and made a bonfire of them (AF). Yet his devotion to painting undoubtedly contributed to the quality of his writing. An observation of Flannery O'Connor's suggests how it did: "I know a good many fiction writers who paint, not because they're any good at painting, but because it helps their writing. It forces them to look at things."[11] Humphrey never gave up his love for painting, and years later he would acknowledge in a 2 November 1958 letter to Blanche and Alfred Knopf that the realization that he could not be a painter "was a very bitter thing, and I really think I still care more for [painting] than even for literature" (Knopf Coll.). He picked up the brush one more time, in 1957, to paint a self-portrait and a still life with irises, which is displayed at the Humphrey house in Hudson, New York.

During Humphrey's senior year at SMU, Grabstald was already in Southwestern Medical College. On a night when he was externing at St. Paul's Hospital as anesthesiologist in the delivery room, he invited Humphrey to don a gown and

10. Au Int.; Harry Grabstald, interview by author, tape recording, Little Rock, Ark., 24 April 2000.

11. Flannery O'Connor, *Mystery and Manners: Occasional Prose*, ed. Sally Fitzgerald and Robert Fitzgerald (1969; reprint, New York: Farrar, Straus and Giroux, 1970), 93.

mask in order to observe a birth. When the obstetrician inserted a huge tool that looked like an iceman's tongs into a young woman and began twisting like a carpenter trying to loosen a stubborn screw, Humphrey grew faint, helped by the fumes of chloroform. Being witness to a high forceps delivery cured Humphrey of all desire to enter the medical profession. Abandoning his plans precipitated something of a crisis. Humphrey put it this way: "my cocoon split and I wriggled out of the shuck." This event occurred during a German class. In something of a daze he rose from his desk and made his way up the aisle. "Humphrey?" called Dr. Schuessler to his prize pupil. "*Was ist? Wogehen sie?*" Humphrey had not known until asked: with his hand on the knob he uttered, "Chicago." And so he went to Chicago for nine months, living in the YMCA and then in a mean hotel at 3210 West Arthington Street. He applied to the University of Chicago, but the dean opposed his application when he learned that Humphrey would be working in a defense factory at night. In 1945 Humphrey returned to Dallas for five months, working for the *Southern Weekly.*[12]

Before he had left Dallas for Chicago, Humphrey had written a five-act historical play entitled "Ambassador Ben," which portrays the aged and decrepit (from gout and rheumatism) Benjamin Franklin, living in Paris in unrepublican luxury, pursuing efforts to raise money for the American Revolution, manipulating political adversaries as though engaged in a chess match, and all the while pressing his interest in the chambers of attractive young ladies. The play seems an imitation of Bernard Shaw—replete with clever exchanges and studied flirtations. When one of the young women upon whom Franklin has set his sights remarks that her heart is his, he responds: "Madam, your heart is in the hands of a holding company—mine is but common stock. But tell me, when do my dividends accrue? . . . It seems unfair that you, to whom I have given so many days, will not in return give me at least one of your nights."[13] With "Ambassador Ben" tucked under his arm, Humphrey traveled to New York City toward the end of 1945 with the great expectation of getting it produced; he brazenly knocked on the door of Broadway producer Brock Pemberton. Although Humphrey has said that the play was unproducible because of its cast of 340, there are in fact only thirty speaking parts (*WST*, 10). The play has some merit and is especially good work from a twenty-year-old college student; its main significance, however, is that it shows Humphrey early on demythologizing American history.

Instead of taking Broadway by storm, as he had planned, he found himself working at various menial jobs—or out of work and nearly starving. In those

12. AF; Humphrey to Grabstald, undated, in HG Letters.
13. "Ambassador Ben," unpublished play, p. 33, in WH res.

early days, Humphrey said in a 1989 interview, "I . . . fell in with a crowd of Village bohemians and learned that my attitude toward the arts was dated and I'd better catch up with the avant-garde. I never did."[14] An accidental decision led to his initial encounter with the woman whom he would love for the rest of his life. It was V-E Day in New York. He said to a friend as they stood in Times Square, "Let's throw up our lousy damned jobs and get out of here." They hitch-hiked to Woodstock, where Humphrey's friend had friends. A week later Humphrey strolled into the woods with his host's wife and seduced her—or she him. Humphrey confessed his sin to his host and was shocked by his response: "We're all civilized people. We can have a little *ménage à trois*." Although Humphrey had only known the woman for a week, he replied: "Well, I think I don't wanna share your wife with you; I think I want her to myself" (Dunwell Int.). She was Dorothy Feinman Cantine, who at the time was calling herself Dorothy Paul; she was an artist's model and painter and for nine years the wife of Holley Cantine, also a painter, who was a leader in the pacifist-anarchist movement and editor, with Dachine Rainer, of *Retort: An Anarchist Review*, published between 1942 and 1951. Dorothy was eight years older than Bill and the mother of a baby daughter, Antonia.[15] So enamored of Humphrey was she that he was able to persuade her not only to leave her husband but her daughter as well. Before the summer was well along, they headed for Guadalajara and Lake Chapala but, having spent their seventy-five-dollar "honeymoon wad," were immobilized by absolute penury in Dallas. Bill got a job as a milkman for Borden Milk Company. His sixteen-hour route depleted him rapidly. He passed out on a Dallas street from malnutrition.[16]

Somehow the couple managed to return to New York City in 1946. It and the next were hard years for them. Bill arrived in time to enter St. Clare's Hospital for hernia surgery, after which he spent thirteen days flat on his back.[17] Having returned to Woodstock to "kidnap" her daughter (whom Dorothy had left with the girl's father and grandmother when she ran off with Bill), mother and daughter now moved in with Dorothy's parents at 65 Ft. Green Place in Brooklyn, and

14. Jose Yglesias, "William Humphrey," ed. Sybil Steinberg, *Publishers Weekly*, 2 June 1989, 65.

15. Dunwell Int. Dorothy's maiden name, Feinman, was a name that her grandparents had as-sumed when they got off the boat from Russia (they had been told that their name, Maistrovoy, would not be suitably American and that Feinman was a good name because there was a well-known Yiddish actor with that name). Dorothy's father was fourteen years old when they arrived. He imme-diately went to work in a garment-district sweatshop (Humphrey to Theodore and Renée Weiss, 19 November [1969], Weiss Coll.).

16. Dorothy Humphrey to Katherine Anne Porter, 14 January 1969, KAP Coll.; Grabstald to Humphrey, 28 November 1977, HG Letters.

17. Humphrey to the Weisses, undated, Weiss Coll.

Bill, upon leaving the hospital, lived in the janitors' quarters at the United States Marine Hospital on Staten Island, where Harry Grabstald, a medical intern there, had got him a job as assistant librarian. During the winter and spring of 1946, while he was still working at the hospital library, Humphrey wrote a short story entitled *"Noli Me Tangere"* ("I am unwilling that you should touch me"). He presented the manuscript to Grabstald, but years later demanded its return and presumably destroyed it—except for the title page, which Grabstald retained.[18] The only clue as to the never-published story's nature, other than its curious title, is the following quotation from Thoreau's *Walden,* which he copied below the title: "If the condition of things which we were made for is not yet, what were any reality which we can substitute?" Humphrey must have felt the appropriateness of this observation with respect to his own life and therefore tried to make a better reality. Mrs. Feinman had threatened to inform Holley of Dorothy's and the child's whereabouts if her daughter did not give up Humphrey or "get out of her house." She got out of the house and with Bill moved into a fifth-floor walk-up on Tenth Avenue, although he had to hock his coat at a Bowery pawn shop to pay rent. Grabstald brought them Thanksgiving dinner in his pockets, which he had gathered in the interns' dining room at the hospital, and the next day paid to get Bill's coat out of hock.[19]

At some point in the first half of 1947, Humphrey lost his job at the hospital library. Dorothy and Toni were forced to move back in with the Feinmans. In despair, Bill secured a passport and contemplated shipping out as a merchant seaman, but unable to be away from Dorothy he hung on in New York by working thirteen-hour stints as a dishwasher, for which he was paid $3.50.[20] On 13 May 1947, he wrote of his destitution to his friend Harry, who had moved on to Pass Christian, Mississippi:

I am sorry I have not written. I just didn't want you to know how hard up I was. I have exactly 44 cents. My rent is paid up till Saturday. I have sold all the books I had in New York with me and sold everything else I own. For the last 2 weeks I have lived on one meal a day. There seems to be absolutely no hope of a job in the country. I gave that up long ago. I have been turned down by every hash house in New York, Staten Island and Brooklyn. I have a job in Doctor Mahoney's V. D. lab [in the Staten Island Marine hospital]—but it doesn't begin until July 15th—for they

18. Grabstald, interview.
19. Ibid.
20. Humphrey to Grabstald, undated, HG Letters.

have overshot their appropriations for the fiscal year ending that date and can't hire anyone until then. . . .

Wrote my mother—not one cent could she dig up. Sold her car, hocked her silver, fur-coat, everything she owns to support her child [Tommy] while her drunken husband has been out of a job for months. Will go tomorrow to try to sell a pint of blood—doubt they'll take it—I am skin and bones. . . .

Even in 1930 you could get a day's work as a bus-boy. Not now apparently.

I am ready for the East River. So is Dorothy. It seems a pretty good idea. I am not being dramatic, purely pragmatical. (HG Letters)

Then unexpectedly, before Grabstald's check arrived, Humphrey had a job—at the Gotham Book Mart on 51 West Forty-Seventh Street. It paid forty dollars a week, and he was excited as well to be working in the "most famous book-store in the world since 1920—very avant-garde—my kind of literature," he wrote to Grabstald in an undated letter. Now he, Dorothy, and Toni were able to live together, if only in a furnished room "with a sort of kitchenette" at 232 Cumberland Street in the Clinton Hill district of Brooklyn, two doors down from Marianne Moore (HG Letters).

Humphrey was only at the Gotham for three months, a record time for anyone working for Frances Steloff, the founding owner. This was in the summer of 1947. He later claimed that he was the three-thousandth clerk Steloff had had up to that time. In a letter to Katherine Anne Porter, a writer he was soon to begin a long-term relationship with, Humphrey exposed Steloff's deficiencies: she was illiterate but for Yiddish and knew nothing of the actual work of those avant-garde poets and novelists she sold, an assessment that is supported in Mary Dearborn's biography of Henry Miller.[21] She read only "smudgy pamphlets on theosophy," but according to Humphrey she was a shrewd businessman, buying up Shakespeare and Company first editions of *Ulysses* for $1.50 from starving writers and selling them for $500. She was demanding and peculiar. Humphrey persevered in this job as long as he did, not because he managed to get along with the "harpy," as he labeled the owner, but because Dorothy, Toni, and he himself would have been starving otherwise. Eventually, in exasperation, Humphrey threw three 100-watt light bulbs at her feet and walked out.

21. Humphrey to Porter, 5 November 1968, KAP Coll.; Mary V. Dearborn, in *The Happiest Man Alive: A Biography of Henry Miller* (New York: Simon & Schuster, 1991), says that Steloff never finished reading any of Miller's books, but being "a shrewd business woman, . . . knew that banned books sold well" (187–88).

Before this valedictory gesture, however, Humphrey had managed to have some fun at Steloff's expense. When she heard that Cyril Connolly—then literary editor of the *New Statesman,* one of the founders of *Horizon,* and author of the novel *The Rock Pool*—was coming to America "on his postwar literary safari," she planned a party at the Gotham Book Mart to welcome him to New York. Steloff did not know what Connolly looked like, but Humphrey had seen a photograph of him. He was, wrote Humphrey, the ugliest man that "God ever wattled a gut in," giving the appearance of an ape. Meant to arrive about 7:00 P.M., he crept into the shop three hours early. Alarmed by the appearance of this browser, Steloff was convinced that the strange-looking man was intent upon stealing something. "Go back there and pretend to be doing something and keep an eye on that man," she said to Humphrey, instructing him to report to her every five minutes. "What's he doing now?" she would say; Humphrey would reply, "Going through that file of Little Reviews last time I looked." She could stand it no longer, was sure that he had stuffed valuable books into his shabby briefcase, and instructed Humphrey to fetch the police, a request that he complied with, grinning all the while. When he returned with the policeman from the corner, "she was chatting with Mr. Cyril Connolly who had obviously introduced himself to her in my short absence, trying to be affable with him and keep an eye out to forestall me. 'Here's that policeman you sent me for, Miss Steloff,' I announced as loud as I could, and looking very puzzled at her frowns and warnings. She could have killed me," he told Porter. Years later, when he saw Connolly in the streets of Lewes, the Sussex village where he lived, Humphrey was tempted to tell the man how close he had come to being falsely arrested for shoplifting in the Gotham Book Mart.[22]

In the same 13 May letter to Grabstald in which he had lamented his destitution, Humphrey announced that he had mustered the daring to approach W. H. Auden and Randall Jarrell with a story he had written. They were unimpressed by the story itself but recognized that he was talented, and so they encouraged him to continue. Humphrey was ecstatic: "Auden promises he'll have me living off my writing in two years—if I can just manage to stay alive for the next 6 months," he wrote; in his next letter to Grabstald he reported that Jarrell had been equally encouraging and had promised to help him as well.[23] He then looked for a way to eke out a living that would allow time to write.

22. Humphrey to Porter, 5 November 1968, KAP Coll.
23. Yglesias, 65; Humphrey to Grabstald, undated, HG Letters.

2

FIRST STORIES—NORTH AND SOUTH
(The Last Husband and Other Stories)

> I lent some stories to a country lady who lives down the road from me, and
> when she returned them, she said, "Well, them stories just gone and shown
> you how some folks *would* do," and I thought to myself that that was right;
> when you write stories, you have to be content to start exactly
> there—showing how some folks *will* do. . . .
> —FLANNERY O'CONNOR, *Mystery and Manners*

I N AN effort to escape the pinched existence that they had been leading in
New York City during 1946–47, and above all to secure a way to live so that
Bill would have time to write, Bill and Dorothy advertised themselves in the
23 August 1947 issue of the *Saturday Review:* "COUPLE-ARTIST, writer, seek country home, subsistence; exchange part-time services. Experiences: farming, tutor-
ing, librarian, kindergartener." A week later Donald Peterson, who had produced
and directed *The Ave Maria Hour* since 1935 as well as such programs as *The
Land of the Free* for WMCA radio, responded. Peterson had a farm in Brewster,
New York, and commuted by train to the city. He offered Bill and Dorothy a
house (with studio, balcony, bedroom, kitchen, and bath), the use of a jeep, and
twenty-five dollars a month for tending a vegetable patch, feeding and milking
five goats, and taking care of a horse and some chickens. They moved to Peterson's farm during the third week of September 1947. Bill found that he could
earn eight dollars a day for doing additional work.[1]

And work indeed Humphrey did—at the outset, earning as many multiples
of eight dollars as he could stand, "getting up at 6 in the morning, working like
mad and falling dead asleep right after supper" (HG Letters). He planned to cur-
tail the day work as soon as he could in order to make time for reading and
writing; but before he could shift to a daily routine that allowed a mix of physical
labor and literary efforts, pregnancy threatened to destroy all expectations—at
least that is how the couple saw it. When her period was nine days late, Dorothy

---

1. "Personals," *Saturday Review,* 23 August 1947, 38; Ben Gross, "Looking and Listening," *Sunday
News,* 25 June 1950, sec. 2, p. 22; Dorothy Cantine to Harry Grabstald, undated, HG Letters; William
Humphrey to Grabstald, undated, HG Letters.

commenced scalding baths and frequent horseback riding in an effort to shake loose the hitch in her regular cycle. On 4 November 1947 Humphrey wrote an anxious letter to Grabstald, who was then a resident in urology at the United States Marine Hospital in Baltimore, asking where Dorothy might obtain a cheap abortion (HG Letters).

When the one doctor they saw in New York City announced a fee of four hundred dollars, which they could not afford, Humphrey wrote again to Grabstald: "what can we do? Oh God! Could you possibly find anyone trustworthy in Baltimore?" Grabstald responded with the admonition that Bill was being hysterical, that he and Dorothy might think of having the baby and then giving it up for adoption. If Bill were not truly hysterical before, he became so upon receipt of his friend's effort to divert his and Dorothy's intention. Humphrey's next letter begins—not "Dear Harry" but "Harry": "What in the world are you thinking of? . . . I don't want one and Dorothy doesn't want one—but, holy God!—do you think I could give it away? . . . [The abortion has] got to be done—if I have to get out my Cunningham [an anatomy book] and do it myself. . . . Now don't think I'm hysterical. I'm anxious, of course. That seems permissible enough under the circumstances. But you're our only hope. You've got to help us" (HG Letters). Grabstald relented and put his friends in touch with a doctor who would perform the undercover procedure.

On 22 December 1947 Dorothy arrived in Baltimore and spent the night in Grabstald's rooming house at 2828 North Calvert. On the next day she underwent a protracted ordeal, passing "the last piece of stubborn placenta" on the train back to Brewster. "Don't worry about its being incomplete," she wrote afterwards to Grabstald: "I *saw* the evidence—to my horror." Dorothy continued to bleed for days and was bedridden for three weeks, during which time Bill, forgetting altogether about writing stories, ran the house and was "a wonderful devoted and untiring nurse—though a bit panicky," she told Grabstald. As Dorothy gradually became stronger, Bill began to make time to write short stories based upon his experiences on the Peterson farm and on observations made during his stint on Staten Island. The main impediment he faced now was the constant and distracting presence of Toni. What was normal childhood behavior he found to be pathological: "The poor kid is getting horribly neurotic and blabs to her make-believe friends without interruption all day." As the summer of 1948 neared its end, he found great relief in the prospect of Toni's starting school in September: "We're looking forward to the freedom it will give us, I must say." But the child's Christmas holiday brought artistic production to a halt and this complaint: "Toni goes back to school tomorrow after a 12 days vacation during which we, of course, have managed to do no writing or painting."[2]

Keeping Toni in his and Dorothy's custody led Bill to devise an unusual method for submitting stories to journals and magazines. Because they had in effect kidnapped the child, Bill could not divulge their location to editors and risk Dorothy's husband's learning their whereabouts. Therefore Bill mailed his stories to Grabstald, who submitted them on Bill's behalf from Baltimore. The first story Bill finished was "In Sickness and Health," which is "based on a couple I knew during my tenure as assistant librarian at the Merchant Marine Hospital on Staten Island" (Au Int.).[3] His success in getting the story published was anything but immediate: three months after submitting it to *Accent*, he had not heard a word, and the editors of *Partisan Review* and *Sewanee Review*, to whom he had also sent stories, were unresponsive as well. The glum weather reflected the anxious writer's overcast spirit: "What with this depressing rainy weather . . . my thoughts turn rather naturally to unpleasant things and I've been very sad and discouraged lately about not being able to get anything accepted anywhere and having to sit here and not hear anything from any of those damned editors." Four months after his submission to *Accent*, six weeks after a letter inquiring after it, and just as he was about to send a "nasty" letter to Charles Shattuck, one of its editors, Humphrey got a letter accepting "In Sickness and Health."[4] His first published story was to appear in the Winter 1949 issue of *Accent*.

"In Sickness and Health" is a probing portrayal of an unfortunate marriage. One of the promises that a man and a woman make to each other in the solemnization of matrimony is that they will have and hold each other "in sickness, and in health." Humphrey plays upon this traditional vow to produce a domestic horror story. Mr. and Mrs. Emmett Grogan are miserably married, bound together only in the perverse pleasure they take in subverting and contradicting each other. The hearty but profoundly overweight Mrs. Grogan, with a persistent German personality, impresses upon her 121-pound Irish husband that he is indeed sick and in need of her care, which she administers with a vengeance. The third-person narration reflects Mr. Grogan's view of his menacing wife; his defiance in the face of her haughtiness is effectively portrayed, as in the following example that ends with a fine Dickensian exaggeration: "Mr. Grogan lay there

2. Telegram from Dorothy Cantine to Grabstald, 22 December 1947, Dorothy Cantine to Grabstald, undated, and Humphrey to Grabstald, undated, in HG Letters.

3. According to Grabstald, the real-life Grogan was a plumber who worked at the hospital (interview by the author, tape recording, Little Rock, Ark., 23 April 2000).

4. Humphrey to Grabstald, undated, in HG Letters.

with [the thermometer] poked out defiantly at her, making it seem there was so much of her that he had to look first around one side of it, then around the other, to take her all in. She stood over him regally; she did every chance she got. Mrs. Grogan carried her head with great pride of ownership, as though she had shot it in Ceylon and had it mounted on a plaque" (*LH*, 74).

This story reveals more than trivial conflict between longtime mates. There is an undercurrent of intentional cruelty. The humor of this conflict gives way to a fearfulness and a sinister depth as the story progresses, revealing a malady of the spirit more serious than Mr. Grogan's wasting illness. Mrs. Grogan takes far too much delight in putting her husband's sick body on display to her friends and in reporting to them elaborately on the severity of his illness. A dance of contrariness emerges, with more at stake than is at first apparent, when Mr. Grogan undertakes to undermine his wife's assessment of his condition. The details suggest that he is very ill: "Mr. Grogan gave himself a shake to unstick a joint or two, threw the covers back and carefully watched himself get up, afraid of leaving something behind"; when he puts his pants on "he knew how much he had shrunk" (*LH*, 82). But he digs up the energy to "trot briskly by" his wife and an assortment of guests, all of whom she has informed of Mr. Grogan's grave condition; he is off to McLeary's tavern to meet up with his own friends, who have not been primed to expect his imminent demise. Since the narration follows only Mr. Grogan, we are left to wonder at what astonishment and embarrassment must fall to the wife who cannot help but now appear to be a spreader of falsehoods about her husband's physical condition. But, in fact, she has been absolutely correct about Mr. Grogan, as the trip to and from the tavern confirms.

The story's conclusion makes clear the deadly struggle in which they are engaged. Mrs. Grogan is willing to make her husband pay the ultimate price for outraging her in front of her friends earlier in the afternoon. Making his way home, Mr. Grogan moves from apprehension to fear to terror: "Something had him by the throat, no air was getting in, he was turning hot and cold, his joints were rusting fast" (*LH*, 84). Reaching home he confesses to Mrs. Grogan that she was right: he *is* dying. In response she drains her tea and—this is Humphrey's perfect detail, which signifies how little regard she has for her husband—she flicks "a leaf off her tongue." She then assumes a position contrary to her former one, jeering vindictively: "You're well enough to swill with the pigs at McLeary's, you're well enough to bring me up a scuttle of coal from the cellar" (85). As he takes to his deathbed, she begins a concerted campaign to endorse his erstwhile insistence on fitness, being last heard telling Grogan's friend Mr. Duffey that her husband is not at all seriously ill, for "he's just come in from McLeary's where he spent the whole afternoon" (86). She knows that Mr. Duffey will not see him again. The matrimonial pledge is given a chilling ironic twist in this dark, disturbing comedic story.

In a letter (28 September 1950) to Katherine Anne Porter, Humphrey proclaimed of "In Sickness and Health": "I stole my first printed story completely from A Day's Work (as you no doubt know)."[5] He meant this "confession" to be a tribute to the inspiration that her stories had given him, for he continues in the same letter: "I wrote for you. You were the only person whose approval I wanted, and my wife and I asked each other constantly, 'Do you think she will like it?'" (KAP Coll.). Joan Givner, however, accepts literally Humphrey's statement that he stole the story from Porter. Indeed, one could say of Mrs. Grogan (as Porter says of Mrs. Halloran in "A Day's Work") that "she was a woman born to make any man miserable." Like Mr. Grogan, Porter's Mr. Halloran frequents an Irish pub, and both stories end with the husband in bed and the wife talking on the telephone about her husband. There are these and other superficial similarities, but Humphrey's and Porter's stories are vastly different in action: while Humphrey's story focuses relentlessly on the marriage of his couple, Porter's scope takes in politics and social corruption. Porter responded to Humphrey by remarking that "In Sickness and Health" was only "something on the order of A Day's Work"—and that, in any case, the marriage-as-battle theme "is certainly in the public domain, and the human situation was happening any where, to all sorts of persons: why should I have been the only one to write about it?"[6]

The second story that Humphrey managed to get into print was "A Man with a Family," which was at the *Sewanee Review* lying around when "In Sickness and Health" was at *Accent*. It is about Humphrey himself: "That's me, me at the time I was working for Donald Peterson, milking his goats and raising his vegetables, and I kept having so many accidents that I decided there must be story in it; I was so accident prone" (Au Int.). In one of his early undated letters from Brewster, he mentions, for example, that he had "just got over a rib contusion—sustained from the fall of a tree I was chopping" (HG Letters). While "A Man with a Family" was under consideration by the *Sewanee Review*, life seemed intent upon imitating art when Humphrey opened the letter from *Accent* saying that "In Sickness and Health" had been accepted; he started up the steps "yelling for Dorothy, got tangled in [his] bedroom slippers, lost them both, fell down and nearly broke

5. Almon's statement that "A Day's Work" inspired instead "Man with a Family" (64) is mistaken.

6. Joan Givner, *Katherine Anne Porter: A Life* (New York: Simon & Schuster, 1982), 374; *The Collected Stories of Katherine Anne Porter* (New York: Harcourt, Brace & World, 1965), 390; Katherine Anne Porter to Humphrey, 30 September 1950, KAP Coll.

one of [his] fingers"; he and Dorothy spent the rest of the day "laughing and giggling" (HG Letters). In "A Man with a Family," accident-prone Dan grabs a milk pail to take it in the house, "took three steps and a corncob rolled under his foot, twisted his ankle and turned him end up in a puddle of milk. It was so funny they [Dan's wife is named Laura] rolled on the ground laughing" (LH, 126).

This story about Dan—like most of Humphrey's stories—is ultimately no laughing matter. Indeed, Humphrey seems to adhere precisely to Hemingway's dictum that "all stories, if continued far enough, end in death."[7] Transplanting the setting from a New York farm to a cotton-growing one—in his letters to Grabstald he says it is in Texas—he transforms the opening laughter over the husband's clumsiness, following a course of increasingly more serious accidental injuries, into the ineluctable horror of Dan's realization that he is dying after being thrown in front of a mower blade. The humor dissolves into poignancy as he begins to resolve back into nature: "He started poking around in him for the strength to get up, but a wave of pain and sadness bent his will like the wind coming over the grass. . . . He tried to rise. But the grass came up cool and crisp, rustling like a fresh bedsheet, and tucked him in" (LH, 151), a figurative depiction of death that Humphrey was to apply (somewhat altered) forty-three years later in "Buck Fever," where a hunter is "covered with [snow] from top to toe as though while he slept a sheet had been drawn over him" (SS, 177). There is good writing in "A Man with a Family"; Humphrey had struggled mightily to trim it down to its shapeliness. His notebook entry for 13 April 1948 reads: "Heavens— how did I let the Dan story get so away from me—so cluttered up? so inflated beyond it's [sic] proper scope? Too many scenes—they dissipate the steady pro- gression, make it jerky—it bumps along. So much to be cut out" (WH Coll., UT). James Lee judged the finished product to be one of the best of Humphrey's early stories,[8] but it is a story based on the Hardy-like relentlessness of fate's pur- suit, the chief interest being in the striking incidents rather than in the relation- ship between the characters.

After "A Man with a Family" was rejected by the Sewanee Review, Humphrey sent it to Accent, where it was published in the Summer 1949 issue. Determined to get a story into the Sewanee Review because he believed it to be "not only the most beautiful magazine, but the most respected in the entire world," he played the highest card he had yet held—"The Hardys," easily the most engaging of the

7. Ernest Hemingway, Death in the Afternoon (New York: Scribner, 1932), 122.

8. James W. Lee, William Humphrey, Southwest Writers Series, no. 7 (Austin, Tex.: Steck-Vaughn, 1967), 11.

early stories. Sure at first that it would "take that schnickel [John E.] Palmer [editor of the *Sewanee Review*] 6 mos to read and reject it," a month later he was sure that an acceptance would be coming any day; and indeed in his next letter to Grabstald Humphrey announced the story's acceptance.[9] It was published sooner than Palmer had at first led the author to believe—in the April 1949 issue.

"The Hardys" is another story about an old couple living on uneasy terms with each other. But they are unlike the old husband and wife in "In Sickness and Health," who are so single-minded in their mutual distaste that no tender emotions could have tempered their geriatric disquietude. The old couple in "The Hardys" love each other a great deal after fifty years of marriage. But Humphrey's story reveals that even love maintained through decades is insufficient for happiness. The perversity of the human heart can figure out a way to undermine the sure foundation of any love, this unusual little story seems to imply. The title of the story probably reflects Humphrey's interest in Thomas Hardy, whose views on human experience are commensurate with those of the story.

The basis for "The Hardys" is the relationship between Humphrey's maternal grandparents. His grandmother, Cora Moorman Varley (1873–1951), was Edward Varley's (1860–1943) second wife, the first, Ellen J. Parkson (1859–ca. 1894), having died giving birth to a son.[10] In a 1982 interview, Humphrey remarked that his grandfather "was the most doting—doting to the point of being uxorious—husband that I've ever seen. . . . But she lived all her life seething with jealousy of that dead first wife, for no reason whatever. . . . [Y]ou had to be extremely careful in Mama's presence not even to mention that dead first wife. And on graveyard cleaning day . . . she had appointed herself the one to clean that grave; and she gradually allowed the mound to grow higher and higher and higher until you could no longer read the legend on the tombstone" (*WST*, 22).[11] The perverse jealousy theme, then, Humphrey took from real life; he had next to create a dramatic situation that would accentuate the wife's debilitating, pointless jealousy. To this end, he set the story in the house that the couple had lived in for their fifty years of marriage—and on the day before their move from the farmstead and as they are tagging their household goods for auction.

The focus of interest is Clara Hardy, whose heart is "sending out to borrow . . . trouble for itself" (*WST*, 23). But the story is conveyed to the reader through

---

9. Humphrey's letters to Grabstald are undated, HG Letters.

10. *Red River Recollections* (Clarksville, Tex.: Red River County Historical Society, 1986), 373.

11. In *FOFH*, Humphrey says that "Ed Varley . . . had never given his wife cause for a single one of the countless pangs she had suffered over him—which in itself must have caused her the sharpest pang of all, for it suggested to her mind that he had been just as singly attached to that dead first wife of his, who was the woman of whom she was jealous" (136).

two minds—that of both husband and wife. This technique of an alternating point of view, unusual in the stories that would be collected in *The Last Husband and Other Stories*, effectively shows how one person can misperceive the thoughts of another. These ironic juxtapositions of the minds reveal the baselessness of the wife's profound unhappiness.

The story begins from Mr. Hardy's[12] point of view. Two things are immediately established: one is that he is an especially thoughtful husband (a quality of his later confirmed by his wife); the other is that his memory of the first Mrs. Hardy is absolutely no threat to the second. Mr. Hardy's first thought upon awakening is that "today he ought to be especially nice to Clara" (*LH*, 221). Clara awakens, however, possessed of an inordinate fear about what Mr. Hardy might find in the attic of his house—and of his mind. Humphrey offers contrasting photographic images to accentuate Clara's jealousy and verify its unfoundedness. In the story's opening, Mr. Hardy had made an unsuccessful attempt to recollect Virgie: "When he rummaged around in his mind for a picture of her, Mr. Hardy found that Virgie's face and Clara's, like two old tintypes laid face to face in an album, had come off on each other. What would Virgie have come to look like, he wondered, if she had lived? The only way he could picture her was about like Clara looked now" (222). Though Mr. Hardy could find no mental picture of Virgie, Clara digs out an actual old photograph of Virgie and, "gazing at it, spent hours wondering . . . which loved him the most" (228). But, of course, what she is really acutely anxious about is which of them *he* loved the most: "Watching him ponder over a lamp that had been brought out for Virgie all the way from St. Louis, then break off suddenly to come in and pat her head and say a word, she felt she was getting only the crumbs that fell from the table" (230).

The one anecdote that might slightly substantiate Clara's jealousy ironically contradicts it. That recollection is of a delicately beautiful Spanish "mantle" that Mr. Hardy had bought for Clara at a county fair when they were a young married couple: "Of all the moments in her life that had been one of the happiest" (*LH*, 235)—that is, until Mr. Hardy explained its significance:

In the wagon that night riding home, she laid her head on Mr. Hardy's shoulder smelling the good smell of him and listening not so much to his words as to the gentle sound of his voice. He was saying he had known beforehand she would like that shawl. . . . Then he said he never forgot

12. In *FOFH*, Humphrey notes that his maternal grandmother always called her husband "Mr. Varley," explaining: "that usage was common among their generation in that part of the world, and was intended to instill respect for the father in the children" (124).

how crazy Virgie was over the one he had given her just like it. He hadn't seen another one and thought he never would. They buried Virgie in hers, as she asked to be. Smiling, he turned and told her that as if he expected it to make the shawl all the more precious to her. (236)

The "mantle" has a symbolic meaning—perhaps an unconscious one for Mr. Hardy—but it is not unconscious for Humphrey, for a mantle is a robe signifying a person of "exalted and defined station" and one who has assumed an important role in life *(OED)*. Mr. Hardy's providing his second wife with the same mantle worn by the previous wife symbolically signals that the role of wife is now entirely hers. This meaning is missed by Clara, who has nursed an unhappy memory of the incident for almost fifty years.

There is a lasting agony in Clara, an agony compiled from a lifetime of small, foolish sufferings. The powerful conclusion to the story might be humorous if Clara did not really believe in hell. But she surely does, for she has lived in it. At the end of the story, Mr. Hardy innocently remarks, "It takes you back, a day like this," he said, "makes you think. Brings back things you hadn't thought of for years." As he is about to offer an example,

> He looked up and there was Clara, her fingers pressed white against her temples. "Oh, what's the use," she cried, "of thinking over things past and done with?"
>
> She started to say something more, then turned back to her dishes. Mr. Hardy got up and quietly stole off to bed. At the door he scratched his pate and thought to ask which of them was it that was always thinking over things long ago done with, but decided not to.
>
> She had to sit; her backbone was like spools on a string. She rocked her head in her hands and wondered would all this misery never end. She thought of Virgie, safe in Heaven these fifty years, safe in Mr. Hardy's mind, forever young and pretty. Surely, she thought, shuffling a finger across her withered lips, surely when the Lord called you you didn't have to come as you were. What else could Hell be? *(LH, 238–39)*[13]

Something more pernicious than a simple-minded religious belief has led Clara to begrudge her husband a memory he has already lost. "The Hardys" is the earli-

13. In his autobiography Humphrey said of his grandmother Varley: "One metaphysical question that vexed [her] . . . was whether in Heaven she would have to share her husband with that first wife of his" *(FOFH, 125)*.

est instance of one of the most persistent themes in Humphrey's fiction: that perverse attention to a faded past sabotages the present.

The sad irony of this well-focused little *tour de force* was hard won, for Humphrey's notebook shows that he was a hard taskmaster, ruthlessly crossing whole pages of proposals to himself about the direction that the story might take, then, when he began to write, crossing out elaborate elements of the story, scribbling in large characters across the page "HOOEY" and pronouncing himself a "pompous Ass" when he judged the writing inauthentic.[14] When the *Sewanee Review*'s payment of $195 for his hard work arrived, Humphrey was ecstatic: "Some check!! Of course I didn't expect that. I had figured on about 60 dollars. Holy Jesus! Of course, when you think what I put into that thing—it comes to about 15 cents an hour. Still, who's complaining?" (HG Letters).

Humphrey was fairly pleased with his life as a goatherd and handyman on the Peterson farm and with the measure of success that he had gained in getting three stories published and another on the way to being published. "I get a little more satisfaction from my writing now—what little time I have for it—and that helps me keep up my spirits," he wrote to Grabstald. Humphrey's spirits received a special boost when the Macmillan publishing house nibbled at the bait that he had dangled in the notes on contributors in the Winter 1949 *Accent*; there he had announced that he was "working on a novel." There was no novel, however. Humphrey desperately tried to persuade Harry Grabstald that the most basic of preliminaries constituted "working on a novel": "Well, you know I haven't got a novel, but I do have a fairly well-formulated plan for a novel, and a rather large collection of notes. It's not a nebulous thing but one fairly well along. I haven't written any of it and there are *parts* I haven't thought out completely but I have my theme, my main characters, my title ("Commuting Distance") and Dorothy [and I] have spent literally months talking it out."[15] Actually, Humphrey began his "Journal for a Novel Commuting Distance" on 18 June 1948, his twenty-fourth birthday (and we find on 1 July "new beginning—of the novel"). To Macmillan, Humphrey offered to send "a written discussion of my novel" (WH Coll., UT).

In the meantime another publisher, William Morrow, expressed an interest in publishing Humphrey's writing. On 6 May 1949, he went to New York City to have lunch with the Macmillan people and dinner with a woman from Morrow. The Macmillan interview proved disappointing ("The man thought there was plenty of time later to get down to business—meanwhile we should just make

---

14. Humphrey, notebook, entry for 12 May 1948, WH Coll., UT.
15. *Accent* 9, no. 2 (Winter 1949): 66; Humphrey to Grabstald, [1949], HG Letters.

this a social call"). That evening, however, the woman from Morrow "wanted to get down to business right off" because she was "wild about my work and about the outline for . . . 'Commuting Distance' . . . that I had sent her." She wanted ten thousand words on the novel by 1 August, and she was confident, based on the summary Humphrey had given her, that Morrow would offer a five-hundred-dollar advance and one hundred dollars a month while he wrote it.[16]

As Humphrey digested this bit of welcome possibility, one of the editors of *Accent,* Charles Shattuck, who was teaching at nearby Vassar College, set in motion additional happy prospects. Shattuck had come to visit him in Brewster on 18 March 1949. When Humphrey showed him the stories and the notes for a novel that he was working on, Shattuck invited him to give a reading and lecture before students and faculty at Vassar. So impressed was Shattuck by Humphrey's performance that he wrote to Theodore Weiss, chairman of the literature department at Bard College, Annandale-on-Hudson, New York, saying "that if he ever heard of a job teaching creative writing to let [Humphrey] know." Weiss wrote immediately to Humphrey, inviting him for an interview with him and the president of the college. Having no suit for the interview, Humphrey found one on sale that he could afford, a heavy herringbone one—which he wore to Annandale on a hot June day. Although he perspired profusely throughout the grueling two-hour interview with the president, he did hear by 15 July that the job was his. His starting salary was $2,800 for the year. Humphrey expected to teach at Bard for only a year, because he contemplated going ahead and accepting the five-hundred-dollar advance from Morrow and requesting that the monthly stipend not begin until he "set out once again on [his] own."[17] As it turned out, Humphrey would remain at Bard for nearly a decade, and so this particular arrangement with Morrow was later abandoned.

The summer of 1949, then, was Bill and Dorothy's last in Brewster. Before they left, she contacted Holley Cantine, and they signed a separation and custody agreement. The divorce, being handled by Dorothy's brother Seymour, an attorney, was made final. Humphrey's undated letter informing Grabstald stated: "Dorothy is now a divorced woman! You can imagine how that strikes us—after 4 years" (HG Letters).

With the divorce and job to celebrate, Humphrey butchered a goat for a feast, and they left Brewster for Annandale-on-Hudson on 1 September. Donald Pe-

16. Humphrey to Grabstald, [June 1949], HG Letters.

17. Humphrey to Grabstald, [March 1949], HG Letters; Antonia Weidenbacher, interview by author, tape recording, Hudson, N.Y., 22 June 1999; Jean Lambert, journal, 28 October 1984, Lambert Coll.; Humphrey to Grabstald, undated, HG Letters.

terson, who had always been extremely kind to Bill and Dorothy, did everything he could to help them prepare for their move to Annandale. He "lent," i.e., gave, Bill money to buy clothes to teach in and books to prepare from, and then he moved them to Annandale himself.[18] Once he received his first paycheck, Bill felt financially secure for the first time in his life.

Moving put a quietus on writing, and the chances for writing did not improve when the semester began, for Humphrey put in hours a day preparing for classes. He hardly had time to make a quick trip to New York City on 10 October to marry Dorothy in Brooklyn City Hall. Among the courses Humphrey taught at first were basic writing and eighteenth-century prose and soon after courses in the Russian novel, the Italian novel, Dickens, and nineteenth-century American literature. One of his students, Sherman Yellen, now a playwright, remembers him as a scrawny Robert Redford with a great mane of hair and a mischievous twinkle in his eye, peering through his cigarette smoke. Yellen said he had "the sharpest mind and wit going" and was "the best teacher I ever had. . . . He made a kid like me feel smart and mature and capable of doing anything. . . . His influence, for good or ill, made me the person I am today." The outdoor writer and publisher Nick Lyons, who had also been a student of Bill's, recalls that Humphrey often conducted a short-story class as he and his students walked through the lovely Hudson Valley landscape: "I was absolutely stunned by his memory. We would talk about stories by D. H. Lawrence, Faulkner, Hemingway, and Flannery O'Connor, and he could recite long sections of them, show me where the tone modulated, show me where the mystery was, show me just about everything that was going on in the stories almost as if he knew them in their entirety by heart. I have never seen anyone else do that with prose."[19] Humphrey proved ideal for bright, engaged students, but he had no use for dull sluggards. According to Theodore Weiss in a 7 October 1997 letter to the author, Humphrey's relationships with his students were, on the whole, very good. He took them and the work he did with them altogether seriously. A number of them, said Weiss, were "everlastingly grateful and devoted to him and became lasting friends."

One of Humphrey's students during 1949–50 was Joan Williams from Memphis, who was later to become William Faulkner's mistress and to write *The Wintering*, a roman à clef about their relationship and, later still, to become the mistress of Humphrey's last publisher, Seymour Lawrence. She met Faulkner be-

18. Humphrey to Grabstald, undated, HG Letters.

19. Humphrey to Grabstald, August 1949 and undated letter, HG Letters; Sherman Yellen to author, 11 December 1999; Nick Lyons, telephone interview by author, tape recording, 28 July 1999.

tween her junior and senior years at Bard and upon her return told Humphrey that she could arrange for Faulkner to give a reading and meet with Bard students and faculty. Humphrey, who at the time had read only one of Faulkner's stories, declined to sponsor the visit. Williams arranged for Faulkner to read at Bard anyway, and Humphrey did not bother going to hear him. When Williams reminded Humphrey, during a 1994 visit to Hudson, of his dismissal of Faulkner, he regretted his foolishness.[20]

Humphrey had the company of some distinguished colleagues during his nine years on the Bard faculty, among them F. W. Dupee, Ralph Ellison, Anthony Hecht, Saul Bellow, Dwight MacDonald, and Theodore Weiss, with whom Humphrey became lasting friends (*A Time and a Place* is dedicated to Weiss). Bill was chairman of the literature department during the year that Saul Bellow, between novels, taught at Bard. Humphrey might have brought Bellow together with the real-life character who was to become Henderson the Rain King: Chandler Chapman, a new friend of Humphrey's. Bellow allowed in a recent interview that Bill "may have taken me out to the house of Chandler's I rented and tried to live in." Bellow went on to say that, although Humphrey made him very welcome, the two writers did not become friends: "he and I were very different types, and there wasn't much I could do to change that. He was an outdoor man, and I was not. He was a hunter, and I took no interest in hunting. He had guns all over the place, and I didn't know how to pull a trigger." Humphrey actually preferred the company of the college's groundskeeper to that of many of his colleagues on the faculty. The groundskeeper, a man named Dick Bard, was a hunter, a fisherman, and a gunsmith. Bill would escape the irritations of campus life to sip Southern Comfort and talk for hours at a time with Dick in his gun shop in the woods of Milan, just a few miles from Annandale. In season they would hunt—mostly geese and deer.[21] In Humphrey's second year at the college, Andrews Wanning—a type of outdoorsman, for he was a sailor—joined the literature department; he and Humphrey became lasting friends.

Humphrey's relationships with his colleagues on the faculty in general were not as good as they were with his students. Bard was in financial crisis, and the entire faculty were on edge wondering, year after year, if the doors would open the next fall. Humphrey admitted that he "stepped on every corn in sight, because I'm just made that way" (AF). During faculty meetings "Bill at times ex-

20. Joan Williams to author, 14 September 1999. Humphrey also expressed the same regret in a letter to Norah Smallwood, 18 October 1972, C&W.

21. Saul Bellow, telephone interview by author, tape recording, 22 March 2000; Helen Bard, interview by author, tape recording, 29 August 2001, Milan, N.Y.

pressed himself on the issues with a fervor I found troubling," Weiss said: "his strong stands left little room for compromise or even negotiation." Because Humphrey had no academic degree, he felt a strong need to justify his post through publication. Thus he was particularly sensitive to any criticism of his writing, and this caused problems with his colleagues. He had quickly become friends with Irma Brandeis, who was generally admiring of Bill, but she made the mistake of questioning some aspect of one of his stories, and to her astonishment she was immediately stricken off the Humphrey list of friends. Although he was not always on good terms with his colleagues, he nonetheless worked hard on the committees that he was appointed to—even though he hated that kind of life-wasting work.[22]

Though claiming no interest in Faulkner at this time, Humphrey was very much taken with the fiction of Katherine Anne Porter, and he arranged for her to visit the campus and speak informally to the English students at the beginning of his second year. Randall Jarrell had recommended that he read her, and he had once bought a secondhand copy of *Flowering Judas and Other Stories* with his penultimate dollar. While living at Brewster, Humphrey had urged Grabstald to send him a copy of Porter's *Pale Horse, Pale Rider.* "That good simple direct prose opened up a whole world to me," he said. In an early letter to her, he wrote: "Reading you was my great revelation; I knew then what I wanted to do. You were my one teacher." Porter also gave him confidence to overcome what he took to be the stigma of being from Texas: "your being from Texas was very important for me: it had always seemed to me that a *writer* had to be from England, or France, possibly from New England, but I thought that being from Texas ruined my hopes. You were a blessing to me." Porter also helped Humphrey by critiquing his stories and offering to assist him in finding publishers. Though she meant well, Porter did not always provide her young protégé with appropriate advice. In one instance she misunderstood what motivated his mania for revision. Regarding his extensive revising of "Report Cards," one of the stories eventually appearing in *The Last Husband and Other Stories,* she admonished: "I am shocked beyond words to know that you have re-written your story every time it was refused" (Humphrey had written to her on 10 October 1950, in his typically hyperbolic mode, that the story had been turned down by nearly every magazine in the country [KAP Coll.]). Porter assumed that he was merely trying "to meet the demands of some editor who has a special kind of public . . . and wants something written to order for it." Humphrey responded immediately to disabuse Porter of her misunderstanding of his aims and methods, pointing

22. Theodore Weiss to author, 7 October 1997.

out that he was not editorially astute enough to know what any individual editor wants and further that he was inclined to "sin in the direction of refusing to take any constructive suggestions for my work, being the most bull-headed person I know, so much so that when I've been contemplating a certain change in one of my stories I refuse to make it for the longest time if someone else suggests it." He then paid her his supreme compliment: "Myself, my wife, and you are the only three people in the world I will listen to for criticism."[23]

Humphrey tried relentlessly and unsuccessfully to find a magazine that would take "Report Cards," meanwhile revising the story repeatedly, working harder on perfecting that recipe than the rather ordinary ingredients warranted. Turned down by *Atlantic Monthly, Harper's Magazine, Harper's Bazaar,* and *Mademoiselle,* the story was never published outside the company of the more distinguished stories that comprise *The Last Husband.*[24]

In his first year at Bard, it was not until the long break between semesters that Humphrey found time to write again. At this time he turned to a story that he had half finished before the move from Brewster—"The Fauve," which he had in mind from its start to send to the *Sewanee Review:* "it's as good as 'The Hardys,' and in fact better," he told Grabstald.[25] The story was not published in the *Sewanee Review* until July 1951. Like the first three stories he had published, "The Fauve" presents a marital relationship, although its concerns are broader. It focuses on a social misfit with an uncontrollable knack for offending everyone—everyone except his wife, who possesses a peculiar immunity to his irksomeness: she is protected by a mixture of devoted love and obtuseness. The cause of James Ruggles's disagreeableness is his sad perception that the other painters in the Redmond artists' colony to which he belongs possess no artistic integrity, produce a vulgar art that panders to popular taste, and thereby achieve tremendous worldly success (they wear fine clothes, live in attractive houses, and drive new Buicks). Ruggles, considering himself the only true artist in town, resents his obscurity and his poverty (he wears the same suit he came to town in twenty years ago, lives in an only slightly converted chicken house, and walks in a worn-out pair of shoes).

Humphrey had finished "The Fauve" by the beginning of his second year at Bard. The title "The Fauve" applies to Ruggles in two senses, both seemingly

23. Humphrey to Porter, 20 September 1950, KAP Coll.; Jose Yglesias, "William Humphrey," ed. Sybil Steinberg, *Publishers Weekly,* 2 June 1989, 65; Humphrey to Grabstald, undated, in HG Letters; Humphrey to Porter, 28 September 1950, KAP Coll.; Porter to Humphrey, 6 January 1951, KAP Coll.

24. Humphrey to Theodore and Renée Weiss, [1953], Weiss Coll.

25. Humphrey to Grabstald, undated, HG Letters.

ironical. He likes to think of himself as a wild beast, as one who stands outside the conventional attitudes and behavior of normal society, yet he desires the benefits of conventional behavior. "Fauve" also denotes a disciple of Matisse, although no one in the story perceives Ruggles as such. His *Still Life with Pineapple,* which he thinks is "epoch-making," has been "rejected by every major exhibition in the country," while his contemporaries are winning prizes at exhibitions and finding recognition in major museums (*LH,* 179). Is James Ruggles truly the one great artist among a colony of mere pretenders, or is he no better than they but afflicted with *bovarysme?* However we answer this question, another remains: How do we explain the sad piece of humanity that Ruggles has become, abusing his wife and offending his fellow artists? The crux of this story's mystery—and the marriage that it focuses upon—is a question of authenticity.

The tone of the story becomes crucial in answering these questions. Is the narration sadly humorous? Perhaps, if James is a great artist. But if James merely thinks too well of his abilities and is really without talent and artistic integrity, then the story is satire. "The Fauve" is ambiguous in its tone and ultimate intent; one can follow the clues presented by the objective third-person narrator and reasonably settle on either side of the issue, or even remain frustratingly between the two.

The truth is that Humphrey meant the story one way, but it has been understood in quite another. Sometime between 1 and 7 October 1950, before he actually met Katherine Anne Porter, Humphrey had sent her the manuscript of "The Fauve," apparently when he was making final revisions for the story's publication in the *Sewanee Review,* requesting her comments and criticisms prior to a dinner during which they planned to discuss the story. Her immediate response was acute: "I venture to say this now and please tell me if I am wrong: that you have begun from real people and a real situation . . . and have not yet cut yourself away from what you *know* enough to let your imagination range freely in re-creating them."[26] Porter was correct. The character of James Ruggles is in fact based upon a real man. Humphrey explained in a recent interview:

His name was John Nichols. He was a person that I met just once, long enough to have a cup of coffee with in a little restaurant in Woodstock, New York. Dorothy had known him *very* well and for a good many years. She regales me with stories about his outrageousness. But also the story is about his work as a painter. He was a very good one. In fact, I'm looking right now in this room where I'm sitting at a picture of his on my wall

26. Porter to Humphrey, 8 October 1950, KAP Coll.

[unnamed, it depicts a seated nude]. A very fine picture it is, too. I'm proud of owning it. He was somebody who figured very much in Dorothy's early life when she had gone up to Woodstock as a young artist on the WPA artists' project. He was the one artist in the town, indeed outcast of the town, whose work she could admire. The rest of them are just what I describe in the story—fuzzy, soft-focused stuff. His was bold and daring and in touch with European tradition. The others were just sort of Hudson Valley School and in many cases [their paintings were] just calendar art. But John was a good bit more than that. He's dead, by the way, and though I made a kind of comedy out of him when I wrote, his life was a tragic one. He had a son commit suicide, and then nearly all of his pictures were burned up in a storage place where he had put them, destroying all his life's work. (Au Int.)

Although Humphrey would probably have denied it, both in character and in some details Humphrey is himself James Ruggles. First of all, Bill had the capacity, not infrequently drawn upon, to be as obnoxious as Ruggles, and Humphrey (remember that he was a painter for several years) was at the time that he wrote this story a devoted writer who had met with scant worldly success, and he was married to an artist who was a Brooklyn-born Jew (like Rachel). Until very recently their financial straits meant that they scrimped on a daily basis. Their one-room kitchenette in Brooklyn had not been superior to the converted chicken house of the Ruggles, and Humphrey's "wardrobe" resembled Ruggles's almost precisely. When we first encounter Ruggles in "The Fauve," his clothes are worn out: his "ancient" jacket "seemed to have sprouted a mold. The sleeves came down no further because they had grown frayed and been turned back more than once" (LH, 175). His faded trousers are too short for the same reason. When Humphrey dressed Ruggles, he must have recalled his own unaccommodated condition when he wrote the following request to Harry Grabstald: "Do you have any civilian clothes to spare? The old blue suit of yours has fallen completely to pieces after being worn night and day for the last three months. . . . [T]he old blue suit of mine is much too small." Furthermore, Humphrey and Ruggles share an admiration for Matisse. Ruggles is "the fauve" of the title, the follower of Matisse—at least that is how he sees himself. At the Redmond artists' colony Ruggles "entered upon his Modified Fauve period" (LH, 179). After Humphrey had given up painting, he waxed ecstatic over a Matisse exhibit in 1966, a show that revealed Matisse to be a greater master than most previous American shows had suggested because it emphasized the "Fauve period portraits" and "those beautiful Nice odalisques, portraits, interiors and still-lifes of 1918–29."[27]

Ruggles is not the only character in the story drawn from life: Homer, a misfit friend of the Ruggles, is a "spotted portrait of my wife's first husband"; according to Humphrey, "he [Holley Cantine] was a bore; [John Nichols] put up with him because the two of them were the town outcasts" (Au Int.). Moreover, according to Humphrey's notebook entry for 29 July 1948, Nichols's wife Leila did in fact win a prize for painting, which greatly distressed her husband. Other elements of the story's plot are only slightly disguised real-life events: for instance, "John's decision to . . . attend a class reunion at Amherst to interest all his old buddies in his painting" (WH Coll., UT) parallels Ruggles's similar decision to attend a reunion at Bowdoin in the story.

Porter's initial response to "The Fauve" goes directly to its unintentional ambiguity and suggests why it might easily be misunderstood. Though Ruggles is based upon a real man who was a bold and accomplished painter, Humphrey does not unequivocally make his corresponding fictional character bold and accomplished. He makes it clear that Ruggles *thinks* he is, but it is impossible to portray a painting in a short story so that the reader can judge it. It seems, too, that Humphrey faced the same problem that the painter does in Henry James's "The Real Thing." James's narrator fails in depicting the Monarchs (who are "the real thing") because there is no latitude for his imagination: "When I drew the Monarchs I couldn't, somehow, get away from them—get into the character I wanted to represent."[28] Indeed the limitations put on "The Fauve" by the facts of John Nichols's life are a small instance of the big problem we shall see in chapter 8: the burden of historical fact in *No Resting Place*.

When Humphrey and his wife were Porter's dinner guests on 13 October 1950, Porter was astonished to discover that Humphrey's intention in "The Fauve" was altogether at variance from her own reading of it. To William Goyen, another Texas writer (*The House of Breath* [1975] and *Arcadio* [1983]), who was invited for drinks before dinner, Porter confided the following account of her conversation with Humphrey:

> To my dismay, I had completely misunderstood the intention of . . . the story. . . . Reading it twice, I took it for granted as a story about a third-

27. Humphrey to Grabstald, undated, HG Letters; to Leonard Woolf and Ian and Trekkie Parsons, 12 June 1966, Woolf Coll.

28. Christof Wegelin, ed., *Tales of Henry James: The Texts of the Stories, the Author on His Craft, Background, and Criticism* (New York: Norton, 1984), 253.

rate painter with a bad case of megalomania, a natural born cad and boor. . . . The filthy nuisance he proceeds to make of himself before God and everybody was, I thought, a remarkably fine job of satire.

Oh, Lord, how wrong I was! It was meant to be the story of an unappreciated genius among slick successful artists.[29]

Yet "The Fauve" contains clues that recommend a reading in line with Humphrey's intent and sympathetic to Ruggles. The story opens on a light and comic note. The account of his wife Rachel's shopping expedition—filled with delusions of lamb chops and artichokes when her light purse can only underwrite, as usual, the makings of "lung stew"—is delightful, as is James's teasing of Rachel in their first scene together (*LH*, 169). In subtle ways Humphrey suggests Ruggles's superiority as an artist. The narrator draws a connection between the landmarks of Redmond—the Putnum Tavern, the Inn—and the work of the local artists, taken as a lump: "Soon, thought Rachel, all the old landmarks would be known only in pictures. In the early days there had been so many things in Redmond to paint. That was why it had been chosen as a colony. One of the most popular subjects was the Inn. James was perhaps the only painter in town who had never done a picture of it. Among the artists the saying was, you can always sell a picture of the Inn. Rachel herself had painted it many times" (172). Every painter in the colony is painting trite subjects, those that "you can always sell"—all except James. James's contemporaries achieve renown and the kind of success that allows them to wear suits marked by "soft, dark flannel, glowing brown with a tasteful light stripe," but we are told that they do not really respect each other's art: "More than one was resentful that to those close to him he was not as legendary as he had become to the world at large" (181, 182). In fact, the only painter in the story mentioned as being appreciated by any of the others is Ruggles: "David Peterson had always admired James Ruggles' painting" (186).[30]

Ruggles's steadfast devotion to art is pointedly contrasted with the attitude of an erstwhile Redmond artist, Muriel Johnson, once an arty type: "eyes puffy and ringed, hair blowzy," which was "meant to show that she was too taken up with her art to bother" (*LH*, 203). Muriel, now the wife of a wealthy wholesale grocer, has returned for a visit. At a party the Ruggleses give, "she was greatly amused at the distance she had come. It seemed to astound her afresh each moment that people still lived like this, still took seriously the things these people did" (203).

29. Porter to William Goyen, 19 October 1950, KAP Coll.

30. Humphrey gives to this colleague of Ruggles the last name of Humphrey's benefactor in Brewster, Donald Peterson.

Muriel, who once feigned concern for art, in her worldly success is astonished at Ruggles.

In the design of the story, Rachel functions as a parallel to Muriel and as a foil to James. Prior to winning a five-hundred-dollar prize, Rachel seems a true artist; she performs the traditional role of artist, which is the transformation of base reality into the ordered and the beautiful. Rachel's talent converts a decaying chicken house into a work of art: "nothing seemed cramped or incongruous or makeshift. One was struck by the repose of the room, the balance of light and dark, the pleasing arrangement of rich colors. Light from the windows was directed to fall upon old-looking, rare-looking things. Softly glowing, suggestive objects rested in the shadow of the corners. It was like stepping inside a Vermeer" (*LH*, 190). Although the title of her winning painting, *Mother and Child*, suggests a less-than-original artist, the main point is that money corrupts her taste, which becomes clear when James "shows off" what he calls their new "prize money bedroom suite!"—a visual cliché: "The little room looked positively embarrassed. In it stood a huge highboy, a vanity with an oval mirror tinted blue, a padded vanity seat covered with glossy satin and a bed with a gleaming headboard, covered with a bright blue chenille spread" (207). James identifies the headboard as "pine with a coat of maple syrup" (208). The objective narrator, in support of James's attitude, observes that "Rachel thought it was beautiful," explaining: "Rachel had taste only so long as she had no money. When her resourcefulness was demanded, when she had to make shift, she made beauty" (207, 208).

"The Fauve" concludes with James preparing to put his own integrity to the test of worldly success. Rachel has bought him a fine suit of clothes and got him a haircut with the rest of her prize money. Now James, possessing the trim appearance of success, prepares to attend his Bowdoin College class reunion with the sure and certain hope of selling a raft of his paintings to the successful tycoons and corporation heads that he expects to fraternize with: "I can ask any price from men like those" (*LH*, 211). Whether he ventures on to lose his soul as an artist is beyond the perimeter of Humphrey's story.

Humphrey sought to make the story "humorous mostly, but with very bitter and big implications," explaining, in his 29 July 1948 notebook entry, the challenging concept of buffoonery upon which he based his characterization of Ruggles: "A buffoon is one who knowingly makes a fool of himself in the effort at once to make light of his sufferings and to feel them more powerfully." In the notebook entry for 2 February 1949, he compared Ruggles to Christopher Isherwood's heroine Sally Bowles, an eccentric and iconoclastic singer in the novella *Sally Bowles* and in the collection of stories entitled *Goodbye to Berlin* (1939): "John's story has got to be comical. Comical in the way say Sally Bowles is" (WH

Coll., UT). Three years after their misunderstanding about the story and after the publication of the book of stories that included "The Fauve," Humphrey, on 21 October 1953, received a letter of vindication from Porter: "you really did pull off that story of the Fauve, which I had misunderstood so thoroughly, so that it was perfectly clear at last even to me!" (KAP Coll.). Whether Porter's change of mind is owing to her generosity or to Humphrey's revisions is unknown.

Writing and revising stories for his first collection and meeting the demands of teaching (which occupation Humphrey had decided to stick with for the foreseeable future) left Humphrey with insufficient imaginative fuel for carrying on with the novel for Morrow. Instead, he found a substantial short story embedded in "Commuting Distance." So he extracted it and let the novel die. The twenty-page "outline" indicates that he had meant in "Commuting Distance" to portray the convergence of the "station-wagon set" (professionals who commute to New York City) and the simple farm folk who have lived in and around the town of Cressett for generations, with the result that each group takes on characteristics of the other. In the outline, an account executive, Andrews Scott,[31] has a cold wife who does not love him, and like other commuters who "are liable to be unusually dissatisfied with the emptiness of their lives," he seeks to find something fundamental in life by embracing farm life. He builds a barn, acquires a herd of goats, and gets up at five in the morning to milk them before traveling by train to the city. Andrews's return to the land is also an attempt "to find some inviolably *male* endeavor, to establish and prove his virility," which he has been trying and failing to do through philandering. The subplot moves in the opposite direction: Henry Toby, the son of simple farm people, feels totally inadequate as a man until he marries, goes into advertising, and becomes a commuter.[32]

From this rather complex outline, Humphrey drew cohesive elements and developed them into the remarkable title story for his first volume of stories, "The Last Husband." He took the just-married Henry Toby from the proposed novel, changed his name to Charley, and placed him in Cressett, a community of mainly advertising artists, a world that Dorothy no doubt gave Bill insights into when two years earlier she had a short-term contract to do commercial art for the second largest advertising agency in New York.[33] Charley, the narrator, begins the story as he steps into the passenger coach on his first day as a rail commuter; he remarks: "The coach was empty when we came in and each man and woman

31. Perhaps Humphrey took this name from his new colleague Andrews Wanning.
32. "Outline of *Commuting Distance*," esp. pp. 15, 18, WH Coll., UT.
33. Humphrey to Grabstald, undated, HG Letters.

took a seat to himself, like a herd of milch cows trained to go to their separate stalls" (*LH*, 11). This quaint rural analogy (left over from the farming background of Henry Toby) effectively suggests the rote lives of the ultimately alienated, those somnolent beings no longer capable of an authentic life. "The Last Husband" is an intensive examination of a man that Charley meets on the train, a man who wages a valiant campaign to achieve authenticity in a hopeless setting. The story is remarkable for the intricate ironies binding together lives that show the unfulfilled quest for meaning.

The initial irony emerges from the ambiguities of the title. The epithet "the last husband" at first applies to the narrator Charley, who has most recently married. Not only is Charley the last in the story to become a husband, but he seems to be the last—we soon observe—to be a husband in a traditional marriage, one in which the man goes to work and the wife stays at home. On his first day as a commuter, he notes, "I was the only man whose wife kissed him, and I waited with Janice to be the last on the train. Then I saw why no other man got a kiss— nearly all their women got on the train with them; they were going to work, too" (*LH*, 9). Charley will soon learn that there are other reasons that a husband and wife would not kiss good-bye.

Charley is a "young man" full of great expectations about his marriage and his work. The disillusionment begins as he observes, in the commuter car, the ranks of advertising artists that he has joined, a "double row of grumpy, unrested faces" and others obscured by newspapers; his disappointment devolves into deflation as he gets to know them better at the tea parties that he soon begins to attend regularly (*LH*, 10). Charley at first appears not to belong to this assortment of the living dead: "from the start I felt myself obscurely unsuited to that crowd. This seemed unnatural, for they were the people with whom I ought to have felt most in sympathy, so I kept going in an effort to overcome it, or at least to determine whose fault it was, theirs or mine. And finally I went back because Alice [the hostess] was so importunate" (28). In the beginning, Charley fails to perceive fully the empty lives of these people or his collusion with them. This failure leads to his shedding his distinction as last real husband, for he repeatedly attends tea parties without his wife and visits unauthentic people of whom he purports to disapprove. In the end his wife Janice takes a job, and Charley begins to put in overtime at night. He gradually becomes what he initially disdained. He turns out to be no real husband at all.

There *is* a last husband, however—that last of the real husbands, a man whom Charley encounters on the train populated mainly by the living dead: he is Edward Gavin,[34] a man whose actions for a long time absolutely confound Charley.

34. Humphrey appropriates the name of his childhood acquaintance Gavin Watson.

Gavin is one of Humphrey's most intriguing central characters. He is not one of the cows sliding mindlessly into its appointed stall; rather, he is a man who fights the death of the spirit with every ounce of imaginative power he can muster. He fights passionately for his dream of the perfect marriage, a good soldier to the end, whose compromise and final defeat challenge the spectral forces, legal and conventional, that overwhelm his efforts.

Aside from the character of Gavin, what distinguishes this story is the limited narrator device Humphrey employs. Charley as narrator of Edward Gavin's story is reminiscent in some respects of the innocent Dowell, the narrator of Ford Madox Ford's *The Good Soldier,* for Charley tells a story full of imperfectly seen images that sharpen and fade according to his faulty perceptions. Charley as narrator cannot maintain an altogether steady understanding of a man who makes such extraordinary demands of life. Though there is much that Charley misses, Humphrey covertly manipulates the narrator so effectively that we come to know Gavin and Charley as subject and observer. This technique makes for a complex and rich reading experience. "The Last Husband" is a story that the reader comes eventually to realize the full sadness of, even though its narrator does not.

Charley is slow to probe the depth of Gavin's struggle to gain an authentic life. For example, when he learns that Gavin conducts extramarital affairs and makes not the slightest effort to hide them from his wife Alice, Charley at first believes that Alice only pretends not to care about her husband's philandering and wonders if "her vanity should not have been at least a little wounded by her husband's escapades"; then comes the true perception "that she was just as happy to have Edward busy himself . . . elsewhere" (*LH,* 22). (Alice is the spiritual sister of Eunice Renshaw, who in *Proud Flesh* will not care about the unfaithfulness of her husband.) At first Charley believes Gavin's effort to transform his life is just a pretense, like putting on a smile that alters his appearance: "his smile performed the most amazing transformation on his face, as when a photographic print lies in the developer and the washed-out features of a face suddenly collect themselves into life" (*LH,* 12). The reader, however, understands before Charley does that Gavin means to change more than his face: he means to transform a passionless existence into a passionate life.

Humphrey provides a foil for Gavin to help the reader see what Charley is incapable of fully understanding. Gavin's foil is Robert Hines, the husband of Victoria Metsys (she uses her maiden name), who has "allowed himself to be made over into a kind of decorative, thoroughbred-looking hearth dog" (*LH,* 55). Victoria keeps this acquiescent little man around as an object upon which to exercise her natural proclivity to demean others. She abuses him with gusto and delights in explaining to company that his failure at music, sculpture, playwriting, anthropology, and everything else is owing to "Robert's weakness[,] . . . a lack of persistence" (33). Robert's acceptance of failure as a man and as a husband serves to emphasize Gavin's opposite insistence that marriage be a man's way of fulfilling his life. (The one exception to Robert's lack of resolve is the persistence with which he has hated Gavin for twenty years—because of the enormous difference between them.)

Although generally bewildered by Gavin's unusual and imaginative strategies to prime his wife's cold heart, Charley manages moments of insight. For example,

> I realized that Gavin had never been trying to conceal his philanderings from Alice, but to make her take notice of them. . . .
>
> I saw him suddenly as a kind of inverted sentimentalist, a believer in marriage—the old-fashioned kind—a man with pride enough left to care if his wife ignored him. He was out of place and out of time, with a pride not to be bent and pacified by the memory of one glamorous, martial, male moment of escape from his routine of meaningless work which any other man could do as well as he and any woman as well as any man, nor in finding something—like gardening—which he could do and his wife couldn't. He took entirely too much pleasure in the mere fact of being unfaithful to his wife, though, who knows, I asked myself, but what in perverse times like ours, perhaps the only way left to honor a thing is in the breach rather than in the observance. (*LH*, 40)

Though Charley sees this much, the reader can conclude even more. A discussion of gardening among the husbands at one of Alice's tea parties clarifies Gavin's predicament. The discussion involves artificial (chemical) versus natural fertilizers. When one of the husbands says, "What chemical fertilizer did to a tomato was blow it up, force it. But the food value was nil," we have an implied commentary on Gavin's artificial efforts to stimulate the growth of love in Alice (37).

Gavin himself eventually comes to realize that his rather perverse efforts to honor his marriage to Alice, like those to inflate the tomato, can only fail. He then opts for a more authentic approach: he finds a woman who proves to be as devoted to him as he is to her and as willing as he to create an ideal marriage with all the trappings—except in the legal sense. When Edward invites Charley "home" to meet his ideal "wife"—Katherine is her name—she comes out to the car to greet Edward in her calico dress and frilly apron. She participates in every way in Gavin's "dream of domesticity" (*LH*, 51). The pretend marriage is more real than the actual one.

Humphrey gives the complex narration of this story further ironic dimensions. While Charley as narrator is tracking Gavin's domestic bliss, he himself belongs to a marriage that has disintegrated. Charley's disillusionment with his marriage is revealed primarily in the tone of his narration. His voice assumes a superiority when he makes fun of the "ultra middle-class respectability" that Gavin has created out of his "life of sin" (*LH*, 50). Gavin's dream relationship— this perfect love, which includes an affectionate little daughter—is judged by the now sophisticated and spiritually jaded Charley to be sentimental rubbish:

> They treated me . . . to all the traditional foolery which newlyweds feel called upon to amuse older people with. There was a little skit in which he burlesqued his own easy householder air, one in which she demonstrated her wifely interest in his business day and her inability to understand the devious workings of the masculine world; then he tried to fix the iron which he must do if he were to have a clean shirt for tomorrow, and there was, of course, his disastrous attempt, in the costume of her apron, to mix the salad dressing.
>
> While she prepared the dinner and he and I sat in the living room, he tried not to let me see how completely she absorbed him, tried to pay some attention to what I said, would engage me in earnest talk—only to break off and dash into the kitchen to get down from the shelf something for which she had only just begun to reach. (51)

The reader comes to experience Charley's contempt exquisitely: it replaces the very happiness that Charley has lost through neglect and single-minded devotion to his work during the course of his narrative. Gavin becomes the happily "married" man (the last husband) that Charley no longer is. The visit to Gavin's love nest is the story's climax; only now is it altogether clear why Humphrey chose to present Gavin, his exuberant, larger-than-life, Henderson-the-Rain-King sort of embracer of life, through the eyes of a deadened commuter. Charley's cynical observation allows Gavin's passion to emerge all the more convincingly, for when Charley reports the actual happiness on Gavin's face we are compelled to believe in it.

The story concludes with an array of ironical twists. Gavin's "climacteric," the truly critical stage in his life, ominously awaits him when he tries to legitimate his new happiness by asking Alice for a divorce so that he can marry Katherine. The crushing irony of Gavin's life is that when he is ready to cash in on his wife's disregard, she refuses him freedom; for Alice has experienced her own "climacteric," having faced the fact of failure in her profession, and she suddenly feels grown old. Life is a sad disappointment for her, and she finds some consolation in forcing Edward to share in that disappointment: "Alice was determined that for every lash she felt she would make Edward feel two. He had something now that he really wanted, something through which she could hurt him" (*LH,* 54–55). Despite Alice's legal hold on him, Gavin means to preserve his double life as long as possible, though he is resigned to eventually losing the woman he loves: "What he had found at last seemed to him from the start too good to last and he is convinced that to move would merely postpone the inevitable end of a happiness which is more than he deserves" (56). With this disillusionment, the story ends. But even in his defeat, Gavin is a monumental character; he overflows with loving-kindness because of the love he has found, and so he "has softened a great deal towards Alice. No doubt this is partly tactical but mostly it is genuine. He knows now how much she missed in life and he is tender with her" (55).

Several of the fictional personages in "The Last Husband" are based upon actual people that Humphrey knew well at Brewster. Edward Gavin is a fictionalized version of Donald Peterson, who had given Bill and Dorothy employment working his farm. Peterson was a skirt chaser but a man of enormous kindness (Au Int.). Peterson's sister-in-law, Ilonka Karasz, the model for Victoria Metsys, designed many covers for the *New Yorker* from the 1930s through the 1970s and lived just up the road from the Humphreys and the Petersons. Her husband, Wim Nyland, was the model for Robert Hines, Victoria's husband. Even so, Humphrey grafted a detail from Peterson's life onto Nyland when he depicts Nyland as repeatedly playing the only music he knew, thirty measures of Bach's *The Well-Tempered Clavichord,* whenever the dog barks signaling a guest. Peterson had done the very same thing when Humphrey escorted Harry Grabstald to Peterson's front door in 1947.[35]

When Ilonka advertised for a typist in the local newspaper, Humphrey answered the advertisement and was installed in the Nylands' house for an extended period in 1948. He typed the first installment of Georges Ivanovitch Gurdjieff's *All and Everything,* which contains "Beelzebub's Tales to His Grandson," published in 1950 by Dutton.[36] While typing the Gurdjieff manuscript, which Humphrey considered insidious rubbish, he observed the sad treatment given the Nyland children. Thus another early story, "Sister," originally appear-

35. Grabstald interview, 25 April 2000.
36. Gurdjieff (1877–1949) was a Russian-born Greek American New Age cult leader who had many followers among artists and intellectuals in the United States and England, among them Katherine Mansfield. In 1922 he established the Institute for the Harmonious Development of Man at the Prienne d'Avon, in Fontainbleau.

ing in *Harper's Bazaar* (May 1950)—and for which he was paid $350—is based on what he observed about the lives of these children. Humphrey contemplated kidnapping the children—as a means of rescuing them from the mistreatment they endured (Au Int.). In "Sister" he makes the brother, whom he calls Edmond, the darling of his parents, especially the favorite of his mother, who calls him "dear" and "Sweet" and hugs him frequently. Sister's presence generally goes unnoticed. But the parents do penance for neglecting the girl by allowing her to keep nineteen cats, which urinate in hard-to-clean places, stinking up the house. The cats apparently serve as an extension of herself, enhancing her presence in the family. At a deeper psychological level they represent her protest against her mistreatment, even as they give her the affection and sense of importance that she naturally desires.

Because Bill and Dorothy were legally married now and Toni legally in their care, the elaborate scheme whereby Bill posted his stories to Grabstald who then sent them on to journals for publication was abandoned. As a result, we have almost no record of when Humphrey wrote the remainder of the stories that would appear in *The Last Husband and Other Stories*. It is safe to say that "The Shell," "Quail for Mr. Forester," and "A Fresh Snow" were the final three that Humphrey wrote because they represent a maturing of style and mastery of his material.

"The Shell" and "Quail for Mr. Forester," rather than being based in the author's recent experience or recent observation, reach back to Humphrey's growing up in Clarksville for their inspiration. "The Shell," which was not published prior to the collection of stories, contains the best lyric passages in the volume. Humphrey achieves in its style the grace that he had clumsily promised to Grabstald in an early letter: "I am constantly working toward a purification of my style. Eventually I want a style which will be more convoluted, long flowing sentences, but I feel that I won't really know how to do that properly until I am able to write simply. It is like modern painting in which the artist does not feel able to progress to abstraction until he has mastered realistic painting" (HG Letters).

The title "The Shell" comes from an actual shotgun shell that had belonged to Humphrey's father: "My mother found a shotgun shell that had been left by my father by his bed. It sat on my worktable for some time until one day I was tinkering with it, and I said there's a story in this" (Au Int.). That story is based in part upon his father's principle that quail was men's game; Humphrey writes extensively in "The Guns of Boyhood" (OS, 275–77) of his early ineptitude at hunting quail and of how he finally achieved success on the last day of quail season in the presence of his expert father. These facts and attitudes, combined with the subsequent death of his father, provide the basic ingredients from which Humphrey constructed "The Shell."

This story concerns a sixteen-year-old boy who, like Hemingway's Nick Adams and Faulkner's Ike McCaslin, must grow to claim his manhood. It bears an especial similarity to "The Bear" in that Joe's heritage (the shell), like Ike's heritage (the silver hunting cup that is exchanged for a tin coffee pot), turns out, as we shall see, to be a dud. The most significant difference between Faulkner's and Humphrey's versions of this universal theme is that Humphrey defines the quest of manhood according to the dominant theme of his fiction—the separation of father and son by death. Joe is seeking self-definition by measuring himself against his dead father, a not uncommon course. Thomas Carlyle, in his *Reminiscences* (1881), records precisely this effort: "I had the example of a real Man. . . . Let me learn of *him*. Let me write my books as he built his houses." Then Carlyle says, "I can *see* my dear Father's Life in some measure as the sunk pillar on which mine was to rise and be built; the waters of Time have now swelled up round his (as they will round mine); I can *see* it (all transfigured) though I *touch* it no longer. I might almost say his spirit seems to have entered into me (so clearly do I discern and love him); I seem to myself only the continuation, and *second volume* of my Father."[37] As "The Shell" opens, Joe anticipates that "This would be the season, the year" when he would be able to fulfill his father and define himself as a man: "he would have the reach of arm to snap the big gun easily to his shoulder. This fall his shoulder would not be bruised black from the recoil. The hunting coat would fit him this season" (*LH,* 57). To Joe, the revered old twelve-gauge shotgun shell that had belonged to his father is the sacramental means by which he can fulfill his father's life: he can extend his father's life into himself if he manages, in firing this shell, to meet the standards of that most accomplished of hunters.

The story's intent, however, is to undermine the whole enterprise of seeking identity in the father. Humphrey makes this point through the image of the boy in his father's hunting coat. Though we are told twice that the "coat fit now," Joe wears it "with greater dread and with even less sense of possession than when it came halfway down to his knees and the sleeves hung down to the midjoints of his fingers and the armpits looped nearly to his waist" (*LH,* 60, 61). In *Farther Off from Heaven,* Humphrey produces an identical clothing image to describe himself on the day after his father died: "it was another indication of the premature wisdom, or, at least, the suspiciousness, the mistrust, which, like some hand-me-down suit of clothes far too big for me and too grown-up in style, but which

37. Thomas Carlyle, *Reminiscences,* ed. C. E. Norton (London: J. M. Dent, 1932), 33.

I must grow into, I had put on in these past few days" (191). In "The Shell" such a ludicrous picture represents Joe's present feeling about dressing "in borrowed robes," reminding us of Shakespeare's picture of Macbeth when he dresses himself in the costume of the king: "Now does he feel his title / Hang loose about him, like a giant's robe / Upon a dwarfish thief" (1.3.109; 5.2.20–22). Humphrey's conscious allusion to *Macbeth* is made clear when he writes that Joe "felt himself a pretender, a callow and clownish usurper" (*LH*, 64).

"The Shell" is a lyric expression in which Humphrey's mature style is realized. His description of Joe's quail hunt with his father's bird dog Mac in this 228-word sentence is one that Faulkner might have envied:[38]

> Now he felt the leash strain against his belt loop and heard the dog whimpering, and out in the field, rising liquid and clear into the liquid air, he heard the first bob-white and immediately heard a second call in answer from across the field and the first answer back, and then, as though they had tuned up to each other, the two of them fell into a beat, set up a round-song of alternate call and response: bob bob white white, bob bob white white, and then others tuned in until there were five, eight separate and distinctly timed voices, and Joe shivered, not ashamed of his emotion and not trying to tell himself it was the cold, but owning that it was the thrill which nothing else, not even other kinds of hunting, could ever give him and which not even his dread that it was the day when he would have to shoot the shell could take away from him, and knowing for just that one moment that this was the real, the right feeling to have, that it was the coming and trying that mattered, the beginning, not the end of the day, the empty, not the full game pockets, feeling for just that moment in deep accord with his father's spirit, feeling him there with him, listening, loading up, unleashing the dog. (*LH*, 62–63)

Then he flushes the quail, which Humphrey presents in a sentence whose construction mimics the movement of the covey: "It was as if he had kicked the detonator of a land mine. There was a roaring whir as the birds, twenty of them at least, burst from the grass at his feet like hurtling fragments of shell and gouts of exploding earth, flung up and out and rapidly diminishing in a flat trajectory, sailing earthward almost instantly, as if, though small, deceptively heavy and traveling with incredible velocity" (65).

The upshot of the story, of course, is that the shell has no sacramental value

---

38. Clarence Humphrey's bird dog was named Mack (*FOFH*, 106).

at all: it is a dud. Thus Joe finds himself free from an obligation to fulfill his father's existence by discharging the father's shell with expertise equal to the father's. Joe's epiphany is the recognition of his freedom from his dead father, freedom to be the hunter that he is, the man he has become: "Then he felt himself soaring as though in a burst of wings like the cock bird, as though he had been shot at himself and gone unscatched [*sic*], free" (*LH*, 71). The experience has defined him. His new freedom allows him to make mistakes—to drop shells on the ground and stick one in the chamber backwards—without feeling that his manhood is undermined by his father's. Earlier on in the story, "his voice did not seem his voice at all but his father's" (64). At the end, he has found his own voice: he speaks to Mac "in a voice he could just recognize as his own," and the dog knows it is his "master's voice" (71).

The sexual dimension of coming of age is also present in "The Shell." The curious connection between quail hunting and sex was laid down in Humphrey when he was a boy. When he first went quail hunting with his father, Humphrey recalled, "The joy of shooting over field dogs had been impressed upon me but it was something that until now I had had to take on faith from my father, just as I took on faith (although about this I had reservations) that the time would come when I would enjoy doing what he had recently told me men did with women"; that the boy would ever drop quail as consistently as his father "seemed as unlikely for [him] as did that other business" (*FOFH*, 106–7). The idea to make hunting a metaphor for sex might have jelled in Humphrey's mind when he taught D. H. Lawrence at Bard, for Lawrence's *The Fox* (1923) does just that. In giving "The Shell" a "metaphorical sub-existence . . . about sex" Humphrey acknowledged years later he had "strained credulity" and that "stickler-hunter readers of *Sports Afield*" would object to his method.[39] But Humphrey did not write just for *Sports Afield* readers.

The story's sexual suggestiveness begins with hints and then becomes explicit. The "Peters Victor," trade name of the shell, Joe at first keeps in his pocket, "his hand fingering it inside his pocket," and then it is "stand[ing] . . . by his bed" (*LH*, 57, 58). He hears his father's voice saying, "Do it," but he does not want to until he can be "as good as his father had been" (58). An Oedipal element enters the story as the boy's mother, fingering the shell, makes a connection between hunting and sexual attraction:

"It's the hunters the girls really go for, isn't it? Us girls—us Southern girls—like a hunting man! I did. I'll bet all the little girls just—"

39. Humphrey to Nick Lyons, 23 March 1975, Lyons Coll.

He hated it when she talked like that. She knew that girls meant nothing to him. He liked it when she let him know that she was glad they didn't. He liked to think that when she teased him this way it was to get him to reaffirm how little he cared for girls; and yet she should know that his feeling for her was, like the feeling he had for hunting, too deep a thing for him to be teased into declaring.

He took the shell away from her.

"You're good enough now," she said. . . .

"You're good enough for me," she said.

"No. No, I'm not. Don't say that," he said. (59–60)[40]

The boy knows that this is a conversation about sex: his Oedipal condition traps him in sexual competition with his father. Thus with "pounding heart" he is unable to act his father's part: he can only get his gun "half-raised," for the burden of his father's shell weighs down his barrel, and he is repeatedly "paralyzed" and "lower[s] the gun unfired" (64–65). He finds himself "hunting now in a grim, cold fury of impotence": for a time he can hold the gun "erect and steady" but then must lower it in spite of his "desperate urgency" to shoot (67).

As the final day of quail season approaches, the concerns of the story become overtly sexual. As "the whole town . . . [awaits] the climax of his single-minded pursuit," a *double entendre* comes into play. When the young people of the town gather at the Greek's confectionery on the night when Joe works there, they tease him about his apparent lack of interest in girls, asking if he had been "[g]etting many" as he hunted for quail and warning him to "[w]atch out for those San Quentin quail" (*LH*, 67–68). "Quail," of course, is an age-old slang term for a sexually attractive girl or young woman, and "Getting many?" suggests its rhyme "Getting any?" "San Quentin quail" is a girl too young legally to have sex, i.e., jailbait. This ribbing registers at some level with Joe, for now he "wanted it" (69). He will now "[l]et it get hard enough"; he will go through the "stiffened grass [that] parted and closed" (69). When he does, he has entered the place of consummation where he will get beyond the need to fulfill his father's role with his mother. He will use his own shells, not his father's, even if he drops "them all over the ground at his feet" (71). He is no longer impotent. He is entirely his own man, sexually free.

The main theme in "The Shell" anticipates the theme of another early story

---

40. The mother's pleasure in observing signs that her son does not care about girls is an element in *Home from the Hill* as well. When Libby Halstead is unable to attend the dance with Theron, "[h]e could see that it did not displease his mother that he was apparently so little displeased" (*HFH*, 123).

about quail, "Quail for Mr. Forester," first published in the *New Yorker* on 11 October 1952. This story has absolutely nothing to do with sex but concerns again the theme of the ineffectual past's impinging on the present, which was broached in "The Shell." "Quail for Mr. Forester" demonstrates the dead hand of the southern past laying itself upon the present day. This theme is of personal concern to Humphrey, and the story is based upon an incident from his own childhood. Humphrey has said that the actual incidents happened just about as they do in the story. After his father had shot some especially plump quail, his parents decided to invite to dinner Mr. Marable, the remnant of Clarksville's antebellum aristocracy and father of Miss Ruth, Billy Humphrey's schoolteacher. The story is not reset; Clarksville is merely given the imaginary name of Columbia.[41]

"Quail for Mr. Forester" portrays an adult's recollection of an evening during his childhood; the account provides insight into his family and the South in general. The family in the story believe the past was better than the present and revere "the faded sovereignty of the Foresters," the family at the upper end of the long-gone social order of the Old South (*LH*, 88). In the New South, Columbia has had to cobble a provisional social hierarchy, given that families once above engaging in trade or business now had to do so: "To deal in notions was probably the lowest, and dry goods was pretty low. Groceries was acceptable . . . furniture almost genteel" (87). Although wholesale was generally socially superior to any retail, an exception was made in the case of Mr. Forester: he had opened a hardware store, and therefore hardware was automatically elevated (Marable's Hardware Store was on the square in Clarksville). Humphrey sensed these conventions in the Clarksville of his youth, but a literary source for his humorous presentation might well be Dickens's *Great Expectations*, wherein Miss Havisham's father's social prominence is explained similarly: "it is indisputable that while you cannot possibly be genteel and bake, you may be as genteel as never was and brew."[42]

The breakup of the antebellum order had broad ramifications, almost like an affront to the Great Chain of Being. Thus the father notes that years ago quail were "like to the present-day birds as a Brahma rooster [is] to a bantam pullet" (*LH*, 89). And to the boy, who in adulthood is the retrospective narrator of the story, present-day girls are not what girls of the last century were. When he passes "bold country girls" as he walks downtown, they "say even coarser things than their brothers" (89). His usual way of dealing with this disagreeable present-

---

41. Humphrey, telephone conversation with author, 2 August 1995.

42. *Red River Recollections*, 29; see Charles Dickens, *Great Expectations*, ed. Angus Calder (London: Penguin, 1985), 203.

day crudeness is to "fix [his] thoughts upon some moment out of history" and to create an ironic distance between himself and these girls: "It was thanks to these girls that I had some idea what the word *violation* meant and I was fond of imagining that I had only lately saved these unworthy girls from violation at the hands of Union soldiers, and of enjoying the irony of their ingratitude" (89).

Living in a time that they consider to be diminished, the family—indeed the whole community—have made Mr. Forester, in the phrase of John Grammar, a "living monument" to a glorious, lost past.[43] The past would really burn bright in the present, the narrator's mother thinks, if her family could entertain Mr. Forester for supper and do it in the way to which he had once been accustomed. When her husband and son come home one morning with a "mess of birds . . . about as near worthy of a Forester as you would come nowadays," they decide to risk a rendezvous with history, even though Forester runs a hardware store to make a living, selling pots and mops, cow salves and horse collars, ropes and seeds to the lower orders of society, even those country folks with "snuff stains at the corners of their mouths" (*LH*, 89).

"Quail for Mr. Forester" gives explicit expression to Humphrey's recurring theme in the Clarksville novels—the unpreservability of the southern past. Early on in the story, the boy looks at the decrepit veterans of the Civil War with disappointment: "Certainly I could never believe that those remains of men, more like ancient women, who were reverently pointed out to me as Confederate veterans, could ever have been the men of the deeds with which my imagination was filled" (*LH*, 90). The point is in keeping with Flannery O'Connor's "A Late Encounter with the Enemy" (published a year after Humphrey's story), in which Sally Poker Sash wants to have her grandfather, a Confederate veteran, on the stage for her college graduation "because she wanted to show what she stood for, or, as she said, 'what all was behind her,' and was not behind them. This *them* . . . was just the upstarts who had turned the world on its head and unsettled the ways of decent living."[44] This dream of countering the mean present with evidence of the glorious past, with which she wishes to associate herself, turns out to be a nightmare.

Humphrey's story exposes more subtly the vanity of the revivalist's effort. Initially, Mr. Forester seems to be everything that the nostalgic family could have wished for. He arrives gallantly bestowing a cone of flowers upon the hostess; his

---

43. John M. Grammar, "Where the South Draws Up to a Stop: The Fiction of William Humphrey," *Mississippi Quarterly* 44 (Winter 1990/91): 8.

44. *Three by Flannery O'Connor* (New York: Signet, 1964), 233–34. "A Late Encounter with the Enemy" first appeared in *Harper's Bazaar* 77 (September 1953): 234, 247, 249, 252.

graciousness extends to the boy, to whom he brings and says just the right thing: "It was a pearl-handled knife, and as he went into the living room he said, 'I thought you might like that one because I was very fond of one just like it when I was about your age. It was given to me by a Mr. J. B. Hood'" (*LH*, 92). The very mention of General John Bell Hood, who led the Confederate resistance to Sherman's march to Atlanta, seems to further Mr. Forester's association with a glorious past. But Hood is in fact one of those propped-up Texas heroes who were in real life basically incompetent: his greatest debacle occurred at Franklin, Tennessee, where he foolishly ordered a head-on assault on breastworks; his loss of seven thousand men was three times what the enemy lost, and it included a dozen Confederate generals and fifty-four regimental commanders; it was, as one contemporary put it, "fearful loss and no results."[45] Mr. Forester himself diminishes the "great soldier" when he divulges that he was "a cagey cotton buyer" and then unsuccessfully tries to rehabilitate him by confusing him with Jeb Stuart, a true southern hero.

Mr. Forester further undermines his status as a "living monument" by alluding during the dinner conversation to the benefits of progress, the fruits of industrialization: electric lights, the telephone, the automobile, motion pictures. Though, according to the mother, these are "[d]oubtful blessings" for "people with what we have to remember," Mr. Forester is Humphrey's mouthpiece as he impatiently counters the mother's position: "But times change and ways of life must change and we must accustom ourselves and make the best of it" (*LH*, 96, 97). When he praises the innovative gas heater that his hosts have in their cozy living room, followed by the admission that a small house like theirs "would more than suit his needs" (he thinks it practical now to sell his grand old eighteen-room mansion), Mr. Forester proves that he is not "different enough" from the family he visits—not different enough to suit them (99).

He is, however, different from them in that he has shed the pretense that the past can be a substitute for the present. The other difference is that Mr. Forester really does have a memory of a glorious past when his family was the center of life in the community. The meal that the silly nostalgic pretender has prepared for him reminds him of a true past that he does remember, and he is moved by nostalgia—but only in its original sense: sadness prompted by a long absence from home. Like Odysseus upon hearing the Lay of Alcinous, he "recalls the past

45. James M. McPherson, *Battle Cry of Freedom: The Civil War Era* (New York: Oxford University Press, 1988), 812–13; quotation from Edward Younger, ed. *Inside the Confederate Government: The Diary of Robert Garlick Hill Kean* (New York: Oxford University Press, 1957), 181.

and weeps," although the narrator imagines that Mr. Forester's eyes might be "filled with tears" only from gas pains (*LH*, 100).[46]

"Quail for Mr. Forester" makes the point that the past is dead—and that it is silly to pretend otherwise. As Grammar has astutely pointed out, this story is a striking contradiction to that southern tradition of literature that holds by main force to its past. Tate, Warren, Lytle, and others have celebrated the past as a "source of power in the effort to resist history," the habit of retrospection being a strategy by which to deal with the emptiness of modern experience. Humphrey's modest little story deflates this southern myth, makes it seem laughable. When Jean Lambert, his French translator, proposed in 1960 translating "Quail for Mr. Forester" for publication in *La nouvelle revue française* in conjunction with Gallimard's edition of *Home from the Hill*, Humphrey swelled with pride as he approved the idea: "I think it is my best."[47]

It might seem that "A Fresh Snow," the first of Humphrey's stories to be published in the *Quarterly Review of Literature*, edited by Ted Weiss, Humphrey's friend and colleague at Bard, is meant to clarify the difference between an insidious nostalgia, like that felt by the family in "Quail for Mr. Forester," and a genuine and sympathetic nostalgia. "A Fresh Snow" examines an ardent homesickness for a home and homeland willingly given up. A young woman has married a northerner, an employee in a bolt factory, and has moved to a northern city. She longs for a South that is still there, not a southern past, and so we are inclined to feel that she is justified in her longing. Humphrey's own experience of leaving the South for Chicago and New York City provides some of the emotional tenor of this story, but it was his own mother that he was thinking about when he wrote it. She had remarried again and moved to Cleveland, Ohio; Humphrey's sympathetic imagining of Nell Moran's homesickness in that big, cold, strange city was the thought that gave rise to the story (Au Int.). Still, he drew upon his own childhood memories of going out after a slight snow, scooping it into teacups and "pour[ing] vanilla extract and sugar on it" (recalled in a 4 January 1973 letter to K. A. Porter [KAP Coll.]) when he writes that the mother in "A Fresh Snow" remembers from her childhood that "everyone went out with soupbowls. Each looked for a drifted spot to fill his bowl. . . . They ate it sprinkled with sugar and flavored with vanilla extract" (*LH*, 213–14).

The imagery of the story seems to owe something to Joyce's "The Dead": the vision of the graveyard, the snow viewed through a window, the contrast of warmth and cold, the contrast of regions (North and South in Humphrey's, the

---

46. *Aristotle's Poetics,* trans. S. H. Butcher (New York: Hill & Wang, 1961), 85.5.

47. Grammer, 8; Humphrey to Jean Lambert, 29 January 1960, Lambert Coll.

East and West in Joyce's). As in "The Dead," the snow in "A Fresh Snow" plays an ambiguous role. Melted snow—water—represents life, while ice represents death, and the snow in Humphrey's story unites the living and the dead through memory. Warmth is associated with the woman's abandoned homeland, a place of strong affections and sense of community, and cold is associated with her northern environment.

The story opens with the mother at the window watching for her son to come home from school. What she sees through the window are images of the oppressive life she now lives: the snow is "dingy with soot," the "street ran with slush," and "the mass of buildings opposite looked black and close" (*LH*, 213). Suddenly, large flakes of fresh snow begin to fall; as her breath condenses on the glass, obscuring her view of her bleak world, she recalls "the thrilling, rare snows of her childhood" in the South—a happy memory colliding with her present ugly urban reality (213). Memory leads to memory, and the expatriated southerner is soon reminiscing about the southern ritual of graveyard cleaning day (which will become a prominent feature of Humphrey's next two books); she recalls the fellowship of the living attending to the dead and contrasts it with the cold indifference to such matters that marks her present circumstances:

> By night the graves had been raked and swept and the headstones straightened, and by then all the men had gone a few times out to the woods where a bottle was kept, so everyone went home feeling tired and happy, pleasantly melancholy, and good friends with the whole community. It seemed you were born knowing the names of every member of every family and when they were born and died, and after a while it came to seem that you had known them all personally all your life and their loss was a personal loss to you. (216–17)

This sense of community among all the living and the dead is missing in her alien northern environment: "Often she had wondered where the city dead were buried and how they were looked after. . . . Surely they could not be as forgotten as they seemed to be. In George's [her husband's] family they never mentioned their dead. You would think they had no kin beyond the living ones" (217). There is no sense of community among the living either. The individual is just "caught in the shrill, jostling store crowds" (217). One is pushed, rushed—as by the chain store butcher: "Mek up yer mind, lady, mek up yer mind!" (217). But even as Humphrey paints a contrast that makes the South of memory seem preferable, he nonetheless implies the danger in such reminiscences; as the mother indulges in nostalgia she forgets the son she was waiting for. The breath that condenses on the window glass obscures the present; when her son bounds in she does not recognize him. Further, "When he neared her she felt the cold which surrounded him and it seemed to penetrate to her heart. She stood up in an impulse of fear" (218). Even after her reverie fades, her memory causes her son to seem alien to her: "his voice seemed stiff with cold. What kind of talk was that, so sharp and nasal? That was not the voice she had given him!" (219).

Thus in an effort to justify memory, to warm the northern coldness with "the slow warm liquid flow" of a southern voice, she makes warm cocoa, places her son on her lap, his head on her breast, and tells him "all about the South, where he was born" (*LH*, 218, 219). This closing tableaux seems an image of genuine and unpretentious solace in the face of a bitter blight of circumstance—yet the mother has had to forbid her son from playing with his friends (they had made plans to go sledding in the very present time that is being replaced by memories of a lost past). Humphrey makes the reader feel uneasy over the mother's effort to shut out the present, however cold and uninviting, and replace it with a warm memory.

In 1948 Humphrey had viewed the acceptance of his first story for publication as an earnest of his future as a writer, and he wrote to Grabstald at the time:

> I don't think that even you realize what this may mean, can mean, has meant to others, actual, demonstrated cases. I'm hoping (I'm pretty sure, in fact) it ["In Sickness and Health"] will get reprinted either in the O. Henry collection of best stories of the year or the Martha Foley collection. . . . There's more money. It means I can get accepted other places, and when you've been accepted by a couple—Partisan, Kenyon, Sewanee, you can easily get some of that big luscious "Harper's Bazaar" money or "Mademoiselle"—neither of which places you need feel ashamed of appearing in. Then comes a collection of stories in book form—then, a Guggenheim. Then, a job teaching creative writing in some university. All these things have happened from just such a little start—not once, but many times, believe it or not.
>
> Don't say—There goes Billy again. (HG Letters)

Whatever his friend might have thought about these dreams of success, the fact is that Humphrey had essentially made his dream come true in six years: he had published stories in the *Sewanee Review, Harper's Bazaar,* and the *New Yorker;* he was in his fourth year of teaching at Bard College; *The Last Husband and Other Stories* was about to be published by Morrow; and his work would soon appear in *Best Stories.* Only the Guggenheim would remain elusive.

Before he sent the final manuscript of the first volume of stories to his publisher, however, Humphrey carefully revised those stories that had already been published in magazines. He took special pains with the first one, "In Sickness and Health," pruning the suckers of comic exaggeration, allowing the harsh reality of the story to flourish. The major revisions were simple deletions, and they began in the first sentence. As the story appeared in *Accent,* it begins: "Mr. Grogan's bald head broke unexpectedly through the covers like a stone heaved up by a hard frost. An eye thawed open and he experimented with his nose."[48] The version published in *The Last Husband* begins more simply: "Mr. Grogan's bald head broke through the covers. He experimented with his nose" (*LH,* 73). In revising "Quail for Mr. Forester," Humphrey made numerous minor changes. In the magazine version of the story he is specific about dates: the setting was "twenty-five or thirty years ago," that is, between 1922 and 1927; 1910 was the year in which the Forester property was auctioned. Also in this version Mr. Forester is said to be sixty years old. For the collection, Humphrey eliminated all of these specifics; he also omitted an extended description of Mr. Forester's likeness to General Beauregard. He made some more significant revisions as well. For example, in the version published in the *New Yorker,* as a response to reminiscing about days gone by, Mr. Forester "ducked his head again, and when he looked up, his eyes were filled with tears."[49] In revising for the book of stories, Humphrey added a phrase: "his eyes, whether from gas or from emotion, filled with tears" (*LH,* 100). It might seem that Humphrey made this change in order to escape the risk of sentimentality, but I think there is a better reason in the motive of the narrator. Since he has concluded that Mr. Forester is not really a living monument to the past, he would be inclined to doubt that the man is capable of finer feeling and thus would think it likely that what appears to be deep emotion is really just gas pains.

Humphrey had not submitted "The Last Husband" for magazine publication but had saved it as the lead story for his first book of stories, which became a substitute for the novel that he had talked about with Morrow. There was a slight delay in the volume's publication because Humphrey objected to two clauses in the contract (which tied him too definitely to Morrow for publication of the novel that he had already begun work on—*Home from the Hill*).[50] *The Last Husband and Other Stories* was published on 8 April 1953. On 17 November Chatto and Windus published a British edition, whereupon Humphrey asked that com-

---

48. *Accent,* 91; MS (WH Coll., UT).
49. *New Yorker,* 11 October 1952, 32, 36.
50. Humphrey to Grabstald, undated, HG Letters.

plementary copies be sent to V. S. Pritchett, T. S. Eliot, Graham Greene, John Lehman, and Cyril Connolly. "I'd like the good opinion of all your countrymen . . . but of [these] in particular," he wrote on 28 December 1953 to Ian Parsons, president of the firm (C&W).

This first volume of fiction contains all of the stories Humphrey wrote in Brewster and Annandale except for a lost one that he had sent to the *Partisan Review.* An undated letter from Humphrey to Grabstald alludes to "the first story about the pregnant woman with the anarchist mother-in-law"—obviously based on Dorothy and Josephine Arosamena Cantine, who was, with her son Holley, a leader in the pacifist-anarchist movement of 1940–50. No title is mentioned, and no such story can be found among Humphrey's surviving papers.

Even though the ten stories in *The Last Husband* did not begin as part of a design, they ended up clearly comprising one, for the stories more or less alternate between ones set in the rural and small-town South (where Humphrey grew up) and others set in the often sophisticated world of the Northeast (where he moved for good in 1946). There might be a thematic motive behind this arrangement, but it also accentuates Humphrey's diversity and his early resistance to being limited to writing about the South. (Even when writing on southern topics, he believed that he transcended the setting, remarking in 1969 when he received an honorary degree from Southern Methodist University that his hometown was for him an "inherited summary of human life nearly anywhere.")[51] These stories, whether located in North or South, take as their themes marriage, parenthood, and the struggles of adolescents.

The final story in the volume, "The Hardys," is a deliberate counterpoint to the title story. "The Last Husband" portrays the failure of marriage because of an absence of love, and "The Hardys" demonstrates that an abundance of love is no insurance against an unhappy marriage. In addition to these stories' mirroring marriage themes, they are linked by a character in "The Last Husband" who actually mentions in conversation having read a story entitled "The Hardys" (and, in fact, "The Hardys" was published four years before "The Last Husband").

The most important feature of Humphrey's fiction that is established in these stories is that he writes about ordinary life. His people struggle to resist a world that moves their lives in undesirable directions. They suffer unmet needs and large or small losses. Sometimes the ordinariness prevents the stories from appearing to be of much account, as in "Sister" and "Report Cards"; but some of

---

51. Lon Tinkle, "For Bill Humphrey a Degree at Last," *Dallas Morning News,* 1 June 1969, sec. C, p. 7.

these stories achieve distinction either because of their lyric depiction of a universal theme ("The Shell"), because of an effective storytelling technique ("The Hardys"), or because he put down the essential marks of character and established an emotional climate that we can easily identify with ("The Last Husband").

Furthermore, in these first stories we see the acorns from which will grow Humphrey's novels. A predominant theme in these stories is the disappointment of marriage—precipitated perhaps by Humphrey's anxiety that his happy relationship with Dorothy might transform into the marital horror he observed around him ("In Sickness and Health"). A number of the stories in *The Last Husband* could be used as evidence to support Thomas Hardy's view that "a marriage should be dissolvable as soon as it becomes a cruelty to either of the parties—being then essentially no marriage."[52] Hardy was speaking of marriages devoid of affection, but the history of Humphrey's family made him more pessimistic than Hardy, for his depiction of his grandparents' marriage ("The Hardys") shows love turned to misery. Probably Humphrey gave to his sad couple the name Hardy because he was consciously intending to out-Hardy Hardy. At any rate, these stories represent groundwork for the more fully developed pictures of the sorrows of marriage in *Home from the Hill, Proud Flesh,* and *Hostages to Fortune.*

Many writers build characters from people they know; a few seldom bother to put a disguise on their real-life originals. Humphrey—like Hemingway, Fitzgerald, and Bellow—is one of these. The stories in *The Last Husband,* which appropriate aspects of the lives of Donald Peterson, Ilonka Karasz, Wim Nyland, Holley Cantine, John Nichols, Cora and Ed Varley, Ruth Marable's father, and several others, establish a practice to be followed through to the last volume of short stories, *September Song*—a practice that caused great heartache for some of Humphrey's friends who appeared in his fiction—and ended some friendships.

Humphrey's own life is not omitted from his practice. A dead father is featured in two of these early stories, "The Shell" and "A Fresh Snow," and the motif of separation (usually by death, usually father and son) runs throughout Humphrey's novels. This theme becomes almost an obsession in his life as well as his art. When his father's birthday rolled around each 22 September, Humphrey would write in the notebook at hand how old his father would have been; and when 5 July came round, he would make a note to the effect that on this day, so many years ago, "my father lay dying" (WH Coll., UT). The sorrow of his early loss never left him. His fiction seems a self-teaching in loss and surren-

---

52. Thomas Hardy, *Jude the Obscure* (London: Macmillan, 1974), 25.

der—of the father, of the past, of life itself. First appearing in "The Shell," this theme of loss will be developed in a southern context in the first three novels, but it will occur at a more universal and yet personal level in *Hostages to Fortune*.

Although these first stories are clear precursors to the novels to come, they offer little hint about the nature of his two subsequent volumes of short stories. For in each of these, as we shall see, Humphrey will focus upon a specific problem in life: in *Time and a Place* he will depict the failures and illusions of success experienced by Dust Bowl victims during the Great Depression, and in *September Song* his imaginative alliance will be with the aged as they face the failures of their bodies and the failures of other people to treat them as fully human. Nonetheless, there is one link between *The Last Husband* ("The Fauve") and *September Song* ("Vissi d'Arte"): each contains the story of an artist who is in one way or another a failure yet supported by a faithful spouse.

The Last Husband attracted a generally favorable response from the reviewers. Pearl Kazin in the *New York Times* said that these "ten remarkably fine stories" demonstrate that Humphrey "has the kind of skilled and persuasive originality which only the most respected practitioners of the short story art can claim." Kazin praised the stories in *The Last Husband* for their "unique freshness," their freedom from "tame obedience to the unending formulas of this or that magazine. . . . All of [Humphrey's] characters have the plain and richly complex dimensions of life which are more often expected—if not often found—in the wider room of a novel." Finally, Kazin praised Humphrey's skill: "detail, gesture and incident are manipulated with such deftness that the stories leave the deep, sure mark of mature comment and craftsmanship."[53]

David Culhane in *Commonweal* was less impressed. He saw a "very uneven book" whose pervasive flaws stem from a "usually awkward match of satire and sympathy." Culhane complained about the very thing that Kazin had praised the stories for—that they were not in fashion: "Mr. Humphrey is not moving with the short story in any of its several directions." Seeming to answer Kazin point for point, the *Commonweal* reviewer said that a "larger form" seemed required for Humphrey to achieve sufficient character development: "The people need more room. . . . These are characters in search of a novel." And instead of seeing well-crafted stories that hit their mark, Culhane saw only "a looseness of construction which tends to dissipate the final effect."[54]

The briefer commentaries tended to fall in line with Kazin's high estimate. *Booklist* noted that Humphrey achieves "his effects with a few suggestive details"

53. Pearl Kazin, "Faltering Casanova," *New York Times*, 12 April 1953, 29.
54. David M. Culhane, "Too Small a World," *Commonweal*, 8 May 1953, 127.

and is successful in "switching . . . from one mood to another." The reviewer saw Humphrey as "a young writer working in the tradition of Mansfield and Chekhov" and showing "a kindred talent for exposing human limitations with a modicum of plot." *Library Journal* recommended the "penetrating," "urbane and modern short stories" in *The Last Husband* and noted that "stories of this quality have both importance and appeal."[55]

Encouraged by these responses to his first book, Humphrey bent over his typewriter and wrote *Home from the Hill,* the second book to come out of his Bard days. Its publication would free him to write for the rest of his life.

55. *Booklist,* 3 April 1953, 269; *Library Journal,* 15 April 1953, 732.

[3]

WALKING INTO OBLIVION
(Home from the Hill)

They stood fixed, their baffled hearts looking out of their eyes with a joylessness
pitiful to see. Both seemed to implore something to shelter them from reality.
—THOMAS HARDY, *Tess of the d'Urbervilles*

> There's no love song finer
> But how strange
> The change
> From major to minor.
> —COLE PORTER, "Ev'ry Time We Say Goodbye"

I N BARD'S "STORE," the coffee shop and mail room, Humphrey would often
take time out from writing and regular college duties to talk with groups of
students who wanted to become writers. Grace Schulman, now a poet, recalled one such occasion when Humphrey was reminiscing, in his soft but intense southern voice, about his travails in New York City during 1946–47. Low
on funds, this day's story went, he had applied for a low-level job at a publishing
house: "It was raining outside. I was wet and hungry. They still didn't give me a
job."[1] The publisher was Alfred A. Knopf—and now Knopf wanted to publish
Humphrey's first novel, *Home from the Hill,* he told the students. That Humphrey would be caught telling an "inspirational" story when his nature was to
emphasize the dark side of every experience is an indication of just how exhila-
rated he was to have this success story to tell.

During the years since the publication of *The Last Husband and Other Stories,*
Humphrey had had to steal time to write on his novel. He had applied, immediately after finishing the book of stories, for a writing fellowship offered by the
Sewanee Review. He was turned down because he already had a book published.
Monroe K. Spears, the journal's new editor, had written on 18 June 1953, according to Humphrey, as follows: "I need hardly say that all the judges thought extremely well of you and your project. But we felt that we ought to help other
young writers who are less well established and who appear to be in more desperate straits."[2] An interesting aside to this failed application is Humphrey's noticing

---

1. Grace Schulman to author, 12 December 1999.
2. William Humphrey to Harry Grabstald, [23 June 1953], HG Letters.

that a reviewer's description of Andrew Lytle's *The Velvet Horn,* published a few months ahead of *Home from the Hill,* bore some striking similarities to Humphrey's own novel, a detailed summary of which he had submitted to the *Sewanee Review* a few years earlier as part of his fellowship application. On the copy of Charles Poore's review that Humphrey sent to his editor at Knopf, Herbert Weinstock, he had marked several curious parallels between his and Lytle's novel—for example, "At the heart of [the novel] lies the tragedy and comedy of ancestral ways that a boy must accept or cast aside on his way to achieving maturity"; also the boy is drawn to a shanty girl, and his father, Captain Joe Cree, is "increasingly estranged from his wife." Humphrey remarked to Weinstock: "It's obvious even from the review that the differences between the book and mine are greater than the similarities—so much greater, indeed, as to cancel out the similarities, were it not for the fact that Mr. Lytle was one of the three judges to whom I was invited to submit a scenario of my proposed novel for a Sewanee Review Fellowship four years ago."[3]

It is a wonder that Humphrey finished *Home from the Hill* in the next three years. Prior to the summer of 1953, he had written about fifty pages on it and during that summer wrote a hundred more, and then he submitted the lot to Morrow. Once the fall semester began, the novel had to be put aside. Ted Weiss was on sabbatical in 1953–54, and Humphrey was put in charge of the *Quarterly Review of Literature.* It was a time when the Bard campus was in an uproar over a severe financial crisis. The college was in danger of losing its accreditation, and the general atmosphere on campus was poisonous. Humphrey wrote to Weiss, who was in England, that he had given up all hope of writing during term, admitting that he had not looked at his novel for months. By November Humphrey heard from Morrow. They did not like his 150 pages. Actually Humphrey had come to like them even less than they.[4]

When summer came the long period of forced neglect drove him to write with a fury. "I worked so damned hard on my book I got up reeling and staggering from the desk," he wrote to the Weisses. Occasionally, he would escape from the novel and fish or play the jazz clarinet. Eventually he gave up the latter diversion. By summer's end he had rewritten everything and added sixty pages. But then all writing came to a halt with the start of the fall semester. He was now chairman of the Division of Literature, Weiss having extended his sabbatical for

3. Charles Poore, "Books of the Times," *New York Times,* 15 August 1957; Humphrey to Herbert Weinstock, 15 August 1957, Knopf Coll.

4. Humphrey to Theodore and Renée Weiss, two undated letters, one of November 1953, Weiss Coll.

another year. Academic life had the effect of making him feel that he was not a writer. When he tried to resume writing during the Christmas holiday, he was frustrated from being out of practice, and he said to Ted and Renée Weiss: "Well, I am writing. It's not very good I'm afraid, but it's the best I seem able to do. More and more I come to realize that the only way to learn to live with the knowledge that you're not going to be a great writer is to work hard and honestly and try not to care."[5]

It is impossible to chart accurately the uncertain progress of *Home from the Hill*'s composition, for the letters that could have made that possible are undated. At any rate, by 15 March 1955 Humphrey had written 254 pages and had resubmitted to Morrow for formal consideration. Humphrey hoped Morrow would reject it because he had hopes for connection with a more prestigious publisher. When they did, of course he declared himself furious, but not so furious that he could not give hard thought to improving his novel. In the same letter to the Weisses in which he announced the rejection, he said that he was "feeling not too hopeless," that in fact he had "had a moment of complete illumination, and suddenly saw the solution—a single solution—to all the problems that have been vexing me about my novel." He went on to say that he would radically alter the plot so as to get full use of the "materials already there."[6]

It was a couple of months before Humphrey found time to touch pen to paper, but he had been allowing his insight about a radical plot change to gestate. He seems also to have had an insight into his main problem as a writer: "I always make the mistake of beginning to write before I know where the thing's going, and I determined I wouldn't this time."[7] But of course he already had and was paying the price of heavy revision, a lesson that would be forgotten, learned, and forgotten again when he took to writing *The Ordways* and *Proud Flesh* in the years to come. For the present, however, he had indeed found the right way to go with *Home from the Hill*, and he worked as steadily as other responsibilities would allow.

In 1956, during the field period—a long vacation between semesters at Bard—Humphrey wrote to Harry Grabstald, saying: "I'm out of school now and working on my novel—now have about 335 pages more or less finished and am praying I can get the thing wound up at long last this spring and summer" (HG Letters). Confident of what he had accomplished during the vacation, Humphrey

5. Humphrey to Alfred Knopf, 26 October 1961, Knopf Coll.; to Katherine Anne Porter, undated, KAP Coll.; to the Weisses, [1954], undated, and [December 1954], Weiss Coll.

6. Humphrey to the Weisses, 15 March [1955] and an undated letter, Weiss Coll.

7. Humphrey to the Weisses, undated, Weiss Coll.

sent an enquiry to Alfred A. Knopf; and toward the end of March Knopf asked to see what he had. Because the spring semester was about to begin, Dorothy delivered the manuscript to the prospective publisher. Knopf's response was quick. On 11 May Henry C. Carlisle Jr. set forth the proposed terms of a contract: one-thousand-dollar advance on royalties of 17.5 percent to 10,000 copies, 21 percent to 12,500 copies, and 23 percent thereafter.[8] In a letter of 15 May 1956, Humphrey suggested to Carlisle more generous terms: "With $1000 now in the bank and $1000 on delivery of the MSS, I'd feel a lot more secure about a roof under which to finish the book," and the publisher accepted the counteroffer (Knopf Coll.). Humphrey signed the contract on 28 May.[9]

He agreed to finish the novel by the end of the summer vacation, but back pain, caused by long hours in the typing position, forced a request for a postponement of the deadline—to 15 January 1957. As soon as final papers and examinations were out of the way, Bill commenced the push to complete the novel. He worked "in a high euphoric frenzy" as the novel wound itself up "using him as a recording machine." That is how the process seemed to Dorothy, who was probably a bit closer to what actually occurred when she later wrote that he worked "16 hrs a day almost effortlessly as all the movements set going [started] working themselves out to their . . . inexorable end." On 26 December 1956 he walked into the kitchen where Dorothy was cleaning up and announced that his first novel was finished. Being finished, however, proved to be an elusive state, for on the next day Humphrey was busy making changes to the manuscript. At the end of the day, he crossed out the date of completion that he had written the day before and substituted "27th." Then Dorothy might have suggested more revisions, or there might have been a deal of retyping to do, for Humphrey did not in fact receive the second thousand dollars of his advance until 15 February 1957 when the MS had been delivered to the publisher.[10]

A month later as he was revising his manuscript in light of suggestions and questions from his two editors, Herbert Weinstock and Carlisle, Humphrey's back trouble re-presented itself.[11] "Please forgive my silence," he wrote to Weinstock on 21 March 1957. "I've been trying to finish the book, write a lecture on the Russian Novel which I must deliver (tomorrow evening) to the young ladies of a posh junior college nearby, start the new term at school—and all these things

8. Also see Humphrey to Vaudrin, 22 March 1956, Knopf Coll.

9. Humphrey to Ian Parsons, 28 May 1956, C&W.

10. Humphrey to Henry C. Carlisle, 28 August 1956, Knopf Coll.; Dorothy Humphrey to the Weisses, 9 January [1964], Weiss Coll.; Humphrey, telephone conversation with author, 7 December 1996; Carlisle to Humphrey, 15 February 1957, WH Coll., UT.

11. For a discussion of these and other revisions, see pp. 105–7 below.

became really urgent since I lost two weeks (the last two) with an attack of rheumatism . . . in my back—so severe I was reduced to going to one of those quacks, osteopaths (who, I must own, helped)." But four days later he wrote that "the book is, as of today, almost finished" (Knopf Coll.). All told, he had taken four and a half years to write the novel that would eventually be called *Home from the Hill.*

Although the novel was written and revised, the struggle was not over: Humphrey had yet to provide a title, and as with all of his Clarksville novels, he was indefatigable in his search for the right one. Not only had he, in 1956, read all the major poems of all major English poets from Shakespeare to A. E. Housman, two collections of folk songs, two dictionaries of proverbs, and the Book of Common Prayer, but he had also read both the Old and New Testaments twice. He had considered and rejected "The Children of Wrath." When pressed by Weinstock, all he could offer—and with no enthusiasm—were "The Hunnicutts" and "The Hunnicutt Tragedy" (the latter, in fact, Carlisle's suggestion). Although Alfred Knopf himself did not take to either of these suggested titles, he was not at all pleased with Humphrey's offer to re-search the Bible; the title issue needed to be settled by the second week of April 1957 to avoid delay in publication. Knopf wanted a title that referred to hunting and to the hero Theron.

In five days' time Humphrey submitted a list of nine possibilities, none of which met Knopf's stipulations. Those tentative suggestions were "A Forest of Trees"; two from *Hamlet*—"The Common Theme" (1.2.103) and "Seek in the Dust" (1.2.71)—and one from *Love's Labor's Lost,* "Infants of the Spring" (1.1.101); "Brief Garland," from Housman's "To an Athlete Dying Young"; "Near in Blood," from John Lyly's "Mother Bombie"; "The Best Men" or "The Wilderness," from Thoreau's *Walden;* "More than the Living," from Ecclesiastes; and "With All These Powers," from Darwin's *Descent of Man.*[12] Of these, Knopf and Weinstock preferred the one that Humphrey inclined toward, "With All These Powers," and Weinstock proposed including the quotation from Darwin on the verso opposite the title page: "With all these exalted powers Man still bears in his bodily frame the indelible stamp of his lowly origin." On the bottom of Humphrey's 9 April letter, however, Weinstock or Henry Robins, another editor, had scribbled three additional possibilities: "The Second Hunter," "Steps of the Hunter," and "Another Hunter." Weinstock suggested the middle of these to

---

12. Humphrey to Weinstock, 25 March; 2, 4, and 9 April 1957, Knopf Coll.; notebook on *Home from the Hill,* WH Coll., UT.

Humphrey: "This has several meanings, as you will see at once, and it seems to me memorable and easy to say, two desirable qualities for a title."[13]

Meanwhile, Humphrey hit upon *Home from the Hill,* from Robert Louis Stevenson's "Requiem":

> Under the wide and starry sky,
> Dig the grave and let me lie.
> Glad did I live and gladly die,
> And I laid me down with a will.
>
> This be the verse you grave for me:
> *Here he lies where he longed to be;*
> *Home is the sailor, home from the sea,*
> *And the hunter home from the hill.*

This title met with approval all around, but a May sales conference at Knopf led to Weinstock's request that Humphrey accept "a much more distinctive title," "The Hunter Home from the Hill"—which Humphrey declined to do.[14] Since Stevenson's poem is widely anthologized, Humphrey might have felt that readers would supply "The Hunter" from memory. At any rate, he wisely stuck with the shorter and more striking title.

The title's relevance to the story is tenuous at best, a far remove from the rich relevancies that we shall see in the title *Proud Flesh.* Stevenson's poem might confirm that Theron does indeed die "Under the wide and starry sky" and "Lies where he [often] long'd to be," deep in the mysterious and dangerous Sulphur Bottom. But the poem seems remote from the novel in almost every other way. Since Theron disappears in the deep woods, no one digs a grave for him to lie in, though his tombstone is in fact "graved." And even if Theron does experience gladness, that gladness is smothered by sorrow and suffering; laying down his life willingly in the pursuit of his father's murderer, surely he does not "gladly die"— for in dying he gives up his own son, so recently recognized and claimed, and the woman he loves immeasurably. So Theron does not lie where he altogether "longed to be." Nor is he, in the end, home from any hill. The home he desires but does not live to have is the one he and Libby had meant to make. The allusion to Stevenson at least conveys an eerie irony.

13. Weinstock to Humphrey, 10 April 1957, Knopf Coll.
14. Weinstock to Humphrey, 29 May 1957, Knopf Coll.

Home from the Hill was published in the United States on 1 October 1957, and on 27 February 1958 in Great Britain by Chatto and Windus, delayed by the hope—unfortunately not realized—of its being a Book Society Choice.[15] Fretting over the title, however, did not end with the publication of the American and British editions. Gallimard was determined to entitle its edition *Celui par qui le scandale arrive* (The One by Whom the Scandal Arrives), which was to be the French title of the Hollywood film loosely based upon the novel. Gallimard intended to benefit from the hoped-for popularity of the movie, while Humphrey had no intention of being "known as the author of the book that was the script of a wretched Hollywood production." Confident that "the book will be remembered after the picture has been forgotten," he pressed for a title gleaned from Alfred de Vigny's "Le Cor," "a poem rich in associations for the book." He vigorously campaigned for one of the following: "L'Adieu du chasseur" (The Hunter's Farewell), "Au fond des bois" (In the Depths of the Woods), and "Le cor au fond des bois" (The Horn in the Depths of the Woods); he got the first.[16] Humphrey hoped that a phrase from Vigny's poem would bring to the French reader's mind other lines from the poem, "Tous les preux etaient morts" (All the valiant knights were dead) and especially the poem's final line, "Dieu! Que le son du cor est triste au fond des bois!" (God! How sad the sound of the horn is in the depths of the woods).[17]

The stop-and-go struggle—which is what writing would always be for Humphrey—that eventually led to *Home from the Hill* must have begun to seem worth the agony when he received from Alfred Knopf an earnest of how the reading world would respond to his novel; on 31 July 1957 Knopf wrote: "Last week coming back on the Mauretania from England I gave myself the very great pleasure of reading a set of proofs of your novel. It is a magnificent work, and I congratulate you most heartily on it. It is a pleasure and a privilege to be able to publish so distinguished a novel, and I am very hopeful indeed that you have a great future to look forward to" (WH Coll., UT). This praise was not mere flattery, because Knopf wrote on 4 December to Myra Rosenau, enclosing a fifty-dollar check as a finder's fee, that he regarded *Home from the Hill* "as one of the best American novels we have ever published" (Knopf Coll.).

Before the first review had found print, Humphrey was ecstatic over the nov-

15. Alva E. Flood to Parsons, 29 August 1957; Peter Calvocoressi to Humphrey, 9 January 1958, C&W. Chatto and Windus tried very hard to get *Home from the Hill* serialized in several British publications, including *John Bull, Daily Express,* and *Argosy* (Calvocoressi to Dudley Barker, 23 October 1957, and to John Thompson, 15 November 1957, C&W).

16. See Alfred de Vigny, *Poèmes* (Paris: Louis Conard, 1914), 123.

17. Humphrey to Jean Lambert, 2 October 1959, Lambert Coll.

el's publication: "I like its shape, I like the color and the texture of the cloth, I like the not-exactly-white paper, I like the stamping and the dust wrapper—in short, I like it. In fact, I love it." When the reviews began to appear, he had even more cause for rejoicing, notwithstanding a little carping. Taliaferro Boatwright, writing in the *New York Herald Tribune*, said that "this dark and beautiful first novel . . . combines pure narrative magic, exquisite sensibility and an uncompromising masculinity." William Goyen, in the *New York Times Book Review*, praised the novel for its eloquence, its brilliant plan, and its "epic grandeur," declaring *Home from the Hill* to be "one of the most distinguished firsts by a young writer . . . to appear in some years." Bill Koshland of Knopf was ecstatic: "it is the book of the year that is being talked about."[18]

The British reviews were, in some instances, even more laudatory. The greatest praise came from the Irish novelist Elizabeth Bowen, who proclaimed Humphrey "a writer of genius," his novel "a tragic masterpiece." Bowen found much to recommend in Humphrey's narrative strategy: "Foreshadowed on the first page of *Home from the Hill*, the crisis is only revealed to us on the last. Meanwhile we have watched the characters, all unconscious, advance to the doom which we know awaits them—though neither they nor we know what the doom will be. . . . A bold method, surely, of story-telling! And one which only a novelist of genius would dare adopt."[19]

Reviews on both sides of the Atlantic noted a connection between Humphrey and William Faulkner. In Britain the connection was merely observed.[20] But in the United States, critics made an issue of the connection. As Louis D. Rubin Jr. was later to put it, "getting out from under" Faulkner, was the mark of authenticity that, from the perspective of northern and some southern commentators, few southern writers manage to achieve, without disconnecting themselves from the southern past and dwelling on the isolated present. Though Humphrey would later achieve that severance in, for example, *Hostages to Fortune*, in *Home from the Hill* the South and its traditions are central, and the influence of Faulkner is evident; and for this "indiscretion," some reviewers could only ridicule Humphrey, as when Walter Havinghurst in the *Saturday Review* asserted that "the tale is from William Faulkner": "For a hundred pages the reader is in Yoknapatawpha County with its summer somnolence and its winter chill, with pigeons scratching

---

18. Humphrey to Knopf, 18 October 1957, Knopf Coll.; Taliaferro Boatwright, "Under the Wide and Starry Sky," *New York Herald Tribune*, 12 January 1958, 1; William Goyen, "Tragedy Awaited," *New York Times Book Review*, 12 January 1958, 4; William A. Koshland to Norah Smallwood, 6 February 1958, C&W.

19. Elizabeth Bowen, "Texas beyond the Oil Wells," *Tatler and Bystander*, 12 March 1958, 506.

20. See, for example, Walter Allen, "New Novels," *New Statesman*, 12 April 1958, 480.

horse dung under the Confederate soldier in the square and back roads leading where the wild game run."[21]

After the initial reviews, however, comparisons of Humphrey with Faulkner were not always derisory. James W. Lee, in the first commentary of any length (a pamphlet on Humphrey in the Southwest Writers Series) observed: "He is a regionalist in the same sense that Faulkner was. That is, he uses regionalism, not as an end in itself, but as the framework for a larger discussion of human life and problems." Lee declared that *Home from the Hill* was the best novel ever written by a Texan, and with his subsequent novel, *The Ordways,* established Humphrey as on his way to becoming "perhaps the best novelist to come out of Texas."[22]

More recent commentary on *Home from the Hill* acknowledges Humphrey's accomplishment. While allowing that the novel has some weaknesses, Bert Almon sees its return to print in 1996 as an earnest that it is "likely to endure as a southern standard" (Almon, 127). Other commentators have been dismissive, Mark Royden Winchell, for example: "Even admirers of *Home from the Hill* must be troubled by the number of coincidences and improbabilities that move the plot toward the end of the novel. It is easy to believe that Thomas Hardy is one of Humphrey's favorite novelists. However, even at his most preposterous, Hardy handled his material with a conviction that Humphrey lacks. When incredibility destroys empathy, as it does by the end of *Home from the Hill,* we are left with a potboiler aspiring to high art. And it is an unusually nihilistic potboiler at that." Perhaps there is some measure of truth to this accusation, but Winchell never gives an example of a coincidence or improbability that offends him, apart from his statement that the Hunnicutts' "marriage could have worked had husband and wife been less the people that Humphrey's plot requires them to be,"[23] a passing shot that ignores the complexities of character. Winchell might have sought support for his point in the sudden appearance of a wild boar when one was needed to prove Theron's mettle, or in Opal Luttrell's coming to seek Captain Hunnicutt's help just after Theron learns about his father's philandering, or in Opal's sudden appearance when Libby Halstead comes to tell Theron that she is pregnant, or that Libby is being married at the courthouse at the very moment that Theron takes Opal there to secure her annulment. Winchell might be trou-

---

21. Louis Rubin, *The Curious Death of the Novel: Essays in American Literature* (Baton Rouge: Louisiana State University Press, 1967), 284; Walter Havinghurst, "Prelude to Violence," *Saturday Review,* 41 (11 January 1958): 15.

22. James W. Lee, *William Humphrey,* Southwest Writers Series, no. 7 (Austin, Tex.: Steck-Vaughn, 1967), 21–22, 43.

23. Mark Royden Winchell, *William Humphrey,* Western Writers Series, no. 105 (Boise, Idaho: Boise State University, 1992), 16.

bled by such intersections, although most readers are unlikely to be bothered by synchronousness driven by exclusive imperatives. The best argument to set against complaints about the tyranny of the novel's plot is in Humphrey's own words, written some years before he began *Home from the Hill.* He had been thinking about the plots of E. M. Forester and Kafka, and he said: "A novelist may use the most fantastic plot . . . and if in doing so, he enables himself to give us some new and real information about human motives, then he is quite justified" (HG Letters).

Winchell's other complaint is that there is neither rhyme nor reason for the shifts in point of view—between the anonymous citizen who uses the collective "we" and the omniscient narrator—and he suggests that Humphrey ought to have opted for clearly designated "multiple points of view," as Faulkner had done in *Absalom, Absalom!*[24] But Humphrey does indeed offer the advantage of a combination of points of view. He begins with a representative member of the community observing events with much more curiosity than understanding, thereby establishing immediacy and engaging the reader. The second reason for beginning as he does is to establish a distance between the community narrator and the author. Jean Lambert remarks astutely, "le narrateur est distinct de l'auteur," but this distinction between the narrator and the author is a feature of the novel that Winchell fails to recognize.[25] Consider the following passage, which contains proud Texas imbecilities that Humphrey hardly subscribes to: "We—at least we small-town Texans . . . have a name abroad for violence: grown men still playing guns and cars. Well, and it must certainly be owned that even those of us who have gone away to college, lived in the East, and ought perhaps to know better, never quite get over admiring a man who is a mighty hunter—and who, for the two things go together, takes many trophies poaching in the preserves of love" (*HFH*, 10–11). Humphrey does admire a skilled hunter, but the attitude and personality of the narrator are out of accord with the author's sensibilities altogether. In fact, Humphrey ultimately makes it clear that Wade Hunnicutt's "poaching in the preserves of love" is the great tragic fault that brings the family down.

The point of view of *Home from the Hill* is not a simple matter of the narrative "we" set against an omniscient narrator, for the all-knowing narrator moves from character to character in shifting points of view that reveal misunderstandings that various characters operate under. For example, in chapter 11, when The-

---

24. Ibid., 17.

25. Jean Lambert, "Presentation de l'auteur," in *L'Adieu du chasseur* by William Humphrey, trans. Lambert (Paris: Gallimard, 1960), 10.

ron's parents disagree on whether he ought to be allowed to hunt in lieu of attending school, a misunderstanding of motives transpires through a shift in point of view. Hannah's section lets us know that her support of Theron's hunting has an ulterior motive, "to make hunting something Theron owed to her" (*HFH*, 72) instead of to his father, the boy's mentor in hunting. Then the chapter goes into Wade's mind, revealing that he assigns more noble motives to his wife's position than she in fact deserves: "Hannah amazed him. Let him live to be a hundred, he would never understand Hannah. But understand her or not, he knew how to appreciate her. You would not find many women who would go so far in understanding what a thing like hunting could mean to a boy his age" (73). It also becomes clear, from the alternating perspective of the narrative, that Wade is mainly concerned with what is best for his son, Hannah with enticing her son to prefer her to her husband. The shifts from the consciousness of one character to another and then to the objective point of view throughout the novel are handled adeptly so as to foster a deep understanding of the tragic conflicts. And at appropriate times throughout, the limited viewpoint of the townspeople makes an appearance, like a Greek chorus giving its perspective on the action. (The town is surely a character in the story, and the attitudes of the community affect the action—for example, when the townsmen mistakenly believe that Wade is the father of Libby's child, they supply Albert Halstead with a motive to murder the Captain.) Often the shifts in point of view occur at the chapter breaks, but if they occur elsewhere, Humphrey signals the change with a triple space between paragraphs.

Along with the alternating points of view, Humphrey exhibits a broad rhetorical range, from the poetical references to the "fresh-plowed and seed-sown land," almost the voice of Dylan Thomas, to the attentive depiction of the "turpentine twang" of the farmers who cleared that land (*HFH*, 84, 124), in particular the farmer who reports having seen the "wile hawg" that had rooted up his winter turnips and busted his chicken coops:

> "Hit's a wile hawg, sho nuff, Cap," he said. "I mean, one that never wuz nothin but wile. One lak that other un ye got that time. Not no barnyard pig run wile. Musta worked his way ovah f'om Loozyanner. I seen him. Hit uz Monday a week when I uz runnin mah line. I skeered im up f'om whur he uz bedded down an ef I hadn' th'owed im the two dead possums I uz totin, why, I doubt he'd a et me. I doubt he'll run ye ever bit ez big ez you other un, Cap." (*HFH*, 80)

The "I doubt" to mean "I do not doubt" is true to Humphrey's subject, as is his partially phonetic rendering of the farmer's pronunciation.[26]

Black characters are distinguished in their speech from the poor whites, as one black is from another. Chauncey, companion to Captain Hunnicutt and the storyteller of the novel, has his own voice: "Well, all this bout them trappers was unbeknownst to yo's truly. Cap'm say we goin huntin so I desume we goin after squirrels" (*HFH*, 53). Melba, the cook and maid of the Hunnicutt house, sounds very much herself as, for example, when she prognosticates the future of Theron's love affair by using apple seeds to represent Theron and Libby Halstead:

"I gonna hold this spade over the heat," she pronounced. "Ef the heat make *Theron* move away from *Libby*, it means that's what the real Theron gonna do, gonna be untrue to Libby. Ef *Libby* move away from *Theron*, she gonna be untrue to you." (148)

Attesting to the effectiveness of Humphrey's characterization of Melba's speech, James Lee remarks: "With few tricks of spelling, he makes the black woman speak accurately. She is just far enough off grammatically to be right—but not exaggerated and made ludicrous." Jean Lambert was stumped when he faced such passages: how could he find a French equivalent for even two kinds of southern dialects—white and black? Humphrey's suggestion was for Lambert to consult the French translations of Mark Twain's *Huckleberry Finn:* "if he has been well done in French, you might profit from studying them. Do not be offended by this suggestion. After all, he helped me write it; why shouldn't his translators help you translate it?"[27]

Humphrey reaches the upper range of the rhetorical scale in passages such as the one preceding Albert Halstead's first visit with Captain Hunnicutt to talk about his daughter and Theron. The literary shine is heightened by the biblical touch and by the allusion to Hardy's poem "Hap":

Mr. Halstead, dizzy and dismayed, plumbed the vast indifference at the heart of things. He was not to be steeled by the sense of ire merited or

26. A clue to the origin of this usage is in Hardy's *The Mayor of Casterbridge,* ed. Robert B. Heilman (Boston: Houghton Mifflin, 1962), 180: the Scot Donald Farfrae says "I doubt" for "I do not doubt."

27. Lee, 31; Humphrey to Lambert, ? [*sic*] November 1958, Lambert Coll. Humphrey could offer no suggestions about how Lambert might represent in French the dogs of the novel: "those breeds of dogs probably do not exist anywhere outside the South. So that poses a problem."

unmerited. If all the adages were lies, the opposite of them would have been another set of lies. If the meek inherited nothing, neither, necessarily, did they suffer. Jeff Traver, sitting there in his cozy home unbuttoned and unperplexed and ignorant of his blessing in having no daughter, had not come to grief through his goodness, the equal, Mr. Halstead knew, of his own. For Mr. Halstead no voice came out of the whirlwind at the hour of his destiny. The wind that blew on all alike blew softly at his back as he walked down the quiet residential street through an unexceptional November evening. (*HFH*, 231)

While Winchell complains mainly about Humphrey's technique, Gary Davenport objects to what he assumes to be the author's values. He calls the novel a failure because, he says, Humphrey is too much the advocate of the vanished southern aristocracy; his "owed pieties" amount to "ancestor-worship." He is overly fascinated with the code of the gentleman hunter: "*Home from the Hill* is spoiled for me by Humphrey's uncritical fascination with . . . Captain Wade Hunicutt [*sic*], who is the embodiment of the hunter's code in the novel, is an object of adoration to his son, but also, I think, to Humphrey: the Captain's only real vice is a kind of lordly philandering, and it is treated with indulgence, almost as if it were the *droit du seigneur* of a gentleman hunter." More recently Almon has sought to correct Davenport's misreading: "Humphrey's book is a finely-crafted work which seeks to destroy the Myth of the Hunter."[28] But surely Theron and Humphrey do indeed admire the Captain's ability as a hunter (though Humphrey does not admire him wholeheartedly). Nonetheless, it is a mistake, as important a figure as he is, to speak of Captain Hunnicutt as though he were the central character of the novel. The central story is Theron's. While we are meant to find the Captain an attractive character in some respects, Humphrey takes pains to display his faults as far from inconsequential. Theron, on the other hand, is meant to be an utterly sympathetic character. Still, Humphrey shows that, however admirable, Theron is of an earlier aristocratic age and has no place in the modern world. Upon the death of his father, Theron chooses the ethos of a lost time, and therefore he dies. He could have chosen differently and returned to Libby and his son and lived in the present day.

Home from the Hill has as intriguing genesis. It was formed by the melding of elements contained in two of the stories from *The Last Husband*: "The Shell" and "Quail for Mr. Forester." From "The Shell" Humphrey took the theme of the

---

28. Gary Davenport, "The Desertion of William Humphrey's Circus Animals," *Southern Review* 23, no. 2 (April 1987): 496; Almon, 99.

boy's progressing through the mastery of hunting to manhood, coping as he does with the help and hindrance of an esteemed father. The separation of father and son, broached in the short story, becomes a significant element throughout the first novel—and will prove to be the red thread that runs through all of Humphrey's novels. From "Quail for Mr. Forester" he took the theme of the relationship between the traditional South, with its aristocratic values and way of life, and the new age of the middle-class and the impropriety of efforts to revive a lost past. The result of the melding is a moving tragedy whose ramifications affect and reflect the social arrangement.

The other obvious source for *Home from the Hill* is Humphrey's own father. In his notebook for *Farther Off from Heaven,* Humphrey refers to his father's "notorious mistreatment of my mother. His philandering" (WH Coll., UT). The real-life philandering auto mechanic who killed an alligator in Sulphur Bottom is turned into the philandering gentleman farmer who kills a powerful razorback hog in Sulphur Bottom. Like Theron, Humphrey himself developed in the ways of the woods under his father's tutelage and grew into an accomplished hunter. Like Theron, Humphrey was in awe of his father's ability as a hunter. In fact, the descriptions of his father in *Farther Off from Heaven* overlap with those of the Captain in *Home from the Hill.* For example, Clarence Humphrey "could glide through the woods in those old tennis shoes he hunted in as silent as a shadow. How many times had I, so much smaller and lighter than he, followed in his footsteps, treading on every twig he had avoided!" (*FOFH,* 232); Theron's father, indistinguishable from the real-life father, except for the absence of the inelegant old tennis shoes, "could walk in the woods in no other way except as noiselessly as ever, seeming to glide across the clearings like the shadow of a bird overhead and to melt into the shadow of the trees" (*HFH,* 61).

Finally, Humphrey has taken from Faulkner the meaning of the southern family and the larger social issue that family signifies. *Home from the Hill* has in common with Faulkner's *The Sound and the Fury* the theme of the disintegration of an aristocratic southern family. Humphrey emphasizes that this family, a holdover from the Old South, must end in destruction for the same reasons that the Old South ended in destruction—because of a moral corruption at its center, but also because another social force is poised to take over. The aristocratic family in Humphrey's novel is not allowed to carry on into the future. All efforts to preserve this remnant of the past fail; the new world of middle-class go-get-ism is in the ascendancy.

Home from the Hill opens a hundred years after Appomattox. A "dusty long black hearse" passes "under the shadow of the Confederate monument" (HFH, 3). The

odoriferous fumes of cottonseed fill the air, and in demonstration of the importance of cotton to the East Texas town, the first bale of the year is displayed
"upon a wooden platform wrapped in red bunting" in the center of the square
(3). Though it is not named, the town is clearly the Clarksville that Humphrey
left when he was thirteen. The names of the people he knew there populate his
novel—Wheeler, Bradley, Stiles, Holloway, Pritchard, McCarley, Latham, Brannon, Benningfield, and so on. Occasionally Humphrey altered a name slightly:
Ramsey becomes Ramsay; Dinwiddie, Dinwoodie. He also rearranged the combi-
nations of last and Christian names; Peyton Stiles, for example, gets his first
name from Peyton Storey; Otis Wheeler his from Otis Latham.[29]

The observing townsmen's curiosity over the contents of the hearse infects
the reader, yet once the townspeople learn that it is Hannah Hunnicutt who is
to be buried, the perspective shifts to that of the hearse driver and his companion—thus they who began by mystifying are suddenly mystified themselves when
Marshall Bradley tells them that they will not "have to dig" in order to bury Mrs.
Hunnicutt; "[h]e said no more, and of course they did not know what to make
of that" (HFH, 9). The mystery behind this bizarre fact lingers, and the opening
chapter concludes with the townsmen dashing about to inform all the rest that
Hannah Hunnicutt has come home to be buried. The chapter's final statement
creates mystery by telling a little but withholding much. The reader is left wondering why one of the tombstones will never get the body that belongs under it
and wondering, too, about why there are unacknowledged Hunnicutts about and
who they might be. The acknowledged ones, at any rate, have "passed into
story"—which story the reader feels compelled to know (10). Margaret Lane engaged in no overstatement when she declared on the BBC radio program *The
Critics*, "I don't remember for years reading a first chapter of an unknown novel
which fixed my attention so immediately."

Instead of proceeding to answer the questions proposed in the first chapter's
last sentence, Humphrey gives the attention of chapter 2 to the subject of Captain
Wade Hunnicutt, the husband of the deceased. A townsman gives a biased and
laudatory account of the Captain, concluding with the conveyance of his body
into town fifteen years earlier in the bed of a pickup truck, his head shot off.
Only one reference in the several-page account bears upon the last sentence of
the previous chapter—namely, the question of publicly unacknowledged Hunnicutts, and that reference is this: the Captain "takes many trophies poaching in
the preserves of love" (HFH, 11).

29. *Red River Recollections* (Clarksville, Tex.: Red River County Historical Society, 1986), 22, 29,
217, 280, 361, and see index.

Chapters 3 and 4 take us to the graveyard and the central image of this episode: the three Hunnicutt gravestones in a row. Arranged as they are on the page, they achieve an almost pictorial presence; indeed, this effect was Humphrey's aim, for the manuscript contains the following marginal note: "note to printer: please, if possible, set all 3 of these inscriptions on one page"—and then he (or someone) underlined the instruction in red ink (MS, p. 37, in WH Coll., UT). (The compositor's following of Humphrey's request is responsible for the large type and leaded opening paragraph of the novel.) Rather than supplying answers to the questions that we already hold, these stones engender additional questions: Why has Hannah's grave already been dug? Why does her gravestone say she departed this life on May 28, 1939, aged thirty-nine years—fifteen years earlier— when she has just died in 1954? Why do her husband's and her son's headstones contain the same date of death as hers? And why the gravestone color scheme— black marble for the husband, white marble for the son, and red granite for the wife?

The reader wants to speculate as intensity builds. Perhaps the red stone next to the gaping hole in the earth is an image representing the great wound that she felt because of "the tragedy," "the catastrophe," repeated phrases in chapter 4 (*HFH*, 22–23). We learn that Hannah has spent nearly all of the years since the as-yet-unidentified catastrophe in a mental institution. And then we learn further that Theron's body is not under his gravestone. Slowly, surely, as a roller-coaster climbs to its greatest height before the thrilling descent, Humphrey's narrative moves forward with mounting anticipation. What we will know is inevitable; there is no turning back. Though the clock is ticking—the courthouse clock chimes the quarter hours throughout the novel—we know that Humphrey has moved the hands back, so that what is and shall be already was.

The central achievement of *Home from the Hill* is that it is a modern tragedy in novel form and built of the standard tragic elements. It is a literary tragedy in the precise sense, not in the revised modern sense in which *Death of a Salesman* is said to be a tragedy. This authentic expression of classical tragedy has seldom been attempted since Hardy, and achieved, I believe, in contemporary American fiction only by Humphrey. The novel's tragic characters are elevated above the common herd; they are marked by hubris; they have tragic flaws, make tragic mistakes that lead to reversal and catastrophe; they undergo tragic recognition *(anagnorisis)*, "a change from ignorance *[agnoia]* to knowledge, producing love or hate"; and their fate has implications for the whole of society. The end of

Theron Hunnicutt, the tragic protagonist, "a virtuous man," is sorrowful, heart-breaking; the presentation assumes solemn dignity and excites pity and fear.[30]

Humphrey's first job is to establish the eminence of the main characters. He selects a name for the family that has an aristocratic ring to it: Hunnicutt, a name in marked contrast to the family name he gives to his representative of the rising lower middle class: Shumway. Years later, without recalling Humphrey's novel at all, William Styron used the name Hunnicutt in *Sophie's Choice*—and to produce the same effect as Humphrey. "Hunnicutt was a well-to-do family in Tidewater Virginia," Styron said, "and I simply appropriated it."[31] Humphrey's Captain Wade Hunnicutt is the head of a well-to-do family in a cotton-growing community of East Texas. The townsman who first limns his portrait uses terms that connect him to the aristocrats of a feudal age (that could be Anglo-Saxon England or the Old South). He holds a "title of rank," is

> our biggest landowner, and even gave his name to a day in the calendar, the first Saturday in October, still called Hunnicutt Day, when his tenants from all over the county came into town for their shares in the year's cash-crop money. And though men have grown rich and men have died memorable deaths since him, none has been remembered as he is. You would have to go back to an earlier, more spacious time, say to something like the days of the opening of Kentucky, when a landowner took personal care of his vast plantation and took the lead in its defence against whatever threatened it, man or beast, or to Tudor England and the times before the gentry grew exquisite, to find another man like Captain Wade. (*HFH*, 10)

Furthermore, he is "a mighty hunter" whose guns "might, any one of them, have stood proxy for the man, as the sword of a king off fighting a war in olden times could stand proxy for him to be married back home" (11).

The Captain is in charge of protecting the community. When a wild boar runs amuck, destroying crops and domestic animals, it is the Captain who ventures into the deep danger of Sulphur Bottom to slay the beast, a deed for which many bestow upon him laud and honor. The townsman narrator describes a hunter's pecking order that puts the Captain at the top: "The Captain had the center place in that circle of men where you will find us all on any Saturday afternoon"; the

---

30. *Aristotle's Poetics*, trans. S. H. Butcher (New York: Hill and Wang, 1961), 72.2, 75.2 (Aristotle alludes to "the stately manner of Tragedy" [57.14]).

31. William Styron to author, 5 May 1999; see *Sophie's Choice* (1979; reprint, New York: Bantam, 1982), 15.

year-round hunters from Sulphur Bottom, however, "are the men for whom the rest of us make place"; and they are the ones who move over "to make a place for just one man—'the Cap'n'" (*HFH*, 13).

It is a mark of Wade Hunnicutt's class that he carries no money, does not care about it, though he is a man of enormous wealth. Nor does he carry a watch ("Time would wait on him") (*HFH*, 12). A Richard Cory to the townsmen, Wade "was a very comfortable looking man, without looking as if he strove for comfort. He was always very trim and sleek. His pockets never bulged" (11). With "hair black and smooth as the breast of a crow and those sharp black eyes and that skin too weather-lined ever to show a wrinkle of age," he possesses a brilliance, a perfection, and a grace that are unusual.

Already the Captain has passed into legend, for the townsman who is narrating assigns a perfection that anyone who has ever set foot in Texas in summer knows is impossible: every day he wore "fresh khaki trousers with creases that even at the end of a wiltering August day still seemed honed to an edge" (*HFH*, 12). The reader senses, as was the case with E. A. Robinson's "always quietly arrayed" figure, that there is more to the Captain than meets the eye. The townsmen, "We people on the pavement," are too envious to see beyond the superficial: "Winter and summer he wore the same felt hat, cream colored, of stockman pattern, and it never seemed to age, just as it had never seemed to be new. He had paid a hundred dollars for that hat, it was said—the sort of extravagant small gesture of which legends are made in Texas" (*HFH*, 12). This is the sort of statement that reveals Humphrey's narrative strategy. It prompts the reader to back away from embracing altogether the exalted picture that the townsman paints. While not precisely undermining the stature of Wade Hunnicutt in the community, Humphrey creates a distance between mindless hero-worship and the reality of the object.

This reality centers on the hero's great flaw. At the end of the narrator's encomium, he divulges that the Captain is a philanderer, a fault that fails to dull his luster for the narrator. Nonetheless, he allows that Wade's "taste ran to married [women]," and he speculates that "Maybe they knew better how to appreciate him. Certainly they were safer from certain complications and entanglements" (*HFH*, 14). Whatever the reason for preferring married women, it was a good one, according to the narrator, for Captain Wade always knew what he was doing and was "free from the indecision that troubled other men" (12). In fact, it is the Captain's epic fornications that are to a great extent responsible for his and his family's tragic undoing; and Hannah is Wade's handmaiden in moral corruption, the ultimate source of the destruction of her family. Thus Humphrey portrays Wade Hunnicutt as a mere man and as a larger-than-life figure at the same time, this dual aspect being suggested by the image that Harvey Brannon observes on the night of Albert Halstead's disastrous meeting with the Captain: "he saw Captain Wade Hunnicutt standing on his front porch in the light with his legs spread, the giant straddling shadow of him flung out upon his yard, looking down at the gate through which poor distraught Albert Halstead had just passed" (275).

Wade is chronicled in epic style by his black retainer, Ole Chauncey, who functions as the poet of his master's heroic life, telling a cycle of tales with titles like *How Cap'm Wade Hunnicutt Killed the Last Wild Boar in East Texas, Cap'm Wade's Most Famous Shot,* and *Young Wade's First Trip through Sulphur Bottom,* "an epic in itself . . . in twenty books" (*HFH,* 50). Humphrey may well have included the element of epic to illustrate Aristotle's observation that "Epic poetry agrees with Tragedy in so far as it is an imitation in verse of characters of a higher type" (*Poetics,* 60.4). Chauncey's main auditor is the Captain's son Theron, who develops an awe of his father that exceeds the esteem of "those men in whose midst his father reigned." Each of the tales contains

> the beginning of the next, so that they were not so much separate stories as a kind of run-on legend, a heroic cycle, set always in Sulphur Bottom, a kind of Sherwood Forest, with all the men becoming, in the endless re-telling, figures as lovably invariable as Friar Tuck or Little John, each enshrined in an anecdote or two, staunch members all of his father's merry band, each unique, but all equally possessed of courage, endurance, fidelity and a kind of comradely awe of their Captain. Romantic, no doubt, but without any yearning for such days of old when knights were bold, because he had Texas, not little England, and Sulphur Bottom, bigger and infinitely more mysterious and dangerous than any Sherwood Forest, a crew of lesser heroes of legendary marksmanship with guns more beautiful, more powerful, and more accurate than any stick with a string tied to it, and he had his own indomitable father, Captain Wade, a hero as much better than a Robin Hood as Robin himself was better than the Sheriff of Nottingham. (*HFH,* 50–51)

From Theron's perspective his father's Purdey shotgun is "fabulous": it "was a magnum 10 gauge double with barrels thirty-three inches long and weighed just under fourteen pounds" (46). "No man but the Captain, it was said, could take the punishment it dealt the shoulder in a day in a duck blind," and when fired it sounded "like the boom of a cannonade" (46, 47). Theron, similar to Joe in "The Shell," worries about how he can ever be worthy of such a father, a man clearly larger than life to him.

Yet just as clearly the illustrious father is not the shining knight that his son thinks he is. Nevertheless, during his childhood Theron is protected from any knowledge of his father's iniquity, the knowledge of which, when it comes, nearly destroys his life. Insofar as Wade represents the traditions of the Old South, Theron's "misplaced adoration" of his father is, in part, a misplaced adoration of the Old South and its traditions. Theron intends to carry on the spirit of the past into the present. In fact, he exceeds his father in the virtues that the father possesses, and the father knows it: "the boy was such a very fine boy that the Captain stood in some awe of him"; "his share in his son made him rise in his own esteem" (*HFH*, 65). Both parents are confident that Theron "was going to be a better man than his father" (65).

Almon's view that the "son is more a victim of his parents' troubled marriage than a tragic hero" (Almon, 87) regards as trivial a character whose fate is tied to the central concern of the novel. Humphrey has taken a cue from Mark Twain to place confidence in the serious integrity of a youth as opposed to his elders.[32] Theron lives with a great seriousness, with more seriousness than his parents. He is the sestet that follows the father's octave. Therefore, from the outset Humphrey takes special care to exalt Theron, even in his uncommon name that sets him apart from others. His ranking above others is a common perception of the townspeople: "he sits high in all the people's hearts," as Casca says of Brutus. The opening voice of the people speaks of him as though he were Prince Hamlet, imagining that "Mrs. Hannah thought Theron had been choiring with the angels these fifteen years," saying also that "At twelve he had all the certainty of a crown prince" (*HFH*, 15, 39). The narrator understands that Theron has derived his sense of manly goodness from reading nineteenth-century fiction and southern history and that he conveys his vision of proper conduct by telling "us stories about ourselves" that contain "words like *courageous, valiant,* even *fortitude,* even *steadfast,* words he got from his reading in Scott, Marryat, Cooper, and Southern historians of The Lost Cause" (38). The narrator describes how the whole tone of male gatherings in the town changes instantly when, at age fifteen, Theron first accompanies his father in sitting with the men on the corner of the square. Before this, though the men mainly talked about hunting, they would utter spontaneous crude remarks when a girl passed. Theron's presence, however, puts a quietus on coarseness, "because the boy himself made us feel ashamed to do it,

32. When Lambert made this observation about Theron in his introduction to the French translation ("Presentation de l'auteur," 12), Humphrey expressed his gratitude for "your understanding of my intentions in the character of Theron. . . . [You go] straight to the heart of the book, to my basic intention" (Humphrey to Lambert, 29 January 1960, in Lambert Coll.).

and this he did not so much by making us feel that he was too good, as that we ourselves were" (38). Theron himself is always a gentleman in the presence of women. Libby Halstead, whom he invites to a dance, is amused by his old-fashioned manners: after issuing her invitation he says, " 'Till tomorrow then,' . . . and, of all things, he tipped his cap to her" (96). Later on "he was almost tongue-tied in his propriety," and she is charmed by "his old-fashioned respect, amounting almost to an awe, of women, his impeccable manners and decorous expressions, his stiff, almost comical propriety," and she does not fail to recognize Theron's superiority: "The boys she had known who were manly were also rough. Theron was manly, but so well-mannered that he sometimes made her feel crude" (158, 166). She admires him because he is "thoughtful and tender, . . . chivalrous, protective, kind" (156).

Theron adheres to an "ancient code," a romantic "code of honor," and to the code of the hunter (*HFH*, 157, 156). When he fights for the honor of his father after a crude bully named Dale Latham casts a slur upon him, Theron engages in what is perceived as medieval trial by combat: "He had won this fight, which would prove to him that the charge had been a lie" (64). Through such tests Theron gains and maintains the manly integrity that tradition has prepared him to walk in. Adherence to the true meaning of hunting also enhances his manliness: "For he knew, had always known, that it was not just being able to line up the front sight in the rear one, not just the meat you brought home for the table. It was to learn to be a man, the only kind of man, to learn it in and from the woods themselves and from the woodsmen, the hunters, who had learned it as boys from their fathers there—and so back through the generations, making you a link in the long strong chain of men of courage and endurance, of cunning and fairness, of humility as well as becoming pride. It was not to be confused with sportsmanship" (49–50). Knowing what hunting means, however, is not sufficient; he must become a hunter—and he does become expert, anticipating the fly-fishing expertise of Anthony Curtis in *Hostages to Fortune*. When Theron hunts, he "picked his buck, passing over half a dozen, as carefully as a housewife picks over all the butcher has on display for the tenderest young fryer. He had gone in for finesse. His squirrels were all shot clean through the head. His quail were hardly ruffled and had never more than three or four pellets in them to annoy the eater, for he took them upon the very edge of the shot pattern" (77).

Although it had been thought that Captain Wade had killed the last wild boar in East Texas, another appears, providing an opportunity for Theron to equal his father, to carry the tradition of the hunter into the next generation. Indeed, Theron, alone, hunts down the "[g]ray-pelted and mud-caked" 340-pound boar, which looks as if it were "forged of cast-iron": "It was majestic in its brutal ugliness and serene self-assurance, and it caused Theron a gasp of surprise, respect, and fear" (*HFH*, 89).

Humphrey not only provides the excitement of the external event—the dramatic killing of the boar—but he also portrays the hunter's feelings and the ultimate meaning of the acute moment during which he stands his ground as the beast hurls itself toward him "like a guided torpedo" (*HFH*, 90). To provide this additional dimension, Humphrey adopted for his own purposes Henry James's strategy in "The Beast in the Jungle" (1903). James, in order to lay bare John Marcher's sudden realization of the emptiness of his wasted existence, externalizes the shocking fact lurking in his unconscious: "The Beast had lurked indeed, and the Beast, at its hour, had sprung."[33] Humphrey modifies James's technique to fit his own character's situation. Theron, passing the obvious test of his manhood by standing his ground unflinchingly as the wild boar charges and falls slain only just before trampling him, now unexpectedly encounters the ulterior motive lurking in the background of his consciousness. He must recognize the fact that his compelling motivation has been "envy of his father's prowess." Immediately upon killing the actual beast, Theron faces and kills the troubling envy that he has unexpectedly discovered:

> Suddenly it seemed to regain its feet and come at him again, to hurl itself at him with a force, a weight, a momentum, which even the living beast had lacked. . . .
>
> Yet even as he shrank from the charge, he heard in his mind a gladdening explosion. He felt the recoil. He felt no need of a second shot. His envy of his father's prowess lay stretched out, mud of the swamp caked upon its tick-infested hide, shuddering, peacefully sighing its life away, at his feet. (*HFH*, 92)

The picnic celebrating Theron's killing of the wild boar is one of the many absorbing instances of local color that enrich Humphrey's novel, but the picnic is also significant for the novel's presentation of Theron's character in that on this occasion he is raised higher in the community's esteem: "He felt many hands on him. He felt himself lifted off his feet. *He was raised above the heads of the crowd*" (*HFH*, 109; italics mine). And then Chauncey commences his "storytell-

---

33. Henry James, *The Beast in the Jungle, The Birthplace, and Other Tales* (New York: Charles Scribner's, 1937), 126. It is a certainty that Humphrey had read James's novella by the time he wrote this passage because in a 1953 letter to Ted Weiss he remarked that Fred Dupee reminded him of John Marcher, the main character in "The Beast" (Weiss Coll.).

ing chant," enthralling children with the exploits of Theron (117). Yet killing the boar—together with killing his envy—and the manly distinction that he achieves in his community do not end Theron's quest for manhood. As we shall come later to see, he must learn about sex, responsibility, fatherhood, and, above all, forgiveness.

With the father and son established as exalted characters, the novel naturally turns into a love story, and out of the conflicts of this love story, tragedy will emerge. Theron falls in love with the town's great beauty, Libby Halstead, his intended partner for the dance following his celebratory barbecue. Though her father has forbidden her to see Theron, Libby visits him on the day after the dance, dazzling him like a woman in a Petrarchan sonnet. Humphrey alters Petrarchan convention to the requirements of a realistic novel: "He looked out the window, and the glare struck him full in the eyes, dazzled him. He shielded his eyes and ducked under the beam. After his vision had returned, and after a moment's search, he discovered its source. At the focal point of the beam, near the hedge across the lawn, stood Libby, semaphoring to him with something round and small and bright, a mirror no doubt, held at her breast" (*HFH*, 131). Their innocent morning in the attic closes with the sharing of an apple—a perhaps too-obvious sign that Theron's innocence is about to end.

Humphrey takes the lovers through the many awkward moments, embarrassments, and ecstasies of their courtship; the love story is effectively told in every respect, in spite of Humphrey's admission that "writing about love is hard for a sour bastard like me."[34] In anticipation of the moment when Theron and Libby consummate their love, Humphrey draws upon Thomas Hardy in portraying Libby's reluctant desire, which is reminiscent of Tess Durbeyfield's in *Tess of the d'Urbervilles*. When Tess hears Angel Clare playing his harp, she enters an uncultivated garden to be near him. The overflowing of her feelings of love and her natural desire are objectified by the description of the garden into which she wades:

> [it] was now damp and rank with juicy grass which sent up mists of pollen at a touch; and with tall blooming weeds emitting offensive smells—weeds whose red and yellow and purple hues formed a polychrome as dazzling as that of cultivated flowers. She [ventured] through this profusion of growth, gathering cuckoo-spittle on her skirts, . . . staining her hands with thistle-milk and slug-slime, and rubbing off upon her naked arms. . . .

34. Humphrey to the Weisses, 15 March [1956], in Weiss Coll.

[T]he rank-smelling weed-flowers glowed as if they would not close for intentness, and the waves of color mixed with the waves of sound.[35]

There can be no doubt that Humphrey alludes to this passage when he conveys Libby's readiness for a love that, like Tess's, is beyond the rectitude of the cultivated:

For she had become fascinated with the mysteries of spring. . . . After the long rains the ground had burst from the thrust of impatient life. Violets and columbines and yellow ladies' slippers had come through, and the woods were shrill with the mating of birds. . . . Daisies budded and burst in the fields and frothy toad spittle appeared on the stalks like a super-abundance of vital sap bursting out. She had gotten some of it on her ankles and on the hem of her skirt as they crossed the field. (*HFH*, 158–59)

The damp fecundity, the burst of wild-flower color, the spittle and sap on skirts and appendages, the blending of sights and sounds, the mating of plants or birds, the general tone and effect of the passages verify the link between Humphrey and Hardy, revealing that Humphrey means to draw a parallel between two fictional women, two fictional couples. The sad misunderstandings and mistakes that Libby and Theron will suffer take on depth and added sadness in being a further instance of a tragically ruined relationship that seemed in its fresh beginning destined for happiness.

Humphrey employs next, and very effectively, a mechanical device as an objective correlative for the irresistible desire that directs Libby and Theron into the motions of love. The device is a windmill, and Humphrey places his young lovers upon the "platform which went around the derrick just beneath the fan blades" (*HFH*, 159). The lovers seem to respond to each other as automatically as the fan blades respond to the breeze:

A light breeze turned the creaking fan blades above their heads. Together they turned to each other, and there was a sudden breathlessness, like an inhalation, a diastole of nature, and the vanes overhead suddenly hushed. They heard the sibilant murmur of the woods. Then, as suddenly, the breeze freshened; the tree tops rustled, the field shimmered, the windmill stirred, and they felt the wind in their faces. One common current seemed

35. Thomas Hardy, *Tess of the d'Urbervilles*, ed. William E. Buckler (Boston: Houghton Mifflin, 1960), 108–9.

to animate all that quickening life, pulsating, tingling, electrical. You could almost feel it, almost hear it. And then she did feel it. Then it was as if her own wintry, sluggish blood had fermented and ran drunk with warmth through her veins. Then the beauty of all things was an ache not to be borne alone. The windmill spun faster and faster, and they looked at each other in the clear, high, earth-free light, and she saw that yes, he had felt it too, was waiting for her to feel it, to turn to him. (159)

Humphrey expands the individuals' physiological manifestations of passion—their breathing and heartbeat—into the energetic processes of all of nature through a play on the term *diastole*. Their sudden diastole, as the term applies to the pause just before dilation of the lungs in inspiration, expands to a "diastole of nature." Their own breathing is associated with the expiration and inspiration of the breeze that stops and turns the windmill. They are attuned, in their own breathing, to the larger breath of nature: they are a part of the general quickening of life. The term diastole also refers to the beating of the heart, the pulse that itself is literally quickened by their passion. Thus, as the lovers are attuned to the new life that comes in spring, they feel as though they are being reborn; Libby's "wintry, sluggish blood" is soon "pulsating"; it "ran drunk with warmth through her veins." As the windmill spins "faster and faster," Libby sees that the same quickening of breathing and pulsation takes place in them: "she felt his heart beat against the sweet intolerable ache in her breast" (*HFH*, 160).

Yet because "the misery of approaching separation" hangs over them, her father having arranged for her to attend college far away, the emotional effect of oneness passes (*HFH*, 165). This profound sense of separation Humphrey portrays especially well in a late-August fishing episode. Libby, being lighter of heart and more capable of finding pleasure in the moments they have, is separated in temperament from Theron, who is "alone and untouchable in his melancholy" (166). Humphrey ties their contrasting emotions to the physical surroundings:

She sat in the prow, he in the stern of the still boat. Though the sun was getting low, the brilliant heat rained down. She wore an old straw hat of his, and the sun came through the cracks in the brim, freckling her face. His bare head was reddish-black in the dying sunlight. The boat was motionless on the water, which seemed to have jelled, so still that even the bobbers, little red and white bubbles, set as though in a solid. Then she saw his jig, bob, jig again, bob under. She looked up and around and saw that though his eyes were fastened on it he did not see it. (167)

Various elements of their emotional relationship are contained in the physical features of this paragraph: their separation is marked by Humphrey's placing them at opposite ends of the boat and by one's wearing a hat, the other not; time is running out ("dying sunlight"); their relationship is stagnant (the boat is still, and the water seems "jelled"); failure to attend to Libby will result in Theron's losing her (self-absorption causes Theron to lose the fish he has hooked). Though Theron and Libby do indeed love each other, do not want to be separated, the tone of this fishing episode resembles the one in Hemingway's "The End of Something," when Nick means to break off his relationship with Margarie; the effect of the resemblance is ominous.

Theron, we come to see, is thoroughly capable of overcoming the emotional difficulties caused by Libby's father, who means to place his daughter out of Theron's reach; but Theron's own mother turns out to be the unwitting agent of this love's destruction. Though it is the father who, in taking over the son's tutelage at age fourteen, steeps him in the ancient code of the hunter, it is the mother who is in charge of forming Theron's character up until that time, and it is she who "had been the smith of that armor of ideals" that he wore (HFH, 64). Further, she fosters Theron's illusions about his father: "Theron worships him. And who has taught him to? Who has lied herself into eternal damnation for his sake, letting his son believe he is the very model of mankind?" (29). This effort is ostensibly to make Theron a better man than his father, but there is an insidious dimension to her benevolence. Although she plays the role of an aristocrat's wife and maintains a strong sense of her own superiority to everyone with whom she has contact (note, for example, her disdainful treatment of the high school principal in chapter 11), she is in fact the only character in the novel whose self-absorption and perversion drive her to the verge of absolute evil so that her husband's sexual indulgences, by contrast, seem almost peccadilloes. Hannah is the chief flaw in the armor of the family, her effect on the Hunnicutt family being no less pernicious than Caroline Compson's on her family. Hannah, then, in the process of destroying the relationship between her son and Libby, destroys her own family.

Hannah does not love her husband, having withdrawn emotionally and physically at the first sign of his infidelity, yet she remains his wife and undertakes to aid and abet the infidelity that she deplores. In short, she pimps for her husband ("Some of us in town came to feel that she just about selected them for him, had them up to the house and first brought them to his notice" [HFH, 27]). By filling in the names on the dance cards of Wade's promiscuities, Hannah assumes a deeper moral responsibility than he, for the one who covertly encourages another to do wrong is more culpable than the one who merely acquiesces. Yet she pretends to a higher moral position and condemns him and does not acknowledge that she is a principal in the setting up of events that move ineluctably to her son's destruction—and her husband's, and her own. In fact, she does not know that all her life as a wife and mother she has been laying the groundwork for catastrophe.

Hannah nurtures in Theron an excessive trustfulness—a trait that is presented humourously in the snipe hunt episode, but it is Theron's credulity, we come to see, that leads to his and his family's downfall. His disposition "to think too well of people in general" makes him susceptible to the most profound disillusionment. Wade, foreseeing the possible unhappy effects that such innocence might lead to, reluctantly goes along. He keeps from "tampering with it" because "this very trustfulness certainly got some amazing practical results," which confirm the early observations of the townsman; Wade "had seen at least one mighty shiftless specimen on one of the farms respond as though determined not to betray this sudden and unexpected confidence, and hold his head up and look people in the eye for the first time in years, all on the strength of Theron's friendship" (*HFH*, 65–66).

While the father worries about the well-being of his son ("he did not want his disappointment to be too keen when, as was inevitable, he was suddenly disillusioned about one" [*HFH*, 65]), Hannah deliberately fosters a romantic idealism and then shatters it. The occasion of her disclosure is the night on which Theron returns at 2:00 A.M. following sexual intercourse with Libby. Wanting but unable to confess what he considered perfidious behavior, he blurts out, as an alternative confession, that Mr. Halstead had turned him away on the night he had intended to pick up Libby for the dance. This confession is a natural alternative to the one that Theron is unable to utter, for Theron now feels that Libby's father's suspicions about him have been justified: he has done to Mr. Halstead's daughter the very thing the father had feared. This scene contains the novel's first moment of tragic recognition and reversal, and it almost seems that Humphrey had Aristotle's *Poetics* open before him as he wrote, because the action of his characters mimics the example of reversal that Aristotle gives in chapter 11: "in the *Oedipus*, the messenger comes to cheer Oedipus and free him from his alarms about his mother, but by revealing who he is, he produces the opposite effect" (*Poetics*, 41.1).

At this moment in *Home from the Hill*, Hannah bites her lip, holds her breath, and then, for the purpose of cheering her son and freeing him from the fear that Libby's father had reason to think ill of him, destroys the image of an ideal father that she herself had cultivated: Albert Halstead "didn't trust his daughter with you because of your father," she utters, and then: "Your father is not what you think" (*HFH*, 182). One of Humphrey's editors at Knopf, Henry Carlisle, objected to this handling of the scene, particularly to the words just quoted: "It is difficult to believe that she would say this at this point. She has good reasons to but you do not make them apparent, at least not at this moment." Carlisle then suggests that the entire paragraph in which Hannah commences her life-shattering announcement "should be greatly expanded, perhaps by a page or so, of review of all Mrs. Hanna[h] feels at this point, toward the Cap't, Theron, and people like Halstead. This is a moment of truth and the most important recognition scene in the book. We should see swiftly and yet clearly what passes through Miz Hannah's mind just before she is drawn to break the years of silence. . . . If we do the scene will assume its proper emotional intensity and drama."[36]

Humphrey changed not a syllable of the passage in question, sending the following carefully worded explanation:

> Because you express yourself with such conviction and urgency on this point (and because I agree that it is a major moment) I have tried especially hard to see it your way. After much trying, though, I still cannot agree at all that the moment is not prepared for. No moment, no matter how dramatic, can ever be regarded as something isolated—and a part of the moment, even of this instant, is the preceding chapter dealing with Mrs. H's stultification. About the related criticism—that some of the explanation of her motives comes *after* she has made her revelations—I must say that this is my way—I might say, my technique—and it still seems to me better. It shows uncontrollable emotion and action resulting therefrom better if you shoot first and ask and answer questions later. (Knopf Coll.)

And, to be sure, it is inherently clear that Hannah's motivation in telling Theron about his father's promiscuity is a mixture of hatred of Wade and concern for her son. Her disclosure is reluctant in the beginning, but then it takes on an outrageous dimension, a wantonness, as she presses upon Theron the truthfulness of her allegations:

> "Oh, he's famous!" she said. "You've told me what an eye he has for squirrels, but they'll all tell you what an eye he has for the girls. That everroving eye! You've only seen him hunting in the daytime, but night-hunting, that's really his sport!" (*HFH*, 189)

36. "William Humphrey Untitled Novel, Suggestions for Final Revision," WH Coll., UT.

This first moment of recognition moves Theron from ignorance to knowledge, in the manner outlined by Aristotle, and produces hostile feelings (*Poetics,* 72.2). The omniscient narrator observes that Hannah considers "the impact her disclosure would have on Theron, . . . the severity with which he would judge such things as she had disclosed," for she had, after all, given him that "fine, high moral sense" (*HFH,* 191).

But Hannah fails to consider what Theron has learned about manhood from his father. It is beyond her imagination "how despicable he [would find] the kind of man she had revealed his father to be": "for him there were the men who behaved with *noblesse oblige,* with a hunter's honor and courage, and there were the others. The others, represented in his own generation by Dale Latham, were coarse and vulgar, selfish, cruel. Subject to their own appetites, they were without dignity; their cheap bragging did not disguise their lack of self-respect. They preyed upon weaker creatures who were trusting by nature (for so, in his boyish, his Southern idealism, he thought of women). They were above all cowardly" (*HFH,* 191–92). Lambert recognizes the full significance of Theron's disillusionment: catastrophe is born at the moment that Theron's admiration for his father is exposed as undeserved, and Humphrey takes great pains to make clear the damage done to Theron by his mother's disclosure.[37] On the following afternoon, when his father suggests that they go hunting on the next day, Theron sobs, "I'm never going hunting again!" (195). But it is in the chapter devoted to Graveyard Cleaning Day that Humphrey boldly objectifies the devastating sense of loss and alienation that Theron feels. As the Drunken Porter's speech in *Macbeth* and the gravedigger's monologue in *Hamlet* comically accentuate the serious issues of those plays, so does Theron's participation in Graveyard Cleaning Day mix the solemn and the comic in such a way as to enhance the sense of overwhelming sadness that chapter 37 closes on. The heartsick Theron, who flushes a "pair of furtive lovers from behind a crypt"—a reminder of the parallel between Romeo and Juliet and Theron and Libby, including the rift between their families— comes upon an isolated grave that possesses a peculiar relevance to his own situation. It is the grave of Hugh Ramsay's leg, the stone for which stands "just about above where the knees of the occupant of the grave would have lain": "HERE /

---

37. Lambert writes, "[T]out le drame, on le verra, prendra naissance le jour où cette admiration sera déçue: il se précipitera alors vers sa fin tragique[;] . . . nous assistons impuissants, consternés, mais non surpris, [au] perte inévitable" (The entire drama, we shall see, is born the day when this admiration is exposed as undeserved: the story rushed towards a tragic ending[;] . . . powerless, dismayed, but unsurprised, we witness the inevitable loss) ("Présentation de l'auteur," 8–9).

AWAITING HIM, / LIES / THE LEG / OF / *Hugh Ramsay* / lost / June, 1927" (196).[38] His leg had been amputated because of a house-painting accident, just as he was about to be married. The grim joke that I think Humphrey means to make here is that Theron feels that, like Hugh, he does not have a leg to stand on any more: the standards upon which he had long stood straight, those for which he thought his father stood, have been lopped off, and so he is morally crippled.

In various other ways Theron's plight parallels Hugh's. The "perverse flair for self-punishment that had made [Hugh] erect the little stone had made him choose, with the money he was awarded in compensation, to set himself up in business as a shoe cobbler" (*HFH*, 196–97); a similar perversity prompts Theron to embrace the profligate life of drinking and fornicating that he thinks is his father's and thereby maintain a perverse accord on a new, depraved basis. Further, as Hugh Ramsay broke his plans for marriage because of his sudden loss and as he "had the bitter satisfaction of seeing [his intended] married inside a year," so does Theron in his profound disillusionment "[cease] to believe in [his and Libby's] love" and therefore tells Libby that they "ought not to see each other anymore" ("I've changed," he says), and within a few months Libby is married to Fred Shumway (197, 244).

Also during the graveyard episode Theron recalls the account he had heard of Hugh Ramsay's shouting, during the trial in which he sued his employer, that "he didn't want their damned money": "I want—justice! Ain't this a court of justice? It's justice I want" (*HFH*, 197). Now that Hugh's loss parallels Theron's loss, Theron for the first time understands Hugh's demand. He did not mean that he wanted to see his employer's leg amputated but that monetary compensation was not compensation. What Hugh wanted is the same "impossible thing" that Theron now wants: "right for the wrong that can never be righted, reparation for loss that nothing could make up for. He wanted things not to be what they were" (198).

Watching from a distance as Hugh tends his leg's grave, Theron recognizes that the man appears to be worshiping his loss at the shrine of his sorrow: "Hugh raked the grave and raked outside the chains for eight or ten feet, making piles of leaves at the four corners. Then he lighted them, hobbling from one to an-

---

38. Clyde Edgerton might have this episode in mind when he tells of Timothy Cook's leg preceding him to the grave in *The Floatplane Notebooks* (1988; reprint, Chapel Hill: Algonquin, 1998), 76. Humphrey based Hugh Ramsay on a cousin named Frank Smith. When Smith was an adolescent, a rifle accidentally discharged and shot his leg off just below the knee. Like Ramsay, Smith afterwards worked in a shoe shop, and he erected a marker over the burial place for his leg (Earl Humphrey, interview by author, tape recording, Clarksville, Tex., 4 May 2002).

other. The thick smoke stood up like four gray columns on the windless air. Hugh dragged himself inside the temple they made and sat, his stiff leg flat out before him, on the grave; it was like some ritual observance, torches at the corners of a catafalque or a votive offering to some strange god" (*HFH*, 198). Theron discovers in himself a strong fellow-feeling for Hugh, who cannot be "reconciled to loss." Nonetheless, Theron's loss seems worse to him—for "You could stump along on a wooden leg, but where could you get back your respect for yourself or for your father, once it was taken from you?" (198). Therefore, in grim—but verging on comical—bitterness Theron, taking his cue from Hugh, imagines "a grave that he might erect, with a stone just over the place for the heart, saying, Here, Awaiting Him, Lies the Happiness of Theron Hunnicutt" (198). At a more serious level, this fantasy prefigures the tombstone marking the burial place that Theron will never occupy. The Hugh Ramsay episode is hardly "a little digression," as Almon judges it (112).

Theron flies from this absurd fantasy to another quarter of the graveyard, where he finds an image that even more properly accords with his heartache. He comes across what we understand to be a perfect objective correlative of his condition—"a shallow valley overgrown with scrub and weeds, a neglected and desolate place" (*HFH*, 199). This location takes on added significance as Theron stumbles and falls on the marker for a reprobate's grave. Then, finding many such markers in "this desolate back-slums of the graveyard," he learns that this is Reprobates' Field, "where people who are not fit to be buried with Christians are put" (200, 201). Humphrey's omniscient narrator assumes a foreboding, Hardyan solemnity, even down to the litotes, in order to suggest Theron's belongingness with those for whom "it would have been better if they had never lived": "A hush hung over this deserted village of dead, who were remembered with no stones or epitaphs, nothing but that uniform and official notice that they had lived and had died. Such was his own mood, however, that he felt himself no unwelcome intruder upon their poor privacy" (200–201). Theron's undertaking to clean up this overgrown, long-neglected purlieu has particular significance. In part it means that he symbolically casts his lot with those excluded from respectability. When Hannah finds Theron "furiously chopping" weeds in Reprobates' Field, she comprehends almost immediately that his theatrical gesture "somehow symbolized a rejection of her" (202, 203).

Yet Hannah continues her campaign to discredit her husband. Her wrongheaded effort is signified by the image of the mirror, a device that Humphrey will use much more extensively in *Proud Flesh*. When Opal Luttrell, the sharecropper's daughter who has left her abusive husband, comes to the Hunnicutts for help, Hannah observes her with her baby as she uses a shaded window as a mirror. This moment of mirror reflection signals a disastrous misprision: Hannah concludes that Opal is the very thing that she is not—the mother of Wade's child. Hannah invites Opal to stay in their home so that she can, she imagines, embarrass Wade and hold up before Theron the ocular proof of his father's guilt. The effect of Opal's presence is that Theron's "throbbing brain" imagines "the scene of intimacy between his father and Opal" (*HFH*, 216).

A mirror plays a more significant role in Theron's brief reunion with Libby upon her return from college, the same mirror that she had used in semaphoring to Theron at the innocent beginning of their relationship. The reflective spots on the ceiling of the den sent by Libby with her mirror should draw Theron's attention away from the gross illusions that infect his mind. Indeed, his heart jumps as he rushes to meet Libby. Though Theron manages to see the importance of Libby to him, Humphrey conveys the complexity of Theron's emotions with an insubstantial blur, an illusion: "His eyes filled with tears and her figure swam. But it was as if he had been blind to her till then. All liquid and shimmering, she seemed to float before him, a vision come in answer to prayers" (*HFH*, 245). The vision is easily shattered as Libby drops the mirror: "At his feet, in splinters, sparkling as if still trembling from the shock of breakage, lay the compact mirror with which today and that first day she had beckoned him out to her" (245–46). Libby, seeing Opal with her baby walk from the house and call Theron's name, looks to Theron to deny that they belong to him. Seeing the mistaken perception, Theron fails to correct it: "he faltered, looked down, saw again the glinting splinters of silver, and so let the moment pass when he might have claimed her" (246). Libby's and Theron's life together, which might have been whole, complete, and fulfilled, is now shattered.

In the ultimate act of perversity, Theron then elects to create a reality out of a distorted, broken reflection; in short, he makes real the illusion that Libby had derived from her easy misreading of reality. Theron's decision, grounded in a despair that Libby had almost saved him from, is itself based upon the illusion that his mother has paraded before him—Opal as the woman wronged by his father, her son as Theron's unacknowledged brother. Theron determines that he can put right his father's wrong and embrace his brother by marrying Opal. Knowing nothing of his own son that Libby is carrying, Theron marries Opal; and Libby, in a parallel to Sue Bridehead's marriage to Phillotson in Hardy's *Jude the Obscure*, marries Fred Shumway out of desperation. Blindness prevails. Humphrey said that Hardy "throws a dark shadow over this book," and indeed it is a Hardyan scene, right down to the reversal, in which Hannah learns that she is mistaken in her assumption about Wade and Opal and confesses her mistake to Theron.[39] His life is suddenly more intolerable than ever, his reason for sacrificing himself in marriage to Opal having vanished. In this second recognition scene, the pattern from *Oedipus* is repeated: the messenger intends to provide a piece of good news and cheer the recipient, but the opposite effect is once again achieved; Theron says to his mother: "When you told me what you did about Papa that night, . . . you took away from me both father and mother. Now what you tell me takes away the brother I thought I'd found"—and then he announces that he is "going to join his wife and step-son" (*HFH*, 264). Humphrey produces an unusual twist on the Oedipal pattern that Aristotle cites. Instead of the moment of enlightenment revealing an unexpected kinship that leads to suffering, Theron's recognition frees him from a false perception of kinship—yet this understanding increases his suffering exponentially, for he finds that he has married a woman that he does not love in order to right what was never wrong.

This is the disappointment that Theron has just suffered when Humphrey sets him at table with Opal and serves his life up on a platter during the crucial chapter 50. The setting is the shabby-genteel dining room of the Norris House,[40] which clearly represents a faded glory: "in Henry and an antique few of the staff there lingered a faint memory, or a fiction, of grandeur, and they kept up a few of the rituals" (*HFH*, 265). Theron's request for adjoining rooms Opal takes to be a pardonable extravagance, for she can hardly suspect that her bridegroom has already resolved to sleep alone behind the locked door of one of these rooms. Theron, we come quickly to understand, is suffering a despair beyond her understanding.

A champagne ritual preceding the nuptial dinner establishes the tenor of the occasion. The waiter, Henry, who has known Theron all his life, in serving a bottle of champagne that had "lost much of its youthful enthusiasm," seems "about to shed tears" of commiseration that reflect Theron's own misgivings: "To Henry this particular bottle seemed to share his own reluctance and disappointment. Its tired pop was to him a sad gratification" (*HFH*, 265).

Humphrey next offers the objective portrayal of the newlyweds' dinner to convey tellingly the subjective world of Theron's emotions. Theron's outer and inner worlds coalesce in the serving of the meal. Humphrey also sets Theron's inner suffering against his new bride's vapid happiness. It is a scene reminiscent

---

39. Humphrey to the Weisses, 15 March [1958], Weiss Coll.

40. There was in Humphrey's day a hotel on the square of Clarksville, and there was also a large house known as the Norris House; Humphrey turned the two into one (*Red River Recollections*, 29, 183).

of one in Flaubert's *Madame Bovary*, a mealtime conveyed through Emma Bovary's perspective: "But it was above all the mealtimes that were unbearable to her, in this small room on the ground-floor, with its smoking stove, its creaking door, the walls that sweated, the damp pavement; all the bitterness of life seemed served up on her plate, and with the smoke of the boiled beef there rose from her secret soul waves of nauseous disgust. Charles was a slow eater."[41] While her husband is satisfied in his marriage, Emma Bovary feels the full force of the terrible mistake that she has made in marrying a dull and unsuitable mate, as her life is reduced to the circumference of her plate. In a similar scene at the Norris House, Theron finds his dinner and his future life served up on the same platter: "The soup plates were removed and in the interval of waiting for the next course, suddenly he felt her hand upon his. He shivered. He looked at her. Her eyes were glazed with pleasure and she said, 'Oh, Theron, honey, I just can't believe it!' Fortunately at that moment Henry came with the entrée. Theron bent over his plate, and he seemed to see in it his future life served up to him. Before him lay nothing but existence. 'Ummmmh!' she said, smacking her lips" (*HFH*, 266). Like Flaubert in his portrayal of Emma, Humphrey deepens the impact of Theron's moment of epiphany by contrasting his mood with his spouse's. When Humphrey writes, "Before him lay nothing but existence," an abstract declaration that would otherwise produce little impact possesses force and emphasis because the limiting of his life resides visually in the confined circumference of the plate before him, and he sees what all his great expectations in life have been reduced to. Of course, what looks unappetizing to Theron is a pleasing prospect to Opal, who smacks her lips. Although the scene is reminiscent most of Flaubert, the psychological parallel to Hardy's Jude Farley in his disillusioning marriage to Arabella Donne is also strong. Like Jude, Theron sees his dreams shattered because of a mistaken notion that he must give a child a legitimate father.

Libby is just as unsuitably yoked to a spouse who can never measure up to her expectations: "She shuddered to think what she and Fred had in common for conversation" (*HFH*, 248). Her husband, Fred Shumway, along with Libby's father, are the main figures who portray the middle-class "vision" of life that stands in contrast to the lofty aristocratic, traditional, supposedly high-minded vision of life that Theron, even more than his father, represents. It is this middle class that displaces the aristocracy, which resolves into irrelevancy by the novel's end.

Humphrey might be accused of wielding a heavy hand in his depiction of

---

41. Gustave Flaubert, *Madame Bovary*, trans. Paul de Man (New York: Norton, 1965), 47.

the worst attributes of the middle class as vulgar philistines. Freckle-faced Fred Shumway is "[s]hallow, self-satisfied, pushing" with "the soul of a Yankee peddler," yet "steady, . . . middle-class and conscious of the need to rise in that class"; for he "was going to be somebody, to amount to something" (*HFH*, 272). Only a fire-extinguisher salesman at the time of his marriage to Libby, his "determination," his "ambition and enterprise," quickly win for him "the local dealership in a new make, off-brand car . . . [with] a showroom of sorts in a disused livery stable on the south edge of town" (248, 270). Fred displays a "happy vulgarity," is always "beaming with satisfaction," oblivious of the ridicule directed at him for being a fool (272, 281). Unmindful of his wife's despondency, Fred is himself very happily married—and comically uxorious.

Albert Halstead anticipates Timothy Bingham, the father of Jo-Lea in Robert Penn Warren's *The Cave*, published two years later. Halstead undergoes a similar change to Bingham's early on in the novel and is established as a satisfied member of the middle class: "he feared guns and was morally shocked by anybody, no matter how little need he might have for getting on in the serious business of life, who allowed some hobby to become his whole existence. Mr. Halstead had a middle-class hatred of all the so-called quality—who took rights unto themselves, especially the right to their neighboring subjects' women-folks" (*HFH*, 115–16). Slopping around the house in his worn-down bedroom slippers, with the newspaper dragging beside him, Mr. Halstead "welcomed growing old because it was expected of the young that they make a show of passion" (112). He exhibits no masculinity, being "distinguishable from [Libby's] mother by such secondary characteristics as that his towels were blue, hers pink" (158). Though he stands for respectability, Halstead is as principled as Ben Jonson's Corvino; he at first wishes to protect Libby's virtue by keeping her out of Theron's reach but then reverts to encouraging that association when he thinks that a slick college man has impregnated his daughter.

Toward the end of the novel, Humphrey arranges for Halstead to undergo a crucial transformation. When Halstead meets the Captain in his den in a failed attempt at emotional bartering on behalf of his pregnant daughter, he becomes "something of a stranger to himself," and this new self is "much more interesting than the old acquaintance" (*HFH*, 272). It is not at first clear how Halstead changes, only that he spends some considerable time pondering "on the transformation he had undergone so late in life" (273). Humphrey is gradually readying his homely creature for a larger part in the tragedy. The reader begins to suspect that Halstead has been so impressed by the Captain's manner that he is appropriating some aspect of the traditional, aristocratic, and manly way of life that he had not been born to, trying to make it his own. The consequence of such a man's appropriation of a past that does not belong to him will prove disastrous, not just silly as it is for the middle-class family in "Quail for Mr. Forester."

All preparations are made for the crucial scene in which all possible destinies are held in the balance before fate suspends hope. This scene is set in the tiny Episcopal Church where the Shumway baby is about to be baptized. (One of Humphrey's notebooks suggests that he had difficulty figuring out how to make the scene work. Because many pages have been excised, we cannot know the full extent of his deliberations, but the notebook does tell us that initially Humphrey did not plan to have Theron go to the church for the baptism; once he decided on the church as the setting for the crucial scene, he considered making it an Anglo-Catholic Church, with holy water in the vestibule [WH Coll., UT].) Though the Shumways are "camp-meeting Baptists," Fred's pride has "made him reckless" enough to swarm "right to the top" of "the religio-social ladder" (*HFH*, 279, 280). On this particular Sunday morning the Baptists, Methodists, and Lutherans have crammed themselves into the Episcopal Church to observe Fred in his overweening and ludicrous pride, for he is the only one who does not know that he is not the father of his wife's baby. The gawkers and hecklers interrupt the priest's solemn intoning from the Book of Common Prayer with rude murmuring and laughter.

At this point in the narrative Humphrey employs the technique of simultaneity, a delaying tactic that, as John Gardner says, "tortures the reader with alternative possibilities" and thereby enhances the impact and significance of the ultimate outcome.[42] Albert Halstead overhears some of the townsmen assert that Libby's baby is the Captain's—the second baby that Wade has been falsely accused of fathering—and so resolves to kill Wade: "He'd done it again, I God. Well, he'd done it for the last time" (*HFH*, 290). Although his "I God" represents the Texan dialectical pronunciation of "By God," the absence of an apostrophe in front of the "I" ("'I"), opens the possibility that Halstead is making an inadvertent admission that he is usurping God's prerogative in the punishment of sinners. Then Humphrey backs up in time to the point where Albert overhears the false accusation but shifts the point of view to Theron and Libby during their reconciliation in the vestibule of the church. Here in a moment's time Theron recognizes his son, knows "the fierce passion of paternity," and he and Libby repair the rift between them, resolving to make themselves into a proper family (294). Theron determines to reconcile with his father and mother, for "Love at last had banished all judgment from his heart and filled him with wonder" (298). Thus he goes straightway to his old home, embraces and kisses his father, and

42. See John Gardner, *On Moral Fiction* (New York: Basic Books, 1978), 115.

departs only to run to his temporary dwelling that he had celibately shared with Opal (who has just left town on a bus) while his father tells his mother that he has returned. This third recognition scene promises another reversal and produces the other emotion that Aristotle associated with such scenes: the first recognition scene had produced hatred, the second one despair, and this one love.

But Humphrey has arranged chapters 57 and 58—the one in which Libby's father resolves to kill Theron's father and the one in which they commit their love to each other—to occur simultaneously, and one resolution will cancel out the other. As the supreme happy moment of the story—in which love of every kind (filial, paternal, maternal, sexual)—is all but achieved, the dark shadow of misapplied judgment in the form of Albert Halstead intervenes. Influenced by the Captain whom he both admires and hates, driven by a vague notion of what a true man would do even though he is not one, Halstead repudiates his middle-class womanish existence by committing the ultimate evil of the novel: he blows the captain's head off, an act that is all the more shocking and terrible because Halstead acts out of ignorance (see *Poetics*, 80.8). Then Theron pursues the killer to their common doom. The novel ends with Deputy Sheriff Bud Stovall concluding that Theron's "body could not be recovered" (*HFH*, 312). One of Humphrey's Knopf editors, Henry Carlisle, suggested that the conclusion leaves Theron's ultimate fate unclear, especially since his grave remains empty; but Humphrey countered that "I say [that Theron dies] here on page 11 and you should have (from many different places in the book) a picture of Sulphur Bottom such that you know that in disappearing therein he is bound to have died."[43] Indeed, in *Farther Off from Heaven*, Humphrey presents Sulphur Bottom as a place that "you could get lost in . . . and never be seen nor heard tell of again" (80).

The publisher objected to another aspect of the novel's conclusion, the absence of a neat "tieing-up of the story" with the opening descriptions of the graves of the Hunnicutts. Herbert Weinstock remarked on this to Humphrey on 29 March 1957, when there was still time to revise the conclusion: "Mr. Knopf, Jr. also felt the lack at the end of the book of any return to the events leading up to Mrs. Hunnicutt's funeral at the beginning of the book" (WH Coll., UT). On 2 April Humphrey replied in part:

Now to Mr. K's recommendation about the ending of the book. What Henry tells you is correct: I'm not in favor of that idea of framing the story inside the funeral episode. I'd thought about it, and Henry and I talked

43. "William Humphrey Untitled Novel, Suggestions for Final Revisions," WH Coll., UT.

about it briefly. Obviously it has its attractions. But to me it seems too expected. From the point of view of information, the book doesn't need it: the "history" is complete. From the point of view of form, I think your phrase describes exactly what I had in mind in rejecting it: "tieing up" the end. It would tie it up—all too neatly, in my view. I hope that you will see this my way. (Knopf Coll.)

The editors and publisher concurred, and there was nothing more said about the question. In fact, there is another reason that *Home from the Hill* should not end neatly tied up, and that is that its ending is a sad undoing: the planned marriage, "the tie," between Theron and Libby, comes undone, and the promised fulfillment of love is cancelled by the working out of the fate that we remember from the beginning.

Chatto and Windus wanted to substitute Anglicisms for Americanisms in the English edition. To their proposed substitution of, for example, "bonnet" for "hood," or "pavement" for "sidewalk," or "hairdresser's" for "barber's shop," Humphrey objected strongly, especially to the latter. He explained to Peter Calvocovessi that in America a hairdresser's shop is strictly for women, and "I cannot reconcile myself to Capt. Wade's going to be shaved in what, to my mind, is synonymous with a ladies' beauty parlor." Humphrey also made a more general point: since in America the charm of English books lay partly in the different vocabulary, why should the reverse not be true?[44]

While Humphrey was adamant in his refusal to revise according to some of the suggestions made by his editors, he felt no reluctance to revise on his own. In fact, as late as 1997 he made an effort to make some corrections and alterations in the text. He wrote out two pages of "corrections" for one of the many reissues of the novel, but they were never used because the first edition was photocopied for all subsequent printings. Although most of the changes on Humphrey's list are to fix typographical errors, a few are interesting—for example: "P. 122 [paragraph] 6. 'The band had been rounded up in niggertown.' That is what the unnamed narrator, writing at that time, would have said. But it is offensive. Change to read: The band had been rounded up in the town" (WH Coll., UT).

The revisions that Humphrey made on his own volition before publication were, as one would expect, much more sweeping. At the time of his preliminary submission of the manuscript to Knopf, he had not completed the boar hunt episode, which, as we have seen, is essential to the development of Theron's character. At the point in the typescript where this scene was to appear, Humphrey

---

44. Humphrey to Calvocoressi, 24 October 1957, C&W.

penned the following: "This episode is unfinished; moreover, it has not been integrated into what follows it as presented in this version. The idea for this episode was a comparatively recent one and since writing this much of it I have not had time to smooth over the joints between it and the parts following. My friends, however, think that even in this fragmentary form it is too good to be left out. My plan is to have Theron rescued by his father, yet to even out the adventure with considerable personal glory too" (WH Coll., UT). It turns out that the character of Theron required that he kill the wild boar entirely on his own, with proficiency and in such a way as to display profound courage; eventually Humphrey wrote the episode according to the demands of the character who had taken on a life of his own. When, then, the complete boar hunt episode in chapter 16 succeeded in elevating Theron to the heroic level of his hunter-father, Humphrey found that there was no reason to include the chapter that followed, whose sole function was to demonstrate Theron's bravery. Therefore the entire episode of Theron's going back into Sulphur Bottom in pursuit of a fugitive murderer is eliminated. Hard as it was to throw out thirty-three manuscript pages, Humphrey consoled himself in his notebook with the thought that "I could make a nice novella out of that part of Home from the Hill that got scrapped. . . . Rather Conradian in theme—a boy's testing himself out—coming through. Like *The Shadow Line*."[45]

Even after Humphrey had initially declared the novel finished on 26 December, he spent a large part of the next day revising and crossing out superfluous passages. Two instances will illustrate the nature of his attention. Just after Hannah finds her murdered husband's body—after the statement "Her mind split as if halved by an axe" (*HFH*, 302)—Humphrey crossed out the following monologue presumably meant to demonstrate her mental collapse: "Some husband. It wasn't me. I wonder it had not happened before. Some husband. I didn't do it. I wonder it wasn't me. I didn't do it before. It wasn't some husband. A wonder I didn't. I didn't. I didn't" (MS, p. 402 [WH Coll., UT]). These incoherent utterances more or less succeed in portraying a divided mind, but Humphrey found a clearer method of conveying her mental state; he incorporates some of these spoken words into an account of her thoughts: "Some husband, she heard a voice say in her mind. It was the voice of her mind, but it sounded distant and strange"—and so on (*HFH*, 302).

45. Humphrey, notebook, entry for 3 January 1958. Later Humphrey wanted to use this discarded chapter when he was writing *Farther Off from Heaven:* "Could I not use some of that in this—with my father as Theron?" (WH Coll., UT). Does this notebook entry suggest that an episode from Clarence Humphrey's life had made its way into the MS of the novel—or that discarded fiction will make its way into the memoir?

Perhaps a plainer indication of Humphrey's thoughtful and precise deletions is in the scene in chapter 59 when Theron returns home to his parents. When his father, who meets him on the lawn, invites him to go in and tell his mother of his return, Theron "remembered the comforting, faintly soapy smell of her breast when she had hugged him to her as a child"—a brief interjection that lets us know that he loves his mother and wants to do what his father suggests—but Theron, having just come from the joyful reunion with Libby, knows the part a son can play in renewing a relationship, and that is the part he means to play with his parents. Therefore, he quickly replies to his father: "No. You tell her," for he knows that his mother will feel gratitude toward the husband who brings the happy news; Theron makes the excuse that he must go back to his house to get his things so that his mother can experience joy in the presence of her husband ("Theron did not want her to be able to see him right away, to see him and forget his father as soon as he had told her" [*HFH*, 299, 300]). What Humphrey saw as superfluous to this scene was the prolonged happy recollection that followed the memory of the comforting "soapy smell of her breast" above; therefore all of the following, originally in the manuscript version, he crossed out: "He remembered hours together over the kitchen table at night when she helped him with his school work. He remembered that sequined dress which, to please him, she had worn among other women of the town to an afternoon children's party" (MS, p. 397 [WH Coll., UT]). The one sentence from the passage that Humphrey retained accomplishes the task required at the moment; all the rest was excess and would have obscured the real point of the episode. By carefully revising the passage, then, Humphrey brings two generations of the Hunnicutt family to the ultimate point of fulfillment: Theron and Libby and their son have resolved to unite, and the promise is held out that Wade—who ceased his philandering when Theron left home—and Hannah, too, are about to achieve a true marriage. But the plot—saddled as it was from the start with an as yet undivulged catastrophe—denies all fulfillment for everyone in the Hunnicutt family.

Yet from the beginning we know that the fate of these characters represents a larger issue: the aristocratic Hunnicutts are defeated by representatives of the middle class. It is a southern theme familiar from Faulkner. Albert kills Wade, and his son-in-law Fred, we assume, keeps Libby. The would-be scion of the Hunnicutt dynasty will have Fred for a father. The boy will not be an accomplished hunter, will not be highly regarded, will not stand head-and-shoulders above everyone else, because his chief model in life will be a buffoon. He will no doubt blend with the new age in which he is born.

And although Theron, carrier of the southern family tradition, seems fully willing to embrace the reality of the present, in the end he cannot escape the traditional code of honor; as he had faced Dale Latham in the past to defend the honor of his father, he now pursues to the death the latest assaulter of his father, and this pursuit takes him back to his old hunting ground, Sulphur Bottom. There the last best remnant of Clarksville aristocracy walks into oblivion, fulfilling to the last his devotion to the old order that must die with him. As Theron undertakes this final gesture, we are overwhelmed by the pity of his ultimate sacrifice. It is indeed terrible that he, so deserving of a better fate, is forced by his own character and circumstance to accept oblivion. Theron, however, laid the groundwork for the tragic end when he fathered the child that was mistaken for his father's. Thus, it is strangely fitting that in avenging the murder of his father he die himself.

The "future had already passed into the past," Libby believed, and here she is surely Humphrey's voice (*HFH*, 249). When the old high way of life becomes an impossibility, Humphrey does not offer up a salubrious alternative. He cuts down the right rose tree because he recognizes that it is infected inwardly; even its shadow proves deadly. However much Humphrey might find a lost way of life preferable to the present—and surely he did, given the nobility of Theron as a character—he declines to embrace the lost cause, the false hope, that the Old South has become.

Home from the Hill (1958), in Knopf's judgment the finest novel to come out of Texas, was helped in its commercial success by being an alternate selection of The Book-of-the-Month Club. By the third week in February it had made the *New York Herald Tribune* best-seller list, and by 3 March it had made the *New York Times* list. Such success prompted *Vogue* to include Humphrey, together with Sir Edmund Hillary, Leonard Bernstein, John Kennedy, Peter Lawford, and others, in its photographic "gallery of international charmers among men"—an honor about which Humphrey was much embarrassed.[46] *Home from the Hill* was made into a bad motion picture in 1960, starring Robert Mitchum, Eleanor Parker, George Peppard, and George Hamilton, and directed by D. Vincente Minnelli. Humphrey never saw the movie. He was even less impressed by the $250 award from the Texas Institute of Letters for the best first novel by a Texan, complaining about it to Knopf on 27 March 1959 as follows:

I'm afraid I don't take much stock in their prize. In fact, it only makes me mad. When I needed encouragement (so badly that I'd have been glad

46. Humphrey to Calvocoressi, 18 February 1958, C&W; "*Vogue*'s Eye View of International Charm," *Vogue*, 15 March 1958, 53. On his copy of the magazine, Grabstald scribbled Humphrey's reaction to the "honor" (HG Letters).

even of theirs)—years ago, when I published my first book—they ignored me. Now there would have been little enough distinction in winning their top award. As it is, it comes much too little, much too late. I've never received any literary handouts before, and I hate to think of losing my virginity to the redneck literati of the Texas Institute of Letters.

Before Knopf knew how Humphrey felt about the award, Knopf had "gone down there and made his speech and accepted the thing in my name," Humphrey complained.[47] The Texas Institute granted Humphrey a similar award seven years later, and there is no record of his objection on the latter occasion.

The financial success of *Home from the Hill* and of the Metro-Goldwyn-Mayer film (Humphrey received ninety thousand dollars for the movie rights) enabled him to take a leave of absence from Bard. In fact Alfred Knopf told Humphrey he was not to sign his Bard contract for the next year but to devote himself full-time to writing.[48] According to Grabstald's notebook entry for 1 March 1958, Humphrey had a guaranteed income of between seven and eight thousand dollars a year from book royalties and the film. But in the autumn of 1958 the flow of funds had not yet begun, and he found himself in a financial pinch as he went from receiving a monthly paycheck to depending upon royalty checks, and so he wrote with some urgency mixed with humor to William Koshland at Knopf on 7 July 1958:

Help! I have received my last check from the college and will be living on nothing. And living means going to Europe, paying for a car there, leaving behind a daughter with tuition to be paid, etc., and no MGM-oney until Jan. 1. Where's that July 1st royalty statement?

Don't write. I'll be in this Wednesday and will call or drop by. (Knopf Coll.)

47. Humphrey to Knopf, 27 March 1959, Knopf Coll.; to Grabstald, undated, HG Letters.
48. Annie Laurie Williams, interoffice memorandum, undated, Williams Coll.; Humphrey to Grabstald, 28 January 1958, HG Letters.

[4]

LOOK AWAY! LOOK AWAY!
(The Ordways)

Duty is the sublimest word in the English language.
—ROBERT E. LEE

The appetite for Texas was from the first a Western passion.
—JOHN QUINCY ADAMS

KATHERINE ANNE PORTER encouraged Humphrey to spend the summer of 1958 at Yaddo, the artists' community in Saratoga, New York, which he declined to apply for, saying in a 28 February letter to her that he "couldn't stand" that sort of thing: "Among all that many writers I would feel like the one dry cow among a herd of milchers" (KAP Coll.). He did not want to buy a house and settle down with Dorothy either, "because his mother may want to live with them," Harry Grabstald wrote in his notebook on 1 March. Therefore on 24 July, supported by the proceeds from the success of *Home from the Hill*, the Humphreys set sail for Europe, where they would spend most of the next six years living a gypsy existence. During this time Bill would write and rewrite the book that became *The Ordways*. Their first stop was London, where they could not sleep for the noise, so after two days, with visions of thatched cottages beside trout streams in mind, they headed for Dorset, the county of Humphrey's favorite writer, Thomas Hardy. They picked Wareham, Hardy's Anglebury, but found, to their disappointment, that because it was a popular holiday spot for the English, the thatched cottages, though in abundance, were all occupied. The determined Humphreys took a room in an inn and set off afoot, "much like a couple of Thomas Hardy characters," in search of accommodation to suit them. They wandered for a week ("Our best day was sixteen miles") and eventually found two rooms at West Mills Farm. In his August report to Blanche and Alfred Knopf, Humphrey wrote: "It's an old mill on the edge of the village [Wareham] common, a dairy farm and chickens and a stream, and the Mears, he a wonderful man with a thick Dorset tongue who keeps us in stitches, and she a wonderful cook who keeps us overfed." Bill's and Dorothy's rooms overlooked flowerbeds on one side and a pigpen on the other.[1]

---

1. William Humphrey to Alfred and Blanche Knopf, 29 August 1958, Knopf Coll.

The practice of grounding his fiction in real places was a feature Humphrey shared with Hardy, and he enjoyed tremendously exploring the real-life settings of his British counterpart's novels. He and Dorothy walked down Egdon Road to Wildeve's inn, The Silent Woman; went by train to Wool Bridge (Hardy's Wellbridge), and saw the house in which Tess Durbeyfield told Angel Clare of her scarlet past on their wedding night. Eventually, on 1 September, the Morgan automobile that Humphrey had ordered before sailing from America and that was supposed to have been ready for them upon arrival in London was delivered, and he and Dorothy immediately adopted the practice of driving to Marnhull on Saturday nights to drink with an assortment of mechanical and agricultural friends at the Pure Drop, the pub frequented by Tess's father. They reminded themselves of Scott and Zelda, crisscrossing the Hardy country in their sporty two-seater. Humphrey became enamored of the rural people of Dorset, whom he characterized as follows in a 29 August letter to the Knopfs:

A more delightfully humorous, irreverent, irrepressible and scampish lot I have never imagined. And where on earth did the American stereotype arise of the Englishman as unapproachable, cold, remote, formal? Just stand on a street corner looking a little uncertain, and someone comes over, asks to help, gives you his address and phone number, and says he'd be delighted to take you rowing next Sunday afternoon if you're not already engaged. A country oughtn't to be too big, I've decided. When people are squeezed together a bit they learn, as they say here, to rub on together. They're not just polite. They're decent. They're not suspicious, but trusting—not close, but curious, not always comparing your ways to theirs and despising you for your difference. They have the great virtue of patience. And they're not a race of god-damned sentimentalists like Americans. And they are not ashamed to be able to speak their tongue. I keep saying to myself, so that now the phrase has come to mean more to me than I can make it express to anyone else, that they are civilized. (Knopf Coll.)

Years later Humphrey recalled that in those days Egdon Heath was free of pine trees, and they could hear the heather bells when the breezes blew. Living in Dorset, Humphrey was as happy as he was ever to be: he liked the country, he liked the people, and his writing was going well. He had started his third book on board the *Liberté* as he and Dorothy sailed to England. In the beginning he thought he was writing a novella, but by the time he had established himself at his writing table at West Mills Farm, his story had expanded. By the end of August Humphrey had written forty pages, "with which," he said, "I am right well pleased."[2]

In October, according to plan, the Humphreys left England to pass the winter in France. They spent two weeks in Paris, devoting their attention to museums where, complained Humphrey in his humorous and hyperbolic mode, "we could see almost nothing, since they depend not on Edison but on his predecessor in the lighting field, and He often shuts off His current." Nonetheless, they acquired a new appreciation of Nicolas Poussin, the French Baroque painter whom they had never much liked. They developed no appreciation for Parisians, however. Having bought a French grammar with the intention of learning the language, Humphrey chucked it in the waste basket after two days, saying, "I don't like these bastards and I'm not going to learn their lousy language."[3]

At the end of the month Bill and Dorothy traveled on to Provence, first to Grasse (which they found unattractive), then to Nice (they were horrified), and finally they scampered into the mountains; the first place they came to was Biot, a quiet little pottery town perched on a mountain about halfway between Cannes and Nice, and here they settled for a while. They found a top-floor apartment with railed balconies overlooking a small courtyard with a palm tree and mimosa in bloom and an orange tree laden with fruit against the wall of the house. Humphrey found pleasure in the rustic simplicity of the town's inhabitants: "We live in the valley just below the southwest side of the town proper, and to go up to shop we climb cobble steps, up and up, through streets that are closed over by long low arches which are really rooms of the houses cut through. One turns a corner and there are the public laundry basins and the women jabbering Italian and Italianate French. The washing is of course done with cold water and a bat." The "streets"—at least forty-five degrees, "some nearer 90," he wrote to Grabstald—"are about wide enough for two starved cats to pass," and he added: "Just this instant outside my window there is passing a herd of milk sheep and their shepherd. He seems to have stepped out of the middle ages." Humphrey was delighted to have found this sleepy, "undiscovered" town before its deflowering by the masses, which he foresaw. A museum was just then being built in honor of the "Tubist" painter Fernand Léger, of all the modern French painters, the one he despised most, because his paintings looked like billboards "advertising plumbing fixtures."[4]

---

2. Humphrey, telephone conversations with author, 18 April 1992 and 8 August 1995; Humphrey to Ian Parsons, 29 August 1958, C&W; to Theodore and Renée Weiss, [19] September 1958, in Weiss Coll.; to the Knopfs, 29 August 1958, Knopf Coll.

3. Dorothy Humphrey to Fred and Barbara Dupee, 12, 13, 14 November [1958], Dupee Coll.

4. Humphrey to the Dupees, 7 January 1959, Dupee Coll.; to the Knopfs, 2 November 1958, Knopf Coll.; to Harry Grabstald, 18 November 1958, HG Letters. Le Musée Fernand Léger, created by Nadia Léger and Georges Bauquier, opened in 1960.

The Humphreys were lonely because they spoke no French. Dorothy had studied the language at Brooklyn College, but her knowledge deserted her in the strain of trying to listen and understand and respond. Therefore Bill was forced to relent in his refusal to make an effort; his early attempts to speak French often ended in amusing noncommunication, as when "in Aix-en-Provence, having made the pilgrimage out to Cézanne's studio, I found myself saying to the custodian, pointing to a paint-box, 'We are the veritable brushes of the master, are we?' " Bill confided to the Knopfs that he sometimes felt so completely stultified and helpless that he could scream, although at other times he coped pretty well by taking a humorous view of his situation. When uncertain about whether to use "le" or "la" he would just blush, certain that the French would "ascribe it to the well-known Anglo-Saxon reticence on this subject," and he tried using hands as a substitute for verbs, eventually learning to get along with the second person singular present tense of three verbs, the past participle of four others. Thus he was able to develop a semblance of communication: "My voisin [neighbor] and I meet over the back wall for about a quarter of an hour every day and converse on a variety of topics, and when done we shake hands extremely vigorously and part in the friendliest frame of mind imaginable. He doesn't know what I've said and I don't know what either of us has said."[5] There were times when Bill would have been pleased to have a conversation in English even with a clergyman or a book reviewer, though generally he inclined to avoid engaging people belonging to these professions. By the time Humphrey left Biot, he had written about ninety pages on *The Ordways,* although during his first month there he had laid it aside and had started what was to become *Proud Flesh.* At this point he had decided that *The Ordways* was going to be somewhat of a picaresque involving a man's search for a lost son.

The Humphreys' Christmas letter (20 December 1958) to the Knopfs, in which they reported on their communication problems in Biot, was two pages, single-spaced, and typed; Alfred's brief response expressed the peculiar wish that Humphrey double-space his letters from then on. Thereupon Humphrey—trying to get under Knopf's skin for no other reason than that he felt his publisher lacked a sense of humor—retyped, double-spacing, the very same 20 December letter and re-sent it (Knopf Coll.). Knopf never acknowledged this retyped letter, and Humphrey's subsequent letters to him were sometimes double-spaced, sometimes not.

Because their French visa was about to run out, the Humphreys had to move on at the end of January. They had earlier planned on going to Vienna but at the

5. Humphrey to the Knopfs, 2 November 1958, Knopf Coll.

last minute decided to give Italy a try, though Bill was predisposed to dislike it. Intending at the outset to remain there no longer than a couple of weeks, they drove first from Biot to Florence, then to Rome, Siena, and Arezzo, then back through Florence to Venice and finally to Lago di Farda and Lugano. About the first week of March, they settled in Lenno, on the western shore of Lago di Como. By this time, Bill had fallen deeply in love with Italy and the Italians, so much so that he had begun—as had Dorothy—nightly lessons in Italian and daily periods of extended study. Soon they were both fluent. On 27 March 1959, he wrote to Knopf that were it not for their daughter Toni and their friends, he would remain in Italy for the rest of his life. He "liked England and the English, liked France (though not the French) . . . but liked Italy and the Italians so much that I don't like the thought of leaving; . . . there is something quick and alert and alive and life-loving in the very glances of the Italians" (Knopf Coll.). He loved them all, from the counts—especially an ironic fascist count who took meals in their hotel—to the "no-counts, more my kind of people," he told Knopf in a letter of 22 April (Knopf Coll.).

Bill's affection was especially directed toward Lenno, and he spent two weeks in mid-March writing a travel essay about the place—"The Mountain of Miracles," which was published in the *New Yorker* in 1960. That done, he returned to *The Ordways* and wrote well on it until the end of April 1959, when he and Dorothy, according to a long-held plan, departed for Spain, with the intention of stopping off at Biot for a day or two on the way. They then drove to Perpignan and went by train to Barcelona. Humphrey liked neither Spain nor the Spaniards, writing to Blanche and Alfred on 17 July 1959: "What we should have done was turn around right [at the start] and headed back to civilization, to the 20th century." What they did was buy railway tickets for Madrid, Toledo, Seville, Granada, Alicante, Valencia, and for return to Barcelona. Humphrey was both eager and hesitant to leave each of these cities—eager because of his revulsion, hesitant for dread of what he might encounter next—and he likened Spanish trains to dromedaries, neither being capable of reaching a speed above five miles an hour downhill. Part of Humphrey's disgust was owing to his left-wing sensibilities, which were offended by the ubiquitous *tricornio* worn by the Franco regime's *Guardia Civil;* he did not really consider the fascist state inappropriate for the people, however: "I had expected to dislike the evidences of the state in Spain, and did; I also came to feel that if any nation deserves such a government it's the Spaniards. A cheerless lot, sour, dour, bigoted, backward, unhandsome, unmusical and suspicious. And ignorant. No, for me the bell did not toll" (Knopf Coll.).

Shaking the dust of Spain from their shoes and returning to France brought the Humphreys much relief. Bill was happy to be behind the wheel of his Morgan again, driving to "lovely Perigord" and Illiers, Marcel Proust's Combray, where they toured Aunt Leonie's house, which was being restored, and where they walked in Proust's garden with the famed aubepines. In charge of restoring this house was an old man named M. Larcher who, dressed in the morning costume of the Third Republic, guided them through it. He played the part of Proustian characters, quoting passages from the novels. The Humphreys spent three days in Illiers, which Bill termed a "lovely town, rather poor and a little sad, and quite unconscious of its fame." They were so happy there that the prospect of Chartres was hardly enough to draw them on, but their week-long stay in Paris proved thrilling. In a letter to the Knopfs, Bill evokes one special night, when after a splendid dinner at Quasimodo's, "a rocket burst over Notre Dame and showered it with falling gold. Instantly thereupon liquid strains of music floated up, and from down below, as if the Seine itself were geyser-ing, great spumy jets of water arched into the sky, veiling the lighted dome of the Pantheon which rose above the tree tops. It was Handel's 200th anniversary, and The Water Music played and the fountains arched and slowly waved over one another like liquid ostrich plumes and the rockets streaked up and burst and showered down."[6]

Leaving France for the United Kingdom via St. Malo, the Humphreys made their way to Penzance, Cornwall, arriving on Bill's birthday, 18 June 1959, and they settled down comfortably in a four-hundred-year-old mill cottage. Everything about the setting—the wheeling gulls, the jackdaws' "weird and wonderful racket on settling to roost," the "rocky, gorsy cliffs above," the bare lonely granite forms below and the "monstrous boulders in heaps running down to the sea, like what was left over when they built England"—pleased him. He also found the setting conducive to getting down to serious work, and he was back to making progress on his second novel.[7]

In a few weeks' time Bill grew restless, and so they moved on to Somerset and spent two weeks at Alfoxton, the Queen Anne manor house two miles from Bristol Channel in which Wordsworth lived in 1797–98 with his sister Dorothy while he and Coleridge were writing *Lyrical Ballads*. There the Humphreys had the pleasure of a park of over a hundred acres on the northern slopes of the Quantock Hills, a salubrious environment that helped Humphrey to write more than the 150 pages on *The Ordways* that he had promised himself to leave with in August.[8] They then returned to London, and he and Dorothy took lodging near the Tate Gallery, where he was disturbed by the noise of a crew digging up a

6. Humphrey to the Knopfs, 17 July 1959, Knopf Coll.
7. Ibid.
8. Humphrey to the Weisses, 5 August 1959, Weiss Coll.

suspected German bomb in the garden of the Tate. Even so, they found the city much more agreeable on this return visit; writing to Knopf on 26 August 1959, Bill allowed that he "could never live in any city for very long—but this one I could imagine for a time" (Knopf Coll.).

On 12 September the couple sailed back to New York on the *Mauretania,* arriving on the eighteenth, having arranged to rent an apartment for two months at 241 West Twelfth Street. Living in the stifling, claustrophobic city, anxious about the chaos that surrounded him, Humphrey got little written. By 30 November they had moved on to Stockbridge, Massachusetts, where they knew nobody and saw nobody. Here Bill hoped he could find the quiet place in his mind that would enable him to make progress on *The Ordways.* Their Morgan, which they had brought back from Europe, was broken down, so they went nowhere. In the next year they moved to Glendale, Massachusetts, where they lived a similarly lonely, uneventful life. In this forced isolation Bill made some headway on the novel. The only significant break from his isolated work was a quick trip to Lexington, Virginia, at the end of 1960 to give two lectures at Washington and Lee.[9]

Humphrey found his sprawling novel hard to contain. He had sent his "hero" on a series of adventures all over Texas in search of his kidnapped son. The technical problems that Bill soon faced stymied him. How, for example, was he to overcome "an incompatibility of tone between the 'funny' and 'serious' sections?"[10] There were no fictional models for Humphrey to follow, for he was writing an original book. Therefore he had to approach and re-approach the writing before he settled all of the small and large issues. His progress was uncertain. He would feel discouraged for months at a time; then he would make a breakthrough and his work would go "rather well again"—but then he would find his fictional house of cards once again collapsing.[11] Over and over, Humphrey escaped the anguish of *The Ordways* by turning to other writing projects until he felt ready to try again.

Bill and Dorothy returned to Italy around year's end (1960) on a freighter. As they looked forward to their Italian sojourn, Bill experienced a sudden seizure of patriotism—or was it a desire to secure an alternative occupation to writing *The Ordways?*—that led him to look into the possibility of lecturing on American literature while abroad. He was, however, apparently discouraged by the detailed planning of his itinerary that would be required by the Bureau of Educational and Cultural Affairs of the State Department.

9. Humphrey to Grabstald, 13 December 1960 and 9 October 1962, HG Letters.
10. Humphrey to the Weisses, 31 January [1960], Weiss Coll.
11. Humphrey to Jean Lambert, 28 April 1960, Lambert Coll.

The remarkably beautiful Etruscan city of Perugia, perched on hills above the Tiber River Valley, was the Humphreys' intended destination, but they were unable to find a house or apartment there. They resorted to Siena, where about the middle of March they found what they at first judged to be felicitous accommodation—Villa Solaia, owned by the Vivantes, a literary and artistic family who took in a few guests. The elder Vivante was the famous philosopher Leone Vivante, author of thirty-three books and whose *English Poetry and Its Contribution to the Knowledge of a Creative Principle* (Faber and Faber, 1950) has a preface by T. S. Eliot; the mother, Elena, was a painter; and their son Arturo Vivante was an erstwhile physician who eventually published several volumes of fiction and poetry and contributed over seventy short stories to the *New Yorker* (Arturo was "always holding his head in his hands, speaking in a kind of eternal wail, sensitive in an outmoded fashion—rather Shelley-like"). Humphrey was particularly fond of Elena, who died two years later. Arturo remembers his mother's and Bill's animated conversations around the dinner table about the baroque, which Bill at first scorned; but he changed his mind after Elena had talked about its exuberance and spirit.[12] Humphrey then embraced the Baroque with enthusiasm, reading the thick tomes on it by Rudolph Wittkower. He became particularly passionate about Borromini.[13] On other evenings at Villa Solaia Humphrey read from his work in progress to the Vivantes. Bill's and Dorothy's room in Siena overlooked a formal garden; everything on the large farm—including apricots, cherries, peaches—was in bloom, and over the haystack in the distance rose the spires of the cathedral and the Palazzo Pubblico. In this fertile setting Bill was unable to advance *The Ordways*. One of his former students who had become a friend, Sherman Yellen, who with his wife Joan visited Bill and Dorothy in Italy, observed that Bill seemed "less confident about his work than before he left for Italy." Then a kidney stone in the spring brought all writing to a stop. His frantic letters to Grabstald, who was a urologist, are marred by ill-formed and incomplete sentences, proof that Bill could not write during this period of excruciating illness.[14]

As enthralling as Villa Solaia was at first, this large house full of various people

12. Arturo Vivante to author, 25 December 1997. It turned out that Arturo and his wife Nancy were the members of the family that Bill and Dorothy saw in future years. They met a few years later in Rome and much later in Wellfleet, Massachusetts, where Arturo lives today.

13. Humphrey to the Weisses, 14 September 1961, Weiss Coll. Humphrey focused on Wittkower's *Art and Architecture in Italy, 1600–1750* (Harmondsworth and Baltimore: Penguin, 1958).

14. Humphrey to Alfred Knopf, 27 March 1961, Knopf Coll.; to the Dupees, 9 May 1961, Dupee Coll.; Tom Rockwell to Grabstald, 5 January 1961, HG Letters; Humphrey to Grabstald, 3 May 1961, HG Letters.

coming and going soon got on the Humphreys' nerves, so after Bill was fully recovered from the bout with a kidney stone, he and Dorothy moved on to Rome on 23 May, where they obtained an out-of-the-way old palazzo with a constant breeze, which they leased for a year. Situated at Corso Vittorio Emanuele 24, Humphrey liked being within a block of the Pantheon, the Campidoglio (the area where it was once thought Julius Caesar was assassinated), and the ghetto. Here, everything seemed to conspire to help Bill's writing on *The Ordways*. Since they knew no one in Rome, there was at first no social distraction. Taking a break from work on his birthday, he and Dorothy went to the Alban Hills, and there he sprained an ankle so severely that he was confined for almost a month.

In the middle of July Jean Lambert, his French translator, arrived for a week's visit, and Humphrey took a holiday from writing, venturing out with the help of a cane. Knowing that Lambert was a sophisticated and knowledgeable traveler, as his book of travel essays, *Le plaisir de voir* (1969), would make evident, Humphrey was therefore alarmed when Lambert said one day, "Bill, today we are going to the Victor Emmanuel monument." Humphrey explained his alarm:

Something had gone wrong with my poor friend. The Victor Emmanuel monument! As all the world knows, that immense vulgarity in garish white marble which the Romans themselves derisively call The Wedding Cake is perhaps the only ugly structure in Rome. I reasoned with Jean, I argued, I refused to go. He was determined. There was nothing to do but humor him. Fortunately—or rather, unfortunately—the thing was not far from the apartment, at least. I had avoided it and had never approached it nearer than a city block—it did not improve upon closer acquaintance. Yet Jean's enthusiasm for it seemed to grow with each step nearer. The absolute end was when he suggested that we mount to the top of it. So we climbed it; he was my guest, after all. There below us lay the Forum. Beyond that the Coliseum. There the Palatine. Off there, the dome of Saint Peter's.

Jean said, "Well?"

I said, "Well, what?"

Jean said, "Wasn't it worth it? Just look! From up here we have the only view of Rome in which you don't see this thing."[15]

15. From a tribute to Lambert presented at Smith College, 7 April 1977 (WH res.) on the occasion of Lambert's retirement party; Andrée Demay, "Jean Lambert," *Smith Alumnae Quarterly,* August 1977, 27.

Writing to Knopf on 7 August 1961, Humphrey forwent mention of his week's holiday from work: the ankle-spraining "was a productive accident," he declared. "I have never worked so well in my life" (Knopf Coll.). Yet he wrote without reluctance to his publisher about the compensation for his hard work that he found in the Roman evenings. After a hard day's writing, he and Dorothy would dine in Piazza Navona, with the Borromini Church in the background; as they listened to the spray of the fountains, the clatter of horse carriages, and the songs of strolling musicians, Humphrey felt that he was "as near heaven as one can expect to come on earth, and explains I suppose why Peter chose this town to set up in" (Knopf Coll.). The onset of the three-week August holiday meant an even quieter Rome, ideal for writing, which Humphrey did from nine till six, seven days a week. He felt so fixed to this place that he was tempted to buy a plot in the Protestant Cemetery. During the autumn Humphrey reread *Tom Jones* for the nineteenth time, read Bellow's *Henderson the Rain King* ("a very good book!"), and the complete works of Faulkner, "who is both worse than I had thought, and so much better that I'm ashamed of ever having run him down. He can be tremendous."[16]

In 1961, four years out from the publication of *Home from the Hill,* Humphrey had written about 500 manuscript pages of *The Ordways* (about two-thirds, he judged, because he foresaw that culling would be needed) but also 120 pages of *Proud Flesh* (about 40 percent), and he had begun eight of the ten stories that would appear in *A Time and a Place* (but had finished none). Alfred Knopf irritated Humphrey by claiming that he could hardly tell which book had the right of way. To mollify the nagging Knopf, who understandably wanted another book from an author in whom he had placed great hope, Humphrey pointed out that it had taken him four and a half years to write *Home from the Hill;* he bid to buy indulgence for even more time for the new novel by remarking modestly on his first novel: "I now think that with a little more time I might have made a pretty good book out of it." He required this time because, he argued, "I am very ambitious. I don't want to write a pretty good book. I want to write a great book." He did not "want to create a season's stir" but to add something to comic literature—and then he avowed, "I want to be remembered after I'm dead."[17] In the same letter Bill made the point to Knopf that *The Ordways* was a harder kind of novel for him to write than *Home from the Hill,* which has a unified plot; *The Ordways* is episodic—which meant that new adventures and new characters must be repeatedly invented without an intricate plot to provide a natural context: "in

16. Humphrey to the Weisses, 30 November 1961, Weiss Coll.
17. Humphrey to Knopf, 26 October 1961, Knopf Coll.

a way it is like writing a great collection of short stories, so that you start afresh, with little help from what has gone before, with each new episode. And yet it must all the same not seem episodic."[18]

Reynolds Price has addressed the same writing problem, noting that he can, with "careful maintenance," keep a narrative engine running for years. All he has to do, while writing a novel, is stop at a place where he knows what will happen next; then he is ready to write the next morning; "it [is] a great joy to wake up, six mornings a week, and to hear the engine running; it [has] been working all night." With short stories, however, "the engine warms up, runs, and stops and goes cold very fast" (*WST*, 61, 60). Such, then, was one reason that writing *The Ordways* was slow-going for Humphrey: he awakened regularly to a cold engine. He was forced to develop patience, learn to wait upon time for inspiration. And he learned, too, that inspiration sometimes proves a Chimera: "Often you spend a week or two writing an episode, only to find, once you surface and get your breath and look around, that you have gotten into very shallow water—or to drop the metaphor, that it's no goddamned good, and into the waste basket goes two weeks of your life."[19]

For most of the first three years of writing *The Ordways*, Humphrey cut around the maggots in his novel's cheese and then filled in the gaps left. But a great crisis occurred in the winter of 1962 in Rome; he saw that carving and fixing would no longer suffice. His work and consequently his state of mind "went completely to hell" when he suddenly felt certain that his novel was "simply awful."[20] The realization plunged him into a deep depression.

A severe and prolonged illness of Dorothy's contributed to Bill's inability to work. She had been ill since about the first of December 1961. After being treated inappropriately for influenza for three weeks but only growing weaker and weaker, she was eventually rushed to the hospital a few days after Christmas and found to have hepatitis. She was required to remain in the hospital for two months and to rest at home for another two. During his wife's recuperation, Bill was very attentive; hour after hour, day after day, he read Shakespeare's plays to her. He found relief from his duties by attending various musical performances. Although he had been disappointed by the opera he saw during the summer, "in which every singer wopped up his role and the whole thing seemed to be a contest as to who could hold all his notes longest," the official opera season brought "the most glorious performance" of Verdi's *Otello*, with Tito Gobbi playing Iago,

18. Ibid.
19. Ibid.
20. Humphrey to Grabstald, 9 October 1962, HG Letters.

"the slinkiest thing you ever saw or heard," and a fair performance of *Entführung aus dem Seraglio*. Being two blocks from the Academy of St. Cecilia, he found it easy to get away for concerts, enjoying especially one by the Parrenin Quartet of Ravel's "Quartet," the last Beethoven quartet, and Alban Berg's *Lyric Suite*.[21] Throughout the winter and spring, Bill hardly approached his writing desk.

But by June 1962, he fell back upon himself, started over again, and recaptured his confidence: "Bill has had very serious trouble with his work and was in a very deeply depressed state . . . but he seems to have pulled out of it now and is tackling anew that which seemed hopeless," explained Dorothy.[22] In a letter from Rome on 1 June 1962, he confessed to Knopf:

> I am just coming out of a kind of crisis arising from a collapse of confidence in my writing the most severe I have ever suffered. Quite suddenly a few months ago I saw that everything I had done on my novel for the past two years was all wrong, worthless. You wouldn't think a grown man could fall into a trance for two whole years, would you, but I did, and the realization has been pretty shattering.
>
> I still have faith in the material and I believe I know where I went wrong and that I can return to that point and (salvaging about 150 pages out of the wreck) still make something out of it. (Knopf Coll.)

One cannot help wondering if Humphrey, in writing these lines, thought of the hubris in the letter of only seven months earlier, where he acknowledged that a picaresque "is perhaps precisely the sort of book which I, with my Flaubertian fretting over each word and over the carefully cadenced rhythm of sentence and paragraph, and with my dependence on plot [see *Home from the Hill*], ought never to attempt. Which is precisely why I am determined to do it. But, as it goes against whatever natural gifts I may have, it does not come easy."[23]

Later in the summer of 1962, the recovered Bill and the recovered Dorothy established themselves in England—in Telscombe, an isolated hamlet in a wooded vale of the windswept Sussex Downs between Lewes and Brighton—where, as Dorothy saw them with her painterly eye, the hills "roll suddenly like an ocean in a heavy swell, treeless but beautifully patterned in every shade of green and gold."[24] Telscombe was the country home of Ian Parsons of Chatto

---

21. Ibid; Humphrey to Knopf, 2 and 28 January 1962, Knopf Coll.

22. Humphrey to Grabstald, 9 October 1962; Dorothy Humphrey to Harry and Milly Grabstald, 1 June 1962, HG Letters.

23. Humphrey to Knopf, 26 October 1961, Knopf Coll.

24. Dorothy Humphrey to the Grabstalds, 4 July 1962, HG Letters.

and Windus, Humphrey's English publisher; he lent the Humphreys his car two days a week when he and his wife Margaret (Trekkie) went to London by train, and this kindness enabled Bill and Dorothy to lay in provisions. Otherwise, they were on foot.

During his depression, Bill's only gesture toward any work had been to dabble among the unfinished stories of *A Time and a Place*. In Telscombe, however, he began to work through the day again on *The Ordways*. His confidence was renewed. Having "got too ambitious and ruined it," Humphrey set about to "cut it down to its just and proper scale."[25] We have a pretty good idea of the revisions that he undertook because of a twenty-page outline that he had submitted in January of 1961 to Anne Laurie Williams, the agent who had sold *Home from the Hill* to MGM. The main scaling down that Humphrey undertook was to limit Sam to one excursion in search of Ned, his kidnapped son. According to Humphrey's "Outline of Untitled Novel," Sam goes west and comes home to find himself dismayed by the resentment he feels toward the son born in his absence because he looks like Ned (WH Coll., UT). Sam prays: "I didn't want another boy! . . . Maybe he'll be a better boy—I don't want a better boy. I just want my boy, my boy!"[26] And so in the earlier form of the novel Sam goes a second time, this time southwest instead of west, in search of Ned. In the final version Sam makes only one excursion and prays a different prayer—with a different result: "A man can have many sons and love them all. Only why did you have to make this one look so much like the other one, to remind me of him a thousand times a day? I know you sent me this boy, Lord, to console me, to take the other's place. But I didn't want to be consoled—at least not just yet. I didn't want another boy. I just want my boy back." The most significant difference between the earlier and the later prayer is that here Sam adds: "Oh, Lord, teach me to love this child of mine" (*O*, 337). This he remains home to do and eventually manages to "put Ned away in the attic of his mind as he had put away his clothes and his toys in the attic of the house" (335).

Sam has many of the same adventures in the earlier version as he does in the final version, though some are different and some are differently ordered. In the final version, Sam encounters the pecan-pie-baking widow Mrs. Eubanks, who is hungry for a husband, at the beginning of his quest, though this humorous incident takes place much later in the earlier draft, after Sam's speech at the political rally in Paris, Texas. Originally Sam takes a train to Paris and buys a horse and buggy there; in the final version he leaves Clarksville in his own wagon, pulled by his plow horse Dolly and the mule.

25. Humphrey to Knopf, 8 June 1962, Knopf Coll.
26. Humphrey, "Outline of Untitled Novel," WH Coll., UT.

In trimming down the novel, Humphrey reduced the number of people who respond to Sam's public speech. He keeps the political backer who tries to persuade Sam to run for lieutenant governor, the swindling "Baptist preacher," and the retired Pinkerton man in search of a case, but he eliminates a Negro who tells Sam "he thinks he might have seen the Vinsons but prays not, for he doesn't want to get mixed up in white folks [sic] affairs" ("Outline," p. 8). Humphrey also eliminates a girl who offers Sam her bastard child to take the place of his lost son. In addition, before Sam gives up for the second time, he helps a young boy named Dick run away from home. Humphrey says, "from this boy Mr. Ordway learns much" ("Outline," p. 12).

Humphrey makes other changes in the final version that help to delineate a consistent picture of Sam Ordway. When Sam finally realizes *two days* after the Vinsons have left that they have left for good, he hurries to the sheriff to make a report. In the original version, we see why Sam had to take a train to Paris to commence his quest: "Terrified, he dashes into town, riding bareback on his old plowhorse, whom he leaves dead in the road a mile outside of Clarksville, having ridden her to death" ("Outline," p. 4). In the published novel Humphrey tones down this account, making the action accord with the attributes of his character, for Sam is a man who would never ride a horse to death—but he is a man who would feel keenly guilty for his own tardy response: "So it was not until the afternoon of . . . the *third day* . . . that my grandfather came into Clarksville, to the sheriff's office—afoot, having left the wagon and his broken-winded team a mile outside of town, and in the wagon bed the frayed piece of harness strap with which he had punished Dolly and the mule for his own slow suspicion" (*O*, 133; my italics).

Sam's preparations for his westward quest are significantly different in the two versions. In the final one much is made of the fact that Sam "traveled light, trusting to the luck of the road, the hospitality of people" (*O*, 153). In the earlier one, however, Sam buys himself two items, a new overcoat and a pistol; the townsmen think that Sam means to gun down Will Vinson and therefore "give him a hero's send-off" ("Outline," p. 8). Significantly, in the final version Sam leaves home quietly, reasoning that the fewer who know about his venture, the easier it will be to return empty-handed. Also, in the early version, Sam has packed his belongings in "the only piece of luggage in the house, a relic of the only trip any Ordway within memory had ever taken. It had been Sam's father's valise, his name, painted thereon when Private Thomas Ordway, C.S.A., set off to war in 1861, still discernible along the side, and it had come west with him" ("Outline," p. 14). This valise, then, leads the earlier version to the rather long account of his father's role in the battle of Shiloh and the family's subsequent emigration to Clarksville, the ninety-seven-page story of the earlier generation that the finished version of the novel begins with.

There are some minor differences in the way individual scenes of this section about the Thomas Ordway family are presented. For example, in the original plan the family mule was killed and cooked but not eaten: "hungry as they all were by then, none of them could eat a bit of [the mule], the children out of old affection, the father out of shame" ("Outline," p. 15). In the final version only the father is unable to eat the mule: with tears swimming in his eyes, he staggers away from the table and out of the house. But in both cases the killing of the mule precipitates the decision to leave Tennessee and go west. In the final writing, the digging up of all the family graves is part of the preparation for leaving, done after the farm has been sold and a wagon obtained; originally, however, Thomas Ordway immediately arises from the mule meal and goes to the family burial ground; he is found an hour later digging up his father's grave: " 'We're leaving!' he had screamed at them. 'And we're leaving nothing behind!' " ("Outline," p. 15). In the published novel Thomas makes the announcement at the table: "I won't live in a country where things have come to such a pass the folks have to eat their mules" (*O*, 54).

The most significant revision is that in the final version Sam does not purchase a pistol but takes with him the seventeen-and-a-half-inch-long Civil War horse pistol that a brevet major had presented to his mother after the battle at Shiloh. Humphrey takes pains to convey the mock heroic nature of Sam's westward venture: when he says that Sam "packed" a pistol, he adds, "I mean packed it on the bottom of his gladstone bag" (*O*, 150). The pistol, we are told, has not been fired in thirty-six years, and it will not cock. It is the first indication of the great irony of the title for Part 3: "Sam Ordway's Revenge." He is, of course, utterly incapable of revenge, though Texas "is a place where a man, where even a boy is expected to find quarrel in a straw when honor is at stake." Like Hamlet, Sam "admired men who could take fire at a spark, who were not to be mollified by anything short of blood, who handed down the torch of their wrath to their descendants, but he could not emulate them. Now, like Hamlet, he had had a cause, and been unpregnant of it" (152). The pistol, then, which had been taken into battle at Shiloh and had been used heroically in the last generation, is a prop that symbolizes the present generation's incapacity to function heroically. When the pistol explodes accidentally in a courtroom, all notions of Sam's "heroic" revenge go up in smoke. But the novel's intention is not to be critical of Sam's inadequacy but rather to show how inappropriate the old code of heroic honor is to a civilized man in the present day. Sam's inadequacy is his virtue, for he possesses a sympathetic perceptiveness that allows the novel to expand the generous spirit.

There are additional more or less significant differences between the early and final forms of *The Ordways*. Instead of the entire family sans Ned returning to Clarksville after the reunion in Del Rio, Humphrey originally had Sam, "surrounded by his children, . . . quietly and happily" die ("Outline," p. 19), an ending too obviously contrived and out of keeping with the otherwise comic conclusion. One other difference bears mentioning: in the early version the narration was in the third person, switching to the first-person only in the final section when Joseph—Tom in the final version—Ordway appears and meets his uncle Ned. Humphrey's decision to rearrange the order of the novel and to have it all told by that same first-person narrator not only solves many of the narrative problems stemming from the outlandishness of many of the episodes, but it also lends a unity to the whole: as the narrator gains insights into his grandfather from listening to his stories, and as he looks back on those stories from thirty years away, he gains insights into himself, and he grows in the understanding of life.

During the time that Humphrey was carrying out these massive revisions, he worked steadily and happily: after he had put away his work for the day, he and Dorothy frequently took afternoon rambles through the Sussex countryside, exploring the public footpaths that crisscross the landscape. In addition to socializing with Ian and Trekkie Parsons, Humphrey delighted in the company of Leonard Woolf, who had been Virginia Woolf's husband. Humphrey found him, he told Knopf in a 12 July letter, "a gracious and courtly man who in his time has known everyone and tells amusing anecdotes of Thomas Hardy and Henry James and rather scurrilous ones of Bertie Russell and others" (Knopf Coll.). Bill often visited Leonard, and they would talk through the night about music.[27] Before the summer of 1962 was over, Blanche and Alfred Knopf paid the Humphreys a visit at Telscombe. Knopf wanted to make sure that his writer was writing.

Leaving Old School Cottage in Telscombe in mid-October, the Humphreys headed back to Rome with the expectation of finding an apartment as easily as they had done eighteen months earlier. In the meantime, however, all had changed: galloping inflation and a severe housing shortage turned the couple desperate. Rental agents laughed in their faces, and they walked the streets day after day searching for a sign that said "*da affittare.*" Just as they were about to give up and move on to they knew not where, they found what they thought must be the most pleasant apartment in all of Rome. It was near St. Peter's Basil-

27. Jose Yglesias, "William Humphrey," ed. Sybil Steinberg, *Publishers Weekly,* 2 June 1989, 65.

ica, at Salita Sant' Onofrio 23. The four-room apartment had two terraces, and the drawing room was glass on two sides, providing views of the Tiber and the domes and rooftops of the city.

Rome was not the peaceful city that it had been several months earlier. Social and political turmoil was breaking out into violence on a regular basis. Communists, monarchists, fascists, and social democrats all demonstrated in the streets and clashed with each other as well as with the authorities. The day before the Humphreys moved into their apartment, an estranged husband had bashed his wife's head in with a paving stone just outside their door. Seeking relief from the social discord in the musical offerings of the city brought mixed results. Bill did not like Stravinsky's conducting a program of his own works ("I'm not much for Stravinsky anyhow, nor for any reputation based on making concert music out of ballet music," he wrote to Knopf on 5 November), although the Humphreys were enthusiastic about a fine concert given by Nathan Milstein (Knopf Coll.).

On 7 February 1963, Phyllis McGinley wrote to Humphrey informing him that he was to be given an award of $2,500 by the National Institute of Arts and Letters "in recognition of your creative work in literature"—which did indeed surprise him, for only a week before he had read an article in *Time* magazine "on all the writers worth watching and every dog and his body was mentioned except yours truly," he wrote to Alfred Knopf on 11 February (WH Coll., UT; Knopf Coll.). Humphrey informed McGinley, who was chairman of the awards committee, that though he appreciated the award, he would be unable to attend the presentation ceremony in May in New York City.[28]

On the day that he received McGinley's letter, Humphrey wrote to Ted and Renée Weiss that he had read Dorothy the first two hundred pages of the new version of the novel, and for the first time, he said, "we thought it was good" (Weiss Coll.). His subsequent letters to the Weisses suggest that he continued to make good progress and, further, that he was enjoying the work. On 20 March 1963, he told them about Sam Ordway's reaction when Topsy the circus elephant dies:

> Well, for a time a dead elephant has been a good drawing attraction. However, the engagement is understandably of limited duration. Now the town fathers are insisting that Topsy be removed. But Topsy as I said weighs 15000 lbs. And remember, that's dead weight. Well, it is Mr. Ordway who solves the problem. . . . "Well, as I see it," he says, "we have either got to get that elephant away from this town, or—" "Or what?" "—Or get this

28. Sanka Knox, "Honors Bestowed by Arts Academy," *New York Times*, 23 May 1963, 37.

town away from this elephant." So today I have got to move a town. So must close and roll up my sleeves. (Weiss Coll.)

After all of the extensive revisions and rewritings, Humphrey had four hundred pages that he was satisfied with, about three-fourths of the projected novel. Feeling in need of a holiday, he and Dorothy, living in Rome at the time, decided to visit Florence for three days and take the manuscript along to read aloud at the end of each day's sightseeing. On the morning of 15 March 1963, the Humphreys boarded a crowded Rome-Milan express. The only copy of the mostly finished novel was in an expensive new briefcase, which Dorothy placed on a seat while she searched in vain for a seat for Bill. "Damned if I'll pay first class to stand up for four hours," bellowed Bill: "Let's get off. There's another train in forty minutes. Only hurry. This one is about to pull out." Fifteen seconds later, as Bill and Dorothy stood on the platform, they remembered the briefcase. At the end of the day, having received no news about the briefcase's recovery, Humphrey sat down at his typewriter to begin rewriting the novel, according to his letter of 20 March to Pete Lemay (Knopf Coll.). The resiliency that this letter portrays is probably posturing. Humphrey had forgotten all about this brave pose when he gave Geoffrey Stokes an account of his feelings about the lost manuscript twenty-one years later: "I remember my hands trembling all the time I walked through [Rome] at the thought—no, not the thought; I wasn't thinking—it was simply from the wound that had so devastated me. That was my stock in life. I was a done man. I was finished."[29] Before the day of the loss was over, the stationmaster called to say that the briefcase had been found in Milan. The next morning Humphrey began making a copy of the manuscript, with eleven carbons. Following the novel's dedication, there is an unusual note of appreciation for the Italian National Railways, especially for the stationmaster in Rome, Michele Fortino.

In the same month Humphrey bought a Volkswagen, intending to drive to England; but he was not altogether happy with his concession to practical considerations: "I do hate to contribute to german prosperity, especially having just read a 1000 page biography of Hitler and being anyhow strongly anti-german—a feeling which is daily enforced by the fact that we live in a buildingful of Germans, but what is one to do—Italian cars are junk." The only consolation was that, as Dorothy said, the Volkswagen "*looks* Jewish."[30] On 30 April they headed

29. Geoffrey Stokes, "Literature Is Hell: The Strange Success of William Humphrey," *Village Voice Literary Supplement* 28 (September 1984), 1.

30. Humphrey to Weisses, 29 March 1963, 10 April 1963, Weiss Coll.

for England, going by way of the Italian lakes, through Jura and Alsace-Lorraine, and bypassing Paris. Bill was looking forward to a week's trout fishing in Wales: "I've earned it," he wrote to Knopf on 19 April: "In fact, I need it. The past 15 months I have worked so hard that I'm in a state of near exhaustion, one evidence of which is that I have had four really nasty, really three-to-six-days-of-utter-incapacitation colds these last six months" (Knopf Coll.). After Bill's fly-fishing, the Humphreys returned to Old School Cottage in Telscombe, where Bill bent his shoulder to *The Ordways*. Time away from the manuscript helped him now to see problems with it. Insisting on writing the best book he could, he described his novel's problems and the need for further revisions to Lemay on 4 July 1963:

> It is too episodic, that's one thing that worries me (I am speaking of the picaresque section); each adventures [*sic*] stands off too much by itself, they don't lead into one another as they should. And it's too imbalanced in the direction of humor and satire. The adventures which Sam Ordway has are too external to him. That he should see something of the larger world is right and proper, something of the world which has little or nothing to do with the reason for his setting out; but his personal quest, and the effect of that larger world upon his state of soul as regards that quest and his motives for it, this has been neglected in the author's interest in the world itself. I don't know if I am making this clear, but at least I know what I mean. More importantly, I think I know a few ways to correct it. But Lord oh Lord, how endlessly difficult this book has been. I am delighted, amazed, that you should say it seems done with ease. (Knopf Coll.)

The Humphreys remained in Telscombe until September, even though the derelict cottage had become so leaky that Bill had to wear a raincoat while working at his typewriter. Knowing that later in the month he would be assuming the Visiting Glasgow Professorship at Washington and Lee, which entailed four public lectures to be given in the fall and winter, he felt compelled to put his manuscript of *The Ordways* aside and work on the lectures: he managed to read five thousand pages of James Fenimore Cooper in preparation for his lectures, roughed out one lecture, and made a good start on the second before he and Dorothy sailed on 11 September for New York on a Dutch liner, the *Statendam*.[31]

31. Humphrey to Leonard Woolf, 12 March 1964, Woolf Coll.; to Harding (Pete) Lemay, 5 August 1963, Knopf Coll.; Dorothy Humphrey to the Weisses, 16 August 1963, Weiss Coll.

One of those lectures, "Ah, Wilderness! The Frontier in American Literature," would be published in 1977 by Texas Western Press.

Although Humphrey was expected in Virginia, he and Dorothy could not resist spending a few joyful days with the Weisses at Bard before making their way south. When they put up in the Robert E. Lee Hotel in Lexington, Bill was still working on those first two lectures and becoming more and more nervous about the whole thing, perhaps in part because Katherine Anne Porter had preceded him as the Glasgow professor. It was a striking irony for Humphrey, of all southern writers the most bent upon debunking the Old South and all that it stood for, to find himself ensconced in Lexington, Virginia, and lecturing in the very Shrine of the South. He was to present his allotment of public lectures in the university chapel dedicated to the memory of Lee, which Humphrey jokingly referred to as "the Robert E. Lee Episcopal Church—the only one in the world not named after some saint or other." The display of Lee's horse Traveller's bones, like the relic of a saint, struck Humphrey as comical. Rather than feeling in accord with the sentiment of reverence toward Lee's shrine—and the one to Stonewall Jackson near the abutting campus of the Virginia Military Institute—Humphrey felt himself more in harmony with his former colleague Ralph Ellison, who would soon speak before a desegregated audience in the same chapel that Humphrey would be lecturing in.[32]

When he delivered his final lecture at Washington and Lee near the middle of January 1964, Humphrey returned frantically to *The Ordways*, the completion of which he had promised by 15 April. He actually finished the novel on 1 March, the eve of Texas Independence Day. The official publication date for the novel had to wait until 1 February 1965 for promotional reasons.[33] That Humphrey had taken every bit of six years to write *The Ordways* did not please Alfred Knopf, especially since Humphrey had reported as early as 1960 that he had written three hundred pages of it. Bill's long letters to Knopf explaining why it was taking so long, especially ones offering the excuse that inspiration was failing him and that he had put *The Ordways* aside to work on another novel *(Proud Flesh)* and on some short stories *(A Time and a Place)*, had not set well with the practical-minded Knopf, who had begun to lose confidence in his bright young writer. In 1961 Knopf had been uncertain whether *The Ordways* was going to have the right of way over "The Renshaws," which was the working title of *Proud Flesh* and had urged, "I hope you won't take too much longer to finish [*The Ordways*] up, be-

32. Humphrey to Knopf, 18 November 1963, Knopf Coll.
33. Humphrey to Lambert, 1 February 1965, Lambert Coll.; to the Weisses, 5 April 1964, Weiss Coll.

cause I think a writer doing this kind of book runs a distinct risk of going stale on it [if] he lives with it for too long a time. And you've been with it quite some time now." When Humphrey finally sent Knopf an early version of both novels, only to have Knopf remark that he could not offer much in the way of useful comment "considering the shape they are in," Humphrey began to feel out of sorts with his publisher. Knopf had also made some remarks about the improbable adventures in the one and the far-fetched humor and brutality of the other. He had closed this letter with yet another prod: "Six years has become the minimum lapse that we can hope for between drinks, and in the contemporary writing and publishing world, that's a long time." With nose out of joint, Humphrey had replied: "I must say I am puzzled and rather disconcerted by your statement, 'considering the state they are in, I don't know that I can make a great deal of useful comment.' I thought both of them well enough along to give a pretty good idea of what they will be when finished."[34] By the time, then, that Humphrey got round to submitting the finished novel, he and Knopf had lost the luster that each had once found in the other.

At the end of 1963 there was another problem with *The Ordways*. Humphrey had submitted all but the final section to his publisher, but events occurred in Dallas that caused him great anxiety about one of the features of his novel. President John F. Kennedy was assassinated on 22 November 1963, and Lee Harvey Oswald was murdered two days later. These events provoked concerns about the novel's satire on the Texas tradition of lawlessness. Humphrey was on the telephone to Pete Lemay about this and expressed his reservations all over again by post "that nothing about Texas justice is now a fit subject for wit, and that a satire on the common Texas expectation that a man revenge his own wrongs outside the law is, after the events of last week, a sort of gallows humor and hardly in decent taste."[35] Humphrey was particularly disturbed about such passages as the following, containing Texas views that Sam Ordway hears on the streets of Dallas: "Let me give you a word of advice, Mr. Hathaway [one of the aliases that Sam assumes]. . . . Don't let on to nobody that you have had the law working on this for you. I'll overlook it myself 'cause you're a stranger and don't know no better. But hereabouts you get the law out after a feller, why folks that never even liked him before start pulling for him. Out here in Texas folks do look down on any man that goes to [the law]" (*O*, 267). Sam has heard it before and will hear it again: in Texas a man has to take the law into his own

34. Humphrey to Knopf, 11 February 1960, 26 October 1961, 1 June 1962, 13 June 1963, Knopf Coll.; Knopf to Humphrey, 4 June 1963, WH Coll., UT.

35. Humphrey to Lemay, 3 December 1963, Knopf Coll.

hands, right his own wrongs ("A man wore his law strapped round his waist out there" [88]).[36]

Humphrey continued in his letter to his editor: "I can't help feeling that these observations of mine might have seemed illuminating were the book already in print, but that now it is going to look as if they've been made—and made in altogether too jocular a tone—as a result of last week's happenings. Satirizing Texas now seems a bit unseemly." Lemay had already assured Humphrey that he "should not be concerned about this matter"; the novel "is an illuminating examination (if you'll pardon the critical jargon) of certain attitudes about life, law, and revenge which reveals more about what happened in Dallas last week than anything I have read or probably ever will read."[37] Additional correspondence eventually assuaged Humphrey's anxiety, and he refrained from revising his novel further.

The world might have expected Humphrey to fail in his second novel—a common fate of American writers whose first novels are greeted with great acclaim. "With that 'major American novelist' label stuck to him," wrote James R. Frakes in *Book Week*, "the slaughterhouse seemed the inevitable next step." But instead Frakes found that Humphrey's "brilliantly comic" second novel "invalidates quite a few such theories"; instead of being the expected poor imitation of *Home from the Hill*, it is "a strongly independent work evincing growth and sureness." On the same day, Elizabeth Janeway declared on the front page of the *New York Times Book Review* that *The Ordways* is "better than the first," an assessment based partly on the contention that "real" comedy is harder to write than tragedy. She allowed that *The Ordways* "isn't a perfect book. It's just a terribly good one, expansive, exploratory, with breathing space for its characters and their humors." Janeway had special praise for "the way Humphrey handles the language": it "is astonishing and individual." While Janeway found the shifting in tone, as the novel moves from the heroic past to the ordinary present, appropriate, Eleanor Dienstag, writing in the *New Republic*, saw that shift as "curious and abrupt," complaining further that "the extremes of comedy and tragedy suddenly make you suspicious of both, and at that moment the magic circle of art is broken and

36. This attitude has its origin in the early years of the Texas Republic; in 1838 the Texan had no confidence in local law enforcement. According to Elithe Hamilton Kirkland, rings of outlaws, "disguised as honest voters, had managed to gain control of local elections and place their fellow outlaws in office to persecute the innocent and release the guilty. . . . The honest minority, to circumvent the lawless law, resorted to personal vengeance for depredations" (*Love Is a Wild Assault* [New York: Doubleday, 1959], 343–44).

37. Lemay to Humphrey, 29 November 1963, Knopf Coll.

you feel robbed of that final and complete pleasure which each masterfully written section led you to expect would be ultimately yours."[38]

Newsweek was impressed by the extent to which *The Ordways* was out of step with contemporary fiction and was especially pleased by the absence of sex: "While novelists are descending, like so many oceanographers, to new and ever more improbable depths of sexual frankness, Humphrey has written a book without a single kiss, but full of love—a man's love for his wife and son, a boy's love for his grandfather, a whole family's affection and piety for their forebears." This reviewer concluded by promising Humphrey what he most desired— readers in future generations: "It is . . . a celebration of character, of goodness, and of honor as they are defined by, and as they define, a place in the American landscape. One is not only pleased but proud to read 'The Ordways.' It is that rarest of volumes, a novel to keep for the children to read—as soon as they can."[39]

While *The Ordways* was receiving mostly rave reviews, Humphrey was five thousand miles away—in Alassio, Italy, writing on *Proud Flesh*. He had given instructions to his publishers and friends that he did not want to see any reviews—"no matter how good they might be." He complained to Ted and Renée Weiss that "well-intentioned friends, sure that they know me better than I know me, have been sending them to me in batches, despite my prohibition."[40] The Weisses were two of those "well-intentioned friends," and they did indeed know that Bill's assertion that he cared nothing for the reviews was mere posturing and based on a fear that the reviews would be bad. Several months earlier he had admitted this very fear when he wrote to them about "how hard I have worked on the book, and how long, and how discouraged I got, and how suicidally self-critical I was while on it, and now I have got to hold my breath for months waiting for it to come out so that the reviewers can demolish it. Lord o Lord, wait till those people at the NY Review of Books get done with me! And the silence with which it will be treated by all the little mags, as before. One of the most felice things about Alassio is its distance from American newspapers and magazines!"[41] Bill's position might seem self-protective in the following way: not hearing anything, he could work on *Proud Flesh* without facing the discourage-

38. James R. Frakes, "An Abundance of Life in the Graveyard," *Book Week*, 31 January 1965, 5; Elizabeth Janeway, "Journey through Time," *New York Times Book Review*, 31 January 1965, 1, 40; Eleanor Dienstag, "West from the Graveyard," *New Republic*, 27 February 1965, 24, 25.

39. "Horizon Everywhere," *Newsweek*, 1 February 1965, 77, 78.

40. Humphrey to Woolf, 8 February 1965, Woolf Coll.; to the Weisses, 7 February 1965, Weiss Coll.

41. Humphrey to the Weisses, 10 September 1964, Weiss Coll.

ment of critical reviews of the last book; he did not have to assume that the reviews were bad if he did not receive any, but surely if they were really good his friends would know to send them, and he would be pleased. Such a strategy would have made sense, but for Humphrey nothing could be this simple. Once assuming the posture of not caring about the reviews, he perversely played it out, and when the batches of excellent reviews began to arrive, he poured over them, recording every remark that he could imagine any offense in. On successive days he complained in the same terms to Leonard Woolf and to the Weisses:

> Oh, Lord, Lord, I am so deepdown weary of their game of counting up my literary debts, of being made to feel like an anthology, a textbook for Modern Lit 101! Wm. Faulkner they have hung around my neck like an albatross, but beyond him the count, to my knowledge, now comes to 23 writers whose stepson I'm said to be, ranging from James M. Cain to Angus Wilson, and including 7 I've never read, 7 to whom I'm indifferent, and 7 I can't stand—meanwhile never mentioning the writers to whom I am, and would be proud to acknowledge I am, indebted. What the hell is a pat on the head worth from them? Who wants their opinions, good or bad? There is nothing more heartsickening than imperceptive praise.

A week after this whining and ranting, Humphrey owned up to being pleased by the reviews—at least to Ian Parsons and Jean Lambert: "The reception the book is getting flabbergasts me. Even I don't think it's all *that* good."[42] When Pete Lemay forwarded copies of reviews on a regular basis, Humphrey never sent letters of objection.

If Humphrey had only waited, he would have had something reasonable to be upset about when he saw Walter Sullivan's review in the *Sewanee Review,* the only truly sullen response in a national publication—and in one that had published two of Humphrey's early stories. Sullivan denounced Humphrey in an unusually strident manner. "Reading *The Ordways,* one gets the feeling that Humphrey has missed the point of what literature is all about," he said, but did not explain what literature is all about. Sullivan did, however, stipulate the novel's main faults as he saw them: "The tone is pompous, the descriptions are too long, the characterization is largely flat, and the dramatic force of various scenes is often dissipated. The plot is neo-picaresque, the search by a father for his kidnapped son, and the circumstances of the kidnapping are rather incredible, even

42. Humphrey to the Weisses, 7 February 1965, Weiss Coll.; to Woolf, 8 February 1965, Woolf Coll.; to Ian Parsons, 16 February 1965, C&W; to Lambert 18 February [1965], Lambert Coll.

for a novel outside the realistic tradition." Sullivan complained, too, of hackneyed southern images—"the same images we have seen for forty years." Surprisingly, this reviewer did in fact get the point of *The Ordways*—it was just not a point that he liked: that the past must be eclipsed if we are to live authentic lives in the present with hope for the future. For Sullivan this was not an agreeable theme, and he therefore attacked Humphrey as wanting in feeling: "He seems isolated, cut off from the past that he writes about, emotionally deadened. He knows from the newspapers and magazines what he ought to think. But nobody has yet made clear to him what he ought to feel, and so he feels nothing."[43]

The only other unsympathetic reviews were, not surprisingly, from Humphrey's home state. The *Houston Post*, the *Dallas Times Herald*, and the *Dallas News* formed a dismissive chorus: the book lacked "any ultimate meaning about Texas itself." Humphrey never uttered a complaint about the Texas response, which was just what he had expected it to be. In fact, he seemed to enjoy it. In a letter to Ian Parsons, he quoted from a letter that he received from a Texas-born "lady": "Yours is the dullest and most boring book I ever read. I can't imagine why anyone should want to read it. . . . I hope that you and Knopf share my $5.95, as there will be few others to donate same." Humphrey then commented: "Bless her hard little old heart! I hope there will be many more like her. My satire is finding its target, and nothing sends people (or Texans, at any rate) to the book stores in greater numbers than the expectation of being outraged."[44]

The strained personal relations between Humphrey and Alfred Knopf notwithstanding, the Knopf firm pulled out all the stops in promoting sales of *The Ordways*. Following a full-page advertisement in the *New York Times Book Review* on 31 January (repeated on 6 June), Knopf advertised extensively in newspapers (book pages and book sections) across the country. The firm also arranged for the book to be discussed on radio programs, and its commercial success was helped by its being selected by the Literary Guild, even though Humphrey somehow felt that this was not as good as the Book-of-the-Month Club. The publication of about sixty manuscript pages in the *Saturday Evening Post* on 7 November 1964, under the title "The Monument and the Shadow," surely primed the public's appetite for the novel. Moreover, once the book had been sold to Columbia Pictures and scheduled for production, Knopf and Columbia teamed up to sponsor a national bookstore window-display sweepstakes, the prize being a week's

43. Walter Sullivan, "Worlds Past and Future: A Christian and Several from the South," *Sewanee Review* 73 (1965): 723, 724.

44. Lon Tinkle, "Is Bookworm Now a Status Symbol?" *Dallas Morning News*, 14 February 1965, sec. 6, p. 10; Humphrey to Parsons, 23 January 1965, C&W.

holiday in Los Angeles. Humphrey wrote to his English publisher—no doubt to imply that Parsons might do the same—to avow that no publisher could do more than Knopf had done to insure that the book sold well.[45]

Although the motion picture was never made, the advertising and other promotional efforts, together with the excellent reviews, helped to place *The Ordways* on the best-seller lists by 5 March (the *New York Times,* the *Herald Tribune,* the *New York Post,* and *Time*).[46] Pete Lemay wrote to Humphrey on 22 March 1965 that the novel was in its sixth printing, with 31,500 copies in print (Knopf Coll.).

Since its initial reception *The Ordways* has received only scant attention. Bert Almon in *William Humphrey: Destroyer of Myths* rightly saw that the novel takes critical aim at the myths of the South and the West (159–82). Gary Davenport, in the *Southern Review,* found much to praise in the account of Samuel Ordway's westward trek: the "grotesque hyper-reality . . . puts the reader in mind of Dickens or Kafka or perhaps Garcia Marquez." But he judged the novel deficient for a reason quite the opposite of Sullivan's. In Davenport's mind, Humphrey wrote *too* feelingly of the past. He objected in the extreme to Part 1, "In a Country Churchyard," which contains the story of Thomas and Ella Ordway's migration from Tennessee to Texas and the events leading up to it. Davenport's objection is frankly as mystifying as Sullivan's. His complaint is identical to the one he lodged against *Home from the Hill*—that Humphrey possesses an "uncritical loyalty" to his subject, in this case to "Southern history and clannishness."[47] The passage that aroused Davenport's special disapprobation is the every-southern-boy-and-the-Civil-War passage, which in its essentials derives from Faulkner's *Intruder in the Dust:* "For me, as for every Southern boy, it was learning that the Civil War was lost which started it all over again; from that time onward each battle had to be refought. The finality of it being inadmissible, my mind drew up short, clinging to that last moment when there was still time. For me it was always noon of July 2 at Gettysburg, and now that the cost of delay was clear,

---

45. The Weisses to the Humphreys, 8 November 1964, Weiss Coll.; Knopf promotional materials, Knopf Coll.; Humphrey to Parsons, 16 February 1965, C&W.

46. Why the novel was not made into a motion picture is unclear, but it might have had something to do with Humphrey's response to the screenplay by Daniel Taradash, who was also supposed to have been the producer—assuming that Humphrey conveyed his feelings to Taradash; on 26 January 1966 he said to Woolf and the Parsons: "The man who is writing the screen version of The Ordways just sent me his adaptation. It is of an ineptitude and a vulgarity that shocked even me, who expected the worst" (C&W).

47. Gary Davenport, "The Desertion of William Humphrey's Circus Animals," *Southern Review* 23, no. 2 (April 1987): 499.

Longstreet would delay no more. Pickett's charge still moved forever up Cemetery Ridge" (*O*, 65). Davenport asserted that in passages like this Humphrey "ceases to speak as a particular man and strives to speak for mankind," and, Davenport claimed, "Not only are such sentiments inorganic to the novel, they are arguably not even true: they tell us less about every southern boy than about the author's compulsion to speak for every southern boy."[48]

The error in such a judgment derives from the critic's failure to discriminate between the author and the narrator. Had Davenport noted that the narrator's name is Tom Ordway, after his great-grandfather, he might have been saved from failing to make the very real distinction between writer and narrator, and then he would have seen how absolutely organic such a passage indeed is to the novel. The narrator is the main unifying factor in *The Ordways*, and an essential one, since the novel comprises four generations of the Ordway family. The first part of this family album is about the narrator's great-grandparents, Thomas and Ella, who removed the family from Tennessee to Clarksville, Texas. The next two parts are about his grandfather Samuel: Part 2 is about the loss of his son Ned, stolen when he was three years old, and Part 3 is about his search all over Texas for Ned, who is half brother of the narrator's father. (The grandfather tells the story of his parents and himself to the narrator when he is a boy.) Part 4 of the novel, an account of the entire family's visit to Uncle Ned's Angora goat farm in southwestern Texas, is based on the narrator's boyhood experience.

The setting for the narration in Part 1 is the Ordway family plot in the churchyard of a white clapboard church in Mabry, Texas, about ten miles west of Clarksville; the day is a Saturday in October, after the crops are in and after hog killing, known as graveyard working day, also a central element of *Home from the Hill*, "A Fresh Snow," and *Farther Off from Heaven*. Reminiscent of the enduring sense of place found in Marygreen that is described in chapter 2 of Hardy's *Jude the Obscure*, *The Ordways* portrays a strong sense of the timelessness of the setting and an awareness of the relationship of one generation to another: "Younger grave-tenders were not noticeably oppressed by the thought that others would someday do the same office for them. Many a mating in the community, later solemnized in the church, had had its beginning as boy and girl pulled weeds side by side on graveyard working day" (*O*, 7).

As each grave is tended, the story of its inhabitant is retold—it is a yearly ritual—and so we know that the narrator has heard the family stories repeatedly.

---

48. Ibid.; Bert Almon, "William Humphrey's 'Broken-Backed Novel': Parody in *The Ordways*," *Southern Quarterly* 32, no. 4 (Summer 1994), provides a summary of other critics' complaints against the novel (107).

Some of the stories are amusing anecdotes, others tragic. The point is that there are many and that our narrator has selected certain ones to give special attention to in his own narration. Tom has chosen particular ones because they entertained him greatly as he grew up, because they pertain in an essential way to his own identity, or because they make a keen observation about American history. These stories he fleshes out in remarkable detail with all the imaginative power at his disposal. It is important to keep in mind that many of the "facts" of this imaginative retelling are doubly filtered—modified in Samuel Ordway's telling of the history to his grandson, who in turn tells the story to the reader. The grandfather's telling about his parents' lives in Tennessee involves events that were told to him, for they occurred prior to his own birth. Although these circumstances suggest unreliable narration, historical reliability is more or less beside the point in this story: of moment is the effect that the story has on the narrator and his grandfather.

These graveyard stories develop in the narrator a desire to give life to the dead, even those belonging to other families, the Jervises in particular, who had "died out": "though strongly impelled to hurry past [their plot], I used often to linger, trying to give features and a voice to the host of spirits who hovered there, beseeching me, on that day when all the dead were resurrected by the memories of those who had known them, to grasp their hand and save them from sinking deeper and deeper into oblivion" (O, 11–12). Regarding his own ancestors, this impulse to give life to the dead applies even to those remote predecessors whose bones were dug up in Tennessee and transported in barrels by his blind great-grandfather; knowing no stories that animate their memory, the narrator resorts to personifying the gravestones: "The gray stone faces of my ancestors—how clearly I see them still! Bearded with moss, freckled with fungus, bathed in tears when the rain fell, inclining this way and that as though in whispered conversation with one another. . . . [H]ere a high bald dome, pinched features formed by the cramped and scanty epitaph, here a crack like a scar across a cheek, a pair of small round old-fashioned spectacles formed by a double O in the text: my family album in stone" (19–20). Breaking down the barrier between the quick and the dead, the narrator, alluding to Hamlet's "Remember thee!" soliloquy (1.5.98), remarks that these stone images of his ancestors are "carved upon the tablets of [his] memory as with a chisel" (O, 20). Thirty years earlier when those memories were being fixed, the doctrine of the communion of saints was a lively belief that made the dead enduringly real to him, for he then believed that he would "one day sit down and converse" with "my dead." Yet even in his present telling he knows that "to them [he] owed [his] features, [his] voice, the strengths and weaknesses of [his] mind and body" (20). It is clear, then, that the narrator proceeds out of an ontological impulse: "Before I could become myself, . . . I would first have to live through the lives of those who had produced me" (20). From this effort flows the entire narrative that constitutes the novel.

But the narrator's imaginative attachment to the lives of his forebears began when he was a boy. From his adult perspective he perceives that his imaginative reliving, during his youth, of Civil War battles is an indispensable aspect of knowing his forebears so that he can in turn know himself:

> I had to lose each of those heart-breaking battles not once but countless times. So it must have been for my great-grandfather. Each day as the sun rose he must have had to lose his sight anew and reconcile himself again to the loss. Listening to the story of his return to Shiloh, I felt I understood him. He could neither accept nor deny his fate, and he went back there out of an irresistible, childish, forlorn hope of either retrieving that terrible day, or of ending it once and for all. The minuteness with which he was said to have toured the battlefield resembled that of a later-day Civil War "buff." He was searching for some flaw in the sequence of events which would cancel it, which would declare that day void and bring it back to be played over again. (O, 66)

During the battle of Shiloh Thomas Ordway lost his sight and received leg wounds that would stink offensively for the rest of his life. In revisiting the battle site on his family's way to Texas, in standing for "a long time . . . upon the spot which was the last he was ever to see," this Confederate veteran wishes that he had run, as others had done; "as he had not, he found himself obliged to take pride in the courage, or that variety of fear called courage, which had blacked out his life past and to come and transformed him into a running sore" (67, 68). The narrator, then, grasps the full ambiguity of his forebear's life and sacrifice; more importantly he knows that reliving the past is childish, and so he must resist embracing the "forlorn hope" that it represents (66).

There is a further profound ambiguity in Thomas Ordway in that he both rejects and embraces the South, and this ambiguity has significance not only for the narrator but for society at large. Thomas feels compelled to abandon the desolate and defeated South and head toward Texas, but when he reaches the new land, he retreats into the little corner of Texas that is still the South, suggesting an abiding attachment. Living on in the westernmost outpost of the South, he is viewed as "the broken idol of a discredited creed" (O, 30). He might even be a symbol of the defeated South trying to hang on to life, however diminished: he has no vision to see beyond his spoiled condition, and his running sores are a constant reminder that the horrible events of history cannot be escaped. Thus symbolically he undermines the backward-looking rituals that celebrate "the glorious cause" that the South fought for, even though he embraces occasions like Confederate Memorial Day in a sentimental way: "They did not know that to those speeches which his presence alone was enough to render tawdry and indecent, no heart among them swelled more enthusiastically than his" (31).

Thomas Ordway's movement westward and his role as mute critic of the backward-looking South become telling influences on his great-grandson Tom. For the narrator, his great-grandfather becomes the statue of the Confederate foot soldier that stands atop the marble shaft in the town square, where it casts "a twisted shadow" on Clarksville (see O, 28). As he thinks about what both his great-grandfather and the statue mean to him, Tom alters reality: the actual statue in Clarksville faces northeast; the narrator, however, says that the soldier "gaze[s] over the rooftops towards the southwest, in which direction the view is almost limitless" (4). Humphrey inserted the phrase "towards the southwest" between the lines on the manuscript, an alteration suggesting that his narrator's alteration reflects a definite vision for his family as well as for himself.[49] Indeed, the story he tells moves southwesterly: it begins in the Old South during the Civil War; the Ordway family intends to leave the South but ends up on its westernmost boundary; then three generations later one member of the family resides on the very southwest rim of Texas, almost in Mexico, in new country altogether. The representative of the fourth generation of the family, the narrator, is captivated by the meaning of this southwesterly movement.

But of course the narrator knows that he has not made a complete escape from the South, since his great-grandfather's attachment is still an acknowledged part of him. He writes of the southern character as though he were telling it in the company of amused and perplexed northern friends, an imagined context that conveys a certain liberating self-awareness. There is irony in his attachment to a past that he knows is passing out of memory, and he does foresee the day when southerners will be free of their Confederate past: "I reckon the active life of a Southerner to extend three generations past his death. He lives on in full vigor in the minds of those who as children heard about him from those who know him in the flesh. As mine is the last generation to whom the Civil War is a told story remembered in the accents of familiar and kindred voices, I calculate

49. MS, p. 2, WH Coll., UT. On p. 8 of the MS Humphrey makes another interlinear addition emphasizing westward movement: the sounds emanating from the iron-rod triangle shared by the one-room schoolhouse and the church are described as "rolling westward unobstructed into infinity."

that it will come to an end when the last of us is gone" (*O*, 41). *The Ordways*, then, moves toward forgetfulness and freedom from tradition, but it is a wrenching movement, especially hard going every step of the way for the first generation headed by the Confederate veteran Thomas Ordway.

It is in Part 1 of the novel that the West, as contrasted to the South, comes to the fore: "When a man decides to pull up his roots and set off in search of a new life, he instinctively heads west. No other point of the compass exerts that powerful pull. The West is the true magnetic pole" (*O*, 54). The West means the future (it "lies farther on, in time as well as space" [4]), as the South means the past ("in the direction from which [the Ordways] had trekked, lay your family's past, yours and everybody else's you knew, that place of the past, the South" [119]).

West to the future—and yet Thomas cannot sever all connections with his past, especially his family connections, a sentiment demonstrated by the family's dislodging the marble tombstones in the family graveyard, digging up the graves, packing the bones in assorted containers, and loading them all in the wagon. They are quite literally carrying the past with them into the future—an objective correlative to which a profound ambiguity attaches. On the one hand, the burden of the past impedes their progress: "those stones caused them to bog down in places where others got through" (*O*, 58). On the other hand, when the family must cross into Texas over the swollen Red River in October 1863 and the oxen must swim while pulling the wagon, the tombstones steady it against a powerful river current: "They had their ballast of tombstones to thank that they were not tipped over" (78). But when the wagon gets almost to the Texas side, it sinks from the weight that it carries; thus the wagon is "[s]aved by the same thing which sank it, those stones" (80). It appears that, the drawbacks being fully acknowledged, the past does have its value. Indeed, the harrowing river crossing, during which five-year-old Dexter is drowned, would have wiped out the entire family had they not packed the past in their wagon. In a very real sense, the past frees the Ordways for the future.

Pulling the sunk wagon out of the shallows, the Ordways test an unfamiliar future that opens before them. They march onto the plains where the sounds and smells of things "turn unfamiliar and frightening to that lost veteran of a lost cause" (*O*, 85). The narrator imagines that the following question arises in his great-grandfather's mind: "In that parched and alien soil, would the bones of his ancestors take root and flower?" (85–86).[50] Yet the question of whether to carry on, stay, or retreat to the South is determined by a consideration for the

---

50. A reference perhaps to Ezekiel ("can these bones live?" [37:2]) and therefore here a hint of regeneration for the Ordways.

living, not the dead: his groping hands discover a child in his wife's "ripening belly," and he thinks, "No man wants his children to be born foreigners. One of his strongest desires is that his sons have the same boyhood, the same memories, only maybe happier, as his own" (86–87). Thus, in retreating to Clarksville, where "the South draws up to a stop" (3), Thomas Ordway preserves his family's attachment to the South and its traditions. But this attachment becomes less fixed in the next generation; the son for whose sake he returns to Clarksville proves unsuited in temperament to living according to the requirements of a demanding tradition; he is pulled to the West that his father had avoided.

The rest of the novel unfolds a gradual opening up to the future as new patterns of life take hold and as new places make new people; the third generation will see one of its members escape to the far West. But it is the narrator's grandfather, carried from Tennessee in his mother's belly, who takes the first true strides westward. This story of Samuel Ordway comprises the two central sections of the novel. For this venture away from the South and its past to take place, father and son must be separated. Thus Samuel's son Ned is stolen by a neighbor when he is two and a half years old, taken west, and reared there. Ned, unaffected by the culture of the South, is altogether a man of the West. In searching the West for Ned, Sam himself discovers a new self in a new place. The narrator, absorbing his family's history, which he learns as a boy on graveyard working day and later during a summer with his grandparents, consciously rejects the southern myth and embraces the western myth. His imaginative identification is no longer with the dead past but with his vision of his living Uncle Ned, for he discovers that there is an alternative to living "with the chronic dyspepsia of defeat":

> I had, right on my doorstep, another myth to turn to. When the last bugle call went echoing off into eternity and the muskets were stacked and the banners lowered and that star-crossed flag hauled down—in short, when Appomattox came to me and I was demobilized and disarmed and returned home, filled with wounded pride and impatient with peacetime life—like many another veteran—I began to face about and look the other way, towards Blossom Prairie, where the range was open and the fancy free to roam. In my fashion I was repeating not only the history of my family, but of the country. For the West provided America with an escape from the memory of the Civil War. (O, 89)

Two factors prompt Sam Ordway to spin for his grandson the story about his adventures in search of his kidnapped son: one is that he perceives a physical resemblance between the grandson and Ned, and the other is that he "discovered the secret cult I had made of my missing uncle" (O, 333). The narrator as a boy makes Ned into a hero of the West, imaginatively dressing him in fringed buckskin and Nocona boots, rounding up cattle all day. Another factor bearing upon Sam's willingness to tell his adventures is that they had occurred thirty-five years earlier, and the topic of his loss and failure to find his stolen son is "no longer painful to him" (333).

The reliability of Sam's tale is compromised, but it is a better tale as a result. In conveying the contents of these told adventures, the narrator considers Sam's position in life as it altered and enhanced his narration: "His wife was old and his children gone from home, the friends of his youth dying off. His work was done, and now as the restlessness of old age came upon him his mind turned to the great adventure of his life, flooding it in a blaze of remembered light. The palette of his memory was spread with pure prismatic colors and the pictures he painted were of a land of perpetual summer" (O, 334). All of this suggests that his real experiences of thirty-five years ago are probably simplified and improved through memory. Even were he not intentionally to alter the events of his excursion, his telling them long afterwards assures unreliability.

In addition, the real quest surely entailed dangers that Sam had not chosen to disclose to his grandson, preferring to conjure a comic adventure. A lone man wandering about in the untamed desert of West Texas in 1898, carrying with him a good sum of money and a pistol that had been loaded in 1862 but not fired since then, would have been a sitting duck for disaster. That he survived for several months to return home safely is remarkable. Instead of acknowledging his dire circumstances, Sam must have decided to turn his ordeal into a rollicking comedy and done so through the power of his imagination. And of course it is proper, since he did not meet with catastrophe in the desert, that the story he tells be a comic one. Thus the entire novel becomes a comedy, its resolution the happy fulfillment of the catastrophic beginning at Shiloh—for the Ordway family escapes cleanly from the Civil War and its life-denying aftermath. Given that there are confusing mistaken identities, daydreams that disrupt reality, possible additional misadventures that are averted, and at the end the joyous celebration of the family reunion, *The Ordways* is as much a traditional comedy as *Home from the Hill* is a traditional tragedy.

Two other observations serve to put Sam's narrative in focus. First, Sam carefully shapes his expression for his intended audience, his young grandson (for example: "She was not so old as the woman who lived in the shoe, but like her she had so many children she didn't know what to do" [O, 164]). Second, his tales are intentional exaggerations, embellished for the sake of entertaining his grandson and to exercise his memory-sweetening imagination. Indeed, the narrator acknowledges that what his grandfather tells is "lovingly embellished" (336). Another factor that skews the accuracy of Sam's tales is the traditional practice of men from the country to cast themselves as the butt of the joke, for "only in this way could a story in first person singular be rendered unegotistical" (336). It is safe to conclude, for example, that Sam was not so susceptible to the confidence trick conducted by the fake Baptist preacher (a literary descendent of Twain's Duke and Dauphin) as he makes out that he was.

The most elaborate of Sam's tales concerns the time when he joins the Dickey Brothers Circus and is assigned to attend an outlandish elephant named Topsy. Sam's joining the circus is in fact a smart move, directly to do with his search for Ned: the circus, which travels from one Texas town to another for one-day stands, attracts more children than any other event, and the elephant is the circus's primary attraction—everybody who comes to the circus comes to see Topsy. Sam recalls that he "would stand beside her trying to see over the faces in front to catch sight of Will or Mrs. Vinson [the couple who kidnapped Ned] among those in the back before either of them should recognize me" (O, 258). As day after day brings Sam no success in his quest, Topsy serves as antidote to his disappointment. The wonderful elephant is a much-needed solace and entertainment for him: "There is nothing like an elephant for keeping you from brooding," Sam confesses (256). And then he goes on to offer a picture of himself in a pea-green majordomo's uniform perched upon Topsy's head, whereupon he remarks—revealing how transported he is by recollecting the experience—"if Ned could see his daddy now Will Vinson wouldn't stand much of a chance!" (257).

But then Sam overleaps the real experience on the wings of exaggeration: he reports that for roughage the elephant's diet requires paving stones, brickbats, and scrap iron; Topsy runs away, eats an apple orchard, knocks over six or eight apple trees, drinks half a mill pond, gets stuck in the pond, gets pulled out, escapes again, drinks the whole run of a still as well as the open vats of mash, passes out for thirty-six hours, and then dies from the effects of the rotgut whiskey. Topsy's corpse starts rotting, and the circus moves the town of Zodiac several miles away as an alternative to digging a hole big enough to bury a 15,000-pound elephant. Sam's motive in telling such a tale is just to produce peals of laughter in his grandson. Similarly, Sam gives accounts of a man who "et a town" (O, 292) and many other tales—all of which, while fleshing out his extensive search for Ned, supply a large measure of humor. It is raucous, slapstick, and hyperbolic—a storyteller's indulgence.

Although some readers have complained that aspects of Sam's episodic narrative are purposeless (the very complaint, by the way, often made of Faulkner's *The Town*), they might be applying to *The Ordways* an unfair standard. A picaresque does not need to meet the same standard of plot relevancy that a novel like *Home from the Hill* must. As Humphrey once said, "humor is a holiday from appositeness."[51] Nonetheless, most of the episodes that Sam tells are clearly part of his quest, understood either as a search for Ned or for himself. In his outward search for his stolen son, Sam discovers unknown aspects of his own being and redefines his relationship to his family. Furthermore, some of what Sam tells appears to be no exaggeration for effect at all.

Sam's character is the emotional center of Parts 2 and 3 of *The Ordways*. Hopelessness is the primary emotion that Sam feels as his search begins. Every fork in the road means a choice that is haunted by "the road not taken" (*O*, 182). Sam persistently makes inquiries of slit-eyed and open-mouthed people who either cannot or will not assist him. The pecan-pie-baking widow proves only a temporary distraction, and he carries on until utter hopelessness gives way to hopeful signs of his own development. He moves beyond wondering how anyone could love Ned. Sam's meeting in Paris, Texas, with R. C. Loftus, a retired Pinkerton detective, introduces the possibility that Ned might have been harmed by the Vinsons, thereby occasioning the first step in the growth of Sam's concern for his son: at night "his heart rose on tiptoe to await the small mangled ghost that walked nightly in his dreams" (219). The tour of the orphans' home represents another step along the way to emotional fatherhood; though he goes to the orphanage in hopes of finding Ned, he is relieved not to find him in that miserable setting. Thus he begins to embrace the idea that Ned's welfare is more important to him than possessing him.

Although Sam's encounter with a lost boy in Paris in a sense turns the quest on its head (for Sam spends a day looking for the boy's father instead of searching for his own lost son), the episode nonetheless affects Sam's growth in consciousness in a couple of ways that are directly related to the novel's main concerns. First, the incident facilitates the enlargement of Sam's affections. He can see a boy who is not Ned as though he were: "This [boy] was one of his own kind"; "he looked, alas, a lot like Ned" (*O*, 210). Second, Sam enlarges his understanding of Will Vinson, for Sam finds himself in a position vis-à-vis the lost child that is parallel to the position of Will Vinson and Ned: once the boy's father is found, Sam tries to save the boy from a father who does not treat him properly, a parallel that hints at an understanding of why Will stole Ned from Sam. Yet the episode ends up giving Sam confidence that if a boy and his father

51. Humphrey to Lemay, 27 March 1964, Knopf Coll.

can be united, the boy will always prefer the father, however much kindness and concern another man might have bestowed upon him.

Sam's internal changes are not all caused by his interaction with other people. The western landscape, which in a sense becomes a character in the novel (in the tradition of Twain in *Roughing It* [1872]), is itself a significant force in his growth.[52] When Sam's quest first takes him into the desert, he is struck by a new sense of isolation and feeling of being lost in a sea of sameness: "In such a landscape to come upon an ant hill was a welcome diversion" (*O*, 287). His account of a prairie-dog town reveals his deeply felt need for human contact, sorely missed in this especially desolate territory, which nonetheless fosters imagination and thoughtfulness. Hence he personifies the prairie dogs: "Comically human-like, two or three of the creatures would collect on the front stoop of one of their neighbors' houses and gossip, their heads bobbing in solemn agreement, jerking up all together at anything untoward happening down the street." As Sam recognizes their similarity to humanity, he thinks of the advantage of being absent from society: "Quick, nervous, excitable, they could not keep still for a moment. With their queer little bark and their humorless, almost petulant expression, they appeared to be destroying reputations and always lecturing one another, and constantly taking offense, abruptly turning their backs on their interlocutor and going off in a huff into their holes" (288). That Sam whiles away the better part of an afternoon allowing himself to be entertained by parallels between people and prairie dogs tells us something additionally about him: that he has grown weary of his search and is in need of distraction.

Even though Sam does not himself place a great deal of emphasis on his loneliness as he roves the vast stretches of Texas—"endless as the bare boundless sky above"—the narrator proves sensitive, in the metaphors that he employs, to the loneliness that he suspects his grandfather must have felt (*O*, 286). Humphrey has his narrator draw upon a long tradition, going back to Josiah Gregg's *Commerce on the Prairies* (1844), of seeing the Southern plains as the "prairie ocean." Gregg apparently meant the metaphor to convey the lack of variety in the landscape, but Tom Ordway here uses the metaphor in a context that clearly conveys loneliness. First, he explains that a phenomenon known as seiche causes the longtime traveler on the prairie to think that the land "rock[s] slowly from side to side like the wallowing of a lake" (*O*, 286).[53] This fact establishes that the em-

52. See David W. Teague, *The Southwest in American Literature and Art* (Tucson: University of Arizona Press, 1997), 54.

53. Josiah Gregg, *Commerce of the Prairies: A Selection*, ed. David F. Hawke (1844; Indianapolis: Bobbs-Merrill, 1970), 25, quoted in Teague, 26. Water imagery appears early on in Part III: Sam "was like a fisherman casting over a stretch of water . . . in search of Ned"; a wagon in the distance seems

phasis here is on the internal response of the man to the landscape; the prairie makes him feel different. Then Tom says that Sam encounters "a naked little house floating on the plain like a solitary chip on the ocean." This "solitary chip"—interestingly not a ship—is a parallel to Sam's own sense of smallness and solitariness. Sam actually "boards" this lonely vessel, going to the "leeward of the house" where he observes the dingy wash on the clothesline "whipping and popping like loosened ship sails in a storm" (292). As Sam navigates the sea of land, his loneliness gives rise to thoughtfulness and insight into himself. He asks himself questions that he had never thought to ask before: Did he marry Hester without caring for her just to provide a mother for his first wife's children? Does Will Vinson love his son Ned more than he does? Does he love his son? The prolongation of aloneness, in part, enables Sam to focus attention on these and related questions.

When Sam passes beyond the uncertainty of loneliness and begins to see land as land, not as sea, he responds to the new land with a new sense of being. For the first time in his life, he feels the ground under his feet. In a letter to Alfred Knopf, Humphrey says that his character "must, like every picaresque hero, find himself while searching for something else"; Humphrey "hope[s] to effect through a sense of the discovery of a place" the psychological alteration that settles his character's being, his "last alteration of soul."[54] Venturing out into unknown terrain, then, beyond the familiar borders of convention, Sam escapes the clannishness that was a part of the ripened Old South culture that had begun to rot, of which his father was an emblem. Thomas Ordway's unhealing wound was the South's wound; his son recovers from that wound by escaping that place and acquiring a new way of seeing in a new place.

In the West, Sam opens himself to a large experience that enlarges him. The meaning of family expands beyond that mad devotion to one's own that prompted his father to dig up the bones of his relatives. The breaking down of the usual familial demarcations is instigated by the Vinsons' loving Ned as though he were their own child; Mrs. Vinson is more Ned's mother than his lawful stepmother. When they take Ned west, the Vinsons erode familial distinctions by assuming the name of Ordway; further, before Sam learns that they have taken his name he has in fact assumed the name of Will Vinson as a cover. Although their motives are incompatible, nonetheless symbolically they have become each other and thus one. What is more, on his deathbed Will tells Ned

---

"not much bigger than a bobbing cork when he first glimpsed it"; then the wagon is "creaking and wallowing like a sailing ship all but becalmed in an ocean of grass" (O, 178).

54. Humphrey to Knopf, 13 June 1963, Knopf Coll.

who his biological father is; Ned returns to Clarksville to claim kin, and when he tells Sam of Will's death, Sam feels as though a member of the family has died. Thus Sam's understanding of family has expanded to include the man whom he once viewed as a destroyer of his family. Humphrey suggests that the enlarged mind and spirit are a result of Sam's sojourn in the open, expansive landscape of southwestern Texas.

The additional ramifications of the West as metaphor are several. Sam is struck by what he perceives to be the newness of the West; even before he reaches the hardly inhabited areas, he is attracted to the "all new" towns; he "enjoyed the sense of being present at the beginning. Like every son, or every son of a son of the old South, he had had enough history. The less history a place had, the happier its past" (O, 298). Immersing himself in the "new West" enables Sam to escape not only the undertow of the historical past and his family's part in it but the pull of his personal past as well. Upon vividly reliving the death of his first wife, he finds himself then able to forget, to tuck the image of that first wife away into the irrelevant past. When he accomplishes this renunciation of Agatha, he senses "that his life [is] about to take a new turn, to close a phase and enter another one." Now he can live in the present, without interference. "Hester is my wife now," he tells himself. "But this was a new Hester," the narrator explains, "different from the former one, nor would she reassume her old shape. Outwardly she was unchanged, yet in some important but indefinable way she had been transfigured. My grandfather did not know this yet, but it was not Hester who had changed; it was himself. A new love for his wife entering into his heart had made him a different man" (313). He therefore vows to return home before she delivers the child she was pregnant with when he left in search of Ned.

Sam undergoes a similar epiphany regarding his feelings for Ned. When the picture of Ned that he has handed to hundreds of people during his half-hearted search becomes so creased and cracked and tattered that the image has disappeared, he suddenly discovers that he possesses a clear picture of the boy "in his mind, an image which, oddly, seemed to have grown sharper as the picture faded and peeled" (O, 315). And then, as he probes his own mind, "his child all but stood before him," and he knows "at last why the Vinsons had been unable to give him up," for he now loves him in the same way and knows the extent of their love for the boy (315). Sam assumes the mantle of fatherhood in a much more subtle way than Theron does in the vestibule of the Episcopal church in *Home from the Hill.*

These competing affections—the new love for his wife back in Clarksville, the new love for the lost son—cause disquietude in Sam. His intimate response to a new landscape will enable him to resolve the conflicting demands on his affections, and he will know peace. Additional change occurs in Sam as he drives "into another landscape, another season, another world, finally into another age" (*O*, 316). Sam undergoes an intense spiritual identification with a place that awakens him to himself in a very similar way to that expressed by Tom Outland in Willa Cather's *The Professor's House* (1925), a book that Humphrey read while writing *The Ordways*.[55] Like Cather's hero, Humphrey's becomes a new man. After Sam crosses the Concho River, he is enthralled by the sense of discovering another civilization; he is "astonished by an unexpected, an awesome sight":

> The river there was banked by steep rock cliffs and along the face of one of these cliffs, near the top, in the shelter of an over-hanging cornice ledge, ran a frieze of hundreds of savage figures painted in red, black, orange, and white, so uniform as to seem to have been stenciled on the rock, or as if in addition to serving as art they served also as the alphabet of a primitive tongue.... Though their colors had retained their strength, their great antiquity was felt nonetheless, felt powerfully in the wild stillness of those surroundings. (*O*, 316)

Similarly, Tom Outland in *The Professor's House* discovers beneath the overarching top ledge of the Blue Mesa "a little city of stone, asleep. It was as still as sculpture—and something like that. It all hung together, seemed to have a kind of composition: pale little houses of stone nesting close to one another, perched on top of each other.... It was beautifully proportioned.... It was red in colour, even on that grey day." Tom is struck by the aura of "immortal repose," the "silence and stillness" that the "composition" affords. Describing the scene's effect upon him, Tom says, "Something had happened in me that made it possible for me to co-ordinate and simplify, and that process, going on in my mind, brought with it great happiness."[56] Sam also has a deep experience of settling into himself as he continues to discover this "[u]ndiscovered country" (*O*, 318), a term that the grandson-narrator attributes to his grandfather. From Hamlet's soliloquy, the phrase is remarkably appropriate. One "grunt[s] and sweat[s] under a weary life," then afterwards goes to the "undiscovered country, from whose bourn / No traveller returns" (3.1.76–79). The allusion suggests that the place Sam has come to is a place where his old self dies and he becomes a different man.

55. In a letter of 25 April 1958 to William Koshland, Humphrey says, "Got and read the same day, *The Professor's House:* a wonderful book" (Knopf Coll.).
56. Willa Cather, *The Professor's House* (1925; reprint, New York: Vintage, 1973), 201, 250–51.

The valley of the Rio Grande is another healing place for Sam; he knows it as "the place to which all men yearned to come" (*O*, 319). A "mood of peacefulness . . . steal[s] over him," and he feels "reconciled" (320). He enters the spirit of another culture: "beneath that clear sky, he felt not only better reconciled to the loss which life had recently brought him, but felt himself eased of some lifelong, some inherited deep, dull ache. This land, because it lay outside your own bloody national past, . . . seemed, despite its great age, strangely new, fresh in its very antiquity" (320). The wound of his father and all it symbolizes is healed in Sam: "Exposed daily to this hot sun, that old unhealed historical wound seemed at last to dry up and to cease to ache" (320). This peace, this relief, Sam discovers in himself while on his quest to find Ned. Now, however, he finds he can leave Ned to this new place; he is reconciled to his loss of Ned because he believes this new land can be for Ned what it is for him:

> "If I had to lose him, if I just had to lose him, I'm glad at least to think that Will made it to here." It was a land of strong contrasts, of bright sunlight and deep cool shadows, of dry rocky hills and lush verdant valleys. A land so old it had come round new again, lost its records, forgotten its age, and started over. Whose battles had been fought in forgotten tongues by vanished races over dead issues, where the bitterness of old divisions lay buried in unmarked graves. It was good country to grow up a boy in. (323)

Sam's view on the rearing of his son is in marked contrast to the view of his own father, who had retreated from the West to Clarksville because he did not want his son to grow up with different memories from his own. Sam, however, is free of this need. His second wife, Hester, hoped that Sam would be "a man whose life lay in the future, not buried in the past" (117). Sam realizes that hope, one shared by Humphrey himself, who spoke modestly of Sam's growth: "I should have liked Sam Ordway to attain more inner stature than he does; he could only acquire as much as his maker could give him, and his maker is not Cervantes, nor even Mark Twain. I do think he comes to some self-knowledge and some knowledge of the world in the end."[57]

The grand finale of *The Ordways* is entitled "Family Reunion," a title with strong associations for the next novel, which Humphrey had already begun, this title in fact taken from T. S. Eliot's play, one of the sources for *Proud Flesh*. The family reunion in the upcoming novel is a grim, grotesque affair; in *The Ordways*, however, it is as joyous as the wedding that concludes Hardy's *Under the Green-*

---

57. Humphrey to the Weisses, 30 January 1965, Weiss coll.

wood Tree or any of Shakespeare's romantic comedies. The entire Ordway family journey to Ned's Angora goat farm in the Rio Grande valley, in a caravan of fourteen cars. Although they encounter the worst horrors of the oil boom— roads black and slick with oil, oil in their food and on everything they touched, even oil in the air they breathed, the hellish "glow of the sulphur fires"—yet they are full of joy (*O*, 351). In biblical fashion, Ned slaughters twenty goats for the family feast, which is followed by games and leisure and the melding of affections.

We expect the narrator's affections to be with the West, for Tom Ordway the younger is the beneficiary of the long family history, which is a record of people trying to escape the limiting perspective of the South. As Tom Outland's story affects Godfrey St. Peter in such a way as to enable him to escape the demands of a cloying social arrangement and discover his essential self and thereby live authentically, so does Sam Ordway's story of two generations of his family affect his grandson. Tom learns of the past in order to leave it behind. What his great-grandfather had tried and failed to do, what his grandfather had glimpsed the value of, he will do. He is already free from the dead hand of the southern past— and free as well from one aspect of the myth of the West, which came unraveled when Ned turned out unromantically to be a goat farmer instead of the cowboy on the range that the narrator had, in his childhood, dreamt him to be. Patrick B. Mullen has rightly pointed out that Sam's account of an encounter with two homosexual cowboys riding off together into the sunset had already smudged the silver-screen luster that had entranced his grandson.[58] The myth exploded, the real meaning of the West emerges in the Ordway family's trip and in Tom's desire to return to the West: the last line of the novel confirms that Tom will go West to see his uncle Ned "and his part of the world" again.

To a limited extent *The Ordways* is based on Humphrey's family. He had a few planks of real (or imagined) family history to begin his novel with, though nothing like a scaffolding. How to move from these few facts to the finished novel cost Humphrey, as we have seen, a great deal of agony. The factual material is this: one of Humphrey's great-grandfathers on his mother's side was blinded and crippled in the battle of Shiloh. "How he got to Texas I haven't the faintest idea," Bill explained (*WST*, 24). His maternal grandfather lost his first wife in childbirth, married for a second time, and lost a child to kidnappers. According to Humphrey, his grandparents left the little boy "whose coming, birth, had caused the mother's death" with neighbors for one day. "When they came back

---

58. Patrick B. Mullen, "Myth and Folklore in *The Ordways*," *Publications of the Texas Folklore Society*, 35 (1971): 143.

that night the family was gone." The conclusion of Part 4 is also drawn from Humphrey's family history:

> When I was four years old, this man turned up. The person he'd thought was his father had died and on his deathbed told him he was not his son, told him who he really was. He came back; he claimed kin with my people. We all piled into cars—this is the year 1928—and went from Clarksville, which is very near Texarkana, and drove all the way to Del Rio. That was quite an undertaking in 1928, to drive that far. A great, huge family. We had a great big bash of barbecue. He turned out to be an Angora goat rancher right on the Rio Grande. (*WST*, 24, 25)

Humphrey's maternal grandmother's jealousy of her husband's first wife is also represented in *The Ordways* as well as the short story "The Hardys."

There is a fairly clear literary predecessor for some features of the story. In certain ways *The Ordways* resembles Katherine Anne Porter's "The Old Order," which is about an old southern family that moves from Louisiana to Texas after the husband dies of his wounds received in the Civil War; this story also deals with the oppressiveness of the southern past, a circus as a route of escape, and a family reunion. Humphrey, of course, had read Porter's story. But the central elements of the novel—the digging up of the family bones, the revisiting of the battlefield, the father's search for his son across Texas—are sheer invention.

The Ordways is a more bountiful cache of rich figures of speech than either of Humphrey's previous two books. Reflecting the life of simple country people, the language accords with their actual experience—as when rain is seen to be "sputtering on the hard-packed ground like grease in a skillet," or when swollen milk cows are described as follows: "their teats stiffened and rose outward like a bunch of carrots drawn together by the tops," although I suspect that this figure owes something to Humphrey's many readings of Hardy's *Tess of the d'Urbervilles*, which contains a reference to "the teats" of cows as being "hard as carrots" (*O*, 259, 123).[59] On other occasions, Humphrey's figures are vividly tactile, as in: "The hand he proffered was boneless and moist and cool as a curd, tender as a mushroom" (*O*, 219). Sometimes a broader figure captures the precise nature of collective movement. When Sam Ordway stops at a house to inquire if the Vinsons have passed by, the offspring of a woman with so many children she did not know what to do are captured thus: "They all came and gaped at the stranger

---

59. Thomas Hardy, *Tess of the d'Urbervilles*, ed. William E. Buckler (Boston: Houghton Mifflin, 1960), 107.

like goldfish flocking to the side of the bowl. . . . 'None of you children saw any folks like that, did you?' my grandfather asked, and they fled like goldfish at the movement of a hand" (164).

One of the best descriptive passages is a still life of Haines's grocery, where the Samuel Ordways purchase essentials; the store

> was dark as a root cellar, and even more redolent. The first thing to hit you on entering was a tingling sour smell which was not the smell of pickles but of the pickled oak of their barrel. The coffee and the strong yellow smell of soap in unwrapped bars laid up like masonry and the slightly rancid smell, like a new copper penny, of the leathery bacon flitches hanging from the rafters, between which hung spiraling flypapers encrusted with dead and struggling flies. Beneath the long counters on each side ran rows of bins with sloping hinged glass covers containing cookies and dried fruits. On the floor, squat barrels of salt cod like flakes of slate; fat sacks with tops rolled back of beans and rice. On the counters sliced hams the color of cedar, the yellow bone like a knot in the wood. (*O*, 122)

Obtaining food was a different matter for the earlier generation. Avoiding sentimentality altogether, Humphrey portrays the feeling that Ella Ordway has for the mule that she must kill in order to save her family from starvation:

> That night after a still more wretched supper, and after the house was asleep, she got up and slipped outdoors. She took from underneath the washstand outside the back door the things she had secreted there earlier: the knife, two raw turnips, and one wrinkled apple. She went out to the barn. She fed the mule the turnips and the apple and listened to him munching in the dark. She waited until he had finished, then as he nuzzled her begging for more, she felt along the bony ribs until she discovered the beat of the heart. She placed the knife between two ribs and shoved with both hands, then fled from the barn and ran to the house, where for the rest of the night she lay shivering on her pallet on the floor. Next morning she found herself spattered with blood. (53)

The generic portrait of country women is as true to his subject as Mike Disfarmer's remarkable photographs:[60]

60. Cf. the portrait of the frail old woman on the back cover of *Disfarmer: Heber Springs Portraits, 1939–1946*, ed. Jack Woody (Santa Fe: Twin Palms, 1996). In 1983 Humphrey was instrumental in arranging for the exhibition of Peter Miller's collection of Mike Disfarmer's photographs at Hendrix College. At the time, Humphrey remarked that the people in Disfarmer's photographs look like the people he came from.

the women [were] bent like the rare prairie trees beneath the prevailing wind, gnarled, sinewy, dry, with pale, wind-cracked, chapped and peeling lips, more than one of them with that lichenlike splotching of the skin which denotes Texas sun cancer, and which may end by eating away the septum of the nose right up to the very bone. From long seething in caustic homemade lye soap, and from a lifetime of scrubbing the overalls of a family of working men against a washboard, their hands looked as if they had been cooked, and when they extended them in one of their shy, faint handshakes, they felt feverish to the touch. They spoke a different language, too. Slow-talking, unused to having to shout to make themselves heard, speaking little in any case, they spent their hoarded and antiquated words as my grandfather in town in the stores counted out his old-fashioned Indian-head pennies and his nickels and dimes from deep in his long stocking-shaped purse and stacked them in neat deliberate stacks on the counter. (*O*, 10–11)

Humphrey is on his mettle in many such passages of precise and vivid description—another that comes to mind is the chilling account of Agatha Ordway's dying in childbirth, which is remembered in telling detail by her husband many years later.

The Ordways is the only one of Humphrey's books that does not have an attractive title, but that does not mean that he did not go through what had become his usual prolonged ordeal to find one. The title he first tentatively gave it, "The Quest of Samuel Ordway," had to be abandoned because its reference was too limited for a novel about four generations. Bill's editor at Knopf, Pete Lemay, wanted a title that would "evoke that spread of generations," but he wanted one as well that would capture "the sense of time passing and the curious strength of kinship which Humphrey so neatly defines in the first section as the peculiar quality of the South." When this editor's expectation was passed on to Humphrey, he concurred generally: "I agree with Pete in wanting an expressive title—but where's it to come from? I welcome any suggestions."[61]

By August 1963 Humphrey came up with an expressive and attractive title, "Look Away, Look Away!"—from "Dixie."[62] This title would have alluded to the Civil War, a major factor in Part 1, and it would also have taken into account the narrative standpoint of the grandchild, "who is taking a long, long view of

61. Humphrey to Knopf, 26 October 1961; Lemay to the Knopfs, 3 June 1963; Humphrey to Knopf, 13 June 1963, Knopf Coll.
62. Humphrey to Lemay, 5 August [1963], Knopf Coll.

the past and where he comes from. I was thinking of the sort of visual sense, looking backwards," said Humphrey (*WST*, 27). Indeed, his narrator early on remarks, "these were distant kin, and all that was long ago and far away" (*O*, 24). The phrase also signals the novel's looking away from the past and into the future and the West, like the statue of the Confederate soldier in the town square. Humphrey liked the title immensely, but was concerned that MacKinlay Kantor, who wrote historical fiction (especially about the Civil War), had already used the title. It turned out that Kantor had not used it, and so Humphrey considered the title search over. But just before the Knopf catalog offering that title was to go to press, Ben Haas did publish a novel entitled *Look Away, Look Away* (New York: Simon and Schuster, 1964).[63]

Humphrey found himself once again searching for a title. He mused, "It is like being told you must rechristen a two year old child, only worse, because children's names are easier to find than one for a book with too many themes for any one title ever to include them all"; just as he was expressing this lament in a 10 April 1964 letter to the Weisses—it was a Friday evening—the telephone rang: the Knopf firm urgently insisted that "they must have a title by Monday." Returning to the letter, Bill told the Weisses that Knopf has suggested he settle for "A Little More than Kin" (from *Hamlet*), giving him forty-eight hours to come up with an alternative: "Oh, Jesus! 48 hours when it took me 3 years to find that other one!" (Weiss Coll.). Humphrey refused to submit to the forty-eight-hour stipulation. That is not to say that he did not feel the urgency of the situation. He thought hard and in four days' time produced a plethora of possibilities, most of which he rejected for one reason or another: "The Sunset Regions," from a song quoted in Hamlin Garland's *A Son of the Middle Border* ("I'm certainly not wild about it"); then seven phrases from the novel itself, "The Outskirts of Heaven," "That Very Blood," "A Kindred Accent," "The Company of Kin," "The Men Our Fathers Were," "Kin and Causes," and "Thicker than Water"—all of which he objected to either because they have "hardly any appositeness" or are "[t]oo flippant." He also considered "The Rites of Autumn," alluding to the graveyard working day, but he thought it "[t]oo literary"; and he considered "Rest in Peace" merely tolerable. "Farther Off from Heaven," which later became the title of his memoir, was also in the running, but here rejected as being "too poetic." Explaining his failure to light on an altogether appropriate title, Humphrey wrote to Lemay: "I tried very hard to find a title which would somehow include that soldier atop the monument in the square and the shadow he casts on the paving stones, and then, in the same title, connected by an *and*,

63. Humphrey to the Weisses, 10 April 1964, Weiss Coll.

something about the other story, the farther west, Sam Ordway's paternity, the narrator's romanticism towards the Western myth. . . . This idea is attractive, but I've failed to come up with anything." But then urgency inspired another possibility, a phrase slightly altered from "Dixie": "But Not Forgotten."[64]

The search—involving many others—continued until the end of May. Rust Hills, then editor of the *Saturday Evening Post,* which was publishing a sixty-page excerpt from the novel, was also anxious for a title and became involved in the search. He suggested "A Sense of Times Past" and "The Flux of Time," a phrase that Humphrey had used in Hills's office when they were discussing the publication of the selection from the novel. Hills also proposed "Times Not Forgotten," a variation on Humphrey's preferred proposal. Humphrey's English publisher, Ian Parsons of Chatto and Windus, also assumed a keen interest in the title of this book. Initially, he suggested "The Search" and "The Far Search," but Lemay rejected these, "The Search" because of C. P. Snow's book by the same name. The title would probably have been "But Not Forgotten" had Parsons not objected, saying, "I really *don't* think [it] would be possible here, because the phrase from 'Dixie' would be lost on the English"; he preferred the Shakespearean phrase "A Little More than Kin" that Alfred Knopf favored. Though it was not essential that the American and English editions have the same title, the publishers agreed that it would be preferable. In the end, writer and publishers settled on *The Ordways.* Though it incorporates more than one generation of the family, it is unremarkable.[65]

The Ordways is by most measures a successful novel and represents a noteworthy comic achievement. Reynolds Price characterizes its tragicomic power accurately when he observes about southern comedy that it is "comedy in spite of itself, like all great forms of comedy. It's comedy that arises out of a tragic sense of life or a sense of the pain and difficulty of life" (*WST,* 50). His comment applies to Humphrey's novel precisely. The novel's comic episodes grow out of tragic events—the blinding and horrible wounding of Sam's father at Shiloh (which eventually leads to the family's difficult journey to Clarksville, during which a son drowns), the death of Sam's wife in childbirth, and the kidnapping of his only son. But these disasters give rise to the wild and often grotesque hilarity that marks the episodes of Sam's peregrination across the vastness of Texas in search of his stolen son. It is a rich mixture—from its beginning with the gather-

64. Humphrey to Lemay, 14 April 1964, Knopf Coll.

65. Rust Hills to Lemay, 26 May 1964, Knopf Coll.; Lemay to Parsons, 5 May 1964, Knopf Coll.; Parsons to Lemay, 14 May 1964, C&W.

ing of the Ordway family on graveyard working day to its ending in the raucous far-west reunion full of comic exuberance. The combining of genres would prove treacherous for Humphrey in *Proud Flesh,* but here he seems to have maneuvered successfully. *The Ordways* might be the most enjoyable of Humphrey's novels, and certainly his most lighthearted.

William Humphrey at age twelve
Courtesy Harry Ransom
Humanities Research Center,
The University of Texas at Austin

Clarence Humphrey shortly
before he died in an automobile
accident at age thirty-eight
Courtesy Dorothy Humphrey

Confederate memorial in the town square of Clarksville, Texas
Photo by the author

Red River County Courthouse, Clarksville
Photo by the author

Former Episcopal church in Clarksville, inspiration for the setting of
Theron and Libby's reconciliation in *Home from the Hill*
Photo by the author

Humphrey and friend Harry Grabstald, ca. 1957
Courtesy Dorothy Humphrey

Jean Lambert, translator of Humphrey's works into French
Courtesy Isabelle Bowden

Humphrey in New York, ca. 1960
Courtesy Dorothy Humphrey

Dorothy Humphrey in the 1960s
Courtesy Dorothy Humphrey

William and Dorothy Humphrey, Andrew Wanning, and Ted and Renée Weiss
Courtesy Esther Wanning

Humphrey in 1980
Photo by Stan Wayman

One of the last photos of Humphrey,
taken in the 1990s
Courtesy Toni Weidenbacher

[5]

WIND WITHOUT RAIN
(A Time and a Place)

Ever' good man gits in hard luck sometime.
—WOODY GUTHRIE

BECAUSE THE rent was paid through the spring of 1964, Bill and Dorothy stayed on at Rose Hill, the elegant country mansion in Lexington, Virginia, after Bill had discharged his duties as Glasgow Professor at Washington and Lee. He had thought about taking a rest after the hard push to finish *The Ordways*. But then he realized that there was some risk in becoming, even for a short time, a man of leisure in the conservative southern setting to which he could not make himself accustomed. If he were not working hard on his writing, then he stood in danger of getting drawn into what he and Dorothy considered to be syrupy southern social gatherings involving dull conversations with complacent bigots. "Lord God and little pickaninnies, have I had enough of my fellow southerners in these six months," he complained: "the people are hopelessly sunk in piety and superpatriotism."[1] Needing to be too busy to socialize, he therefore wrote—yet sneaked off a few times during his last days in Virginia to fish the streams of the Blue Ridge Mountains.[2]

Following a brief trip to Bard College (where Bill gave the annual "literature" lecture), the Humphreys set sail back to England, this time on "a World War II" ("or was it [World War] I?" he wondered) supply ship, anything so as to avoid the inanities of ocean liners—Cuban marimba bands and paper hats at gala dinners. Humphrey was returning to Telscombe especially in response to his aged friend Leonard Woolf's plea: "Without you here the summer dies out of the year for me. I cannot get through it if you do not come."[3] After the eleven-day voyage to Liverpool, Bill and Dorothy drove through Shropshire and the Cotswolds to join their friend, who was then eighty-four years old. They did not stay in the

1. William Humphrey to Harry Grabstald, 1 April 1964, HG Letters; Dorothy Humphrey to Ian and Trekkie Parsons and Leonard Woolf, 4 October [1963], Woolf Coll.; Humphrey to Theodore and Renée Weiss, 22 March 1964, Weiss Coll.; to Annie Laurie Williams, 1 April 1964, Williams Coll.
2. Humphrey to Woolf, 11 March 1964, Woolf Coll.
3. Humphrey to the Weisses, 22 March and 24 April 1964, Weiss Coll.; to Woolf, 12 March 1964, Woolf Coll.

leaky Old School Cottage this time but in the much more elegant black-beamed and ivy-covered fourteenth-century Oak Cottage, which the squire of the village provided rent free.[4] The beams and ivy, along with diamond-paned leaded windows, a large garden, an ilex tree, cooing pigeons, and a steady rain, provided the very image of Englishness.

Though Humphrey had finished and published in magazines some of the stories he had started several years ago in Italy and though he looked forward to finishing the others, he nonetheless set aside the unfinished short stories and worked happily on his long-time writing project *Proud Flesh* in this agreeable house, enjoying at the end of the day the company of Woolf and Dame Peggy Ashcroft, the famous Shakespearean actress. After a good summer's work, during which time Bill moved the novel along (getting about two-thirds of it written), he and Dorothy toured Scotland and East Anglia with Ian and Trekkie Parsons. About thirty years later Trekkie would recall that "there was [n]ever before so much laughter packed into so small a space."[5] They left on this tour on 11 September 1964 and returned on the twenty-fourth, in time for both couples to leave for France on the twenty-sixth; the Humphreys were going to Paris and the Parsons to Bordeaux, but on the morning of the planned departure, the Humphreys discovered that their passport was missing, and so they had to remain behind. When they went to the American embassy in London to apply for a new one, they found that someone had found their passport in a pub in Lincolnshire and posted it to the embassy. The delay had prevented the hoped-for eleven-day stay in Paris; therefore the Humphreys went straight to Alassio, Italy, where they had booked an incredibly cheap house called Villa Felice on Via Solva 38. Once they had settled in, Bill left his manuscript of *Proud Flesh* in its folder and turned his attention to a new short story—"Mouth of Brass." He worked hard but was distracted by an element of his setting. In spite of the villa's pleasant garden of carob trees, palms, great aloes, cacti, and a pool with a dripping fountain, Alassio at first proved disappointing because it was a German settlement. But a couple of months later Humphrey discovered some redeeming features—wonderful footpaths back into the hills among cascading olive terraces—and he became enamored of the view of the blue sea. His basic reason for deciding to like the town, however, was that by November the Germans had all gone back to their "northern mists and marchen," or as he put it to Harry and Milly Grabstald, "the Huns began to leave and Alassio began to look a lot better."[6]

4. Humphrey to Grabstald, 1 April 1964, HG Letters.

5. Humphrey to Alfred Knopf, 24 June 1964; to William Koshland, 10 September [1964]; to Harding Lemay, 31 August 1964, Knopf Coll.; Trekkie Parsons to Humphrey, 30 July 1992, WH res.

6. Humphrey to the Weisses, 20 October and 11 December 1964, Weiss Coll.; to Harry and Milly Grabstald, 16 November 1964, HG Letters.

Humphrey still did not get much written during this time because he was distracted by other considerations. While residing in Alassio Humphrey received, as he wrote to Pete Lemay on 15 January 1965, a vague feeler from Boston University, which was interested in his being writer-in-residence for 1966. Although Humphrey had already refused Bard's offer to be reinstated on the faculty, he was amenable at first to the Boston offer because "these things can sometimes be very lucrative, and with usually very little work attached" (Knopf Coll.).[7] Knopf foresaw that the university administrator had a *quid pro quo* up his sleeve. On 1 February Humphrey reported to Knopf that he had heard nothing further from Boston University about the job:

> But even before offering it to me, they are already, as you foresaw by some strange power of divination, after me to donate my manuscripts, as well as all my other private papers. They wish, they say, to make their university a great center for the study of outstanding contemporary literature. The "nucleus" of this would be what they would like to call "The William Humphrey Collection." I could rest content that my papers were being preserved for future generations, for they would be "housed and curated under optimum archival conditions." I have replied as soberly as I could that nothing on earth would make me feel so fatuous as knowing that somewhere there was something called "The William Humphrey Collection"; that it would inhibit me so that I would write still less than I do; that my manuscripts, along with my collection of rejection slips, repose in one small cardboard carton in the loft of a friend's barn in New York State, where they will stay until, seeing the end approach, I burn them up. (Knopf Coll.)

Apparently Boston University was, in the end, not deterred and agreed to accept a writer-in-residence with no papers.

In the same letter to Knopf, Humphrey wrote that he and Dorothy were tired of roaming and wanted to find a house somewhere and settle down and plant a flower bed. They remained in Alassio until about the middle of March, then left for a week in Rome and almost two weeks in Sicily before sailing on the *Christofor Columbo* on 20 April for the United States to begin the search for a place to call home. They took up a temporary residence at 89 Lauer Road in Poughkeepsie, in a Cape Cod cottage belonging to Norman Rockwell, and by the second week of May 1965, were in the throes of house hunting, concentrating their ef-

7. Humphrey to the Weisses, 30 December 1964, Weiss Coll.

forts in "the literary belt of nearby Connecticut." By 18 June house hunting had become not just a problem but a nightmare.[8]

In the meantime, Bill turned down the offer from Boston University and accepted a teaching position at Massachusetts Institute of Technology for the forthcoming academic year (1965–66). It was, from his perspective, the perfect post: a fabulous salary with minimal duties. He would teach one course—whatever he wanted it to be—each semester. To the extent that money could ameliorate some of the unpleasantness of searching for a house, the position at MIT (which Bill kept wanting to refer to as IBM) provided at least a temporary fix, and Bill did not feel that the light teaching load would drain energy and time required to make progress on his third novel and his second collection of stories. Nonetheless, the lecture notes for his fall semester in "The Origins of the Novel," with a reading list including Cervantes, Defoe, Richardson, Fielding, and Sterne, show that he took his position seriously. In the spring his class was called "The Frontier in American Literature."[9]

In June of 1965 the Humphreys had bought a house—an antique one, built in 1795.[10] The house sat on a 165-acre tract with an apple orchard, a stream flowing through it, and about fifty acres of swamp. The place, called High Meadow, is situated about five miles outside of Hudson, New York, on Gahbauer Road. The purchase of this house near Hudson created a complication because of the teaching position in Cambridge that Bill had just accepted. He and Dorothy thus found themselves moving into two houses at once, the Cambridge one being at 8 Francis Avenue. They spent Tuesdays through Thursdays in the city, the extended weekends in the Hudson Valley.

When Jean Lambert visited High Meadow on 27 December 1966, he noted in his journal that the house had two large front rooms furnished with Regency Anglo-American antiques (which Bill had restored himself) and oriental appointments; running between these rooms of wide-planked floors was a broad hall with a natural wood staircase. Behind the front rooms was an enormous dining room with simple early American furnishings and a large fireplace. In a letter of 10 January 1967, Humphrey described the house's setting to Katherine Anne Porter: "You've heard of that fabled valley where ailing elephants betake themselves to die—well all old sick autos seem to turn instinctively to the Hudson Valley when their headlights grow blear and their crankshafts stiffen and

8. Humphrey to Lemay, 11 May and 8 June 1965, Knopf Coll.; to F. W. Dupee, 1 March 1965, Dupee Coll.; to Williams, 8 March 1965, Williams Coll.

9. Humphrey to Lemay, 8 June 1965, Knopf Coll.; to the Weisses, 17 February 1965, Weiss Coll.

10. Knopf interoffice memorandum, 22 June 1965, Knopf Coll.

their shock absorbers won't absorb the shocks any more and hardening of the fuel line overtakes them, and this happy rural seat is now littered with their rotting carcasses and skeletal remains" (KAP Coll.). There was a trailer camp, or "mobile homes estate," as it styled itself, nearby. Junk cars and mobile homes might, in part, account for the location's attractiveness to Humphrey: what else could make a displaced southerner feel more at home? Yet the real beauty of the location, in spite of a few eyesores, was its main attraction, which Humphrey went on to describe to Porter: "From the high meadow that gives this place its name you can see the Catskills and the Berkshires and the Helderbergs all without turning on your heel and in all that not even a telephone wire to bisect the vision." He invited Porter to visit in the spring when the apple orchard blossomed.

During the previous several years of living here and there in Europe, Humphrey had lost touch with Katherine Anne Porter (she had been moving frequently as well). But a month before the Humphreys returned from Italy to begin the search for a permanent home, Porter's request that Humphrey be her literary executor reached him in Alassio, and he accepted. Once he and Dorothy had moved into their two residences, Bill began to seek a proper repository for Porter's massive array of papers, ruling out Harvard straightaway because "women are not allowed inside Harvard's main library. . . . I must find some way to let them know they're not getting your papers, and just why! Medieval!" he wrote on 22 September 1965 (KAP Coll.).

Once Bill's year at MIT was over, he and Dorothy settled into a routine of cocktail parties and dining with the literati of Columbia and Dutchess counties, New York. Hilary Masters has noted that the women in this set were "all handsome and marvelous cooks, and the men were writers and artists." The congenial, smug group included Richard Rovere (who wrote the *New Yorker* column "Letter from Washington" for thirty years) and his wife Eleanor, Martin and Alice Provensen (famous book illustrators), Hilary Masters (whose first novel, *The Common Pasture*, was about to be published) and his wife Polly, Gore Vidal (whose *Julian* had spent a recent summer on the fiction best-seller lists and whose *Myra Breckinridge* was in the works), and Mary Lee Settle (whose *All the Brave Promises* was about to be published). Humphrey felt connected to Settle even before he met her because they were "partners in one man's disesteem"— Walter Allen's, who in 1964 had written that Settle's and Humphrey's unhappy melding of Poe and Erskine Caldwell was "what is wrong with the Southern novel." Settle and Humphrey surely laughed at Allen's unsuccessful effort to brand their books "Southerns" (cf. "Westerns"). At the dinner parties that all of these people had together, wine, whiskey, and brilliant talk were plentiful; jokes were regularly "passed with the cassoulet and the flan." Bill held his own as an entertaining raconteur, spinning astounding reports of dinners with Alfred and Blanche Knopf at Chappaqua and with Katherine Anne Porter in Washington. When he and Dorothy hosted the group, he always served "the best of bordeaux," and dessert was always served in one of the formal parlors.[11]

Having escaped from poverty, Humphrey was determined to indulge himself in the best of everything and to show it off. He had his suits made on Saville Row, his shoes in Florence, his shotgun in England. When he bought a fly rod, it had to be a Leonard. No longer was S. S. Pierce's Gold Coast pipe tobacco good enough for him; his tobacconist in St. Louis mailed him a pound of Heywood mixture every month. Humphrey recommended his suppliers to his friends, less to be helpful than to inform them of his good taste and high standards. When he strolled onto the field to hunt quail, he looked as though he had stepped forth from "the pages of an Abercrombie & Fitch catalogue. His costume looked freshly pressed, a sporty tweed cap cocked on his head, and puttees expertly fixed around his calves. His bird dog belonged in an ad for expensive bourbon."[12]

While Humphrey had been house hunting in Connecticut, he had stopped at Roxbury to see William Styron, who gave him some unexpected financial insight. He told Humphrey that Kathleen Winsor, author of the historical romance *Forever Amber* (Macmillan, 1944) and the just-published *Wanderers Eastward, Wanderers West* (Random House, 1965), was getting 70 percent of the profit from the sale of paperback rights and that Bennett Cerf of Random House, recently merged with Knopf, had offered him (Styron) 66 2/3 percent on his as-yet-unfinished third novel even after a previous agreement to split the profit fifty-fifty. Knopf had recently sold the paperback rights to *The Ordways* to Bantam for $57,500, an amount to be split fifty-fifty between Knopf and Humphrey. With the knowledge that Styron had provided, then, Humphrey wrote to Pete Lemay on 11 May, mentioning Winsor's lucrative arrangement while withholding the name of Styron, but alluding to Cerf's generous offer to increase that author's share in the paperback rights:

> This latter [Styron] is no Kathleen Winsor but a serious writer, whose two previous books have won much acclaim—though as a matter of record,

11. Hilary Masters, "Proud Flesh: William Humphrey Remembered," *Sewanee Review* 108, no. 3 (Spring 2000): 256, 258, 257; Gore Vidal, *Palimpsest: A Memoir* (New York: Random House, 1995), 404; Humphrey to the Weisses, 11 December 1964, Weiss Coll.; Walter Allen, *The Modern Novel in Britain and the United States* (New York: E. P. Dutton, 1964), 307.

12. Masters, 258; Humphrey to the Weisses, 30 November 1961, Weiss Coll.

no greater than mine, and whose sales have been no larger, if as large, as mine. What is more, only one of his two previous books (and this the less successful, critically and commercially, of the two) was published by Random House. As a matter of principle—and even more as a matter of money—I feel that I deserve the same sort of consideration, and I do not mean on my next book, I mean on *The Ordways*. In fact, considering that I have sold as well if not better than the writer in question, and remembering that I gave Knopf 10% of the movie rights (which as we both know, and as I pointed out at the time, most publishers do not share in) I deserve the 70% that Miss Winsor is getting. (Knopf coll.)

Lemay responded on the next day that the officers of Random House and Knopf had already decided at a meeting the previous week to offer Humphrey (as well as Styron) two-thirds of the income from the sale of paperback rights. He added that Kathleen Winsor was not getting 70 percent and that the *Saturday Review,* the original source of this misinformation, would be printing a retraction in its next issue.

Humphrey did not entirely buy this version of events—otherwise, why had Styron been informed of the increase and not Humphrey? He appreciated Styron's providing the information for leverage, and he wrote to Styron thanking him. Styron replied on 14 May: "Bravo! It pleasures me greatly to think that I may have been instrumental, or at least a help, in getting you 10 grand or so—even if Lemay's letter was on the level. I won't breathe a word to Kathleen Winsor. Do keep in touch and we'll have more evenings" (WH Coll., UT). On 24 October 1997 Styron wrote that he "didn't have more than a couple of evenings with Bill. This was largely due to geography; New York is a surprisingly big state and I discovered that his place up the Hudson was really a very long haul. Distance more than anything prevented us from becoming better friends."[13]

The haggling over paperback rights created a distance between Alfred Knopf and Humphrey, coming as it did hard upon those distempered exchanges between the two men about the long delayed novel *The Ordways*. Further, such disputatious dealings (as far as Knopf was concerned) were out of accord with the spirit of 1965, a year that marked the fiftieth anniversary of Alfred A. Knopf's founding of his publishing house and featured major celebrations, lauds, and honors. For all of these festivities Humphrey remained on the sidelines. The

13. William Styron to author.

Lotos Club,[14] an institution with a long tradition of honoring prominent figures, put on a dinner for Knopf at its building on East 66th Street, to which Humphrey declined an invitation. In October admirers of Knopf gave a dinner at the Astor Hotel, for which occasion the two-volume work *Portrait of a Publisher, 1915–1965* was produced.[15] Humphrey was not among the 276 diners. He contemplated the fallout from his nonparticipation in these celebratory occasions, as well as his general feeling of being on the outs with Knopf, on a page in one of his *Proud Flesh* notebooks:

> It's six months since I've heard from Alfred. He's an unforgiving man and I suspect that our exchange of letters about the unfinished manuscripts of The Ordways and the Renshaws still rankles him. Also my declining invitations to the Lotos Club dinner for him and the 50th Anniversary Dinner for him. And I think he never really liked the Ordways. So he gives interviews with the Saturday Review in which he praises Home from the Hill but doesn't mention the new book. The interview with Life in which he praises all his writers but me—singling out especially Updike as his best young writer. Then comes the anthology of Knopf's 50 years with nothing of mine in it. So I'm afraid relations between Alfred and me have not just cooled but congealed. I ought to mention the dust-jacket quarrel. Oh, Alfred would be very gracious again if the Ordways should win one of the prizes. But it's not going to. Isn't even in contention for the NBA. Funny the career of this book. Such bruhaha on its appearance—forgotten by the end of the year. (Notes, 90–91)

The "interviews" to which Humphrey refers are not really interviews. The *Saturday Review* piece "How Alfred Knopf Saw His Authors" features photographs that he had taken of some of his writers, and beneath their portraits are brief quotations drawn apparently from *Dialogue,* a motion picture on Knopf and his authors that was soon to be released. Under Humphrey's picture is the following abbreviated comment: "*Home from the Hill* is the best novel that has ever come out of Texas." The *Life* magazine "interview" in the following month is in fact a record of Alfred and Blanche Knopf's reminiscing about their roster of authors.

---

14. The Lotos Club, founded in 1870, has as its object "to promote social intercourse among journalists, artists and members of the musical and dramatic professions, and representatives, amateurs and friends of literature, science and the fine arts . . ." (*Club Men of New York* [New York: Republic Press, 1896], 18).

15. Harry Gilroy, "Knopf Gets a Surprise 2-Volume 'Portrait,'" *New York Times,* 30 October 1965, 33.

Humphrey was cut to the quick not just by the praise of Updike and the absence of praise of himself but by what Knopf praised Updike for: "John Updike is the most remarkable young man we have on the list. In terms of sheer volume he makes the others look like slouches." Humphrey, having been poked and prodded by Knopf to get *The Ordways* finished and then having taken six years to do it, felt himself the greatest slouch of the lot—or at least smarted to think that was how Knopf thought of him. And then to have been left out of Clifton Fadiman's *Fifty Years: Being a Retrospective Collection of Novels, Novellas, Tales, Drama, Poetry, and Reportage and Essays (Whether Literary, Musical, Contemplative, Historical, Biographical, Argumentative, or Gastronomical) All Drawn from Volumes Issued during the Last Half-Century by Alfred and Blanche Knopf* (New York: Knopf, 1965) when Updike, Elizabeth Bowen, W. H. Hudson, and a host of others were included made Humphrey feel *persona non grata* at the house of Knopf. As for *The Ordways* "dust-jacket quarrel," Humphrey had complained fiercely about its design and about the designer, Rudolph Ruzicka, who was an old friend of Knopf's.[16] In spite of the cooled relationship with his publisher, Humphrey nonetheless remained with the firm for another decade.

This period of Humphrey's life was characterized by a grumbling mood in which he felt forsaken by fate and by man, yet he maintained a reserve capacity to carry on. He saw a general lack of appreciation for his work. He complained, for example, about Updike's "The Bulgarian Poetess" winning the O. Henry Memorial Award for 1966 while his "A Job of the Plains" and "A Good Indian" were not included in *First Prize Stories, 1919–1966* (1966). Despondency over such issues often overcame Bill, as his letters frequently attest. Ted Weiss said that Humphrey's dejection could usually be traced to two sources: writing blocks and rejection. When he felt neglected and ignored, he often asserted with great conviction that he was through with writing. But his rage quickly abated, and usually in a day or two he would be back at it as intensely as ever. Likewise, oppressed by the uncertainties of writing and publishing and doubts that he could continue to make a living by writing, he would usually bounce back quickly. Although his underlying sense of life was that it was tragic, "his zest and his wry wit, his passion for hunting, fishing, art especially, literature and music (his taste in music always expanded) all lent a wonderful comic side to his nature." Humphrey always loved to talk, to spin anecdotes that his friends knew to be enhanced by his

16. Margaret R. Weiss, "How Alfred Knopf Saw His Authors," *Saturday Review*, 12 June 1965, 26–28; "Golden Anniversary of Excellence," *Life*, 23 July 1965, 37–38, 40; telegram from Humphrey to Lemay, 26 October 1964, Knopf Coll.

fictional powers.[17] A perfect example of Humphrey's "wonderful comic side"—
and his proneness to tell an embellished tale—is the magical account of his generosity to poet Robert Lowell on Christmas in 1965, when Humphrey was still at
MIT. Hearing that Lowell was trapped for the holidays in McLean's, a mental
hospital outside Boston, on a ward populated by juvenile drug addicts,[18] Bill,
who had met Lowell only once, arranged to have him as a guest for Christmas
dinner. Humphrey told the story to Katherine Anne Porter on 7 January 1966:

> I was to come for him at 12 noon. This I did, leaving Dorothy at home
> whipping up oyster soup and roasts and other goodies. When I got there
> I found Lowell lying in bed in anything but his going-out-to-dinner
> clothes. Poor man, I said to myself, he has forgotten about it. So I said,
> come on, get dressed, dinner's ready. He very docilely did this, and only
> when he was finished voiced his doubt. "Are you sure it isn't for tomorrow?" he said uncertainly. I said I was sure, and he agreed it was likely, that
> time didn't have any too much meaning inside there. As we were going out
> of his room he said, "Are you sure I've been given permission to go out?"
> I assured him that it had all been arranged. "Let's just make sure," he said.
> I went to the office, leaving him outside. "Mr. Lowell has been given permission to go to my house for dinner today," I said to the young man.
> "Fine. I'll just check on it," he said. He went into another room. He returned with a big notebook in his hand and in his eye a very queer look
> for me. "It's for tomorrow," he said. "Isn't this Christmas?" I said weakly.
> "No, it isn't. Tomorrow is Christmas." He felt more embarrassed for me
> even than I did for myself. "That is too bad," I said. "Because my wife has
> got Christmas dinner ready now." He said, "Well, it's been approved in
> principle that Mr. Lowell may go out with you; I don't see that it matters
> much which day, so go ahead, and have a good time." I returned to Lowell,
> and tried to hustle him out fast. Two doors had to be unlocked for us. "It
> is all right?" he asked. "Am I allowed out?" "Yes, you're allowed out," I
> said. "The question now is, whether they're going to let me out or not."
> At last we were outdoors. "Tomorrow is Christmas, isn't it?" he said. I
> admitted that it was. "And they have let me out in your care?" he roared.
> "Well, this is a treat! To be let out of there to go to Christmas dinner with

17. Notes, 94; *First-Prize Stories, 1919–1966* (New York: Doubleday, 1966), 723; Theodore Weiss to
author, 7 October 1997.

18. Lowell had been admitted on 7 December; see Ian Hamilton, *Robert Lowell: A Biography*
(New York: Random House, 1982), 343; Humphrey to Woolf, 7 January 1966, Woolf Coll.

the only man alive who doesn't know when Christmas comes!" We all had a marvelous time, and vowed to celebrate Christmas a day early every year from now on. (KAP Coll.)

After Humphrey's year in Cambridge, he had little occasion to cross paths with Lowell, but another acquaintance that he made at that time—publisher Seymour Lawrence—eventually became a friend. Lawrence had for years sought, unsuccessfully, to lure Humphrey away from Knopf; and Humphrey used Lawrence's interest, as well as that of other publishers, to press for more favorable financial arrangements with Knopf. On 11 March 1966 Lemay was prompted to offer Humphrey, on behalf of Knopf, an advance of $75,000 on his next novel and a royalty of 15 percent as well as two-thirds on the sale of paperback rights. Humphrey then came down to the city and allowed himself to be taken to lunch by the Knopf firm; apparently after more than a few drinks, Lemay declared that Knopf would match *any* offer made to Humphrey by any other publisher. In his memorandum of 12 April 1966 to Bennett Cerf, Lemay revealed that he did not remember many of the details of what was discussed at the luncheon with Humphrey, but recalled that the firm had agreed to match Delacorte's offer of an $85,000 advance on *Proud Flesh*. Humphrey's growing reputation surely helped in those negotiations. In 1966 he was appointed to the writers' panel of the Foundation for the Arts and Humanities, and the next year Katherine Anne Porter named him, along with Eudora Welty and Robert Penn Warren, to the committee overseeing the Katherine Anne Porter Foundation "for the occasional alleviation of the perennial miseries of gifted writers."[19]

While serving on this foundation board, Humphrey enjoyed especially his relationship with Welty, but in 1970 he seemed ready to dismiss her for the merest slight. He interrupted his work on *Proud Flesh* on 11 April to record in his notebook that Welty's new novel *Losing Battles* had just been reviewed in the Sunday *Times* and that an accompanying interview "mentions her receiving a phone call from friends in New Mexico to whom she had sent a copy of the book." Humphrey then writes: "None to me, and it reminds me that she never thanked me for sending her a copy of my last." Next Humphrey places this observation in the context of their relationship: "I don't understand this. She seems, whenever we meet, so very friendly and open. She and I are always in agreement at those KAP foundation meetings. Is this hypocritical? It must be. I must cease thinking of her as a friend of mine" (WH Coll., UT). Such observations, such sensitivity, such deductions many people might—under similar circumstances—have enter-

19. Katherine Anne Porter to William and Dorothy Humphrey, 13 April 1967, KAP Coll.

tained as passing thoughts. The best light that might be put on this paragraph in his notebook is to say that he is more honest than most people in owning up to his feelings. Furthermore, that he wrote his feelings down certainly does not mean that they were preserved in his mind. There were no ill feelings remaining about Welty in October 1976 to prevent his attending a cocktail party in her honor at the home of Kenneth Connelly in Northampton, Massachusetts.[20]

Because upkeep of High Meadow, house and grounds, had become an all-consuming occupation for Humphrey, he and Dorothy planned an escape to England for the autumn of 1967; they looked forward to 14 November, when the first rumbles of the engines of the *Ile de France* would cut them "thoroughly from the pesty responsibilities of home" and thus enable Bill to devote his energies to finishing *A Time and a Place* and working on the long-delayed *Proud Flesh*. From the end of November until the end of January, they lived first just outside the Dean's yard at Westminster Abbey, in a "filthy, dark, shabby," and depressing little flat—not the "handsome and comfortable flat" that Dorothy had asked Trekkie Parsons to try to find for them. Bill did not feel comfortable in the neighborhood either, being surrounded as he was by such establishments as the Society for Christian Dedication and the Christian Mothers' Union. Before the Humphreys had had a chance to unpack, their flat was burgled and the contents of their suitcases scattered about. The intruders took just four of Bill's cigars from a new box of fifty, which he thought was "jolly decent of them." About the only feature of English culture that cheered Bill was the omnipresence of mini-skirts worn by the young women of London. The Humphreys enjoyed Christmas with the Parsons in the country, even though Bill felt that his dissatisfaction with the London flat put a strain on the friendship.[21]

Between September 1963 and the autumn of 1965, five of the stories that would go in *A Time and a Place* had appeared in magazines, and Humphrey had seven fragments of stories (including three he never finished). They are "A City of the Plains," "Mr. Sensabough's Drunken Negro"—at one point simply titled "The Drunkard" (*Sensabough* was the name of the man Humphrey bought firewood from in Lexington, Virginia)—and "Jake Clark" (at other times called "John Clark's Sons") (Notes, i). Among Humphrey's papers at the University of Texas is a two-page summary of this last story, which is about a man here named Ernest

20. Humphrey, notebook, entry for 4 October 1976, WH Coll., UT.

21. Humphrey to the Weisses, 5 December [1967], Weiss Coll.; Dorothy Humphrey to Woolf, 26 August 1967 and October [1967], Woolf Coll.; Humphrey to the Weisses, 3, 5, 29 December 1967, Weiss Coll.

Clark who strikes oil and then dies of tuberculosis; the title on the summary is "To Settle the Estate." Deciding that these three could never become effective stories, Humphrey agreed to supply Knopf with a collection of only nine stories by the middle of March, so he had four to finish during the winter of 1967–68.

By 3 February Bill and Dorothy had moved to more commodious and salubrious accommodation at 2a Nugent Terrace in St. John's Wood—a former stable "in a garden just off a delightful street of shops" with a studio "the size of a small race track," he had said to Lawrence on 20 September 1967—"as big as a ship," he said on 3 February 1968 to Porter (Lawrence Coll.; KAP Coll.). They were as happy now as they had been miserable in the other place. The local pub had three names—The Heroes of Alma, The Twenty-Third Foot, and The Royal Welsh Fusiliers—this so that "you can go pub-crawling and still stay in the same place," he explained to Lawrence (Lawrence Coll.). Early in February, he still had two stories to finish for *A Time and a Place;* he finished the last of the nine on 21 February 1968 and elected to write another since he had extra time as well as inclination. "The Human Fly" made the tenth story for the volume.

Although Humphrey had felt some pressure to meet Knopf's deadline, he and Dorothy nonetheless made time to soak themselves in the theater, an activity that their rural location in New York hardly allowed. In London, however, they were in the theater almost as much as out of it. He was an enthusiastic fan who would sit there with his mouth hanging open and either laughing or crying loud enough to annoy his neighbors. The Humphreys attended performances of Chekhov's *Three Sisters,* Molière's *Tartuffe,* Shakespeare's *Macbeth* and *All's Well That Ends Well,* and Jonson's *Volpone* at the Old Vic; Vanbrugh's *The Relapse, or Virtue in Danger* ("how long one would wait for a revival of Vanbrugh in New York!" he remarked) at the Royal Shakespeare Theatre; Shakespeare's *As You Like It, Othello,* and *The Merchant of Venice* (with Ralph Richardson playing Shylock) at the Aldwych; and Ibsen's *Ghosts* at the Haymarket. Of these Humphrey seems to have been most impressed by the Old Vic production of *Three Sisters,* which was "enough to make you say I never knew the theater could be this marvelous." At the end of February they were the guests of Peggy Ashcroft for performances of *King Lear* and *Julius Caesar* at the Royal Shakespeare Theatre in Stratford-upon-Avon.

Then theatergoing ceased for a couple of weeks while Humphrey gathered his manuscripts and put them in final order for submission. On 22 March—their first time out of doors in about two weeks—the Humphreys attended a performance at the Royal Court Theatre of D. H. Lawrence's *The Widowing of Mrs. Holyroyd.* This play, which dates from the time of *Sons and Lovers,* was, according to Humphrey, "superb." They did manage one contact with the literary scene when Peggy Ashcroft invited them to dinner with the poet laureate, C. Day Lewis, and Robert Graves. Lewis and Humphrey, both former communists, especially enjoyed one another's company, in part because both loved Thomas Hardy and were in strong agreement that T. S. Eliot would only "make a footnote in the history of English Literature."[22]

At those times when Humphrey felt confident about his success and when he thought he had the ear of someone who might pay attention to him, he did all he could to help other writers secure a wider audience. During this 1967–68 sojourn in London, Bill saw a good deal of his old friend Tim Pember, who had written a novel about life in an English public school entitled *Not Me, Sir*, which had received rave reviews just after being published in England in 1941. The novel was, however, a casualty of the war, and Pember became discouraged. Humphrey had sent the novel to Lawrence in 1966, urging him to publish an American edition, and in 1968 was still promoting the same, arguing that a little encouragement might get a once very good writer to write again. Lawrence declined. Later in February Humphrey was again unsuccessful on behalf of the Polish Jewish writer Adolph Rudnicki. Having sent Lawrence some French translations of Rudnicki's books, he pestered his friend for two years until the publisher declined unequivocally, whereupon Humphrey redirected his efforts to William Koshland of Knopf.

After finishing and mailing *A Time and a Place* while in England, Humphrey and his wife left for the United States on 19 April 1968 from Southampton on the *Ile de France*. Bill came home to find that he had a new editor at Knopf, Robert Gottlieb. Unfazed, he recommended his eternal wrestling match with *Proud Flesh*.

In October or November 1968, Katherine Anne Porter asked Humphrey to organize her essays, together with a handful of poems, for a collected edition of her nonfiction. She was following her publisher Seymour Lawrence's suggestion, made in 1967, that publication of the collected edition of essays need not be delayed owing to her ill health if she asked her friend Humphrey to attend to the preparations. Bill had already informed Lawrence of his willingness. As soon as Porter approached Humphrey herself, he began work on this project for her, devoting his evenings to it. In a letter of 5 November 1968, he proposed using the basic divisions of *The Days Before,* one of Porter's earlier books of essays: Critical, Personal and Particular, and Mexican. He also proposed adding three divisions:

---

22. Humphrey to Porter, 3 February 1968, KAP Coll.; to Seymour Lawrence, 3 February 1968, Lawrence Coll.; to the Weisses, 21 February and 23 March 1968, 29 December 1967, and [12 February] 1968, Weiss Coll.

Biographical, the three Cotton Mather pieces, and Poems. She did not respond in writing to Humphrey's proposal (in fact, there are no letters from her to him between January 1968 and May 1970), but they did talk on the telephone. One would assume that Porter assented to the overall plan, for Humphrey's proposed arrangement is essentially the one he followed. *The Collected Essays and Occasional Writings of Katherine Anne Porter* was published on 23 March 1970. Humphrey tried "to get her to leave out ephemera" but in the end acceded to her wishes, retaining, for example, the piece on Jacqueline Kennedy Onassis. Humphrey took a break from *Proud Flesh* as well as from his Porter project to appear at Princeton University on 13 November, where he read his short story "The Last of the Caddoes."[23]

A Time and a Place, Humphrey's second volume of short stories, was published in November 1968. It is different from *The Last Husband and Other Stories* in several ways. While the earlier collection alternated between stories set in Humphrey's native region and those set in the Northeast, the second volume is comprised entirely of stories set in East Texas or just across the border in southeastern Oklahoma, the area known, according to William Owens's *Walking on Borrowed Land,* as "Little Dixie." And while the stories in *The Last Husband* are set over a twenty-year period, all of those in *A Time and a Place* are set in 1935 or thereabouts.[24]

Humphrey originally wanted to call the collection "Red River Valley," but his new editor, Gottlieb, strongly opposed it because of the song of the same title, which reminded him of television cowboys. Humphrey also suggested "Mouth of Brass," the title of his favorite story in the volume. Gottlieb countered with a revision of Bill's original idea, "Red River Country," but Humphrey did not care for it. Other titles that were bandied about were "Hard Luck Stories," "Hard Luck: 10 Stories by William Humphrey," "Hardscrabble," "Losers," "Sooners and Losers," "Ten Stories," and "A Voice from the Woods—Stories." Then the hint of a title arrived in the positive prefatory remark of a rejection notice from *Atlantic Monthly:* "An effective evocation of its time and place." Bill did not perceive a title in the phrase at the time, but it stuck with him, and several weeks later, casually remarking on the stories, he said to Gottlieb, "Well, they do have some-

23. Humphrey to Porter, 5 November 1968, KAP Coll.; Lawrence to Humphrey, 8 February 1970, Lawrence Coll.; Humphrey to Lawrence, 28 May 1985, Lawrence Coll.; to the Weisses, 17 July 1968, Weiss Coll.

24. The dust storms were at their worst in 1934–36 (Frederick Lewis Allen, *Since Yesterday: The Nineteen-Thirties in America* [New York: Harper, 1940], 199).

thing in common—a time and a place." Gottlieb suddenly shouted that "there we had our title."[25]

The next issue to be resolved was the ordering of the stories. Gottlieb favored keeping the stories with a similarity in matter or tone apart from each other; for example, the stories about the discovery of oil and about banditry would be separated. Catherine Carver of Chatto and Windus saw problems with this as the sole principle, pointing out that Gottlieb's juxtaposition of "The Human Fly" and "A Good Indian" would confuse the reader because both are narrated in the first person but have different narrating personas.[26] Gottlieb conceded, and Carver's revised ordering was adopted, though the separation principle was adhered to after the first three ("The Ballad of Jesse Neighbours," "A Good Indian," and "A Job of the Plains")—all of which are about the discovery of oil. "The Rainmaker," the longest story, was placed in the center of the book.

Common to most of the stories in *A Time and a Place* are two themes: the gullibility of humanity, especially when facing deprivation or other extreme circumstances (in particular the drought of the 1930s and the Great Depression) and the depravity of man as he seeks to increase his fortune at the expense of the gullible and disadvantaged. Into the mix is thrown the discovery of oil. As early as 1961, Humphrey envisioned his volume as a kind of minority report about those who did not participate in the oil boom—or who wished they had not.[27] Taken as a whole, Humphrey's volume remains a fierce attack upon the American capitalistic system, though its concerns also include bigotry and the struggle for personal identity.

Most of the stories in *A Time and a Place* are not based on Humphrey's personal life, as many in the first volume were, but are connected to the experience of the collective mind during the Depression. They are populated by gangsters, a rainmaker, a human fly, more than one overnight oil millionaire, a defeated plowman of hardscrabble, and a snookered Indian—all types common to Depression and Dust Bowl Texas and Oklahoma. John Steinbeck explored this territory with great sympathy, finding loveliness in the midst of deprivation. But Humphrey did not think much of Steinbeck's sentimentality, later posing a question and answer that summed up his general disapproval: "Q: Which is John

25. Ian Parsons was not, however, happy with the Knopf title; when he could not produce a counterproposal, he thought of using a subtitle for the English edition. Humphrey to the Weisses, [12 February], 5 March, 23 March 1968, Weiss Coll.; Robert Gottlieb to Catherine Carver, 2 May 1968, C&W; Carver to Gottlieb, 31 May 1968, C&W; Rita Spurdle to Ellen McNeilly, 19 September 1968, C&W; Humphrey to the Weisses, 15 March 1968, Weiss Coll.

26. Gottlieb to Humphrey, [April 1968], C&W; Carver to Gottlieb, 25 April 1968, C&W.

27. Humphrey to the Weisses, 14 March 1961, Weiss Coll.

Steinbeck's best book? A: None."[28] *A Time and a Place* takes a long, sad look at the worst that man can be. Sometimes Humphrey resorts to humor, which provides a measure of relief from the persistent grimness. This humor is most effective, however, when mixed with profound seriousness, with one mode alternately being surprised by the other.

The volume is a remarkable achievement, especially considering that many of its stories were written during periods when Humphrey needed escape from the tribulations of writing *The Ordways* and *Proud Flesh*. When he reached an impasse in *The Ordways,* he would turn to the other novel; when he lost his way in it, he would turn to the stories that eventually became *A Time and a Place*. Although their writing amounted to therapy for a writer fraught with anxiety about his work, the stories themselves are perfectly controlled. In the end, Humphrey was certainly pleased with the volume and thought it as important as either of his novels. In a rash moment a few months after its publication, he told Parsons that he thought it a better book than either of the novels. He told Ted and Renée Weiss that he especially valued the collection because he had thought his short-story well had dried up and was glad to find it still working. To them he exaggerated that since the publication of his first volume of stories, ten years passed without his having "even a glimmer of an idea for another one."[29]

The reviewers of *A Time and a Place* were impressed by Humphrey's hard look at hard lives and by the unusual unity of this book (not just collection) of stories. In the *New York Times Book Review,* Larry L. King, a Texas novelist, said that the ten stories "are held together by common and interlocking themes; . . . for all their varied treatments, the reader must remind himself he is not reading a novel." Granville Hicks, in the *Saturday Review,* noted that for all their unity of setting and theme, these stories boast a laudable variety in narrative technique: in most of the stories Humphrey used "bold, broad strokes," though he also showed himself "capable of subtler effects."[30]

In the reviews of *Home from the Hill,* Humphrey had often been compared disadvantageously to Faulkner, but reviews of *A Time and a Place* reversed the intent of that comparison. Hicks, for example, acknowledged that because of Humphrey's growing reputation the present volume "will probably get the attention it deserves, and that is a good deal, for Humphrey is a storyteller in the tradition of Mark Twain and William Faulkner." Furthermore, *Choice* declared

---

28. Written on 1 April inside the cover of a 1988 diary, WH Coll., UT.

29. Humphrey to the Weisses, 21 February 1968, Weiss Coll.

30. Larry L. King, "A Setting Mean and Hard," *New York Times Book Review,* 3 November 1968, 5; Granville Hicks, "Hoping for Oil, Hoping for Rain," *Saturday Review,* 9 November 1968, 31.

A Time and a Place "an impressive fictional achievement," saying that "Humphrey is establishing himself as one of America's most promising young writers," for "like Faulkner, [he] transcends the limits of regionalism." "The Rainmaker" was singled out as "the best of its kind since Faulkner." And King concluded his review by saying: "William Humphrey is more than an accomplished raconteur. He has a grand ear; his descriptions of the land's brooding presence, and how it works its moods on its people, is at once reminiscent of Faulkner and William Styron. His cadence is his own as are marvelous subtleties of tone reflecting his awareness of the unending little contests and struggles comprising life. And certainly William Humphrey is more than the 'regional writer' some have named him (a limitation also misapplied to the early Faulkner) because he so skillfully explores themes that are universal in their ironies and degradations." These approving reviews helped the book to sell a great deal better than anyone at Knopf expected a short-story collection to sell. By March 1969 the first printing of 12,500 had sold out, and a second printing was ordered.[31]

The success of *A Time and a Place* in the United States did not at first impress Gallimard. On 19 February 1969, Michel Mohrt shocked Humphrey by turning down the collection and thereby severing the French firm's relationship with him. In less than two months' time, however, Humphrey was even more surprised when Virginia Bradley, his agent in France, telephoned with the astonishing news that Gallimard had just called her to say that they realized they had "made a big mistake" and "could they have the book back." Gallimard even wished to run some of the stories in *La nouvelle revue française* before the book's publication. As Humphrey put it, the "sour note in the French song has been sweetened."[32]

"The Ballad of Jesse Neighbours," the first story in the volume, seems a simply told tale. Its subject and narrative technique derive from the ballad tradition and the folktale. Such old stories from rural communities about a "poor boy, heiress, and her father," involving the tragic consequences growing out of betrayed love, are the stock materials of traditional ballads. Humphrey's narrative voice in sympathy with the story's downtrodden hero, producing strong feelings, is another feature of the ballad. Furthermore, throughout the narrative various ballad techniques are used—repeated chords of music and repeated references, such as to Jesse's resourcefulness in saving balls of tinfoil; and there are abrupt transitions,

31. Hicks, 31; *Choice*, September 1969, 816–17; King, 47; Humphrey to Parsons, 14 March 1969, C&W.

32. Humphrey to the Weisses, 14 April 1969, Weiss Coll.

as when the narrative jumps from Jesse leaning on the plow handles, "sweat dripping from the tip of his nose," to "the story told" (note the ballad phrase) of Bull Childress being knocked off the hole of his outhouse when the oil well blew on his property (*TP*, 9).

Jesse and Naomi are looking forward to marriage, even though they live in Oklahoma, where few marriages are being made in the hard Dust Bowl days. The third sentence of the story contains the ironic understatement that governs the story: "Things might never get any better!" (*TP*, 3). The *might* suggests an inkling of hope, a desperate hope that Jesse lives and dies by, even as he sees that things are not only not getting any better but are in fact worsening for him. Hope seems, however, not entirely unreasonable at the beginning of the story. Though Jesse is the son of a sharecropper, and therefore about as poor as one could be, he is hardworking enough to have won Bull Childress's provisional blessing to marry Naomi. In contrast to Jesse, O. J. Childress is "rich," having a house of his own and clear title to "twenty-seven acres of hardscrabble" (4). Jesse entertains the long-range hope of owning his own land and a herd of Bramers, just as Humphrey's grandfather, also a sharecropper, had "clung to his dream of gathering a good enough crop for a couple of years in succession to make a down payment on a place of his own and 'work for himself'" (*FOFH*, 55).

When the Childresses strike oil, however, the meaning of the word *heiress* appreciates; abruptly the ironic dimension that had attached to the term drops away. Naomi is immediately catapulted beyond Jesse's reach on a gusher of oil. Cries Naomi's father, jubilant over their good fortune: "'The Childresses are headed for the big city. Don't bother packing nothing. We won't need none of this trash'—the sweep of his arm comprehended the sum of their previous life— 'never no more'" (*TP*, 11). Jesse is among the discarded trash. His would-be father-in-law's balladlike refrain "never no more" reverberates into every aspect of Jesse's sad life, beginning with the end of all possibility that he can own his own land: when the Childresses' neighbors start striking oil, the value of land shoots up from twenty dollars an acre to thousands of dollars an acre. Other people's success eliminates the possibility of Jesse's having any success—a classic case of injustice under capitalism: the gulf between the rich and poor necessarily widens.

Humphrey appropriately fills this balladlike story with references to well-known ballads—in fact, ones that he and Grabstald used to sing together during their days at Southern Methodist University.[33] Many of these ballads that Jesse

---

33. In his copy of the *Esquire* version of "The Ballad of Jesse Neighbours," Grabstald scribbled a note identifying these lyrics as ones "Billy and I sang . . . over 20 years before (1940–42)" (HG Letters).

sings anticipate his own troubles. Indeed, "The lore of his class, the songs he sang, were rich in cynical commentaries on such situations as his" (*TP*, 15). The song "Greenback Dollar" expresses his affection for Naomi and anticipates her defection:

> I don't want your greenback dollar;
> I don't want your watch and chain;
> All I want is you, my darling;
> Won't you take me back again?
> (5)

Another song that he sings, "The Crash on the Highway," accords with his life devoid of hope. Jesse reaches the point at which his spirit finds its objective correlative in the "parched soil [with] a crust like dried blood" and the air full of choking dust, when, working fourteen hours at a stretch, "his mind . . . furrowed by his thoughts as regular as a tractored field, throbbed to a beat as insistent as the rise and fall of his hoe" (21); and he sings ballads that reflect his own sad story:

> I got no use for the women.
> A true one can never be found.
> They'll stick by a man while he's winning;
> When he's losing they turn him down.
> (21)

The language of the narrative itself turns strongly balladlike as it alludes to Tennessee Ernie Ford's "Sixteen Tons": "You chopped three acres a day and what did it get you? A plate of greens at night, enough to just keep you going tomorrow. You picked two hundred pounds, dragging the heavy sack after you like a wounded animal its entrails, bent double, blinded by your own salt sweat, no time to mop your brow, other hands quick to pick whatever you missed, half a cent a pound, take it or leave it, and at the end of the season what did you have? Enough to not quite pay your bill at the company store" (21–22).[34] In sympathetic metaphor, Humphrey provides the perfect symbolic picture of Jesse's helplessness: "From every blade of grass, like a viscous black dew, hung a single unfalling drop. A dying songbird staggered about the yard, his wings heavy and use-

---

34. Just after World War I the price for cotton was forty cents per pound; in the next fifteen years the price plummeted (*FOFH*, 170).

less"(11). Jesse is a dying songbird, and the wings that at one time might have carried him where his hopes aspired are now useless; everything is clogged by oil, the cause of his lost possibilities.

In his memoir Humphrey remarks on the "sense of helplessness, of the futility of trying to get ahead through hard work" when conditions in the 1930s were stacked against a man: "desperate men [turned] into desperadoes, and a sympathetic public followed their exploits in the papers and secretly cheered them on" (*FOFH*, 176). When he was a boy the newspapers that he "delivered each afternoon were filled with stories of holdups and getaways, shoot-outs and ambuscades" (*FOFH*, 179). Thus it was natural for Jesse to begin to identify with the "storied outlaws past and present" who are the heroes of those left out of the oil boom—Jesse James, Baby Face Nelson, Pretty Boy Floyd, John Dillinger, Sam Bass, and Billy the Kid, some of whom had already become the subjects of popular ballads. As Jesse's friends talk of these "poreboys" who became famed outlaws, the word "poreboy" reverberates in him as though it were "the bass string which the hand must always strum no matter what the chord, on a guitar" (*TP*, 20). It becomes inevitable, then, that Jesse will associate his life with a different kind of ballad: no longer will he identify with the tragic ballads about men who lose everything in life; he will embrace the music about desperado bank robbers, the heroes of the down and out, and he will become such a hero himself, he resolves. He is perfectly willing to die in a blazing gunfight.

But Jesse is not successful in writing this song for his life. Although he envisions going out of this world in a blaze of glory after years of excitement and years of adulation, his career as an outlaw is all too brief. For on his first attempt to rob a bank in Clarksville, he is foiled by the teller, then grabbed by a bank guard who slugs him senseless with a blackjack. It is all over in a moment. Jesse is electrocuted in the state penitentiary, and his broken parents travel to Texas to bring his body home. The inevitable bass chord—his ballad chord, one might say—that outlives Jesse and that reflects his life is repeatedly sounded. His parents return to Oklahoma on the train, his body on the baggage car, Jesse's "guitar . . . across their laps. And still though they sat, in four hundred and fifty miles it happened now and again that one or the other would brush the strings, drawing from them a low chord like a sob" (*TP*, 27). This "chord, melodious and woeful" from a guitar sounds repeatedly in Humphrey's fiction (*PF*, 83).

A common feature of the traditional ballad is that it is devoid of literary influence. But Humphrey finds a role for the most traditional of literary objects to play in his "Ballad of Jesse Neighbours," a daring move that adds humor to a form that generally avoids it. Humphrey unmistakably alludes to Alexander Pope's *The Rape of the Lock* (1712) to portray the transformation of Naomi Childress when, owing to her newly gained wealth, she lifts herself out of the ballad world of the common man and enters the sophisticated realm of the cultivated Dallas beauty. Naomi's transformation ironically occurs after her family has arrived in the city, like the Beverly Hillbillies in their pickup truck arriving in California.

Naomi commences the rites of beauty in the salon of Neiman Marcus, the "inferior priestess" being "a gorgeous young sorcerer of intermediate sex with bangs and plucked brows, a pout, fluttering hands" (*TP*, 13). As the ministrations at her toilet that call "forth all the Wonders of [Belenda's] face" and produce "A heav'nly Image in the Glass" cause Pope's heroine to worship a beauty that is beyond herself, so is Naomi moved by her reflection to "shyly [touch] the vision in the glass," for "her lips that had blossomed, sweetly sullen, moist, quivering" produce in her "[w]onder, not self-infatuation."[35] Less experienced at the shrine than Belenda, Naomi must be introduced to the "ritual": as she is taught the function of each of the "Unnumber'd Treasures" necessary to her enhanced beauty, Humphrey forces us to think of "The various Off'rings of the World [that] appear" in Pope's poem, especially: "This Casket *India*'s glowing Gems unlocks, / And all *Arabia* breathes from yonder Box."[36] Humphrey's catalog exaggerates Pope's heroic mockery: "This cream, from the beestings of wild Mongolian she-asses. This, with ambergris secreted by afflicted whales and found floating upon tropical seas. A hair rinse of champagne and plovers' eggs. This jelly rich in the hormones of queen bees fed on the nectar of Alpine wild flowers. This lotion, to prevent dry skin, containing morning dew from the Sahara . . . [and all] the guarded secrets of Cleopatra and the Queen of Sheba, precious as virgin's milk" (*TP*, 14). Thus Humphrey boldly introduces a complex literary allusion of a satirical nature into his simple balladlike story. This comic glimpse of the Childresses in Dallas flagrantly living their success has the practical effect of dramatically highlighting Jesse's desperation.

"The Ballad of Jesse Neighbours" was originally published in *Esquire* in September 1963. Even though the story is not a mystery, the Mystery Writers of America nonetheless voted it one of the three finalists in 1963 for the Edgar (a statuette of Edgar Allan Poe), which is awarded the best short mystery each year. Humphrey responded to the organization, confessing his "inexpressible joy at the news, but asking if they can clear up my mystification, for I can't find the mystery in this story of mine."[37] Humphrey never heard from the group again.

35. Alexander Pope, "The Rape of the Lock," in *The Rape of the Lock and Other Poems*, 3rd ed., Geoffrey Tillotson, ed. (London: Methuen, 1962), Canto 1, 143, 125; *TP*, 13.

36. Pope, Canto 1, 130, 133–34.

37. Humphrey to Woolf and to the Weisses, 24 March 1964 (Woolf Coll.,Weiss Coll.).

He found more satisfaction in learning that the story won third prize in *Prize Stories, 1965: The O. Henry Awards* and that Annie Laurie Williams sold the story to Hollywood, together with "The Human Fly." Paul Monash had plans to use both stories in one film, and he offered $22,500, to be paid upon the beginning of photography. But then photography never began on the film, and Humphrey never saw any benefit from the "sale." He was disappointed over more than the monetary loss, for he had envisioned Elvis Presley as Jesse Neighbours.[38]

Humphrey was especially fond of "The Ballad of Jesse Neighbours." On 28 December 1961, he had sent a special little forty-three-page "edition" of the story that he had typed and bound himself to Alfred Knopf as a belated Christmas gift. On the same day Humphrey posted a letter by air announcing that the story was coming by surface mail: "It is a special little copy of a short story, the first to get finished of that group of stories I spoke of in an earlier letter treating of the discovery of oil in my parts when I was a boy" (Knopf Coll.). When Knopf received the packet from Rome on 16 January, he found that it contained "montages made of old newspaper clippings" that, Humphrey explained to Pete Lemay on 20 March 1963, "were cut out of a contemporary newspaper which an aunt of mine found in her attic in Texas" (Knopf Coll.). The headlines of these cuttings announce the death of Bonnie Parker and Clyde Barrow: "Long Hunt for Barrow Ended with Bullets," "Outlaw Pair Inseparable in Crime, Separated in Death," "Clyde Had Bonnie Too Long, Mother Says; Won't Let Her Be Buried Beside Her Lover," and "Gunman Clyde Also Musician; Doubled on Sax." The most amusing feature of Humphrey's very handsome little book is "A Note on the Type": "The text of this book is set in L. C. Smith-Corona, a type face designed by Lem. C. Smith and Uncle Ned Corona, two blacksmiths in Ithaca, New York during the years 1865–70. Smith-Corona belongs to the family of type faces known as dirty-face. It is darker in tone than Olivetti, principally owing to the fact that the holes of all the vowels are filled in solid" (Knopf Coll.).

While Jesse Neighbours has no luck, the protagonist in "A Job of the Plains" (like O. J. Childress) seems eventually to have all of the luck: he strikes oil on his land. Yet his good luck turns out to be at least as bad as no luck at all. In "A Job of the Plains" Humphrey plays one-upmanship with Thomas Hardy. As grim as life often appears in Hardy's fiction and poetry, he always assumes that the catastrophe might have been avoided, happiness not being an unknown possibility. In this story Humphrey seems to up the philosophical ante to the point of saying that the option of happiness is a mere illusion. According to Hardy, "dic-

---

38. Lucille Sullivan to Humphrey, 27 February 1969, Williams Coll.; Humphrey to Williams, 22 November 1969, Williams Coll.

ing Time for gladness casts a moan"—and "purblind Doomsters had as readily strown / Blisses about my pilgrimage as pain."[39] In "A Job of the Plains" gladness is little more than a disguised moan: even as one embraces good fortune, it turns immediately into misery. We see a man enter the Temple of Delight to find that Delight has absconded; Melancholy has taken over. Humphrey's Job, Dobbs, lives the sorrow of his good fortune every day, the only possibility of escape being death. This is an important story because it conveys its author's profound rejection of belief in a good God, but it is not a very good story for the same reason: it sacrifices the protagonist's freedom to struggle toward understanding; he never achieves insight into what is happening to him and is incapable of making any changes in his life. He is a helpless victim of a merciless universe.

The Book of Job is the frame upon which Humphrey constructs this tale of withered consolations in the Oklahoma of the Depression and Dust Bowl era. The first section of "A Job of the Plains" is a close paraphrasing of the beginning of the biblical book: "There was a man in the land of Oklahoma [Uz] whose name was Dobbs [Job]; and this man was blameless and upright, one who feared God and turned away from evil" (*TP*, 47; Job 1:1). Instead of Job's seven sons and four daughters, Humphrey's Dobbs has three sons and four daughters; his substance is much less than Job's, and different: instead of 7,000 sheep, 3,000 camels, 500 oxen, 500 she-asses, and very many servants, Dobbs has "one lank Jersey cow, a team of spavined mules, one razorback hog, eight or ten mongrel hound pups"—and no servants. As Job "was the greatest of all the men of the east," Dobbs "was about as well off as most everybody else in eastern Pushmataha County" (Job 1:3; *TP*, 47).

Humphrey then skips two verses of the Book of Job, picking up again at 6–11 and following the source while altering appropriately (Job's hedge is turned into a single strand of barb wire, for example). Humphrey varies altogether from his source in having Satan conclude that 1929 was a very good year for Dobbs, that "the Lord had blessed the work of Dobbs's hands": "There had been a bumper cotton crop, Dobbs had ginned five bales, and—the reverse of what you could generally count on when the crop was good—the price was staying up. In fact it was rising by the day" (*TP*, 48). Following this interpolation, Humphrey resumes his near-paraphrase of the biblical story at verse 12, thus ending the first section of the story.

The biblical tone is curtailed at this point, and though parallels between Job and Dobbs persist, the story resumes in the immediacy of early twentieth-century

---

39. Thomas Hardy, "Hap," in *The Complete Poems of Thomas Hardy*, ed. James Gibson (London: Macmillan, 1976), 9.

Oklahoma life. When Dobbs quotes Job, it is to cite a familiar aphorism depended upon by any Oklahoman in adversity: "the Lord gives and the Lord takes away" (TP 48; cf. Job 1:21). Once the bottom falls out of the cotton market, followed by the Great Depression, grocer and banker alike suspend credit, and Job's lament "my welfare passeth away as a cloud" (Job 30:15) is Dobbs's as well. In his adversity Dobbs, like his biblical counterpart, refuses to curse God and gives thanks instead. In accordance with God's permission to Satan to increase Job's suffering, Dobbs's difficulties increase. His God allows boll weevils, worms, drought, and dust storms; and instead of afflicting his servant directly, He puts the loathsome sores upon the earth: "Stock ponds dried up into scabs, . . . [and] the land, with the subsoil showing, looked red and raw as something skinned" (TP, 50, 54). Satan appears in the form of a United States Government agent who tempts Dobbs to forsake his integrity and accept payment for not growing cotton and for not fattening his shoats but selling them to the government to be shot. Dobbs refuses the first offer because it "sounded, well, a trifle shady, underhanded": "when it comes to shooting little suckling pigs, like drownding a litter of kittens, no sir, include me out. And if this is what voting straight Democratic all your life gets you, then next time around I'll go Republican, though God should strike me dead in my tracks at the polling booth!" (52, 53). By contemplating voting Republican, Humphrey's Job verges on cursing God and dying.

In "A Job of the Plains" Humphrey takes the biblical happy ending and subjects it to real-life considerations. Although Job endures tribulations for forty-one chapters of the Book of Job and in the end God rewards him for his faithfulness, restoring his fortunes (see Job 42:10, 11), Dobbs's blessing, in the form of oil discovered on his bit of hardscrabble, turns out to be a new twist on his curse. Instead of being restored to his friends, his old friends desert him, those who might be new friends snigger at his unsophisticated ways, his kin are "all crippled by pointed shoes" (TP, 60) (a touch of humor in this grim story), he hates the expensive food he can now afford, and he finds no pleasure in fishing with his fancy level-wind reel and box of artificial baits that he does not know how to use or in hunting with his fine new gun; he even hates his bank statement because it just makes him worry about how much he has to lose. Above all, Dobbs is unhappy because he is bored.

There is one final, elaborate reversal of the blessing mentioned in Job 42:15: "And in all the land were no women found so fair as the daughters of Job: and their father gave them inheritance among their brethren"—the point being that Job's daughters will face no obstacles in marrying well. But when Humphrey writes, "In all of Oklahoma no women were found so fair as the daughters of Dobbs" (TP, 64), he is being profoundly ironical, for the only thing that makes them fair is their "equal inheritance among their brothers." These long-necked, chinless girls, whose "topmost ribs [show] like rubboards above the tops of their low-cut dresses," never receive a second glance from a man until they are rich (60). Humphrey's finale is a chilling, ironic paraphrase of the conclusion of Job, the last words of which are "So Job died, being old and full of days":

> And so the Lord blessed the latter end of Dobbs more than his begin-
> ning. For in addition to his oil wells, he had (he never did come to trust
> oil, and old country boy that he was, converted much of it into livestock)
> fourteen thousand head of whiteface cattle and five thousand Poland
> China hogs.
> He also had two sons and four daughters. And he gave them equal in-
> heritance, though there was not one who didn't believe that the rest had
> all been favored over him.
> After this lived Dobbs not very long. Just long enough to see his sons'
> sons, and despair.
> So Dobbs died, being old before his time, and having had his fill of
> days. (70)

Sylvia Grider and Elizabeth Tebeaux conclude that "A Job of the Plains" ex-hibits the theme that "neither God nor human effort can control events"—that man "is inevitably a victim of a universe that is pitiless, arbitrary, and unjust."[40] Humphrey paints in fact a much darker picture, for he contradicts the Book of Job's contention that if a man keeps his integrity and perseveres, God will reward him in the end for his perseverance. Humphrey's story, from section 2 onwards, is a continuation of the story of Job, beyond what the Bible tells. To think that God truly rewards a good man is to lack full understanding, to misunderstand the irony of rewards. And there is another anomaly in the story: in the biblical account, God comes to Job in chapter 38, and they talk together; Humphrey's God speaks only to Satan, never uttering a word to Dobbs, and Dobbs stops praying to God. The silence of God together with the silence of Dobbs bespeaks Humphrey's empty vision of life.

"A Job of the Plains" was turned down by Atlantic Monthly, Harper's, and Esquire before it was published in the twentieth-anniversary issue of the Quar-terly Review of Literature in the fall of 1965. While "The Ballad of Jesse Neigh-bours," also repeatedly rejected before publication, shows the unhappy effects

40. Sylvia Grider and Elizabeth Tebeaux, "Blessings into Curses: Sardonic Humor and Irony in 'A Job of the Plains,'" Studies in Short Fiction 23 (Summer 1986): 306.

upon a poor man of someone else's striking oil, "A Job of the Plains" is a study
of the unhappy effects of striking oil oneself.[41] Humphrey examines the phenomenon in three more stories. One portrays a novel form of anxious misery stemming from the "luck" of striking it rich, another plays off of the story of Dobbs
and presents a happy couple who were fortunate enough to avoid the "good
luck" of becoming oil rich, and in the final one we see an unscrupulous car salesman practicing inhumanity toward an "oil rich" Indian.

"The Pump," published in *Esquire* (January 1964), considers Jordan Terry as
he strikes oil on his property, and though he avoids all of the sad aftereffects that
subdued Dobbs, Terry ruins his possibility for happiness with no outside help.
Terry possesses the predisposition necessary to misery: his greed and obsessive-
ness assure the death of his humanity before his actual death. From the story's
first sentence, Humphrey portrays Terry as a man whose overwhelming desire
for oil puts him on a par with an oil-guzzling automobile: "For weeks Jordan
Terry had been down on his knees promising God to drink the first barrelful if
only they would go on drilling and not give up, . . ." and then the next section
of the story opens with the observation that Terry's 1921 Durant demands large
quantities of oil (*TP*, 141). Mechanization, which Terry absorbs into his being,
compromises his humanity as soon as the pump is installed on his oil well. He
is fascinated with the movement of the pump, which Humphrey mimics with
repeated short, pulsing phrases: "Up and down it went, up and down, bowing in
frenzied, untiring obeisance"—and again: "Day and night the pump went, night
and day, working for him: rocket-a-bump, rocket-a-bump, rocket-a-bump"
(142). Terry's full identification with the mechanical pump, and thus his utter
dehumanization, takes place as he synchronizes his own movements to it, and
especially when his heartbeat times itself to the mechanical pump: "In the day-
time it went at about the same trot that Jordan went at in his rocking chair, at
night as he lay awake grinning in the dark each stroke of the cycle matched a
beat of his heart" (142). The rocking of the pump, the rocking of Terry's chair,
the rocket-a-bump of his heart—the rhythms of his life—are all connected.
Thus, Terry calculates how much richer he grows "with each rock of his rocker,
each beat of his heart." His repetitive thought pattern takes on a mechanical relentlessness: "Rocket-a-bump: half a cent. Rocket-a-bump: that makes a penny.
Rocket-a-bump, rocket-a-bump—the last thing he heard at night, the first thing

41. Likewise, Cecil Smoot, Humphrey's oil-rich hero of the unpublished "The Horse Latitudes,"
is diminished by his wealth: "*he* felt he belonged to *it*. The more it grew the more he seemed to
shrink, and there were times when he felt, like Job in reverse, that that was God's intention" (MS,
p. 56, WH Coll., UT).

he heard in the morning. Sixty times twenty-five was fifteen hundred. Twenty-four times fifteen hundred times three hundred and sixty-five" (143).

Terry's mechanical existence proceeds without a hitch until his neighbor, Clarence Bywaters, also strikes oil, whereupon he begins to worry that his and his neighbor's pumps are pumping from the same reservoir of oil and that Bywaters's well, which is deeper than Terry's, will drain the supply of oil from the shallower side. Humphrey comically portrays the imagined competition as between two lovers drinking a single ice-cream soda with two straws, an image that gains additional ironic resonance with the frequent references to Terry's heart. Imagining his straw's empty sucking sound at the bottom of the soda glass causes him acute anxiety. Terry's mechanical existence will turn on him with a vengeance when his violent empty rocking movement causes him to seize up like an abused engine: "He was still warm when they got to him but it was as if rigor mortis had set in while he was still alive"—which is a way of saying that Terry had died before his time; he had certainly died to the possibilities of his good fortune (TP, 150). Thus his neighbor, ignorant of Terry's compulsive perversity, conveys the irony of his situation: "A crying shame the poor son of a bitch had only lived to enjoy his wealth such a little while" (150).

"A Home Away from Home," in Humphrey's view the slightest piece in the volume, provides perspective on "The Pump."[42] It is an oil story without oil. Elgin Floyd and his wife Sybil are fortunate in that the roughnecks drilling for oil on their land strike useless natural gas instead, even though the loud hiss of the gas flame and the light it produces disturb their sleep, even though their daughter Geraldine has run off with one of the oil men who looks like an insect, even though the eternal flame from the gas well is like a "flaming sword" that "guard[s] the east gate of Eden," the portal to the tree of life (see Genesis 3:24), and even though Elgin is condemned to till the ground all his days—striking indications that they were expelled from paradise before they could gain it. Nonetheless, the couple find solace in their "health" and in "each other"; they are not going to break their hearts over the loss of a million dollars (TP, 102). The story's imagery makes the point that Elgin and Sybil are not mindlessly enamored of the well's possibilities. Their equanimity contrasts with a company official who is drawn to the derrick fire like an insect (he is depicted as "a man-sized bug" [98]). Many of this company man's human attributes have been burnt away by the well fires that he has put out, while Elgin and Sybil remain untouched and secure in their humanity.

In "A Good Indian," a story Humphrey had allowed to lie around unfinished

---

42. Humphrey, notebook, entry for 16 December 1968, WH Coll., UT.

for two years, a boy who grows up thinking that "the white man's greed and perfidy" has inflicted a great injustice on the Indians turns into an adult who takes every opportunity to practice greed and deception upon Indians (*TP*, 39). About this story and its protagonist, Humphrey commented: "Oooh, is it ugly! But I believe I've created . . . the best, certainly the most repulsive, character I've ever created."[43] Unlike most of the stories in *A Time and a Place*, this tale is grounded in a fact from Humphrey's own life—that he is part Indian. He wrote in his memoir: "there was reason to believe that one of [my great-grandparents], instead of coming [to Texas], had, along with whatever tribe he was of, always been there, though living not in a house but in a tepee" (*FOFH*, 31). The narrator of "A Good Indian" had discovered when he was twelve years old that he was part Indian and "vowed that when [he] grew up [he] would join a tribe and become an Indian," an attitude in tune with that of the adolescent protagonist of "The Last of the Caddoes," the final story in the present volume. When this narrator grows up, however, he finds that he despises Indians, perceiving them as immoral "[d]irty pigs" who cannot hold their liquor, will not work, and "won't help themselves" (*TP*, 33).

The narrator seems to think his change in attitude is just a matter of growing up. But his account of his childhood interest in Indians provides hints of a better explanation, one of which the narrator seems unaware. As he tells of always taking the part of the Indians in childhood play, we note an inchoate meanness, a disregard for other children, for he says, "sometimes I came near to drawing blood with my stone tomahawk in trying to lift the scalp of my fallen paleface foe" (*TP*, 30). His impulse to hurt his "paleface" playmates evolves into a habit when, upon entering adulthood, he reverses his racial alliance. In by-the-way chatty prose, he reveals an early acquisitiveness as being a basis for his interest in Indian artifacts: he procures painted pottery, bones, and grinding pestles from the Indian burial mound on his family's property but gives no indication that he holds the mound or its contents sacred. Were his interest in Indians and the integrity of their way of life as genuine as he makes out in his nonchalant telling, he would have respected their ancient burial mound (as Jimmy Hawkins does in "The Last of the Caddoes").

There are political overtones to this story as well. The narrator grows up in a country that is not finished with its blatant fleecing of the Indian, and his story reveals him to act in the spirit of official United States policies. After every treaty with the Indians, from colonial days onward, the white man discovered that his avarice required the land that the Indian had just been granted, and so he took

---

43. Humphrey to the Weisses, 30 December 1964, Weiss Coll.

it. He concocted many pious-sounding justifications for his unbridled avarice. The acquisitive policies of the federal government continue to be glossed over, as in the following explanation from the *Encyclopaedia Britannica:* "The rapid development of the Far West exposed the inadequacy of the nation's traditional Indian policy and destroyed the illusion that any large area in the West could be permanently set aside for the Indians."[44]

The General Allotment Act of 1887, known also as the Dawes Severalty Act, was based on the assumption that the Indians ought to be "absorbed into American society as farmers and citizens," and the act required the gradual abrogation of tribal ownership of land: over a period of twenty-five years, ownership was to accrue to the individual Indian. The period of transition was extended in some areas. Land grabbers saw the Dawes Act as a windfall. Between 1887 and 1934, when the allotment act was reversed, twenty-seven million acres of land owned by individual Indians passed to white ownership.[45] In 1921, the Commissioner of Indian Affairs observed that two-thirds of the Indians who had received their allotment had been "unable or unwilling to cope with the business acumen coupled with the selfishness and greed of the more competent whites, and in many instances have lost every acre they had." He noted that young Indians were especially prone to "dispose of their land at a sacrifice, put most of the proceeds in an automobile or some other extravagant investment, and in a few months are 'down and out,' as far as any visible possessions are concerned."[46]

The narrator of "A Good Indian" is an exploiter of Indian naïveté. He tells what he believes to be an amusing tale of how he sold two bile-yellow Cadillacs to an Indian without a last name, who had just been tricked out of his land by an oil speculator. The narrator, presenting the Indians' selling of oil-rich land for a cheap price as an indication of their stupidity, jumps on the bandwagon of American capitalism in order to garner his "share." He has opened a Cadillac dealership and sells the finest cars to Indians who suddenly have enough money

44. *Encyclopaedia Britannica,* Expo '70 Commemorative edition, s.v. "United States (of America)."

45. Ibid.; Wilcomb E. Washburn, *The Indian in America* (New York: Harper and Row, 1975), 243. Having already shown that he lacks personal insight, the narrator of "A Good Indian" proves unreliable about his "facts." He says, "In 1935 a law was passed that the tribes could no longer hold the reservation lands in common (which is socialism) but it had to be divided up and parceled out among the members" (*TP,* 34). As we have seen, this law was actually passed in 1887 and was put into effect in various places at various times until 1934, when the mischievous results of the law were clear to all.

46. Laurence F. Schmeckebier, *The Office of Indian Affairs: Its History, Activities, and Organization* (Baltimore: Johns Hopkins Press, 1927), 156–57, quoted in Washburn, 247.

to buy them: "If they didn't have any better sense than to spend it with me, that was their lookout. They wanted what I had to sell, and if I hadn't taken their money, there were plenty more who would have" (*TP*, 35). There is genuine humor in his account of a primitive man's fascination with an unfamiliar but dazzling technological device of the white man:

> To see that Indian come up on that automobile was worth the price of a ticket. He carried the key hidden behind his back, as if it were a halter, and Doyle swore he was talking to that automobile under his breath all the while he sidled up to it, to coax it into standing still. Though he had been behind the wheel for his driving lesson, old habit was strong, and now he did not come at her from the driver's side because, unlike a white man, an Indian mounts a horse from the right. He stood stroking the door panel for a minute, then opened the door, saw he was on the off side, nodded to himself, shut the door, and, holding on to her all the while, made his way around the front end—never go behind them: that's where they can kick you. (38)

There is, however, meanness in the narrator's sense of superiority.

What the narrator tells us about the actual sale reveals that he is dishonest, not a mere opportunist. The amount he charges the Indian for his Cadillac is more than double a fair price. In 1935, Cadillacs were sold "at prices which are well below the figures of 1934," the basic price then being $2,395. The most expensive Cadillac, the Fleetwood, sold for $2,445 in 1935.[47] Humphrey's car salesman sells the Indian, John, a demonstrator with "a few thousand miles on the speedometer"—we can be sure that "few" is an understatement—for $4,200 (*TP*, 37). And after John wrecks the first one, then he turns around and sells him another—a new one—for the same price, while requiring the wrecked one, as well as his wagon and mule team, as a trade-in (he does not tell the Indian that the car he has driven into a tree is repairable).[48] The cost of the two cars equals the Indian's entire yield from the sale of his land.

The story ends on a poignant note that eludes the narrator who tells it. After John, who does not know how to drive, kills himself in the second Cadillac on the day of its purchase, his wife allows that "she ain't got no place to bury him

47. See advertisements in *Fortune* 9 (January 1934): 10; *Time*, 18 February 1935, 57; *Time*, 2 December 1935, 24–25.

48. The car salesman's outrageous demand that the down-and-out customer trade in his mules and wagon has an antecedent in chap. 7 of John Steinbeck's *The Grapes of Wrath* (New York: Viking, 1939), 87.

in" (*TP*, 46); the narrator can only express outrage that anyone would think him responsible: "That was when I blew the whistle. 'What in the infernal hell,' I said, 'has that got to do with me, I'd just like to know? Am I supposed to include a cemetery plot with every car one of these jokers buys from me?' " (46). Thus does Humphrey offer a picture of the Devil as automobile salesman—the devil who "wears as many disguises as there have been model changes," as Humphrey was to write in "The Horse Latitudes" in 1973.[49] "The Good Indian" captures one instance in the long effort of white America to take from the Indian everything— his tribal organization and culture, his land, his money, his few possessions, his life.

The story was originally published under the title "The Gaudiest Thing on Wheels" in the *Saturday Evening Post* for 28 August 1965. The title Humphrey gave the story in the collection is far superior, for it is the boiled-down essence of the common expression "The only good Indian is a dead Indian." N. M. Bo-decker's two-page illustration of the story for the magazine is based upon the following sentence from the narration, which has to do with Indians luckier than the one the story focuses upon: "a few months [after the purchase of a car], after they had run out of money to buy gas to put in them, or after they had driven them without any oil in the crankcase, you might see on a country road one of those Packards or Pierce-Arrows or Cadillacs hitched to a team of mules with the brave sitting on the hood on a blanket holding the reins, while inside, with the windows all rolled up regardless of the heat, sat the squaw and the papooses" (*TP*, 36). Bodecker adds only a background of distant oil wells—presumably on the land the Indian has sold to buy the car.[50] This illustration captures the shallow humor of the story's narrator and serves as a foil for its poignant conclusion.

"The Rainmaker" (also published in the *Saturday Evening Post*, 2 December 1967) and "The Human Fly" (*Esquire*, September 1968) portray other aspects of life in the days of the Depression and the Dust Bowl. These are humorous stories even as they exhibit the meanness, ruthlessness, and desperation that grew so readily in a time when nothing else would grow.

"The Rainmaker" has its origin in traditional culture. A rainmaker was a sorcerer or a magician who claimed to produce rain by supernatural means. Humphrey's rainmaker, however, "THe 1 & OnLY ProF. ORViLLe SiMMs" (as the lettering on the side of his truck identifies him), with his mechanical contraption called Old Magnet—an array of needle gauges, vacuum tubes, and exposed coils—touts himself as a genuine professor who can produce rain by scientific

---

49. MS, p. 199, WH Coll., UT.

50. "The Gaudiest Thing on Wheels," *Saturday Evening Post*, 28 August 1965, 60–61.

means (*TP*, 113). This "modern" rainmaker is aptly illustrated by Jerry Pickney in the *Saturday Evening Post:* Professor Simms is depicted standing atop a windmill with a magnet, wired to his contraption, held in the direction of a great storm cloud to his left.[51]

Simms gulls desperate Oklahomans upon whom it has not rained in three years. Even though he has depended upon *Miles' Almanac* for assurance that "light showers were forecast for the morrow," the almanac's prediction proves false, and he is run out of town in the traditional manner—tarred and feathered for failing to make rain (*TP*, 119). The publication to which the story refers, *Dr. Miles' New Weather Almanac and Handbook of Valuable Information*, was dispensed by Dr. Miles's Laboratories in Elkhart, Indiana. Humphrey apparently bases Simms's "scientific" explanations on this pseudoscientific publication. Dr. Miles's weather almanac for 1934 contains a section under the heading "What makes Rain, Snow, Hail?" (3), which is surely the inspiration for Simms's pseudoscientific speech to his audience on how "every drop of rain contained, was formed around, a single grain of dust": "it was your magnetism that drew all your other elements together. That charged your dust particles and made them draw your atoms of oxygen and hydrogen and form your drops which your clouds then soaked up" (*TP*, 123, 127). This sheer fabrication seems further inspired by the many explanations of how Dr. Miles's various pills and elixirs work. For example, Dr. Miles's Cactus Compound makes "the heart muscles contract more forcibly, thus aiding the circulation of the blood. With better circulation comes . . . better elimination of the waste products" (22).

Humphrey employs the traditional method of portraying his character's degeneracy by turning him into an animal. As Simms makes his escape from Oklahoma following the people's realization that he is a fraud, he begins to look like a turtle to the ferryman who will transport him over the Red River to the freedom of Texas: "his passenger poked his head out. He inched it out cautiously as a turtle and looked back towards Oklahoma" (*TP*, 108). Once exposed, Simms changes from turtle- to chicken-like: "The man's long, red, wrinkled, leathery neck, notched with bones, his crawlike Adam's apple, the wattles underneath his chin and his beak of a nose enforced his resemblance to a chicken—one in molt" (110). After he washes away the feathers that had been tarred to his person, he resumes resemblance to a turtle: "his head stick[s] up like a turtle's on that long seamy neck" (111).

"The Rainmaker" allows Humphrey an occasion to make exaggerated fun of the stupidity and gullibility of the people along the Red River Valley, especially

51. "The Rainmaker," *Saturday Evening Post*, 2 December 1967, 62.

those on the Texas side. The Oklahomans believe only briefly in Simms's rain-making abilities, and then they run him out of the state.[52] But in Texas he en-counters an unyielding confidence in his abilities. Simms hits Texas at just the time when the black blizzards had blown themselves out, when the "rivers went on a rampage," bringing extensive flooding.[53] The Texans give Simms credit for the flood; of course, they are as angry over too much success as his previous customers were over the lack of results.

Katherine Anne Porter called "The Rainmaker" "a *Gorgeous* story,"[54] though a large portion of it is marked by broad caricature and unsophisticated humor. But its descriptive passages are superb. Humphrey effectively limns the drought-stricken countryside where weeds refuse to grow in the ditches; he portrays the wasteland through the imagery of illness. The stock ponds "were dry white scabs" and "the earth pimpled and pocked" (*TP*, 114, 115).

Humphrey finished the nine stories that were originally supposed to comprise *A Time and a Place* ahead of schedule and found he had another story in him. He began "The Human Fly" on 23 February, scrapped the first two day's work and started again on 25 February, finishing the seventeen manuscript pages in record time—on 1 March, still fourteen days before the due date. There was still time for Humphrey to arrange for this story's publication before the collection was to come out; "The Human Fly" appeared in *Esquire* in October 1968. When Humphrey told Ted and Renée Weiss that the additional story was "a jolly little fable about the joys of small-town life," they suspected irony.[55] They were cor-rect. "The Human Fly" takes place in 1935, when Texas had "hit rock bottom": "What the national Depression had left us, our regional dust storms had taken from us" (*TP*, 167). Like "The Rainmaker," this story gives an account of one man's attempt to use other people to save himself from the stifling effects of hard times, and Humphrey thereby provides a compelling account of one more social phenomenon born of desperate times—human flies, people who for a fee would scale tall buildings, more desperate versions of flagpole-sitters, tree-sitters, and marathon dancers. Stan Reynolds, a disgruntled resident of New Jerusalem (one of the fictional names for Clarksville), like many others at the time, has set his sights on California, obedient to the westward bent of America. Under the guise of "The Great Grippo," Stan proposes to the Chamber of Commerce that he

52. Simms makes his escape by using the same back-road ferry on the Red River, manned by the same dirty, tobacco-spitting ferryman, that William Owens portrays in *Look to the River* (New York: Atheneum, 1963).

53. Frederick Lewis Allen, 208.

54. Porter to Humphrey, 1 January 1968, KAP Coll.

55. Humphrey to the Weisses, 5 March 1968, Weiss Coll.

climb the town's colonial gothic courthouse for a thousand dollars. The idea is that advertisement of the climb will attract crowds from miles around, giving a shot in the arm to ailing businesses. Thus Stan and the town conspire to take advantage of each other. Humphrey portrays the climb with excitement—and with characteristic humor. Repeatedly, a woman exclaims some form of the following sentiment: "I can't stand it any more! I'm going home where I belong!" (173, 174). In the midst of our chuckling about the lady who never goes home, Stan falls from the courthouse—not to his death, but to thirty-three years as a helpless cripple. Ironically, he becomes a ward of New Jerusalem, dependent in full measure upon the community he only wanted to escape.

During Humphrey's childhood a tire company hoisted a "human fly" (not a citizen of Clarksville) up the facade of the courthouse in a tire as an advertising stunt; it is this event that Humphrey transformed into a story of desperate hope during the days of the Depression.[56] Most of the stories in *A Time and a Place*, however, do not have this much basis in fact. "Mouth of Brass"—Humphrey first called it "Voice of Brass"—is the most striking exception.

"Mouth of Brass," the volume's best story, has as much basis in the facts of Humphrey's life as any story he ever wrote. It is about the day a black man who sells hot tamales door to door lets a young white boy go with him on his rounds. The black vendor in the story, a remarkably well-drawn character, was actually a childhood friend of Humphrey's named Finus Goodman, called Finus Watson in the story, the same big black man who walks through *The Ordways* calling, "Molly ot! Hot tamales!" The corn shucks in which he wrapped his tamales litter the streets of all the Clarksville novels as well as *Farther Off from Heaven*.[57]

"When I began that story," Humphrey said, "I did not know that Finus might be a corruption of the name Phineas, and I did not know that Phineas meant 'mouth of brass,' and I don't know how I learned that. I guess I just went to the dictionary" (Au Int.). *Webster's New International Dictionary* (2nd ed.) gives "mouth of brass" as the meaning of the name Phineas, and Humphrey surely means to assign the figurative sense of *brass*—"effrontery, impudence" (*OED*, sense 4)—to Finus. On the other hand, *The Name Dictionary* says that Phineas means "negro," "dark-complexioned," and applies specifically to those dark-skinned Nubians from the south of ancient Egypt.[58] The name *Finus*, then, sums up a fatal combination: "He was born loud as surely as he was born black" (*TP*,

56. Gavin Watson, interview by author, tape recording, Clarksville, Tex., 17 July 1997.

57. Au Int. The tamale man's last name in the story comes from Gavin Watson, Humphrey's childhood acquaintance whom he revisited in later years.

58. A. J. Kolatch, *The Name Dictionary*, 2nd ed. (New York: Jonathan David, 1973), 116.

72). These features along with the *place* (Blossom Prairie, which is another fictional name for the southern town of Clarksville) and the *time* (1930) result in Finus's cold-blooded murder.

"Mouth of Brass" is a story of discovery and disillusionment told from the point of view of an adult's remembrance of his boyhood. This narrative technique provides distinct advantages. The adult narrator is able to articulate what a boy might have sensed but been unable to tell clearly. For example, when the boy's father seems to treat him roughly as he is grieving over Finus's violent death, the narrator sees what only years and maturity can provide: "My father was not angry at me but at the world which was all he could give me and which he was as helpless to cope with as I" (*TP*, 88). In explaining that "No matter what Finus said it came out sounding proud and mighty" at a time and in a place when blacks were expected to be self-effacing and quiet around white people, the narrator offers an insight unavailable to a boy: "to be answered by a Negro in that powerful bass brought the blood to some men's cheeks quick as a slap. His size alone was a standing challenge, the silence in which he took refuge easily misinterpreted as surliness; add to these provocations the sound that came out of him whenever he did speak, and Finus was often in trouble of the kind I myself had witnessed one Saturday afternoon on the town square when a sailor knocked him down, saying, 'I'll teach you to talk back to a white man in that tone of voice'" (72). Furthermore, the adult narrator can shift to an elevated diction in order to convey the majesty of Finus's larger-than-life presence; he can say that Finus's stentorian voice "proclaimed his advent in the next street" (74). This narrator can also obliquely acknowledge the title of the volume of stories in which "Mouth of Brass" appears: "In another place, or at some later period perhaps, his voice might have made Finus's fortune" (72). And, finally, the power and significance of the story are enhanced by its being so indelibly etched on the memory of the adult who, years later, tells it as though not a single detail has been blurred by time.

Humphrey produces the presence of Finus through the interplay of sound and image. The story vibrates with the force of his voice calling "Molly ot! Hot tamales!"—a chord which is struck in the first sentence (*TP*, 71). The narrator's rhetoric, including syntax and sounds, mimics the prolonged movement of afternoon thunder: "Down from the top of our street each weekday afternoon that cry, in a voice deeper than any I have ever heard in all the years since, used to come rumbling like thunder" (71). Moments later Finus's "cry, nearer now, would roll out again, sonorous as a chord drawn from the deepest pipes of a church organ" (71). The long consonants in "roll," "sonorous," "chord," "drawn," "deepest," and "organ"—especially the repetition of the *n* sound—

mimic the reverberations of a church organ (church organs, by the way, often have brass pipes), and the analogy to the pipe organ carries on in the vibrations of the subsequent sentence: when Finus sounds his advertisement in front of the narrator's childhood home, "the chimes of our doorbell shuddered softly and teacups rattled on their saucers" (72). Not only does the imagery portray vibration, but so does the thoughtfully selected diction: the double *d* and *t* in "shuddered" and "rattled" represent the effect of bass vibration. Elsewhere we read that Finus "rumbled" as he makes his "rounds" (77).

In the third section of the six-part story, Humphrey displays the observational skill of the painter that he long wanted to be. Here Finus has invited his little white friend to accompany him on his tamale rounds, and the boy's parents have consented. Finus has also invited the boy to help him make tamales early in the morning. The narrator conveys the stark simplicity of Finus's life with a masterly, painterly evocation of what he saw as a boy:

> through the dark opening of Finus's doorway I passed as through a wall. The house consisted of just one room, most of it devoted to the manufacture of hot tamales. A big black cast-iron wood range, heavily scrolled and garlanded, squatted on its paws against one wall. In the center of the room stood a long wooden table, its top as scarred as a butcher's block and bleached colorless from scrubbing, on which was heaped a mound of finely shredded cooked chicken meat. From nails on the walls hung clusters of dried and shriveled red peppers and bunches of dried herbs. In one corner stood Finus's cot. Beside it stood a washstand on which sat a basin and ewer. (*TP,* 75)

The process of preparing tamales is no less vividly realized. Here the figures of speech—an ax handle "boiled white as a bone" and the "roll-your-own" tamales—sharpen the seeing (76).

In fact, learning to see and to penetrate with the eyes of understanding—to have insight—is the real stuff of Humphrey's story. Finus is the source of this knowledge; he knows the town of Blossom Prairie "better than anyone else"; he has "traversed its length and breadth daily"; he even knows each of the 870 dogs by name (*TP,* 77). As the boy travels with Finus, helping him sell tamales, he begins "to acquire a sense of the relation of [familiar] places one to another, of the overall plan of [his] town" (78). Finus helps the boy to see the pattern: "As in those puzzles in which one draws lines between dots until suddenly a recognizable creature or object emerges, I was drawing lines between what before had been disconnected dots forming no pattern or design. It was doubly delightful because it was both new and familiar" (78–79). The boy's excitement about knowing and seeing seems unbounded: "I was a different boy from the one who had left home only that morning. The world had been revealed to me much bigger and much more exciting than I had dreamed. With much of it I was now acquainted, much of it I had yet to explore. For both this knowledge and this promise I had Finus to thank, and as I heard his voice swell up from the bottom of the street my heart swelled with gratitude and affection for my friend, my guide" (79).

Section 5 gives an account of a five-minute event after which "nothing was ever the same for me again" (TP, 81). A drunken redneck named Jewel Purdom, thinking that Finus has cheated his son out of three tamales and insulted by Finus's tone of voice, springs on him with a knife. Ironic in view of Finus's emphasis on observation, the townspeople look on unseeing as Finus is murdered. The boy, who has been playing around the Confederate monument in the square, observes the movement of the crowd and belatedly arrives at the scene of the crime. Fixing on a vivid recollection of Finus's blood, not on his dead body, the narrator conveys the meaning of Finus's life and death with astonishing poignancy:

> By the time I got near enough to see it the wide pool of blood on the pavement where Finus had fallen was, though still wet, beginning to congeal. An iridescence playing over its surface in waves and slow swirls made it appear to shrink from exposure to the air like a living, that is a dying, thing. The way a fish fresh out of water grows more vivid and lustrous as it struggles and gasps, then fades as it dies, so Finus's blood brightened and shone as I watched, then darkened and lay still beneath a spreading dull film. Just before that final stage, however, came another. Struck by the glare of the sun, the pool of blood became a mirror, and in it I saw reflected—and can see still, though this was long ago and Blossom Prairie now far away—the buildings of the square in sharp perspective, the courthouse tower, the Confederate soldier mounted high on his marble shaft, the steeple of the Methodist church that sat a block away on a hill overlooking the creek. (86)

This vivid epic simile involving a caught fish pulled out of its water suggests how Finus's lessons in perception, in really seeing, have developed in the boy who was taught to see by Finus. Early in the story Finus is called a "fixture of the place" (72); his blood, in this final instance, becomes a particular fixture, a mirror—a mirror that offers a new perception of the town, whose people neither come to

Finus's defense nor identify his murderer; the entire town is implicated in the crime by his pool of blood.

The boy is inconsolable. His mother having "given up trying to occupy or divert" him, he is left to contemplate an empty vista that objectifies his inner emptiness: "I sat at the window watching the empty street. The time drew near when down from above had always sounded Finus's cry. In heavy silence the clock on the mantel tolled four. I felt my chin pucker and tremble, my bruised heart swell with pain" (*TP*, 88). The very experience of joy and delight is what gives assurance that the boy's "soul shall taste the sadness of [Melancholy's] might," for the "bruised heart" that "swell[s] with pain" at the end is the heart that had "swelled with gratitude and affection" (79) for Finus, who had opened his eyes to the world.[59]

The boy wishes to mute his own suffering by trying to adopt the racism of his townspeople, as his father has tried to do. His effort to choke off his sorrow with the dismissive aspersion "nigger" turns out to be nothing more than a profound expression of love: " 'What!' I cried, tears for Finus, for myself, for my father, for all the world gushing from my eyes, 'me cry over an old nigger?' " (*TP*, 89). Humphrey contrasts the child's overwhelming emotion at its peak with his mother's muting irrelevance: " 'ssh!' said my mother, drawing me to her own heaving breast. 'You musn't say that, hon. Nice people don't use that word' " (89). "Mouth of Brass" is a tale of crude violence transmuted into the story of a sensitive boy coming to terms with a world that offers joy but much less joy than ill.

Humphrey had started writing "Mouth of Brass" as soon as he arrived in Alassio in October 1964, in response to Rust Hills's request that he contribute a story about childhood for a special children's issue of the *Saturday Evening Post*. In a 19 October letter to Pete Lemay, Humphrey confessed the anxiety that Hill's request had caused him: "I'm beating my brains out trying to do one, deadline November 1. Having already begun three, even finished one, which I don't like, am now beginning a fourth" (Knopf Coll.). "Mouth of Brass" was that fourth, but completing it for good was no easy task. After three false starts on the story—each lasting a week—he worked three weeks steadily on the manuscript, and as soon as he was finished he posted it to Hills. Although Humphrey felt it was the best story he had ever written, he was sure that Hills would reject it. In the first place, it would arrive a month after the deadline; in the second, the story was an unlikely candidate for a children's issue of anything. As Humphrey proudly announced to Leonard Woolf, he had turned out "the grisliest little tale you ever

59. "Ode on Melancholy," in *John Keats*, ed. Elizabeth Cook (1990; reprint, New York: Oxford University Press, 1992), 290.

read, absolutely hair-raising, and with the now-forbidden word 'nigger' occurring just about every other page." Humphrey had in fact enclosed an instruction with the manuscript for Hills to return it, if he were not going to use it in the *Post,* to Ted Weiss at Bard. In a 1992 interview, Humphrey said that no sooner had he sent the manuscript to New York than he realized he did not like the story's second half, and so he wired Hills saying, "reject it" (Au Int.). But in fact Humphrey's second thoughts were slower to come. Apparently he enjoyed some days of basking in the glow of accomplishment. On 23 November he and Dorothy enjoyed breakfast in their pajamas on the terrace in the blazing sunlight and talked of the vacation that they would take to celebrate the happy completion of "Mouth of Brass." They then went upon a five-day jaunt to Florence, Pisa, and Lucca, the latter two for the first time.[60]

According to the written record, it was actually three weeks later when writer's remorse struck. Bill began to have serious misgivings about his story's resolution. Hills had rejected it and returned the manuscript to Weiss, who in turn had submitted it to the *New Yorker,* which Bill had originally requested him to do. On 22 December Humphrey wrote urgently to Weiss, asking him to get the story back from the *New Yorker,* explaining: "It's the first time I've ever sent a story off so quickly after 'finishing' it. I wouldn't have done it this time, only I thought I might still get it in under the deadline for the Post which I had worked so hard against, so hard it dazed me to the defects in the story" (Weiss Coll.). The first half of the story Humphrey still thought was very good, and this made it all the more imperative that he have a chance to make the second half equal to it. He was correct in having qualms about the original version, for it was too close to what really happened to Finus Goodman, and so the imaginative story suffered the drag of reality (like "The Fauve"). Humphrey admitted that he first wrote the story's conclusion close to the way he heard it originally: the deputy sheriff had said, "I'm going to kill me a nigger," and he went out and shot Finus. (Gavin Watson had a different recollection of the actual event: the sheriff had been summoned because Finus was drunk and disorderly, and he was killed when he resisted arrest.)[61]

After Humphrey got the manuscript back, he put it away awhile, for he was then seduced by the fun of getting a start on *The Spawning Run.* But about a year later, early in 1967, he returned to "Mouth of Brass" with critical perspective and transformed it into the moving story that it is. He sent the revised story to the *Saturday Evening Post,* then *Esquire;* both rejected it. He then sent it back to the

60. Humphrey to Woolf and to the Weisses, 23 November 1964 (Woolf Coll., Weiss Coll.).
61. Au Int.; Watson, interview.

New Yorker just before he and Dorothy set sail for England in mid-November. Anxious about the fate of his story, he had written twice by 3 February 1968 asking the magazine for an early decision and had received no reply. He was outraged when the *New Yorker* returned it to him in London by surface mail (which took six weeks) with a form rejection slip; the manuscript was so badly packaged that it had to be retyped before it could be sent out again. Humphrey was never to subject himself to the discourtesy of "those sonsofbitches" again.

Retyping the story convinced Humphrey all over again that "Mouth of Brass" was good work. Therefore he sent it to the *Atlantic Monthly*. After a long wait the rejection came with the comment that "the problem of Negro/white relations has moved so far, and become so complicated since the time of your story that it is something of an antique." Humphrey imagined that the same editor would have rejected *King Lear* because "parent/children relations have moved far, and become so complicated since the time of the story." Has penicillin destroyed Ibsen's *Ghosts*? The story was subsequently also rejected by *Harper's* magazine.[62] Thus, "Mouth of Brass," one of Humphrey's best stories, ironically was the only story in *A Time and a Place* not to have been previously published in a national magazine. Humphrey must, then, have been overjoyed on 20 January 1969 when the movie agent John Forman, representing Paul Newman and Joanne Woodward, said he wanted to buy "Mouth of Brass" together with "A Good Indian" and a couple of other stories from *A Time and a Place*.[63]

"A Voice from the Woods," first published in *Atlantic Monthly* (October 1963), only incidentally touches upon the themes of desperation found in several other stories in this volume: although there is a brief account of a foiled bank robbery, the story is about the importance of a memory to two different people, the narrator and his mother. This story, like "Mouth of Brass," has a basis in Humphrey's own life; it begins with a simple fact from real life. Humphrey's mother, who had remarried for the third time (she was then Mrs. Dan Moran), had moved to Cleveland; in 1952, Humphrey had gone to see her and—to his surprise—enjoyed five days "reminiscing over my little home town and engaging in Southern gossip."[64] For the purposes of his story, Humphrey imported this decade-earlier experience with his mother to New England, having her visiting him and his wife. It comes out in the story's dialogue that the narrator is thirty-seven years old, Humphrey's very age when he wrote it in 1961. The three charac-

62. Humphrey to the Weisses, 3 February 1968, [12 February] 1968, 15 March 1968 [misdated 1958], and 23 March 1968, Weiss Coll.

63. Humphrey, notebook, entry undated, WH Coll., UT.

64. Humphrey to the Weisses [1952], Weiss Coll.

ters are relaxing on a sunporch in spring, drinking beer and talking. The mother chides her son the writer for his story on Finus: "Why anybody should clutter up their memory with him, I don't know!" (*TP*, 153).

They hear a "ghostly sound, defying location, seeming in successive calls to come out of the woods from all points of the compass" (*TP*, 151). It is the "*hoo-oo, hoo-hoo-hoo; hoo-oo, hoo-hoo-hoo*" of a dove, a southern bird as out of place in New England as the mother and son are, the story suggests (152). But of course Humphrey is ignoring a fact to help his fiction, for the mourning dove is not out of place in New England.[65] Still, this fictional mourning dove, crooning "its ceaseless inconsolable lament," is a sound from the past that takes mother and son back to another time and another place, to Texas when she was a young woman and he a very small boy, happy days before the death of his father (152). The dove's sound suggests an essential quality of the experience of remembering: a simultaneous sense of the distance and the nearness of a remembered person or event; thus the dove's call is "Near at hand one moment, far away and faint the next" (151).

The sound of the dove prompts different memories in the son and in the mother but none in the wife, the odd man out in this story of remembrance. And so the convivial three, having enjoyed an afternoon of fellowship, are suddenly isolated from each other by an accidental sound, although a curious parallel emerges in the mother's and son's recollections that they seem unaware of. In a reverie, the son remembers "the long hot somnolent summer afternoons of my Texas boyhood, when the cotton fields shimmered white-hot and in the black shade of the pecan trees bordering the fields the Negro pickers lay napping on their sacks and I alone of all the world was astir, out with my air rifle hunting doves I never killed, gray elusive ghosts I never could locate" (*TP*, 151–52). In the cool of a crisp New England spring, the narrator's memory conjures Texas summer heat, the sun cooking the resin on the trunks of pines and sweet gums, the wheeling buzzards over only apparently empty fields—all prompted by the "visiting" dove's lament. The story's accurate descriptions constitute the world of Humphrey's fiction, a world that he would never have felt the urge to reproduce in words had he not, like the dove of this story, exiled himself in a distant country. Thus the dove has a definite significance for the writer.

Oddly, the narrator recalls that doves "favored cedars, . . . and cedars in turn favored burial grounds, so that I think of the dove's whispered dirge as the voice

65. The mourning dove breeds from Nova Scotia to Florida as well as from Wisconsin to the Gulf Coast, according to Roger Peterson's *A Field Guide to the Birds* (Boston: Houghton Mifflin, 1947), 203.

of that funereal tree" (*TP*, 152). So does the narrator's mother—only she recollects the sound of a dove in a very specific graveyard. It was in her family's graveyard on a Sunday that a long-ago lover met to receive her answer to his proposal of marriage. The narrator is still concentrated on his own recollections, and his mother must dislodge his reverie in order to reveal an experience of her youth that she has never told her son about.

The suitor whose proposal she refused (Travis Winfield) returns to Blossom Prairie years later, in order to rob the bank.[66] In her telling of the foiled bank robbery, the mother gives special attention to Travis's redheaded girlfriend, providing an elaborate account of her espionage to ascertain a layout of the bank as well as information about the timing of major deposits. The mother's admiration for the redheaded lover of Travis is unmistakable, as is her romanticizing of the bank robbers, "[t]hree strong young men cut off in the very Maytime of life" (*TP*, 162). She explains that she had once "gone with" Travis Winfield, and we know that she is thinking that she might have played the role of the romantic redheaded woman had she dared. She might have traded her conventional, circumspect life as wife and mother of a six-year-old boy for a Bonnie-and-Clyde adventure! Thus, as the past is brought to the present by the cooing of a misplaced dove, the mother has an unexpected recognition that she has missed the excitement of life: "life with Travis wouldn't be dull," she says, as though the past were a future possible to her. Then she remarks, "It would be different from life on the farm, or in Blossom Prairie in a bungalow that had to be swept out and dusted every day" (163). Like her son, the mother longs for that which life has denied.

The mother's memory is the story's central concern. The sudden appearance in memory of a boy from her past is reminiscent of Gretta Conroy's powerful encounter with the long-dead Michael Fury in James Joyce's "The Dead." As in "The Dead" it is a song that stimulates the vivid memory: the "dolorous refrain" of the dove causes her to turn in memory to the "cooing of a dove" (*TP*, 163) that she had heard when as a girl she had waited for Travis Winfield, an extremely handsome young man with a reputation for wildness. That is a reputation he shares with Humphrey's own father, and in fact, Humphrey's mother was a redhead. Is the recollection, then, a disguised memory of her lost, exciting life with Clarence Humphrey set against a dull life with her subsequent hus-

---

66. The Clarksville bank robbery took place in the summer of 1927, when Humphrey was three years old (Gavin Watson, "Bill Humphrey Reading," *Clarksville Times*, 22 November 1982, 1). Humphrey recently said, "The bank in my home town was held up, but it happened before my time. I was never taken to see bodies on the street. I just heard about it" (Au Int.).

bands? Perhaps. At any rate, she is moved in the present, as was Gretta Conroy, by a past that still lives within her. She tells it in the past tense, but her emotion is a present one: "There was I, happy, with a good, loving husband and a decent home and a smooth, even life ahead of me and my own child's hand in mine. And yet, thinking of that redheaded woman—even then on her way to prison—I felt, well, I don't know what else to call it if not jealousy. Isn't that crazy?" (164).

Out of his mother's imagined visit to his New England home and the memory of the failed bank robbery, Humphrey created one of the freshest stories in *A Time and a Place*. It is a story that impresses upon us an awareness of the power that the sudden discovery of an almost forgotten memory can have. One is struck by the fact that such memories often emerge according to an accidental stimulus, such as the call of a mourning dove.

When one of the book's editors at the Knopf firm recommended that "the endless mourning doves" be "dispensed with," Humphrey wrote to Alfred Knopf (7 October 1962) an unusually extensive defense of his narrative device, explaining that because "you have taken such a lot of trouble for me, . . . I would hate for you to think I had refused [your editor's] suggestion out of angry pride"; in part, Humphrey argued that the "actual sound of the dove . . . should, for the attentive reader, re-echo as a kind of leitmotiv when towards the end of the story the mother recalls that moment after she had rejected the proposal of her wild lover—something she has always half-regretted, and that mood of half-regret seems to me to be well 'caught' by the peculiar sound the mourning dove makes. Further, in terms of the violence in which the story deals, it is calculated that what the narrator should remember is his (unsuccessful) efforts to kill the dove" (Knopf Coll.). The symbolic dove establishes the relationship among the characters and brings order to diverse experience, past and present. Without it, the narrator's presence in the story would be superfluous, and the short story would be nothing but an anecdote. Leonard Woolf was taken with "A Voice from the Woods" and thought it a "perfectly controlled" story with many dimensions.[67]

The last story in *A Time and a Place* is "The Last of the Caddoes," which originally appeared in *Esquire* (October 1968). One of the most engaging stories in the volume, it derives its title from Fenimore Cooper's *The Last of the Mohicans*. While lacking the poignant emotion of "Mouth of Brass," it nonetheless conveys a power and latent terror of its own, and it plants the theme of matricide that is to unfold fully in Humphrey's next novel, *Proud Flesh*.

"The Last of the Caddoes" has a superficial connection with "A Good Indian"

67. Woolf to the Humphreys, 13 November 1963, *Letters of Leonard Woolf*, ed. Frederick Spotts (New York: Harcourt Brace, 1989), 525.

in that here, too, a twelve-year-old boy discovers that he is part Indian and wants to "become" an Indian. There is no backing away from Indianness in this story, as there is in the previous one; rather, the boy demonstrates a serious and relentless pursuit of his Indian identity. This pursuit is clearly involved in the boy's need to establish his independence from his parents, especially from his mother. But the story is more than one about growing up. For one thing, it suggests that parental possessiveness that denies an adolescent's natural development is evil. Yet in examining the boy's careful quest for identity, the narrative demonstrates the ultimate powerlessness of the mother to obstruct her son's development. As this mysterious process unfolds, the story enters the realm of myth; in this dimension the story operates to transcend ordinary distinctions between the real and the imagined.

The first sentence reads like the beginning of a fairy tale, laying down the possibility that all that follows may exceed reasonable expectation: "By the shores of the Red River, in Texas, lived a boy named Jimmy Hawkins, who learned one day to his surprise that he was, on his father's side, part Indian" (*TP*, 179). This fairy tale element is confirmed a few pages into the story by the explanation of why Jimmy is "a dangerous person, a permanent threat to those who wronged him." The narrator says, "So they must have been warned by the bad fairy (herself Indian) who was not invited to his christening but who appeared at it all the same. 'You may bleach him whiter than the snow, give him a white man's name, and bring him up in ignorance of his people,' she had pronounced in a raspy voice, shaking a bony brown finger at them, 'he is what he is'" (189). This fairy tale element establishes the boy's identity as being tied to his as-yet-undiscovered origins: "He had often wondered who he really was, and had felt that like the changeling prince in the fairy tale he had been cheated of his birthright and brought up in a meaner station of life than fate and his gifts had intended for him" (189).

Jimmy's mother is possessed of an inexplicable reluctance to divulge her son's Indian blood to him; to deny him knowledge that would have so delighted him amounts to a denial of love, a flagrant failure to regard her son. She trivializes his feelings when she rationalizes her reluctance; the superficial language of her interior monologue betrays her lack of sincerity (note her "What's it *to me* . . . ?" [italics mine]):

"But it's only the tiniest little fraction," she would rejoin. "Hardly enough to count." Or, again, "It isn't as if I had deliberately not told him. Heavens! Why on earth would I do that? What's it to me, one way or the other? The subject has simply never come up, that's all. If it ever should, why then, of course . . ." (*TP*, 180)

Eventually, out of anger she blurts out the knowledge of his Indian blood as a mark of deficiency. While on the level of human motivation the mother with-holds—and then divulges—the truth out of meanness, the narrative voice begins to suggest that forces beyond the woman have played a part in her utterance. We are told that Jimmy learns about his ancestry "only by accident," and then parenthetically the following qualification is added: "or so it seemed at the time." Furthermore, Mrs. Hawkins feels "as though she had been tricked into letting it out" (182, 181).

The second section of the story suggests the source of the trick; somehow—no suggestion as yet about how—Indians are the real source of the message: "They had been calling to him, blood calling to blood" (*TP*, 184). Since Jimmy is the last of the Caddoes, the implication is that the message comes from the dead. Before this section of the story ends, the implication finds acknowledgment: "There was an unseen power at work here. The spirits of his long-denied red forefathers had spoken to him at last (ironically enough, through his mother's own mouth) and claimed him as one of their own" (185). As Henry James's *The Turn of the Screw* preserves ambiguity about whether the evil that threatens the children is real or a figment of the governess's sick imagination, so Humphrey's story makes us uncertain whether we are to accept the occult dimension as actual or to assume that the narrative, which is slanted to the boy's perspective, is owing to his derangement.

At least this ambiguity continues until the story's mythical dimension emerges. The fairy tale element gives way to the mythic, which seems to sanction the uncanny. Sacred to the Indians, the snake's image takes a prominent place in their artistic designs. The jug that Jimmy's mother dashes to the ground is snake-like: "diamonds in bands . . . coiled about it shrinking and expanding in con-formity with its shape" as though it were itself a living thing (*TP*, 199). The coiled rope of clay that forms the shape of the pot suggests the snake eating its own tail, the "full circle, returning in the end to [its] source," and is the basic image of life, life continuing even in death (201). Indeed, Humphrey's narrator pronounces: "Unconquerable, the spirit of the people who could produce one such thing!" (199).

When his mother sees that he "belong[s] body and soul to it," she dashes the jug to the ground, hissing, "A snake in your mother's bosom!" (*TP*, 200). On the mythical and symbolic level, then, Jimmy is the living embodiment of the spirit that is expressed in the jug, and he comes fully to life following her act of destroying the image of the snake in the jug. Jimmy becomes snakelike. His new name, Snake-in-His-Mother's-Bosom, "fit him like a skin. . . . It encased him in an armor of scales. It enabled him to slink in silence. It gave to his brain the serpent's subtlety. It equipped him with a forked tongue for speaking to the enemies by whom he was surrounded. It armed him with fangs" (202). The mother's next pronouncement is that Jimmy will be the death of her. When he hears this, he takes it as an exhortation, believing the spirit of his ancestors to be once again speaking through his mother.

Humphrey presents this episode in the context of Indian myth, but he also clearly draws upon Aeschylus's *The Libation Bearers,* which Humphrey had read in connection with his subsequent novel, *Proud Flesh.* "The Last of the Caddoes" is a short and transmogrified retelling of the ancient story of Orestes and his mother, as *Proud Flesh,* we shall see, is an elaborate version of the same Greek story. As Orestes acted out his "wretched tribute to the unconscious dead," so does Jimmy feel called to avenge his "mother's crime against" his ancestors: "she must be made to pay, and Indian justice decreed that her punishment was that her son be a snake in her bosom," writes Humphrey, unmistakably alluding to *The Libation Bearers (TP,* 201).[68] Learning that his mother Clytemnestra had "fancied she gave a serpent birth," which when she suckled it, "gash[ed] her nipple," sucking "Clots of blood . . . with the milk," Orestes says, "I pray this dream comes true in me," continuing:

> If this snake emerges from the place where I came from,
>> was snuggled in my baby clothes;
> if it mouthed the breast that suckled me,
> blent the sweet milk with clotted blood,
> and if she shouted out with pain and shock—
>> then this hideous freak she nursed
> means she surely dies: dies viciously.
> *I* turn snake to murder her.
> That is what this dream forebodes.[69]

Like Jimmy's mother, Clytemnestra recognizes, though it is only when he is about to kill her, that Orestes is the snake in her bosom: "So *you* are the snake I bore and gave my breast to?"[70]

68. *The Orestes Plays of Aeschylus,* ed. and trans. Paul Roche (New York: Mentor, 1962), 128.
69. Aeschylus, 129–30.
70. Aeschylus, 146.

Humphrey's Texas Orestes attempts to avoid his fate by running away from home. When he stops at the burial mound "to forswear his allegiance and bid [the spirits of the dead Caddoes] goodbye forever" (*TP*, 206) and is about to offer his valedictory before departing with the intent, like the Caddoes before him, of being absorbed into another tribe across the river in Oklahoma, a snake makes a dramatic entrance, emerging out of the burial mound upon which Jimmy stands: "Out and out it came: its final four inches were rattles. It was an old snake. Its skin was dull and lusterless, its markings blurred, and it was half blind with a film clouding its eyes. . . . And suddenly with one long stroke, at the part dividing its nostrils, the snake's skin split and out of its dull wrapper popped a bright new head with keen new eyes that blinked at the raw daylight" (206, 207). Out of what appears to be a dying creature emerges a vibrant new life, dazzling, elegant, and transcendent. According to Joseph Campbell, "The power of life causes the snake to shed its skin. . . . The serpent represents immortal energy and consciousness engaged in the field of time, constantly throwing off death and being born again."[71] More particularly, the snake's appearance symbolizes that Snake-in-His-Mother's-Bosom cannot die to his calling but must be renewed and therefore must persevere in his life's mission. Thus, "Snake-in-His-Mother's-Bosom knelt and picked up the cast-off skin. Rising, he saw his mother's face appear over the top of the mound. He felt himself instinctively coil, his lips fly back to bare his fangs. 'Ah-hah,' said his mother's smirk, 'I knew where to find you, didn't I? You can't get away from me'" (*TP*, 207). When his mother utters this remark, Snake-in-His-Mother's-Bosom knows the source (the narrator reminds us of the "sly toothless grins" beneath his feet), and therefore surrenders to his fate, which is to murder his mother. He might have tried to die to his fate, but it renews itself with unusual vigor ("The snake might shed his skin, but only to grow another one the same as before" [207]). The boy rides home with his mother, the old snake skin in his lap. "Now he must wait." One day he will receive a mysterious message, we feel sure: "Then Snake-in-His-Mother's-Bosom would strike, accomplish his mission and fulfill the prophecy; and then at last the ghosts of the Caddoes could lie down at peace in their many-tiered mound and haunt the land and him no more" (208). This statement standing alone, taken at face value, suggests that the boy is on his way to becoming a permanent resident in a state hospital for the criminally insane. But in the full context of the story, allowing the full symbolic and mythic dimension, we see rather a boy who knows he will have to "kill" his mother in order to inhabit the identity that he has uncovered for himself.

71. Joseph Campbell with Bill Moyers, *The Power of Myth* (New York: Doubleday, 1988), 45.

Humphrey also makes it clear that the boy's near relatives on his father's side will not be any help in the achieving of his identity either. Part 3 offers a comic treatment of Jimmy's grandfather Hawkins, who is a buffoon in "baggy, patched old denim overalls," the squalid remnant of the noble savage, who is clearly based upon Humphrey's paternal grandfather (*TP*, 185). About this grandfather, Will Humphreys, a cotton sharecropper, the author has remarked: "He was, it was plain to see, part Indian. Which meant that his father, long dead, had been even more of one. This monosyllabic grandfather of mine, stolid as an Indian, would, or could, satisfy none of my eager curiosity about my Indian great-grandfather [Star Humphreys was his name]. With his own son, when he was a little boy, inquisitive about himself and his origins, he had been just as uncommunicative" (*FOFH*, 65). Hardly aware of his own Indian heritage, Jimmy's grandfather, much like Humphrey's own, is a man of empty words—clichéd pronouncements that mean nothing to the boy who wants to know who he is and is convinced that knowing the life of an Indian ancestor will help him do so. "Son, what a man is born don't matter a hill of beans. It's what you make of yoreself that counts," he says to Jimmy, oblivious of the meaning for the boy of Indian blood (*TP*, 186). As he tries to answer Jimmy's question about his great-grandfather, the ridiculous grandfather sounds like the fool Malvolio reporting on Cesario at Olivia's gate: "Well, he was not what you would call a big man. Neither was he a little man. More what you would call middling-sized" (*TP*, 187; cf. *Twelfth Night* 1.5.150ff.). His name? No Indian name; he was "Mr. George P. Hawkins, same as mine," and the grandfather dispenses the following piece of wisdom: "I can tell you one thing though: I'm grateful I haven't had to go through life named George P. Crazy Horse" (*TP*, 187). This comic episode with the grandfather contributes context for the boy's quest.

In fact, when the story ends in the manner that we have already observed, we have also been made aware of how long and hard Jimmy has labored in his quest. Not only has he read all that he can find about the now extinct (except for himself, he now feels) Caddo tribe, but he has walked the fields along the Red River in Texas with an imaginative perception capable of identifying "the mortars in which his people had ground their maize and the pestles with which they had pounded it," as well as many other artifacts (*TP*, 190). Familiarity with the objects of their daily life eventually enables Jimmy imaginatively to sense their presence in the woods: "In the green stillness he could see their spirits flitting among the trees and in the whispering together of the branches could hear their voices." Recalling the Twenty-Third Psalm, "He knew no fear, for they were with him" (190).

Jimmy accomplishes one astonishing feat: he digs into the Caddo burial mound on his grandfather's farm. Digging, literally, into his cultural and spiritual past becomes as important an enterprise for Jimmy as it is for the Irish poet Seamus Heaney, who asserts that in his poem "Digging" he "had let down a shaft into real life," which amounted to a "revelation of the self to the self" at the same time that it was a "restoration of the culture to itself." Moreover, in *Door into the Dark* Heaney writes with the assumption that the boglands, which contain the bodies and artifacts of ancient Irish culture, constitute the "memory of the landscape"—it was "a landscape that remembered everything that happened in and to it."[72] What archaeological finds in the bogs of Ireland are for Heaney, the Caddo burial mound is for Jimmy Hawkins. His extensive excavation yields beaded medicine bags, clay pipes, corn pouches, skulls, and clay jugs seemingly "fresh from the hand that had made [them] centuries ago"; this dig restores his lost culture to him and tells him who he is: "Jimmy had bared the buried history of the Caddoes, delving backwards in time from their end to their beginning. He had measured the antiquity of his lineage in countless shovelfuls of earth. The handiwork of his tribe had shown him the strangeness of his heritage, his own difference" (*TP*, 199, 193).

Jimmy's mother, however, is repelled by all that is Indian. She is the enemy of his identity. For the last of the Caddoes to live with integrity, then, she must die. It is a terrifying conclusion—one that the boy seeks to run from—but the story carefully makes the conclusion inevitable. We are left to feel that Jimmy, as much as Orestes, is bound to "Learn the reaches of a rage undampable."[73] Humphrey's integration of the Aeschylean factor into his story about a boy trying to grow up in Texas not only makes his reader aware of the universal nature of the theme, but also gives the theme stature, preventing it from being taken lightly.

In 1982, Ken Harrison produced and directed a twenty-nine-minute Phoenix motion picture closely based on "The Last of the Caddoes." It was filmed in Clarksville, and the cast included Humphrey's uncle Bernard Varley as the grandfather; Jim Mills playing Jimmy Hawkins, Paula Craig Williams as Jimmy's mother, and Charles Giddens as his father. Humphrey was pleased at how well his favorite uncle had done in his first acting role. Another Texas writer, William Owens, served as Harrison's consultant on the film, and this role brought him back in touch with Humphrey. The two Texas writers had not seen each other for twenty years. They discovered that they were near neighbors, for Owens was then living in Nyack, New York, about sixty miles from Hudson.[74]

72. Seamus Heaney, *Preoccupations* (New York: Farrar, Straus & Giroux, 1980), 41, 54.
73. Aeschylus, 125.
74. Bill Porterfield, "The Great Writer's Nephew Didn't Understand," *Dallas Times Herald*, 24 June 1981, sec. A, p. 23.

Taken as a whole, the stories in *A Time and a Place* exhibit a remarkable unity, although the *Times Book Review*'s Larry King overstated the case in saying the volume seemed almost a novel. Still, seven of the ten stories focus on the effect of the Great Depression and the Dust Bowl and on the lives and spirits of the poor. In this collection of stories, all promises of escape from hard economic conditions prove to be insubstantial. Efforts to chase wealth through daring exploits end in death or paralysis, and if wealth is achieved it serves only to accentuate a poverty of spirit that prevents enjoyment or felicity. A general degradation prevails through all elements of society during the mean times that Humphrey focuses on: common suffering, in several stories, even seems to encourage more meanness of spirit, a desire to look out for oneself at the expense of one's neighbors. The three best stories in the volume—"Mouth of Brass," "A Voice from the Woods," and "The Last of the Caddoes"—while related to the time and place of the other seven stories, portray a depth of experience that exceeds by far the pictures of life in the five stories about the discovery of oil and the two rather fantastic tales, "The Rainmaker" and "The Human Fly." These three remarkable stories have in common that they evoke childhood in East Texas, a feature of Humphrey's most successful fiction prior to his move to a different mode in *Hostages to Fortune*. In this respect *The Ordways* holds a special place among Humphrey's works, for as Keats warns, unrelieved attention to melancholy images will "drown the wakeful anguish of the soul."

[6]

AS EDWINA LAY DYING
(Proud Flesh)

A dismal pedigree
of inbred pain and jangled fate
dripping with its wound!
—Aeschylus, *The Libation
Bearers,* Strophe 11

We are country-bred people.
—T. S. Eliot, *The Family Reunion*

FTER THE publication of *The Ordways* in 1965, Humphrey was slow to
return to *Proud Flesh.* He was house hunting (1965–66) and immediately
afterwards commuting between Hudson and Cambridge while he taught
at Massachusetts Institute of Technology. Then the completion of *A Time and a
Place* intervened. Even after his life settled down and *Proud Flesh* became his sole
endeavor, he progressed very slowly. The lonely struggle took a terrible toll on
him, physically and psychologically. In the autumn of 1968, just as he was beginning to sort through his heap of notes for the novel, he was overcome by "fear
of this unwritten book"; he treated his fear with whiskey and got little done: "I
waste my evenings drinking myself to bed, and in the mornings my head doesn't
work." He slogged along on *Proud Flesh*—dissatisfied with the results—until
winter. If Humphrey were to make any progress on the book that so depressed
him, he would have to escape the dreary cold of a Hudson winter. Therefore he
and Dorothy took off for a comparatively beautiful and temperate Paris. They
crossed the Atlantic on an airplane for the first time—arriving rigid with terror.
Stumbling off the plane, they immediately made arrangements to return on the
Ile de France on 9 May, and then they settled into their happy apartment on rue
Boursalt in a quarter of Paris that was "petit petit-bourgeois—humming with the
familiar bustle of a small provincial French town." It gave them an especial pleasure to live the real French life. Humphrey soon discovered that Stéphane Mallarmé had for twenty-five years lived just around the corner from their
apartment (on rue de Rome), where he conducted his famous weekly soirées attended by Verlaine, Valéry, Proust, James, Turgenev, Flaubert, Degas, and others.
Humphrey, now deep in the study of French symbolist poetry, was struck by

the mass of railroad tracks alongside Mallarmé's dwelling, and it suggested an imaginative insight into his poetry:

> These [railroad tracks] do more to explain Mallarme's poetry than a book of close explication. No ordinary railroad tracks, these. These are the Grand Canyon of railroad tracks, or chemins de fer, to keep up the atmosphere. These are about 24 sets of tracks with accompanying cinder beds, signals, wires, noise and everything else un-poetic you can conjure up to your mind, in a chasm some hundred and fifty feet deep and about two hundred yards wide. They terminate about two blocks further down in the Gare St. Lazare. These tracks were for 23 years Mallarme's view. What it is to be a poet in the age of steel. So no wonder he dreamed of pure poetry. Of words divorced from things, becoming things themselves.[1]

Humphrey was encouraged to write by the fervent interest in the southern novel that he found in Paris. Thus while Dorothy painted in her little salon, Bill labored at his desk in the bedroom to get back into *Proud Flesh,* but it was like "trying after a long spell to get back into . . . a wet bathing suit." The long hall that separated the two rooms provided privacy, even though the space was small. Every afternoon, they would quit work at about three o'clock and set off into the city to visit museums or just stroll through the streets.[2]

Humphrey confessed some fanciful plans he had for the May departure for the United States—plans that are an index to the high value Bill placed on the small pleasures of living in Paris: "We've got a cabin for three on the France," he told the Weisses, "and do you know who is going into the third bunk? One Monsieur Delesque, our baker around the corner." On the morning of their leaving, Humphrey continues in his 26 April letter, "I'm going to have the taxi stop on our way to Gare St. Lazare, dash in with a handkerchief soaked in chloroform, anaesthetize M. Delesque and take him home with me so I will not have to give up his brioches, his bread, and his gatoaux" (Weiss Coll.).

Nine days after the Humphreys returned from Paris on 14 May of 1969, they flew to Dallas. Humphrey's "old alamo mater," as he called Southern Methodist

1. William Humphrey to Harry Grabstald, 15 July 1966, HG Letters; to Annie Laurie Williams, 31 August 1964, Williams Coll.; to Nick Lyons, 18 December 1971, Lyons Coll.; notebook, entry for 12 December 1968, WH Coll., UT; Dorothy Humphrey to Katherine Anne Porter, 6 April 1969, KAP Coll.; to Theodore and Renée Weiss, 24 February 1969, Weiss Coll.; Humphrey to the Weisses, 21 March and 14 April 1969, Weiss Coll.

2. Humphrey to the Weisses, 7 and 21 March 1969, Weiss Coll.; Dorothy Humphrey to Porter, 6 April 1969, KAP Coll.

University, was to confer an honorary doctorate upon him. This degree, conferred on him on 25 May, was the only degree of any kind he ever received. On this trip back to Texas he, like the salmon in *The Spawning Run* (which he would take up and finish writing before the year's end), returned to his hometown of Clarksville—for the first time since he and his mother had abruptly left following his father's death thirty-two years before. He had been afraid to go back, because he "didn't want anything to have changed." But it "was changed. In that part of Texas everything is changed. When I was a boy it was cotton country, sharecropping, tenant-farming, a hard life whether you were white or black, but as nobody was much better off than anyone else, we didn't complain too much. Now the people, black and white, have left, and the land is used to graze beef cattle and the town has shrunk in size and grown tired and sleepy." Humphrey did all that he could to revisit his origins in the short period of time that he had allotted. When he saw the crumbling old tenant houses that his people came from, he was moved to remember how poor his family had been. He dutifully visited the old country graveyards of his mother's and father's people; and like the salmon with whom he felt a kinship, he decided his final resting place would be his original home. To insure his ultimate reconnection with his origins, Humphrey purchased a plot, in the shade of the old hanging tree, in the Clarksville cemetery. A reception held in his honor was attended by about eleven hundred people.[3]

Returning to Hudson just after the middle of June, Humphrey carried on his struggle to finish *Proud Flesh*, which presented more and more assorted difficulties. On 15 August 1969, he interrupted his extensive note-making for the novel to jot in his notebook: "Leonard is dead. I heard the news over the radio this morning at 8:45." He wrote no more on Leonard Woolf's death, but he did no more note-taking that day either. When he resumed working, it was fitful work. At the end of August he chided himself that if he was "ever to get moving on this book now's the time," and he tried to cheer himself up by remembering that Faulkner had taken fifteen years to write *The Hamlet*.[4]

Outrage over Richard Nixon's prolonging and expanding the Vietnam War took Humphrey, for a time, altogether away from his troubling novel; he actively

3. Lon Tinkle, "For Bill Humphrey a Degree at Last," *Dallas Morning News*, 1 June 1969, sec. C. p. 7; Humphrey to the Weisses, 21 March 1969, Weiss Coll.; to Jean Lambert, 15 April 1969, Lambert Coll.; to Porter, 14 July 1969, KAP Coll.; *FOFH*, 241.

4. Humphrey, notebook, entry for 24 August 1969, WH Coll., UT. Humphrey must have been thinking about Faulkner's difficulty in writing *The Fable*, which he worked on for almost eleven years. Ordinarily Faulkner got out a book a year (Joseph Blotner, *Faulkner: A Biography* one-volume ed. [New York: Random House, 1984], 452, 584).

participated in antiwar protests. On the night of 14 November 1969 he joined the Vietnam Moratorium march to the White House, having been chauffeured to the site of the protest in a limousine provided by Katherine Anne Porter. When he returned home on 17 November Humphrey found another way to sidestep *Proud Flesh;* on that date, in an effort to find pleasure in writing, he dug up a piece he had begun four years earlier, an account of salmon fishing in Wales. He worked well and effectively on it and by 9 December 1969 had completed *The Spawning Run.*[5]

Once his fishing story was completed, Humphrey returned to his novel. There were no more unfinished manuscripts that he could divert his attention with. Drinking once again became his only refuge, and it turned into a serious problem—one that Humphrey himself recognized. It, more than anything else, undermined progress on *Proud Flesh,* but of course the frustrations with the novel contributed to the excessive drinking. Humphrey, however, preferred to think that external events were the main reasons for the lack of progress on the novel. He gave accounts of those interfering events to his friends. In January a big storm deposited so much snow on his roof that when it began to thaw, refreeze, and thaw again, water ran between the walls and through the window frames, keeping Bill and Dorothy up for four nights emptying buckets and wringing out towels. Wanting some relief from the continuing drip, and the constant wiping up, Humphrey hired a neighbor to break up the melting ice on his roof. While steadying the ladder for the man, Humphrey was struck on the head by a chunk of ice, giving him a concussion, raising a knot "the size of a horse apple and . . . opening a gash about two inches long and half an inch wide," Humphrey exaggerated to Katherine Anne Porter. During this dreary winter, the only other human face he saw was Dorothy's—and there were in fact days when he did not even see her, for she had rented a studio in a village fifteen miles away and, for a period, worked there seven days a week.[6]

Humphrey's writing hardly progressed. On a Sunday morning—9 February 1970—he engaged in serious self-communion in one of his six notebooks on the novel: "I have become a nervous wreck, and unless I get a hold on myself I am headed for a breakdown. I am really disintegrating. God, even my handwriting shows it. Dead drunk every night. Sick, hung-over. Shaky half the next day, re-

5. Hilary Masters, "Proud Flesh: William Humphrey Remembered," *Sewanee Review* 108, no. 3 (Spring 2000): 258; Humphrey to the Weisses, 30 December 1964, Weiss Coll.; MS of *The Spawning Run* (a fair copy), last page, WH res. *The Spawning Run* appeared in the next June issue of *Esquire.*

6. Humphrey, notebook, entry for 9 February 1970, WH Coll., UT; Humphrey to Seymour Lawrence, 24 January 1970, Lawrence Coll.; Humphrey to Porter, 15 January 1970, KAP Coll.; Humphrey to the Weisses, 19 November [1969], Weiss Coll.

covering in time to start drinking again. A crack-up. That's what I have had—or am having. The worst may be yet to come. It certainly will be unless I begin to put up a little more resistance. For one thing I must cut down on the drinking. And I must somewhere find the strength and the courage to get back into the novel" (WH Coll., UT). The resolve lasted for some months.

Then another potential diversion presented itself. *Esquire* asked Humphrey to do a 75,000-word biography of Lieutenant William Calley, who had directed the infamous My Lai massacre on 16 March 1968. It was to have been published in three installments. Humphrey seriously considered accepting this task, thinking he might find in it a way to make some contribution to ending the war by making this country look at itself through looking at Calley. He thought, too, that if he could emphasize the innocent victims, the story might help America to achieve a fuller humanity. But the possibility of going ahead with the biography ended abruptly when Lieutenant Calley's representative said to Humphrey: "Now, I've told you what Calley can give you: what can you give Calley? What can you offer him?" Humphrey was amazed and replied, "Why I offer him nothing except my competence as a writer and my dedication to the truth. He has no right to ask more of me or any other writer. Indeed, he'd better be grateful for that." When Humphrey realized that the proposed arrangement did not insure his freedom to write his own book, he turned the job down.[7] The title of Wayne Greenhaw's biography suggests what Calley had expected from Humphrey: *The Making of a Hero: The Story of Lieut. William Calley Jr.* (1971).

Instead of pursuing the *Esquire* project Humphrey went to northern Alabama for *Life* magazine. His essay about Granny Branch in Lawrence County, "Ditches Are Quicker," exposes the environmental disaster wrought by the Soil Conservation Service in its efforts to straighten creeks to alleviate flooding. On his way back to New York, he and the *Life* photographer Stan Wayman stopped in Washington to see Katherine Anne Porter, who was in the hospital. Though the sun was shining, he wore a raincoat so that he could smuggle a pint of Virginia Gentleman into the hospital. After the three of them drank that bottle, Porter took great delight in revealing that she had a whole case more of the same "medicine" under her bed.[8]

When Humphrey returned to Hudson, he went to work on the novel in a serious way, and he eventually seemed to have gotten his drinking under control. On 26 September 1970 he recorded that he had gone eight days without a drink.

---

7. Humphrey, notebook, entries for 9 and 12 April 1970, WH Coll., UT.

8. "Ditches Are Quicker," *Life*, 7 August 1970, 59–61, reprinted in *OS*, 231–40; Humphrey to Lawrence, 20 June 1970, Lawrence Coll.

"I have quit," he claimed. A month later he admitted to his notebook, however, that he had been backsliding. While he might indeed have quit drinking whiskey, he had instead been consuming wine, beer, and narcotics: "I'm substituting, not quitting—must not go on like this." He wrote this on the day that *The Spawning Run* was published as a book: 30 October 1970, "a good day to re-dedicate myself to sobriety" (WH Coll., UT).

But the trouble with *Proud Flesh* continued, and Bill continued pointing to external hindrances to explain his lack of progress. Thus he complained about his expensive new German typewriter: "Another myth exploded: German mechanical efficiency."[9] Then a kidney stone incapacitated him. Once he was rid of the stone, he resolved to "lead a healthier life," declaring to Ian Parsons on 12 October 1970, "I've quit drinking," a resolve that lasted about as long as Falstaff's to "give over" his life as a highway robber (C&W). Seemingly stalked by mishap, Humphrey had another accident during the following year, and it proved to be another impediment to completing *Proud Flesh*, which he himself had come to refer to as his "eternal novel." He had gone to Cape Cod for his birthday and broke his foot while playing baseball with some children. Unable to type because he had to keep his foot propped, all he managed to do was drink whiskey, ingest codeine, smoke his pipe, and scribble in his notebooks. When he finally got off the crutches at the end of the summer, as he would later explain to Katherine Anne Porter in a letter dated 16 June 1972, he "looked at the mound of tattered unnumbered pages of the manuscript" that he had worked on intermittently for fifteen years and said to himself: "You have this choice: throw it away now, or give yourself one more year—it will take that at least—and then throw it away" (KAP Coll.).[10] But then instead of sitting at his typewriter, he hung up a "gone fishing" sign and sailed for the Bahamas. From this diversion he returned to the novel with serious intent—after writing a short fishing piece.

In November the broken foot became tender with the onset of cold weather, and Bill and Dorothy decided that he had better not try to endure another bleak winter on the farm with *Proud Flesh* to face. Therefore, Dorothy went ahead to London and found a flat at 10 Cheyne Walk, three doors from the house that George Eliot had died in. In this neighborhood reeking of literary associations, where lived and worked Swinburne, Rossetti, Smollett, Carlyle, and Moore as well as Whistler, Humphrey at first did not know whether to be inspired or intimidated. But eventually, in this quiet and imaginatively fertile setting, well beyond the embankment and behind a park that had once been part of Henry VIII's

9. Humphrey to Ian Parsons, 13 July 1970, C&W.
10. Humphrey to the Weisses, 19 October [1971], Weiss Coll.

garden, he found himself productive, working all day every day. He was free from the compulsion to overdrink.

In spite of his relentless work schedule—and partly to avoid the temptation to drink excessively after the day's work—he and Dorothy filled their evenings with theater engagements. They went to operas, everything by Verdi, whom Humphrey loved; another favorite was Mozart, especially *Cosi fan tutte*, which had Humphrey weeping with laughter and love.[11] They also enjoyed classic theater: Goldsmith's *She Stoops to Conquer*, Gorki's *Enemies*, Etherege's *The Man of Mode*, and O'Neill's *A Long Day's Journey into Night*; but he refused to attend Albee's *All Over*, even though his friend Peggy Ashcroft was starring in it ("I'd sooner stay home and play mumblepeg by myself than see a play by Edward Albee," he announced to the Weisses on 1 February [Weiss Coll.]).

For six months in London Humphrey worked harder than he had ever worked, and as he approached the end of a fifteen-year ordeal, he was in a state of euphoria. His final push on *Proud Flesh* bore fruit on 8 April, nineteen years from the day that his first book was published. He wrote to Porter that "There were times when I thought it would finish me—and I'm still not sure it hasn't. But in any case I have fought it to a draw." These sentiments are understated. It had been a fight to the finish. Humphrey threw his 368-page manuscript on the floor, placed his foot upon the pile, and—with a bottle of *Moet et Chandon* in hand—shouted, "winnah by a knockout!"[12]

At the end of his stint in London, 29 April 1972, Humphrey headed for the streams and rivers near the Lakes of Killarney in County Kerry, Ireland. *True* magazine, which had paid for his fishing trip to the Bahamas during the previous year, was sponsoring two weeks of salmon fishing. Gales and snow that April meant that the fortnight yielded only one fish—a smoked salmon provided by his hotel as a consolation for his bad luck. But he and Dorothy enjoyed themselves tremendously, and their Irish sojourn was followed by a week of riotous living in Paris before they returned home to deliver the *Proud Flesh* manuscript by hand to Robert Gottlieb, who was then president of Knopf as well as Humphrey's editor. Before he submitted the manuscript, Humphrey listed, at the end of it, all of the locations at which he had worked on *Proud Flesh:* Rhinebeck, Wareham, Biot, Lenno, St. Buryan's, Holford, Stockbridge, Sienna, Rome, Telscombe, Lexington, Alassio, Freedom Plains, Cambridge, Ghent, Paris, Wellfleet, London. In

11. Humphrey to Porter, 27 January 1972, KAP Coll.

12. Humphrey to the Weisses, 8 April [1972], Weiss Coll.; to Porter, 13 April 1972, KAP Coll.; Dorothy Humphrey to Milly and Harry Grabstald, 17 March 1972, HG Letters; Humphrey to the Weisses, 8 April [1972], Weiss Coll.

June he attended to the final revisions, and on 8 March 1973 he received his first copy of the novel. It was officially published in April.[13]

What had Humphrey produced? A hybrid, it seems. It is easy to characterize *Home from the Hill* as a tragedy, *The Ordways* as a comedy, but it is hard to say what the fascinating, puzzling, and quirky *Proud Flesh* is. Its serious and comic elements combined depict lives marked by incompleteness and uncertainty. The comedy itself contributes to the bleak vision of life. What hope there is is outlandish and accentuates the absence of greater hope. It is highly ironic in treating its many flawed characters and their skewed relationships. Yet this basically grim novel contains some of Humphrey's best, most expressive prose—highly polished, perfectly rendered visual images that create an overwhelming sense of reality intensely perceived.

When Humphrey uses words to paint with, "the details [are] all there, and once painted upon the surface of [the reader's] mind they [penetrate] . . . to its bottom-most layer, like fresco on a wall" (*PF*, 46). Humphrey, who failed at being a painter with brushes and canvas, achieves profound painterly effects with language. Here he limns the scene when Edwina, the dying matriarch of the novel, awakens in the night: "At just past ten o'clock a whisper, like rain sweeping over the roof, ran through the house, and the men in the yard saw the sick-light upstairs flare into sudden white. A moment later the lights came on downstairs, the front door flew open and a bolt of light flashed across the porch and over the lawn, throwing into skeletal shadows the craned and twisted faces of the squatting men" (119). His panorama of the cotton pickers at work on the Renshaw farm is a masterly evocation: "In September come the migrant workers [that] settle . . . in a swarm. Bent black figures in clothes darkened and colorless with sweat, dragging their long bolster-shaped sacks behind them, they eat their way across the fields, white ahead of them, stripped bare and brown in their wake, like some plague of great white-bodied, black-headed caterpillars" (29).

Humphrey has an astonishing ability to evoke faces and hands, and also movement. Clovis Dodds, one of the cotton pickers, has a "flat face like a piece of water-worn fountain statuary, dripping sweat"; when she shakes Clyde's hand, she "wrung [it] with her own two twisted claws that were scaly and fleshless as a chicken foot" (*PF*, 36). Clyde, the Renshaw brother who manages the family farm, opens a cabin door and finds "a row of half a dozen pinky-brown children, napping, covered with flies like raisin-sprinkled gingerbread men" (48). Junya

13. It seems that Humphrey failed to include Hudson in his list. Humphrey to Parsons, 30 May 1972, C&W; Humphrey to Lyons, 13 June 1972, Lyons Coll.; Humphrey, notebook, entry for 22 March 1976, WH Coll., UT.

Price, another worker, has "prompt young muscles bunching beneath a skin as glossy as an eggplant's" (57).

Humphrey also excels at portraying small, individual movements. When an old black man, with "work-worn, blackish-yellow, horny hands" reaches in for his snap-top pocketbook to pay for vanilla wafers and canned sardines, it looks, when he draws it out of his "overalls pocket, as if [he] were extracting a vital body gland" (*PF*, 19). And when Edwina Renshaw awakens to utter the one word she speaks in the novel ("Kyle"), her awakening is represented as follows: "Her old eyelids, crinkly and thin as the skin of a bat's wing, fluttered open" (121).[14]

But it is not just poetical perceptions that Humphrey accomplishes with his metaphors and similes: he uses them to convey emotions as well. When Clyde pulls a closet door open with the sure and certain expectation of finding his mistress and her lover crouching naked together behind hanging clothes, his profound awareness of his own foolishness is conveyed by a precise objective correlative: "Blindly he yanked open the door. On the rod hung three bent and empty clothes hangers. Stirred by the wind they tinkled together like distant laughter" (*PF*, 49). Sister Amy's desolation of spirit caused by an enduring recollection of a moment when she knew her mother hated her is poignantly portrayed in the dry winter leaves at the end of the following passage: "Throughout all the succeeding years, extending right up to the present moment here in the same room, there were times when her remembrance of that penetrating glare, that pointed finger, that piercing cry, 'You get out of here!' and even worse, that appeal to the others present to '*Get her out of here!*' stripped all Amy's explanations from her and drove them before it like dry leaves in a winter wind, leaving her bare and huddling" (168). Humphrey finds an apt figure of speech to clarify how Amy's compromised marriage nonetheless fits her unsatisfactory life: "They fitted together like . . . two halves of a broken plate that had gotten dispersed and had miraculously been rejoined. Mended together, they made a presentable plate; they themselves knew that the plate was for display only" (169).[15] And the deepseated racism of divorce lawyer Francis Fleurnoy is revealed in an insightful metaphor showing precisely how his mind is arranged. Were Eunice to name the woman Clyde is having an affair with, Fleurnoy would not know at first that she is talking about a black woman, but then it would dawn on him: "He would look

14. One cannot resist noting that in Faulkner's *As I Lay Dying*, Addie Bundren opens her eyes during the present time of the novel, to utter only one name: Cash (*As I Lay Dying* [New York: Vintage International, 1990], 46, 48).

15. Humphrey says of himself following the death of his father: "My heart, if I ever got the pieces back together again, would be like a mended plate: not for use" (*FOFH*, 234).

blank for a while. He would be expecting a knock on the front door of his memory; it would take a while for him to realize that it was somebody at the back door" (132).

Much of *Proud Flesh* shows evidence of careful shaping. For example, in the introductory chapter, the silence of waiting in the shade of the pear tree is broken from time to time by the drone of wasps, by "the stridulation of a locust like a telephone ringing insistently in an empty house," and by the "mournful chant" of the blacks picking cotton (*PF*, 5). As the chapter reaches its conclusion, these three sounds are brought together, following "another, deeper, longer silence," in one expression: "The wasps drone, the locust repeats its ring, up from the fields floats the Negroes' melodious moan" (7). A few pages farther on, Humphrey orchestrates musical effects that convey a sense of wholeness in the midst and aftermath of violence. Claude Renshaw, riding upon the hood of a car, trying to figure out what is wrong with it, listening to the sounds of its motor, requesting the driver to speed up or slow down, is said to be "directing with the finesse of an orchestra conductor" (20–21).[16] Moments later Claude is shot with a rifle whose report is as "oriental as a brass gong or the twang of a zither string" (21). Finally, when Claude's relatives gather to view his shot-away face, "the nickelodeon in the deserted confectionery down the block" produces "the whine of a balladier [*sic*] and the whang of a steel guitar" (22).[17]

Like *Home from the Hill, Hostages to Fortune,* and *No Resting Place, Proud Flesh* is rich in literary allusions. Sometimes the allusion amounts to little more than the ghostly presence of other writers. In chapter 4 of Part 1, Humphrey glances to Hemingway and Shakespeare in characterizing the relationship between Clyde and Eunice. Like Krebs in "Soldier's Home" *(In Our Time),* Clyde was "the last man ["in his theater of the war"] to get back home." Humphrey is referring to the Second World War instead of the First World War, as he reports: "When the war was over and all those ex-golf caddies and barbers' college students . . . were home getting the good jobs and the girls, Clyde was kept on" (*PF*, 35). Because Humphrey knew Shakespeare's plays thoroughly, he could hardly

16. This picture of Clyde comes from Humphrey's boyhood memory of a car passing frequently through the square of Clarksville "with my father lying on the hood of it listening to the beat of the engine to diagnose what ailed it" (*FOFH*, 53).

17. Another way in which Humphrey's careful planning manifests itself is in how a major theme is reflected in a small image, similar to the way an ecclesiastical architect might imitate, in the design of pew supports, the church's buttresses. Thus the novel's major emphasis on the condition of Edwina's heart, as well as the continuing theme of characters' probing the depths of their hearts, is mirrored in that small image of Claude's riding on the hood of the car and "listening to the engine as a doctor listens to a sick man's heart" (*PF*, 20).

have helped thinking of Othello and Desdemona when he portrayed Clyde telling Eunice about his "Army adventures": "She listened avidly. . . . The telling drew them together as they had not been before. Both sensed this and drew closer still"—then Humphrey adds his own twist that foretells the breakup of their marriage—"[u]ntil both realized that what they were enjoying was the memory of the time when they had not been married" (35).

The effect upon Shug of her initial sexual encounter with Clyde gains standing through its resemblance to Hamlet's

> Yea, from the table of my memory
> I'll wipe away all trivial fond records
>
> . . . .
>
> And thy commandment all alone shall live
> Within the book and volume of my brain.
> (*Hamlet*, 1.5.98–99, 102–3)

Shug hears "herself say that, it was as though her mind were a blackboard and an eraser had just been drawn across it, and all those shorthand symbols she had worked to memorize were wiped away and her mind was a slate-colored blank" (*PF*, 152). Humphrey's own version of Hamlet's gesture might just have been influenced by Hank Thompson's "The Blackboard of My Heart," containing the line "My tears have washed 'I love you' from the blackboard of my heart." The inevitability of Shug's dream (how she would tempt Clyde into killing her and her lover) is also helped by the resemblance between her language and Hamlet's. Hamlet speaks of Providence: "If it be [now], 'tis not to come; if it be not to come, it will be now; if it be not now, yet it will come—the readiness is all" (5.2.220–22); Humphrey substitutes the concept of "ripeness" (from *King Lear*: "Ripeness is all" [4.2.11]) in place of "readiness" and has Shug say: "If not tonight, another night. If not with this one tonight then with one of the others. . . . If not this fall then next spring, if not next spring then next fall. The seed had been sown; now time would ripen it" (*PF*, 147). Shug's thoughts echo Hamlet's at the very point in the play when he has decided to struggle no longer with the question of what he should do; because of the echoes of Hamlet, we conclude that Shug will wait calmly upon fate, as Hamlet had learned to do.

Since writing this novel had inflicted upon the author more anxiety and frustration than any of his other books, it is no surprise to find that its title had also been an agonizing question for him, one that he pursued with meticulous care. John Forster reported that Dickens had a hard time deciding on the title for *Hard Times* and in the end resorted to submitting a list of fourteen possibilities to two friends and allowing them to pick.[18] Humphrey would say that, measured against his experience, Boz had rather an easy time. Humphrey's friends and editors offered to help, Pete Lemay, for example, as early as 25 June 1963 proposing "The Renshaw Boys" (Knopf Coll.). Humphrey began his title search in earnest by copying down a passage from Ecclesiasticus (38:16–23) and culling four possible titles from it: "According to Custom," "Let Tears Fall Down," "Let Remembrance Rest," and "Yesterday for Me." He also considered a fifth: "Children of Wrath." In the same notebook, he contemplated a host of alternatives: "A Time to Mourn" (from Ecclesiastes), "The House of Mourning" (and then "A House of Mourning"), "More than the Living," "Guardians of the Name," "Guardians of the Flame," "Honor Guard," "Among those Surviving," "The Eumenides," "The Mourners," "The Term of Mourning," "The Bereft," and "By Ties of Blood." Next Humphrey made a list of possible titles from *Hamlet:* "More Than Kin," "A Little More than Kin," "Seekers in the Dust," "All that Lives," "The Shows of Grief," "These Mourning Duties," "The Term of Obligation," "The Term of Sorrow," "A Fault to Heaven," "A Fault Against the Dead," and "A Fault to Nature" (Notes, 1, 24).

Unable to make a selection, he resorted to "The Renshaws" but later favored "A Time to Mourn" as a working title. Later he proposed to himself "Whistling Dixie" and "Day of Reckoning" (Notes, 148). Clearly Humphrey was not overstating his experience when he declared, "Titles are devils of things to find"—and then he explained the reason for his indecisiveness: "No author really likes to give a title to his book because any title he gives illuminates only one aspect of the book, and he likes to think that his book has more than one aspect, so that any title is limiting unless it's something straight as *The Ordways*" (*WST*, 27). Since he had been forced to accept the easy solution of a family name for *The Ordways*, he could not very well call this one "The Renshaws," and he could not allow himself to think of "As She Lay Dying" because he was already worrying about echoing Faulkner, not just *As I Lay Dying* but "A Rose for Emily" as well (Notes, 125). Not until after 13 June 1966 did he narrow the choices to two, "A Time to Mourn" and "Proud Flesh," mentioned for the first time.[19] He went back to "Day of Reckoning" on the final page of "Notes on the Orestia." The subsequent notebooks—there are five additional ones—do not concern the title question, yet the title was not decided until Humphrey was ready to submit the

---

18. John Forster, *The Life of Charles Dickens* (New York: D. Appleton, [1880]), 284.

19. In the late 1930s Robert Penn Warren wrote a verse play entitled *Proud Flesh*, which in 1943 he began to turn into the novel that became *All the King's Men* (Robert Penn Warren, introduction to *All the King's Men* [New York: Modern Library, 1946], i–v).

manuscript to Knopf. On the manuscript title page he crossed out "A Time to Mourn" and wrote "Proud Flesh" (WH Coll., UT). In his last letter to Katherine Anne Porter (dated 4 January 1973), he said: "Found a title for the novel. Proud Flesh. It fits somehow" (KAP Coll.).

How does it fit? Its applicability to the novel is manifold, just what Humphrey was looking for. First, the term *flesh* on its own points to the novel's emphasis on family, as in "one's own flesh and blood." Another sense of the word, which refers to the "sensual appetites and inclinations as antagonistic to the nobler elements of human nature" (*OED*, sense 10b), applies particularly to Clyde and his perpetual erection, brought on by the blue film that constantly plays in his head, starring his black mistress Shug. Different associations attach to the word *proud*. On the one hand, the term pertains to the Renshaw family, who hold a "high or lofty opinion" of themselves and are "[d]isposed to take an attitude of superiority to and contempt for others" (*OED*, sense 1). There is nothing lofty about Clyde, except ironically, in that he is "swollen with pride"—always ashamed of his swollen flesh, his erection: he is "[s]ensually excited" and "lascivious" (*OED*, sense 7d, 8).

The two words of the title considered together prove remarkably appropriate, for Humphrey surely means to recall one of Shakespeare's sonnets to *his* Dark Lady, one written out of a painful awareness that she was unfaithful to him, as Shug is unfaithful to Clyde. Shakespeare tells his "gentle cheater" that though he wishes his "nobler part" could prevail, his gross body commits treason, responding unreservedly to the mere thought of her name:

> My soul doth tell my body that he may
> Triumph in love; *flesh* stays no farther reason,
> But rising at thy name doth point out thee,
> As his triumphant prize. *Proud* of this pride,
> He is contented thy poor drudge to be,
> To stand in thy affairs, fall by thy side.
> (Sonnet 151; italics mine)

The sonnet brings to mind a contrast between Shakespeare's and Clyde's situations: because of the disruption in routine associated with Edwina's impending death, Clyde's standing flesh has no opportunity to "fall by [his dark mistress's] side."

Proud Flesh as a title has a cruel import as well. Clyde considers severing his offending member with the razor that hangs around his neck: "In an instant, with one swift surgical stroke, he could sever that malignant growth from him and be free. Free of longing, free of guilt, free of her and all her kind. This was for him the one fitting punishment, atonement, and deliverance. Expiation for his sins as a son, a husband, a father, and a white man, and lifelong deliverance from his thralldom to that thing, that growth, which never had been anything but a running sore since it first rose on him, never any pleasure except the pleasure of momentary relief from its incurable ache" (*PF*, 110–11). Clyde's courage deserts him as soon as he applies the blade to his penis, and Dr. Metcalf, the family physician attending Edwina, is summoned to treat the wound. Thus Clyde's proud flesh in one sense produces proud flesh in another, proud flesh upon proud flesh—for the term in its most usual sense means "Overgrown flesh arising from excessive granulation upon, or around the edges of, a healing wound" (*OED*). Thus "When that wound had healed," it left "an itch—an itch on top of an itch" (*PF*, 288).

The title's actual appearance in the text of the novel is in connection with the combative quarrels between the youngest son Kyle and his mother, which eventually lead to his taking flight: "Nothing was ever left unsaid; they flayed each other raw, reopened every old wound, remembered all their unsettled disputes—and all their disputes went unsettled—in all their painful details. For old injuries from each other they both had total recall. Nor was any injury ever afterward repaired. Neither could bring himself to apologize, neither would give the other a chance to apologize. Over the lacerations they inflicted upon each other, tissue formed like proud flesh over festering wounds" (*PF*, 233). When Kyle drives away after a quarrel with Edwina and never returns, that severance brings to the reader's mind Clyde's near one. Kyle's absence produces an unrelievable itch in Edwina, according to Mrs. Bywaters, a neighbor, who likens Edwina's ten children to her ten fingers: "And her . . . like a person with a finger missing. Trying to keep it hidden from sight. And from her own sight. . . . Trying not to notice the itch. They say a missing limb itches. Not the stump, the limb itself. You can feel it in its old place, they say, itching. It's an itch no scratching can ease" (113).[20] Edwina does indeed suffer from the proud flesh that grows upon the severing wound caused by Kyle's running away, and she and Clyde suffer a longing itch (they just have different longings) that finds no relief.

The care with which Humphrey searched for the right title characterizes his

20. Mrs. Bywaters's commentary about a woman's effort to hide the fact that a finger is missing is based upon Humphrey's mother, who lost a finger in a childhood accident. Nell was so adept at "concealing her disfigurement by holding the bad hand in the good one or carrying a handkerchief always crumpled in it," Humphrey writes, "that my father had been married to her for five years before he learned about it—and my father was not an unobservant man" (*FOFH*, 131–32).

work on the novel in general; he wrestled with every aspect of the book's writing, even to the naming of the characters. The Renshaw daughter who plays the most prominent female part in the story was first Hallie, then Sarah ("I must find a better name for her," he wrote), then Sis, Julia, Alice, Lottie, Rhoda ("I rather like Rhoda. But do I like the two R's—Rhoda Renshaw. I've already had one Rachel Ruggles"),[21] then Dixie, Beryl, Ione, and, finally, Amy (Notes, 39, 107). Amy, which means "to love," proved to be an apt selection.

In 1965–66, Humphrey considered various ways of resolving plot lines that in the end he abandoned. In "Notes on the Orestia," he recorded an elaborate scheme whereby Eunice secures a divorce and embarrasses and ruins Clyde in the community (eventually he turned this episode into an imagined one). At one point Humphrey meant to have Clyde switch from Negro labor to a cotton picking machine in order to cure his "sick fear that he is sharing Shug with Negro men" (Notes, 85–86, 87). The following depiction of Clyde's sense of loss, effectively written, was never put in the novel: "The bleakness of it saddened him—he had watched the machines at work and listened to their roar—no more the singing in the fields—no more the swarming life among the shanties—no more the privileged witnes[s] prying into a rich and violent life lived beyond restrictions, in the freedom of the outcast" (Notes, 88). Humphrey entertained notions of all sorts of developments that do not find a place in the final version—having an angry mob of townsmen arriving at the Renshaws', having Shug run away, having Amy utter bits of profound wisdom from her storm cellar instead of only moaning—or putting into her mouth eloquent lamentations "worthy of Jeremiah or Ecclesiastes" (Notes, 49, 101, 107).

For a time, Humphrey considered making the nurse Amy elect not to assist at her mother's sickbed; at another time he thought that perhaps Edwina would refuse to allow Amy to attend her, resulting in Amy's forcibly entering her mother's sickroom. He also struggled with how Amy would encounter her real feelings about her mother: Would she have a sudden shocking perception that she was the opposite of what she thought she was, in the manner of Conrad's Lord Jim, or would she undergo a series of gradual revelations, layer after layer of her "self-coverings" stripping away in the manner of Oedipus Rex? Humphrey carefully worked out the implications of the two methods before deciding on the former. Yet he retained an aspect of the second by providing Dr. Metcalf with the gradual realization of the feelings that Amy protected herself from until the very end (Notes, 96–97, 100).

On into the late sixties and early seventies, Humphrey continued struggling

21. Rachel Ruggles is the wife in "The Fauve" (LH).

with the overall design. In his notebooks, he wrote out various additional plot directions and discussed with himself the advantages and disadvantages of the various alternatives. He made lists of parts to be redone. His method of working was painstaking: he would spend a morning going through his handwritten notebooks, gathering together all the notes on the relationship between pairs of characters, type them up, and then consider the problems that required solutions. The character of Clyde Renshaw, in an agonizing relationship with his black mistress Shug, cost Humphrey nights of sleeplessness and many pages of exploratory note-making. As Clyde's mother is dying, his mind is occupied by two concerns—his overwhelming sexual desire for Shug and his overwhelming guilt because he can think of little else. Humphrey wondered for many pages of his notebooks how to portray Clyde's conflict. He considered having Clyde demand that Dr. Metcalf castrate him, then having Clyde castrate himself, and then having Clyde lop off his penis. This last possibility left Humphrey wondering if a man continues to have sexual desire in the absence of a penis, and so he consulted his friend Harry Grabstald, then an attending surgeon in urology at Memorial Sloan-Kettering Cancer Center in New York City. In the end, Clyde was allowed to keep his member, making only a half-hearted gesture at cutting it off.[22]

Probably the most outlandish proposal Humphrey contemplated for Clyde was death during orgasm, a death which Shug would not at first notice. She would fall asleep, awaken and achieve orgasm with Clyde's corpse and then fall back to sleep herself. In the end she would die of starvation because she could not extricate herself from under Clyde's dead weight. Humphrey wrote to Grabstald on the physical possibility of all this, but even before receiving a reply seemed to come to his senses. He wrote in his notebook: "I've got a taste for the macabre. But it's a taste I ought to fight"—and then a little later: "Lying in bed this morning at 6 a.m. I had a revulsion against the sensationalism of what turns I've been contemplating in these pages."[23]

One of Humphrey's most involved decisions had to do with how to arrange the chapters; for example: "Problem with placement, timing, when, where does the part come that shows Amy in the storm cellar? In relation to the Doc Metcalf part, where and when?" (Notes, 133). Originally the book opened with what ended up as chapter 3. In other cases, as he was getting close to finishing, he returned to previous arrangements—for example to the old way of ending Part 1—with "God damn the English language!"[24] He at first planned on grouping the

22. Humphrey, notebook, entries for 4 April and 17 July 1968, WH Coll., UT.
23. Humphrey, notebook, entry undated, WH Coll., UT.
24. Humphrey, notebook, entries for 18 June 1969 and 22 March 1970, WH Coll., UT.

chapters into five—or possibly six—parts (he at first thought he would depict Amy's self-discovery in a separate section, deciding later, however, to incorporate it into Dr. Metcalf's section). He finally settled on thirty-eight chapters of widely varying lengths, grouped into four parts as follows:

Part 1 The family gathers as Edwina dies
Part 2 Dr. Metcalf's relationship with the family, lasting until two days following the death of Edwina
Part 3 Amy's self-burial and Clyde's confession
Part 4 Lester and Ballard in New York City, still looking for Kyle

Humphrey's handling of point of view in *Proud Flesh* is technically demanding and is the novel's most distinctive feature. Within the overall arrangement listed above, the chapters range back and forth over time, from past to future to present; and though the chapters are consistently in the third person, they vary in point of view. We enter into the frames of reference of family members, blacks living on the place, townspeople, and neighbors. None of the chapters has an omniscient narrator, though some are objective, providing only what an observer can note. Only chapters representing the perspective of a single character explore the inner reality of a character. Shug, Amy, Dr. Metcalf, and Clyde are portrayed in narratives in which they, at least some of the time, are the centers of consciousness.

The chapters often begin in midconversation, as though the reader were going from group to group eavesdropping, a method that derives perhaps from Robert Penn Warren's practice. The reader must "listen" for a while to get the drift, to figure out who is being talked about. Even so, the reader, who is privy to all of the various narratives, can put together one incomplete narrative with another. Thus the reader can form perceptions that are not explicitly provided in any one narrative.

Neither the chapters nor the larger parts can be depended upon to align. The novel is put together spatially and temporally like a cubist painting: the expected parts are mostly there but are arranged in a fragmented manner, defying ordinary expectations. The narrative begins with "outside" knowledge of the Renshaw family.[25] There are brief excursions into the inner life of Clyde, Amy, and later Shug. Dr. Metcalf, who has known the family for many years, provides probing insights, especially into the relationship between Edwina and Amy.

25. Renshaw is not an uncommon name in Clarksville, Texas (see *Red River Recollections* [Clarksville, Tex.: Red River County Historical Society, 1986], 361, 393).

When Part 2 begins, Dr. Metcalf knows very little of what has been going on in Part 1. Then gradually the time sequences in Parts 1 and 2 align, but only temporarily. The novel moves to a long, probing descent into the jangled nervous system of Clyde, during which he and Amy join as confessor and penitent, then concludes with the briefest of chapters, containing the whimper of Lester pleading with Ballard to give up searching New York City for Kyle.

The style of the novel engenders some frustration on the reader's part, probably because its aim is to mirror or repeat the futility the characters experience. The most obvious futility of the novel is the prolonged search for the missing brother Kyle, but it contains futility on many fronts: conflicts unresolved, loose ends still loose. Amy is left buried alive, eating only bread and water. Edwina is thawing out in a public icehouse, on the verge of stinking. Clyde is in agony over what is probably a fruitless love. What his wife will do with him is unknown. Shug imagines Clyde murdering her and her lover, but what might really happen to her we have no idea. Dr. Metcalf is almost insane over his treatment at the hands of the Renshaws, and we wonder if he will recover. The television cameras have moved onto the Renshaw place, which is turned into a circus-like freak show. How long will people continue to come to worship according to the new religion that has grown up around Amy? Only Clifford's fate is sewn up, the widow Shumlin having got him through trickery. Whether resolved or unresolved, nothing works out satisfactorily for any character. The only sign of hope is in the buds of love and acceptance that break out within Clyde and the people gathered around Amy's hiding place. Whether the buds will bloom or not the novel does not tell.

In spite of the care that Humphrey exercised in arranging this complex novel, one feature of the plot particularly strains credence. When all of the townspeople are frantically worried over the whereabouts of Dr. Metcalf, no one thinks he might be at the Renshaws; yet everyone knows that Edwina had been stricken with her deadly illness on the very eve of the doctor's disappearance. Dr. Weinberg, the other doctor in town, has not been called to the Renshaw house. Are we to believe, then, that the sheriff and the other townspeople would think that the mother-loving Renshaws were going to let Edwina die without calling another doctor if Dr. Metcalf were unavailable? Surely the Renshaws, notorious for running roughshod over the rights of anyone when the interests of the clan are at stake, would be suspected of having appropriated Dr. Metcalf. However, they are not.

The novel is placed in time only indirectly. Humphrey nowhere in the text or in his notes on the novel identifies directly the time setting of the main action of *Proud Flesh*. But some details are suggestive. The first piece of temporal evidence is the pin worn by Junya Price, one of Clyde's cotton pickers. The pin proclaims the motto of the civil rights movement prominent in the 1960s: "Black is beautiful" (*PF*, 57). Stokely Carmichael coined the term in 1966, and Martin Luther King Jr. picked it up in the following year. There are additional clues that place the time in the late sixties: "It was not long since the repeal of the old law which made cohabitation between the races a criminal offense punishable by a prison sentence; the unwritten law against it was as much in force as ever" (*PF*, 64). The allusion here is to the landmark case of *Loving v. Virginia:* the United States Supreme Court unanimously struck down Virginia's law against interracial marriage, which signaled the end of antimiscegenation laws in the sixteen states that had them (Texas was one). This decision was handed down on 12 June 1967, so we know that *Proud Flesh* is set "not long" after 1967.[26]

The history of Lois Renshaw's marriage can help in pinning down a more exact date. She married the same man for the second time in March of 1944, intending to divorce him when the child she was pregnant with reached the age of eighteen. In 1950 Lois found herself pregnant again and so had to start counting again the length of time she felt she had to stay married. She sought a divorce when her daughter married, presumably at eighteen—which would put her divorce, granted three months before the action of the novel begins, sometime in 1969.

The final section of the novel, consisting of a single chapter describing the search by Lester and Ballard for Kyle in New York City, takes place at some far distant future time. Although everyone back in Texas, and the reader too, has regarded the effort by Lester and Ballard to find Kyle as merely perfunctory ("Ballard and Lester were not there to succeed but just to do their best" [*PF*, 311]), Ballard has insisted upon continuing the search; and Humphrey has come up with an effective way of establishing the extent of Ballard's doggedness. He depicts Lester listening to the fifth game of the World Series on a portable radio as he slouches from door to door to inquire about Kyle; the game is between two teams that have yet to play each other, the Cleveland Indians and the New York Mets, and the likelihood in 1969 of their playing each other in the near future (Cleveland was at the bottom of the standings in its division, the Mets at the top in theirs) was remote. In 1973, when *Proud Flesh* was published, Cleveland was still at the bottom. And the players whose actions are described in the play-by-play radio account—O'Toole, Hubbard, Lopez, Turley, and so on—are all imaginary; at least no such players were on the rosters of either team during the times

26. Robert J. Sickels, *Race, Marriage, and the Law* (Albuquerque: University of New Mexico Press, 1972), 1, 107, 110.

in question. At the beginning of the twenty-first century, the teams have yet to play each other in the World Series. Are we are to imagine that Lester and Ballard are still searching for Kyle?

Although the organization of the novel is unusual, *Proud Flesh* nonetheless contains many surface features of a traditional southern novel: men hunker beneath a shade tree conversing intermittently about crops while a tar road boils in the distance; they talk in country diction (he is "as mean a man as e'er God wattled a gut in" [*PF*, 204]); they are named Billybob, Billyjim, Elwood, Harlan, Herschell, and Prentiss; the women are named Clovis, Velma, and Edwina; and the novel exhibits a natural violence expected in southern fiction. The Renshaws, the central family in the drama, reveal their violent natures in their looks, and they all look alike: "identical sets of eyes, or rather of shadowed eye-sockets, which are like the muzzles of . . . double-barreled shotguns" (5).

In fact, however, the Renshaws—nine children and a comatose mother—are actually characters in search of a regular southern novel to be in. They are involved in a fictional effort to preserve the fading South but without their author's blessing. Instead, he uses them to demonstrate what the Old South has degenerated into: a few sorry people relentlessly striving to preserve the trifling remnant of a lost way of life. In answer to a citizen of Clarksville who charged Humphrey with writing about the 1940s instead of the 1960s in his depiction of the Renshaws, Humphrey responded: "I tried in every way I could to say that they represent a way of life whose day was ended, that they knew this though they denied it to themselves and fought to disprove it to the world."[27]

Proud Flesh is truly about the end of things—the end of the twisted family at its center, but also of the old southern hierarchy, hanging on now only in this degenerate family. We can gauge the extent to which the Old South has deteriorated in Humphrey's fiction by noting that Captain Wade Hunnicutt and Theron in *Home from the Hill* represent the aristocratic heritage of the Old South and that in *Proud Flesh* Edwina Renshaw and her children play that role. Clearly the Old South is dead and gone; it's with Jeb Stuart in the grave; and although twitches of it continue in people like the Renshaws, the novel seems to say, if they are what the South has come to, then let us let it go. This perspective finds symbolic expression in Edwina Renshaw's hanging on to life when she ought to go ahead and die. Humphrey himself once stated that *Proud Flesh* is about "the South seen as a family—a family in change, as the old guard dies, and fights it[s] last stubborn fight for values that no longer are viable" (Notes, 32).

27. Pat Black to Humphrey, 27 March 1973; Humphrey to Black [April 1973]. These letters are in the possession of Don Emery, Clarksville, Tex.

The novel opens as the Renshaw family matriarch Edwina is dying. Though she utters but one word in the novel, she is at the center of all the action: all the family, save one lost member, have returned home to sit—or squat—in attendance at her death. We sense that something once large is going down, an era ending. Indeed, "[i]n their mother's passing they foresaw the passing of their way of life" (PF, 245). Not unlike Kathleen Ni Houlihan, the old woman who is the personification of Ireland, Edwina is a country, a personification of the Old South: "Her reign had been Victorian in length, her sovereignty absolute, claiming allegiance at birth from all in whose veins a drop of her blood flowed" (13). Edwina's demands upon her offspring are like those expectations traditionally placed upon southerners by their homeland: "Dutifully, unquestioningly, like offering them up to a religious order or to a draft call, her sons and daughters turned over their children to her" (13–14). Edwina, who "knew what made a man," cultivated in her sons and grandsons those characteristics commonly associated with antebellum southern manhood. They should be "braggardly and bold," "headstrong," "touchy," "wild," "vigorous but idle," "chivalrous but predatory," and reckless with guns and horses and, yes, cars, because the Renshaws are—at least in this way—modern (15).

The Renshaws strive to maintain the practices and codes of behavior of the Old South, especially the one having to do with the separation of the races. Although many farmers in East Texas have "switched from cotton to cattle as pickers got harder and harder to find, Clyde Renshaw [who runs the farm for Edwina] stuck with cotton" (PF, 32). Cotton is associated with stability and continuity, for, as the Renshaw's neighbor Alvah Tarrant observes, "what I like about cotton, it ain't perishable" (62). The abandonment of cotton portends the end of civilization, the coming of chaos: "Well, when folks leave off wearing clothes and take to painting theirselves instead, and when cows start giving grape juice, why then maybe I'll switch to soybeans; meanwhile I'll stick to cotton"—which was "good enough for my old daddy and for his old daddy before him," Tarrant declares (60).

In their own way, the Renshaws strive to be aristocratic. They admire the "bounty, lavishness, waste" often associated with the Old South, and they despise "chinchiness" (PF, 10). Even in the end of the novel, when Amy Renshaw has taken to the storm cellar and has become a character on a television freak show, Eulalie, the black kitchen servant descended of slaves owned by the Renshaws, delivers Amy's supper with "silver and a linen napkin in a napkin ring"; her brother Clyde observes, "That was keeping up the fine old plantation traditions under trying circumstances. A napkin ring, for Christ's sake" (290). Although most of the Renshaws like to think that their consanguinity represents the continuity of southern tradition, we see what Humphrey sees: they are barely above the level of white trash; they have elevated themselves, in the social vacuum created by the actual disappearance of the Old South and never replaced by anything substantial, to a privileged place in small-town East Texas society. They assert an aristocratic prerogative, making unusual demands on everyone, and their outrageous demands and requirements are met with dumbfounded acquiescence, partly because the people who know them fear their outrageousness and partly because the townspeople like the idea of having in their town a privileged family, even if its sullen members would clearly elicit respect nowhere else in the world.[28]

The Renshaws preserve southern racial codes with ludicrous and precise innovations. When a distant relative in a nearby county, Conway Renshaw, opens a grocery store in a black neighborhood and becomes known as "Nig" Renshaw, the men of the family feel compelled to erase this blot upon their family escutcheon. In an account reminiscent of the ad hoc social order in "Quail for Mr. Forester," we are told, "What stung was the thought of a Renshaw waiting on Negroes, serving them, taking orders from them, clerking to them, selling them intimate household items for petty cash, hand to hand, retail" (PF, 18). Therefore, the Renshaws drop in on Uncle Conway unannounced, engaging in "highhanded interference": "Shortly afterward he re-emerged in the business world on a more genteel plane, taking on the local franchise for bottling a new brand of strawberry pop" (19)—wholesale being socially superior to any retail.

The other side of the family coin is that the Renshaws will look out for the interests of any family member, especially one who is assaulted by an outsider—as when, after Malcolm Beatty shoots Cousin Claude Renshaw in the head for seducing his wife, the Renshaw men force Beatty to jump from his fourthfloor office window. When the Renshaws commandeer the town's only icehouse for the purpose of preserving their mother's corpse until the lost son can return for the funeral, some of the townspeople acquiesce in their sense of family "solidarity" and overlook the inconvenience (PF, 166).

Kyle, a chink in the family's armor of solidarity, is "a defector, an escapee" (PF, 230). His abrupt departure strains Edwina's heart, initiating the disintegration of the family. He has left because he could no longer bear the sense of isola-

28. In their little East Texas world they get away with asserting that their "strong, old-fashioned family" with a powerful sense of duty is something special. In various ways the Renshaws show that they are "too good for the town" (PF, 249, 25). They consider themselves "of a caste to find ['itinerant millenarian' preachers] not only crazy but common and comical." They look down on revivals and "the brimstone creeds of the religious underprivileged" (300).

tion from others that his corrupt family cultivated. Because they "run down their neighbors" and "everybody outside the pale," Kyle declares that they suffer from xenophobia (231). Clyde Renshaw, the son whose consciousness dominates the novel, also longs for escape but remains a covert "internal emigre," still in the family but secretly rebelling against all it stands for, especially its racism (230). In fact, "Clyde liked only Negroes" and "longed to be one of them" (32, 33). Not only does he think "of nothing but what he called poontang from waking to sleeping," but he secretly has his own black mistress, Shug (32). Further, he projects his racial obsession outward. Clyde thinks he knows why Ballard and Lester, who have gone to New York to find Kyle, will never find him: they will not think to look in Harlem; but because Clyde sees Kyle as a kindred spirit, he is sure that Harlem is exactly where Kyle is (312–13).

Because Clyde remains at home he is potentially a more serious threat to his family's respectability than Kyle in his defection. Alluding to Conrad's *Heart of Darkness,* the narrative voice tells us that "Clyde had explored the jungle in the depths of his own soul. . . . Those thick lips, pouting with passion, those heavy-lidded liquid eyes, the white shading off into ivory, those broad nostrils dilated with desire, firm bodies smooth as onyx, redolent either of provocative perfume or the quick musk of their responsive glands—white women, after a man had known the other, were as dry and insipid as the white meat of chicken compared with the dark juiciness of the thigh" (*PF,* 313). Clyde imagines that Kyle has married a black woman because it is what part of Clyde really wants to do, even though the other part resists being known by others as well as by himself as a "niggerlover" (38).[29] And so Clyde leads a double life, outwardly married to a white wife, secretly attached to a black lover. He establishes Shug in a cottage behind the Renshaw house and arranges for a safe husband, an old drunk named Jug, putting her, he would hope, off limits to others. Shug does what she can to destroy the appearance of respectability that Clyde has manufactured, breaking the windows, pulling the gate off its hinges, littering the front yard—actions meant as an affront to the hypocrisy of Clyde's "respectability." As the Renshaw saga ends, Clyde is making some headway against his family's pretense; he admits to himself that he loves Shug and that his "heart's desire" and the "desires of the flesh" are one and the same and thus resolves the painful inner conflict that has plagued his heart and mind (110). Edwina's death eases the resolution of the dichotomy between thinking and feeling, leading to freedom.

Edwina's death has a less salubrious effect on the more conventional Ren-

---

29. In one of the notebooks, Humphrey contemplated having Kyle return to Clarksville with a black wife (WH Coll., UT).

shaws. Amy remarks that her mother's impending death "seemed to . . . signal the family's breakup" (*PF*, 85). Dr. Metcalf confirms this assessment when he says, "In their mother's passing they foresaw the passing of their way of life" (245). In their view, her death signals a general trend; the "waywardness of today's youth" is owing to "the decline of families with a strong, old-fashioned family sense" (249). Thus it is that young men on a bus will not relinquish their seats to ladies; that there is a general "disappearance of decency, manners"; that youths wear long hair and use drugs; and that unmarried girls give birth (249). The Renshaw sisters are alarmed at the decline in their own children: "Comparing notes, each found that her sisters had also begun, coincident with Ma's coming down sick, to detect in their children signs of the disobedience, the ingratitude, the independence, the disrespect for age and authority and tradition so prevalent among the younger generation" (249).

In *Proud Flesh* Humphrey is clearly seeking higher ground for a resolution on the issue of the southern tradition. A sense of hopefulness emerges when the family's disintegration gives rise to reconciliations that embrace a moral dimension, hinting at a better future. Clyde's—and possibly Kyle's—breaking through racial barriers finds parallels in society at large. The town's united intent to bring the kidnappers of Dr. Metcalf to "justice" produces "the first racially integrated lynch mob in the town's history" (*PF*, 204). And whereas at the beginning of the novel we are told that black people still adhere to the old practice of going to the balcony of the cinema, even though the law no longer requires racial separation, at the end, when many are gathered around the storm shelter where Amy has buried herself, the old racially based seating pattern has dissolved:

[I]t was hard for the colored people to know where their place was. Lacking directions, they disposed themselves throughout the audience; and as everyone, black and white alike, took his seat as softly as though coming late to church, their manner was not noticeably more self-apologetic than the others'. Remarkably, no one challenged them, despite the fact that among the whites were many from the class ordinarily the most sensitive to the nearness of a Negro. Perhaps it was the lack of seats for all equally that made the difference. Under a roof, at a table or a counter or in a pew, or on a public conveyance, a man might feel he had to be more particular about whom he let sit beside him than beneath the sky and on the ground. It was not the time or the place to raise a fuss. There was a feeling that the sorrowing woman underground had no race or color; she belonged equally to all. (292–93)

The novel clearly endorses the reconciliation of the races. Carefully drawn parallels between black and white characters contribute to this effect. Clyde's raping of Shug is carried out in the same low-key manner as the Renshaws' kidnapping of Dr. Metcalf. Shug's narrative records that "He gave her no commands; there was no need for him to" and "She made no protest; it would have done no good" (*PF*, 153). Similarly, Dr. Metcalf remains "prisoner" of the Renshaws, not because they threaten him, but because he anticipates their unspoken threats. He refrains from telephoning his wife to tell her where he is, for example, because, as he tells the sheriff later, "I didn't know what they might do to her to keep her from telling you" (224). Black and white alike are joined in their susceptibility to the quiet intimidation of the Renshaws.

A parallel between Shug and Eunice, Clyde's wife, accentuates the congruity of black and white experience. The narratives belonging to these women record similar experiences at the hands of Clyde. After he rolls off Shug on the day he picks her up after school, "She could not bring herself to look down at herself. She had sensed before it happened that she was about to be taken from her family, her friends, her own people—now she learned that she had been taken from herself. She did not belong to herself any more" (*PF*, 154). The same reaction occurs in Eunice when Clyde rapes her. When they had stopped sleeping together as man and wife, Eunice was pleased: "her body was restored to her ownership" (128). She then begins to attend to herself, awakening every loveliness in her capacity by assiduous cosmetic attention: "never had she seen such loveliness, and it was all her own" (129). In her mind she is "Sleeping Beauty with no fear of being wakened by the kiss of any Prince Charming" (129). When Clyde rapes his wife on the first night of his mother's illness, Eunice loses possession of the self that she has created; she feels "the indignation of an artist whose work had been vandalized" (129). The significant similarity between Shug's and Eunice's experiences is not that they are both raped by the same man but that each feels strongly the loss of her self as a result of the rape. The inner experiences of black and white are the same.[30]

To be sure, the purpose of the parallels is to blur distinctions, but Humphrey also manages to accomplish the same effect by creating sharp contrasts that dissolve before our eyes, cancel each other out, or terminate in resolution. Like a Zen prophet, Humphrey observes the oneness of opposites: he embraces all. Black cotton pickers turn white before our eyes: "They inch along the rows more

---

30. Shug and Kyle have similar responses to violence. After the rape, Shug "wanted never to go home again" (*PF*, 154); Kyle leaves home in the face of Edwina's violent emotional storms and never returns.

and more slowly as their sacks swell. Bit by bit black hands and arms, sticky with sweat, turn white from the lint that fills the air, clogs the nostrils, chokes the breath, sprouts white moustaches on sweaty lips, turns hair and eye-brows griz-zled; and soon all of them, bent as they are, look hoary and stooped with age" (*PF*, 29–30). Clyde undergoes "a black-and-white paradox of the mind," longing to change races (38). When the black field workers come in the spring to chop cotton, Clyde undergoes "a quickening of self-renewal, like the surge of sap in the trees" (37). He envies the blacks their natural ability to reject respectability and stability, conditions unavailable to them anyway. Clyde wonders, "How could the master envy the slave, and envy him precisely his freedom?" (38). But he already knows the answer to this paradox, for he understands that they alone, "the despised, the outcast, were free. The prisoners of life were their lords and masters, hostages to their possessions and their reputations" (37).

In the area of characterization, Humphrey fills the novel with scenes and im-ages of contradiction and opposition. These scenes and images introduce uncer-tainty about the characters' ability to know truth and reality. An example of such an oppositional scene occurs when Edwina is in travail during the birth of Kyle and Dr. Metcalf has requested Amy's assistance:

> When she saw her eldest child at the foot of her bed Edwina Renshaw shot her such a hostile glare that all the women—Dr. Metcalf was too occupied just then to notice—snapped around to look. Gasping with pain and un-able to speak, Edwina tried to rise, pushing back against the headboard, clutching for the bedclothes to cover herself with, pointing a finger at arm's length at Amy. She gave a growl, then in a voice that must surely have carried to her men down around the pear tree, she yelled, "You get out of here! Get her out of here! *Get her out of here!*" (*PF*, 162)

And then when Amy is so wounded by her mother's response as to become bed-ridden herself, the mother-daughter roles reverse:

> There was [Amy] in her sickroom with Dr. Metcalf attending her when the door opened and there, with her baby in her arms, stood Ma. Amy had shot her a glare, had pushed back against the headboard, had clutched at the bedclothes to hide herself. She had almost yelled, "You get out of here!" (170)

Oppositions and contradictions manifest themselves within characters as well. Clifford, the oldest son, is like a woman (see 31); Hazel is a mannish woman, who is rich but lives—and makes her family live—as though she has nothing (see 52), and who "found more enjoyment in being wronged than she found in having her wrongs righted" (53). In her job, Amy sleeps while the world is awake, and she works while the world sleeps (158). Amy, the "one with the least to reproach herself with, . . . would be the one to reproach herself the most" (212). And Amy is born to the one mother who will not appreciate her (168). Clyde jokes, "Poor Ma was dead from hardening of the arteries and he was dying of arteries of the hardening" (290). Dr. Metcalf "had been forced to do [the Renshaws'] bidding without their having to bid him do it" (243), and when he makes his escape, he observes: "The mad intensity inside made the quiet reality outside seem unreal" (278, 279).

The novel's imagery adds a sense of mystery and insubstantiality to the relationships among its many opposites and contradictions. As three Renshaw men crouch in the shade of a pear tree in the opening scene, "their sweat-soaked clothes" make them "look like survivors from a capsized boat just washed ashore" (*PF*, 4–5). Yet before long "[t]he shadow of the pear tree" is no longer an island but "a drying water stain" (70). As more men, neighbors, join the Renshaws, the "shade of the pear tree" becomes "a pond" (25). When Dr. Metcalf leaves the pond, "he wades through the shimmering heat waves on the far shore of which stands the house" (6). This shifting of elements produces an eerie uncertainty about reality and the relationship among the elements of the world.

The first chapter told from the daughter Amy's perspective (Part 1, chapter 11) begins to fathom the mystery of the relationship among contraries. "What if the truth about everything was just the reverse of what it seemed to be, of what we were taught was true?" she wonders—and then she introduces the image of the mirror, which is central to the issue: "The one thing a human being never sees is his own face. When he looks in the mirror what he sees is exactly the reverse of what the world sees. Life was full of evidence that things were just the reverse of what they appeared to be" (*PF*, 174). Sometimes Amy feels that she has "stepped through the looking-glass and seen the other side of things" (175), shattering the glass and destroying the illusion that appearance is reality. As a child, Amy had cupped her hands to her eyes so that she could see through a pane of glass, which has been turned into a mirror by the darkness of a sudden storm. What she saw was a horse struck by lightning; the instant of death when "the horse hung Pegasuslike in the burst of light against the livid sky" produces, in memory, "a sense of deepest shame" (91). This episode is an earnest of Amy's will and capacity to see what light might be contained in the depths of her darkness.

Amy wonders if there is a distinction between the innocent and the guilty—or if the distinction is so slight that "a single word would shatter it forever" (*PF*, 176). Clyde puts the relationship between such opposites another way: "heads and tails: opposites, but not separated from each other by very much" (307). Dr. Metcalf offers yet another analogy as he seeks himself to fathom Amy, to comprehend how the loving, devoted daughter can also desire her mother's death. The vengeful Amy, full of hatred, "was a reverse image," he opines; "perhaps it was the one from which the first had come—as in photography the print comes from the negative" (258). If knowing one thing, being one thing, is dangerously close to its opposite, the entire enterprise of probing the human heart, of the individual attempting to know himself, becomes treacherous. Yet characters' searching for their true hearts is a concept central to Humphrey's novel. The very fact that Edwina is dying as the result of a heart attack and the hearts of her children are affected by this event symbolically places the human heart at center stage.

Proud Flesh is replete with references to the hearts of its characters. Early on, the moan of the cotton pickers in the Renshaw fields is "like the concerted groan of all the separate aches crying in [Clyde's] heart" (*PF*, 42). The love that Clyde feels for his dying mother shares disconcertingly a space in his heart with his persistent longing for Shug: his "grief" is not pure, then, but "foully adulterated in that slop-pail he called his heart" (42). The link between the physical and emotional illnesses of the heart is established in Clyde's second chapter (Part 1, chapter 8): "The trouble with him—all this obsession with sex, this mad urge to unmask himself—was, he was not well. Not well at all. He had not been for some time. Today was just more of the same, aggravated by worry over Ma and shame for the unseemliness of feeling what he felt while Ma was sick. He was not well. A constricted feeling in his chest, centering around the heart, making breathing difficult. Ma's trouble was heart, and those things could be hereditary" (65).

The achings of the human heart grow as the novel progresses, until in the end Amy's heart groans not only with the ache of her own guilt for having, she believes, killed her mother but also with the aches of thousands of people who venture to her living tomb to open up their hearts to her, then join together to produce a world-filling moan in sympathy and accord with her: "ooooooo-OOOOOOH. Like a wind over some desolate waste it rose to a howl, a shriek: aaaaaaaAAAA-EEEEEEEH" (*PF*, 318).

Amy and Clyde, the only two characters whose hearts are explored in depth in the novel, are unplumbed as the action begins. Amy is destined to face the darkest shadow in her divided self. She depends upon authority to determine what she knows about anything, including herself and what she feels. Just as she had once been bewildered by a wrong answer in the back of her mathematics book, she is, as an adult, perplexed in the extreme when she looks into her mother's eyes and does not find the reassuring love she needs: "What she saw was: nothing. What she saw was perplexity to equal her own. What she saw was a mirror image of her own distress" (*PF*, 171).[31] Amy's recognition of her mother's fear and revulsion comes within a hair's breadth of providing insight into her own hatred of her mother. In spite of Amy's efforts to suppress it, this hatred nonetheless demonstrates itself. Though Amy, who is a registered nurse, appears as attentive at her mother's bedside as any devoted daughter could be, Amy repeatedly—but without self-awareness—withholds medication required to stabilize her mother's heart. Before Dr. Metcalf arrives in the dead of the night, Amy has pulled a sheet over her mother's face, after failing to administer the ampule of adrenalin that the doctor had left. Conducting herself in the "indigo obscurity" of the sick room, Amy is oblivious of her inadequacy.

When she realizes what she has done, Amy immerds herself in cow dung, even cramming it Yahoo-like down her throat, her self-punishment for nearly killing her mother. She is close to self-knowledge at this point, knocking on the door of her heart's chamber. But then she backs away. The next day she returns to duty, acting as though nothing has happened—and proceeds to withhold medicine once again, and yet another time hands the doctor the wrong medicine, an act which would have been fatal had he not detected the "error."

Ultimately, some part of Amy realizes what another part of her denies. In her most crucial scene, just as Dr. Metcalf is about to give Edwina a shot and as Amy is rubbing alcohol on her arm, Edwina suddenly awakens and "A look . . . passed between them" (*PF*, 264). "The look on [Edwina's] face declared more loudly than words, 'You have murdered me.'" Dr. Metcalf glances at the look on Amy's face: "He looked away barely in time to keep from being turned to stone by that face. The last thing she saw, it did just that to Edwina Renshaw" (265). This passage clearly lends a Medusa-like quality to Amy. Exactly what Dr. Metcalf is witness to is uncertain, and that was Humphrey's intention, according to his notes on the novel: "Doc sees something but it's mysterious to him and to us" (Notes, 95).

Yet the image of the mirror suggests the nature of Amy's new knowledge: in the moment of death Edwina's face is a "mirror . . . held up" to her daughter (*PF*, 265). What Amy thereby is forced to see is that she has indeed hated her mother and has indeed wished her dead: she steps through the looking glass and shatters her illusion of being a devoted daughter. Dr. Metcalf sees, too. His insight cuts through the distinction between love and hatred; he comprehends the

---

31. Cf. the mirror image discussed on pp. 98–99, 242, 247, 248, and 251*n*.

coin of truth turned on its edge: "As in that most dread disease of the body, an organ enlarged itself through gross reproduction of its own cells and became malignant. This was what had happened to Amy's love for her mother: through overenlargement of itself that vital organ had become malignant" (275). Because Edwina had always rejected the love offered by the daughter whose name means "to love," Amy's love had to grow more and more to overcome the rejection, and thus it turned malevolent. Amy had thought the unwanted emotional growths could be managed: "Ah, yes, she knew what bitterness was, though praised to her face so often for her sweetness. Hers, too, was a human heart, and in that poor soil grew more weeds than flowers. The weeds of resentment and jealousy, the weed—most noxious of them all—of self-righteous selflessness. She had tried simply to be a good gardener and root them out while they were still only seedlings" (170). Amy, then, is horrified when she suddenly gazes into her heart of darkness and recognizes that the weeds have taken over.

Humphrey's notes on the novel suggest an apt parallel for Amy's self-discovery—Conrad's *Lord Jim:* "Jim . . . knows that should a dangerous situation ever arise—. . . lives in hopes that one will—he will behave heroically, and . . . in his first test is a coward" (Notes, 55). Likewise, Amy is a "woman who has spent her life in service to an ideal, her love of her Mother, and to an image of herself as a dutiful and self-sacrificing daughter, and must suddenly see herself as a matricide" (Notes, 55). Then Humphrey quotes a paragraph from Dorothy Van Ghent's famous essay on *Lord Jim:*

> Jim's shocking encounter with himself at the moment of his jump from the *Patna* is a model of those moments when the destiny each person carries within him, the destiny fully molded in the unconscious will, lifts its blind head from the dark, drinks blood, and speaks. There is no unclarity in the shape that Jim saw at that moment: he had jumped—it is as simple as that. But because the event is a paradigm of the encounters of the conscious personality with the stranger within, the stranger who is the very self of the self, the significance of Jim's story is our own significance, contained in the enigmatic relationship between the conscious will and the fatality of our acts. Jim's discovery of himself was a frightful one, and his solution of the problem of "how to be" was to exorcise the stranger in a fierce, long, concentrated effort to be his opposite. The oracle spoke early to Oedipus, too, in his youth in Corinth, telling him who he was—the man destined to transgress most horribly the saving code of kinship relations—and Oedipus' solution of the problem of "how to be" was the same

as Jim's: he fled in the opposite direction from his destiny and ran straight into it.[32]

These observations "touch me deeply," says Humphrey; and indeed the ideas inform his presentation of the character of Amy (Notes, 56).

Amy's psychology provides a real test of the novel's scaffolding. Her excesses strain credulity. She is practically grotesque. Knowing that her mother always feared being buried alive, Amy expiates her own guilt by burying *herself* alive in an underground storm shelter. Although this *seems* an insane act, Humphrey maintains that she is not insane: "When she enters the storm cellar with instructions that she is never coming out again, that minimal food is to be left outside at dark for her, she is going not in madness but in self-imposed penance" (Notes, 44). Humphrey has Jug provide his version of Amy's words to him: "She say she know her own soul better than any preacher and her own mind better than any psychiatrist. She say she is where she belongs and where she wants to be" (*PF*, 306).[33] However much logic and clear planning support her retreat from life, it remains that Amy's life is perverted in the extreme by an exaggerated guilt over her hatred of a mother who, from all evidence, is altogether deserving of that hatred. Still, Amy is a brittle and limited character with whom it is difficult to sympathize or identify. She is not really adequate to carry the moral weight of the novel's conclusion.

But Humphrey persists in assigning Amy this role, by extending his theme of contradiction and opposition to the very end. She unexpectedly, ludicrously, finds herself trapped in her narrow cell, listening to thousands of people who come from all over the United States and foreign countries to whisper their unspeakable sins to her through the air vent in the storm cellar. Clyde pictures his sister facing what lay moldering in the cellars of human hearts: "Listening to confessions had always been Amy's second career, and he could see her, out of a sense of duty—misplaced—and out of her own sense of guilt—mistaken—taking

32. Dorothy Van Ghent, *The English Novel: Form and Function* (New York: Rinehart, 1953), 229, quoted by Humphrey (Notes, 56–57).

33. When a local preacher tries to coax Amy out of her tomb, Humphrey takes a rare misstep. "The preacher's text was from Ecclesiasticus," writes Humphrey, and then the preacher sermonizes to Amy about "the deadly sin of idolatry" (*PF*, 294). Only a Roman Catholic or an Episcopal priest would be likely to quote from Ecclesiasticus, or Sirach, as it is sometimes called, for the apocrypha are not recognized by Protestant sects, one of which the "preacher" haranguing Amy obviously represents. Humphrey, who attended the Episcopal Church as a boy, would naturally know Ecclesiasticus, but one would expect him to know that the Protestants in Clarksville paid no attention to those "Catholic" texts. See p. 227 for Humphrey's searching in Ecclesiasticus for a title for this novel.

her hands from her ears and forcing herself to listen . . . in her horror and disgust" (*PF*, 304). Unable to forgive herself, Amy ironically becomes confessor to many suffering souls who then carry on with their lives, keeping their sins but feeling better for having confessed. A new religion for the times springs up spontaneously around Amy's burial place—the inverse of Christianity: "confession without absolution" ("Their sins were the only thing that made them interesting to themselves. Absolve them and they would have nothing left"); "a god who instead of rising preferred the tomb"; a god who "instead of offering her followers hope and life offered them despair and death" (315). In his "Notes on the Orestia" Humphrey remarked, "I want hers to be a very un-Christian lament. She has lost her God and knows there is no one to pray to" (49). Clyde embodies Humphrey's view: a strong desire prevails for a religion without hope and all the fretfulness associated with hope.

The notes Humphrey made while he was writing this section of the novel strongly suggest that he intended a critique of those off-brand versions of Christianity designed especially for the down and out. Amy will not insult people by telling them that their troubles are blessings in disguise: "She won't tell you to look for no silver lining. She just somebody like you suffering more than you are. And ready to take yours along with her own" (Notes, 50–51). *Proud Flesh* ends with Amy still listening, horrified. The people keep coming.

Clyde, like Amy, has a self-encounter, but his is a happier experience of self-discovery—though he is nonetheless staggered by it. Like Oedipus, he "rounds a corner and collides with himself going full tilt in the opposite direction" (*PF*, 316). Like Amy, Clyde, too, looks into a mirror—a television camera. On television he sees a tramp who, like Kyle, has exiled himself from home; Clyde sees himself as this very tramp coming home for the first time in years, confessing his life's history down the pipe to Amy, "hoping by telling it to her to gain readmittance not just to his own family but to the human family, if only as the poorest of poor relations" (308). After a commercial—the rites surrounding Amy's ensconcement are being telecast on Lone Star Television (Channel 6)—Clyde takes another step toward wholeness: he encounters what he imagines to be himself confessing to Amy that "he loved a nigger," not "Just that I go to bed with her," but "I love her" (317). Because Clyde is bound by the long-held taboos of his southern family, he understands his confession to have the magnitude of the other confessions going down the pipe to Amy: his is a great sin.[34] Clyde's sense

34. "Lechery, adultery, fornication, even miscegenation were things that held no terror for Clyde. They could be sniggered at. Everybody did it: what terrified, what appalled Clyde was what he now was forced to admit, to give that name to, was that he loved a nigger, and as if that wasn't bad enough, that the one loved did not love him but was a tart who would bed down with anything male, preferably black," Humphrey commented (Notes, 137–38).

of sin puts his confession in the category with Huck Finn's decision to be a sinner and not turn in the runaway slave Jim: "All right, then, I'll go to hell."[35] Both Huck and Clyde transcend the southern social prohibition against interracial love, though both are bound to feel that they have transgressed.

Amy and Clyde, then, are enabled to join a larger humanity because they possess an ability to see beyond the surface reflection encountered in a mirror, to probe deeply, taking into account the reversals involved in exploring the self. The other members of the Renshaw family are unable to escape the superficial family traditions: "In observance of custom the house was being darkened, the light of day shut out. They were rubbing soap on the mirrors and shrouding all other reflecting surfaces with bedsheets, for according to the old superstition, whoever sees himself in a house where death is will die before the year is out" (PF, 211). Typically, of course, the Renshaws protect themselves from the dangerous business of encountering their own selves.

Lois, Amy's sister, represents the family's general unwillingness to aspire to personal insight. When Amy has unwittingly found a larger significance, her sister Lois vainly tries to pull her back to the confines of the family and its myth of solidarity. Speaking into the storm pipe, she pleads with Amy to "come out and rejoin your family who love you" (PF, 304). Making her speech as part of a show for television, Lois allows—she is unaware of how wrong she is—that she knows how Amy feels: "Like you just never want to set eyes on another human face, knowing you'll never see Ma's dear loving face again" (304). These "unctuous phrases" of Lois's are an attempt to perpetuate the myth of the family, while Amy now knows full well that her own devotion to her family has been "hypocritical"; she has lived nearly "a lifetime of . . . self-delusion" (Notes, 127). Members of her family are actually striving to counter insight.

In 1965, while Humphrey was at an impasse, unable to figure out how to go on with Proud Flesh, he happened to read one of the Oresteian plays; he then read others and found in them not only a way to end his novel but also the means by which to give it additional depth of meaning. Humphrey discovered his tale of the Renshaws to be a modern version of the story of the House of Atreus; seen in this light, Proud Flesh joins the fictional family of Dostoyevsky's The Brothers Karamazov, Hardy's The Mayor of Casterbridge, and Joyce's Ulysses—even if as a poor relation. Probably inspired most by Hardy, whose novels show the pervasive influence of Greek tragedy, Humphrey has hung his East Texas story on a well-known classical frame provided by Aeschylus's The Libation Bearers and

35. Samuel L. Clemens, Adventures of Huckleberry Finn (San Francisco: Chandler, 1962), 272.

Sophocles's *Electra*, drawing upon them more thoroughly than O'Neill did in *Mourning Becomes Electra* and more than Eliot did in *The Family Reunion*.

In his "Notes on the Orestia," begun in June 1965, Humphrey remarks that "[t]he other day I began idly reading The Orestia [of Aeschylus]. What I found led me on to read the plays of Sophocles and Euripides relating to the house of Atreus. It has been an almost uncanny experience. I had previously read only The Agamemnon; now I find that without knowing it I have been retelling, in modern times, the story of the Orestia. What is more, this reading has suggested ways out of the impasse I have been in with my book" (Notes, 2). Once he had realized his story's kinship with ancient Greek drama, Humphrey worked at expanding the connections and thereby gave weight to his endeavor: "the book is becoming a lot more serious"—and then he added, "I wanted to be somber again, and I see I am" (Notes, 44).

It appears that Humphrey also depended upon Eliot's *The Family Reunion*. Early on in his "Notes on the Orestia," he jots the following note: "T. S. Eliot's The Family Reunion is a retelling of The Orestia. I ought to look into it" (27). Although he leaves no record of his response to *The Family Reunion*, he must have read it and have been as astonished as when he read Aeschylus, because in some ways it resembles *Proud Flesh* more than *The Libation Bearers* does. Since Humphrey did not like Eliot, mainly because of Eliot's unfair and wrongheaded views on the works of Thomas Hardy, it is no surprise that he would refrain from acknowledging that he borrowed from a poet he considered an intolerable Christian prude.[36]

The basic situation in Eliot's play is that an elderly woman with a bad heart dies surrounded by her family except for one son who has left. She is attended by the longtime family physician. That basically is what we have in *Proud Flesh*. Further, the mother in *The Family Reunion* is named Amy, the name that Humphrey ultimately gave to the eldest daughter in the Renshaw family. In the play the oldest son, Harry, does not know if he has pushed his wife overboard and drowned her: "Perhaps I only dreamt I pushed her." Harry's uncle Charles says, "I suspect it is simply that the wish to get rid of her / Makes him believe he did." Another relative suggests "that Cousin Amy—I almost believe it—had killed her by willing. Doesn't that sound awful?"[37] The suggestion that a buried resentment

---

36. See especially T. S. Eliot, *After Strange Gods* (London: Faber & Faber, 1934), 54–58, and Martin Seymour-Smith, *Hardy* (New York: St. Martin's Press, 1994), 393.

37. T. S. Eliot, *The Complete Poems and Plays, 1909–1950* (1952; reprint, New York: Harcourt, Brace & World, 1962), 275, 237, 245. O'Neill's *Mourning Becomes Electra* also contains a self-accusing character: Orin accuses himself of murdering his mother even though she actually had committed suicide.

might give rise to the assumption of guilt for murder is, as we have seen, an important element in Humphrey's portrayal of Amy Renshaw, and this feature, in so far as the general concept can be traced to a literary source, stems from Eliot's play, not from Aeschylus's.[38]

Still, the main thrust of Humphrey's mid-1960s efforts on *Proud Flesh* was to strengthen the parallels to Aeschylus beyond those in his earlier drafts of the novel. Humphrey was not, however, in the least concerned about the events of *The Agamemnon*, Clytemnestra's motives for the murder of her husband, or any of the gory details of cannibalism that are its background. His main interest, rather, was in a modern telling of *The Libation Bearers*. In both the ancient play and the modern novel, family members find that family traditions and practices must be thrown over if there is to be any escape from life-denying limitations.

Humphrey's Agamemnon (Alonzo Renshaw) has been "dust and a handful of anecdotes for twenty years" (*PF*, 15).[39] Strictly speaking, his Clytemnestra did not murder him; he died of illness. Yet Humphrey, in his notes, holds that "My Agamemnon was ritually murdered by his wife" (Notes, 6). The novel only hints at this, however: "Tame as a tabby cat with his wife, with all the rest of the world he had been quarrelsome, self-opinionated, abrasive"; in their wedding picture he looks "like the consort to a queen" (PF, 15, 16). The strongest evidence of her total dominance, though, is in her superior role as a parent: "People were in-clined to feel that Alonzo Renshaw had been dead even longer than he had. In conversation his widow managed to convey the impression that she had raised, if not conceived, her ten children single-handed. And it was true that even during her husband's lifetime she had been both mother and father to their boys, leaving him to the girls" (17). Some of the mannish superiority that Aeschylus's Clytem-nestra exerts over her husband is expressed when Alonzo is "Unremembered now in the lineaments of his offspring, in all of whom down to the fourth genera-tion [Edwina's] pattern was distinct and assertive" (16). Edwina's features are as assertive as her character was in all its aspects; she is, like Clytemnestra, "the

38. Eliot's family's discussion of the "undoubtedly decadent" "younger generation" (226) might just represent another way in which *The Family Reunion* added to Humphrey's portrayal of the Ren-shaw family. When the Renshaw sisters bemoan the "waywardness of today's youth," they remind us of the Monchensey family as they lament that

The younger generation

Are not what we were. Haven't the stamina.

Haven't the sense of responsibility. (Eliot, 227)

39. Sophocles's Electra says that her father "is earth and nothing, / poorly lying" (*Electra*, in *Sophocles II*, ed. and trans. David Grene [1954; reprint, Chicago: University of Chicago Press, 1957], 135).

most brazen / of all of womankind."[40] Thus, in a sense, Humphrey's Agamemnon has a quietus put on him less dramatically but no less effectively than his ancient Greek counterpart.

Although Edwina never remarries, Humphrey gives her an ersatz Aegisthus, her eldest son, Clifford, "who rules the house along with his mother—who remembers his father with hatred for his violation of his mother" (Notes, 5–6). In fact, he had been an accomplice in his mother's displacement of Alonzo from his role as husband. After his mother had gone through the agony of giving birth to her tenth child, Kyle, Clifford had threatened to kill his father if he ever touched his mother again: "If she had died I would have killed you. Now leave her alone. Don't ever go near her again. She's taken all of that off of you she should have to" (PF, 102). Kyle is the last child. But though Clifford "rules the house along with his mother," the emphasis needs to be on the phrase "along with," for he goes "along with" whatever she says (31). Like his Greek counterpart, Clifford is not a man inside but an "old maid" (31).

As Proud Flesh begins, Edwina-Clytemnestra is dying of a heart attack; the medical evidence—"a certain bluish swelling around the bases of her fingernails"—confirms this (PF, 89). Humphrey's parallel to The Libation Bearers, however, implies another reason for her death—that his Orestes and his Electra cooperatively assault Edwina's life. These expectations are born out. His Orestes is Kyle, who, wearying of arguments with his mother, leaves home. Instead of coming home and killing his mother, as the Aeschylean Orestes does, Kyle kills his mother by staying away. His going away in the first place severely wounds Edwina's heart, but his continued absence after her attack is, according to the loyal children, a death blow.[41] Humphrey's Electra, Amy, attends to her mother's death more directly, and so he associates her with the image of the snake, which Aeschylus connects with Orestes. In The Libation Bearers, he "turn[s] snake to

40. Sophocles, 143. Concern over female dominance also occurs in Euripides's Electra: "O what perversion when the woman in the house / stands out as master, not the man" (Electra, trans. Emily Townsend Verneule, in Euripides V, ed. David Grene [Chicago: University of Chicago Press, 1959], 49).

41. Humphrey had trouble figuring out whether he wanted Kyle to return home or not. One reason he decided not to bring him home was that Kyle "is less important in himself than he is as a mirror for his various sisters and brothers (particularly [Amy]) to see themselves in. . . . A mirror must not come alive" (Notes, 8). Thus Humphrey put a good deal of emphasis on the chorus of townsmen speculating on whether Kyle is dead or alive, even whether he might be in the penitentiary, or maybe that "he's risen to think he's too good for his folks, for his old hometown" (PF, 24, 25). The chorus makes it clear that Kyle's brothers are very much embarrassed about the disappearance of their brother and are closed-mouthed about him when others are so indiscreet as to ask about him.

murder" his mother; in *Proud Flesh* Dr. Metcalf opines that Amy, who is alone with her mother in the moment of death, is "a snake in disguise."[42]

Humphrey's portrayal of Amy depends upon Sophocles's Electra. In his "Notes on the Orestia" he remarked that "the correspondences between Sophocles' Electra and my [Amy] Renshaw are uncanny. It is as if I had read the play before and patterned my book on it" (Notes, 15).[43] The uncanniness extends even to the seemingly purposeful departures from Sophocles. One of the most prominent features of this classical Electra, from the outset of the play, is her "never ceas[ing] . . . dirges and sorrowful laments."[44] In striking contrast, Humphrey's Amy, while her sisters engage in extensive lamentations over the condition of their mother, "could not utter a sound—not one monosyllable of woe" (*PF*, 85). Sophocles's Electra has as companion to her sorrows the "Itys, Itys" of the nightingale, the "bird of crazy sorrow."[45] Though Humphrey supplies his own bird of sorrow, the "plaint of the mourning dove" never has any association with Amy (*PF*, 244–45). The classical Electra complains about the limitations of her wardrobe and the unsatisfactory food: "Like some dishonored foreigner, / I tenant my father's house in these ugly rags / and stand at a scanty table."[46] Again, reversing this portrayal, Humphrey allows Amy to indulge her expensive taste in attire at Neiman Marcus, and he supplies a sumptuous banquet, including baked ham with cloves and pineapple rings, roast beef, leg of mutton, an extensive assortment of vegetables and desserts, for her and the entire family (*PF*, 116; Notes, 18). Whereas Electra suffers mainly from seeing Aegisthus's occupying the throne that had belonged to her father, Amy has no thought of her father but suffers lamentably at the hands of her abusing mother. Finally, Amy is not well-enough acquainted with her feelings to feel full of sorrow until the end, when she undertakes her perpetual lament. The condition, then, that Sophocles gives Electra at the outset is the very condition that Humphrey gives Amy at the conclusion. To be sure, Electra's early words speak for Amy's position at the end:

> With terrors around me, I will not hold back
> these mad cries of misery, so long as I live.

---

42. *The Orestes Plays of Aeschylus*, ed. and trans. Paul Roche (New York: Mentor, 1962), 129–30; *PF*, 276. Humphrey had portrayed a son as the snake at his mother's bosom in "The Last of the Caddoes"; see chap. 5, pp. 210–11.

43. Humphrey noted that "the Electra of Euripides is of no value to me; it suggests nothing. It's mainly lyrical, not psychological" (Notes, 23). Yet he exaggerates the play's uselessness to him; see p. 251*n*. In quoting from "Notes," "Amy," the final choice for the character's name will be used (she was sometimes called Hallie, then Sarah).

44. Sophocles, 130.

45. Ibid., 132.

46. Ibid., 133.

For who, dear girls, who that thought right
would believe there were suitable comforting
words for me? Forebear, forebear, my comforters.
These ills of mine shall be called cureless
and never shall I give over my sorrow. . . .[47]

More precise parallels obtain. Electra exclaims, "I am one wasted in childlessness, / with no loving husband for champion." Amy is childless and, though she is married, her husband is far from being her champion, the quality of their marriage being indicated by the fact that when they dine out together, "they asked for separate checks."[48] The submissive and patient Chrysothemis, sister of Electra, becomes in *Proud Flesh* an inward aspect of Amy herself. In *Electra* Chrysothemis encourages her sister to lower her sails and get along with Clytemnestra and Aegisthus. When Electra responds, "Do not teach me falseness to those I love," her sister counters, "that is not what I teach, but to yield to authority."[49] Humphrey's response, recorded in his Notes, makes clear his purpose for his character: "For me this line is really hair-raising. It's [sic] relevance to what I have *already* written for *my* Electra, my [Amy] Renshaw[,] is amazing. Mine is an Electra who has obeyed the injunction of an inner Chrysothemis, a *modern* Electra, and who has out of guilt, psychological compensation, made herself the slave of all authority" (Notes, 19–20; italics Humphrey's). The novel represents this aspect of Amy's character as follows: "Amy's patriotism, her politics, her religion, all resembled her piety toward her mother and her allegiance to her clan. A fundamentalist, she believed in a hot hell, a chilly heaven. A royalist with a worship of authority, she voted always for the incumbent" (*PF*, 87).[50] Commenting further on this resemblance, Humphrey said: "I wrote this without ever having read Sophocles' Electra! Merely remembering my Aunt Gertrude. She is clearly a classic, an archetypal case!" (Notes, 20).

Humphrey goes on to explain what Sophocles suggested to him about the fate of Amy, which he found in the following warning that Chrysothemis offers to Electra:

47. Ibid., 134.

48. Ibid., 133; *PF*, 85; Notes, 17.

49. Sophocles, 140, 141.

50. Humphrey's notes contain a slightly different version of this passage, probably copied from the working manuscript, which I quote to provide an indication of the extent to which he revised wording (here I shall quote Amy's MS name): "Hallie'[s] patriotism[,] her politics, her religion all resembled her piety towards her Mother and her loyalty to her family. A fundamentalist[,] she believed in a hot hell, a chilly heaven. A royalist with a passion for authority, she voted always for whoever was already established in office" (Notes, 20).

they will send you where
never a gleam of sun shall visit you.
You shall live out your life in an underground cave
and there bewail sorrows of the world outside.[51]

From this passage Humphrey might well have got his idea to put Amy in the storm cellar to play out her larger purpose. Yet it is hard to believe that Humphrey was not also thinking of Robert Penn Warren's *The Cave* (1959), for in this novel Jasper Herrick, buried in a cave, attracts a large congregation of watchers who sing and confess their sins at the mouth of the cave. The attending Baptist preacher vows that Jasper (like Amy) "is suffering for us all."[52] What is more, in Warren's novel the singing and praying mob is telecast, and, as in *Proud Flesh*, the participants in the proceedings observe themselves on the television screen.

Humphrey's own larger purpose in the novel, which Amy in the storm cellar plays a significant role in furthering, is related to Aeschylus's main theme, "the quest for justice," which is discussed in Philip Vellacott's introduction to *The Oresteian Trilogy*. According to Vellacott, the old law, especially as it has to do with family loyalty, comes in conflict with the new law, which emphasizes the community and the requirements of the public good. Humphrey, then, found in Aeschylus and in Vellacott's discussion of the theme of justice clarification of his own purpose in *Proud Flesh:* "For it is by this concern that Aeschylus lifts his domestic tragedy of the house of Atreus onto the public and thus the mythic-philosophical level. Thus does he implicate, involve all humanity in the fate of a single family, touch the very core of human experience. I aspire in my small way to do something like that in *[Proud Flesh]*."[53] Humphrey does, indeed, demon-

51. Sophocles, 140.

52. Robert Penn Warren, *The Cave* (New York: Random House, 1959), 270.

53. Philip Vellacott, introduction to *The Oresteian Trilogy* (Harmondsworth: Penguin, 1959), 22–23; Notes, 12. Humphrey also meant to establish a parallel between the condition of women in fifth-century Athenian society and the condition of women in the modern South. Vellacott's introduction to Aeschylus discusses "the respective rights and status of a man and a woman in marriage and parenthood," making the point that Athenian society did not grant women power equal to men and that this discrepancy led to "the poison of resentment and perverted ambition" (20, 21). Clytemnestra is, then, "a symbol of all women and mothers who suffer from the inferior status of women in marriage" (22). Humphrey comments that this is "All wonderfully rich in its applicability, and it[s] suggestiveness to my case. For the Southern woman is in exactly the situation described here as the lot of Athenian women, and my Edwina has responded in the same way to her lot as Clytemnestra to hers" (Notes, 11). I do not, however, believe that Humphrey's analogy between Clytemnestra and Edwina works out. We sympathize with Clytemnestra's outrage over her husband's preemptive appropriation of Iphigenia, their daughter, for sacrificial purposes (merely to gain favorable winds for

strate the clan mentality of the Renshaws as it comes into conflict with the community. Their appropriation of the most popular doctor in the town, keeping him for several days to watch over their dying mother—and even two days beyond to make sure she is dead—without a moment's thought about the doctor's well-being (he has a heart condition himself), without a moment's thought about his wife (who has no idea where he is), above all without a moment's thought about his many other patients who are crowding his waiting room and seeking his attention in the hospital, constitutes an arrogance reminiscent of Faulkner's Thomas Sutpen when he kidnaps the French architect and keeps him prisoner until the mansion on Sutpen's Hundred is completed. The Renshaws commandeer the icehouse, meant for the use of the entire community for food storage, in order to preserve Edwina's corpse. Even before the crisis of Edwina's heart attack and subsequent death, the Renshaws had exercised a family prerogative that ran roughshod over the law of the larger community. Their threats against a distant relative, Conway Renshaw, because his grocery business threatened the dignity of the Renshaw name, and their vigilante "execution" of the killer of their Cousin Claude signify their antisocial deportment. Going further back, Clyde's military history in World War II is a precise example of the family's "indifference to—the contempt for—the common welfare" (Notes, 27): although his superiors viewed Clyde as an exemplary soldier, he actually "had about as much patriotism as a green pepper" (*PF*, 35). His sole motivation in killing Germans was self-preservation. Clyde's emphasis on his own welfare, as well as his lack of regard for others, is an example of the Renshaw clan's general insularity from society.

Humphrey shows that there is a connection between the disintegration of this old-order family and an increase of justice in the community, especially among the blacks. New laws have been introduced to prevent discrimination against black people, though the old practice of treating blacks as inferiors has not disappeared. For example, Shug does not have enough standing as a human being to be considered a correspondent in a suit for divorce, and blacks continue to follow the old patterns of sitting separately in the balcony of the movie theater in town. Set against these attitudes is the novel's conclusion; even as Clyde renounces the old law that said he could not love a black woman, blacks and whites mingle and sit together casually around Amy's tomb. Amy, then, is the agent of both Clyde's transformation (she draws forth his self-recognition) and the change in the general attitude toward racial commingling.

---

the Greek ships). But there is nothing in Edwina's life to explain her insidious appropriation of power and control over her family. Further, the main conflict in *Proud Flesh* is not between Edwina and her husband but between Edwina and her daughter Amy.

Amy's devotion also undergoes an expansion. She had always limited her ministrations to the family, serving as confessor for her wild brothers for years and helping them when they were in trouble. When Amy divorces herself from the Renshaw family and enters the storm cellar, she "become[s] a public figure," indeed a "sacred figure" (*PF*, 293). As confessor to thousands, in her own bizarre way she is contributing to the general welfare. Thus her "dreary chant" is not expressive of "her woes but of the woes which oppress the world." She becomes "a sufferer for all of us" (Notes, 21–22).

Humphrey presents these changes only as gestures in the direction of a properly ordered society. No new order establishes itself, and he was not confident that he had dealt effectively with the concept of justice that he found so important in Aeschylus. He had wanted to make *Proud Flesh* "a parable of progress," but in the end he felt that he had failed. His comments place some of the blame on the country he was writing about—the South: "Do I really believe that justice is on the way in the South? Do I not really believe instead in the contrary? A country where injustice is condoned and violence not only tolerated but admired?" (Notes, 60).

While Aeschylus, Sophocles, and Eliot are the literary sources of *Proud Flesh*, Humphrey found, as in *The Ordways* and in "The Hardys," a near-at-hand original for the Renshaws: his mother's family, the Varleys. Like the Renshaws, "The Varleys did not much approve of anybody who was not a Varley," Humphrey says in *Farther Off from Heaven* (120). Although he has said that the real-life counterpart of Edwina Renshaw is his grandmother Cora Moorman Varley, his accounts of her in his autobiography yield few resemblances except that like Edwina his grandmother was an object of the religious devotion of her twelve children, but she shared this position equally with Humphrey's grandfather Edward (Au Int.; *FOFH*, 127).

Though Humphrey did not acknowledge it, Clarence Humphrey, his father, supplied a significant ingredient in *Proud Flesh*. The novel records the destruction of the settled, traditional Renshaw family. Clarence served this function in real life. He courted and won the favorite daughter of the Varleys, Humphrey's mother, suggesting to her the never-before-known freedom from restraint, the "striking off [of] old shackles," the emancipation from old-fashioned family propriety that also moves the novel *Proud Flesh* along (*FOFH*, 134). In his wild rage against the proprieties of the old order, Clarence seems the brother of the fictional Clyde—especially in his challenge to traditional racial attitudes. Clarence was "just enough of a maverick, and enough of an outsider . . . to test the code [governing relations between the races] to the breaking point": Wylie West, the black man who worked in Clarence's garage, "was the one man he liked, trusted, and respected" (*FOFH*, 83). In fact, William Humphrey's own experience seems to contribute to the characterization of Clyde, for the young Billy also "liked Wylie to an unacceptable degree, beyond what was tolerated"; and his liking bothered him, in the same terms as it did Clyde: "I had heard the term 'nigger-lover' and the contempt and hatred with which it was spoken. I had to be on guard against letting my fondness for Wylie show" (*FOFH*, 84).

The protagonist of *Proud Flesh*, Amy, is based upon Humphrey's aunt Gertrude Ridgeway, who "had caged her true nature and patrolled it unceasingly" (Notes, 46). Gertrude was so enamored of her career as an administrative secretary that she had five or six abortions in fifteen years. Humphrey gives three reasons for her attachment to her work: "She would not have wanted to give up her earnings and been dependent upon those of my uncle Tom. She would not have wanted to be a housewife, dependent for a sense of purpose in her life upon the notice and praise of my uncle Tom. She would not have wanted to give up the power over her mother and her brothers and sisters that her independent earnings gave her" (Notes, 42). Humphrey had at first considered making three abortions part of Amy's background, but he decided to approximate his model by making her merely childless. Also, like Gertrude, Amy "earned good pay" and kept herself financially independent of her husband. Having amassed a "considerable sum" by investing regularly in blue chip common stocks, Amy is "always available [with] an emergency loan fund for her brothers and sisters," thereby keeping them "in her debt for favors rendered them" (Notes, 144; *PF*, 85, 86). Amy maintains a position superior to her mother, handling the problems of the family and forcing Edwina to feel beholden to her.

Humphrey had enormous ambitions for *Proud Flesh;* he wanted it to have the kind of spellbinding effect that *Home from the Hill* produces in readers. *Home from the Hill* had succeeded in being a "modern Greek tragedy," and he hoped that *Proud Flesh*, based on two Greek tragedies, would do the same. Eventually, however, he realized that the tale was too outrageous to achieve tragic stature. The inclusion of sublime and grotesque elements finally leaves the novel in a state of unresolved tension. Humphrey admonished himself to "cut down the comedy, build up the sense of doom and disorder." But then he admitted, "The idea of this thing is already so wild that to get timid now is too late" (Notes, 102, 103).

A timid book *Proud Flesh* is not—and it is not a failure. The combining of the sublime and the ridiculous elements reflects the novel's primary theme and accords with the irreconcilable opposites upon which it is constructed: love and hate, black and white, illusion and reality, innocence and guilt—a double vision that is paralleled even in its somewhat irreconcilable sources (classical Greeks and familiar relatives from East Texas) and in its broken narrative format. The novel fails to reconcile its opposites, to resolve even its tonal tensions, to put itself together into a clear, consecutive narrative. Ultimate wholeness—for the novel, for the individual characters, and for the larger society—is beyond Humphrey's vision.

Proud Flesh is the only one of Humphrey's books to be panned by most of its reviewers. It is a difficult book. It can be hard to tell whether an incident is actually taking place or is merely imagined in the mind of a character. A certain amount of reader confusion is designed into the book, and *Proud Flesh* is clearly not a book that can be read once and understood. Humphrey insisted that it "must be read twice. Not every reader is going to do that, I realize, but the ones I am after will."[54] Christopher Lehmann-Haupt, who in the late 1990s was on the college lecture circuit speaking to students on the dubious subject of how they can read five thousand books a year, was the lead reviewer for the *New York Times* in the 1970s, and clearly he would not give *Proud Flesh* even one careful reading. He wrote a devastating denunciation of the novel, declaring it "hands down the worst piece of fiction I've read so far this year." It is "dreadful," a "tricked up . . . parody of William Faulkner," the "Southern gothic imagination gone rococo." Although Humphrey writes "up a dust storm," he does not create any characters: "the Renshaws, especially Edwina, don't even exist, except as a kind of half-hearted premise at the top of Mr. Humphrey's plot outline." Lehmann-Haupt admits to being "dumbfounded" by the novel: "I simply can't believe that the author of 'Home from the Hill,' 'The Ordways,' and 'The Spawning Run' . . . could have produced such an awful mess as this." Toward the end of his lengthy and detailed assault, which incidentally contains inaccuracies reflecting a careless reading of the novel, he asks, "Do I make it all sound awful?" His quick answer is that "It's worse. The only hopeful comment I can think of to make is that Mr. Humphrey has now gotten out of his system a problem that he neither understood nor cared about to begin with—or maybe he did care a little about it to begin with, for what else but some obscure obsession could have kept him writing such balderdash?" Lehmann-Haupt cavalierly remarked that "the title stinks a little."[55]

Hilary Masters says this review "is probably the most viciously constructed condemnation of a writer's work in modern history." Jonathan Yardley, one of the most respected book reviewers in the United States, recalled in 1977 how angry Lehmann-Haupt's "asinine" review made him: "There is nothing like a Northern 'critic' sneering at a Southern writer he doesn't understand." A recent

54. Humphrey to Norah Smallwood, 7 June 1972, C&W.
55. Christopher Lehmann-Haupt, "More Meat for the Boycott," *New York Times,* 4 April 1973, 41.

admission by Lehmann-Haupt leads one to wonder if the outrageous review were not owing to something more than arrogance, obtuseness, or careless reading. Lehmann-Haupt has admitted to functioning as a hit man, taking his "orders directly from the top" (i.e., from then *New York Times* executive editor Abe Rosenthal) to give a book a bad review. Lehmann-Haupt has admitted to destroying Seymour Hersh's *The Price of Power*, just a few years after the crippling review of *Proud Flesh*.[56] Humphrey was a prickly character, and he would step on people's corns. Could he have offended the executives at the *Times*, or even a friend of Lehmann-Haupt's? One has to wonder. Yet, to be fair, Lehmann-Haupt reviewed *My Moby Dick* favorably in 1978, which argues against ulterior motives with respect to Humphrey.[57]

At any rate, the review of *Proud Flesh* had a devastating effect on Humphrey. When his editor from Knopf, Robert Gottlieb, telephoned on the morning of the review to warn Humphrey not to read it, Humphrey took out his fury on the messenger in the form of astonishingly abusive language. The Reverend Elliott Lindsley, rector of St. Paul's Episcopal Church, Tivoli (since his days as a Bard student, a friend of Humphrey's), anticipated trouble when he saw the review in the morning paper and immediately called on Bill; neither said anything about the review for a while. When Bill finally asked Elliott if he had seen it and the priest out of kindness lied that he had not, Bill broke down in tears; beyond blaming the reviewer, he was in despair. A few days later Bill wrote to Lindsley: "I am deeply touched to know that you made that trip up here early that morning because you were concerned over me and wanted to comfort and support me. I shall never forget it." Nick Lyons, another former Bard student who had remained a friend of Bill's, telephoned him every day for three weeks, trying to comfort him because Lyons "was absolutely positive he would blow his brains out because of it." Another friend who called Humphrey "immediately and often" following the *Times* review was Ted Thomas, who also recruited Andrews Wanning to help the thin-skinned Humphrey survive the review. Humphrey tried to drop Thomas, who never read any of his friend's books except *The Spawning Run*, but Thomas refused to be dismissed and remained Humphrey's friend for life. Other friends of long standing such as Richard Rovere and Fred Dupee were appalled by Lehmann-Haupt's review and did commiserate with

---

56. Hilary Masters, "Proud Flesh: William Humphrey Remembered," *Sewanee Review* 108, no. 3 (Spring 2000): 258; Jonathan Yardley to Humphrey, 21 July 1977, WH Coll., UT; Dennis Johnson, "Reviewing the Reviewers: Was the Times 'Decadent'?" *Arkansas Democrat-Gazette* (Little Rock), 21 May 2000, sec. J, p. 6.

57. Smallwood to Humphrey, 29 November 1978, C&W.

Humphrey, but the friends who were not loud enough in their praise of the be-leaguered book were dropped, according to Sally Thomas.[58] Friendships did end, but it was not so simple as Humphrey's cutting off those who did not meet his standard of support. He felt, as Lyons explained, like one who had "farted in church." Humphrey wrote to Grabstald: "Except for exactly five, every friend I thought I had has dropped me following the failure of my last book. All the world loves a winner, but nobody knows you when you're down and out." It appears that Humphrey was correct in taking the measure of his local friends. Hilary Masters admitted that many in Humphrey's social set were secretly pleased by the savagery of Lehmann-Haupt's review, which some of them felt had "evened the score . . . for Bill's occasional hauteur, his self-made and self-taught criteria that few of us could meet." He thinks that Humphrey sensed these feelings, which accounted for his failure to answer their letters of commiseration. Dorothy intercepted phone calls, and Bill "posted no trespassing signs around that ele-gantly furnished house in the apple orchard" (though it is not clear whether Mas-ters is being literal or figurative here).[59] For months afterwards, Humphrey sat in his big silent house where the telephone never rang and the postman stopped only to leave bills and junk mail.

Had someone brought Humphrey's attention to Clifton Fadiman's denuncia-tion in the *New Yorker* of Faulkner's *Absalom, Absalom!*, he would have been reminded of how wrong a reviewer in a hurry can be when faced with a literary work that challenges his assumptions: "Mr. Faulkner . . . gets quite an interesting effect . . . by tearing the Sutpen chronicle into pieces, as if a mad child were to go to work on it with a pair of shears. . . . Seriously, I do not know what to say of this book except that it seems to point to the final blowup of what was once a remarkable, if minor, talent." A few years later Nick Lyons sent Bill a detailed comparison of Lehmann-Haupt's review of *Proud Flesh* and reviews of the late Rembrandts and the last Cézannes.[60]

But there were other reviews of *Proud Flesh* to be endured. The *Times* review, because it was the first one and because that paper had unrivaled power of influ-

---

58. Robert Gottlieb, telephone conversation with author, 16 May 2001; Elliott Lindsley to author, 20 August 1999; Humphrey to Lindsley, 18 April 1973 (letter in Lindsley's possession); Nick Lyons, telephone interview by author, tape recording, 28 July 1999; Sally Thomas to author, 13 December 1997 and 2 January 1998.

59. Lyons, interview; Humphrey to Grabstald, 16 January 1974, HG Letters; Masters, 259.

60. Clifton Fadiman, "Faulkner, Extra-Special, Double-Distilled," *New Yorker*, 31 October 1936, in *Faulkner: A Collection of Critical Essays*, ed. Robert Penn Warren (Englewood Cliffs, N.J.: Prentice-Hall, 1966), 290; Lyons to Humphrey, 11 December 1977, WH Coll., UT.

ence, established a tone and position that almost all the rest followed.[61] Before April was over the *New York Times Book Review* gave the book a cool reception, not as disapproving as the one in its parent paper but still a poor one. Allowing that it "has passages of magnetic description, detours of absorbing story, glints of original characterization," Richard Brickner concluded that *Proud Flesh* does not hold together as a novel. Humphrey "is not at his best," for the readers' "emotions are exhorted but never persuaded," and thus it is hard to care about the characters: "the Renshaws are a bunch of maniacs; and in fact Humphrey finally says this himself, but not until long after we've given up hoping Humphrey knew it too." In July *Best Sellers* hit *Proud Flesh* with Lehmann-Haupt's caliber of abuse: "This travesty of the English language is almost unbelievable." *Time* did not take Humphrey's novel seriously, seeing *Proud Flesh* as a variation on the usual formula for the southern novel: instead of "Big Daddy" signaling "the passing of a way of life," Humphrey gives us "Big Mommy." *Library Journal* stood alone in finding nothing in *Proud Flesh* to complain about and much to praise. According to Lee Sullenger, *Proud Flesh* gives evidence of Humphrey's artistry: "The characters, both major and minor, are extremely well drawn, and the use of descriptive detail is virtually flawless." The dismissive reviews notwithstanding, *Proud Flesh* had by 14 July 1973 sold 24,500 copies, exactly the number sold of *Home from the Hill,* though 4,000 fewer than *The Ordways.*[62]

When the assault was over, Humphrey took stock. The disastrous reception of the novel in the United States as well as in England left him stunned, bewildered about what had happened to his career as a writer; he felt uncertain about the future and was unable to write. He sent two distressing letters to Ian Parsons, who became alarmed over Bill's despondency. He thought for a while of returning to full-time teaching in order to make a living.[63]

61. Smallwood wrote to Humphrey: "that opening review did the damage; it is damnable the effect that one review can have" (8 January 1974, C&W).
62. Richard Brickner, *New York Times Book Review,* 29 April 1973, 26, 29; *Best Sellers,* 15 July 1973, 250; Melvin Maddocks, "Ten-Gallon Gothic," *Time,* 30 April 1973, 94; Lee Sullenger, *Library Journal,* 1 April 1997, 1192; Humphrey to Parsons, 14 July 1973, C&W.
63. Humphrey to Nick and Mari Lyons, 27 April [1973], Lyons Coll.; to Smallwood, 21 December 1973, C&W; Parsons to William Koshland, 4 July 1973, C&W.

A PALPABLE DARKNESS
(Hostages to Fortune)

Of the people who commit suicide, some do violence to themselves; others, on the contrary, merely give in to themselves and appear to follow some unknown and fatal line of destiny.

—PAUL VALÉRY, *Occasions*

Death . . . was now a daily presence, blowing over me in cold gusts. I had not conceived how my end would come. In short, I was still keeping the idea of suicide at bay. But plainly the possibility was around the corner, and I would soon meet it face to face.

—WILLIAM STYRON, *Darkness Visible*

The heart of another is a dark forest, always, no matter how close it has been to one's own.

—WILLA CATHER, *The Professor's House*

IT WAS in the midst of Humphrey's deep sorrow over the reception of *Proud Flesh* that his twenty-year relationship with Katherine Anne Porter came to an end. She did not desert him because he had been pommeled by the reviewers. Their breakup, ironically, was on account of her reaction to Humphrey's kind assistance in the organization and selection of the contents of her *Collected Essays*, which had been published in 1970. She apparently had expected the fact of his assistance—as well as that of others who helped by reading galleys and searching out the texts of poems—to remain unknown to the world. But her publisher Seymour Lawrence judged that those who had labored on Porter's behalf deserved recognition; therefore, when the book was published it bore the following acknowledgment: "The publishers wish to express profound appreciation to Robert A. Beach, Jr., George Core, William Humphrey, Rhea Johnson, and Glenway Wescott for their help and guidance in the preparation of this volume." According to her biographer, Porter was "mortified" when she saw the book, objecting to selections made during her illness as well as to its being published without her being able to do the proofreading. Porter took every opportunity to write outraged commentaries in books that people brought her to autograph. Typical is the following: "The damndest piece of impudence I ever encountered in my long war with such idiots as Seymour Lawrence. In this group of five misled men, there is not one I would have ever in all my life asked for a word about my work. K. A. P."[1] Years later Humphrey noticed, in the catalog for a sale on 2 May 1985 at Swann Galleries, an inscribed copy of the *Collected Essays* in which Porter had crossed through Lawrence's acknowledgment and written the following: "The mystery remains—what gave the Publisher and these men the notion that they could give me help and guidance, even if I had needed it? KAP." Humphrey sent a photocopy of the page from the catalog to Lawrence, who responded on 19 June 1985 with the observation that Porter "was egomaniacal, paranoid, vindictive, an injustice collector, devoid of loyalty, etc." (Lawrence Coll.).

At the time of her initial outrage, however, Porter seems not to have expressed her feelings to Humphrey;[2] their correspondence continued on a friendly basis until early in 1973, his last letter to her giving no hint that the relationship was about to end. In fact, he and Dorothy had decided to take a vacation in Key West in March, and he proposed to visit Porter on the way down or back. But then it seems likely he got wind of her caviling. He never made the visit and never wrote again, nor did she. In a letter to Lawrence dated 23 June 1985, Humphrey looked back on his long relationship with Porter: "As for Katherine Anne, I try to remember what she meant to me, the good times I had with her, but she did leave behind some poison. You must get Dorothy to tell you someday about the 10 days she spent looking after her. I am afraid I have to say that she came home hating the woman" (Lawrence Coll.). After Porter's death, Humphrey avoided recognizing his connection with her. When Joan Givner asked for his help with her biography of Porter, he refused.[3] In 1989, when Blanche T. Ebeling-Koning invited Humphrey to "share" his memories at the celebration for the hundredth anniversary of Porter's birth to be held at the University of Maryland, Humphrey practiced his response on the back of the invitation: "I cannot plan for an event a year and a half off, so do not count on my presence at your Katherine Anne Porter conference" (WH Coll., UT). He then revised his refusal, removing the sharp edge. Although Humphrey wanted to forget his personal relationship with Porter, he recognized her contribution to literature, commenting on Larry McMurtry's slighting of her in the *Texas Observer* as follows: "though slender her gifts were real and lasting and to them he is obtuse."[4]

1. William Humphrey to Seymour Lawrence, undated, Lawrence Coll.; Joan Givner, *Katherine Anne Porter: A Life* (New York: Simon and Schuster, 1982), 490–91.
2. Nor did she complain to George Core. Lawrence had asked Core "to look up the text of a poem (perhaps more than one poem)" (George Core to author, 14 April 2000).
3. Givner to Humphrey, 4 October 1977, WH Coll., UT.
4. Humphrey to Nick Lyons, 29 December [1981], Lyons Coll.; Larry McMurtry, "Ever a Bridegroom: Reflections on the Failure of Texas Literature," *Texas Observer*, 23 October 1981, 8.

Before the disastrous reception of *Proud Flesh* and before the subsequent breakup with Katherine Anne Porter, Humphrey had been in high spirits for a while. He was basking in the illusion of success, just having completed *Proud Flesh,* and he had begun another novel in December of 1972. He was so sanguine that he felt up to staying at home for the winter of 1972–73, and in an effort to enjoy the season in Hudson, he and Dorothy bought cross-country skis.[5]

The first sign of the new novel's emergence appears in an old notebook that had been devoted to *Proud Flesh.* After a few pages of scribbling about a character named Cecil Smoot, Humphrey pasted a copy of an article by D. S. Savage on Dostoyevsky's *The Gambler,* which he thought would help in the development of the Smoot character. After a few more pages on Smoot, Humphrey jotted a note to himself acknowledging that Dorothy was encouraging him to make the story of his father's death his next book, but Humphrey decided to stick with Smoot because he had a clear idea of the character, whose views ("the world has gone completely to hell") closely resembled Humphrey's own. He already had a title for it (it was the first time he had ever started a novel with a title), "The Last Refuge," from Dr. Johnson's dictum about patriotism; but he soon changed it to "The Horse Latitudes."[6] Even when those devastating reviews of *Proud Flesh* burst Bill's ebullience, he nonetheless tried to press on with his story of a cranky, rich redneck who "had gotten where he was in life by noticing things that other people overlooked" ("The Horse Latitudes," in WH Coll., UT).

Humphrey's dejected plowing in the hardscrabble of Smoot gave way to joy—at least temporarily—when the French reviews of *Proud Flesh* began to praise the book unstintingly. He was "lauded to the point that it is downright embarrassing. It is the sort of embarrassment that I can use," he told Ted and Renée Weiss. *Les liens du sang* (1975) got the sort of reception in Paris that Humphrey had hoped the novel would get in America and England.[7] The effect of the laudatory French reviews was to give Humphrey new—though short-lived—confidence in "The Horse Latitudes."

5. Humphrey to Theodore and Renée Weiss, 8 December 1972, Weiss Coll.

6. Humphrey to Ian Parsons, 22 November 1972, C&W; Humphrey, "The Horse Latitudes" (MS, WH Coll., UT; another copy in WH res.); Humphrey to Norah Smallwood, 2 December 1972, C&W.

7. Humphrey to Nick and Mari Lyons, 27 April [1973], Lyons Coll.; to Smallwood, 21 December 1973, C&W; Parsons to William Koshland, 4 July 1973, C&W; Humphrey to the Weisses, 24 October 1975 and 16 January 1976, Weiss Coll. For the French response to *Proud Flesh,* see Philippe R. Hupp, *Le Républicain Lorrain,* 31 January 1976; Ugné Karvelis, "Le «Faulkner» du pauvre," *Figaro,* 24 January 1976; Alain Bosquet, "Pour comprendre le Texas: William Humphrey," *Magazine littéraire,* November 1975, 49; François Wagener, "William Humphrey: un Texan «old fashion,»" *Le Monde* (Paris), 30 October 1975.

There were early indications that this troubled project was not destined for success anywhere. On 14 January 1974 Jean Lambert, visiting at High Meadow, recorded in his journal: "Bill speaks to me of his new work—a rather violent satire of Nixon, for which he records all that happens each day; he reads some of the pages to me. I do not believe that I will ever translate this book, but I am happy to see that he has overcome the disappointments that the preceding gave him" (Lambert Coll.). In May, Lambert complained to his journal that Humphrey read to him the same chapter again, an indication that Humphrey was not making progress. Lambert objected again to the novel's excessive timeliness: "The danger, for Bill, is that he wants to integrate into his book all that appears each day on television." Lambert did not think much of the Smoot book and *vowed* that he would never translate it.[8] By the end of 1974 Humphrey had managed to write only 125 pages on the new novel. Melancholy had resumed its place in his life. Even so, he could make out that Cecil Smoot was no more than a mouthpiece for his own railing against Nixon and his toadies and that, placed beside the other book that he had begun to work on also *(Farther Off from Heaven)*, it did not measure up. This insight might have been helped by Robert Gottlieb's unequivocal rejection of "The Horse Latitudes" on 18 January 1975, based upon the pages that Humphrey had submitted. Bill stopped typing in the middle of the third line on an unnumbered manuscript page when the rejection notice arrived (WH res.). He would find, however, that he could not cut himself loose from the Smoot book so easily. He was still weighing its merits on Easter Sunday, 1975, saying to Seymour Lawrence: "After working all last year on a novel and accumulating nearly 300 pages of it, what I have got is a mess I myself don't know what to make of and which I may just walk away from. In the meantime, I am nearly 100 pages into a memoir of my first thirteen years. With this I am well pleased" (Lawrence Coll.).

Justifiably so. *Farther Off from Heaven,* which centers on the thirteen-year-old Billy's reaction to his father's death, marking his loss of innocence and ending his whole way of life, was to become one of Humphrey's best books. The painful dimension of his memories assured a degree of reluctance to carry on with this writing project, yet it was obviously a task that he felt compelled to do—and to do with artistic integrity. He did not want to produce a standard chronological account of his early life. He wanted his memoir to have the kind of shapeliness that a good novel has, though he wondered how it could have that and truth too. Eventually he worked out a way to use some of the techniques of the novel—for example, withholding information early on because it would produce a greater

---

8. Jean Lambert, journal, entry for 30 May 1974, Lambert Coll.

impact later or portraying a character as he seems, only to demonstrate later that his reality is different from his seeming (*WST*, 21).

Much of the writing of *Farther Off from Heaven* was done at the country house of Jean Lambert, in Souvigny-en-Sologne, about fifteen miles from Lamotte-Beuvron. Lambert's library, a converted outbuilding, was a happy setting for writing, and from October until the end of 1975, Humphrey added a hundred pages to the hundred that he had written by Easter. There was very little else to do in Souvigny. Since the Humphreys did not have a car and there was no bus or train, their outings were confined to an occasional dinner at Auberge de la Croix Blanche, the only hotel in the village. Bill's relief from hard work was confined to drinking, and Dorothy joined him: in four months' time, they filled Lambert's garage with empty wine and whiskey bottles. There was, however, one perfect, happy event during Humphrey's largely uneventful autumn: about the middle of December, he was taken on a wild boar hunt. He had never seen a wild boar (when he had required one for a character to kill in *Home from the Hill*, he had had to import the boar from Louisiana), and he had "the time of [his] life" and wrote it up for *Sports Illustrated*.[9]

Claude Gallimard, head of the Paris firm that published all of the French translations of Humphrey's books, offered the Humphreys a means of escape from weary rustication: they could move into his father's apartment (Gaston Gallimard had died during Christmas) in Paris (39 rue Saint LaSare) for January and February. "It would give me great pleasure to know that you finished, or had written some part of this book [*Father Off from Heaven*], in my ancestral home," Claude said to Humphrey. Bill and Dorothy remained in Gaston's apartment until the end of February, when they visited friends in England before returning to America on 18 March. Bill delivered the manuscript of the memoir to Knopf by midsummer.[10] Before doing so, he took time to contribute an eloquent tribute to Ian Parsons on his seventieth birthday (3 June 1976). Humphrey's contribution to the festschrift took its place along with those from Quentin Bell, William Empson, Graham Greene, Basil Willey and others (C&W).

Later in 1976 Humphrey was the Elizabeth Drew Professor of English for the fall semester at Smith College, where his longtime friend and French translator Jean Lambert was on the faculty. Humphrey offered one course in the writing of short stories and gave a series of public readings and lectures. He and Dorothy

---

9. Jean Lambert, interview by author, Paris, France, 19 July 1998; Humphrey to the Weisses, 30 December 1975; "Royal Game" is collected in *OS*, 305–23.

10. Humphrey to Smallwood, 16 January and 25 February 1976, C&W; to the Weisses, 16 February, Weiss Coll.; to Lambert, [12 July 1976], Lambert Coll.

came down in the middle of the week, staying over for two nights, and returning to Hudson before the weekend. According to one of his colleagues, Professor Frank Murphy, some of the English faculty who knew Bill's work well arranged a luncheon party for him and Dorothy each week. Often they were joined by Victor and Dorothy Pritchett, who were frequent visitors to Smith in those years. Talk ranged from Italian painting to fishing and life in Texas. Murphy remarked that Humphrey was good company and "a wonderful blend of urbanity and earthiness."[11] Humphrey's workload at Smith was light; in fact, he spent most of his time there attending to the queries from his Knopf editor on the manuscript of *Farther Off from Heaven*; the manuscript was in such a mess when he finished those revisions that he retyped—in his own rapid-motion, two-fingered manner—the entire 250 pages. His mother's birthday letter (2 November) noted that he had by then proofread and posted the revised version to Knopf.

At the end of his stint at Smith, Humphrey returned to the Smoot book; on 12 December 1976 he told Pierre Affre, one of his longtime fishing companions, that he had about 360 manuscript pages. He thought much—maybe all—of it would have to be thrown out, but he resolved to make one more effort to salvage it, in spite of Gottlieb's rejection of it almost two years earlier. There is an unsigned contract between Knopf and Humphrey in which the author would have received a $45,000 advance and royalties of 15 percent, with the stipulation that the manuscript be completed by 1 January 1977 (WH res.). Since Knopf apparently would not sign this contract, Humphrey sent a 225-page, trimmed-down version of the Smoot novel to Doubleday, Simon and Schuster, and Macmillan—getting no happy results. Humphrey wrote on 21 January to Ted Weiss that "this sad and certainly-not-destined-for-the-blockbuster-list book" was not likely to find a sponsor. Six days later he lamented, "I have lived to see a time when every publisher wants a large and immediate return on his every title. I feel like one of the last specimens of a species on the verge of extinction" (Weiss Coll.).

A few days later Humphrey did not know what to do with himself. He was certain that he would write no more memoirs. But what, if anything? Short stories? Essays? Another novel? He confided his ambivalence to his "Smith College Journal": "The very fact that the novel *is* dead—or in the hands of clowns like Vonnegut, unimaginative men like Bellow—means I could have it to myself, if I wanted it. The fact that the world didn't want my last novel means I don't have to care whether it wants another." On the next page Humphrey was telling himself that the Smoot book "*is* worth writing, and I should get to it." At the same time, he recognized that "The Horse Latitudes," even in its revised and trimmed-

11. Frank Murphy to author, 19 December 1997.

down condition, required a great deal more work: "Just to start retyping the Smoot book is not going to solve my problems. I've got to have some ideas for making a novel out of the book. More character, more action. Something to re-place all that Nixon-Ford stuff which must be scrapped."[12]

A new notebook begun on 4 February 1977 signaled a serious psychological downturn. Humphrey seemed desperately to hold on to Smoot: "It's all I've got," he declared (WH Coll., UT). But his frustration over how to turn his ventings on Nixon into a real novel turned his life into a shambles. That he was indeed depressed is clear from everything he said about his feelings—either in his note-books or in letters to friends. In February 1977 he wrote:

> Time to begin a new notebook. Only out of habit. Only because I don't know how to stop. Surely the time to stop has come. My ideas for writing have dried up. My personal life is a wreck. I am alone, friendless—just about—isolated. I feel old and used up.
>
> But what am I to do with myself? How get through the day? Though I believe it's hopeless, absurd, I must try to write. I don't know anything else to do. (WH Coll., UT)

He worked on the manuscript some more, but he could not finish it. After some additional pages of such jottings as "It would add to Smoot's woes to have to blame himself for Nixon," Humphrey realized that "The Horse Latitudes" had rotted on the vine, and he finally gave up the idea of a harvest (WH Coll., UT).

The onset of spring did nothing to lift Humphrey's spirits. He would awaken to flowering and songbird mornings, but it would be a damp, drizzly November in his soul. The clouds persisted nearly into summer, eventually lifting when *Farther Off from Heaven* was greeted with unanimous enthusiasm by the reviewers. The *Saturday Review* called it "a magical and touching memoir," and Reynolds Price paid tribute to Humphrey's effective narrative structure: the mother's and the son's long vigil beside the broken body of the husband and father "becomes the barely glimpsed spine of the story, from which long and short nerves of memory and knowledge probe into past and future action."[13] The general enthu-siasm registered at Knopf. William Koshland wrote to Michel Mohrt of Galli-mard: "Everybody who has read the book seems to be of a single mind as to its being the best Bill has ever done" (Gallimard). With confidence in his publisher,

---

12. Humphrey, journal, entry for 25 January 1977, passim, WH res.

13. Peter Shaw, *Saturday Review*, 28 May 1977, 30; Reynolds Price, "Homecountry, East Texas," *New York Times Book Review*, 22 May 1977, 31.

Humphrey wrote to Ugné Karvelis, an editor at Gallimard, on 2 March: "Things are looking very good for *Farther Off from Heaven*. There is great enthusiasm for it in the offices of Knopf, and that means a great deal in how a book gets promoted" (Gallimard). Humphrey was even willing to do something he had never done before: in conjunction with a lecture at the University of Texas at El Paso, he made a triumphal tour involving book-signings, luncheons, and dinners in San Antonio, Austin, Fort Worth, and Dallas; the excursion ended with an autograph party held by the people of Clarksville (the guest book was signed by 123 couples).[14]

While the author made extraordinary efforts (for him) to promote his book, his publisher did nothing; although the book initially sold 13,000 of the first printing of 15,000, Knopf did not buy an inch of advertising for the book, and it quickly became unavailable in bookstores. Humphrey was horrified, sent into an emotional tailspin, to see a book that had collected lauds from all quarters treated by his own publisher with such little regard. His first impulse was to try to write something quickly that would reach a large audience. Therefore, he proposed to do a feature on Guy Fawkes's Day in Sussex for *National Geographic*, but the magazine turned down his proposal—a small rejection but one he felt keenly. At this point, he misplaced his wristwatch—which had the odd effect of easing his troubled mind. It was as though he had got free from time while the watch did not bind his wrist. He was again depressed upon finding it, for its small face once again reminded him of the passage of time and the small allotment that remained for him to achieve what fame he could. His anxiety drove him to hound Robert Gottlieb, the new president of Knopf, to lend some measure of support to *Farther Off from Heaven*. His arm-twisting got two advertisements in the *New York Times Book Review* and the *New Yorker* in October, but then the firm wearied of Humphrey's complaints about their neglect and no longer returned his calls. Norah Smallwood of the English firm Chatto and Windus commiserated: "I am not a great believer in vilifying another publisher, even if he is on the other side of the Atlantic, but I do think the behaviour of yours is quite inexplicable." Looking back on this controversy, Gottlieb's comment was: "nine out of ten writers think publishers don't advertise enough." On the other hand, Humphrey's English firm's president, Ian Parsons, seemed to want to do everything possible to promote the book; he even wrote a panegyric for the memoir in the *Bookseller*

---

14. Dorothy Humphrey to Becky and Bernard Varley, 23 March 1977 (letter in possession of Don Emery, Clarksville, Tex.); guest book, WH Coll., UT. At this time, the Texas Western Press published *Ah, Wilderness! The Frontier in American Literature,* one of the lectures that Humphrey had originally given at Washington and Lee University in 1963.

(7 January 1978, 45). The Texas Institute of Arts and Letters granted Humphrey one of its yearly awards for the third time, declaring *Farther Off from Heaven* the best nonfiction book of 1977.[15]

This award and his English friend's effort notwithstanding, Humphrey fell back into the slough of despair. Dorothy was even worse off than he, for in early October she was hospitalized for severe depression. She was very "skeptical that help will help—They can't change this shitty world," she told Harry Grabstald on 6 October 1977 (HG Letters). Bill remained in the big house alone with his own discouragement, which expanded to include "the way the world is going."[16] It is hard to say what he might have meant by this blanket groan. The Watergate episode and the Vietnam War were over, both of which had greatly distressed him. The energy crisis, even though he heated with fuel oil, was not the sort of issue to trouble Humphrey. Perhaps disgust over Judge Sirica's reduction of the prison sentences of Mitchell, Haldeman, and Ehrlichman could have pained the old Nixon hater, and there was plenty of political mayhem ruining the lives of ordinary people throughout the world—Idi Amin's wave of terror in Uganda, civil war in Nicaragua, bombings in Belfast. But in truth, Humphrey was already depressed; it was only natural that world events would feed his depression.

The end of November brought an occurrence much closer to home that drove both Dorothy and Bill farther toward despair: she was diagnosed with colon cancer. After she underwent immediate surgery, Bill, for the third time in their long life together, assumed the roles of nurse, cook, and housekeeper during his wife's prolonged convalescence. By 27 December Dorothy was pronounced cured, but then early in January her incisions became infected, and Bill's period of nursing was extended.[17]

As angry as Bill was with the Knopf firm over its mishandling of *Farther Off from Heaven* (even many years later he would say in an interview that they might as well have "shredded" and "pulped" it), he was much angrier over Gottlieb's failure to express any concern for Dorothy during her life-threatening illness. Nick Lyons had told the Knopf firm about Dorothy on 28 November; on 3 December Humphrey recorded his disappointment over not hearing from anyone in the firm: "I've still heard nothing. This is really inexplicable. It can only be

15. Humphrey to Smallwood, 14 July 1977, C&W; Humphrey to Lambert, 16 October 1977, Lambert Coll.; Smallwood to Humphrey, 28 November 1977, C&W; Robert Gottlieb, telephone interview by author, 16 May 2001; Humphrey to Smallwood, 23 February 1978, C&W.

16. Humphrey to Smallwood, 29 June 1978, C&W.

17. Humphrey to Smallwood, 22 November 1977, C&W; to Lambert, 15 December 1977, Lambert Coll.; to F. W. Dupee, 27 December 1977, Dupee Coll.

interpreted to mean that Gottlieb for some reason just wants to forget me. Very well. I'll certainly let him."[18]

Farther Off from Heaven was the last of Humphrey's books to be handled by Knopf. He got a literary agent, an Englishman by the name of Toby Eady, a fishing companion of five years who had come to the United States. Eady soon had Humphrey talking with every major publisher in the United States. In the meantime—and without informing Knopf—Humphrey made arrangements with his friend Nick Lyons for the publication of *My Moby Dick*, his story of fishing for a much-respected, giant one-eyed trout in a small stream near Great Barrington. Lyons had recently established a press specializing in outdoors literature; he published Humphrey's fishing book in cooperation with Doubleday in 1979.[19] Still needing a new general publisher, on 30 July 1978 Humphrey wrote to Seymour Lawrence, his longtime friend:

> I have grown unhappy with Knopf and, after 24 years association, am looking for another publisher. Or rather, I really am not looking for another publisher: I am so disgruntled with publishing I'd as soon quit. But a lit. agent has talked me into letting him make this proposal to publishers: support me with an annual stipend for the next 10 years and see what I produce. I've had interviews just recently with half a dozen and will be seeing a few more soon. It's a proposal that anybody will want time to think over, and I've told them I'm in no hurry. If you think you'd be interested, my agent is Toby Eady Associates. . . . But right now he's in Africa and won't be back until early September. At which time I'll be on Nantucket for a couple of weeks. (Lawrence Coll.)

Not long after sending off this letter, Bill and Dorothy retreated to Nantucket—Ted Thomas had lent them a wonderful 1641 house built with the timbers of wrecked ships—in order to await the outcome. Lawrence made a note in the left margin of the letter to call Eady in September. When they talked Eady proposed a stipend of $25,000 a year for ten years; this figure, or something like it, was agreed upon, for on 26 September 1978, Lawrence sent Humphrey a telegram saying, "It would be a singular honor and privilege to publish your work." By this time, however, two more publishers—E. P. Dutton and Methuen—had taken an

---

18. Geoffrey Stokes, "Literature Is Hell: William Humphrey's Strange Success," *Village Voice Literary Supplement* 28 (September 1984), 21; Humphrey, notebook, entry for 3 December 1977, WH res.

19. Humphrey to Smallwood, 12, 17 December 1977 and 9 January 1978, C&W; to Lambert, 25 June 1978, Lambert Coll.

interest in Humphrey, he explained to Norah Smallwood on 6 November, and so Humphrey elected to hold out for an even more favorable offer than Lawrence's. Eady, declaring the Smoot book a masterpiece, reported that he obtained an offer of $200,000 advance from Larry Dent of Methuen. This offer was based on Dent's hearing forty or fifty pages read over the phone; apparently when Humphrey presented the entire manuscript the offer was withdrawn.[20]

In the end Bill decided to go with Lawrence. Thus just a month after Knopf had prematurely remaindered *Farther Off from Heaven*, in January 1979, he signed with Lawrence—a long-term contract that involved at least four books. What possibly clinched the matter was that Lawrence was the only publisher that wanted to buy all of the old titles from Knopf and issue a uniform edition. But of course Humphrey's having known Lawrence for many years and his liking and trusting him surely weighed into the decision, especially in light of his conviction of having been betrayed by Knopf.[21] Norah Smallwood, by then president of Chatto and Windus, wrote to Lawrence on 19 March: "I am very pleased about you and Bill Humphrey because I know you will look after him and cherish him. And Heaven knows, he is worth cherishing" (C&W). Although Bill held on to the hope that Lawrence would arrange for the publication of the Smoot book, which he said he "finished" (the quotation marks are his) on 2 May 1979, Delacourt would not publish the curious novel and returned the manuscript on 5 June 1979 (WH res.). Well after author and publisher had agreed to set aside "The Horse Latitudes," then, Lawrence declared: "I'll publish anything you write and that's not just loyalty, it's my astute literary judgment (!) and good sense. I know the real thing when I see it," he wrote on 22 February 1989 (WH res.). Indeed, Lawrence proved over the years to be a loyal supporter of his writer. This relationship with Lawrence would continue until Lawrence's death in 1994, not long after he had moved to Oxford, Mississippi, with Humphrey's former student and Faulkner's former mistress, Joan Williams, to live in a house within sight of Rowan Oak.

While all of the interviewing and hand-wringing over securing a new publisher was going on in 1978, the Humphreys decided to sell High Meadow; on 1 December they put it on the market for $200,000.[22] They thought of buying a smaller house in New York and—as a part-time residence—a grand house in

20. Humphrey to Lambert, 14 August 1978, Lambert Coll.; to Smallwood, 16 September 1978, C&W; Lawrence, telegram to Humphrey, 26 September 1978, Lawrence Coll.; Humphrey to Smallwood, 6 November 1978, C&W; Humphrey, journal, entry for 7 December 1978, WH res.

21. Lee Goerner to Humphrey, 12 December 1978, WH Coll., UT; Humphrey to Smallwood, 26 January 1979 and 28 September 1978, C&W.

22. Jerome A. French (realtor) to the Humphreys, 1 December 1978, WH res.

Clarksville. It would seem that Humphrey envisioned himself, in part, as imitating Shakespeare's return to Stratford and purchase of the second largest house in town as proof that the small-town boy had done well in the wide world. Even though Bill wanted to return to Clarksville for only part of the year and though Dorothy knew that "his feeling for that town is very deep," she was nonetheless apprehensive about the effect that being "down there" would have on her: "how would this Brooklyn Jew manage?" It was very hard for her to picture herself in that environment. The house Bill had in mind was the old and elegant but somewhat faded DeMorse house, built in 1833—one of the first in Clarksville—for Charles DeMorse, founder of the *Northern Standard* newspaper; this colonial house was available, although its trustees were bound by a covenant that dictated restoration requirements.[23]

Whether Humphrey was amenable to the restoration requirements is unknown, how much Dorothy's apprehension was a factor is also unknown, but what is clear is that completing the other half of the real-estate equation failed: although the Humphreys had found a buyer for High Meadow in the fall of 1979, they had been unable to find another house in New York state appropriate to their needs. They then decided to try to purchase a small lot and build a house to suit them, a plan that faced disillusionment on two fronts: first, they were dismayed to find that land in smaller parcels costs not less but more than a big holding like theirs; second, after talking with an architect, they realized that instead of coming out of the sale of High Meadow with money enough to build and some left over, it would cost them more than they would get. After the architect left, Bill and Dorothy were in such a state of stupefaction that when they finished preparing supper they left a burner on under a pan of oil, resulting in a fire that severely burnt both of Dorothy's hands as she tried to extinguish it. They decided not to sign the contract offered by their buyer and instead set about making repairs to the kitchen and the four rooms damaged by smoke. By Christmas Dorothy's hands had healed.[24] The DeMorse house in Clarksville was forgotten.

While the house hunting had been going on, Humphrey had begun to work on his fourth novel. The universal praise for *Farther Off from Heaven*, which might have countered the pain from the disastrous reception of *Proud Flesh*, was muted by Knopf's refusal to promote the memoir, even to supply bookstores

23. Dorothy Humphrey to Grabstald, 11 May 1978, HG Letters; Pat C. Beadle to Humphrey, 23 June 1978, WH Coll., UT; *Red River Recollections* (Clarksville, Tex.: Red River County Historical Society, 1986), 29.

24. Humphrey to Lawrence, 26 December 1979, Lawrence Coll.

with it, and by the firm's remaindering it prematurely in 1978. "Knopf's treatment of me," he had said in a letter to Norah Smallwood, has "had me constantly
depressed for months now and I can't shake it."[25] Clearly his cast of thought
was colored by the disappointment of lost possibility and the disintegration of
relationships. Humphrey very naturally followed his turn of mind to a work of
fiction that would be a metaphor for his own saddened existence. And so, in 1978,
he began to think of the tragic story that he would name *Hostages to Fortune*. He
wondered if he could write the story he was putting together in his head, if he
had the strength, the will, the imagination to get it written. On a particularly dark
day—the date in his notebook is not given—he concluded that he was bereft of
the requisite attributes (WH Coll., UT).

If the tale that he was then contemplating was the typed scenario among his
papers in Austin—an early version of the material, which would have resulted in
a very different novel—then it is just as well that he was not up to writing at the
time. For he had concocted an outlandish tale about a man's son committing
suicide and the father's retrieving his son's body, wrapping it in a bed sheet, and
placing it in the backseat of a rental car—and then proceeding as though he were
a New Jersey Anse Bundren bent on conveying that boy to the place he would
like to be buried. This contemporary version of *As I Lay Dying* would have involved various adventures along the way, such as the father's being arrested by a
state trooper and accused of murder. The central day in this scenario is the one
the father spends digging his son's grave on his prep school's campus, all the
while reviewing his life and his son's. In keeping with this outlandish conception,
Humphrey planned to provide a comic dimension to the father's suicide attempt.
In his notebook the following extraordinary comment about "the comic failure
of his suicide attempt" appears: "Remember: it's not comic to him. At least not
at first though making it *then* comic to him could give him a human dimension."
When it eventually occurred to Humphrey that he ought not to try to write the
story as he first conceived it, he was again loose from all moorings: "What do I
do in order simply to stay alive[?] Not that I want to stay alive. But here I am."[26]

Humphrey was still here in 1979, and by then he had begun to refine his conception of the novel about a father whose son has killed himself. He found that
he had the attributes needed to write a very different novel from the one he had
at first imagined. More optimistic about writing and publishing because of his
new affiliation with his longtime friend Seymour Lawrence, Bill had 140 pages

25. Goerner to Humphrey, 12 December 1978, WH Coll., UT; Humphrey to Smallwood, 19 December 1978, C&W.
26. Humphrey, notebook, entry in 1978, WH Coll., UT.

written by year's end. In 1980 progress on the novel was hampered somewhat, however, by the fishing excursions that *Sports Illustrated* sent him on. Yet it happened that it was a *Sports Illustrated* connection that provided Humphrey with an opportunity to work on *Hostages* nearly distraction-free for two months during the coming winter. Pierre Affre, Humphrey's veterinarian friend in Paris who spent most of his time off fishing in some remote part of the world and who was the subject of one of Humphrey's fishing essays in *Sports Illustrated,* had been house-sitting for his friend Jean-François Gaillard. Affre was off to the Amazon and offered Gaillard's elegant apartment with a private garden situated on a private ally near Place Pigalle. It was a pleasant environment for work, the only drawback being the daily vocalizations of their neighbor upstairs, soprano Regine Crespin.[27]

It was Humphrey's custom to work on more than one book at the same time, as when he moved between the manuscripts of *The Ordways, Proud Flesh,* and *A Time and a Place.* This was less the case, however, with *Hostages to Fortune.* Though *No Resting Place* did share space with *Hostages* on his writing table, it was only for a brief period. Once Humphrey sensed the way to go with *Hostages to Fortune,* he went at it single-mindedly. This decision disregarded the advice of his new publisher, Seymour Lawrence. On 30 December 1980 Humphrey had sent from Paris a fairly large chunk of *Hostages* (140 pages) and a lesser portion of *No Resting Place*—"The Cherokees," as it was then called. On 23 January 1981 Lawrence responded with enthusiasm, but with a surprising preference:

> HOSTAGES TO FORTUNE moves extremely well and held my interest throughout. It is hard to say more at this stage until, as you expressed it so well, the characters tell you what is to become of them.
>
> But what really excited me were the first 26 pages of THE CHEROKEES. It's beautifully told and has a depth and rare quality not to be found in contemporary fiction. I wish you would drop everything and concentrate on this book. These opening pages tell me so much already and promise even more. . . . There's a world in this book and I urge you with all my heart to recreate it.
>
> I am sure that HOSTAGES TO FORTUNE will be a good book, and a very thoughtful one. But THE CHEROKEES has magnificence and a forceful appeal. (Lawrence Coll.)

27. Humphrey to Lambert, 19 December 1980, Lambert Coll.; to Smallwood, 19 December 1980, C&W; to Lawrence, 28 December 1980, Lawrence Coll.

Humphrey's response was immediate; on 28 January he explained that he had hit his stride with *Hostages* and would have to put the historical novel aside:

> Your response to the MSS. is immensely gratifying and I am glowing from yr. praise. It will mean much encouragement to me as I go on. I didn't choose to work 1st on Hostages—it just happened that way. But now I'm well into it and it absorbs my thoughts and it's going well (I'm working here—hard) and it would seem a mistake to drop it at such a time. You may be right that the Indian book is the better one but I've got this one in me and I must be grateful for it and attentive to its dictates. Don't you agree? I'm not sure I could divert my mind from what I'm doing right now if I tried. (Lawrence Coll.)

After an account of the kind attentions the Gallimard firm was showering upon him, Humphrey closed his letter with an effort to appease Lawrence: "I can't do as you'd like and switch horses now but don't be disappointed. Everything will come of its own and in its own time" (Lawrence Coll.). The serenity of this expression tells that the kind of agony that Humphrey faced with the previous two novels was behind him. In the writing of *Hostages to Fortune* Humphrey was master: he was in cool control of his material, and he created the most moving novel of his life.

In 1981 Humphrey was a visiting professor at Princeton University for the fall semester. Princeton worked him a good deal harder than he had been led to expect, for he had thirty students turning in short stories for him to read and ponder and criticize every week. When deer season came round, Humphrey made an escape and hunted for seven days in Hudson with his friend and neighbor Bob Fisher and Dorothy. Nonetheless, Humphrey felt that he earned his $18,000 salary. According to Ted Weiss, who was then a full-time member of the faculty at Princeton, Humphrey formed friendships with several students that went on after his leaving Princeton, and when he gave a very successful public reading of *The Spawning Run,* a number of the faculty were taken with his writing—and with him. Although Humphrey had a pleasant time during his term at Princeton, he thought the cocktail and dinner parties were "too much," even though he was glad to have gotten to know some of the people he met on those social occasions, especially the English poet Charles Tomlinson, who dedicated his poem "Of the Winter Ball Game" to Humphrey after he had persuaded Tomlinson to attend a football game with him. The demanding post at Princeton had left him little time to write, but that academic setting did provide the details for an important scene in *Hostages to Fortune:* the father's visit to the campus where his son had hanged himself. After Humphrey's tenure at Princeton, he and his wife spent most of the winter of 1982 in Paris, during which time he pounded on his typewriter eight to ten hours a day. He made excellent progress on *Hostages* even though on 27 January the accident-prone Humphrey broke the third finger of his right hand, no great handicap for one who typed with two fingers.[28] In fact, he had written two hundred pages before 9 February, when he and Dorothy departed from Paris to spend a week—as they had done the previous year—with Trekkie Parsons in Sussex, after which they went to London for a week before returning to Hudson.

Once home, Humphrey continued working steadily and by July 1982 could see the end—a time in the writing process that was always exhilarating for him. Opportunities to fish, travel, and lecture, however, intervened. In the early fall of 1982 he accepted an invitation from Toby Eady to fish the Itchen and the Test, "the world's two most storied trout streams,"[29] after which he traveled to Hendrix College in Arkansas on 9 November, where he participated in a program on contemporary southern fiction with Reynolds Price, Andrew Lytle, Harry Crews, David Madden, Cleanth Brooks, and Robert Drake. On 12 November, Humphrey boarded a Trailways bus in Conway, Arkansas, and headed for Clarksville, mainly to visit his uncle Bernard Varley. On 17 November he gave a reading at the Red River County Public Library; to the home folks there he read "A Voice from the Woods," which is based on a noontime robbery of the Red River National Bank in 1927. His old acquaintance Gavin Watson put him up in a little house at the Clarksville country club. When he returned to Hudson, he and Dorothy went deer hunting, and she shot a roe between the eyes. They met Jean Lambert at the train station with the deer tied to the car, and that evening they all ate the liver and then had the kidneys for breakfast. On Thanksgiving Day Humphrey read passages from his novel in progress, *Hostages to Fortune.*[30]

Humphrey received an invitation in 1983 that compelled him once again to lay aside the manuscript of *Hostages*. On 25 April he wrote the following amusing message to Yannick Guillou of Gallimard:

28. "Deer Season, 1981" (notebook), WH Coll., UT; Aaron Lemonick to Humphrey, 21 July 1981, WH Coll., UT; Humphrey to Smallwood, 26 October 1981, C&W; Weiss to author, 26 November 1997; Charles Tomlinson, *Collected Poems* (Oxford: Oxford University Press, 1985), 368 (in addition, Tomlinson's *Annunciations* [New York: Oxford University Press, 1989] contains a poem based on the Tomlinsons' visiting the Humphreys at High Meadow: "Hudson River School," with the dedication "*for Dorothy and Bill*" [18]); Humphrey to Lawrence, 28 January [1981], Lawrence Coll.

29. Humphrey to the Weisses, 24 August 1982, Weiss Coll.; Dorothy Humphrey to Lambert, 13 October 1982, Lambert Coll.

30. Gavin Watson, "Bill Humphrey Reading," *Clarksville Times*, 22 November 1982, 1; Jean Lambert, journal, entry for 24 November 1982, Lambert Coll.; Lambert, interview.

We are about to go off soon on another fishing expedition for Sports Illustrated. . . . To South America? No. To Alaska? No. After all, it is not just big fish that a fisherman is after—especially this fisherman. For as you will have noticed in my essays, I don't ever catch any fish anyway. What I look for when I go fishing is a beautiful river. Scenery. Tradition. A river which inspires such dedication in its fishermen that they don't really care whether they catch any fish. A river in some place where there is something to do with yourself when the fish are not biting. What does this begin to sound like to you? To me it sounds like the Seine in Paris. And so that is where I am being sent. (Gallimard)

He would be gone for a month, sitting under the Pont Neuf and the Pont Sully to fish for gardons and goujous. When Humphrey returned he quickly wrote the article "The Fishermen of the Seine," which was published in *Town and Country* instead of *Sports Illustrated*, and then went back to *Hostages*. He finished the novel (265 typewritten pages) during the second week of October. "Oh, how glad I am to be done with this painful book!" he wrote to Jean Lambert on 11 October. By 21 May he had returned the proofs, and the book was due to be published on 21 September 1984.[31]

Hostages to Fortune is both like and unlike Humphrey's previous novels. *Home from the Hill* and *The Ordways* focus on the relationship between father and son and the gulf created between them. In *Proud Flesh*, though the father is long absent, an extensive family remains. The title *Hostages to Fortune* would seem to signal yet another portrayal of traditional family relationships, for it is taken from Francis Bacon's maxim, "He that hath a wife and children hath given hostages to fortune" *(Essays).*[32] At the opening of *Hostages to Fortune*, however, fortune has already levied her ultimate claim, and the protagonist, Ben Curtis, is left with no family. Following his son's suicide, he is a man who has lost everything—as Humphrey says in his notebook, "reduced to nothingness, which is to say, to himself" (WH Coll., UT). He has undergone an extended period of isolation, the likes of which appear nowhere else in modern American literature.

Unlike the characters who belong to the extensive southern families of the Clarksville novels, Ben has no wife (she has left him), and he is an orphan, his parents and sister having died in a fire when he was only ten. Nor is Ben a south-

31. *OS*, 205–29; Humphrey to Lambert, 11 October and 4 November [1983], Lambert Coll.; to Pierre Affre, 11 October [1983] and 21 May 1984 (letters in Affre's possession, Paris, France).

32. Humphrey found his title early, seriously considering only two others: "The Savour of Salt" and "All Good Things" (notebook, WH Coll., UT).

erner: he was born in Kansas and has lived in Blairstown, New Jersey, for all of his married life. In providing a northeastern setting for the novel, Humphrey revived a feature of his first collection of short stories, half of which are set there.

Hostages to Fortune is like the other novels in that it is based upon real people and some real events. In an interview years ago Humphrey said that this novel "is based on two terrible events in the lives of two dear friends of mine. My friend Ted had a son hang himself in his first semester at Harvard. And his friend, and my friend, Andy, had a daughter kill herself by jumping off a building in Philadelphia in the second year of her marriage. . . . Many of the events in the novel are very much as they happened" (*WST*, 28). Blanche Knopf, in a letter expressing her appreciation for what Humphrey accomplished in *Hostages to Fortune* (even though it was not published by the Knopf firm), added a postscript that provides a fairly clear indication of Ted's identity: "What a gift you have made Ted Thomas." Edmond G. Thomas owned a medical advertising agency called Ted Thomas Associates and was an old fishing companion of Humphrey's during and after the years that he taught at Bard and is the real-life basis for the character Ben Curtis. It was in August 1960 when they were both sailing off Penobscot Bay in Maine as guests of Andy and Pat Wanning that Humphrey first met Ted. The Wannings had a thirty-nine-foot yawl with five sails, and during the week on the boat while Humphrey learned the rudiments of sailing, he made a new and lasting friend. Andy, the original for the character of Tony Thayer, is Andrews Wanning, who was Humphrey's colleague at Bard, having joined the faculty two years after Humphrey; he was a specialist in seventeenth-century English prose.[33]

Soon after Humphrey met Ted and Virginia (Jinny) Thomas, their son Michael, twenty, was found dead in a dormitory room at Harvard. It was some years later that Wanning's daughter, Margaret Sommer, committed suicide in Philadelphia. On 16 October 1970, Humphrey records in one of his notebooks for *Proud Flesh,* Andy telephoned to say that Margaret, who was twenty-three years old, had killed herself the night before in Philadelphia. When Bill and Dorothy succeeded in luring the Wannings out of the house where for a week they had sat alone together in silence, they learned that Margaret had in fact thrown herself from the Lippincott Building, where she worked as a copy editor.[34] "I was

33. Blanche Knopf to Humphrey, 16 September 1984, WH Coll., UT; Sally Thomas to author, 13 December 1997; *The Bardian,* Fall 1997, 32; Dorothy Humphrey to Harry and Milly Grabstald, 30 August 1960, HG Letters. Eight years later Bill and Dorothy once again sailed the waters off Maine as guests of the Wannings (Dorothy Humphrey to Grabstald, 17 July 1968, HG Letters).

34. Humphrey to Lyons, 26 and 28 October 1970, Lyons Coll.

drawn to the subject from the start," Humphrey has said, "but I did say to both I meant to write about it, but I wouldn't if they objected. One of the two said, if you can make anything out of it, it will make it that much less painful for me" (Au Int.). The friend who said this was Ted, a large, robust man who could accommodate himself to the fictional portrayal of a painful event in his life; also, twenty-four years had elapsed since the event. Wanning, on the other hand, apparently did not give his blessing to Bill's idea for a novel—or else did not realize that the actual events surrounding his daughter's suicide would appear unaltered. Much less time had passed since the event, and so his and his wife's feelings were more sensitive to the public display of their personal loss and suffering. After the publication of the novel, Wanning, who had been Humphrey's friend for almost thirty-five years, withdrew somewhat, though there was no formal breach, according to Nick Lyons. Wanning's son Rufus, however, recalls no such diminution.[35]

Humphrey sets out in *Hostages to Fortune* to assume the pain of his friends, both of whom he was seeing regularly as he began work on the novel.[36] It "doesn't really give a picture of either of those two men," Humphrey explained— "both of them are me, and how I would feel if I had a child kill himself" (*WST*, 28). Indeed, elsewhere, in a catalog of the many lives that he has assumed as a fiction writer, he remarked, "I have been a father (I who am nobody's father) suffering the agony of his young son's suicide" (*WST*, 187). Bert Almon says that Humphrey's own experience is tied to the suffering of his character Ben Curtis. The agonizing struggle to finish *Proud Flesh* and the struggles with "The Horse Latitudes," he argues, provided the personal suffering that Humphrey brought over to his fictional character (Almon, 305). Almon's suggestion seems incredible, for to pose a direct connection between the suffering attendant upon writing a book and the suffering of a father over the loss of a child by suicide seems outrageous (even if Ted Thomas had also made such an equation [see Almon, 306]). But Almon's theory might in fact get close to the truth. A passage in Jean Lambert's journal explains convincingly the link between the father of a suicide and Humphrey's life. When Lambert expressed astonishment that Humphrey could represent so believably a father's loss of his son, he explained that he had drawn upon his reaction to the reception of *Proud Flesh* and life in its wake—the life of silence and isolation. Humphrey even says that he depicted the sinister

35. Lyons, telephone interview by author, tape recording, 28 July 1999; Rufus Wanning, telephone interview by author, 1 September 2001.

36. Humphrey to Lyons, 18 February 1979, Lyons Coll.

environment of his own home in portraying the life of Ben and Cathy before their breakup.[37]

To be sure, there are many indications that Humphrey imaginatively became the character based upon Ted Thomas. The novel's description of the prep school cemetery where Tony buries the ashes of his son comes directly from Humphrey's experience. Bard College has its own cemetery (studded with old oak trees like the one at the fictional prep school) on the edge of campus where long-tenured faculty members and old graduates are buried. In fact, Humphrey's notebook says that the campus in the novel is based on Bard. Furthermore, like his character Ben, who in the opening scene of the novel is protecting himself against insect stings, Humphrey was allergic to bee stings, his letters containing frequent references to his being laid low by them ("I am highly allergic," he said).[38] Bill also attributes his own family history, while not to Ben, to Ben's wife Cathy, who is "only a generation removed from southern sharecropping" (HF, 174). Finally, Ben's shotgun, with its highly polished walnut stock and the subtle engraving of the metal, is obviously based upon Humphrey's own best shotgun, which he bequeathed to his friend Bob Fisher two days before he died.[39]

The old house ("totally rural") that Ben and his wife Cathy buy and restore sounds very much like the old house that the Humphreys bought near Hudson in 1965 and spent years fixing up, doing much of the work themselves as money became available after the publication of each book; this is the modus operandi of the Curtises as well (see HF, 172). Both the real and the fictional couple furnished the house in the same manner: they searched through shops in nearby towns and attended household auctions, buying antiques at bargain prices. The particular antiques that Humphrey places in Ben and Cathy's house belong to High Meadow, including a mahogany window seat by McIntyre of Salem (which was in Bill's library as he wrote Hostages), a Launnier pier table, and a rosewood washstand stenciled in gold. The author and his wife had in common with the fictional couple a special interest in early Empire style (HF, 173). Finally, the Humphreys', like the Curtises', was a "neglected house" surrounded by "neglected grounds"; both Humphrey and Ben Curtis "planted shrubs" and "laid out a rose garden and beds of cut-flowers."[40]

Ben, also a fiction writer, says that "the house was written into his books,"

37. Journal of Jean Lambert, entry for 28 December 1984, Lambert Coll.

38. Humphrey, notebook, entry for 22 December [1982?], WH Coll., UT; HF, 176; Humphrey to Lambert, 13 July [1977], Lambert Coll.; to Lyons, 10 August [1977], Lyons Coll.; to the Weisses, 25 August 1977, Weiss Coll.; Alistair Whitton to Humphrey, 25 August 1977, WH Coll., UT.

39. Humphrey to Bob Fisher, 18 August 1997 (note in Fisher's possession); HF, 39.

40. Humphrey to Lawrence, 24 January 1969, Lawrence Coll.; HF, 172.

and in the same way, Humphrey makes his house Ben's house—and he writes it into his book about Ben Curtis. For Ben, the house "and its furnishings had been his storehouse of metaphors," the narrator explaining: "Whenever he felt the need of one to convey his meaning, a stroll outside or a session in the kitchen usually suggested one" (HF, 174). Thus Humphrey has Ben ask, "People who killed themselves on the doorsill of life were ones to whom life's challenges seemed too great for the effort, weren't they?" (97). Similes as well come from observations in the house: "Above the ground a low-lying luminosity, like the crack of light at the bottom of a curtain, gave presentiment of day" (106). And as Ben walks about the empty house after Cathy has walked out on him, Humphrey writes on behalf of his character: "On her desk a revolving calendar showed the date on which she had left. He reset it not to the day's date but to that of Anthony's death. It was like the inscription on the burial vault of a family that had perished all together, for this room in which he had been conceived was now the tomb of the love that had died on the day Anthony killed himself" (169–70).[41] Further, one of Humphrey's sessions in the kitchen, in all likelihood, provided the manner of Ben's perception of his own life: "His clumsiness in the kitchen would have been comical to watch. To see a man near fifty, trying to mop up an egg dropped on the floor, suddenly seeing in it the wreckage of his life and, on his knees, with tears in his eyes, begging 'Cathy, come back to me,' would have been amusing to someone else perhaps but not to the poor fool himself" (168).

The fictional character and the real author share another habit of composition. As Ben says the characters in his books "took over their destinies from his direction and went their own self-willed ways" (HF, 205), so had Humphrey, before the publication of Hostages to Fortune, remarked in an interview: "if the book is going to be any good, you have got to be ready to abandon your original ideas about it about half-way through. If it's any good, then the characters start telling you where it's going to go, instead of you telling them"(WST, 19).

In many other ways Humphrey lends the habits of his life to his characters: he and his wife worked at home, meeting occasionally during the day, and eating every meal together, as is the habit of the Curtises; Bill and Dorothy's five o'clock sherry becomes the habit of Ben and Cathy; Humphrey's standard whiskey at the time of the novel's writing, Jack Daniel's, is Ben's; and, as Humphrey and his

41. At first Humphrey had planned for Ben to burn the calendar but decided that was melodramatic and childish; see notebook, entry for 23 September [1983], WH Coll., UT. The final version resembles the description of the Hunnicutt inscriptions, which indicate that all members of the family had perished on the same date (HFH, 30).

wife often dressed up in unusual clothes and pretended to be other people, so do Ben and Cathy habitually dress up for dinner and pretend to be "landed gentry" in their ancient, dilapidated house (*HF*, 163, 173). One of Humphrey's favorite bon mots was that "a writer was somebody for whom writing was harder than it was for other people," and indeed that is one of Ben's pet witticisms as well (*HF*, 188). Also, the account of Ben and Tony's annual rite of dipping and hoisting nets loaded with thousands of spawning herring on the banks of the Hudson River is based on Humphrey's own annual rite, usually in the company of Dick Bard (see *HF*, 35–37). Harry Grabstald, who accompanied Bill on one occasion, described the very procedure set forth in the novel: "he would just get at the edge of the Hudson where he knew they were, and he'd dip the screen down, pick up herring, toss them over on the shore, and then repeat that procedure over and over, and then put them in a big container still wriggling. The Hudson was just full of herring." In his relationship with Ted Thomas, Humphrey was in the habit of frequently saying, when they were drinking, "Just one more before we have another one," and this is the running joke between Ben and Tony.[42] Finally, Humphrey said on many occasions the very words that explain why Ben leaves behind all of his published books when he moves to his moated dwelling after Anthony's burial: Ben was "never one to reread his books once the proofs had been corrected" (*HF*, 188).

One thing remains to be said about Humphrey's portrayal of Andrews Wanning's loss in the novel. Although the character of Tony Thayer is based upon what *happened* in the life of Wanning, the personality of Tony is actually based upon another friend of Humphrey's, Chandler Chapman, who had died in April 1982. Humphrey once remarked that Saul Bellow, in *Henderson the Rain King*, did not succeed in getting all there is of Chandler down on paper, and so apparently Humphrey tried to capture some more of this "storm of a man" in print.[43] Rather than the self-contained, retiring Wanning, Humphrey used Chapman as his model for Tony Thayer, a bear of a man, exuberant and overflowing with gusto, laughter, raillery, and song. Like Chapman, Thayer was an early riser, "restless for each day to begin" (*HF*, 38). It was certainly not Wanning (though it was his sailing vessel) who inspired the account of Tony's doing "a back somersault over the rail" of the boat, hitting the water feet first, sinking from sight and

42. Helen Bard, interview by author, tape recording, 28 August 2001, Milan, N.Y.; Harry Grabstald, interview by author, tape recording, Little Rock, Ark., 23 April 2000; Sally Thomas to author, 2 January 1998.

43. Humphrey to Lambert, 13 January 1967, Lambert Coll.; Humphrey, "Storm of a Man," *Barrytown Explorer* 24, no. 2 (April 1982): 2.

resurfacing "with his drowned pipe clenched between his teeth" (70). Thayer's constant quoting of poetry is suggested by Chapman's practice of printing poetry, some of his own devising, in the newspaper of which he was publisher and editor, the *Barrytown Explorer*. Chapman came from an aristocratic Hudson Valley family (his father was the famous scholar and reformer John Jay Chapman, and his mother, Elizabeth Winthrop, was related to the Astors), and this is a feature of the patrician Thayer who was connected to the Astors and the Livingstons.[44] His great country estate is modeled upon the one Chandler inherited (located near the Bard College campus). The confident display of eccentric behavior that everyone who knew Chandler remarks on is a feature of Tony's personality. For example, "His first act on getting up in the morning was to step outside and, while relieving himself, assess the weather. Not even a blizzard could stop him" (*HF*, 39). This is probably a practice that Humphrey observed in Chapman.

Humphrey used other friends to complete his cast of characters. He might have been thinking of his friend Nick Lyons's son when he gave Thayer's son the name of Anthony, and it is extremely likely that he was recalling the fishing expertise of Pierre Affre in creating Ben's description of Anthony's fly-fishing technique. Like Anthony, Pierre was obsessed with fishing, and Humphrey believed him to be one of the "most knowledgeable fishermen alive."[45]

Thus, in a rather complicated but still very real way, Humphrey makes his own life the life of Ted Thomas and Andrews Wanning, taking on the suffering that his friends had undergone. This undertaking was a risky one, because the opportunity of taking an inauthentic step, of sounding the wrong emotional note, of seeming false and overdramatic, of lapsing into sentimentalism presented itself at every turn. Yet Humphrey avoided these pitfalls. After reading Humphrey's manuscript, Nick Lyons told its author that he knew of nothing ever written that captured so perfectly the anguish that human beings are capable of. Mary O'Rourke's assessment of Thomas Hardy's treatment of human suffer-

---

44. *HF*, 34. When Chapman was on his deathbed, Humphrey visited his friend, who was rambling on about his family connections: "You know, Bill, I am an Astor." Humphrey's reply was "No, Chandler, you are a half-Astor" (Brooks Wright to author, 12 July 1999).

45. Humphrey to the Lyonses, [February 1976], Lyons Coll. Though Humphrey wrote in detail about Anthony's expertise as a falconer, he had no experience with the sport beyond going with his friend Dick Bard once or twice to feed his son Robby's pet falcon, Harriet. As Stephen Bodio, author of *A Rage for Falcons* (New York: Nick Lyons Books, 1984) says, "Bill never knew any falconers. He imagined it right" (Humphrey to Lyons, undated, Lyons Coll.; Bodio to author, 6 September 1999).

ing applies equally to Humphrey: "He is spiritually nailed to the Cross whose mind is crucified through compassion for his neighbour."[46]

Fishing, a favorite metaphor of Humphrey's, plays the same role in *Hostages to Fortune* that it does in Hemingway—as a point of focus for a man trying to steady himself after a staggering psychological ordeal. Like Hemingway's wounded men, Ben Curtis is an emotionally ravaged man who has returned to fish in the clear waters of what is to him "the good place," to borrow an apt term from Hemingway's *In Our Time*. The trout brooks represent a clear past that Ben desires to recapture: "During his year away from it, on nights when he lay awake in bed, he had retraced it, sometimes from the top down, sometimes from the bottom up, recalling as closely as he could individual trees, boulders, shallows and pools, bends where the bank was undercut, fish he had caught and fish he had hooked and lost" (*HF*, 19). This passage is strikingly similar to the following from Hemingway's "Now I Lay Me": "I had different ways of occupying myself while I lay awake. I would think of a trout stream I had fished along when I was a boy and fish its whole length very carefully in my mind; fishing very carefully under all the logs, all the turns of the bank, the deep holes and the clear shallow stretches, sometimes catching trout and sometimes losing them."[47] The details of the day on which Ben returns are in many ways reminiscent of Nick Adams in the two parts of "Big Two-Hearted River," a story that Humphrey knew well; for in the manuscript of the unpublished novel "The Horse Latitudes" (written between *Proud Flesh* and the present novel), his character Cecil Smoot succumbs to Cooper's Vintage Oxford Marmalade "in the spirit of Hemingway's Nick Adams with the canned spaghetti on that fishing trip of his to the Big Two-Hearted River"—and then Humphrey quotes from Hemingway's story (MS, p. 26, in WH Coll., UT).

Although Ben is much older than Nick, both men return to fish for trout in a stream that remains unchanged when each of them has undergone an ordeal that has profoundly affected his mental stability and changed him utterly. As "Nick's hand was shaky," Ben's has a "steady tremor."[48] Having left much behind that is troubling, both men assiduously attend to simple rituals of preparation that keep their minds from "starting to work."[49] For Ben the "fussy little ritual

46. Lyons to Humphrey, 18 October 1983, WH Coll., UT; see Martin Seymour-Smith, *Hardy* (New York: St. Martin's Press, 1994), 795.

47. Ernest Hemingway, "Now I Lay Me," in *The Short Stories of Ernest Hemingway* (New York: Charles Scribner's Sons, 1953), 363.

48. Ernest Hemingway, *In Our Time* (New York: Charles Scribner's Sons, 1958), 204; *HF*, 4.

49. Hemingway, 191.

of readying for a day's fishing reined in the mind, kept it in a channel between narrow banks." As he attends to the threading of the line through the guides, the clipping off of the old leader and replacing it with a new one, the tying of a blood knot, he checks on his mental equilibrium:

> "How we doing?" he asked himself.
> "Doing all right but it's better not to ask," he answered himself. (*HF*, 4)

Once Nick completes his tasks that have controlled and channeled his thoughts, he feels shaky: "He had not been unhappy all day. This was different though. Now things were done. There had been this to do. Now it was done."[50] Then "he saw a mist rising"—a sign that clarity of mind is on the verge of giving way to confusion; Ben, too, observes the "mist rising off the water."[51]

Yet in returning to the places that represent to them their previously whole selves, each man is restored to some extent. As Nick "felt all the old feeling," Ben "wait[ed] for the old thrill to rise in him, to see whether it would once again."[52] Nick is surprised by happiness as he goes into the water: "He stepped into the stream. It was a shock. His trousers clung tight to his legs." Likewise, "The shock of the icy water on [Ben's] feet and legs sufficed to dispel from his mind" the fragments of his "divided world."[53]

Humphrey even uses some of those short sentences that Hemingway is famous for and that portray effectively a mind making an effort to hold steady in the presence of an impulse to give way to confusion. Both authors employ this technique when they portray their characters at their eating rituals, or in anticipation of them. First, Nick: "While he waited for the coffee to boil, he opened a small can of apricots. He liked to open cans. He emptied the can of apricots out into a tin cup."[54] Ben, his morning of fishing ending, anticipates his break for lunch, and he thinks of the thermos of martinis in his lunch basket: "Today he would have just his one. That was more than he was used to having in midday now. He was looking forward to it" (*HF*, 111). The style in each passage portrays tight control, the deliberate attention of the mind, the need for simplicity. Ben "was still in training and must guard against rushing his sensations. They got out of hand when he tried to deal with too many at a time" (112). Similarly, Nick "did not want to rush his sensations any."[55]

50. Ibid., 186.
51. Ibid., 188; *HF*, 15.
52. Hemingway, *In Our Time*, 178; *HF*, 22.
53. Hemingway, *In Our Time*, 199; *HF*, 21.
54. Hemingway, *In Our Time*, 189.
55. Ibid., 204.

Why has Humphrey gone to the trouble of making Ben a "two-hearted person" (the term actually appears in Part 1 of *Hostages*), of reproducing the patterns of Hemingway's story? For more reason than to offer tribute to his predecessor's technique, for more reason than to give readers some pleasure in noticing the parallels. Because we feel the pervading presence of Nick Adams in *Hostages*, something of his youthful effort to steady himself against the currents of thought and feeling that would undermine his sanity comes to Ben Curtis, who in his middle years struggles to right himself following months of being mentally out of equilibrium. In other words, the integration of Hemingway's hero into the form of the present depiction lends weight and depth to it. Our certainty of the heroic effort, our sense of the energy and concentration needed to still the dangerous emotions, is amplified in Humphrey's character because of the shadow presence of Hemingway's.

At the end of the day's fishing, both Nick and Ben are pleased to have landed one good trout. Neither requires more. But here all similarity between these characters ends. Nick Adams succeeds in keeping his mind from turning to what he came to the trout stream to escape. Ben Curtis does not: "His thoughts turned [to them]—no stopping them" (*HF*, 26). This profound difference is why "Big Two-Hearted River" is merely a two-part short story and why *Hostages to Fortune* is a novel. It is all of the "before" that lies behind Ben that gives substance and depth to Humphrey's novel.

In fact, that "before" is alluded to metaphorically in the opening description of Ben:

> He stood with his eyes shut tight and covered by his hand, holding his breath while the icy insect repellent dried on his skin. He had sprayed himself down to the waist, avoiding the palms of his hands, for the stuff could take the varnish off a bamboo fishing rod. He was allergic to the sting of bees, wasps, and hornets and to the bite of deerflies, of which, now in June, the woods were full. Unlike other people, he did not absorb and shed the venom; in him it accumulated, and he had been stung so many times now he was full of it. More stings, maybe just one more, could prove fatal to him, his doctor had warned. After all he had come through, that would be a senseless way to go. The doctor's advice was that he not take up fishing again. (*HF*, 3)

Having been stung repeatedly by the bitter assaults of life, and feeling the cumulative effect of those assaults, he is now anointing himself "against his enemies," and thus we see that he has a will to live and means to protect himself (3). The metaphorical dimension of the stings is unmistakable, for later on the narrator comments: "For him [fishing] was a dangerous recreation, fraught with too many memories of a life now lost. Already he had been stung repeatedly on this outing and not by insects, as his doctor, who was not an allergist but rather an analyst, had warned him he would be" (20). The memory of what he has lost is only part of the danger Ben's mind faces; there is as well his overwhelming guilt for his part in the loss. Thus Humphrey's metaphor mutates to disclose a further dimension of Ben's suffering: "It was not against people that he needed protection. What he needed was a spray for protection against himself, against the stings of remorse. He had had many, and he did not shed the venom. In him it accumulated" (153).

The structure of *Hostages to Fortune* is similar to that of *Farther Off from Heaven*. The memoir's central event is the death of Humphrey's father when the son was only thirteen; stemming off that core event, like nerves connected to a spinal column, are a ganglia of before-and-after memories that show how the boy's life was forever changed by a car wreck. Humphrey alters chronology in *Hostages to Fortune* in a similar yet significantly different way. The nervous center of this novel is the day on which the protagonist reenters life after being for two years on a descent into darkness, and the ganglia of memories offer startling contrasts of exhilarating happiness and life-defying emotional agony caused by the suicide of his son and worsened by his wife's leaving him and the suicide of his best friend. (Theoretically, this contrast might be too stark, the blue sky of the happy days too blue to believe in, which could possibly have the unfortunate effect of casting doubt upon the dark days of despair that follow, yet this effect seems hardly ever an aspect of readers' responses.) The gradual disclosure of the impact of a variety of events on Ben's consciousness bit by bit limns his emotional constitution. Sometimes Humphrey merely obliquely alludes to events that had assaulted Ben's consciousness, then clarifies and fills in later on. These techniques, in addition to the strategy of not revealing the calamity of his life until the time when he is on his way to recovery, creates a distance between the character's deep personal suffering and the reader; yet this distance has the reverse effect of drawing the reader into the suffering. Another way of speaking of the structure's function is to say that the account of Ben Curtis's being swamped by sorrow requires containment, and the frame is the artful container, a kind of structural understatement. The structure grows less evident as the novel plunges deeper and deeper into Curtis's mind, and some readers might recoil from the turmoil, feeling that they have been cut loose from the steadying effect of the artful construction. But the frame's final importance is that it informs the reader that the central character has survived his ordeal and that perhaps there is something to be learned from it about how to live.

The overt action of the novel, then, takes place in one day, a day of fly fishing, Ben having returned on the previous evening, after a hiatus of two years, to the fishing club that he has belonged to for twenty years. (The fishing club in the novel is based upon Pohoqualine in the Pocono Mountains of Pennsylvania, to which Ted Thomas invited Humphrey several times every year.)[56] The main substance of the novel consists of Ben's memories of events (as well as his analysis of and reaction to them), many of which occurred between his last and this sojourn at the fishing club. Like the real-life man upon whom Ben's life is based, his son has committed suicide during his first semester at college (Princeton in the novel, Harvard in the case of Ted Thomas's son). Ben's closest friend's daughter, Ben's godchild, has jumped off a skyscraper (New York in the novel, Philadelphia in real life). To these real-life facts Humphrey adds three fictional circumstances: Ben's wife Cathy leaves him after the death of Anthony; Ben's friend Tony Thayer, the father of his godchild, himself commits suicide; and Ben attempts to kill himself as well but is saved—how, we never know. Ben has been so close to death that he exhibited "no outward sign of life, no pulse, no discernible respiration, no reaction to the prick of pain" (*HF*, 216). The events leading to his attempted suicide and the physical and mental effects of the event itself have left their mark on his appearance—so much so that people who have known him for years think that he is a guest at the club, or a new member. At age forty-eight Ben had black hair and weighed 205 pounds; at age fifty he has white hair and weighs 170 pounds. Ben is defined in the present through this strong contrast to his past.

Hostages to Fortune is obviously linked to Shakespeare's great monument to a father's agony and regret, *King Lear*. The structure of the novel in fact has a double tragic plot as does Shakespeare's play. Lear contains a double dose of calamity, strife, and outrage—that of Lear's family being doubled by Gloucester's. In the same way, Humphrey presents first the suicide of Tony Thayer's daughter, the crumbling of his marriage, and Tony's suicide and then the suicide of Ben's son, the breakup of his marriage, and his interrupted suicide attempt. Humphrey integrates the parallel lives more thoroughly than Shakespeare, for he gives us Ben puzzling over the suffering of his friend Tony and his wife, observing the effect of the catastrophe on them, and never being able to enter into their

56. Thomas to author, 13 December 1997; Humphrey, notebook on *Proud Flesh*, entry for [September 1970], WH Coll., UT; Humphrey to Affre, 21 June 1979 (letter in Affre's possession, Paris, France).

suffering. All the while, Ben's own calamity awaits him. With no warning Ben suffers the very same fate as his friends. Ironically, Ben attains what he had wanted—full knowledge of the extent of his friend's agony. And as he is puzzled by the disintegration of his friends' marriage, so does he experience the same puzzlement over the disintegration of his own. The method works like a turbo, giving the novel added emotional horsepower.

The reader stands with Ben outside Tony and Pris Thayer's suffering; like Ben we are interlopers "in the close presence of inconsolable loss" (*HF*, 64). Ben's thoughts on his friends, after the first day of a cruise meant to mark their first effort to reenter life after their daughter's suicide, reveal the chasm between the observer and the participant in loss ("It was presumptuous enough of him to try to imagine the father's grief and guilt; the mother's, she in whose body had ripened that one smashed by itself out of all human semblance—at least he had the humility not even to try to imagine that" [57]). What Ben observes in his friend will be amplified in his own experience: the white strands in Tony's hair will come to fill Ben's head; the "unanswered question" will become a plethora of unanswered questions.

An important function of the parallel-couples structure is to allow Ben and the reader to observe the rift between the formerly happy Tony and Pris. Ben is astonished at the lack of sympathy between them: the loss that he had imagined would join them more solidly to each other has instead created an unbridgeable distance. Ben concludes that "suffering was not ennobling" as it is so often thought to be; "on the contrary, it was demeaning. Suffering distorted the heart, perverted its impulses" (*HF*, 54). Ben's probing memory and analysis tell him also, however, that "nonsuffering too" distorts the heart (59), and he knows from hindsight that his satisfaction in his illusion of immunity was a failure of insight. The call from Princeton that tells of Anthony's suicide awaits Ben's return from the cruise. Even then he feels that he and Cathy are not subject to the fate of Tony and Pris: "it was unthinkable now that there ever be another cross word between them" (126). The shrill irony is that there is hardly a word of any sort between them before she is gone, never to be heard from again.

The ever more pressing fact is that Tony's fate is Ben's fate. In a profound sense Ben becomes one with his longtime friend, in the way that Hieronimo sees himself in Bazulto in Thomas Kyd's *The Spanish Tragedy:* "Thou art the lively image of my grief" (3.13.160). Just before Ben receives the news that will initiate the duplication of their experiences, Humphrey employs an unusual rhetorical device to bring the two characters together as one. The third-person singular pronouns in the following passage seem to refer in each instance to Tony, but in the first of the following two paragraphs, starting with the sixth sentence, they actually refer to Ben. Anchored inside the harbor of the marina, the friends stop for what turns out to be their last meal together:

> They had had a drink and were having just one more before having another when Tony became dissatisfied with his fire. He went below to the galley and returned with a paper cup full of alcohol. When he poured the alcohol on the charcoal it flared and the stream became a fuse leading to the cup. It was not the first time this had ever happened. Tony was used to it. But he was not and when Tony set the cup on the deck to burn itself out he stamped on it. Tony did a back somersault over the rail, hit the water feet first and sank from sight. All this happened in a second.
> Tony surfaced with his drowned pipe clenched between his teeth. He was wearing shorts and when the cup was stamped his bare legs had been spattered with drops of burning alcohol. Tony's leap into the water had been as instinctive as was his stamping out the fire. (*HF*, 70)

The point of this curious ambiguity is that the suffering and absence of suffering that marked the distance between these two friends is to be circumvented, for they are soon to be one in the same in suffering—in the loss of their children by suicide, in the loss of their marriages, and in their own suicides. The motif of "stereo picture[s] whose halves refused to merge," but which "merge and become one" when one stares at the halves, supports the mutuality of experience that develops between these friends (6, 217).[57] Humphrey's technique of employing the ambiguous pronoun, then, emphasizes the characters' common humanity—as much as Will Vinson's and Sam Ordway's exchange of last names does the same in *The Ordways*. The mutuality of the friends' experiences is, however, lived by neither of them. Humphrey holds out common experience as a possibility for mutual understanding, and then he snatches away that redemptive morsel. Parallels to the contrary notwithstanding, Ben must now face in isolation what Tony has faced in isolation. Only the reader possesses the lenses that make in imagination the one image of suffering out of the two.

After the superintendent of the marina sends a skiff out to the anchored sailboat, Ben dials the New Jersey number that he is given, and his ordeal is underway. He is cast alone into the unplumbed salt-estranging sea, which has been prefigured in his friend's jump overboard. Ben feels the impossibility of "straining across the unbridgeable gulf that had opened all around him" (*HF*, 73). Being especially unable to face the commiseration of his friends, he sees a greater gulf

57. Other instances of "two eyes making one in sight" appear on pp. 21 and 86 of *HF*.

between them and him than he had known. Previously Tony's sorrow stood between them; now his does as well. Ben sees, too, that just as the mutual sorrow had come between his friend and his wife, so would it come between friend and friend: "The last persons on earth who would want to see him now were the dear friends who would understand only too well what he was going through. Nor did he want to see them. Only now did he realize how little he had really felt, how shallow his sympathy had been, how trite and beside the point his efforts to console them when they were enduring what he was enduring now. This bond had not brought them closer, it had sundered them" (74). The dominant theme in Humphrey's symphony of sorrow, then, becomes isolation. The lesson that Humphrey himself learned as a boy, his "first lesson in life's essential loneliness," was that "the grieving heart grieves all alone, in unbridgeable isolation," and this is the lesson that Ben learns as a nearly-fifty-year-old man (*FOFH*, 153); the inability of people to "reach and succor one another" brings home to Ben "the irremediable isolation in which we were each born to live and to die" (*HF*, 121). And so Ben does not look for any comfort from his wife, for "[i]t was a loneliness that nobody, not even Cathy, was going to be able entirely to fill" (92). As it turns out, she fills it not a jot. Upon learning of her son's death, Cathy locks herself in her room, venturing out only long enough to echo Pris's constant refrain to her husband: "Must you have *another* drink?" (159), and then she disappears. Unable to remain in his former family's house, Ben rents a house in Stone Ridge, on "an island of one solid rock," which is connected to civilization by a slim footbridge. His isolation is complete at this point.

In his isolation Ben can fixate on the innumerable unanswerable questions that flood his mind—questions about the cause, and the reason for the method, of his son's suicide: "His every trait must be reexamined for signs of morbidity. Harmless, even endearing little quirks of character were now seen as having been potentially pathological" (*HF*, 95). And so Ben questions and requestions:

What was Anthony demonstrating to the world by the way he had chosen to leave it? (132)

Had the end come when he discovered his likeness to humankind in one particular above all, and had he declared his difference in the only way possible, by not awaiting the common fate but by anticipating and thus forestalling it, taking matters into his own hands and making himself master of his? (140)

Did it make you seem more mature? If maturity was age and age was prox-imity to death, what better way to steal the march, overtake and outstrip your elders, get there before they did and repay them for what the poet called the ignominy of childhood? (134)

Why not? (135)

These are but a small sampling of the questions that rumble in Ben. He had begun the questioning rather dismayed by the "hopelessness of finding a motive" for his son's suicide; "he was dismayed now to discover the fertility of his mind in finding them" (134).

Ben does achieve some imaginative insights into his son's everyday behavior that yield a measure of understanding. As a boy his son would inflict punishment upon himself—confining himself to his room all day, for example—if he had done something wrong. This observation, put together with what Ben sees in the boy's relationship with the hunting falcon named Jezebel that he had trained, suggests a worrisome potential for self-immolation: "Not disgrace in men's eyes—disgrace in her own eyes. So it was with the boy; for the world's he cared nothing, it was his own disapproval he could not endure" (*HF,* 103). Anthony's relationship with another hawk, his first one, which he had found wounded, is also suggestive of how he viewed himself. He nursed the hawk in the bathtub; however, "When it was plain to see that the bird would never fly again but would be a dependent cripple he broke its neck with one quick snap. As he had broken his own rather than live on in whatever way it was that he felt himself impaired" (98). Had the boy failed at tasks set before him at Princeton, or found himself unequal to his own expectations, and concluded that failure was unendurable? Such questions Ben cannot hope to answer, and so his understanding is severely limited. Humphrey appears to have been portraying his character according to the truth that William Styron was soon to discover about himself—that "the greatest fallacy about suicide lies in the belief that there is a single, immediate answer—or perhaps combined answers—as to why the deed was done." The fu-tility of trying to ferret motives for a suicide might have been suggested to Hum-phrey by Leslie H. Farber's "Despair and the Life of Suicide," a work that Humphrey lists in his notebook on the novel. Farber might in turn have re-minded Bill of his own impulse to determine the cause of Margaret Sommer's suicide—was she depressed over a job that was working her to death so that her husband could "play around in his darkroom, play at being a photographer"? Or did she lack self-regard because when she was a child her mother remarked in her presence that she was her dumb child, her sister Esther the bright one?[58] At any rate, Humphrey's fictional father knows better than to accept easy answers and therefore allows himself only the most general of conclusions, namely, that Anthony knew "how deeply he was about to hurt his parents" and thus he must have been overwhelmed "with an unhappiness too deep for that to deter him" (*HF*, 138).

Although a definitive explanation of Anthony's suicide remains elusive, Ben moves ineluctably to the definitive reason for his own. The rather horrifying conclusion that *Hostages to Fortune* moves toward is that little understanding of a suicide can be gained without undergoing the experience of suicide oneself. Ben's first step in this direction is to isolate himself in every way possible: after moving to the island, he loses his glasses, so that he cannot see beyond his very immediate surroundings, and he drinks as much Jack Daniel's as he can hold. Detached from the world as thoroughly as he can make himself, Ben nurtures a deep melancholy and plunges into "desolation and despair" (*HF*, 193). He feels himself moving closer to his son as he hastens to the doorstep of suicide.

Like many others in the face of "desolation and despair," Ben seeks consolation in Holy Scripture. Ben turns to the Gospel of Matthew, to the consoling Sermon on the Mount, which contains the beatitudes that assure that "the poor of spirit" and "they that mourn" are not only blessed but are to be comforted. But like Dr. Faustus, Ben eschews the context of the biblical verses he quotes, for he is capable of seeing only what reflects his own despair. And so from the abundance of comforting words in chapter 5 of Matthew, Ben plucks the most despairing utterance: "*When salt has lost its savor wherewith shall it be salted?*" (Matthew 5:13; *HF*, 193). Like most of the quotations that Ben frequently resorts to, this one applies precisely to his predicament, indicating that he is no longer himself—for salt that has lost its savor cannot fulfill its proper function, is useless, and its saltiness can never be restored: thus the hopelessness of Ben's condition.

The section of the novel in which the protagonist moves ever closer to suicide because he is convinced that his condition is irreversible must have been especially difficult for Humphrey to write. On 23 March 1977, he requested that a friend send him a copy of Paul Valéry's *Various Occasions,* saying, "I remember from years ago that he makes in an essay on Stendhal's Julien Sorel, some inter-

---

58. William Styron, *Darkness Visible* (New York: Vintage, 1990), 39; Leslie H. Farber, "Despair and the Life of Suicide," in *Lying, Despair, Jealousy, Envy, Sex, Suicide, Drugs, and the Good Life* (New York: Basic Books, 1976), 65–66 (Humphrey would not have been impressed by the tangled formulations of Farber's opaque prose); Humphrey, notebook, entry for 16 October 1970, WH Coll., UT.

esting speculations on suicide" (Knopf Coll.). Humphrey's memory was faulty on two counts. Valéry's essay on Stendhal (not in *Occasions* but in *Variety: Second Series*) contains no speculations on suicide. There is, however, an essay entitled "On Suicide" in *Occasions*, which is likely the source to which Humphrey eventually turned for help.

Valéry's opening sentence observes that while some people intend to "do violence to themselves," others "merely give in to themselves and appear to follow some unknown and fatal line of destiny." It appears that Humphrey might well have followed this observation, individualizing it for his character, for Ben learns that the "means [of his suicide] was provided before the intention was discovered. . . . In his case he had been filling prescriptions for sleeping pills and hoarding them for weeks without questioning why, without letting himself observe what he was doing" (*HF*, 201). In this connection Valéry also observes that the method of suicide is predetermined: "A potential suicide who imagines himself hanging will never jump in the river." Humphrey elaborates on Valéry in depicting Ben's discovery that attitudes throughout life "dictate the mode of death": "The lifelong hydrophobiac will not drown himself nor the hater of fire arms blow out his brains" (*HF*, 201).[59] Having questioned why Anthony had hanged himself, and close to suicide himself, Ben answers "his old question about the suicide's choice of method, why one person chose to do it one way and another a different way." His discovery is that "One did not choose, one was chosen, predestined. For this person a gas oven waited, for that one a razor blade" (201). Yet another of Ben's insights is owing to Valéry—that some suicides "are like drug addicts"; they "practice the same secrecy and deceit as an addict in pursuit of his drug."[60] Thus Ben learns that "Suicide was an addiction"; in his experience, which he feels is a general experience among suicides, "you ended by becoming dependent upon it as your only way of keeping alive. You hugged it to you, afraid that it might be taken away" (*HF*, 202).

Valéry's most significant influence on Humphrey's account of the acute phase of Ben's life is in the suggestion that potential suicides have a double who stalks them. They "carry in the dark of their soul," says Valéry, "a sleepwalking murderer, an implacable dreamer, a *double* who must carry out an irrevocable command."[61] From the moment Ben takes up residence in Stone Ridge, he feels

59. Paul Valéry, *Occasions*, trans. Roger Shattuck and Frederick Brown (Princeton: Princeton University Press, 1970), 202, 203. Valéry points out that it is the person fascinated by guns who would become "*the slave of the pistol*" (204).

60. Valéry, 203.

61. Ibid.

haunted by an uninvited houseguest. At first Ben recognizes that the shadow he sees is a hallucination: "That was what was so terrifying about it, that you could see something as real as life with one half of your mind while the other half told you that you were seeing things" (*HF*, 197). The dramatic presentment of the double, or shadow, becomes one of the ways in which Humphrey demonstrates how Ben is no longer himself, has become a "textbook case of what is called disintegration of the personality" (199). Moreover, his shadowy other self encourages him toward his "unavoidable destination" with its penetrating refrain: "with nothing to live for, why do you go on living?" (194, 199).[62]

Oddly, as long as the uninvited guest remains an other self, Ben resists its importunings, thinking of the effect that his suicide would have on his friend Tony, who suffers from the same calamity, the death of a child. But when Ben travels to New York City and learns that Tony has already killed himself, his final reason to resist his alter-self vanishes. The stalemate between the self that urges suicide and the resisting self ends, two yielding to one, and he is alone. Humphrey presents this resolution dramatically. Ben leaves the Princeton Club, where he has received the news of Tony's death, and walks to the Oyster Bar, in the building that Tony's daughter had jumped from. When the headwaiter at the Oyster Bar asks, "Are you alone, sir?" Ben replies, "Yes. I am alone." The "door to [his] future had been flung open on a vista as flat and featureless as an arctic waste," and so "he turned and walked away" (*HF*, 210). The word *alone* knelling in his mind brings up the lines that mark his easy turning to death:

> When true hearts lie withered
> And fond ones are flown,
> Oh, who would inhabit
> This bleak world alone?

Here Humphrey vouchsafes his character to draw from the very dregs of "his fatal fund of verse" (211). These four lines conclude " 'Tis The Last Rose of Summer," a sentimental, laughable piece of verse written by the inconsequential Victorian poet Thomas Moore. This poem, insufficient to hold the weight of Ben's distress, begins as follows:

> 'Tis the last rose of summer,
> Left blooming alone;

62. Styron also experienced a division of the self: "I, the victim-to-be of self-murder, was both the solitary actor and lone member of the audience" (*Darkness Visible*, 65).

All her lovely companions
Are faded and gone;
No flower of her kindred,
No rose-bud is nigh,
To reflect back her blushes,
Or give sigh for sigh![63]

It would be unlike Humphrey to have his character act upon sentiments contained in such a poem. Yet perhaps Humphrey suspected that when one finds himself in the darkest waters of feeling and thought, the last thing he is concerned about is proper literary taste. The simple expression of what is most deeply felt is all that matters. Moreover, I think it unlikely that Humphrey expected his readers to recognize the source of Ben's quotation; he counted on the dramatic context out of which Ben utters Moore's words to uphold the sentiment expressed. When Ben makes "Oh, who would inhabit / This bleak world alone?" *his* question, the final tolling of *alone* tells us that it is no rhetorical question posed for sentimental effect: he will answer it with a decisive act that means "not I."

The ease with which the words from this bad poem slip out of the literary man Ben Curtis is suggestive of the casual ease with which Ben takes the final step. Humphrey might have recalled Valéry's remark that sometimes a suicidal man "simply allowed himself to act, and his death occurred like a slip of the tongue."[64] At another level, Valéry's comment suggested to Humphrey how suicide is a sudden freedom from all inhibition: thus Ben, in thinking of his son's—and anticipating his own—suicide, knows that at that "absolutely last moment [when] you were alone with the death you had courted, . . . then it would lose its terror and between you and it the barrier would drop and there would be nothing to prevent you from stepping over the borderline to consummation" (*HF*, 208).

Religion usually plays an incidental role in Humphrey's fiction, when it plays any role at all. A baptism in *Home from the Hill* is merely the occasion upon which Theron Hunnicutt recognizes his son and reconciles with Libby. Sam Ordway goes to church and prays on one occasion, but this action is merely part of the cultural setting of *The Ordways*, not part of its meaning. Also in *The Ordways*, Humphrey compares Thomas Ordway to Moses when he leads his family out of

---

63. *Poetical Works of Thomas Moore* (Philadelphia: Crissy & Markley, [1858]), 534.
64. Valéry, 204–5.

Tennessee to the promised land of Texas, but that is not how the character thinks of his action, and Humphrey does not develop the comparison into significance. In commenting on Walker Percy, Humphrey once quipped that he was "not a great big fan of all this Christian interpretation of life" (*WST*, 6). In fact, in the two works in which Humphrey treats religion extensively—"A Job of the Plains" and *No Resting Place*—he obviously means to undermine religious belief.

In *Hostages to Fortune*, however, religion has a subtle and significant part to play. Ben Curtis is not a religious man. In fact, he has made a conscious decision not to be. He professes no creed, attends no church—nor do the other members of his family. He "had believed that by bringing up his child in a household free of religion he was giving him an advantage. He still believed that" (*HF*, 117). But then he wonders: "maybe he had denied his child the thing that might have *saved* him" (italics mine): "Maybe what had once restrained people from laying violent hands upon themselves might have restrained Anthony: the belief that in so doing they were destroying the image of God, in which they were created. People killed themselves in greater numbers nowadays than ever before; was that because they had ceased by and large to believe in God?" (117). Although Ben does not really mean "saved" in the theological sense, the word begs to undermine the limitations he would place on its meaning. With such considerations Ben is inclined to hang upon his memories the wreath of religion.

Hostages to Fortune does not contradict Humphrey's rejection of Christian fiction; on the other hand, religious allusions, including quotations from the Bible, occur with unusual frequency in this novel, and at least two episodes are unmistakably invested with powerful religious symbolism. Thus it is fair to say at least that Ben Curtis thinks of his ordeal as a spiritual struggle: he loses himself and finds himself; and his death and rebirth, even when they are described in the broadest possible terms, cannot help but suggest a religious journey. Though Ben is not a religious man, the novel's account of his experience is replete with the language, images, patterns, literature, and symbolism of religion.

Throughout, Ben's actions are represented with language based in a religious consciousness. The opening depiction of his applying insect repellant concludes with the observation that he is "[a]nointed against his enemies" (cf. Psalm 23). Then when he contemplates the halls of Princeton University, they become "Temples of learning into which you entered like an infidel in disguise, faked the responses to the ritual by taking your cue from the true believers and sometimes failing to take your cue" (*HF*, 79). Giving his attention to Canada geese, Ben observes that they have a "white throat patch like a clergyman's collar" (44). Further, Ben sees "the zealous, beleaguered little band" of falconers, among whom his son Anthony counts himself, as a religious sect: "A band of coreligionists, proscribed, dispersed, but still stubbornly devout, keeping their ancient rites and rituals in a secret brotherhood" (99).[65] Such passages in the aggregate show a mind inclined, perhaps subliminally, toward a religious perspective.

The scene in which Ben buries Anthony's ashes acquires weight and solemnity through religious allusion. At the scene's outset, the religious diction reflects Ben's sense of the inadequacy of his individual obsequies, which he views as a "furtive, hole-and-corner, outcast and excommunicated . . . proceeding" (*HF*, 177). The observance is, to be sure, a "one-man ceremony in which [Ben] was the entire cortege, the gravedigger, the preacher, and the congregation" (176). His recognition of his own inadequacy to play all the roles that the occasion requires leads him to wish for that which only the traditional church can provide: "until now his one thought had been to get it over with quickly; now he felt the contrary urge to slow it down, do something more, dignify it, not let the boy go so unregretted, put forever out of sight with this indecent haste, this lack of ceremony" (178). As ready as Ben is to apply lines from the entire range of English and American poetry (and Dante as well) to the circumstances of his life, one wonders why Philip Larkin's "Church Going" fails to enter his consciousness at this point; for Ben seems very much to feel that in the church's "blent air all our compulsions meet, / Are recognized, and robed as destinies" and that the major events of life, "marriage, and birth, / and death" are bestowed their just significance by its ceremonies.[66]

Even when Ben quashes his impulse for the aliments of religious ritual, he does it with a passage from Job: *Let the day perish wherein I was born* (3:3). Putting his son's ashes in the little hole that he has dug with his pocket knife, he is "overwhelmed by the bitter appropriateness of this bare, bleak ceremony to that lonely death" (*HF*, 178). The line and subsequent passages from Job are the ones uttered by Jude Farley as he lies upon his deathbed. In *Jude the Obscure*, Hardy juxtaposes the sad verses from Job with celebratory shouts associated with Remembrance Day at Christminster, an irony that presses upon the reader the full force of Jude's disappointed dreams. The effect of Humphrey's double allusion is to pile Jude's anguish on top of Job's. Humphrey's version of Hardy's method also serves to contrast Ben's present despair with his lost happiness. The ultimate effect—because the happiness is lost—of Ben's remembered glimpses of happi-

65. Additional passages in which Anthony appears as a priest in an ancient cult appear on pp. 99–100 and 102 in *HF*.

66. His mind an anthology of verse, Ben quotes extensively from Wyatt, Spenser, Shakespeare, Milton, Thomas Moore, Emily Brontë, Bryant, Wordsworth, Keats, Poe, Hardy, Housman, Robinson, Yeats, T. S. Eliot, and Frost. See Philip Larkin, *Collected Poems*, ed. Anthony Thwaite (1988; reprint, New York: Farrar, Straus, & Giroux, 1989), 98.

ness is to compound the sorrow. Following his voicing of "*Let the day perish wherein I was born,*"[67] Ben recalls the sunny day when Anthony was born three days early, how "glad" his parents were at his birth (*HF*, 178). Following "*and the night in which it was said, There is a man child conceived,*" Ben recalls an "enchanted night," an especially memorable "spasm in the groin" that has "begotten this boxful of ashes" (Job 3:3; *HF*, 179). Following "*As for that night, let darkness seize upon it. . . . Because it shut not up the doors of my mother's womb*" and "*Why died I not from the womb?*" (3:6, 10, 11), Ben focuses upon that birth in which he delivered his son in the snow, and he remembers—heightening his present helplessness—his shameless pride in his ability to tend to the needs of both mother and son in that emergency. Ben's closing words from Job are "*Why did I not give up the ghost when I came out of the belly? For now I should have lain still and been quiet, I should have slept; then had I been at rest*" (3:13); they represent darkness closing in: "He knelt and lowered the carton into the hole. With those hands of his that had been the first and the last to hold his child he crumbled a clod of dirt on the lid of the carton, saying, 'Earth to earth, ashes to ashes, dust to dust'" (*HF*, 180).

The terms of religious experience assert themselves as a straightforward counterforce to Ben's downward movement when he retreats to the house in Stone Ridge, leaving behind all of his old associations, in order to achieve perfect isolation. His desperate need for the solace of religion manifests itself in the location and in the way he perceives the features of the house that he has selected for his ultimate isolation. The house is on a rock, a biblical metaphor for God Himself (Deuteronomy 32:18); and the house, furthermore, rests on that quarter-acre "rock like the Ark on Ararat," a simile representing perhaps deliverance from ultimate destruction (*HF*, 186). The worn stone steps leading up to the door remind him of "holy-water fonts"; the house has "permanently tinted" glass, the panes "mullioned with lead"; and "it seemed to him that he was entering something like a one-man monastery" (187). His observation with the most significant religious association is that "[t]he thick slates of [the house's] gambrel roof were ragged and flaky at the edges like the worn scales of an old, old fish" (186). The religious symbolism of the sacrificial fish, hinted at here, develops fully on the day Ben returns to the fishing club and rejoins the eternal round of life. At this point, however, Ben holds that "in work lay his one hope of salvation"; though the narrator, reflecting Ben's consciousness, means less than he says, he nonetheless appropriates the vocabulary of religion to present Ben's sad circumstance (187).

67. This sentiment is also the gist of Michael Henchard's will (Hardy, *The Mayor of Casterbridge*, ed. Robert B. Heilman [Boston: Houghton Mifflin, 1962], 289).

Work, his writing, soon proves an inadequate salvation, and he finds that he stands repeatedly on the doorstep of suicide. Yet "something would intervene" on these occasions: "The telephone, so long silent, would ring, a salesman would knock or some self-appointed door-to-door peddler of salvation. . . . The urgings of some cultist to mind his eternal soul would teach him how final a fate he had been flirting with" (*HF*, 205). Though there is some measure of contempt in these words, they nonetheless acknowledge the efficacy of the intervention.

Part 3 of the novel celebrates the return to life. That the despairing man can return to life from the "farthest country of despair" is the premise that Humphrey bases *Hostages* upon, and if he got anything from Farber's essay on suicide, it would be this concept.[68] Some ultimate intervention—never explained and thus mysterious—brings the lifeless Ben back to life. Humphrey begins to eke out hope even as he gives a pessimistic turn to one of the famous phrases from the Book of Common Prayer: "The attraction of death was diminished by the thought of how very little we could ever gain on it. By shortening your years yourself how few at most you were able to subtract, how few add to the many you would be dead. Man that is born of woman has a long time to be dead. There was no such thing as a long life. There was such a thing as too long a life—eighteen years could be a weary lot; but there was no such thing as a long life" (*HF*, 222). Thus Humphrey gains for Ben the small measure of acceptance and perspective that will enable him to reenter the stream of life.

On the day we first encounter Ben, when he has endured the worst that life has to offer, he has given up the desire for oblivion, seeks wholeness, and realizes that he requires help beyond himself. And so he seeks community in the old fishing club, which assumes a religious meaning for him: "To this temple of the fish and the fly, people came for the weekend as though to a religious retreat, leaving behind them all worldly cares and concerns" (*HF*, 6). Surely meaning to draw upon the traditional religious significance of the fish, Humphrey portrays Ben recalling the club members' participating in a divine service as they attend to the bringing in of "Old Jumbo," the famously big trout who has occupied the stream for years:

> So as to be less visible and thus less alarming to the fish, Tony sank slowly to his knees. . . . On this signal, as though they were his congregation and he their priest, every member of the audience already beginning to gather promptly knelt. In this prayerful posture was the contest fought and witnessed to its finish.

68. Farber, 83.

And they were as hushed and reverent as though silently at prayer. . . . They were there to observe a master, or rather, a match between two masters: the fish, the idol of their common cult, and the man performing, the celebrant of the rite that bound them together. (31–32)

Before the speckled brown trout gives himself up to the hook, he secures "the sanctuary of a sunken log"; then, requiring no *coup de grâce,* he is laid out on the grass, and the people gather "around . . . in respectful silence look[ing] down at him with bowed heads" (32). In recalling this event of many years ago, Ben lends to his memory the coloring of religious experience, but in the late afternoon of the present he actually participates in the sacramental observance of the fish, which ceremony renews his life—a life that he perceives in the full context of the processes of nature and the eternal round of life and death, his part and his son's part acknowledged, accepted, the *Benedicite* concluding, appropriately, with the *Gloria Patri.* He wades into the water of life, commencing to fish—and we are reminded of the epigram from Thoreau's *Walden* for Humphrey's *My Moby Dick,* the story of a man and an especially important trout: "Time is but the stream I go a-fishing in."[69] Here Ben attains an encompassing perspective:

A hatch of mayflies, the evening rise, was beginning to come off the pool in ever-thickening numbers. Splitting and shedding their nymphal shucks in their swift ascent from the bed, they exchanged elements, surfaced, and rode the current for the seconds required to dry their wings for flight. A miniature armada about to take off. It was these seconds in their life cycle that the dry-fly fisherman imitated with his artificial, for it was then, during their period of immobility and helplessness, that the trout preyed upon them. Those that escaped found perches for themselves among the leaves and branches of the streamside bushes. There overnight they attained their maturity. One last function of their brief lives remained to them. Hovering above the stream out of reach of leaping trout, males and females, a cloud of them, met and mated on the wing—fulfillment fatal to the males. The females dipped again and again depositing their fertilized eggs upon the surface, rose when all were shed in a last flutter of release, then fell thick as snowflakes to the water, spent, their carcasses now feeding the fish. Their winged lives would have lasted for a day. Next year's trout, those of that third of their kind that survived the winter, would feed on the nymphs

69. This quotation is absent in the 1979 Penguin edition, but Humphrey added it when *My Moby Dick* was reprinted in *Open Season* in 1986.

and the duns that hatched from those eggs, they in their turn to feed the fishermen who made it back, licensed for another season. Ol' man river, that ol' man river, he don't plant taters and don't plant cotton, and them what plants 'em is soon forgotten, but ol' man river, he just keeps rollin' along. The water he had waded through this morning was miles downstream from him now and somebody else was fishing it. By this time tomorrow it would be part of a different river and by next week an ocean wave. And even now, over his native Kansas, were forming clouds that would replenish the stream with raindrops that once before, even more than once, times out of number, had mingled in it, when one of those old mustachioed members of the club, and after him his son, even that latter worthy's last cast framed and hanging on the wall, had stood where he stood now. The amount of moisture in our atmosphere and on our planet was constant, fixed at the creation, perpetually being recycled, ours on loan in our time and place. Izaak Walton, fishing his River Dove, had fished this very water. And what was it we were told? That the human body was seventy-five percent composed of water. Around his feet now flowed a droplet condensed from the vapors of that one, flesh of his flesh, reduced to its components in Princeton on that October day. As it was in the beginning, is now, and ever shall be: world without end. Amen. (223–24)

In this stream, in the failing light, Ben undertakes skillfully to hook the trout that will miraculously give him new life. As the mayflies die to renew life, so must the fish die to give Ben renewed life. Therefore, Ben must resist the temptation to intervene in the natural order by returning the trout, once caught, to the stream; he perceives that his role is to accept the way nature works—and also that out of death comes life:

The fish could be saved, and game as it was, it deserved to live. It looked lifeless but it was not, it was just exhausted from the fight, and if he held it head first into the current and gently rocked it back and forth its respiration would be restored and it would revive. He extracted the hook from its palate using his hemostat and submerged it. Then he changed his mind. Holding the fish as he would hold a club, he knocked its head against a rock. It quivered, then stilled and stiffened.

He changed his mind because into it had come thoughts of the moment on the clubhouse porch when everybody laid out his day's catch. If he appeared there with nothing they would all feel sorry for him, and God knew, people were tired of having to feel sorry for him. But if he brought

in the day's finest fish—and it was unlikely that anybody had caught a
better one than his—it would seem that he was proud of himself and
pleased with his day. Nobody would envy him his luck. They would all be
relieved. They would congratulate him and want to stand him to a drink.
At supper Eddie would serve the fish to some party with his compliments
and from across the dining room they would gesture with thumbs up and
he would respond in kind. Then it would seem to all that he had really
rejoined the club. (*HF*, 226–7)

He has. Thus, out of emotionally harrowing material Humphrey has wrested the
most hopeful conclusion in all of his fiction.

When Humphrey was awaiting the publication of *Hostages,* the thought of
launching it with the likes of Lehmann-Haupt waiting to assault it made him
anxious, but Dorothy encouraged in him a very high opinion of his literary
worth, which enabled him—at least temporarily—to feel immune to the opinions of mere journalists. He was also heartened that Delacorte would be reissuing
all of his old books in paperback. For all of his books to be in print on his sixtieth
birthday was almost enough to make Humphrey think that all was right with the
world. *Hostages to Fortune* was in fact an astonishing critical success. It was not,
however, a commercial one. Though by 31 January *Hostages* had sold out of the
original printing of fifteen thousand and though Delacorte had ordered a second
printing, the novel did not continue to sell well. Ros Kaveney, who read the
manuscript for Chatto and Windus, foresaw the novel's fate and made the rather
appalling comment—which nevertheless might be true from a publisher's perspective—that the story "is so deeply uncommercial as to be rather irritating."[70]
Nonetheless, it is awesome and terrible in the root meanings of those terms. It is
horrible to endure and was no doubt difficult to review. *Hostages to Fortune* is
one of the most painstaking, evocative, and articulate literary works about suicide ever written. That it does what it means to do—present the full measure
of agony attendant upon the loss of a child by suicide—assured its commercial
failure.

In 1984 Nick Lyons, then a professor at Hunter College, wrote sixteen letters
to various publications encouraging them to assign a review of the book, and

70. Jean Lambert, journal, entry for 31 October 1983, Lambert Coll.; Humphrey to Affre, 21 May
1984 (letter in Affre's possession); to Yannick Guillou, 31 January 1985, Gallimard; "Reader Report,"
20 December 1983, C&W. Chatto & Windus followed Kaveney's advice, and Secker & Warburg then
became Humphrey's British publisher; *Hostages* came out in Britain in 1985.

indeed it was widely reviewed—and extremely favorably. Yet the praise heaped on *Hostages to Fortune* by the critics makes it clear why many people were reluctant to read it. Almost all spoke of the "harrowing" tragedy, "the fierce reality of Ben's Gethsemane." "It is explicit and unsparing in its thorough exploration of a grim theme," wrote Elaine Kendall in the *Los Angeles Times*. Richard Lipez in *Newsday* declared, "To pick up Humphrey's extraordinary new novel is to hold an embodiment of grief in your hands. The unrelenting anguish that suffuses this story . . . is almost unbearable to behold. It is possible to get through it because the stark poetry of Humphrey's work is enthralling." The *Plain Dealer* said that this "searching novel," this "unsparingly honest book puts the reader through the emotional wringer." This "story of heartbreaking dimensions" *(Publishers Weekly)* is "probably too wrenching and too painful a novel . . . to achieve mass popularity, but no one who reads it can help being profoundly affected by it and made more appreciative of Mr. Humphrey's abilities," vouched the *Kansas City Star*. A reviewer for the *Arizona Daily Star* was also deeply affected by the novel, but his response was anger at what Humphrey had done to him. Indeed, *Hostages to Fortune* found "a place deep within" Leo W. Banks: "It digs down and clamps itself on a nerve and you know it will be a long time before it releases you." Banks avowed that he would rather have had a stroke than to have read Humphrey's novel, explaining: "It is so wretched, so thoroughly morbid and diseased in intent and execution, that I shall be an old man before I am able to discuss it without feeling a flush of anger rise to my face." As Mark Royden Winchell remarked, "Nothing that its author had written previously would prepare a reader for the emotional catharsis of this extraordinarily harrowing book."[71]

Without doubt, some reviewers stopped reading when they realized what they were in for. *Hostages* is the sort of book that many readers might lay aside before completing, not because it is not engaging but because the emotional cost of continuing is too high. As Ben Curtis remarks in the novel, "No one liked to be reminded of the dark disasters of life" (*HF*, 119). Such readers are, indeed, like the friends of Housman's Terence, who complain,

71. Seymour Epstein, "Gone, Inexplicably," *New York Times Book Review,* 14 October 1984, 9; Elaine Kendall, "Dad's Struggle to Survive Teen Suicide," *Los Angeles Times,* 20 September 1984, 26; Richard Lipez, "A Son's Suicide," *Newsday,* 9 September 1984, 15; Walter Berkov, "Searing Look at the Emotional Debris of Suicide," *Cleveland Plain Dealer,* 18 October 1984, 49; rev. of *Hostages to Fortune,* in *Publishers Weekly,* 13 July 1984, 44; Theodore M. O'Leary, "Pain of 'Hostages' Makes Its Power Even Greater," *Kansas City Star,* 7 October 1984, sec. F, p. 9; Leo W. Banks, "Hostages Truly Wretched Past Belief," *Arizona Daily Star* (Tucson), 30 September 1984, sec. C, p. 6; Mark Royden Winchell, *William Humphrey,* Western Writers Series, no. 105 (Boise, Idaho: Boise State University, 1992), 39.

Pretty friendship 'tis to rhyme
Your friends to death before their time
Moping melancholy mad. . . .

Humphrey's reply might well be Terence's:

But take it: if the smack is sour,
The better for the embittered hour;
It should do good to heart and head
When your soul is in my soul's stead;
And I will friend you if I may,
In the dark and cloudy day.

That *Hostages to Fortune* proved a friend to readers in their dark days is attested to by an unusual packet of letters among Humphrey's papers at the University of Texas; these letters are from readers whose friends or family members had committed suicide or who had attempted it themselves. Typical is the following, from a young woman in Madison, Wisconsin, whose fiancé had killed himself: "Ever since he died, I've been looking for something or someone to know that pain. . . . [I]t was unsettling to me not to have found someone who knew something of that pain—as if to find that would somehow purge me of the remainder of it. . . . [I]t was your Ben Curtis that touched me." A woman in Ketchum, Idaho, the unwilling survivor of a serious suicide attempt, wrote to thank Humphrey for writing "with such compassion about those of us who want to leave." When Humphrey received this letter, he immediately telephoned the woman to assure her that though he tried to understand the workings of a suicidal mind, he did not condone suicide. They talked for a long time and remained in touch.[72]

72. *The Collected Poems of A. E. Housman* (1939; reprint, London: Jonathan Cape, 1966), 63, 64; letters to Humphrey, 27 August 1985 and 7 September 1999; the identities of the authors of letters (in WH Coll., UT) are withheld.

[8]

THE RED AND THE WHITE
(No Resting Place)

... the lost Eden, the better time that once was ...
—DALE VAN EVERY, *Disinherited*

nvdagini alsdisqi
—CHEROKEE FOR "THE TEXAN,
THE TROUBLE MAKER"

A MONTH AFTER completing *Hostages to Fortune,* Humphrey boasted to Jean Lambert that he was getting down to work on another book: "No rest for the weary," a private joke lost on his correspondent, who had not yet been informed that the next novel was to be called *No Resting Place.*[1] Actually, *No Resting Place* was the project that Bill had abandoned against the advice of Lawrence in order to focus solely upon *Hostages to Fortune.* He found that it was not so easy, nearly three years later, to pick up where he had left off. In fact, he was unable to apply himself to the resumed novel owing to a debilitating depression. "I have not been able to settle down to serious work since finishing the novel last October. I have been in a state of constant mental depression. I am always depressed after finishing a book, but seldom has it lasted this long and been so profound," Humphrey wrote on 30 March 1984 to Pierre Affre. In May Nick Lyons reported to Affre that Humphrey's depression had not abated. It was not till August of 1984 that Humphrey threw off "the persistent deep depression that had gripped [him] all winter and spring." Nonetheless, getting back to work on the Cherokee novel was still a struggle.[2] The most that can be said of his progress is that he began to write in his notebook about writing the novel; he continued in this semifunctional mode for another year or so.

The first sure sign that Humphrey really had recovered—at least tentatively—from this bout with depression is in his lively response to an appeal from a Clarksville resident. John Harrison wrote to him on 31 January 1985 to inform him that the Red River County Courthouse—a landmark in Humphrey's stories—was in danger of being razed to make way for an efficient new courthouse;

1. William Humphrey to Jean Lambert, 4 November 1983, Lambert Coll.
2. Nick Lyons to Pierre Affre, 5 May 1984, Lyons Coll.; Humphrey to Lambert, 19 August [1984], Lambert Coll.

he concluded with a suggestion as to how Humphrey might help: "If you informed us that we would be barbarian rubes to endanger Old Red, the preservationist point of view would gain respectability" (WH Coll., UT). Humphrey enthusiastically embraced the cause of preservation, writing on 6 February to Gavin Watson, editor of the *Clarksville Times*, asking him to run "the following—prominently—in your next issue":

Dear Gavin,
Will you, should the necessity arise, please run this ad in your paper—full page:

FOR SALE

LAST UNOCCUPIED PLOT

IN

OLD CLARKSVILLE CEMETERY

BENEATH LIMB OF THE HANGING TREE

DUE TO CHANGE IN OWNERS' PLANS

and forward all interested inquiries to me? The necessity will arise if and when the County Courthouse is razed or abandoned. It was with the thought in mind of hearing the chimes of its clock in eternity that I bought that plot, and, after it stopped chiming on the midnight, of getting up and ambling over there to gaze at its tower by the light of the moon. Without these satisfactions to look forward to, I might as well be just anywhere, because without its courthouse Clarksville will be just anywhere. Half of this decision was taken by my Brooklyn-born wife, destined to lie alongside me, who loves that unique old pile every bit as much as I do. She adds, and I agree, that we won't want to associate till Judgment Day (when the courthouse will be resurrected along with us) with people so indifferent to their greatest treasure.

Yours,
Bill Humphrey
(WH Coll., UT)

The courthouse is still there.

Later in the year, Humphrey was distracted by the prospect of being a candidate for the directorship of the M.F.A. program at Louisiana State University. Daniel Fogel offered a salary of $40,000, assuring Humphrey that it would be increased promptly. He thought seriously about the offer, finding it more attractive than many of the other offers that he had turned down in recent years, but in the end he declined this one too, not wishing to leave his occupation as full-time writer for an extended period. Then summer brought an emotional blow that kept Humphrey out of commission a while longer: his friend of thirty-five years, Dick Bard, died suddenly on 16 July. The depth of Bill's affection for this man is indicated by his willingly performing the eulogy at Dick's funeral, the only time Humphrey ever participated officially in a funeral.[3]

Humphrey did not get down to serious work on *No Resting Place* before the first of December 1985. During the months of floundering he arrived at an understanding that he needed to do a great deal of research and reading before he could write. At this time, then, he set about to put his hand on every printed source available in order to gain as balanced and as encompassing a sense of the historical context as he could of the story he meant to tell. In the small orange notebook that he titled "The Detention Camp," he noted that the Cherokee Trail of Tears was the worst of many episodes in the ten-year period of Indian removal. Resolving to reread all the accounts of all the expeditions, he began with Grant Foreman's *Indian Removal.* His friend Nick Lyons, who was then still on the English faculty at Hunter College, was Humphrey's main means for obtaining books. He would give a list of titles to Lyons, who then would request the books on interlibrary loan through the Hunter library and mail them to Humphrey. Donald L. Symington of Brewster got books for him at the New York Public Library as well. Among the library books that Humphrey used are Foreman's *Indians and Pioneers* and *Advancing the Frontier, 1830–1860,* Wendell H. Oswalt's *This Land Was Theirs,* Ruth Underhill's *Red Man's America,* Walter H. Blumenthal's *American Indians Dispossessed,* Louis Filler and Allen Guttman's *Removal of the Cherokee Nation: Manifest Destiny or National Dishonor?,* Wilcomb E. Washburn's *The Indians and the White Man,* Marion Starkey's *The Cherokee Nation,* and Herbert Gambrell's *Mirabeau B. Lamar.*[4]

In addition to those borrowed, Humphrey purchased Jean Louis Berlandier's *Indians of Texas in 1830* (1969); Jack Gregory and Rennard Strickland's *Sam Houston with the Cherokees, 1829–1833* (1967); Helen Jackson's *A Century of Dishonor: A Sketch of the United States Government's Dealings with Some of the Indian Tribes* (1900); Alvin M. Josephy Jr.'s *The Indian Heritage of America* (1968); W. W. Newcomb Jr.'s *The Indians of Texas* (1961); Charles C. Royce's *The Cherokee Nation*

3. Humphrey to Daniel Fogel, 28 May 1985, Lawrence Coll.; Helen Bard, interview by author, tape recorded, 28 August 2001, Milan, N.Y.

4. Humphrey, "The Detention Camp" (notebook), entry for 5 December 1985, WH Coll., UT; Nick Lyons, telephone interview by author, tape recording, 28 July 1999; Humphrey to Lyons, 21 March [1978], 6 and 9 May 1978, Lyons Coll.; to Donald L. Symington, [1978], WH Coll., UT.

of Indians (1975); Thurman Wilkins's *Cherokee Tragedy: The Story of the Ridge Family and the Decimation of a People* (1971); Clark Wissler's *Indians of the United States* (1940); Grace Steele Woodward's *The Cherokees* (1976); and Elémire Zolla's *The Writer and the Shaman: A Morphology of the American Indian*, trans. Raymond Rosenthal (1969).[5]

Humphrey's main sources for *No Resting Place* were Dale Van Every's *Disinherited: The Lost Birthright of the American Indian* (1966) and *Chief Bowles and the Texas Cherokees*, by Mary Whatley Clarke (1971). He marked passages and scribbled in the margins and blank pages in his own copies of Van Every's and Clarke's books, as well as some of the others, Woodward's *The Cherokees*, for example. The notes he made from these sources filled three notebooks: "The Detention Camp," "On the Trail," and "The Bowl" (WH Coll., UT).

Humphrey also obtained historical publications such as *The Chronicles of Oklahoma*.[6] His papers at the University of Texas also contain photocopied pages from *A History of Upshur County, Texas* (1966) as well as newspaper cuttings of stories about the Trail of Roses planted by the Cherokees and a transcript of the Official Texas Historical Marker erected by the Moody Foundation in Upshur County to identify the "Cherokee Trace"; these items might have reminded Humphrey of facts that he already knew.[7]

By 18 January 1986 Bill had written 180 pages. He had planned to take a break and go to Europe in the spring, but he and Dorothy fell victim to the American hysteria over the Hezbollah's taking of thirty-nine American hostages on a TWA airliner and the Palestinian terrorists' shooting of passengers at the airport check-in counters in Rome and Vienna the year before. Humphrey was afraid that an Arab might shoot him when his Indian book was only half done.[8]

5. Humphrey's own books were sold to Howard Frisch Antiquarian Books, Livingston, N.Y., after his death.

6. Some of the articles Humphrey read are Anna Muckleroy, "The Indian Policy of the Republic of Texas," *Southwestern Historical Quarterly* 25 (April 1922), 26 (July 1922), 26 (October 1922), 26 (January 1923); John H. Reagon, "The Expulsion of the Cherokees from East Texas," *Quarterly of the Texas State Historical Association* 1 (July 1897); John Ridge, "The Cherokee War Path," *Chronicles of Oklahoma* 9 (September 1931); Dorman Winfrey, "Chief Bowles of the Texas Cherokees," *Chronicles of Oklahoma* 32 (Spring 1954); Ernest W. Winkler, "The Cherokee Indians in Texas," *Quarterly of the Texas State Historical Association* 7 (October 1903); Albert Woldert, "The Last of the Cherokees in Texas, and the Life and Death of Chief Bowles," *Chronicles of Oklahoma* 1 (June 1923).

7. Doyal Loyd, *A History of Upshur County, Texas* (Privately published, 1966); Frank X. Tolbert, "Following Trail of Roses Planted by 1821 Cherokees," *Dallas Morning News*, 8 June 1969; Sarah Greene, "Roadmap for Trip in Time—Backwards," *Gilmer (Texas) Mirror*, 28 May 1970.

8. Humphrey to Theodore and Renée Weiss, 6 March 1979, Weiss Coll.; to Affre, 30 March [1984] (letter in Affre's possession); Lyons to Affre, 5 May 1984, Lyons Coll.; Humphrey to Lambert, 18 January 1986, Lambert Coll.

Therefore, Humphrey stayed at home and continued work on *No Resting Place*. He was making good progress when in September he had to suspend his work on the novel to deliver a speech at the Texas Governor's Sesquicentennial Conference on the Literary Arts in 1986, a task he accepted not so much to celebrate his home state's anniversary as to collect an honorarium of three thousand dollars. To swell his purse, he also accepted an invitation to give the Texas Writers Lecture at the University of Dallas a few days before the Sesquicentennial Conference began on the twenty-fourth.[9] After these literary events, the Humphreys visited Clarksville for five days, residing in Robert Story's lakefront cabin. Humphrey spent time talking with Gavin Watson, who recently told what Bill said about why he had hardly ever returned to his childhood home over the past forty-five years. His reason concerned his fiction, much of which drew upon the town's 1930s appearance; he did not want to see the old picture painted over, obscuring the original that was fixed in his memory at age thirteen. Humphrey also told Watson that he would not be back because his mother's racial views embarrassed him. He had just visited her, and she had said to Bill in the presence of her black caretaker: "This nigger woman takes care of me." Humphrey told Watson that his mother embarrassed him: "She's Old South and I'm not. I just can't stand it." Thus although he said to Watson that he loved his mother, he was not going to see her any more. The mixed feelings about his mother are emblematic of his mixed feelings about his hometown and the South. Shortly after Humphrey's death Ted Weiss offered the following perspective: "Bill had a love-hate relationship with Clarksville (and the South): he loved it for the world it gave him, for his father and a few other relatives, for its providing the source of his being and his writing. He hated it for its intellectual and artistic poverty, its desert-like dinginess. Yet he wrote mainly out of memories and imaginings about it."[10]

A year after his last trip to Clarksville, Bill completed his last novel—on 18 October 1987. A month later Seymour Lawrence informed him that he was dissatisfied with the way the first chapter connected with the main body of the narrative. Humphrey at first resisted making any revisions, and Lawrence told him

9. A photograph dated 18 September 1986 testifies to Humphrey's participation at the University of Dallas; Joseph Rice to Humphrey, 23 May 1986, WH Coll., UT; Almon (23–25) has given a full account of Humphrey's criticism of the Texas "literary barbecue," although he does not mention that Humphrey's lecture on 26 September was entitled "Why Do I Write?" published in 1990 (*WST*, 183–89); the lecture was really a preface to a reading of a short story entitled "Dolce Far' Niente."

10. Dorothy Humphrey to Lambert, 8 August 1986, Lambert Coll.; Gavin Watson to Humphrey, 4 May 1986, WH Coll., UT.; Watson, interview by author, tape recording, Clarksville, Tex., 17 July 1997; Weiss to author, 7 October 1997.

that the book was his and if he felt that he had accomplished what he had set out to do in the book, then he was not required to change anything. The author's ultimate trust in Lawrence eventually prevailed, however, and he retrieved the manuscript and undertook extensive revisions. The manuscript in Austin provides a clear record of the revisions. Humphrey inserted additions and substitutions on six different colors and kinds of paper—beige, blue, green, white, lined notebook paper, and Princeton University "Program in Theatre" stationery; some additions are written in pencil, some in ballpoint, some in ink, and some are typed (on old and new typewriters). These variations suggest several stages in an extensive process of revision. On 5 April 1988 Humphrey sent the revised manuscript to Lawrence, who praised him for the "superb revisions": "The book is greatly improved and I congratulate you. I withdraw any reservations I may have had." Humphrey was always game for one-upmanship, and so it was not long before he demanded the manuscript back: he felt compelled to do *more* revising—which he completed by 6 August. Though the revisions were obviously done at different times, it is impossible to tell what—if any—significant revisions occurred during this final stage. *No Resting Place,* a novel on an issue that Humphrey had deep feelings about, was published in May 1989.[11]

Hostages to Fortune had been a departure from a body of fiction that dwells primarily upon southern family relationships, especially the family's vain efforts to survive, to hold together, but *No Resting Place* is rather an expanded version, almost a redefinition, of the theme of the family's effort to endure. As Seamus Heaney has expanded his sense of racial consciousness from Ireland to include the far-flung Viking countries whose blood, in varying amounts, flows in all Irishmen, so does Humphrey in this novel expand his cultural and racial consciousness from Anglo-Saxon southern to embrace the Indian blood that he believed flowed in his own veins and in the veins of many East Texans. Thus in a sense *No Resting Place* is as much about Humphrey's people as are his Clarksville novels.

Before *No Resting Place* Humphrey's fiction had on three occasions briefly treated the white man's destruction of Indian civilization. In *The Ordways,* when Sam Ordway crosses the Concho River, he encounters a frieze of hundreds of figures near the top of steep cliffs; painted over time, they represent a strong and

11. Humphrey to Seymour Lawrence, 18 October 1987, Lawrence Coll.; Lawrence to Humphrey, 18 November 1987, 1 December 1987, Lawrence Coll.; Humphrey to Lambert, 2 April [1988], Lambert Coll.; Dorothy Humphrey to Lambert, 5 April 1988, Lambert Coll.; Lawrence to Humphrey, 27 April 1988, WH res.; Jackie Farber to Humphrey, 26 July 1988, WH res.; Toby Eady to Humphrey, 7 June 1988, WH res. Eady arranged for British publication through Barley Alison.

persevering Indian culture. Then Sam notes that the earliest figures are hunting and dancing and that they are superseded by crude representations of "a mission church, a priest in a cassock, and a Christian devil with pointed tail and a pitchfork. After that, bare rock" (*O*, 317). *The Ordways* continues with its business, which has nothing more to do with the white man's destruction of Indian civilization. There are two stories in *A Time and a Place*, "A Good Indian" and "The Last of the Caddoes," that briefly present the white man's betrayal of the Indian. In *No Resting Place* Humphrey comes back to the white man's destruction of the Indians, making it the central concern of the novel. Yet, like *The Ordways*, *No Resting Place* is about several generations of one family—in this case, a Cherokee family whose name begins as Ferguson but becomes Smith. As *The Ordways* is, in part, about how and why a white Tennessee family migrates as far west as East Texas, *No Resting Place* is about how and why a Cherokee family in Georgia—indeed, their entire tribe with them—migrates to the same place in East Texas. These two families—the Ordways and the Fergusons—represent the two bloodlines that merge in Humphrey himself, although the characters and family relationships in *No Resting Place* are altogether imaginary.

Going west has a starkly different meaning for the two families. For the Ordways the West represents new hope and freedom and an escape from the past, but the opposite is true for the Fergusons. According to Cherokee myth, the West is "the region ruled by evil in which the sun died, the abode of the Black Man, the personification of death. Their country in the East on the other hand was the Sun Land, where light was born, presided over by the benevolent Red Man, the personification of life, and people[ed] by innumerable lesser gods and the spirits of their ancestors."[12] Yet the West is the place to which the Cherokees are expelled. Then, after they adapt to their new place, they are expelled from it. The West is no place of escape for the Cherokees. *No Resting Place* is therefore different from *The Ordways* and the other Clarksville novels in the way it treats the past. In those novels, the cooked-up myth of the South's glorious past is rejected, but in *No Resting Place* the hard reality of the Indian past is dealt with in a different manner. Humphrey's Indian narrative intertwines the past with the present in such a way as to demonstrate the enduring effect of the past. Indeed, at the beginning of his early notes for *No Resting Place*, Humphrey copied these famous lines from Faulkner: "The past is never dead—it isn't even past."[13]

12. Dale Van Every, *Disinherited: The Lost Birthright of the American Indian* (New York: Avon, 1966), 40.

13. The saying belongs to Gavin Stevens in *Requiem for a Nun* (New York: Signet, 1961), 229. Humphrey also copied the Faulkner quotation on the front inside page of his copy of Van Every's *Disinherited*.

A century and a half after the march along the Trail of Tears, the descendent of Noquisi (Amos Ferguson I), having heard the long story of his Cherokee ancestors, the telling of which is the novel's dominant present, is now visiting the grave of his great-great-grandmother in Beesville, Tennessee. Although the motel owner has said that there is "nothing in Beesville to see," Amos Smith IV, using the meticulous map drawn by Captain Donovan, the United States Army officer who led the Cherokee march out of Georgia, finds a piece of earth in Beesville with enormous significance to him, the mass grave where Anne Ferguson is buried. As Amos IV stands at the grave site, the narrative—without missing a beat—merges into the past, and it is Amos I (Noquisi) who stands at his mother's grave: "There was no time for him to mourn. That was an indulgence that would have to wait. The train was already in motion under a steady cold rain, and keeping up with it demanded all one's strength of will. There was no time and there was no allowance. He had his duty the same as everyone to the spirit of the group" (*NRP*, 169). What Amos IV learns is that he, too, has a duty to the spirit of the group, which includes both the living and the dead. This is the lesson in responsibility that he acquires in "going to the water" with his father in Part 1 of the novel. "Going to the water," a significant motif in the narrative, always involves knowing and assuming one's identity; this process is repeated throughout all the generations of this Indian family.

It was finding and knowing his identity that compelled Humphrey to write *No Resting Place*. In March 1978 he told Norah Smallwood that his "foolish mind" kept running on the idea of a novel set in Texas in 1839, shortly after Texas won its independence from Mexico, when "the riff-raff started pouring in and began exterminating the Indians." In pen Humphrey annotated two of these terms, indicating that among the "riff-raff" were "my white ancestors" and among the Indians "my non-white ancestors."[14] The conflict that the novel ends with involves both sides of Humphrey's own family and thus is tied to his sense of self. As he began research for the novel, he seemed at ease with his mixed ancestry, but as the full story of the wrong done his Indian ancestors emerged, his sense of self shifted to a Cherokee one.

Humphrey had written the introductory section of his Cherokee novel in 1978, the first investigations into the subject being on 7 March when he copied into his notebook a description of the Cherokee Rose from Katherine Anne Porter's "The Flower of Flowers" and a day or so later when he copied passages from

14. Humphrey to Norah Smallwood, 6 March 1978, C&W.

John Graves's *Goodbye to a River* (1960). Bill found that Graves's imaginative consideration of Texas history and tradition described the very character of his own concern about the culture in which he had been reared. Although Humphrey's Clarksville novels had dramatically demonstrated the necessity of southerners' swimming free from the undertow of their history, he found in Graves a perspective that justified his own strong impulse to embrace another aspect of his cultural past:

> If [a man] wants in some way to know himself, define himself, and tried to do it without taking into account the thing he came from, he is writing without any ink in his pen. The provincial who cultivates only his roots is in peril, potato-like, of becoming more root than plant. The man who cuts his roots away and denies that they were ever connected with him withers into half a man. . . . It is, I think, necessary to know in that crystal chamber of the mind where one speaks straight to oneself that one is or was that thing, and for any understanding of the human condition it's probably necessary to know a little about what the thing consists of.

In *Goodbye to a River* Humphrey found and copied into his notebook references to little-known aspects of Texas history that pertained to the Indian side of his own family—references, for example, to Sam Houston's objections to the greedy white man's attacks on peaceful Indians and to the "official removal of all Indians from Texas, farmers and fighters alike, up across the Red [River] and into the Territory."[15] Humphrey's notebook gives special attention to Graves's allusion to the bogus accounts of Texas "history" in the prejudiced "brag-books" of the "boosters" who take delight in resurrecting old bloodshed in festivals that ignore the "rough-edged realities of the past." Graves's comments set Humphrey to thinking of "the abundant mindless hoop-la" associated with San Jacinto Day, the main subject of the introductory chapter of *No Resting Place*.[16]

To write *No Resting Place*, Humphrey had had to renounce a long-held aversion to the historical novel. On 11 December 1963, in the third of his lectures as Glasgow Professor at Washington and Lee University, "Carthage and Moscow," he had denounced any historical novel as a book "trying to do two things at once: be a work of art and a work of information." He insisted that "a novel

---

15. John Graves, *Goodbye to a River* (New York: Knopf, 1960), 145, 50–51. Humphrey copied the passages into his "Graves" notebook in March 1978, WH res.

16. See Graves, 142–44; Humphrey, notebook, WH res.

ought to be a novel, that it should have no secondary purpose, that it should not try to educate me, nor edify me." Furthermore, interest in the historical novel "is evidence of neither an interest in history nor an interest in the novel"; it is a subgenre that sins against factual truth and against imaginative truth.[17]

Before his lecture was over Humphrey had argued that some writers are capable of overcoming the pitfalls of the historical novel. Flaubert was not one, but Tolstoy was and did in *War and Peace,* in which he melded the purpose of the historian and the artist. Perhaps a lack of confidence that he could avoid the trap that Flaubert had fallen victim to in *Salammbo* was a factor in Humphrey's diverting his attention for three years to *Hostages to Fortune.* Eventually, however, he concluded that he could write a historical novel that was more historically accurate than history—more so at least than Texas history as it was taught in Texas schools.

This compelling issue is a concern of Robert Penn Warren in "The Use of the Past," where he remarks on the "[a]ppalling history textbooks [his] children studied"; in those books, he said, "I find embalmed every official lie, idiotic piety, and stereotypical attitude that characterizes our social and political life." Humphrey observed deficiencies in history books for adults as well. One June morning he sat down to take notes for his novel from Arthur Schlesinger's *The Age of Jackson* in a notebook he had designated for this purpose, but he did not get far; on the second page of the notebook he wrote: "This notebook went nowhere. Schlesinger overlooks Jackson's Indian policy!" This appalling omission led Humphrey to mistrust Schlesinger entirely.[18] *No Resting Place* confronts the issue of misleading school texts head on. On the book's first page, Humphrey's narrator says, "History is heavily edited for schoolchildren and, for most of us, commencement puts an end to study. Thus we go through life with notions of our past which, for depth, complexity, subtlety of shading, rank with comic books. Texas history particularly lends itself to this; it is so farfetched that only a child could believe it" (*NRP,* 1–2). The dramatic context for this judgment is a reenactment of the San Jacinto Day pageant, commemorating the victory over Mexico that created Texas as "a redneck republic" (15). The narrator, Amos IV, who is among the audience at the junior high school football stadium, recalls his partici-

17. Humphrey, "Carthage and Moscow," unpublished lecture delivered on 11 December 1963, Washington and Lee University, WH Coll., UT. This lecture was given again at Smith College, 7 October 1976, during his semester as Elizabeth Drew Professor of English.

18. Robert Penn Warren, "The Use of the Past," in *New and Selected Essays* (New York: Random House, 1989), 48; "Notes on Arthur Schlesinger's The Age of Jackson for The Red and the White," WH res.

pation, as an eighth grader, in the first performance of this pageant, done for the centennial of Texas, in 1936. At this time, Amos IV had originally been selected to play "one of the two heroes of the battle, the man with the most resonant name in the annals of the state, none other than Mirabeau . . . Buonaparte Lamar," the second president of the Republic of Texas. But when his father learns that his son is to play "[t]hat sorry rascal" he decides to tell his son some history that will forever prevent him from participating in the patriotic inanities of his contemporary Texans (10). The boy's father knows what a heavy hand the weight of the past will lay upon his thirteen-year-old son—a theme *vis à vis* the southern past in Humphrey's fiction—but in this case, the father feels that the "sordid betrayal" of the Indians by the government of the Republic of Texas, particularly by Lamar, must not be forgotten (13). The entire story of betrayal, which began in Washington, D.C., and Georgia but ended in Texas, had been passed on from father to son or from grandfather to grandson for generations.

And so the father takes his son to the water, to the shore of the Red River, as his father had done for him when he approached manhood, and he tells the story that will mark his son as one set apart from other Texans forever. The father, Amos III, is uncertain about just where the story begins, but he has no doubt about its ending: "it had all ended here on this spot on the banks of Red River on . . . [13] July 1839" (*NRP*, 18). As Amos III sings "Amazing Grace" in the Cherokee language, Part 1 of the novel fades out, with many questions raised and almost none answered. Humphrey does not come back to the perfidy of Texas in its treatment of the Cherokees until the last section of the novel. Between the beginning and the ending, Amos III tells the story of Amos I (Noquisi) and his people, the story of the forced migration of the Cherokees from Georgia to the land that had been promised to them beyond the Mississippi. That story recounts the United States Government's betrayal of the Cherokee. The final section of the novel returns to the issue broached in its beginning: the Republic of Texas's subsequent betrayal of the same people.

Humphrey made a special effort to lend historical authenticity to his novel. For one thing, he drew upon *Dr. Hooper's Physician's Vademecum; or, A Manual of the Principles and Practice of Physic,* which enabled him to depict accurately the diseases that the Cherokees and their United States Army escorts acquired on their long trek westward—and the contemporary treatments of those diseases as well. Not only did Humphrey use information from this handbook, but he actually places a copy of it in the hands of the physician accompanying the Cherokees, Dr. Warren. Humphrey must have used the 1842 edition, for his narrator refers to the book's "Philadelphia imprint," 1842 being the year of the edition published in Philadelphia—a silent anachronism, just three years off.[19]

Giving attention to almost every detail that he could think of that would help to represent historical events accurately and with a sense of presence, Humphrey purchased an old Cherokee language book and studied it; he also consulted Bill Pulte and Durbin Feeling in the Anthropology Department at Southern Methodist University on the meanings and spellings of Cherokee words.[20] He then sprinkled Cherokee phrases throughout the narrative. For example, the Cherokees take a stand against emigration in their own language: "*TLA YIDAYOJADANVSI*" (*NRP*, 98). Earlier Humphrey had thought of the importance of including the exact flora of the Cherokee Trace and so had written to his aunt Becky Varley requesting information about the wild flowers that bloom at the same time as the Cherokee Roses. She gathered and pressed samples of flowers and sent them to Humphrey, but apparently he could not identify them from the pressings and therefore did not allude to other blooming plants in the Cherokee Trace section of the novel.[21]

Humphrey was so successful in melding the historical events and his fictional characters that his publisher, Seymour Lawrence, thought the family story told was a true one; therefore he wrote to Humphrey on 18 November 1987, saying, "I do not think it should be published as fiction but as narrative history" (Lawrence Coll.). The author was compelled to explain the nature of the book:

The characters in it are caught up in an historical experience but they are not, nor are they based upon, actual people. It is not the story of my family, nor of anybody else's known to me. No real-life boy that I know of listened to the story of his people from his grandfather nor cast a magic spell upon a land-surveyor nor served as a doctor on the Trail of Tears nor saw his father shot to death on Red River. No minister known to me lost his faith through that experience. These are fictional characters and events not drawn from recorded facts but imagined as being expressive of an historical happening. Indeed, as history the book is unreliable, for I have taken liberties with known facts and personages.

19. The edition that the novel's doctor would have used was published in 1833 in London; this edition went simply by the title *The Physician's Vademecum*, the author's name not appearing in the title until the 1842 edition.
20. Ruth Bradley Holmes and Betty Sharp Smith, *Beginning Cherokee* (Norman: University of Oklahoma Press, 1924); Bill Pulte to Humphrey, 27 July 1987, WH res.
21. Pat C. Beadle to Humphrey, 5 May 1978, WH Coll., UT.

That Humphrey's novel is so easily mistaken for history might seem a virtue. Because at least the main part of the novel—excepting the frame, which is about a little-known aspect of Texas history—is grounded in historical events that most readers have some knowledge of, the author actually has a leg up in the game of persuading readers to believe in what is written. It is an easy step for them to believe in the novel's ostensible writer, Amos Smith IV, and he is the present-day descendent of Amos I, who came to Texas over the Trail of Tears in 1839. Humphrey's method is similar to the one Geoffrey Tillotson saw in Thackeray: "The story is given out unmistakably as history, as merely a further piece of the history everybody is already familiar with."[22] It is essential to Humphrey's purpose that he make no distinction between the historical persons who populate his novel and the imaginary ones that he has attached to history. We are asked to take Noquisi and O. J. Blodgett as being just as real as Chief Bowles and John Ross, and we feel no reluctance to comply. For Humphrey has taken special pains to lend a historical dimension to his made-from-scratch characters. For example, the Reverend Malcolm Mackenzie, who comes from Scotland "to save the Indians," apart from the convincing dramatic verisimilitude of his role, is afforded the illusion of historical solidity by frequent references to his published letters, entitled *The Missionary in Spite of Himself*, and to the diary that he kept for the length of his association with the Cherokees (*NRP*, 25).[23] This "publication" also gives the ostensible writer of the novel, Amos IV, a source for the inner thoughts and concerns of Mackenzie, which are a part of his account.

The very existence of a missionary to the eastern Cherokees in 1837, when Mackenzie arrives, is an anomaly, but Humphrey is careful with details to prevent his presence from being a historical error. So intense was the State of Georgia's objection to the interference of "northern missionaries" that the state militia had arrested, beaten, chained, and imprisoned three of them on 7 July 1831, and by 1835 the American Mission Board, capitulating to outside pressures, moved its Cherokees mission to those Cherokee who had gone west many years previous.[24] The novel imparts that the last of the New England missionaries had been arrested and beaten in 1828. There had been no clerical presence among the eastern Cherokees, then, for nine years when the Reverend Mackenzie arrives; and, since the New England protestants had abandoned these Indians, Humphrey resorts to making his clergyman a priest in the Scottish Episcopal Church, the name

22. Humphrey to Lawrence, [February 1989], Lawrence Coll.; Geoffrey Tillotson, *Thackeray the Novelist* (London: Methuen, 1954), 75.

23. In his notes for the novel Humphrey called the clergyman MacIntosh.

24. Van Every, 148–50, 228.

taken by the Anglican Church in Scotland after the Presbyterian became the Church of Scotland in the seventeenth century. Humphrey needed for him to be a marked contrast to the New England missionaries, which a nineteenth-century Presbyterian would not have been. To prevent his readers from the easy error of assuming that this Scottish cleric is a Presbyterian, which nonetheless two reviewers were quick to do,[25] Humphrey repeatedly includes detailed references to his clergyman's religious attitudes and beliefs that should leave no doubt as to his affiliation. Not only does his missionary have his Prayer Book always in hand, but he conducts services peculiar to the Book of Common Prayer—for example, "The Churching of Women" and "The Visitation of the Sick"; he expounds on the Articles of Faith, and he makes distinctions between *his* Church and garden-variety protestants: "the Reverend Mackenzie had always thought of nonconformists as misguided at best, nitpickers and hairsplitters, and, at worst, as outcasts for going against the Kingdom's established church" (*NRP*, 30). There is even a hint that Mackenzie is well born: because he was a "younger son," he was "destined from birth for the church"—a detail suggesting the fate of many younger sons of the aristocracy who had inherited neither a title nor the family's wealth and who, because their social position prevented their entering trade, had left to them little choice of vocation other than to take holy orders (26). Apparently, then, Humphrey has made his missionary a man with standing in British society in order to provide him with some degree of immunity against the kind of treatment that the Georgia authorities had meted out to the New England missionaries, for the United States government would have wished to prevent an international incident that might result if a representative of the United Kingdom were to be officially mistreated and thus would likely have urged the Georgians to act with restraint.

Humphrey has a great deal of historical baggage to bring to the reader's attention, but he comes up with some rather clever ways of presenting information dramatically. For example, through Mackenzie's reaction to a newspaper article the reader learns about the provisions of Georgia's legislation designed to undo the Cherokee nation, an omnibus act passed by the legislature on 19 December 1829:

> On reading that they were forbidden to dig for the gold on their own land, and that this land, theirs from time immemorial, was being taken from them and distributed to white settlers while they were forced to leave their

---

25. See Larry R. Bowden, "A Lament for the Vanishing," *Cross Currents* 41 (Spring 1991): 114, and John Ehle, "God Was at Least Partly to Blame," *New York Times Book Review*, 25 June 1989, 19.

ancestral home and move to a far west, as wild to them as to white men, he said again, this time more vehemently, "Shocking!" Then when he read that their missionaries had been expelled and the converts among them, of whom there were many, denied the right of religious assembly, this in a state professedly Christian, the Reverend Mackenzie said, "Now see here! We can't have that!" (*NRP*, 26)[26]

Forced by conscience to answer God's call to go as a missionary to the Cherokees, Mackenzie sails for Georgia with his new wife and sets about figuring out ways to circumvent the restrictions that the laws of Georgia placed upon him and his flock. He gets around the prohibition against congregational worship by administering the sacraments singly or in pairs.

Mackenzie's role helps to clarify the predicament of the Cherokees. Through him the novel emphasizes one of the great ironies of history—that the Cherokee were persecuted as Indians just when they had ceased to appear to be Indians. Mackenzie's outsider European eyes come on the scene expecting to see wigwams, headdresses of eagle feathers, breech cloths, beaded moccasins, and bows and arrows. Instead he sees a cultured and Christian community of farmers, many of whom he would, because of their mixed blood, never have guessed were Indians. The priest's first sacramental act identifies one of the central cultural dilemmas of the Cherokees—that they have become so much like white people that they are uncertain of their identity. We see the dilemma dramatized in the baptism of a boy of about twelve years when, during the river ceremony, the priest asks the boy to state his name: he does not know what name to give, his "white" name, Amos Ferguson, or his "Indian" name, Noquisi, which means "Bright Star" (*NRP*, 32). These names signify two conflicting modes of being, his "civilized" Christian mode and his dreadful warlike Indian mode. For the moment, he gives his white name for the white ceremony, keeping to himself his Indian name received a few days earlier on the occasion of his "scratching," a rite of manhood during which the boy had been scratched with a comb made from the bone of a wolf, a long-neglected ceremony that he and his grandfather had revived because the civilization that they had adopted was turning against them. This Cherokee rite, like baptism, involves going to the river, though for the Cherokee rite the purpose is to wash away the blood from the scratching. The similarity in the ceremonies, however, emphasizes the enduring conflict that resides within Noquisi-Amos, and the question of his identity remains unresolved four generations later in Amos IV, who, as we have seen, has lived with a

26. The provisions of the act are summarized by Van Every, 144.

white identity but who on the occasion of going to the river with his father has his Cherokee identity revived.

Noquisi's Cherokee rite of manhood also involves a "sequestration, in a sort of male purdah," and Humphrey uses its operation as a means of supplying the background for the story of the Cherokees' expulsion from their eastern homeland and the sad death march to Texas (*NRP*, 37). During Noquisi's sequestration, "days he spent sleeping, his nights he spent with his grandfather in the *asi*, the hothouse, his eyes washed with owl-feather-water to keep them open, listening to the stories of the Creation, of the early history of his people and of their recent period of glory, their present peril, the portents of their impending disaster" (37). As the reader "hears" Noquisi's grandfather's nightly accounts, he feels at times in need of owl-feather-water himself to keep awake for this rather tedious portion of the book, but how could the history and the politics of the situation have been presented more effectively? Victor Hugo had no better idea for giving the historical context of *Les Miserables*, though the ratio of history and politics to the life of his characters is much more favorable. One thing to be said in favor of Humphrey's handling of the historical and political background is that it justifies the selective aspect of his use of his sources. First, "there were gaps in the telling of the story," and because the history is told throughout the long night, "there were gaps in the listening" as well: "even the eyewash of owl-feather-water was not proof against the old man's unbroken, low monotone, the darkness, the heat, the flickering flames, the cross-legged immobility; . . . the boy often dozed off despite himself" (47). Then, too, when Amos IV, generations later, produces the story that is the written-down account that we read, additional gaps and compressions are naturally to be assumed. One of the omissions in the historical account that Noquisi hears is that the Continental Congress had proclaimed the seaboard Indians "a defeated enemy who had by their belligerent actions"—they had supported the British against the American revolutionists—"forfeited every right except such as might be restored them by the sufferance of the victors."[27] In some minds, this omitted fact might go a way toward justifying the ruthless treatment of the Cherokees.

In 1836 the New Echota Treaty was ratified by the United States Senate; it provided for the use of military force to compel the Cherokees to leave their ancestral lands. The complex political realities that actually led longtime friends of the Cherokees to vote yea on this bill are omitted in the novel's account. Although John Ross, president of the Cherokee nation, led a campaign of passive resistance, the date for confiscation of all Cherokee lands and for their removal to concentration camps to await the march to the West was set: 23 May 1838.

27. Van Every, 95.

THE RED AND THE WHITE

Even though Humphrey has thought of strategies for omitting parts of the historical record, and even though he has provided a quasi-dramatic framework for its disbursement, a question remains: did the great heap of historical fact that Humphrey felt compelled to include prove to overweight his imagination, preventing it from taking flight? Knowing that Humphrey cared enormously about the subject of this novel, one would like to be generous in assessing it. If Humphrey just had to bind himself to a body of historical fact and tell the story faithfully, then he could not have chosen better. But William Styron's warnings for the writer of historical fiction (which accord with Humphrey's own in "Carthage and Moscow") do apply to *No Resting Place*. Too much historical fact, said Styron, shackles the imagination. "A bad historical novel is like a hopelessly over-furnished house," he said—"fiction requires a disregard of most facts."[28]

Unable to disregard what he considered essential historical facts—in the case of the Trail of Tears, the facts are too well known to be ignored—Humphrey carefully provides the historical background that leads up to his central concern: the famous march to the West. The poignant account of the preparations to leave, the confinement, and the march itself are well told, but the plain truth is that, however affecting the facts of the case might be, the sweep of the historical process is an impediment to the full development of character. Thus we are reluctant to care deeply about the individual characters because we do not know them well enough. This fault in the novel remains even though one of Humphrey's main purposes in revising the manuscript had been to enrich the characters and bring them to the foreground, to save them from being swamped by the historical sweep of events.[29]

But that is not to say that Humphrey fails to give attention to the dramatic revelation of character. In fact, as he had previously taken the occasion of removal as an acute moment for the revelation of character (see "The Hardys"), so here, during the process of packing those few belongings that might be taken to the West, Humphrey dramatizes Noquisi's growth into manhood. He and his mother attend to the packing of the essentials for their family. When his mother observes her son "handling something of his that she knew he treasured," she says more than once: "I'm sure we can make space for that, Noquisi" (*NRP*, 85). His refusal, over and over, to take such items clearly portrays him as one for whom the assumption of the role of manhood is adequate compensation for any sadness about giving up his past pleasures, and the packing process is an earnest

28. William Styron, the C. Vann Woodward Lecture in Southern History and Literature, Henderson State University, Arkadelphia, Ark., 1 October 1997.

29. Dorothy Humphrey to Yannick Guillou, [1988], Gallimard.

of Noquisi's adaptability to the hardships of the forthcoming journey and his ultimate adaptability when he is adopted by the white man who kills his father.

Packing belongings also marks a distinction between the cultivated and educated Cherokees and the ignorant redneck Georgians whose rapaciousness is the primary cause for the expulsion. Agiduda, Noquisi's grandfather, considers what few books he might take with him to the territory beyond the Mississippi. His bound collection of *The Tatler*, he decides, would "be just the thing to make life tolerable in that literary desert"; the narrator remarks, "Its urbanity and polish made him feel that his crude world was not the only world that men had made for themselves" (*NRP*, 101). Agiduda knows that he will find no white buyer for the books that he cannot take with him.

The character of the Cherokee people is sometimes starkly conveyed by the powerful use of precise detail as they react to the sudden appearance of the militia to escort them to the holding stockade; one Indian woman, for example, goes immediately to the front door to call her chickens and feeds them for the last time. Yet these instances do not turn into a sustained development of character. In fact, Humphrey's development of the corporate personality of the Cherokees is at odds with his effort to develop individual characters. He knew that their individuality was lost in the face of their "common threat": they "have no life of [their] own, no more individuality than a raindrop" (*NRP*, 103). Humphrey's aim, then, he explained to Seymour Lawrence, was contrary to the usual requirement of fiction to create fully realized characters: "The right to an individual fate is the first right lost in genocide. It was this that I meant to convey."[30] Hence, Humphrey repeatedly portrays the Cherokees as a lump sum: "While they had been driven from their separate homes and might each have had a different story to tell about what he or she had been doing at the moment of the soldiers' surprise appearance, all divergences among them had been canceled by the common fate that had swept them up and hurled them together. They had been reduced to cells of a single body, with a single purpose and destination, like a column of ants on the march" (126). Subsequently, Humphrey likens them to "a shoal of fish caught in a net," and over and over they produce their "universal groan": "the people cried with a single heart"; a "thousand people cried as one" (133, 132, 175, 176).

Among the Cherokees who are treated as a mass, Noquisi, or Amos Ferguson, later to become Amos Smith, is the most fully realized character. He plays several significant roles, all of which he meets with astonishing maturity, working as the Reverend Mackenzie's translator and assistant, as the assistant to the medical

30. Humphrey to Lawrence, [February 1989], Lawrence Coll.

doctor, and, following the doctor's death, as the march's sole medical official. Humphrey foresaw the danger that such a character presented; in his notes for the novel he remarked, "I don't want him to seem 'heroic.' That would be cheap fiction" (WH Coll., UT). Here Humphrey was remembering one of his principal complaints about the historical novel in his 1963 lecture at Washington and Lee—the profusion of heroes and heroism. By way of preventing Noquisi from seeming superhuman, then, Humphrey dramatizes his failures as a substitute physician: though he does the best he can for them, his patients die one after another, often owing to his inexperience or lack of knowledge. Though Noquisi is constantly present and doing his best with the odds of success against him, and though he stands out from the mass of suffering humanity, his character does not develop inwardly; we get no sense of the depth of his being. He is merely busy fulfilling all the roles that befall him.

The one character that Humphrey makes into a somewhat complex fictional personage is the Reverend Mackenzie. Even though he is as busy as Noquisi— mostly burying the dead—this Scottish priest develops an affecting complexity of being in which his strength is his weakness: he loses his faith as a result of practicing it devotedly. When a well-bred gentleman born for a life of ease in a pleasant highland parish answers the call to take the Church to the Cherokees who are being abandoned by fair-weather friends, and what is more, elects to accompany them on their hazardous march of many months, we know that we are not presented with a man from a common mold (Humphrey is once again in danger of creating a hero). The Cherokees "saw that he was voluntarily endur- ing their hardships"; in this way, he lives his faith to the ultimate (*NRP*, 159). Yet in seeing the suffering that the Cherokees are subjected to, he begins to doubt the efficacy of prayer and to feel a "sorrowful sense of God's disinterestedness" (139). When he preaches to them that "God worked in a mysterious way His wonders to perform," he comes to feel a profound sense of doubt about the va- lidity of his utterance (146). His doubts begin while the Cherokee captives are being confined in inhuman conditions ("bunched together like a bed of mag- gots") where hundreds are dying of dysentery. The concentration camp provides merely a foretaste of hell; for, once the march begins, the deaths are so many that the sky behind the column is darkened with buzzards, and the ever-present wolves at night "serenaded their future fare with hungry howls" (137, 155).

Slowly but surely, the Reverend Mackenzie's uncertainty about God's good- ness grows, and it is confirmed by the death of his young wife, who has hardly been present until she comes to the fore to die on the ground. When she does, her husband abandons the rigid faith that he had been schooled in as decisively as Jude Fawley and with the very verse that Hardy's character utters near the end of his life: "The letter killeth."[31] Praying the prayer of despair, "My God, my God, why hast Thou forsaken me?" and deeply mindful of the origin of that prayer, he rips off his clerical collar, and then buries his wife without ceremony (*NRP*, 211). From that moment on he "felt it was for God, not him, to explain his ways" (212). Thus, the Reverend Mackenzie does not lose his belief in God's existence: "His heresy went deeper than that. Gone from him forever was his faith in God's goodness" (214). Nonetheless, Father Mackenzie spends the rest of his life preaching God's love to the surviving Cherokees: "This life of imposture and deception he defends on the ground that having seen the suffering he had seen he was not only justified but in duty bound to tell whatever harmless lies might alleviate any more" (214).

In painting the portrait of a man who loses his faith by practicing it faithfully, Humphrey makes a nice ironical point. But MacKenzie's character lacks dimension, for we cannot see beyond his religious aspect. We never know anything about his relationship with his wife, for example—what effect does the hardship that he introduced into her life have on their relationship? We have little sense of what kind of husband he is. These and a hundred other questions might have been pursued, and a round, full character that we could care deeply about might have emerged.

Weak though the characterization is, Humphrey's imaginative powers manage to break out of their historical shackles and produce some powerfully perceived moments. When the winding column of Cherokees halts at the end of a day's march, Humphrey will often provide a vivid sense of the individuals who are part of this great historical event. In a "spot without shelter," Noquisi and his grandparents make camp on a bleak midwinter evening:

> When the Fergusons straggled in that evening the boy fetched water from the wagon and put it to heat on the fire. He unlaced his grandmother's moccasins and unwound the rags that wrapped her calves. Her feet, blue with cold, were a mass of blisters, fresh and old, all rubbed raw. While they soaked the boy rubbed them. They puckered and swelled in the warm water.
>
> He tucked her into her blanket, bathed his grandfather's feet, then put him to bed. Their sleeping bodies sought each other's warmth. To get into his place between them the boy had to squeeze.
>
> Sometime later in the night he woke to see his grandfather huddled

---

31. *NRP*, 211; Thomas Hardy, *Jude the Obscure* (London: Macmillan, 1974), 407.

beside the fire. He had put his blanket over the two of them. (*NRP*, 189–90)

The main purpose of such details is to convey a sense of the real presence of the participants in the march; what Humphrey also achieves is a profound sense of the humanity of the Cherokees.

One of the story's most chilling descriptions is of the birds of carrion that follow the marchers. These birds are the beneficiaries of quick, frequent, and necessarily shallow (because of the frozen ground) burials: "Of the buzzards hovering high overhead like kites there seemed at times to be one for each and every marcher. They took their places as did the people on command from the conductor in the morning and there they hung daylong, moving at the people's pace, and when that slowed, dropping expectantly a notch lower in the sky. By night they settled to roost in trees nearby, in such numbers that by morning their droppings had whitened the trunks. There was no stopping the mind from thinking of what those droppings were composed of" (*NRP*, 190). The painterly Humphrey effectively limns portraits, be they brief sketches—"Grandmother, dazed with fatigue, sat gazing dully into the flames, forgetful of the bite of tasteless food unswallowed in her mouth" (182)—or ones more fully filled in with character-revealing highlights, such as the following picture of Chief Bowles:

Now, though he still stood as straight as a gun barrel and his stride was upright and brisk, his sandy hair was streaked with white and his weather-worn and suntanned face was as wrinkled as the rind of an Osage orange, the fruit of the tree of the ark. His eyes were gray with age, it seemed, as though they had once been a darker shade but had been bleached by time, had faded from all his close and wary observation of life. In the Indian fashion, he kept them shut for lengthy periods when he was speaking and when he was listening—they opened, suddenly or slowly, for emphasis, of his words or of yours, and this suddenness or slowness, combined with their paleness, made them unfailingly startling. (222–23)

Humphrey's accurate figures of speech are no less in evidence in *No Resting Place* than in his other books. Though he allows the clichés expected in the portrayal of Indians (they "bury the tomahawk," "smoke the peace pipe," and say "ugh!"), and though he includes an assortment of white-man clichés as well ("they will have to drag me kicking and screaming every inch of the way"), Humphrey offers numerous counters to these lapses (*NRP*, 116, 120, 106). Chief Bowles's voice, for example, is "crackling like the blaze" as he intones the traditional Cherokee war chant; as the battle with the Texas Rangers commences, "Like a volley of arrows he loosed his warriors"; and when the battle is over, "His own men lay like spent arrows that had missed their mark" (235, 244, 245). His most poignant figures convey the collective suffering of the Cherokees even as he sorts their conditions: "As the fittest and the less fit and the least fit and the unfit were sorted out and separated, the column straggled like an old animal whose hindquarters are failing it" (160). And he wonderfully conveys their collective emotion during the heartbreaking march: "the farther they got from [their homeland] the greater was the pain. To them it was like an elastic cord to which they were attached: the farther it was stretched, the stronger its pull" (176).

Part 5, the novel's final section, comes back to the issue of Part 1: why Amos IV should not play the part of Lamar in a pageant that celebrates this Texas hero's participation in the Battle of San Jacinto. Amos's father tells his son of how the survivors of the Trail of Tears joined with the Cherokees, as well as other tribes, who had previously settled in Texas, of how the new Republic of Texas had promised this land to the Indians in appreciation for their cooperation in securing Texas's independence, and then of how that republic's second governor expelled all Indians. When many of them refused to leave, a battle ensued; Amos I and his father, Dr. Abel Ferguson (who had vacated Georgia earlier on a voluntary basis), man the field hospital during this battle between the Texas Rangers and the Indians. Though there are some *Iliad*-like descriptions of battle wounds that convey the effect of large events on individuals, little opportunity for character development presents itself during the novel's final section, and the historical sweep leading up to the battle paints only a large picture with a large cast.

Nevertheless, Humphrey integrates the imagery of the novel's closing into its established pattern. As Amos I, or Noquisi, had gone to the water in Christian baptism and as an aspect of his scratching ceremony, facing in these dual rites the question of his identity, so does that same character at the novel's conclusion encounter a crisis of identity when he goes to the Red River: here, as he and his father seek to flee Texas after the battle, he is adopted by the Texas Ranger named Smith who has just gunned down his father and who thinks the boy is a white captive.[32] That the Texan has no idea that the boy is one of those he hates—that if he had seen the boy's father up close he would not have known him to be an Indian either—is a wry and ironical commentary on the mindlessness of racial hatred.

32. Almon points out that Walter Prescott Webb's *The Texas Rangers* (Boston: Houghton Mifflin, 1935) is Humphrey's source for this incident (381).

Noquisi is forced to abandon his Cherokee identity and to enter white society as Amos Smith in order to live at all. Generations later, Amos Smith IV learns that the Cherokee part of his ancestor survives in him, and, psychologically, he disengages from the white society that he had thought he properly belonged to. He becomes an "internal emigré," a term Humphrey first applied to Clyde Renshaw in *Proud Flesh* (*NRP*, 10; *PF*, 230). The issue of Amos IV's identity, then, is settled when he goes with his father to that same Red River—as his father had done with his—and hears the story that is the story of the novel. And so the present issue of the San Jacinto Day celebration is not merely a contrived frame for the main narrative, but it is a present that proves how the past affects it and thus justifies, gives a rationale for, the retelling of the story of the Cherokee expulsions from Georgia and Texas.

One of the successes of *No Resting Place* is the developing play on the title. When Amos IV's father is struggling with the question of whether he should tell his son the story that will redefine his relationship with the society of Texas, the boy recalls, "The roses were much on my father's mind just then. In fact, for the past several days they had allowed him *no rest*" (*NRP*, 13; italics mine). This intimation of the title finds its full expression at the beginning of Part 2 when the scope of the novel becomes evident. Amos I's grandfather reads to him an article from the Cherokee newspaper, the *Phoenix*, entitled "Remarkable Fulfillment of Indian Prophecy": the article at one point says that the white man "WILL POINT YOU TO THE WEST, but you will find *no resting place* there, for your elder brother [the white man] will drive you from one place to another until you reach the western waters" (38–39; italics mine). As the Georgia Cherokees embark on their long journey to the remote west, Noquisi is reminded of this prophecy—that "even there they would find no resting place" (161; also cf. 104). Once the march is under way, however, the meaning of "resting place" as "ultimate goal" disappears in the face of ever-present need. In the cold, wind, snow, and ice, "no resting place" quickly acquires the practical meaning "no shelter": although the Cherokees "desperately needed rest and recuperation, . . . there was no resting place" (192). As the Cherokees die along the way, they come to see that they will indeed have a resting place—but it will be their final resting place. Noquisi's grandmother plods toward a cross in her mind, which gets bigger in her imagination as her footsteps begin to falter. She perceives that her death will provide a "resting place" (170). This is no proper resting place, however, because the earth "in its frozen state, often refused to receive even their mortal remains" (194).

Enduring the long journey and arriving in Texas, Noquisi momentarily forgets the prophecy that there would be "no resting place" for the Cherokees: he opines, as he first crosses the Red River, that "he had found his resting place"; yet the prophesy proclaimed generations ago in the *Phoenix* proves true (*NRP*, 217). In the end, he learns that there will be no resting place for him as an Indian, that he will only find rest as a white man. Still, Amos, as well as his descendants, retains inwardly his Cherokee identity.

There are only two other titles that Humphrey considered for the novel: "The Red and the White" (referring to the Cherokee Rose, which is streaked red and white) and "The Trail of Tears." Humphrey said he would have used this title, the name the Cherokees themselves gave to the episode in their tribal history, had the phrase not been used for a book title at least twice before. He did, however, want *La piste des larmes* as the title for the French translation. When he learned that Gallimard objected to this title as sentimental, Humphrey was alarmed and wrote to his editor Yannick Guillou assuring him that the title was not sentimental and insisting that it not be changed.[33] The title that he chose for the American edition, however, has the virtue of uniting generations of Cherokees together through a phrase that has multiple meanings.

One of Humphrey's other unifying elements connects the suffering of the Cherokees with the suffering of the Jews. Following the suggestion of some of his sources, Humphrey planted frequent allusions to the similar fates of the Cherokees and the Jews. In *Disinherited*, Van Every, remarking on the unusual aspect of the Cherokee's fate, says, "There have been relatively [few] recorded occasions, as in the instance of the Babylonian Captivity of the Jews, of an entire people being compelled to abandon their country"; and Clarke, following John Henry Brown's *Indian Wars and Pioneers of Texas* (1897), alludes to Chief Bowles as "the Moses of their tribe."[34] Humphrey takes these brief allusions and makes them into a red thread that runs throughout all sections of the novel, there being, all told, twenty-two allusive parallels between the Cherokees and the Jews. Some of Humphrey's references are directly from one of his sources, as when his narrator says, "Now he was seen by many Cherokees as their Moses"; some are minor, as when we learn that a number of the Cherokees, like the Jews, refuse to touch pork; yet other parallels are sweeping, all-defining identifications, as in the following: "They were in truth the Chosen People—chosen to be the scapegoat of the human race, sent into the wilderness to atone for all its sins" (*NRP*, 110, 93, 176). In one instance, Humphrey denies the parallel even as he makes it, suggest-

33. Humphrey to Lambert, 27 October 1990, Lambert Coll.; to Guillou, 27 October 1990, Gallimard.

34. Van Every, 262; Mary Whatley Clarke, *Chief Bowles and the Texas Cherokees* (Norman: University of Oklahoma Press, 1971), 111.

ing in the end that the Cherokees have suffered more than the Jews: the Cherokees are "an entire nation of Jobs, never doubting, though tested without precedent or parallel," and then we see that "[t]hese were truly the Chosen People, wandering in the wilderness" (193). More than once Humphrey refers to the stockades in which the Cherokees were imprisoned to await the forced march to their place of exile as "concentration camps" (98, 130). Those Georgia Cherokees who survive the march join in a confederation with other wandering tribes (parallel to the twelve tribes of Israel?) west of the Red River. Diwali, or Bowles, was chief of these people, and he was aware of another man in another time who had the same role to play: "He knew the story of this Chief Moses. How, long ago and in another world, Moses had led his oppressed people out of a land called Egypt ruled by a tyrant named Pharaoh across a red sea and into a wilderness before reaching the land promised to them" (238). Chief Bowles also knows that his Pharaoh is Mirabeau Buonaparte Lamar—and that he is the ruler who will keep them from their land promised by Sam Houston.

Another significant unifying feature of the novel is Humphrey's evocation of the "trail of Cherokee roses" at its beginning and ending. These roses mark the trail made by the Cherokees when they entered Texas as their Promised Land; it is the same trail by which they sought to escape the white man's ruthlessness in 1839. Those damasked roses represent Sam Houston's dream of an empire in which the white man and Indian would live together in peace, a dream shattered by Lamar when he succeeded Houston as president. Furthermore, these enduring roses serve to unify the generations: "With a wild rose in my buttonhole that my father had plucked and put there, I sat myself down beside the water where he had sat to listen to the same tale when he was a boy like me" (*NRP*, 20). One of these roses, dried and pressed, is preserved among Humphrey's papers at the University of Texas.

Humphrey confided to Jean Lambert that *No Resting Place* would be his last novel—not because of the agony involved in the writing but because of the anguish that he and Dorothy experienced together after a novel's publication. It was the old fear about the reviews—the trauma from having been ganged up on over *Proud Flesh* still troubled him. Humphrey was gratified to read poet Charles Tomlinson's laudatory letter calling *No Resting Place* a "masterpiece," a "literary stunner," a book that was "moving and harrowing without once becoming sentimental."[35] Had Humphrey received published notices of this sort, he might have

35. Jean Lambert, journal, entry for 28 October 1984, Lambert Coll.; Charles Tomlinson to Humphrey, 21 July 1989, WH res. Humphrey was so proud of this letter from England's leading poet that he copied it out and sent it to Lambert (2 August [1989], Lambert Coll.).

331

instantly been cured of the "critic's evil" that Lehmann-Haupt touched him with years before.

While not as enthusiastic about the novel as Tomlinson in his letter, most of the reviews of *No Resting Place* pronounced the novel a thoroughgoing success. The *Chicago Tribune* said that Humphrey makes memorable "the truly horrid . . . rigors of the long walk" to the Arkansas-Texas region and ended by remarking on the subsequent treatment of the Indians, their expulsion from Texas: "Humphrey has taken a little-known tale of the West, illuminated it with his writing and made it come alive." "Humphrey frames his story with intelligence and compassion and the result is superb," said *Time,* and *Library Journal* agreed: "*No Resting Place* . . . is the story of a nation dispossessed and brought to its knees by the greed and power of another. A beautiful story, highly recommended."[36]

John Ehle, in the *New York Times Book Review,* found the novel "nicely understated, sympathetic, yet somewhat romanticized." Ehle, a historian and author of *Trail of Tears: The Rise and Fall of the Cherokee Nation* (1988), blamed Humphrey's book for being slanted in favor of the Cherokee point of view: "Mr. Humphrey's novel effectively lays the blame ["for the horrors they endure"] on both God and the white man's Government but spares the Cherokees, thus rendering a somewhat unrealistic vision of their tragedy." Then he asked, "[W]here are the hundreds of black slaves who were forced to accompany their Indian masters?"[37] Though Humphrey does not assign a number, "a train of slaves—the captives of captives—self-propelled possessions" appears on page 133. Yet it is hard to see how that issue in any way pertains to the presentation of the "horrors that the Indians endur[ed]" on the Trail of Tears, unless Ehle means to suggest that in adopting the white man's ways, including the keeping of slaves, the Indians were therefore deserving of the treatment they experienced in the diaspora. Ehle also asked, "And where are the medicine men, whose sweat-based treatments for cholera, diphtheria, internal bleeding and many other ailments surely increased the numbers of the dead?"[38] In fact the medicine men with their "heating stones" do appear in *No Resting Place* (see 172); what Humphrey emphasizes, however, is the inability of nineteenth-century medicine to affect the outcome of most of the diseases that strike the Cherokees; the medicine men are called in only when the medical doctor has failed, and they do no worse. The physician

---

36. Kerry Luft, "A Foretaste of Hell on the Old Frontier," *Chicago Tribune,* 8 August 1989, sec. 5, p. 3; "Summer Reading," *Time,* 19 June 1989, 65; Thomas L. Kilpatrick, rev. of *No Resting Place,* in *Library Journal,* 15 May 1989, 89.

37. Ehle, 19.

38. Ibid.

attending the participants in the hazardous march sees no harm in the hot stones and rattles meant to scare the evil spirits away. Moreover, Humphrey's narrator allows that witch doctors actually distract a sufferer's attention from his plight, and the Cherokee physician, Dr. Ferguson, Amos's father, early on in the narrative, acknowledges that many time-tested herbal medications came to him from the lore of the witch doctors (*NRP*, 79). Though he makes some unwarranted complaints, Ehle finds the final section of *No Resting Place* "excellent," especially the final passages, which "are a fitting memorial to this little-remembered event from America's past," the Indians' sad and pointless resistance to their expulsion from Texas. "William Humphrey's prose is unadorned and unobtrusive, a pleasure to read—and to read over again," he says.[39]

Larry R. Bowden, in a lengthy review in *Cross Currents*, judges the novel to be an instance of historical fiction that fulfills Scott Momaday's expectations; it is "historically and ethnographically sound, imaginatively engaging, and morally challenging." Bowden points out aspects of the historical record that Humphrey has omitted, yet he says that the novel is "poignantly conceived" and that its "narrative structure . . . is in harmony with tribal and oral traditions": "Its shape is a story told and retold, father to son, over four generations." Robert Morseberger, on the other hand, finds the narrative framework "awkward" and "clumsy"; he is baffled by Humphrey's interplay of past and present, but his dissatisfactions might be owing to his not having given the novel a very attentive reading (on five occasions in his review he calls the character *Amos* by the name *Adam*). Nevertheless, he concludes by saying that "*No Resting Place*, despite some shortcomings, is a compelling and unforgettable retelling of the Cherokee tragedy."[40]

A review also appeared in *Texas Monthly*, where one might expect an ungracious reception, given that Humphrey's novel undoes the reputation of one of Texas's main heroes, Mirabeau Buonaparte Lamar. To be sure, the reviewer begins by taking some broad swipes at Humphrey, accusing him of having merely "gone through the motions of concocting characters and dialogue and a plot"; these "narrative devices" are "halfhearted." The remainder of the review, however, speaks well of the novel—if oddly: "When it slips out of its fictive coat and tie and into the much more comfortable cloak of reminiscence it is a fine and touching book." More significantly, this reviewer acknowledges the validity of one of the clear aims of *No Resting Place*—"that the pat classroom history of

39. Ibid.
40. Bowden 107, 109; Robert E. Morseberger, rev. of *No Resting Place*, in *Western American Literature* 24 (Winter 1990): 392.

Texas . . . does not jibe with the vastly more complicated and often inequitable events of real life."[41]

Humphrey had hopes that *No Resting Place* would become a movie. The Landsburg Company, on behalf of Home Box Office, purchased the television rights for the novel in August 1989 and then extended the option for another year. Although scriptwriting was done, HBO never made the movie, perhaps worrying that the whole state of Texas would be offended.[42]

41. Suzanne Winkler, "Restless Spirits," *Texas Monthly* 17 (June 1989): 115, 116.

42. Michele Pelkey to Humphrey, 4 August 1989, WH res.; Christopher Goff to Victor Paddock, 19 July 1989, WH res.; Michele Hanson to Humphrey, 6 August 1990, WH res.

[9]

SENESCENCE, ILLNESS, AND DEATH
(September Song)

What is it to grow old?
. . . .
It is to spend long days
And not once feel that we were ever young;
It is to add, immured
In the hot prison of the present, month
To month with weary pain.
> —MATTHEW ARNOLD, "Growing Old"

in a modesty of death I join my father
who dared so long agone leave me.
> —JOHN BERRYMAN, "Henry's Confession"

IN ALL his forty-five years as a writer, William Humphrey never came to rely upon habit: he never figured out a method whereby he could work efficiently (it was always by fits and starts), and he never settled upon a kind of fiction that he could comfortably produce. After *Home from the Hill,* a tragedy, the critical world expected his next novel to be an inferior imitation of the first. But Humphrey struggled for six full years to write a comedy the likes of which his reviewers had never seen but which surprised and delighted them: *The Ordways.* He was in no rut when it came to short stories either. Having produced *The Last Husband,* a collection of stories that in their diversity accentuate his resistance to the "southern writer" label, Humphrey then wrote a book of short stories with a single-minded concentration: *A Time and a Place.* These stories concern the depression and drought days of the 1930s (the time) and the Texas-Oklahoma border (the place). Then came his third novel, *Proud Flesh,* another departure from the expected. *Proud Flesh* is so unusual as to defy categorization: it is not just a mixing of the serious and the hilarious, but a melding. Though like the first two novels in discrediting the southern myth, *Proud Flesh* portrays the Old South's final collapse by means of a fragmented form that matches his subject perfectly. His next novel, *Hostages to Fortune,* takes a radical turn toward somber psychological realism. The most tightly organized of Humphrey's novels, it records a man's return to life following an emotional dive to the depths of pain and loss, and it contains merely a drop of humor in a flood of sorrow.

In his last novel, *No Resting Place,* Humphrey undertook what he had long before warned himself against: the historical novel. Recognizing the limitations of historical fiction, he nevertheless forged ahead with *No Resting Place* because America's betrayal of the Cherokees was a subject about which he felt so strongly that he was willing to risk failure as a writer in order to treat it. And he did fail. Yet Humphrey kept to his determination not to repeat himself. He once commented on the variety of his writing, by quoting Tolstoy: "What am I, a cricket, that I should make the same noise all the time?" (*WST,* 32).

As Humphrey turned the final corner of his life—a fairly lengthy life for a man who drank and smoked as much as he did—he began to consider the relationship between his writing and the death that he saw awaiting him. In remarks at the University of North Texas on 26 September 1986, he had said that his aim in writing was to overcome the fear "of going into the grave without having lived as fully as I might." Through the creation of characters, he labored "to cram into one life more lives than one, to experience in imagination adventures I have not, and never will have."[1] He then reviewed some of these other lives that he had lived through his writing:

Thus I have been, with all the intensity I could bring to the role, a young man oppressed by his small town, whose solution to getting out of it is to masquerade as a human fly, attempting to climb his way to freedom up the local courthouse tower—with disastrous consequences. I have been a mountebank rainmaker during the time of the Dust Bowl, who finds that people are gullible even beyond his requirements. I have been an old woman obliged because of age to sell her possessions and leave the farmhouse, still fiercely jealous of her husband's long dead first wife, whom he himself has forgotten. I have been an adolescent girl neglected by her parents in favor of her brother, who exacts her revenge by inflicting upon them a house full of smelly and obnoxious cats. A bank robber, as well as the woman he once courted. A young mother transplanted from her small Texas town to a great, impersonal Northern city, watching the snow fall as she waits for her child to come home from school, and remembering the rare snows of her childhood. I have been a father (I who am nobody's father) suffering the agony of his young son's suicide. (*WST,* 186–87)

1. In his notes for "Portrait of the Artist," Humphrey says his character begins to fabricate in order "To have on record a life he had not lived and thus had not died" (1988 diary, entry for 11 September, WH Coll., UT).

But the talent that led to a fuller life and the creation of many volumes of fiction had a dark side to it: repeatedly Humphrey embraced the deep grief of things, and he fell into debilitating depression. Repeatedly—by sheer will—he pulled himself up from the depths of despair to live imaginatively another tragic life. In the end, in *September Song* (1992), his last book, he turned to the saddest of all aspects of life—old age.

It is true that his first published story forty-three years earlier—"In Sickness and Health"—was on the hideousness of old age, and so in a sense Humphrey returned to his beginning. But in his own old age his gaze into the subject was more prolonged and more penetrating. At the same time, as each book over the years offered something different from the previous, so is there a striking variety among these final stories: some are painstakingly developed and well fitted out with characters, while others are brief, almost like lyric prose poems; some full of the sorrow and pain attendant upon old age, others high comedic adventures. Yet in all of them Humphrey is unwilling to find comfort in what remains behind. He meant to do to old age what Thoreau did to life in general. He meant to drive old age "into a corner, . . . reduce it to its lowest terms, and, if it prove to be mean, why then [he intended] to get the whole and genuine meanness out of it, and publish its meanness to the world." Humphrey's association with Katherine Anne Porter had led him to face "what a hideous time extreme old age can be." He divulged to Seymour Lawrence that Porter had once "showed [him] a 45 caliber automatic pistol in her possession, said she was keeping it to kill herself with should she ever become senile and helpless, and asked [him] to promise to tell her when that time had come if she herself was unable to detect it."[2]

A few years before the sustained look at old age that we have in *September Song*, Humphrey had primed the pump on this subject with two stories that were published in *Collected Stories* (1985). Rather than with *The Last Husband* and *A Time and a Place*, however, these two stories, "Dolce Far' Niente" and "The Patience of a Saint," belong with those of *September Song*. Like a number of the stories in *September Song*, these are based upon real people that Humphrey knew. The protagonist of "Dolce Far' Niente" was suggested by the Humphreys' former cleaning woman, Maria, who lives in Hudson. For several years, she used to come to their house outside of Hudson twice a week, not because she needed to make money but because she needed to escape the company of her old husband, who was a tombstone carver and "the embodiment of his trade: sedentary, solemn,

2. Henry David Thoreau, *Walden and Civil Disobedience*, ed. Sherman Paul (Boston: Houghton Mifflin, 1960), 62–63; William Humphrey to Seymour Lawrence, 21 August 1978, Lawrence Coll.

unsociable, incommunicative—about as talkative as a tombstone and just as humorous" (Au Int.). Humphrey described the predicament of his real-life source as follows:

Maria came to work for us not for the money but out of boredom and loneliness, just to get out of the house and do something with herself, to talk to somebody about something. With us she was able to talk about her native Italy, where we had lived for several years. She was a joy to have around. She sang, hummed and whistled as she went about her work. We spoke Italian, and that was a pleasure for us all.

But as we got to know Maria better what happened was what always happens when you get to know a person better: confidences, complaints—things which she had nobody else to tell to. Over the lunch which my wife served the three of us there would come moments when Maria seemed to gaze across time and space, to her young womanhood in her native village.

Not, God knows, that life there had been easy. She was from the Veneto, the region near Venice, a region even more poverty-stricken than the interior of Sicily. Her family was of the very poorest. For seven children there had been just one pair of shoes, and that is Alpine country, cold, snow-covered in winter. They shivered and starved.

Their diet was cheese and polenta—cornmeal mush. The young men got away if they could, but from this life there was no hope of escape for the young women. Maria could not even marry her way out, for the young man she loved was as poor as she, and always would be.

She was apologetic about her complaints. Life had, according to the standards by which she had been trained to judge, treated her well. She had been miraculously delivered from what the Italians call miseria—misery—crushing and unallievable deprivation. She had had a good life. She had married, had children, a home of her own, a good income, could look forward to a comfortable old age. And yet . . .

She would say, "My Vittorio is a good man. A good husband. A good father. A good provider. But . . ."

She would say, "My children are good to me. But . . ."

She would say, "America has been good to me. But . . ."

She would say, "My neighbors are good neighbors. But . . ."

But: it was around that little word with which we qualify whatever we say that my story formed, as an oyster spins a pearl around the grain of sand that chafes it. (*WST*, 187–89)

"Dolce Far' Niente" seems at first little more than a sketch of Giorgio and Gina Donatis, Italian immigrants who are successful according to American standards but who in the end manage only a mechanical existence. Humphrey, however, produces a poignant conclusion of stifled epiphany. When Giorgio retires from the coffin-making business (his occupation is slightly altered from that of his real-life model), he quickly starts over on a different treadmill existence: he busies himself making little chests "For keeping things in" (*CS*, 182). While Giorgio is satisfied merely to keep busy, to pass time, the life of his wife of many years is as empty as the little chests that he makes. Gina senses that something is missing from her life on the occasion of her husband's retirement. When she gazes upon the silent gold pocket watch presented to Giorgio by his former employees, "it seemed to her that time had stopped, had never begun, that in her gnarled and workworn fingers she held the emblem of her joyless past, her joyless future, her approaching end" (182). The paragraphs leading up to this moment clarify the nature of Gina's emptiness, even as they show that she falls short of fully comprehending the cause. She does perceive, after it is too late to do differently, that her "life" of attending the funerals that her husband made coffins for "dressed in black, always in the presence of grief" was to miss life: "I am tired to death of death! Let us live a little while we are alive, for pity's sake!" she exclaims to her bewildered husband, whose reply defines the limitation of his view of life: "What is it that you would like to do?" (181). Life is merely doing for him, and his response encourages Gina to contemplate the question of life in his terms. The narrator, capturing her in this dilemma, remarks, "A tombstone on her tongue, in neither language [Italian or English] could she find a word to say. How was she to know what she would like to do? What opportunity had she ever had to learn what diversions life offered?" (181). The narrator, attuned to her unexpressed thought, makes it clear that in thinking on the issue in her husband's terms she has lost her sense of what is wrong with her life, for it was not "diversions" that she had wanted; it was a bountiful life itself.

There is, however, in the expression "in neither language could she find a word to say" a clue to the cause of Gina's sense of life's emptiness. For earlier in the story we are told that when her children were young, she found great pleasure in speaking both English and Italian to them, "correcting them in English, reserving Italian for intimacy and affection" (*CS*, 180). When her children face pressures to conform to American life, they refuse to communicate in Italian—which suggests that for Gina intimacy and affection are thereby absented from her life, for Giorgio is not one to whom she wishes to speak in Italian; he is "the one person with whom she would have preferred to speak English"—which means that he is one with whom she finds the language of intimacy and affection inappropriate.

It is, then, the absence of intimacy and affection that accounts for the emptiness of Gina's life, though she cannot articulate this sad fact. She can do no more than feel her emptiness as she gazes at her husband's gold watch. Her friends observe her moment of near-epiphany uncomprehendingly: "Attributing her tears to gratitude and a sense of fulfillment, the guests all smiled at her" (CS, 182). "Dolce Far' Niente," which means "it is sweet to do nothing," is an ironic reference to the sour disappointment of retirement.

The other new story in Collected Stories, "The Patience of a Saint," also has an ironical title. The story is based pretty closely on Humphrey's own hired man, now dead, and is another story portraying the misprision of casual observers. The narrator, who is as close to the central character, Ernest van Voorhees, as anybody in Tracytown, is in the beginning as much in the dark as everyone else. All are convinced that Ernest finds meaning in life by attending to the needs of his incontinent and demented mother, but the truth the narrator learns is that Ernest has for years resented spoon-feeding his dotty old mother, has resented having to take to the laundromat every morning the bed sheets that she had soiled during the night. Ernest finally finds an opportunity to get rid of the cause of his life's misery, and he confesses his "crime" to the narrator: "I seen my chance and I took it. Lord knows it was long enough in coming" (CS, 193).

Although the narrator is at first shocked, he has had enough regular contact with Ernest's mother to make him sympathetic to the son. The narrator is disposed to distance the mother from the reader's sympathies, too, through a comic treatment of her. The full force of the mother's repulsiveness hits the reader in the comic understatement with which the following paragraph concludes: "There was certainly nothing about her deserving of such devotion as Ernest's. I found her spoiled by his attentions, a chronic malcontent and complainer, tiresome, foolish even before her brain began to go soft, misshapen by age, and to sit beside her in the cab of that pickup with the windows shut tight and the heater going full blast was to feel—well, as if you were in, and not alone in, an outhouse" (CS, 185). With a slight reminder of Pip's portrait of Miss Havisham, Humphrey's narrator comically evokes Mrs. van Voorhees: "Her gold brooch, her diamond engagement ring and her wedding band, now as loose on her dried-up finger as the band on a game bird's leg, were the only reminders of the woman she had been. She had shriveled to skin and bones and her hair had thinned to the scantiness of the fur on a coconut" (186). These and other humorous descriptions tend to dehumanize the outrageous old woman and invite sympathy for the son whose life has been diminished by thirty years of trapped devotion. Ernest does

not take any overt action to harm his mother, such as we might expect in a belated follow-up to "The Last of the Caddoes" and *Proud Flesh*. It is hard to equate
old Mrs. van Voorhees with Clytemnestra, and Ernest is no Orestes. He unhero-
ically "murders" his mother by simply refusing, on her behalf, medical help when
a virulent flu strikes. Ernest almost dies of the flu himself, but it is a risk he
is willing to take for the chance to be free, to secure some measure of life for
himself.

Misinterpreting the "sprightlier pace" of Ernest following his recovery from
his own long illness, misinterpreting as well his frequenting the local bar after a
"lifetime's abstinence," the townspeople admire his fortitude to carry on in spite
of his loss. They believe he is drowning his great sorrow in drink. Typical is the
narrator's cleaning woman, Giuseppina: "He may not be quite all there," she
says, pausing in her work, looking out at Ernest in the yard, "but he has feelings
the same as anybody else and he's a brave soul to carry on as he does all alone
in this terrible cruel world with nothing to live for" (*CS*, 195). Humphrey has
always enjoyed reminding us of the terrible and comic ironies of life—as he had
done in "The Last Husband," *Home from the Hill*, and "A Job of the Plains," to
name but a few. More than that, in "The Patience of a Saint" Humphrey keeps
before us the sadness of living what is not life, living is so dear. Though Ernest
is an old man, it is not too late for him to think about living.

These two precursory stories are based on Humphrey's observation of other
people coming to terms with old age. *September Song* reflects the author's own
frustration with growing old and the losses that accompany it—especially his loss
of hearing and the sense of isolation caused by it. When Charles and Brenda
Tomlinson last saw Bill Humphrey in the mid-1980s, his hearing was worsening
alarmingly, and he was understandably very depressed. In the years following, he
grew harder and harder of hearing, and he had great difficulty adjusting. Not
wanting to be noticed and pitied, and not wanting to make people impatient
with him for having to repeat what they said, he avoided people—thereby in-
creasing the silence in which he lived. His letters to friends frequently complained of his growing steadily deafer and of the inadequacies of hearing aids,
which he began trying in 1988. On 9 June 1988 he wrote: "I've just been told by
a specialist in New York City that the time is not far off when I shall need a
hearing aid." When he went to Paris in the fall to write an essay for the *Washington Post*, he was happy to get away from English for a while; it did not bother
him as much not being able to make out French. [3]

3. Brenda Tomlinson to author, 4 August 1999; Humphrey to Jean Lambert, 22 and 23 February
1990, Lambert Coll.; Humphrey, 1988 diary, entry for 30 April, WH Coll., UT; to author, 9 June 1988;
to Yannick Guillou, [30 August 1988], Gallimard; Dorothy Humphrey to Lambert, 26 January 1989,
Lambert Coll.

Having spent a long career mainly writing stories based on the psychic wounds that he had nursed through the years, Humphrey now turned to immediate physical losses, those he was directly experiencing and those that he foresaw in the near future. He had hoped to complete the stories at the Rockefeller Foundation center in Bellagio, Italy. His application for a fellowship, however, was denied on 13 August 1990. Working at his kitchen table—which became his usual place in later years—he completed the collection within a year (on 21 July 1991), in spite of a bout with pneumonia that involved eight days in the hospital in September and a long recuperation at home. Seymour Lawrence had moved from Delacorte to Houghton Mifflin but had secured excellent terms for Humphrey: 15 percent royalty on all copies sold in hardcover and a $25,000 advance. *September Song* was published on 30 June 1992 and in a month's time had gone into a second printing.[4]

In two of the stories—"The Apple of Discord" and "The Dead Languages"— Humphrey likens half-deafness to hearing a foreigner speak English: you know it is English, but you just cannot make out the words. In "The Dead Languages" he presents the revelation of his own deafness, mainlining his own experience into the story: "the discovery that I was losing my hearing happened indeed when I went to try to cover a trial here in the town of Hudson of a boy who had slaughtered his family of four and learned that I really was not hearing what was going on."[5] In the story Humphrey emphasizes the profound sense of isolation that ensues once "the silence thickened around him": "he felt marooned alone on a desert island watching his ship sail off without him into the infinite ocean" (*SS*, 121). He demonstrates the natural urge to try to cope with the adversity through the exercise of humorous incomprehension—cows, not clouds, in the sky, for example—but he succeeds in conveying the great sadness of worsening deafness. "The Dead Languages" concludes with a sentence that tells how much the deaf wish they could regain their hearing: "he would have dashed himself against the rocks happily to have heard the sirens sing" (125).

4. Dorothy Humphrey to Lambert, 30 September 1990, Lambert Coll.; Susan E. Garfield to Humphrey, 13 August 1990, WH res.; Lawrence to Humphrey, 18 September 1991 and 22 August 1990, WH res.; telegram from Lawrence to Humphrey, 30 June and 28 July 1992, WH res.

5. Au Int. The murder and conspiracy trial of eighteen-year-old Wyley Gates began in the summer of 1986 and was not over until October 1987. Although Humphrey's two notebooks at the University of Texas on the trial contain scant notes, he must have arranged for someone to take notes for him in September 1987, for at the Humphrey residence there is, written in an unknown hand, an extensive record of the trial in a shorthand notebook (WH Coll., UT; WH res.). It is possible that Humphrey was contemplating a fictional treatment of the Gates story or something on the order of Truman Capote's *In Cold Blood*.

One would imagine that Humphrey, who had focused on the family for decades (the mere memory of her family being a solace to the woman in "A Fresh Snow"), might offer close family relationships as an antidote to the losses and sorrows of growing old. But not so. Following the perspective of the two stories added for *Collected Stories,* a number of the stories in *September Song* portray the family as a bane rather than a benefit. The enmity between the daughters and father in "The Apple of Discord," the self-serving disregard a daughter shows for the wishes of her aged mother in "Be It Ever So Humble," and a sister's selfish manipulation of her brother in "A Labor of Love" suggest that the larger family offers little comfort in old age. Then in the few stories about youthful folly that serve as counterpoint to those about the aged, family obligations limit life rather than enhance it. In "The Farmer's Daughter," Beth Etheridge gives up school in order to take care of her father after her mother dies, leaving her an improper match for the educated man that she falls in love with, and "Ties of Blood" shows that those ties lead to the shedding of blood when a wife shares her bed with her live-in brother-in-law. In those stories in which the family is reduced to the husband-wife relationship, the effect is often the same; in "Vissi d'Arte," for example, a husband's excessive devotion proves him a fool. Only in the final story, "A Heart in Hiding," do we find a truly happily married couple—but that happiness lasts for only the first few paragraphs; the wife dies before breakfast can be cooked.

Although the overall view of life in *September Song* is grim, Humphrey has infused enough humor into the telling to sugar the sour vision. Nowhere is Humphrey's humor more prominent than in the first story, "A Portrait of the Artist as an Old Man." The Gallimard editors found this story so delightful that they selected "Portrait de l'auteur en vieil homme" for publication in *La nouvelle revue française* prior to the book publication of *Chanson d'automne.*[6] The story is about William Humphrey himself, with hardly any attempt at disguise. A young woman interviewed him in 1988, and that interview is the occasion of this story. It begins with a writer's telling the interviewer some of the basic facts of his life, only slightly altered from the facts of Humphrey's own life. Clarksville, Humphrey's place of birth, becomes Sulphur Flats for the fictional author, but the dates of his birth, his father's death, his mother's and his removal to Dallas, his attendance at Southern Methodist University, his coming to New York City, and the publication of his first short story all accord with the dates of the same events

6. Humphrey to Guillou, 30 March [1992], Gallimard.

in Humphrey's own life. In his notes for the story, Humphrey considered including another fact from life: the reporter insisting on calling a cab because she is afraid to let the drunken author drive her back to the train station.[7]

The author has hardly begun to tell the interviewer about himself when he suddenly realizes that she has been sent to gather facts for his obituary—for he had reached the age, sixty-four, when prudence required that a newspaper put his facts on file. "Here was Death in the guise of a young woman," the writer observes (SS, 4). The remainder of "A Portrait of the Artist as an Old Man" represents Humphrey's manner of dealing with the fact of death—which is to provide a fantastic tale of a life imagined. The author tells a life story that includes how he killed both of his parents and went on to be a pool hustler and failed jazz musician, an account based upon Humphrey's personal essay "The Trick-Shot Artist," first published in Sports Illustrated.[8]

When the reporter had departed and the author's wife—clearly she is Dorothy Humphrey—wonders why he has made up all this rigmarole, his reply provides a real insight into what motivates Humphrey's writing: "Makes mine more tolerable. And as long as I can make up one I'm still here" (SS, 11). As long as he can make up lives that display greater losses and more suffering than his own, his own life looks a little better to him. Perhaps there is some truth to this bit of flippancy, but the writer's second comment contains a more immediate motivation: making up stories is a truly desirable alternative to having that obituary properly written. It also suggests how integral the creation of stories is to his being, for doing so defines his existence: when asked about his life, he immediately makes up a story. Or his response could mean that he wants to be remembered for the stories that he made up. However it is put, the fundamental fact is that by writing Humphrey staves off death, and being called upon by death in the form of a young woman has stimulated him to tell a story in defiance.[9]

Humphrey touches on another aspect of writing in "A Labor of Love"—the pleasure of constructing a well-made story. This story is ostensibly about a sour old woman who tricks her brother into building a house for her and her milk-toast husband. The characters of the hard woman (Berenice) and her husband (Wendell) are, incidentally, based on Humphrey's aunt and uncle Bess and Dewey Sturch, who are not among those remembered fondly in *Farther Off from*

---

7. 1988 diary, entry for 29 September, WH Coll., UT.
8. The essay was reprinted in *OS*, 241–49.
9. In one notebook Humphrey considered making the messenger of death an overworked man in a single-breasted suit with sloping shoulders and carrying a bulging briefcase (WH Coll., UT).

Heaven. In "A Labor of Love," Henry, Berenice's brother, comes out of retirement to build a finely crafted house for his sister, using materials that he had stored up years before. The narrative draws a significant parallel between building and writing: "To cut a board to measure, fit it in place and drive the nail home was as satisfying as putting a period at the end of a sentence that said just what you wanted said" (*SS*, 30). Yet Humphrey knows that when one thinks he has got all the sentences fitted into a story, one begins to find fault and thus revision follows. Henry's "revisions" of the house that he builds for Berenice seem a metaphor for the kind of revisions that Humphrey tended to make: "The truth of the matter was, it was not finished, for he kept finding fault with it. . . . [H]e twice replaced the kitchen cabinet door knobs and drawer pulls. He changed light fixtures. He fussed with this, that and everything" (31).

Humphrey's last house of fiction contains a great deal of variety, even though most of the stories are devoted to the lives of the aged. Two of these are based upon the lives of Humphrey's neighbors. "The Apple of Discord," published earlier in *American Short Fiction* (1991) and the most substantial story in this volume, has its origin in the predicament of the old man and his wife living just west of High Meadow. Phil and Harriet Egan, nearing ninety, were forced to sell their 130-acre apple farm because none of their four daughters wanted it. Property values had risen so markedly in Columbia County that the Egans could not afford to pay their real estate taxes, and so they sold their farm to be turned into a housing development. The Humphreys' property, which they had paid $35,000 for in 1965, had in the 1980s been revalued at $480,000, and their real estate taxes had risen from $5,000 to $9,000 a year.[10] Thus Humphrey saw in his neighbors' fate his own.

Humphrey was getting close to finishing *No Resting Place* when the chainsaws and bulldozers began to rip out the trees on the Egans' farm. Humphrey's property soon faced comparable devastation. The atrocious winter of 1988 wreaked havoc on his own trees, the garden that he and Dorothy had tended for twenty-two years being destroyed. The apple orchard was ruined, and their entire farm was turned into a hideous landscape. In this additional way Humphrey's fate was his neighbors'. And so when Humphrey finished the last fifty pages of *No Resting Place*, he found that "this thing about Phil Egan seems to want to be written."

10. Au Int.; Humphrey to Lambert, 19 February 1988, Lambert Coll.; Humphrey, telephone conversation with author, 7 March 1993. Humphrey heard in February 1988 of a nearby farm of over 1,100 acres that had gone on the market as a housing development.

He began immediately writing what he at first thought would be a short novel, and by the beginning of April 1988 he was well along with it.[11] It turned out to be a long short story.

Onto the fairly commonplace event of "The Apple of Discord" Humphrey grafts four literary parallels, one Chekhovian *(The Cherry Orchard)*, two mythological (the Greek story of the apple of discord and the biblical story of the fall of man), and one Shakespearean *(King Lear)*. He includes as well a few briefer and oblique literary references. Thus there is a mock heroic quality to this domestic story of perceived ingratitude and senile depravity, yet, as in much of Humphrey's work, there is a balance between parody and serious emotion. The basic events and issue of Humphrey's story reflect Chekhov's *The Cherry Orchard*, the parallels to which impart to "The Apple of Discord" a social dimension. The cherry orchard (apple orchard) has to be sold, chopped down (chainsawed and bulldozed), and the land cut up into plots for summer villas (tract housing); and these changes mean that a way of life is passing away. Humphrey found in Chekhov—reflecting the real-life situation of the Egans—the daughters who did not wish to carry on the family's traditional life represented by the cherry orchard. As Chekhov's play records the human suffering that occurs when an old order and old values give way to new values and new ways of life, so does Humphrey's story—even down to the Chekhovian balance between regret for the loss of the old way of life and happiness over new-won freedom from the past.

As Humphrey's story begins, Seth Bennett, a fanatical apple farmer somewhat reminiscent of John Gardner's James L. Page *(October Light)*, is so consumed by his preoccupation with apples that he is comically on the verge of becoming one: "An old apple, a rotten apple, the last one from the bottom of the barrel, shriveled, mottled: that was what his face had come to look like"—and he remarks that had he tried to shave with a blade, "he would have peeled himself" *(SS*, 35). In fact, he perceives his entire family, the living and the dead, as apples, the apple tree standing in the center of his family graveyard being "the family tree" (71). In the mode of Shakespeare's sonnet seventy-three, Seth identifies himself with this fading tree: "it was old now, and time had thinned its blossoms as it had his hair" (70). Seth tends this tree but does not pick its fruit, allowing it to fall on the graves beneath, a sacred "offering to those who rested below" (71).

Having no sons but three daughters, Seth has accommodated himself to the notion that the Bennett family line will end with him—a fate that he can accept

11. Humphrey, notebook, WH Coll., UT; Dorothy Humphrey to Lambert, 5 April 1988, Lambert Coll.

because it happens to apples as well, many varieties having grown extinct (the Rock Pippin, the Repka Matenka, the Buckingham, and others). These apples, however, had been "hybridized with other kinds and in the marriage their names were changed. But their offspring were still apples" (SS, 71). This farmer is possessed of a fond hope that a similar apple-like destiny awaits his name and family.

Seth, like Chekhov's Lyubov, who cannot "conceive of life without the cherry orchard" (act 3), has a deep sense of tradition and a vision of what he feels life should be. More than anything, he wishes to bequeath the apple farm, which has been in his family for generations, to a daughter who will marry an orchard man. None of the daughters, however, is the least bit interested in the apple farm or in marrying an apple farmer.

The mythological title of the story—"The Apple of Discord"—is a comic and ironic reference to the Greek myth in which Eris, the personification of discord, tosses a golden apple inscribed "for the fairest" into an assembly of the gods. Athene, Hera, and Aphrodite contend for this apple, and when Aphrodite is declared by Paris to be the most beautiful, dissension ensues. In Humphrey's story, there are not three goddesses but three daughters, and though a wealth of apples is tossed among them, there is no greedy contention to acquire them; the daughters, rather, contend to avoid them—and all the discord occurs as a result of their lack of interest. Humphrey sets his story on the day of the most intense discord, the day that the youngest daughter, on whom Seth had pinned his last hope that the farm could be passed on to succeeding generations, is married to the real estate broker who has sold the farm to a subdivider. On this day, the air is filled with the bulldozer and chainsaw cacophony of the land-clearing crew who are destroying the farm even as the daughter's marriage is solemnized. The bulk of the story consists of Seth's recollections of the events leading up to this hated day.

The basic conflict of the story is between a man who embraces the status quo (tradition) and his daughters, who embrace change (progress), which of course is the basic conflict of The Cherry Orchard. Seth emphasizes the sense of continuity that apple farming represents to him: "Your grandfather planted that tree, your father that one. They did it for their children, we do it for ours" (SS, 55). Yet it is more than mere continuity; he invests the act of laboring in the orchard with religious standing, and it is a means of achieving eternal life: "I expect to be feeding people long after I'm dead"—and then he contemplates "[t]he work and the faith" (note that these are the theological concepts that lead to salvation) that apple farming consists of (55).

Elements of the Genesis story also find an ironic place in "The Apple of Discord." Seth is in fact unmindful—rather than mindful—of the real significance of the apple in the Garden of Eden myth, "the Fruit / Of that Forbidden Tree, whose mortal taste / Brought Death into the World, and all our woe."[12] Instead of lamenting the fall from grace represented by Adam and Eve's devotion to the first apple, Seth reveres his first parents for caring more about apples than about God. And instead of lamenting the fact that "man must eat his bread in the sweat of his face," which the fall has condemned man to do, Seth construes that original curse as a blessing, and he celebrates the requirement to till the ground and labor all of his days (SS, 62; Genesis 3:19). The Hudson Valley does lie "east of Eden," and "[t]here was no season of rest" for an apple farmer, mowing or pruning or spraying or picking or grading or packing or shipping or repairing, hard at work all year long (60). Far from thinking of such a laborious life as a curse, Seth sometimes thinks of his life as "Paradise regained"; moreover, he calls his farm "Garden of Eden Orchards" (60, 41). He cannot imagine his first parents being sorry that they found an apple irresistible: "If they'd had it to do over again Adam and Eve would have done it. Apple farmers were like that. Born, not made. You inherited it" (53).

In "The Apple of Discord," Humphrey develops a rather humorous conceit based on the Garden of Eden and the forbidden fruit. Having tasted the "fruit of knowledge" at Vassar College, Seth's daughters have lost their primal innocence and have been corrupted by the world; like Grace Melbury in Hardy's The Woodlanders, they have gone off to better themselves through education and are thus rendered unsuitable to lead a rustic apple-farm life.

All of Seth's daughters are fallen: "those girls of mine all fell far from the tree" (SS, 65). Recognizing that they have choices, they exercise them and marry city men. The eldest daughter, Ellen, having married a preacher, has aligned herself with a representative of that God who "had borne a grudge against that forbidden fruit ever since Eve" and therefore "sent His frost and His hail and His drought and His mold and His bugs to blight and destroy" the apples that Seth strove to grow (36). The second daughter, Doris, has married an undertaker whom Seth regards as a collaborator with the preacher (often they team up on a case) and equally contrary to the interests of apple farming: "he now had for sons-in-law one to put him under and another to get him a pass to that nursing home in the sky"—but no son-in-law to carry on the family apple farm (39).

The youngest daughter, Janet, "the apple of her father's eye" (cf. Deut. 32:10), is her father's last hope, and Seth makes every effort to manipulate her, to force her to feel an obligation to adhere to his will. Those efforts are extreme, bizarre,

12. John Milton, Paradise Lost, in The Student's Milton, rev. ed., ed. Frank Allen Patterson (1933; reprint, New York: Appleton-Century-Crofts, 1958), book 1, 1–3.

and elaborate, ending in the kind of inadvertent fait accompli that Humphrey loves so well. Janet falls in love with and marries the slick real estate broker— "him with hair like a meringue"—who finally sells her father's farm (*SS,* 57).

Throughout "The Apple of Discord," Seth hovers between being a bitter, mean, and outrageous bully and being regarded as a misguided yet deeply sad and sympathetic father. Humphrey commented in his notebook on the balance he sought to give Seth: "He's a monster of selfishness—yet it's not personal—it's dynastic. And this relieves him of some of the onus of selfishness."[13] If we descry him as the serpent in his own Garden of Eden (Janet says to him, "Do you realize what you are doing and what it makes you? You are tempting me with the apple" [*SS,* 58]), he is rescued into full humanity by a recollection of deep devotion to his daughters:

> He recalled the many times they had been tucked in bed and allowed to fall asleep before Molly and he went out on the tractor and the sprayer and spent the night in the orchard. They would leave them purring like kittens, yet while they worked they worried every minute that one of them might wake up sick or frightened and wake the others and they not find their parents there to comfort them, and he remembered one night when Molly dozed off at the wheel and woke up inches short of going over the cliff at the edge of the land and they had dashed to the house as if they had indeed orphaned the children. (77–78)

The story's other major literary allusion, to Shakespeare's *King Lear,* evokes a similar ambiguous response to Seth: he is both enhanced and diminished by the reminders of his similarity to King Lear, the prevailing effect resting always just beyond certainty. Like Lear, Seth has three daughters, the older two already married, the marriage of the youngest pending. Seth, too, has a "kingdom," ten thousand trees on 320 acres, and he is prepared at the outset to abdicate his rule in favor of any daughter who will accept his fertile land (*SS,* 43). Since the older ones have disqualified themselves by inappropriate marriages, Seth, in Humphrey's sharp twisting of *Lear,* anticipates bestowing his kingdom upon his youngest ("You always were my favorite," he says [58]).

The discord over ownership leads in Humphrey as surely as in Shakespeare to a destructive war. The apple farm is readied for division and development through the most violent of means, though the effect is mock heroic: there is much "lopping off all the limbs," a "row of stumps" falls under attack, and "[t]he

13. 1988 diary, entry for 11 April, WH Coll., UT.

holes left looked like bomb craters" (*SS*, 63, 64). The horrible groans from the machinery of this war disrupt the marriage ceremony. Seth finds it unbearable that his apple kingdom is being torn to bits while his daughter marries the man whose business transaction sealed the farm's fate. From Seth's perspective Paradise is indeed lost.

Following the marriage, Humphrey provides a surprise shift in Seth's efforts to bequeath his farm to his daughters. If they would not accept any obligation to him with the gift of the farm, he will corrupt them with a gift—he opines—that they cannot refuse, for it has no strings attached. Seth announces, with a Lear-like reasonableness, that he has divided the proceeds from the sale of the farm equally among his three daughters, and he passes out three envelopes containing three checks. They now have their inheritance in advance. Like Goneril and Regan, the older daughters respond to their inheritance with shrouded eagerness, exclaiming "in tones of injured innocence, shock": "Oh, Father!" (*SS*, 80). Only Janet is unable to participate in the charade of emotions. A stripped-down Cordelia, she exhibits only truth and duty, not love. Having been unwilling to accept the farm and its obligations, she will not now accept financial reward from its sale (beyond her husband's broker's commission, that is): "Janet's envelope remained unopened. She now rose, tore it in half and let the pieces fall to the floor" (80).

Seth's final sour gesture is as self-dramatizing as all his other actions. He has been determined to make his daughters take what they have already refused. But his "Cordelia" has thwarted him again. By refusing to allow him to complete his plan of disbursing the proceeds of the farm, which he had meant to follow with his suicide, she renders that final gesture moot. He does make a half-hearted attempt, holding his pistol to his head and pulling the trigger. But he misses.[14] At this close range, a miss is unlikely, even though he is left-handed and is forced to use his right hand because he has a broken left arm. The narrator remarks, "That right hand of his was good for nothing" (*SS*, 82). This closing comment brings to mind an earlier and similar one. Squatting on the toilet seat, he draws from the roll a length of paper: "With that right hand of his he was clumsy at everything" (68). These parallel statements imply that a messy suicide would show about as much dignity as a poor job of ass-wiping. Seth has enough insight to know that his suicide would, after all, not be very noble, but it is Janet's incorruptible integrity that in getting the better of him probably saves his life.

Because of the complexity of the characters, "The Apple of Discord" caused

---

14. Even in this detail Humphrey takes a cue from Chekhov's play, which has a character with a revolver who means to shoot himself.

Humphrey more difficulty than any of the other stories in *September Song*. Both the manuscript and the proofs show significant changes, some of which were in fact suggested by an editor of *American Short Fiction*. This seems the only story, too, that Humphrey had a hard time naming. Before settling on "The Apple of Discord," he considered some inspired by Robert Frost ("After Apple Picking," "Done with Apple Picking," and "Some Human Sleep"), some from the Bible ("The Fruit of Temptation," "Forbidden Fruit," "Daughters of Eve," and "Comfort Me with Apples" [Song of Solomon 2:5]), and only one suggested by a cliché ("Many Happy Returns").[15]

The other story based on a neighbor in *September Song* is "Auntie," a psychological study of a woman, Miss Rebecca, who has what she thought she always wanted—her independence. She "refused marriage" because she has no desire to wait upon a man: "As far as she could see, the wives were the horses and the husbands the carriages" (*SS*, 190, 188). In her old age, however, Miss Rebecca sacrifices the principle upon which she has founded most of her life in order to provide a home for a delinquent grandnephew, who brings heartache, worry, and trouble into her simple life. Perhaps it is the natural perversity of the human heart to borrow trouble, or perhaps it is just the natural urge to find an object of love—the story does not say; yet after a lifetime of avoiding having "to wait hand and foot on a man" she, in her old age, embraces servitude (190–91). Evan, who demonstrates no concern for his "auntie," turns out to be a great deal more trouble than almost any husband or any number of normal children would have been. The story illustrates unreservedly that the affections of the heart prevail over all reason. Humphrey said that the story he tells in "Auntie" is "close to the truth, although [the real woman] didn't spend her life working in a bank" as Miss Rebecca does in this story. He also said that "she actually had a husband, but never any children, and she adopted her great nephew. Last I heard of him, he was back in prison" (Au Int.).

There are two insignificant stories of violent outrage and vengeance in *September Song,* both involving a ménage à trois. "Ties of Blood" is the slighter of these. It is about a young man and his wife, who takes to bed the older brother who lives with them. What is remarkable about the narrator of this two-page vignette is that, though he has already killed the brother who had sex with his wife, he retains an enormous degree of affection and admiration for him. The more well-developed companion piece to "Ties of Blood" is "An Eye for an Eye." Here Humphrey seems to be playing on an expanded definition of family, a sig-

15. Laura Furman to Humphrey, 27 August 1990, WH res.; notebook, entry for 19 October 1987, WH Coll., UT.

nificant feature of *The Ordways.* But in "An Eye for an Eye" the author appears to have made a special effort to come up with the most perverse way that three people could possibly be bound to each other. They are in fact bound by vengeance and guilt, but the dark secrets of the human heart that make the ties that bind are unknown to outside observers, to whom the relationships of mutual dependency appear normal. The story is unusual in that it has three points of view. The telling begins with James, the husband of a blind wife, Irene; then the point of view moves to her, and the story ends with the perspective of Ursula, the wife's live-in companion. All three characters endure a living hell, and the three first-person narrations add up to a full explanation of how they earned their interdependent hells. The domestic arrangement bears a slight resemblance to Edith Wharton's *Ethan Frome* until Irene, who suffers from a degenerative eye disease, undergoes a spontaneous remission and observes her "friend" performing fellatio on James and thereupon tosses half a bottle of sulfuric acid in Ursula's face.[16]

Humphrey worked very hard on this story, filling most of a composition book with various scenarios of how the wronged wife might achieve vengeance on "the other woman" and her husband, one involving the wife's being tricked into a divorce whereupon she arranges to have her eyeballs sent to James and Ursula as a wedding gift. From the trial versions of "An Eye for an Eye," he found the basis for "Last Words," probably the most inconsequential story in the volume—a short suicide note, written by a divorced wife, to her husband on the day he marries his new wife.

When he was writing *The Last Husband* and *A Time and a Place,* Humphrey would have discarded these stories; one can only assume that a senescent and alcoholic haze blurred his judgment. We must wonder why Seymour Lawrence did not suggest that "Ties of Blood," "An Eye for an Eye," and "Last Words" be omitted from the volume. The same goes for "The Parishioner," which is about a clergyman who comforts one of his flock following the death of her mother and who turns out to have had the ulterior motive of seduction in mind from the first comforting pat, and "Virgin and Child," in which a savvy young woman fends off her dirty-old-man uncle bent on molesting her.

Two of the most significant stories in *September Song* have a striking common

16. Humphrey might have recalled a story that the Reverend Elliott Lindsley told him about his aunt and uncle of Morristown, N.J. Mrs. Mack had been blind for years, but one night after supper she was sitting opposite her husband and was suddenly able to read the headline of the *Daily News* that he was reading across the room from her (Lindsley, interview by author, tape recording, Millbrook, N.Y., 25 October 1999).

feature. It is not that they are both studies in marriage—they have that in common with many of Humphrey's stories. It is that the title story, "September Song," and "Vissi d'Arte" are based directly on events in the lives of close friends of Humphrey, the events are largely unchanged in the stories, and the two stories ended long friendships.

If the Wannings' friendship with Humphrey had not been strained severely as a result of his writing about the suicide of their daughter in *Hostages to Fortune*, their lives presented Bill with another temptation to outrage his friends' feelings. He was working on "The Apple of Discord" when he learned about the breakup of their marriage, according to a letter to Jean Lambert:

> Not long ago [the Wannings'] telephone rang. The caller was a lover of hers [Pat Wanning's] from whom she had not heard since their breaking up (his wife found a letter of hers to him) 25 years ago. His wife had died, could he see her? They met, he proposed that she leave her husband of 50 years and marry him. She agreed. She is 78 years old! Her husband consented to the divorce. At the last minute she relented. I know about all this because a friend of theirs who is a friend also of mine has been sending me copies of her letters. My story is finished, but—I can't publish it.[17]

In January 1988 Humphrey records in his diary that he heard this gossip from the Thomases (Sally and Ted), who telephoned from Key West; the call was "followed by Pat's letter to her daughter Esther." (Did Pat Wanning make a copy of her letter to Esther and send it to Sally as a way of explaining herself, whereupon Sally sent a copy of the letter to Bill? Perhaps.) Anyway, Humphrey was sympathetic to Pat: "Why should she not have a final fling? Forty years of her life she had given to one dull man. Was whatever little time left her not hers?" The story accurately depicts the marriage, according to Pat and Andy's son, Rufus Wanning.[18] On 30 January Humphrey began to write the story, jotting in his diary: "I can't resist a little piece of malice," justifying himself by adding: "He began it"—alluding to some real or imagined slight (WH Coll., UT).

Upon finishing "September Song," Humphrey resolved not to publish it, explaining to Lambert that he did not fear a lawsuit, "but I have been unable to depart from the facts of the case, and I don't want to hurt them. It must wait either for their deaths or mine."[19] In fact, Humphrey did depart from the facts

17. Humphrey to Lambert, 4 March 1989, Lambert Coll.

18. 1988 diary, entry for 2 January, WH Coll., UT; Rufus Wanning, telephone interview by author, 1 September 2001.

19. Humphrey to Lambert, 4 March 1989, Lambert Coll.

of the case. Although in his letter to Lambert quoted above he states that "[a]t the last minute" the wife relented, Pat Wanning actually left her husband—as Humphrey explained in a 1995 interview: "the woman in my story sacrifices herself by staying with the man; in real life, she didn't: she left him and married another man, who within a year blew his brains out" (Au Int.). At any rate, Humphrey knew that the story was too close to the truth for it not to have consequences if published. Therefore, when he sent "September Song" to Lawrence, he insisted that it could not be included in the book of stories.[20] But why did Humphrey send this not-to-be-included story to his publisher? So that Lawrence could say, Oh, it *must* be in this collection? Well, that is what happened.

"September Song" has a literary as well as a real-life source. It is a recasting with geriatric lovers of Joyce's "Eveline." Humphrey's story is more fully developed than Joyce's but less emotionally dense. A great-grandmother, Virginia Tyler, aged seventy-six (he made her two years younger than Pat Wanning), has endured forty-nine years of marriage to her husband Toby, who keeps his nose in a book, leaving her to herself. She feeds her husband and helps him put on his clothes, which is difficult for him to do owing to arthritis; but emotionally she lives alone, has lived alone for years. Humphrey adeptly portrays her years of emptiness in a list of paragraphs with no development (each line is a paragraph):

Over the succeeding years:
The children all left home.
Married.
Had children.
Toby retired. (SS, 95–96)

The next sentence, "He grew increasingly hard of hearing," does warrant developing, and that development conveys the sadness and frustration of being in the house with a person nearly incapable of communication (96). A deaf mate renders the other dumb.

Like Joyce's Eveline, Virginia makes preparations to leave her empty life; also like Eveline, she begins to recall the promises that hold her to her present life, and her brother represents the life-denying influence of the past: "On matters of devotion and duty he spoke with the voices of both their dead parents, all their ancestors" (SS, 102). The turning event, Virginia's failure of will that holds her to the life she knows when we know that she desires to be open to a new life of possibility, does not possess the riveting tension that the reader senses when Eve-

20. Humphrey to Lawrence, 10 February 1989, Lawrence Coll.

line undergoes the seizure of paralysis that freezes her into immobility. But perhaps a less dramatic backing away is more fitting for the aged woman in "September Song." Toby, accepting her decision with all the equanimity he can muster, heads off to see their lawyer about arranging for a friendly divorce. However, he manages to look "the picture of rejection," and Virginia asks herself, "Oh, dear, what would become of him without her to look after him?" (104).[21] Thus she undergoes a failure of impulse, a deficiency of power: "She felt her purpose falter as the weight of her years settled upon her" (105). She calls Toby back, and they continue their weary life. It looks as though Virginia concludes that she is too old to really live. That there is nothing noble about her decision is made clear when the narrator observes: "Around her neck she felt a collar tighten" (105). Thus Maxwell Anderson's "September Song" from *Knickerbocker Holiday* (1938) proves to be ironic background music for Humphrey's sad story: Virginia will not spend the "few precious days" that she has left with the man she loves; her last days will be a "plentiful waste of time."[22] That Humphrey produced a story so close to the events in his friends' lives was offensive to them. But his obviously taking the wife's part in the marital breakup put him especially on the wrong side of Andy Wanning, his colleague and friend of forty years.

Just before publication of *September Song,* a passage in "September Song" required quick revision. The copyright holders of Anderson's "September Song" refused to grant permission for Humphrey to quote from the song in a story with the same title. A quotation of four lines, therefore, had to be reduced to two, which would be allowed under "fair use" and not require permission.[23] Bill eliminated the following lines in the song through which Virginia's lover proposes marriage:

> These precious days I'd share with you.
> These precious days I'd share with you. (cf. *SS,* 100)

The other story in *September Song* that is based on Humphrey's perception of the relationship between a longtime friend and his wife is "Vissi d'Arte." The husband has requested that their names not be given. He had been devoted to Humphrey for many years and was deeply hurt to find his relationship with his wife, who is a painter, so blatantly paraded. As Humphrey did with "September

21. The story portrays the husband as totally incompetent and dependent upon his wife, a portrayal at odds with the facts of Andy Wanning's life. According to Rufus Wanning (interview), his father managed well on his own after Pat left him.

22. *The New York Times Great Songs of Broadway* (New York: Quadrangle, 1973), 114–17.

23. Sarah Burnes to Humphrey, 19 April 1992, WH res.

Song," he sent a copy of "Vissi d'Arte" to Lawrence, vouching that it was "so closely based on an actual person" that it would have to be held back from publication, which he was sure would lead to a libel suit; Lawrence replied that he saw nothing "libelous and defamatory in the story." As with "September Song" Lawrence persuaded Humphrey to include the excellent story in the collection: "With your permission we've made a copy for Camille [Hykes] to read and add to the collection." He promised Bill that he would ask "Houghton's legal counsel to review any stories which are based on living people and which you feel might be questionable." Houghton's legal department approved the two stories that Humphrey was concerned about and sent him a copy of the firm's liability insurance contract to assure him that he was protected against lawsuits for libel or slander.[24] Though safe from suit, Humphrey lost one of his best friends by publishing this story. He knew that aspects of the portrait of his friend were offensive: "Obviously I made him a uxorious idiot, and he wouldn't have liked that," he later explained, and then added: "He *is* a uxorious idiot" (Au Int.).

In "Vissi d'Arte," instead of a husband who is all but unaware of his wife's life (as in "September Song"), the husband is excessively attentive to an undeserving wife. In addition to painting a vivid picture of what seems really a perverse relationship, the story also captures the sounds, images, and aromas of New York City, and it is one of the few stories in *September Song* that exhibits a richness of language that compares favorably with Humphrey's previous books.

At the outset of this story, Humphrey creates a sense of the reality of New York City; all the details are right: no taxies free on an evening when it is raining, vulgar graffiti, a man defecating on the sidewalk. He presents a sense of the city with humor, as in the following: "Now on this day in the late afternoon she plucked at his sleeve. To hear what she had to say he steered them into a store, for in addition to the pounding of tires in potholes and the rattle of vans a woman was crying, 'shithead motherfuckers,' as though she were vending them" (*SS*, 200).

The "she" and the "he" of this quotation are Jane Randall—that is her "professional name"—a failed painter who has an endless belief in her artistry, and her husband Allen Sanford, who has a misplaced confidence in her. He functions as her patron during the week and as her agent on the weekend. Solicitous of her feelings in the extreme, he cannot bear to preside over her disillusionment. Jane has been painting full time for years and has never sold a painting; nine hundred of her unsold paintings are in storage at a Yonkers warehouse.

24. Camille Hykes was an editor at Houghton Mifflin; Au Int.; Lawrence to Humphrey, 19 November 1990, WH res.; "Houghton Mifflin Co., Publishers Liability Insurance Coverage (April 1990)," WH res.

"Vissi d'Arte" is similar to "The Fauve," from Humphrey's first collection of stories, *The Last Husband*, in that both depict painters who have a conviction of their worth in the face of rejection by those in a position to pass judgment. The main difference between the two artists who swim against the current of popular taste is that James Ruggles of the earlier story is meant to be an unrecognized genius, while Jane Randall is unambiguously depicted as utterly delusional with regard to her ability and her accomplishments.

The particular Saturday on which the story begins is like all the other Saturdays in the couple's very regular life. They have walked from gallery to gallery and have received rejection after rejection. The proprietors of the Melrose Gallery, with branches in the important capitals of the world and which Allen judges to be "a trendsetter, a weathervane in the winds of artistic fad," is so fed up with the Sanfords' persistent calls that they will not allow them in the door (*SS*, 201). It remains for the reader to determine whether the rejection of Jane's art is deserved or not, but Humphrey more clearly plants clues that provide a basis for such a determination in this story than he does in "The Fauve."

First of all, the imagery casts a derisive shadow on her and her art. As the story opens, Allen and Jane as well as numerous others that have visited galleries and exhibitions—a fact suggesting that there are plenty of potential customers interested in art—are trying to make their way home in the rain. Allen is trying to hail a cab "with a hand raised like that of an overlooked auction bidder"—a figure whose tenor and vehicle characterize him as unfruitful in representing the interests of his wife, who remains in this opening tableau passively waiting under an umbrella by the curb (*SS*, 197). Her immediate context seems not only inhospitable but perhaps should be taken as a reflection of the disrespect that the world pays her as an artist: "Behind her a man was trying to steady himself against the wall while taking a shit. The place he had picked, consciously or not, was especially well suited to his purpose, for on the wall in artistic lettering was sprayed, SHIT PISS FUCK NIGGER KIKE WOP" (197). We may also take it that the defecator's selection of place is "especially well suited" to Humphrey's purpose: the context of a man's defecating asks us to draw a parallel between him and Jane, his product and hers. This hint at the beginning of the story of a connection between Jane's art and excrement is confirmed later on when people enter the gallery that Allen has, unknown to his wife, rented at an exorbitant fee because all galleries have for years refused to allow her paintings to be shown: "During the two weeks the show hung some two dozen visitors came to the gallery. They looked as though they were lost and had wandered in by mistake. They left hurriedly. A few others poked their heads inside and withdrew them as though they had smelled a bad smell" (209). Obviously they think her paintings stink, and she admits to feeling "like the lady attendant of a Paris pissoir" (209).

The figures of speech that apply to Jane's paintings also contain a coloring of disapproval. For example, after her two-week show at the rented gallery, which ends without a single painting having been sold, Humphrey describes those paintings after they are taken down from the walls: "They were stood with their faces to the wall like punished school-children" (SS, 209). Jane's prolonged failure takes its toll psychologically, and Humphrey's figures suggest that the ardor with which she practices her art is a sickness: "As though he [Allen] had a thermometer and a chart at the foot of her bed, he could see that her fever was peaking. It was not that she was painting any less determinedly than before. On the contrary. What was alarming was that she was painting with both hands, like a mariner trying to bail out a sinking boat" (206). And when an Internal Revenue Service agent disallows deductions because Jane's painting is determined to be a hobby, not a business, Humphrey pictures Allen as being depleted by his wife's self-indulgence: "Shaking his head incredulously, as though dealing with someone deluded, the IRS man had read off the figures for the studio rent, the supplies, the models, the storage bill on the nine hundred pictures in Yonkers, etc. Each wove a strand in the web he was tangled in like one of those hapless insects injected with anesthesia by its captor and slowly sucked dry of its juices" (205–6). Allen, however, remains unable to acknowledge what he knows in his heart to be true: that his wife is no good as a painter and that her eager acceptance of his support is draining him both financially and psychologically.

Still, the portrait of Allen, the devoted husband who has given up the pleasures of life for his wife's absurd obsession, is touching. No longer able to fish on Saturdays because of his weekend devotion to promoting his wife's art, he has placed his valuable fly rods in storage. Occasionally, he "sneaked a visit to the warehouse and while nobody was looking joined a rod and flexed it. He felt then like a conductor with a chorus of trout at the bidding of his baton. For in all modesty, he had made himself a maestro" (SS, 210). Humphrey's figure here argues that Allen as a fisherman is more of an artist than his wife is as a painter. He has given up what he is good at in order to make it possible for her to do what she is no good at. And so self-absorbed is Jane that she appears to be unaware of what her devoted husband has given up for her. We wonder at Allen's love for this wife in the same way that we wonder how Henry manages to love his impossibly thoughtless sister Berenice in "A Labor of Love." Humphrey seems to marvel at the mystery of love that is as determined to succeed in the face of odds as insurmountable as those met by the salmon intent upon reaching their spawning waters. Perhaps that is why the story refrains from suggesting why the husband is so devoted to a wife who finds it easy merely to be the beloved. The story's title comes from an aria in the second act of Puccini's *Tosca:* "Vissi d'arte, vissi d'amore" (I have lived for art, I have lived for love)—a perfect summing up of the husband's life.

"Vissi d'Arte" concludes with Allen's daydream of wading "knee-deep in his favorite stretch of the Catskills' Willowemoc" with one of his favorite fly rods, all of which have recently been auctioned to help pay the expenses of renting the Pettingill Gallery for Jane's exhibition (*SS*, 210). His happy dream is interrupted by the appearance of the moving van that is returning all of the paintings, unsold, from the gallery:

> It was just sunrise with steam hovering above the water. So silent was the world that he could hear the big fish rising greedily, unguardedly to a hatch of insects—Hendricksons they were, size 16—forty feet upstream of him. He presented his fly just above and to the left of the fish for it to float down to him on the current. He tensed for the strike . . .
>
> "Here they are," said Jane.
>
> They looked out the studio window. Down on the street two men inside the moving van were handing the pictures to two outside. (210–11)

Humphrey's sympathy is with the husband, whose deep desire remains unacted upon. Only a devoted fly-fisherman such as Humphrey was could really know what Allen has given up for his wife. Humphrey was also a devoted hunter, and he once sold his best rifle in order to buy Dorothy a camera—because she wanted to become a professional photographer. She never did.[25] There might be as much of Humphrey in the character of Allen Sanford as there is of his offended friend.

With "Buck Fever" we switch from fishing to hunting, Humphrey's other favorite activity.[26] Here an aged hunter, with "shortness of breath, stiffness in the joints," looks forward to his last season, his final chance to kill a big buck that he has admired from a distance for years (*SS*, 170). Anticipation intensifies as the old hunter recognizes signs of the buck's proximity, and finally, as the buck charges into his sight, the hunter, perceiving at the last moment a pack of dogs pursuing the buck, fires upon *them*, saving the deer both from the dogs and from himself, for the buck moves out of range. Feeling unsteady and breathless, the

25. Antonia Weidenbacher, interview by author, tape recording, Hudson, N.Y., 12 July 1999.

26. Although "Buck Fever" had many advocates on the staff of *Sports Illustrated*, it was not published there because of the managing editor's antipathy toward fiction, especially outdoors stories (Bob Brown to Humphrey, 10 September 1990, WH res.).

old hunter rests in a "glow of charity" over having spared the buck, and then the hunter fades away in a sudden snowstorm and is swallowed by oblivion (177).

The story's theme seems a Brueghelian one—that men in their seasonal occupations have little significance in the context of the overwhelming motions of nature. Peter Brueghel's *Hunters in the Snow* with its ominous stand of dark trees and images of coldness might well have been in the back of Humphrey's mind as he wrote "Buck Fever." The old hunter, weakening from his long trek deep into the woods and his overexcitement at the encounter with his long-sought quarry, responds to "the hypnotic snow sift[ing] down in . . . silence as deep as sleep" by drifting into a "long hunter's sleep" beneath a stand of trees (*SS*, 177). As he sleeps his last sleep, the snow covers him "from top to toe as though while he slept a sheet had been drawn over him," and he grows one with nature—an image that recalls Dan's manner of dying in "Man with a Family," one of Humphrey's earliest stories: "the grass came up cool and crisp, rustling like a fresh bedsheet, and tucked [Dan] in" (*SS*, 177; *LH*, 151).

The old hunter's pursuing his heart's desire even though it leads to his death brings about a happier fate than would his being packed off to a safe-from-the-world nursing home. "Be It Ever So Humble" faces head on the threat posed by homes for the aged. The heroine of this story, Lily Harper, knows that homes for the aged are graveyards "full of living ghosts" (*SS*, 248). But it is to a nonlife in such a home that Lily's daughter Elizabeth is intent upon consigning her mother. In order to avoid that fate, Lily runs away from her neat one-room apartment. She would rather be homeless than be in a nursing home.

Though in this story Humphrey is utterly sympathetic to a woman who wishes to avoid a nursing home at all costs, he would nevertheless arrange, a few years later, for his own wife to be put in one so that he could die in peace, even though he had declared earlier that "that's the one thing that I've always wanted to prevent; I'd as soon shoot her rather than have that happen." Humphrey admitted that when he expressed these sentiments, "the state police came and took me to the hospital in a straight jacket."[27]

"Dead Weight" is a lightweight tale recounting the adventure of an antique picker—he purchases "finds" for dealers—who on a search for antiques in the byways of Dixie has a friend die on the toilet of his camper. In this sort of Yankee version of *As I Lay Dying,* the picker drives the camper back to New York with the corpse propped upon the toilet. This plot is loosely based upon fact. Humphrey's stepdaughter, Antonia Weidenbacher, who lives in Woodstock, brought

27. Humphrey, telephone conversation with author, 15 July 1997.

to Humphrey an article in the *Woodstock Times* about the camper death and the trek back to New York. She was an old girl friend of the man who died, Jim Matteson (Humphrey knew him too), and she knew the driver, Luke Klementis, well. The two friends had gone south for a vacation. When the diabetic died, his friend panicked and drove straight back to Woodstock, called Antonia on the phone, and said, "What should I do?" She took charge and arranged for the funeral.[28] When Humphrey read the newspaper article and heard his stepdaughter's account, he responded, "I've got a story there"; of course, he invented the purpose for the trip to the South and "had to make up all the adventures on the road and imagine what it was like to be driving with a corpse in a van" (Au Int.).

The adventures are well done, especially the episode in "darkest Arkansas," where the picker trades some new dishes for a valuable set of Chelsea cups and saucers because a hillbilly woman thought they were tacky and because she felt that "longtime ownership of a thing meant you could afford nothing newer" (*SS*, 222, 223). There is an entertaining episode in which he is persuaded to umpire a Little League baseball game while the corpse is ripening. An amusing adventure is what "Dead Weight" is, nothing more.

There are several other titles of varying interest, some merely anecdotes. Of these "A Weekend in the Country" is the most engaging, for it seems to celebrate pretense as a way to inject an element of elegance into a workaday life. A man and his wife pretend on weekends to be rich, busy, and important prospective house buyers, thereby securing access to the most elegant houses in New England. For this story Bill drew upon his and Dorothy's actual experience, for they engaged a real estate agent and under the ruse of looking for an elegant house allowed themselves to be conducted from one end of central New York to the other, enjoying the autumnal foliage and touring beautiful houses. For the story, Humphrey made the instigator of this ruse a postman; no doubt he had in mind his friend Bob Fisher, who is a retired letter carrier. To the real-life episodes, Bill added the husband's pretending to be the author of *Cozy Country Inns*, a pretense that gains him and his wife free accommodation in New England inns and the royal treatment.

Another of these stories that is grounded in Humphrey's own experience is "Mortal Enemies." In 1978 Bill had remarked to Nick Lyons: "Got home to find that damned woodchuck had eaten all my parsnips and green beans. How much work goes into getting parsnips up to woodchuck-eating size you cannot imag-

---

28. Matteson, 57, was the son of a painter in the Norman Rockwell group. Weidenbacher, telephone conversation with author, 4 March 2000; Kenneth Wapner, "Long Road Home," *Woodstock Times*, 23 March 1989, 1, 12.

ine."[29] In "Mortal Enemies" an old man, who hates woodchucks because they have devoured his gardens over the years, finds, upon shooting an old wood-chuck who had just taken up residence on the edge of his lawn, that he is sorry to have killed him. This old man's sympathies are broadened by the perspective of age: "He wanted everything to go on living. What they had in common had made peace between him and his old enemy" (SS, 111).

Two of the stories in this volume are left over from an earlier time, and one of them seems somewhat out of place in a volume mainly devoted to the depic-tion of life in advanced age, even though it might seem reasonable to consider these few stories of youthful folly as a counterpoint to the dominant theme about the effects of aging. "The Farmer's Daughter" and "A Tomb for the Living" are about young people and are set in Texas rather than the Northeast. In fact, Hum-phrey in 1995 said that "The Farmer's Daughter" was begun fifty-two years earlier when he was nineteen years old, living in a Chicago YMCA and working at night in a defense plant. At that time he had only recently "begun to get very serious about writing," he later explained. "I think I began that story feeling that it was going to become a very long novel in the manner of Thomas Wolfe. . . . But when I got around to writing it as a story three or four years ago, I found that the two pages I had written when I was nineteen years old were perfectly printable as they stood and so they were. Actually, the story turns out pretty much as the novel was going to have done in my head" (Au Int.).

"The Farmer's Daughter" is a story that illustrates how life dangles a joy be-fore the eyes just long enough to create a strong desire in the beholder and then snatches the joy away, a sequence that is not unusual in Humphrey's fiction (cf. *Home from the Hill* and "Mouth of Brass"). The farmer's daughter, Beth Ether-idge, and a young law student working in the summer for the telephone com-pany, Jeff Duncan, are briefly thrown together by accident—his accident, falling off of a telephone pole owing to a sunstroke. As he recuperates at the Etheridge farm, Beth—Humphrey had first named her Jill—is fully aware of the irony of her position as she coaxes Jeff into walking: "Come to me. Come to me," she utters, even as she is aware that "Each step towards her was a step away from her" (SS, 22). When she gives him a haircut, she knows that she is grooming him for the world beyond the farm.

Though the two young people have a great deal in common—the love of French, for example—there is a disparity in their levels of education: she had quit school to care for her father after the death of her mother, and Jeff has aspi-rations that will require many more years of education. As she watches the train

29. Humphrey to Nick Lyons, 29 June [1978], Lyons Coll.

pull out that is taking him away, she longs to call those words that had helped him to walk: "Come to me!" (*SS*, 24). But all she can do is retreat into loneliness, repeating a French poem, Paul Verlaine's "Chanson d'automne," which Jeff had taught her and which now fully expresses her profound despair. *Chanson d'automne* is the title of the Gallimard edition of *September Song*, published in 1995.

"A Tomb for the Living" does not seem to belong in *September Song* at all. It must be left over from *A Time and a Place*, for it is set during the 1930s where dust storms were common. While a family are engaged in the hopeless task of planting potato skins (because they could not afford proper sets) in "dirt as dry as gunpowder," a storm comes upon them (*SS*, 161). Taking refuge in a storm cellar, they listen to the wind blowing across the ventilation pipe and imagine the destruction above ground. The scene is very much the same as the early part of "A Job of the Plains," which might be why it had not been included in *A Time and a Place*. This story, however, does not develop; the father cuts his throat before the storm is over. Humphrey should have cut the story from the collection.

"A Heart in Hiding," on the other hand, one of the briefest stories in the volume, "plumbs the quick of tender emotion."[30] Humphrey has designed the story so as to withhold its emotion until the last possible moment. When the great sobs of grief pour out in the end, their authenticity is not only enhanced by their reluctance, but they are brought on so concretely that this story could never be accused of sentimentality.

A couple, who have been married for forty-two years, enjoy lying abed late on Sundays, reading the paper and drinking tea. His turn to make breakfast this morning, the husband plans a special treat. With the breakfast tray, he enters the bedroom singing a song whose refrain is meant to awaken his wife with a fond memory of past happiness, but she has died while he fried kippers. What dismays him is his lack of response to his wife's death: "When the body had been taken away he sat awaiting the onslaught of grief like a man in the electric chair. But the switch was not thrown. He felt nothing. Nothing whatever" (*SS*, 254). The brief details of the story convey his experience of emptiness—but no grief. During the following day, when he goes to have a prescription refilled, he encounters unexpectedly but thankfully his profound grief:

As he was leaving the drugstore he saw an item for sale that stopped him in the aisle. It was a bamboo backscratcher. The sight brought to

30. Crowder, "Humphrey Writes about Old Age," *Arkansas Democrat-Gazette* (Little Rock), 16 May 1993, sec. J, p. 7.

mind the countless times he had asked her to scratch his back. He could feel again the touch of her fingers, the soothing relief. "Higher. There. Ahh . . ."

His tears flowed and, grateful for his grief, he shook with sobs. (256)

The concrete evocation of authentic emotion here is a striking contrast to the mere sentiment conveyed in the long-popular song from which Humphrey's volume takes its name.

The old man's sudden "seeing" that his life's companion is dead and gone and will not scratch his back any more is moving indeed—but the reader cannot be blamed for wondering why the man's emotional juices were so sluggish in the first place. Are we just to think that old people's emotions are as slow to operate as their worn-out bodies? Was the groove of his emotional life with his wife so worn in his consciousness that he could not at first navigate outside it? Perhaps, though, the title suggests an answer to these questions. It comes from Hopkins's "The Windhover," and it suggests that the heart is forever needing to be awakened through insightful perceptions of the things of the world: "My heart in hiding / Stirred for a bird,—the achieve of, the mastery of the thing!"[31]

The protagonist of "A Heart in Hiding" is probably Humphrey's imagined self. As the first story in this collection, "A Portrait of the Artist as an Old Man," contains the author himself and his wife, so are the married pair in the last story William and Dorothy—in the sense that Humphrey is through the story imagining himself without his wife, to whom he had been married for forty-two years at the time he wrote the story, the same number of years his characters have been married. Further, the husband in the story has reminded himself that his relationship with his wife will have its ending, just as Humphrey forces himself to imagine life without Dorothy by writing the story: "After forty-two years it must have come to seem to him that their marriage would just go on and on. It ought to have been the very opposite with each passing day. But when he warned himself that it could not go on forever like this, it was more to scare himself into a fuller appreciation of his good fortune than it was out of conviction. It was not that he took his wife for granted, but rather that he could not imagine—could scarcely even remember—life without her" (SS, 255).

Keenly aware of his physical diminishment in the 1990s, Humphrey seems not to have noted—at least he never admitted it out loud—the dilution of his imaginative powers. No Resting Place and September Song, although there is some

31. Gerard Manley Hopkins, Poems and Prose, ed. W. H. Gardner (1954; reprint, Harmondsworth: Penguin, 1970), 30.

excellent writing in both, appear frail accomplishments when set against the powerful novels and stories that he had produced in stronger days. Nonetheless, the stories in his final volume got Humphrey appreciative assessments from many reviewers, who were almost unanimous in saying that the collection is uneven and that most of it is not equal to his best fiction. Nonetheless, Humphrey's skill as a storyteller was unanimously acknowledged, the *Virginia Quarterly Review* concluding that the stories are "beautifully crafted" and *Publishers Weekly* that Humphrey "proves himself a master of his craft." The stories, taken together, the *Richmond Times-Dispatch* said, produce "a fresh, moving, and unsentimental view of growing old"; instead of giving the aged stock parts to play—as dispensers of a wisdom garnered over a long life or as recluses living a life of memory—Humphrey's "skilled hands" demonstrate that "the elderly do not belong to a separate world from everybody else."[32]

The *New York Times Book Review* held that the "most successful stories are those that deal head on with the insults of old age," which, however, results in "a book steeped in almost overwhelming despair"—a feature alleviated in the best stories by "Humphrey's wry sense of humor," said the *Chicago Tribune*. The *Washington Post* emphasized the understanding of human nature that Humphrey shows in *September Song:* "He knows that life rarely follows the patterns we expect it to, but that this does not prevent us from trying to shape it to our liking." Though he demonstrates this theme effectively, much in *September Song* is minor—

> Minor, but interesting and admirable. It has been a long time since Humphrey has enjoyed a commercial success, but he has dedicated his life to his writing with a fidelity all too rare in a culture that encourages facile success and empty honor. Utterly devoid of fashionable glitz, his books are made of durable stuff that will secure his reputation long after those of the day's "hot" writers have settled into oblivion. In *September Song,* as in all his other work, he demonstrates that he is what has become, alas, an American rarity: a genuinely serious writer of fiction.[33]

If we discard the emphasis on "minor," which Jonathan Yardley means to apply only to *September Song,* this assessment speaks accurately of William Hum-

---

32. *Virginia Quarterly Review* 69 (Winter 1993): 24; *Publishers Weekly,* 18 May 1992, 56; Charles Slack, "Humphrey Avoids Warm Fuzzies on Old Age," *Richmond Times-Dispatch,* 2 August 1992, sec. F, p. 4.

33. Molly Giles, "The Insults of Old Age," *New York Times Book Review,* 23 August 1992, 18; Pinckney Benedict, "The Odd, the Old, and the Mysterious," *Chicago Tribune,* 5 July 1992, Books section, 1; Jonathan Yardley, "Harvest of the Years," *Washington Post,* 5 July 1992, Book World section, 3.

phrey's life's work. Humphrey's final plea to his friend Bob Fisher—"Remember me" (quoting the ghost of Hamlet's father)—places an obligation on anyone who values living prose—perfectly written passages, transparent when they need to be, lyrical and lapidary when polished diamonds are fitting. Indeed, Humphrey has devoted readers. In a column in the *Boston Globe,* Geoffrey Stokes tells of keeping an eye out for the Humphrey book that occasionally shows up at his church's annual book sale: "I set it aside and hand-sell it to someone who deserves it."[34]

Humphrey had extraordinary powers of observation, which he displayed acutely in metaphors and similes that capture apprehension. He created from scratch intricate and artful structures—the laborious alternatives to telling a story simply and straight, as Larry McMurtry so easily does. He explored the depths of loss and pain—without the aliment of religion. He squeezed bitter humor out of tragedy. He escaped the undertow of history and cast a cold, critical eye upon his native South. He sacrificed life, love, and friendship for his writing. *Home from the Hill, The Ordways,* and *Hostages to Fortune,* his best novels—all powerful and unique—are bound to secure an enduring place in American literature for William Humphrey.

Having written all that he would ever publish, Humphrey lived on for another five years in the sear and yellow leaf. He and Dorothy had given up traveling altogether. Whereas in the late 1970s they would dash off to the Boston Museum and attend a Chardin exhibition, by May of 1993 even a trip to New York City was an ordeal that they could no longer endure. Between 1990 and 1993, according to their daughter, Bill and Dorothy did find delight in spending a day buying all sorts of fancy but second-hand old-fashioned clothes and getting dressed up. They were reminiscent of Nathan and Sophie in Styron's *Sophie's Choice* in their bewitching costumes "decidedly out of fashion—his being a white chalk-stripe gray flannel double-breasted suit of the kind made modish more than fifteen years before by the Prince of Wales; hers a pleated plum-colored satin skirt of the same period, a white flannel yachting jacket, and a burgundy beret tilted over her brow."[35]

By 1993 the main activity in Humphrey's life was drinking—perhaps resorted to because of the silent recognition of his diminished powers. He did not merely drink far too much at night, as he had done for years; he now drank all day.

34. Geoffrey Stokes, "In Pursuit of Meaning and Magic to Comfort Us in Our Sorrow," *Boston Sunday Globe,* 13 December 1992, sec. B, p. 38.

35. William Styron, *Sophie's Choice* (1979; reprint, New York: Bantam, 1983), 73.

When Howard Woolmer was cataloging Humphrey's papers for sale to the University of Texas in June, he would be called at ten o'clock in the morning for a vodka break.[36] Later in the day, Bill would switch to whiskey—Ten High whiskey now, the quantities consumed making Jack Daniel's unaffordable. Apparently the heavy drinking was taking a toll on his general health. In a telephone conversation with me on 7 March 1993 he confessed that he had begun to walk unsteadily and that he needed two naps a day; he had been told that he might have had a mild stroke. He paid no attention to the medical advice to refrain from drinking. Bill's neighbor with whom he had hunted and fished for years, Bob Fisher, remarked that now Bill "was drunk all the time" and was therefore too dangerous to hunt with. Humphrey's health continued to deteriorate, abetted by alcoholism. On 8 December 1995, he remarked to me on the telephone that his limbs had begun to ache severely and that he needed to do something to cheer himself up, but he was "not going to any damn doctors: I'm just going to stay home and die."

Although physical ills impeded Humphrey's writing, he continued to work on an occasional short story, but he did not plan another book. He completed an ironical story entitled "The Doctor In Spite of Himself," which is about the burial of a psychiatrist who was a "medical missionary to the privileged and pampered, the Albert Schweitzer of the Upper East Side" (MS, WH res.). Another is "The Sendoff," a three-story series about a Clarksville boy who has to live in the town whose businesses his father has been convicted of burglarizing. The details of this story are imitative of "The Shell" and *Home from the Hill*. The manuscripts for these stories, left in his house, show extensive revising prior to the completion of fair copy. Humphrey's stepdaughter says that he read the three completed stories to her shortly before his final serious illness.[37]

Humphrey maintained into his last years his radical political views, important to him partly because they separated him from the mindless conservatism that he associated with the lower social orders of small-town Texas, though he sometimes approved of conventional figures. He was in despair over what he termed "the idiotic Gulf war" of 1991. In it he saw the country's sad attempt to make up for Vietnam; his disapproval was unequivocal: "Not only does the Gulf war distress me, its popularity disgusts me. Nothing like a nice clean little war a long way from home to buck up the populace. . . . Got something to cheer for this

36. Woolmer to author, 22 August 1999. Woolmer arranged for the University of Texas to purchase nineteen boxes of letters, manuscripts, and photographs; they are housed in the Harry Ransom Humanities Research Center.

37. Weidenbacher, telephone conversation with author, 21 June 2000.

time around."[38] Disgusted with nearly all politicians, he said in a 1995 telephone conversation with me that Eisenhower, whom he voted against twice, was the last president who "wasn't a shit." His frustrations with the political state of the world found extreme expression on the day after he had had three abscessed teeth extracted (2 July 1995): "I wish the world were back the way it used to be," and then he said the world would be more ordered and stable if the likes of Stalin and Tito were still in power. "I'm not a man of my century," he remarked on another occasion. He was certainly not a man who accorded with contemporary American culture. He once remarked that he would rather be stuffed into a barrel of snakes than go to Disney World. Upset about Disney's efforts to put a theme park on the Manassas battlefield in Virginia, he asked Shelby Foote, "Is nothing sacred any more?" Foote replied, "You are nearly seventy years old and ask me a question like that!"[39]

On 13 April 1996, Humphrey received the Lon Tinkle Award for excellence sustained throughout a career from the Texas Institute of Letters. This award meant more to Humphrey than most because Lon Tinkle, a dapper young professor of French at Southern Methodist University back in 1941, was his first mentor. Although unable to attend the awards ceremony in Houston, Humphrey sent the following greeting:

> I met Lon Tinkle when I was 16, a freshman at SMU. I regret that I did not study with him. I took German. I became fluent in German, which I have since forgotten; I speak my homegrown French like a Spanish cow, as the French say. But I was a clean slate for him to write on, and we became friends. When I wrote my first story it was to him that I took it for criticism. He encouraged me. My pleasure in accepting an award named for my early mentor and longtime friend is all the greater for knowing that it would have pleased him, too.[40]

The salutary effect of this recognition was fleeting. Humphrey soon entered a long period of dejection and solitude, taking to his room, communicating with no one, not even his wife. He did not make contact with the outside world for

38. Humphrey to author, 20 January and 27 February 1991.

39. Humphrey, telephone conversations with author, 22 April and 22 May 1994.

40. James Hoggard to Humphrey, 23 February 1996, WH res. (Hoggard was president of the Texas Institute of Letters); Robert Compton, "Texas Institute of Letters Celebrates . . . ," *Dallas Morning News,* 14 April 1996, sec. A, p. 41; program for 13 April 1996 meeting of the Texas Institute of Letters. Humphrey received a check for $1,500 from the institute (Hoggard to Humphrey, 15 April 1996, WH res.).

months; then on Pearl Harbor Day in 1996 he broke the long silence with a somewhat slurred voice, telling me that he had had a stroke and was having to learn to use his right hand again—that he had fallen several times and had broken three ribs and had a concussion. Early in 1997 he began to have difficulty swallowing, and he made an appointment to see his doctor in Hudson but was seen instead by a physician's assistant who did not take his symptoms seriously. So annoyed was Humphrey with the doctor who foisted him off on an unqualified assistant that he resolved not to return. In April of 1997 his health worsened: he could *not* swallow, and his weight had dropped to 103 pounds. At this point he saw another physician, Dr. Neal A. Baillargeon in the nearby village of Valatie, who took Humphrey's symptoms very seriously, ordering an endoscopy and MRI. These investigations revealed an undifferentiated cancer, wildly metastatic and extending into his esophagus. Identified at this point, the tumor was not amenable to treatment. Even so, radiation and chemotherapy were prescribed. Humphrey's main concern about radiation treatment was that it would render him unable to speak: "I'd rather die than not have my voice," he said. These treatments were so hard on him that by the end of May he refused any more. By then he was down to ninety-one pounds and was being fed through a hole in his stomach. Two weeks earlier, when he was invited by the directors of the PEN/ Faulkner Award to give a reading at the Folger Shakespeare Library in the spring of 1998, his only remark was, "I won't be alive then."[41]

Bill was concerned about what would happen to Dorothy when he was dead, for she had begun to deteriorate mentally as he did so physically. There was a general concern among family and friends that he might take his own life and Dorothy's as well—as a kind of final act of their life together. Antonia Weidenbacher and her husband Bill removed all of the guns from the house. Even as Stan Bardwell, a retired physician and friend, was reporting to social services the sad case of a bedridden dying man accompanied only by a wife with senile dementia, Humphrey himself arranged for Abe Badian, his accountant with power of attorney, to place Dorothy in a nursing home. Part of Bill's motivation was to get Dorothy out of the house so that he could die in peace. Badian arranged for two women to stay with Bill, but he soon fired them. When he got to the point that he was too weak to walk to the bathroom, he pleaded with his neighbor Bob Fisher to bring a pistol to his bed. Fisher refused.[42]

41. Humphrey, telephone conversations with author, 7 December 1996 and 4 April 1997; Stan Bardwell, M.D., interview by author, tape recording, 13 July 1999, Hudson, N.Y.; Janice Delaney to Humphrey, 2 April 1997, WH res.; Humphrey, telephone conversation with author, May 1997.

42. Bardwell, interview; Weidenbacher to author, 10 May 2000; Bob Fisher, interview by author, tape recording, Hudson, N.Y., 11 July 1999.

Nonetheless, on the ragged edge of life and "frail and ill as he was, Bill still deeply cared about his work and was at it till very near the end." Indeed Bob Fisher, who daily looked in on his friend during his final weeks, described Humphrey—his scraggly hair shoulder length—as chain-smoking and sucking on ice cubes in his large four-poster bed, lying naked in ashes (when his ash tray was full, he dumped it out, being too weak to do otherwise), and surrounded by papers upon which he had been scribbling.[43] He left eleven manuscripts of short stories, some completed, at his death.

During his final weeks, Fisher and his fishing companion John Liebruk, also a longtime familiar of Humphrey's, would come by at the end of the day to "shoot the shit about hunting and fishing" and have a drink; although Bill had given up eating, he had not given up "drinking" whiskey, which he consumed through his feeding tube. Humphrey's one request of me during his final illness—I was 1,500 miles away—was that I send him a cedar water bucket and a gourd dipper. At first I thought he wished to relive a childhood memory, but then I realized that he was probably trying to merge his life into literature. Surely, he was thinking of Faulkner's *As I Lay Dying* wherein Darl says, "When I was a boy I first learned how much better water tastes when it has set a while in a cedar bucket. Warmish-cool, with a faint taste like the hot July wind in cedar trees smells. It has to set at least six hours, and be drunk from a gourd."[44] Yet he was probably also thinking of his own Sam Ordway when he is offered a bucket full of fresh-drawn water: "The dipper was one of that year's gourds and imparted to the water its own sweet flavor, like new-mown hay" (*O,* 180). I sent him the gourd dipper; the bucket, which I had to have made in Paris, Texas, was ready three days after he died.

As Humphrey was nearing death, the two friends whose tragic losses had inspired the characters of Ben Curtis and Tony Thayer, and whose lives and losses Humphrey had assumed imaginatively in *Hostages to Fortune*—Ted Thomas and Andrews Wanning—also died. Ted died on 10 March, Andy on 25 July. When Thomas's second wife, Sally, traveled to New York for Andy's funeral, she went to see Humphrey at home. "What I saw," she wrote, "was a naked skeleton curled in a fetal position in his bedroom, with no one in the house. Horrible! A week or two later he was dead. A sad and lonely end."[45] On 3 August, Fisher visited Humphrey at night and thought he was near death. When he got home he wrote down the following:

43. Theodore Weiss to author, 7 October 1997; Fisher, interview.

44. William Faulkner, *The Sound and the Fury* and *As I Lay Dying* (New York: Modern Library, 1946), 344.

45. Sally Thomas to author, 13 December 1997.

he said to me in his southern drawl, Bob you've been a good friend. Remember me, you did a lot for me. I said I wish I could do more for you. He said Bless you Bob. I gave him a hug and rubbed his forehead, he smiled and said you're a good friend. Bless you Bob. I gave him a kiss on his fore head, another smile came across his face. He knows he is ready to die, said he was in a lot of Pain so I poured a cup of whiskey down his feeding tube, then he asked me to pour water down tube and said go home now[.]

I returned @ 10PM to check on him the lights were out I turned them on and he asked who it was, he said he was cold and wanted a blanket, he said again you've been a good friend and bless you. Then said I love you Bob. I said I loved him a[nd] that he taught me a lot about wing shooting hunting and fishing and that I will miss you. He always said *remember me*[.]

Such affectionate exchange Humphrey reserved for a select few. It did not extend to his family. When his grandson, Ted Weidenbacher, with whom Humphrey had had a strained relationship since the boy's childhood, wrote to express the desire that they be reconciled, Humphrey's only reply was that it was too late.[46] But he did want to see his friend of sixty years, Harry Grabstald, and so telephoned on 10 August, asking him to come before he died. Grabstald drove from his farm in western New York to Hudson immediately and found Bill in the same condition that Sally Thomas had reported ("he'd got down to seventy pounds")—yet he was reading an unabridged version of Hugo's *Les Miserables,* in French. Grabstald spent two nights with Bill, pouring whiskey down his feeding tube and lighting his cigarettes. In his last days he did not sleep.[47]

Humphrey's wakeful anguish ended on 20 August 1997 at 11:30 in the morning. During his illness he had abandoned the long-held plan to be buried in Clarksville, and on 25 October his ashes were buried in the churchyard of St. Paul's Episcopal Church in Tivoli, the hallowed ground of Dutchess County aristocrats (the Astors, Livingstons, Van Rensselaers), only a few miles from Hudson. The Reverend James Elliott Lindsley, who had been Humphrey's friend since his days as a Bard student, read the office of the Burial of the Dead, using Rite I of the Book of Common Prayer because Bill appreciated the elegant language: "All we go down to the dust; yet even at the grave we make our song." Humphrey could only come back to the Church when he was dead. But the holy ground did

---

46. Ted Weidenbacher, telephone conversation with author, 21 June 2000.
47. Harry Grabstald, interview by author, tape recording, Little Rock, Ark., 23 April 2000.

not get all of his remains. Barbara Tonne, who became Dorothy's caretaker upon her return to High Meadow from the nursing home after Bill's death, had saved some of his ashes in an onion soup can. In the spring of 1998 she, Dorothy, and Bob Fisher drove in Bob's convertible to Cheviot, Bill's favorite place to fish for shad. From the landing the three of them cast the remaining ashes upon the waters of the Hudson River—the fulfillment of the wish that Bill had expressed a week before his death.[48]

48. Humphrey said to Grabstald on 11 August that he did not "care what the hell they do with me" (Grabstald to author, 14 March 2000); Lindsley to author, 31 July 1999; Certificate of Death, signed by Neil A. Baillargeon, M.D.; Fisher, interview; Humphrey, telephone conversation with author, 13 August 1997.

Selected Bibliography

Books by William Humphrey

The Last Husband and Other Stories. New York: Morrow, 1953; London: Chatto & Windus, 1953. Also Lippincott (Keystone Books), 1962; Books for Libraries, 1971; Lifetime Library, 1971; Ayer, 1977; Gallimard (France), 1988.

Home from the Hill. New York: Knopf, 1958; London: Chatto & Windus, 1958. Also Delacorte, 1985; Secker & Warburg, 1985; Gyldendal (Norway), 1959; Gallimard (France), 1960; Bonniers (Sweden), 1960; Henry Goverts (Germany), 1960; Goldmann (Germany), 1963; Sugar (Italy), 1960; Buchgemeinschaft Donauland (Austria), 1960; Stok (The Netherlands), 1961; Frimad (Denmark), 1961; Plaza & Janes (Spain), 1961, 1962, 1965. Paperback: Pocket Books, 1959, 1978; Avon, 1964, 1965, 1966; Bantam Books, 1971; Dell, 1984; Delta/Seymour Lawrence, 1989; Louisiana State University Press, 1996; Pan Books (England), 1960; Garzanti (Italy), 1971; Folio Books (France), 1978; French & European Pubns., 1979.

The Ordways. New York: Knopf, 1965; London: Chatto & Windus, 1965. Also Delacorte, 1985; Plaza & Janes (Spain), 1965; G. B. Fischer (Germany), 1967; Gallimard (France), 1968; Mortensens (Norway), 1968. Paperback: Bantam Books, 1966; Pocket Books, 1967, 1977; Dell, 1984; Louisiana State University Press, 1997.

A Time and a Place. New York: Knopf, 1968; London: Chatto & Windus, 1968. Also Gallimard (France), 1970; G. B. Fischer (Germany), 1970; Europa Konyvkiado (Hungary), 1975. Paperback: Bantam Books, 1971.

The Spawning Run. New York: Knopf, 1970; London: Chatto & Windus, 1970. Also Lindardt (Denmark), 1971. Paperback: Dell, 1979.

Proud Flesh. New York: Knopf, 1973; London: Chatto & Windus, 1973. Also Gallimard (France), 1975. Paperback: Dell, 1985.

Farther Off from Heaven. New York: Knopf, 1977; London: Chatto & Windus, 1977. Also Gallimard (France), 1979. Paperback: Dell, 1984.

Ah, Wilderness!: The Frontier in American Literature. El Paso: Texas Western Press, 1977.

My Moby Dick. New York: Doubleday, 1978; London: Chatto & Windus, 1979. Paperback: Penguin, 1979.

Hostages to Fortune. New York: Delacorte/Seymour Lawrence, 1984; London: Secker & Warburg, 1985. Also Gallimard (France), 1986. Paperback: Laurel, 1984.

The Collected Stories of William Humphrey. New York: Delacorte/Seymour Lawrence, 1985; London: Secker & Warburg, 1986. Paperback: Dell, 1986.

Open Season: Sporting Adventures of William Humphrey. New York: Delacorte/Seymour Lawrence, 1986. Paperback: Delta/Seymour Lawrence, 1989.

No Resting Place. New York: Delacorte/Seymour Lawrence, 1989; London: Alison, 1989. Also Gallimard (France), 1991.

September Song. Boston: Houghton Mifflin/Seymour Lawrence, 1992. Also Gallimard (France), 1995.

UNCOLLECTED PERIODICAL PUBLICATIONS BY HUMPHREY

"The Mountain of Miracles." *New Yorker,* 29 October 1960, 120, 122, 124, 127–28, 130–32, 135–44.

"Storm of a Man." *Barrytown Explorer* 24, no. 2 (April 1982): 2.

UNPUBLISHED MANUSCRIPTS RELATED TO HUMPHREY

Affre, Pierre. Letters from and about William Humphrey. Privately held. Paris, France.

Chatto & Windus. William Humphrey Papers. Archives of Chatto & Windus, University Library, University of Reading, England.

Dupee, F. W. Dupee Collection. Letters from William and Dorothy Humphrey. Rare Book and Manuscript Library, Columbia University, New York.

Gallimard. William Humphrey Papers. Archives de les Editions Gallimard, Paris, France.

Grabstald, Harry. Letters from William and Dorothy Humphrey. Privately held. New York.

Humphrey, William. William Humphrey Collection. Harry Ransom Humanities Research Center, University of Texas at Austin.

———. Letters to Bernard and Rebecca Varley. Privately held. Don Emery, Clarksville, Tex.

———. Papers at the William Humphrey residence, Hudson, N.Y. Includes unpublished MS of "Ambassador Ben" [1944], letters, essays, diaries, notebooks, an autobiographical fragment, MS of *The Spawning Run,* and MSS of several unpublished stories, including "The Sendoff," "The Doctor in Spite of Himself," "The Proxy," "You'd Better Not Go Home Again," "The Tooth Fairy," "The Cat," "Precious Metal," "A Game of Cheese," "The Smokers," and "Tribute to Caesar."

Knopf, Alfred A., Jr. Knopf Collection. Harry Ransom Humanities Research Center, University of Texas at Austin.

Lambert, Jean. Letters of William and Dorothy Humphrey and journal of Jean Lambert. Lambert Collection. Souvigny, Lamotte-Beuvron, France.

Lawrence, Seymour. Lawrence Collection. John Davis Williams Library, University of Mississippi, Oxford.

Lyons, Nick. Lyons Collection. Letters from and about William Humphrey. DeGolyer Library, Southern Methodist University, Dallas.

Porter, Katherine Anne. Katherine Anne Porter Collection. Hornbake Library, University of Maryland at College Park.

Weiss, Theodore, and Renée Weiss. Letters from William and Dorothy Humphrey. Weiss Collection. Princeton University Library, Princeton, N.J.

Williams, Annie Laurie. Williams Collection. Rare Book and Manuscript Library, Columbia University, New York.

Woolf, Leonard. Woolf Collection. University Library, University of Sussex, Brighton, England.

INTERVIEWS WITH HUMPHREY

Compton, Robert. "On Becoming a Writer." *Dallas Morning News,* 8 February 1987, sec. C, p. 8.

Crowder, Ashby Bland. "History, Family, and William Humphrey." *Southern Review* 24, no. 4 (Autumn 1988): 825–39.

———. "William Humphrey: Defining Southern Literature." *Mississippi Quarterly* 41 (Fall 1988): 529–40.

———. *Writing in the Southern Tradition: Interviews with Five Contemporary Authors.* Amsterdam and Atlanta: Rodopi, 1990.

Dunwell, Virginia. Unpublished interview with William Humphrey in 1984 (original at Humphrey residence).

Fortenbaugh, Jennifer. "William Humphrey: The Writer as Witness." *The Paper,* 7 May–3 June 1987, 5–7.

Guégan, Gérard. "A table avec William Humphrey." *Passages* 14 (February 1989): 86.

Ligon, Betty. "Novelist Finds Time Does Not Heal Wounds." *El Paso Herald-Post,* 6 May 1977, 3.

Mitgang, Herbert. "His Main Crop Is Words." *New York Times Book Review,* 18 August 1985, 3.

Shanahan, Edward K. "A Journey into the World of Writing." *Northampton (Mass.) Daily Hampshire Gazette,* 27 June 1992.

Sherman, Carl R. "A Novelist Finds Teaching Gratifying and a Release from Writing's Tortures." *Northampton (Mass.) Daily Hampshire Gazette,* 30 December 1976, 7.

Stokes, Geoffrey. "Literature Is Hell: The Strange Success of William Humphrey." *Village Voice Literary Supplement* (September 1984), 1, 21.

Tinkle, Lon. "For Bill Humphrey a Degree at Last." *Dallas Morning News,* 1 June 1969, sec. C, p. 7.

"Visiting Professor." *A Letter from Smith,* July 1976, 3.

Yglesias, Jose. "William Humphrey." Ed. Sybil Steinberg. *Publishers Weekly,* 2 June 1989, 64–65.

CRITICISM AND PUBLISHED BIOGRAPHICAL SOURCES

Almon, Bert. *William Humphrey: Destroyer of Myths.* Denton, Tex.: University of North Texas Press, 1998.

———. "William Humphrey's 'Broken-Backed Novel': Parody in *The Ordways.*" *Southern Quarterly* 32, no. 4 (Summer 1994): 107–16.

Chaney, L. Dwight. "William Humphrey, Regionalist: Southern or Southwestern?" *Journal of the American Studies Association of Texas* 19 (October 1988): 91–98.

Compton, Robert. "Texas Institute of Letters Celebrates Lone Star Writings." *Dallas Morning News,* 15 April 1996, sec. A, p. 17.

Crowder, Ashby Bland. "William Humphrey." In *American Short-Story Writers since World War II* (Third Series), ed. Patrick Meanor and Richard E. Lee, vol. 234 of *Dictionary of Literary Biography,* 142–52. Detroit: Gale Group, 2001.

———. "William Humphrey." In *Twentieth-Century American Western Writers* (Second Series), ed. Richard H. Cracroft, vol. 212 of *Dictionary of Literary Biography,* 126–32. Detroit: Gale Group, 1999.

Davenport, Gary. "The Desertion of William Humphrey's Circus Animals." *Southern Review* 23, no. 2 (April 1987): 494–503.

Flora, Joseph M., and Robert Bain, eds. *Contemporary Fiction Writers of the South: A Bio-Bibliographical Sourcebook.* Westport, Conn.: Greenwood, 1993.

Givner, Joan. *Katherine Anne Porter: A Life.* New York: Simon & Schuster, 1982.

———. "Katherine Anne Porter: The Old Order and the New." In *The Texas Literary Tradition,* 58–68. Austin: University of Texas and Texas Historical Assn., 1983.

Grammer, John M. "Where the South Draws Up to a Stop: The Fiction of William Humphrey." *Mississippi Quarterly* 44 (Winter 1990–91): 5–21.

Greene, A. C. *The Fifty Best Books on Texas.* Dallas: Pressworks, 1981.

Grider, Sylvia, and Elizabeth Tebeaux. "Blessings into Curses: Sardonic Humor and Irony in 'A Job of the Plains.'" *Studies in Short Fiction* 23 (Summer 1986): 297–306.

Heirs, John T. "The Graveyard Epiphany in Modern Southern Fiction: Transcendence of Selfhood." *Southern Humanities Review* 9, no. 4 (1975): 389–403.

Hoffman, Frederick J. *The Art of Southern Fiction: A Study of Some Modern Novelists.* Carbondale: Southern Illinois University Press, 1967.

Lambert, Jean. "Presentation de l'auteur." In *L'Adieu du chasseur* by William Humphrey. Trans. Jean Lambert, 7–12. Paris: Gallimard, 1960.

Lee, James W. *William Humphrey.* Southwest Writers Series, no. 7. Austin: Steck-Vaughn, 1967.

Masters, Hilary. "Proud Flesh: William Humphrey Remembered." *Sewanee Review* 108, no. 3 (Spring 2000): 254–58.

McMurtry, Larry. "Ever a Bridegroom: Reflections on the Failure of Texas Literature." *Texas Observer,* 23 October 1981, 1, 8–19.

Mullen, Patrick B. "Myth and Folklore in *The Ordways.*" *Publications of the Texas Folklore Society* 35 (1971): 133–45.

Porterfield, Bill. "The Great Writer's Nephew Didn't Understand." *Dallas Times Herald,* 24 June 1981, sec. A, p. 23.

Red River Recollections. Clarksville, Tex.: Red River County Historical Society, 1986.

Rubin, Louis D., Jr. *The Curious Death of the Novel: Essays in American Literature.* Baton Rouge: Louisiana State University Press, 1967.

Spotts, Frederic, ed. *Letters of Leonard Woolf.* New York: Harcourt Brace, 1989.

Steely, Jim. "Clarksville Author William Humphrey Gives Engaging Short Story Reading." *Paris (Texas) News,* 21 November 1982, 1.

Sullivan, Walter. "Southern Fiction in the Fifties." In *South: Modern Southern Literature in Its Cultural Setting,* eds. Louis D. Rubin Jr. and Robert D. Jacobs. Westport, Conn.: Greenwood, 1961.

Tebeaux, Elizabeth. "Irony as Art: The Short Fiction of William Humphrey." *Studies in Short Fiction* 26, no. 3 (Summer 1989): 323–34.

Tinkle, Lon. "Is Bookworm Now a Status Symbol?" *Dallas Morning News,* 14 February 1965, sec. 6, p. 10.

Watson, Gavin. "Bill Humphrey Reading Wows Home Town Crowd." *Clarksville (Texas) Times,* 22 November 1982, 1.

"William Humphrey." *Bardian,* Fall 1997, 32.

Winchell, Mark Royden. "Beyond Regionalism: The Growth of William Humphrey." *Sewanee Review* 96 (Spring 1988): 287–92.

———. *William Humphrey.* Boise State University Western Writers Series, no. 105. Boise, Idaho: Boise State University, 1992.

REVIEWS OF HUMPHREY'S FICTION

The Last Husband and Other Stories

Blanc, Paul. *Le Dauphiné libéré,* 21 May 1988.

Booklist, 3 April 1953, 269.

Chaumont, Thomas. *Révolution,* 22 April 1988.

Culhane, David M. "Too Small a World." *Commonweal,* 8 May 1953, 127.

Descampes, Pierre. *Feuille d'Annonces-Valenciennes,* 14 May 1988.

Favarger, Alain. "Entre fatalité et besoin de grandeur." *La Liberté-Dimanche* (Fribourg), 1 May 1988.

Guégan. Gérard. "L'Amérique en noir et gris." *Sud-ouest,* 10 April 1988.

[Harvey, Elizabeth]. *Birmingham Post,* 29 December 1953.

Kazin, Pearl. "Faltering Casanova." *New York Times,* 12 April 1953, 29.

Kirkus Reviews, 15 January 1953, 54.

Library Journal, 15 April 1953, 732.

Madame Figaro, 1 April 1988.

New Yorker, 11 April 1953, 137–38.

[Nicolson, Nigel]. *Manchester Daily Dispatch,* 11 December 1953.

Peden, William. "From Farmlands to Suburbia." *Saturday Review,* 25 July 1953, 33.

Plomer, William. *London Magazine,* March 1954.

Spectator, 18 December 1954.

Springfield Republican, 19 July 1953, sec. D, p. 7.

Times Literary Supplement, 25 December 1953.

Home from the Hill

Allen, Walter. *New Statesman,* 12 April 1958, 480.

Birmingham Post and Gazette, 18 March 1958, 3.

Boatwright, Taliaferro. "Under the Wide and Starry Sky." *New York Herald Tribune Book Review,* 12 January 1958, 1.

Booklist, 15 December 1957, 219; 15 January 1958, 278.

Bookmark 17 (March 1958): 145.

Bowen, Elizabeth. "Texas beyond the Oil Wells." *Tatler and Bystander,* 12 March 1958, 506.

Brady, Charles A. "Texas Tragedy." *Buffalo Evening News,* 11 January 1958, 8.

Butcher, Fanny. *Chicago Sunday Tribune,* 12 January 1958, 3.

Davenport, John. *Observer,* 2 March 1958, 17.

Goyen, William. "Tragedy Awaited." *New York Times Book Review,* 12 January 1958, 4.

Havinghurst, Walter. "Prelude to Violence." *Saturday Review,* 11 January 1958, 15.

Hogan, William. *San Francisco Chronicle,* 30 January 1958, 29.

Holzhauer, Jean. "Transcending the Limits of a Southern Locale." *Commonweal,* 28 February 1958, 571.

Hughes, Riley. *Catholic World* 186 (March 1958): 472.

Jaccottet, Philippe. *Nouvelle revue de Lausanne,* 10 August 1960, 4.

Kirkus Reviews, 1 November 1957, 824.

La Gazette officielle de la chasse 117 (1 December 1960): 10.

Metcalf, Joan. *Sunday Times* (London), 2 March 1958.

McLure, Millar. "Two First Novels." *Tamarack Review* 7 (Spring 1958): 92–95.

"New American Tragedy." *Time,* 27 January 1958, 94.

New Yorker, 8 February 1958, 133.

Spence, Rhoda. "Contrasts in Life—in the Thirties." *Weekly Scotsman,* 15 March 1958, 5.

Stevenson, David L. "Ceremony of Prose." *Nation,* 22 February 1958, 172–74.

Times Literary Supplement, 7 March 1958, 125.

Villelaur, Anne. *Lettres française,* 4 August 1960.

Walbridge, E. F. *Library Journal,* 1 February 1958, 500.

Wilson, John W. "Revelation in a Texas Town." *Southwest Review* 43, no. 2 (Spring 1958): 170–71.

Wisconsin Library Bulletin 54 (January 1958): 81.

Wyndham, Francis. *Spectator,* 14 March 1958, 336.

The Ordways

Beaux-Arts, 25 January 1969.

Booklist, 1 February 1965, 517.

Bouise, O. A. *Best Sellers*, 1 February 1965, 417.

Bradbury, M. *Punch*, 14 July 1965, 66.

Bulletin critique du livre en français, February 1969.

Choice, 2 (May 1965): 158.

Coleman, J. *Observer*, 20 June 1965, 27.

Cook, Bruce. "West of Yoknapatawpha." *Critic* 23 (April–May 1965): 67–68.

Cook, Roderick. *Harper's* 230 (February 1965): 128.

Corbett, Edward P. J. *America*, 6 February 1965, 197–98.

Culligan, Glendy. *Washington Post*, 12 February 1965, sec. A, p. 12.

Davis, Paxton. "Seven Years, and Worth It." *Roanoke Times*, 7 March 1965, sec. C, p. 6.

[De Sardi, Marie-Audrée]. *La France Australe*, 24 January 1969.

Dienstag, Eleanor. "West from the Graveyard." *New Republic*, 27 February 1965, 24, 25.

Dolbier, M. "Every Page Gives Pleasure." *New York Herald Tribune*, 3 February 1965, 21.

Forgue, Guy. "Sept ans de reverie." *La Quinzaine littéraire*, 1–15 January 1969, 8–9.

Frakes, James R. "An Abundance of Life in the Graveyard," *Book Week*, 31 January
    1965, 5, 66.

Green, Harris. *Texas Observer*, 15 October 1965, 13–14.

Guidicelli, Christian. *Combat Lettres*, 26 December 1968, 8.

Hicks, Granville. "Texas Bound, Bones and All." *Saturday Review*, 6 February 1965, 25–26.

Hill, William B. *America*, 8 May 1965, 676.

Holloway, David. "Nostalgia for Texas." *Book Society*, May 1965, 33–34.

"Horizon Everywhere." *Newsweek*, 1 February 1965, 77–78.

Janeway, Elizabeth. "Journey through Time." *New York Times Book Review*, 31 January
    1965, 1, 40.

Kappler, Frank. "Texas with Another Accent." *Life*, 5 February 1965, 17.

Kitching, Jessie. *New York Post Magazine*, 31 January 1965, 15.

———. *Publisher's Weekly*, 25 January–24 February 1965, 58.

Library Journal, 15 January 1965, 121.

Lister, Richard. "Tough Wives—and None Came Tougher than Ella." *Evening Standard*,
    15 June 1965.

Maddocks, Melvin. *Christian Science Monitor*, 11 February 1965, 7.

New Yorker, 1 May 1965, 189.

Ostermann, R. *National Observer*, 15 February 1965, 21.

Poore, Charles. "Elements of the American Past—and Present." *New York Times*, 2 Febru-
    ary 1965, 31.

Popkin, Henry. *Commonweal*, 26 March 1965, 26–27.

Raines, Charles A. *Library Journal*, 1 March 1965, 1141.

Stéphane, Nelly. *Europe*, July 1970.

Sullivan, Walter. "Worlds Past and Future: A Christian and Several from the South." *Sewanee Review* 73 (1965): 719–26.

Taubman, Robert. *New Statesman,* 11 June 1965, 927.

Time, 5 February 1965, 110.

Times Literary Supplement, 17 June 1965, 489.

Tinkle, Lon. *Dallas Morning News,* 31 January 1965, sec. 5, p. 6.

Virginia Quarterly Review 41 (Summer 1965): lxxxii.

A Time and a Place

Action Politique, March 1972, 122.

Algren, Nelson. "Texarkana Phantoms." *Critic* 27 (April–May 1969): 82–84.

Bailey, Paul. "Miniature Masterpieces." *Observer,* 2 March 1969.

Brown, Karl. *Library Journal,* 15 October 1968, 3798.

Choice 6, no. 7 (September 1969): 816–17.

Clech, Guy Le. "Le Maupassant du Far-West." *Figaro,* 15 April 1972.

Eliott, Janice. "In Sickness." *New Statesman,* 28 February 1969, 302.

Hicks, Granville. "Hoping for Oil, Hoping for Rain." *Saturday Review,* 9 November 1968, 31–32.

King, Larry L. "A Setting Mean and Hard." *New York Times Book Review,* 3 November 1968, 5.

Kirkus Reviews, 15 August 1968, 925.

Kyria, Pierre. *Combat lettres,* 24 February 1972.

Marguerite, Sister M. *Best Sellers,* 1 November 1968, 314–15.

Petillon, Pierre-Yves. "Chronique de la terre rouge et seche." *Critique,* March 1972, 288–89.

Publishers Weekly, 26 August 1968, 264.

Reid, Margaret W. "Depression Years in Texas and Oklahoma." *Wichita Falls Times,* 20 October 1968.

"A Retreat to Familiar Ground." *Times Literary Supplement,* 14 August 1969, 897.

Rhodes, Richard. *Book World (Washington Post),* 3 November 1968, 4.

Scannell, Vernon. "Riches and Rags." *Irish Times,* 5 April 1969.

Turnill, Oscar. "Short Stories." *Sunday Times* (London), 13 April 1969.

Villelaur, Anne. "L'a-bonheur et le souvenir." *Les Lettres françaises,* 22 March 1972, 8.

Proud Flesh

Best Sellers, 15 July 1973, 186.

Bosquet, Alain. "Pour comprendre le Texas: William Humphrey." *Magazine littéraire,* November 1975, 49.

Brickner, Richard. *New York Times Book Review,* 29 April 1973, 26, 29.

Collard, Henri. *France-Soir,* 30 October 1975.

Farren, Ronan. "Irony in the Land of Melodrama." *Irish Independent,* 25 August 1973.

Garmel, Marion Simon. "A Family that Sees Itself above God's Laws." *National Observer,* 28 April 1973, 21.

Guilhon, Philippe. "La fin d'un monde." *Quotidien de Paris,* 21 October 1975.

Hupp, Philippe. *Le Républicain Lorrain,* 31 January 1976.

Karvelis, Ugné. "Le «Faulkner» du Pauvre." *Figaro,* 24 January 1976.

Kirkus Reviews, 1 February 1973, 138.

Lehmann-Haupt, Christopher. "More Meat for the Boycott." *New York Times,* 4 April 1973, 41.

Maddocks, Melvin. "Ten-Gallon Gothic." *Time,* 30 April 1973, 94.

Observer, 2 September 1973, 34.

Publishers Weekly, 26 February 1973, 121.

Reeves, Alfred. "Portrait in Failure." *Times Literary Supplement,* 3 August 1973, 893.

Scott, Michael Maxwell. *Daily Telegraph* (London), 26 July 1973.

Seymour-Smith, Martin. *Financial Times* (London), 26 July 1973.

Sullenger, Lee. *Library Journal,* 1 April 1973, 1192.

[Valmont, Jacques]. *Aspects de la France,* 15 January 1976, 4.

Wagener, Françoise. "William Humphrey: un Texan «old fashion.»" *Le Monde* (Paris), 7 November 1975.

Hostages to Fortune

Alexander, James E. "Novel Probes Fortune's Changes." *Pittsburgh Post-Gazette,* 13 October 1984.

Banks, Leo W. "Hostages Truly Wretched Past Belief." *Arizona Daily Star* (Tucson), 30 September 1984, sec. C, p. 6.

Berkov, Walter. "Searing Look at the Emotional Debris of Suicide." *Cleveland Plain Dealer,* 18 October 1984, 49.

Best Sellers, 44 (December 1984), 327.

Carr, Housley. "Son's Death Forces Painful Reassessment." *Richmond News Leader,* 24 October 1984.

Drabelle, Dennis. "A Disturbing but Defiant Novel about Suicide." *USA Today,* 24 October 1984, 2.

DuVal, Aline. *Le Réveil du centre* (Paris), September 1986.

Epstein, Seymour. "Gone, Inexplicably." *New York Times Book Review,* 14 October 1984, 9.

Favarger, Alain. "Le scandale de la mort d'un enfant." *La Liberté,* 5–6 July 1986.

Fleury, Claude. "La nostalgie américaine." *Le Républicain Lorrain,* 20 June 1986.

Fry, Robert. "Lonely Vigil of a Young Suicide's Father." *Grand Rapids Press,* 30 September 1984, sec. H, p. 7.

Gibbons, Richard. "Through Pain, Humphrey Affirms Life." *Chicago Tribune,* 28 October 1984.

Grisolia, Michel. "Une journée dans la via de Ben Curtis." *L'Express,* 15–21 August 1986.

Guégan, Gérard. "William Humphrey: La mort en face." *Sud-ouest,* 18 May 1986.

Heller, Amanda. "Short Takes." *Boston Sunday Globe,* 21 October 1984.

Kendall, Elaine. "Dad's Struggle to Survive Teen Suicide." *Los Angeles Times,* 20 September 1984, 26.

Kirkus Reviews, 15 July 1984, 641–42.

"Les Paraboles de Humphrey." *Magazine littéraire,* July–August 1986.

Library Journal, 1 September 1984, 1686.

Lipez, Richard. "A Son's Suicide." *Newsday,* 9 September 1984, 15.

Mapes, Terry. "Humphrey's New Novel Echoes His Fine Writing Talent." *Mansfield (Ohio) News Journal,* 28 October 1984.

McCoy, Campbell. "No Escape from Hell." *Chattanooga Times,* 24 October 1984.

Mohrt, Michel. "La symphonie pastorale de William Humphrey." *Figaro,* 20 May 1986.

"Native Son Has New Book Published." *Clarksville (Texas) Times,* 4 October 1984, 1.

O'Leary, Theodore. "Pain of Hostages Makes Its Power Even Greater." *Kansas City Star,* 7 October 1984, sec. F, p. 9. (Originally published in the *Dallas Morning News,* 23 September 1984.)

Owens, William. "The Meaning of Death." *Dallas Morning News,* 23 September 1984.

Profuno, David. "Casting Around." *Times Literary Supplement,* 15 March 1985, 284.

Publishers Weekly, 13 July 1984, 44.

Ritchey, Mike. "The Loneliness in Passing Life's Cruel Examination." *Ft. Worth Star-Telegram,* 28 October 1984.

Syna, Sy. "Humphrey's Hostages a Difficult Read." *New York Tribune,* 13 October 1984.

Whitaker, James. "Tangled Lines." *Texas Monthly* 12 (September 1984): 184, 186.

Yardley, Jonathan. "A Death in the Family." *Book World (Washington Post),* 16 September 1984, 3.

No Resting Place

Antone, Evan Haywood. "Novel Tells of Abuse of Indians Many Historians Ignore." *El Paso Times,* 25 June 1989.

Atwan, Robert. "On the Trail of Tears." *St. Petersburg Times,* 9 July 1989, sec. D, p. 6.

Barth, Ilene. "Tragedy at the End of the Trail of Tears." *Newsday,* 21 June 1989, 11.

Berger, Yves. "La Saint-Barthelemy des Indiens." *Figaro,* 11 March 1991.

Bosquet, Alain. "Humphrey et les Peaux-Rouges." *Magazine littéraire,* April 1991, 82.

Bowden, Larry R. "A Lament for the Vanishing." *Cross Currents,* 41 (Spring 1991): 107–15.

Brown, Dee. "Tale of the Trail of Tears." *Chicago Sun-Times,* 11 June 1989.

Burns, Grant. "Cherokee Plight Crushingly Portrayed." *Flint Journal,* 6 August 1989.

Caroll, James M. "No Resting Place Details Sad Chapter in American History." *Pittsburgh Press,* 27 August 1989.

Clute, John. *Times Literary Supplement,* 1 December 1989, 1338.

Delannoy, Jean-Pierre. *La Tribune,* July and August 1991.

Ehle, John. "God Was at Least Partly to Blame." *New York Times Book Review*, 25 June 1989, 19.

Farndale, Nigel. "The Injuns Reply." *Literary Review* (London), August 1989, 13–14.

Graham, Don. "Canon Fever." *Texas Monthly* 24 (March 1996): 105.

Hunter, Timothy. "A Compelling Look at the 'Trail of Tears.'" *Cleveland Plain Dealer*, 23 July 1989.

Johnson, Charles Blake. "No Resting Place a Tale of Horrors." *Knoxville News-Sentinel*, 10 September 1989, 19.

Jones, Bill. "West of Eden." *Spectrum* (Little Rock), 2–15 August 1989, 31.

Kilpatrick, Thomas L. *Library Journal*, 15 May 1989, 89.

Kirkus Reviews, 15 April 1989, 570.

Lee, James Ward. "Texas' Bloody Role in the Trail of Tears." *Dallas Morning News*, 25 June 1989, sec. C, pp. 8–9.

"Le retour des refoulés." *Le Monde*, 11 November 1991.

Los Angeles Times Book Review, 25 June 1989, 2.

Luft, Kerry. "A Foretaste of Hell on the Old Frontier." *Chicago Tribune*, 8 August 1989, sec. 5, p. 3.

Mauroux, Jean-Baptiste. "Sur la piste des indiens morts pour cause de purification ethnique." *La Liberté*, August 1991, 17–18.

Mohrt, Michel. *Madame Figaro*, 23 March 1991, 34.

Morseberger, Robert E. *Western American Literature*, 24 (Winter 1990): 391–92.

Owens, Louis. "The Slaughter of the Cherokee." *Book Review (Los Angeles Times)*, 26 June 1989, 2.

Perez, Emile. *Le Réveil*, 25 January 1991.

Publishers Weekly, 7 April 1989, 126.

Quinn, Anthony. "On the Trail of Tears." *Independent*, 12 August 1989.

Signol, Christian. *Populaire du Centre*, 20 February 1991.

Taylor, John. "Tale Traces Cherokees' Betrayal." *Wilmington News Journal*, 25 June 1989.

Thomas, Phil. "Recounting Cherokees' 'Trail of Tears.'" *Dallas Times Herald*, 8 October 1989, sec. J, p. 6.

Time, 19 June 1989, 65.

Vervliet, Frédérique. *Indications* 4 (August 1991): 53–55.

Weaver, Will. "The Blood of the Cherokees." *Book World (Washington Post)*, 28 May 1989, 5.

Winkler, Suzanne. "Restless Spirits." *Texas Monthly* 17 (June 1989): 115, 116.

Wordsworth, Christopher. "From the Horse's Mouth." *Guardian*, 11 August 1989.

September Song

Benedict, Pinckney. "The Odd, the Old, and the Mysterious." *Tribune Books (Chicago Tribune)*, 5 July 1992, 1, 10.

Bosquet, Alain. "Un chant de la précarité." *Magazine littéraire*, January 1996.

Cheuse, Alan. "A Collection of Stories about People in Their Later Years." *Dallas Morning News,* 21 June 1992, sec. J, pp. 8–9.

Crowder, Ashby Bland. "Humphrey Writes about Old Age with Vision and Humor." *Arkansas Democrat-Gazette* (Little Rock), 16 May 1993, sec. J, p. 7.

Giles, Molly. "The Insults of Old Age." *New York Times Book Review,* 23 August 1992, 18.

Guégan, Gérard. "Humphrey nous donne de ses nouvelles." *Sud-ouest,* 10 December 1995.

Kirkus Reviews, 1 May 1992, 559.

Pascaud, Fabienne. *Télérama,* 17 January 1996.

Powers, Katherine A. *Boston Sunday Globe,* 26 July 1992.

Publishers Weekly, 18 May 1992, 56.

Rife, Susan L. "*September Song* Direct and Elegant." *Wichita Eagle,* 23 August 1992.

Robertson, William. "In September Golden Years Tinged with Sorrow, Regret." *Miami Herald,* 26 July 1992.

Skiles, Don. "Stories of Life and Literary Loss." *San Francisco Examiner and Chronicle,* 6 September 1992.

Slack, Charles. "Humphrey Avoids Warm Fuzzies on Old Age." *Richmond Times-Dispatch,* 2 August 1992, sec. F, p. 4.

Thomas, Phil. "William Humphrey's Short Stories are Hard to Top." *Intelligencer-Record,* 13 September 1992, sec. C, p. 6.

Virginia Quarterly Review 69 (Winter 1993): 23–24.

Vitoux, Frédéric. "Humphrey le juste." *Le Nouvel observateur,* 20 December 1995.

Wagner, Jean. "Un vrai Texan." *La Quinzaine,* 16–13 January 1996.

Wilhelm, Albert E. *Library Journal,* 1 June 1992, 182.

Yardley, Jonathan. "Harvest of the Years." *Book World (Washington Post),* 5 July 1992, 3.

INDEX

The abbreviation WH refers to William Humphrey in the index.

Horizon, 25

"The Horse Latitudes" (Humphrey), 191*n*41, 264–65, 267–68, 272, 280, 285

Hostages to Fortune (Humphrey): father-son separation in, 1, 66, 274, 278; Northeast as setting of, 7, 215, 278–79; marriage in, 65, 281–83, 289, 290, 292; present versus past in, 75; fishing in, 88, 283–89, 301–4; early plot outline of, 274; suicide in, 274, 278, 279–80, 282, 288, 289–94, 301, 304–6, 353; writing of, 274–78, 316; biographical elements and actual persons as inspiration for characters in, 276–77, 279–84, 370; publication of, 278, 304, 304*n*70; title for, 278; homes in, 281–82, 300; figures of speech in, 282; falconry in, 284*n*45, 293, 298–99; compared with other authors' works, 285–87, 290, 299; sentence structure in, 286; structure of, 288–89, 289–91; literary allusions in, 296–97, 299, 299*n*66; shadowy other self in, 296; religion in, 297–304; reviews and evaluation of, 304–5, 366; sales figures for, 304; readers' responses to, 306

—characters: Ben Curtis as without family, 278–79; Ben Curtis's suffering, 280, 288–97, 299–301, 305, 335; Ben Curtis as writer, 281–83; Cathy Curtis, 281–83, 289, 290, 292; Tony Thayer, 283–84, 289–92, 296, 301–2; fishing by Ben Curtis and Nick Adams, 285–89; reasons for Anthony's suicide, 293–97; Ben Curtis's burial of Anthony's ashes, 299–300; Anthony's birth, 300; Ben Curtis's return to life, 301–4, 335

Houghton Mifflin publisher, 342, 356

The House of Breath (Goyen), 43

Housman, A. E., 9, 72, 299*n*66, 305–6

Houston, Sam, 315, 331

Houston Post, 134

Howe, Irving, 5

Huckleberry Finn (Twain), 79, 248

Hudson, W. H., 173

"Hudson River School" (Tomlinson), 277*n*28

Hugo, Victor, 322, 371

"The Human Fly" (Humphrey), 177, 180, 187, 196, 198–99, 215

Humphrey, Clarence: death of, 1, 5, 15–17, 224*n*15; marriage of, 10, 11, 13, 207, 229*n*20; ed-

ucation of, 11; wild habits of, 11, 12, 13, 15, 81, 207; car repair garage owned by, 12–13, 225*n*16, 256–57; and frequent moves, 12; and hunting, 13–14, 52–53, 55, 57, 81; funeral and burial of, 16–17; photograph of, *following p.* 156; and race relations, 256–57

Humphrey, Dorothy Feinman Cantine: beginning of relationship with WH, 22–23, 24; daughter of, 22, 23; family background of, 22*n*15; in New York City, 22–23, 24, 26, 116; as painter, 22, 26, 42, 217, 219; homes of, 23, 24, 26–28, 42, 116, 167–69, 176, 216, 272–73, 277*n*28, 281–82; at Peterson farm in New York, 26–28, 30–31, 36, 51; abortion for, 27; and WH's plans for first novel, 35; divorce of, from Holley Cantine, 36; move to Annandale-on-Hudson, 36–37; marriage of, to WH, 37, 65; and WH's short stories, 41–42; as commercial artist, 46; and *Home from the Hill,* 71; in Europe, 110–22, 125–28, 132, 165–67, 169, 176–78, 203–5, 216–17, 221–23, 266, 277–78; in Massachusetts, 116; illnesses and injury of, 120, 270, 273; on WH's depression, 121; and *The Ordways,* 126–27; and Volkswagen, 127; in Virginia, 128–29, 165; photographs of, *following p.* 156; in Cape Cod, 167, 271; social life of, 169–70; and reviews of *Proud Flesh,* 260; and Katherine Anne Porter, 263; and cross-country skiing, 264; and Smith College, 266–67; depression of, 270; and hunting, 276, 277; daily routines of, 282–83; and dressing up in vintage clothing, 283, 366; and *Hostages to Fortune,* 304; and photography, 359; and aging, 360, 366, 369, 372; nursing home for, 360, 369, 372

Humphrey, Nell Varley: and son William's birth deformity, 10–11; education of, 11; and frequent moves, 11–12; marital relationship between Clarence Humphrey and, 11, 13, 81, 207, 229*n*20; food canning by, 14–15; singing by, 14; and death of husband Clarence, 16; move to Dallas by, 16–17; employment of, in Dallas, 17, 18; marriages of, after first husband's death, 17, 18, 20, 24, 60, 205; divorce of, from Andy Fleming, 20; and son Tommy, 24; in Cleveland, 60, 205; disfigurement (missing finger) of, 229*n*20; racial views of, 311

Humphrey, Toni. *See* Cantine, Antonia (Toni)

Humphrey, William: and father's death, 1, 5, 15–17, 53, 65–66, 224n15; personality of, 1, 12, 17, 40, 42, 173–75, 259–60, 261, 267; and promotion of books, 3, 269; birth and birthplace of, 5, 10; in New York City, 6–7, 21–26, 60, 68, 116; birth deformity of, 10–11; childhood and youth of, 10–20, 52–53, 57, 60, 185, 199, 207n66, 257; church attendance by, 11, 16, 246n33; near-drowning of and death certificate for, 12, 14, 15; and hunting, 13–14, 38, 52–53, 55, 81, 170, 173, 266, 277, 281; illnesses, health problems, and injuries of, 14, 22, 71–72, 117–19, 219, 221, 277, 281, 342, 367, 369–71; reading interests of, 14, 17–18, 72, 76, 89n33, 119, 120, 127, 148, 148n55, 151, 309–10; and house fires, 15, 273; in Dallas, 16–21, 22, 217–18; painting by, 17, 18, 19, 20, 42; Boss as mentor of, 18, 20; political views of, 18, 19–20, 218–19, 220, 270, 367–68; university education of, 19–21, 183, 368; and medical profession, 20–21; physical appearance of, 20, 37; self-portrait of, 20; in Chicago, 21, 60, 362; beginning of relationship with Dorothy Feinman Cantine, 22–23, 24; finances and publishing contracts of, 22–24, 26, 35, 36, 42, 52, 71, 109, 168, 171, 175, 271–72, 276, 311, 342; homes of, 23, 24, 26–28, 42, 116, 167–69, 176, 216, 272–73, 281–82; at Peterson farm in New York, 26–28, 30–31, 35, 36, 51; and abortion for Dorothy, 27; relationship with Antonia (Toni), 27–28, 114; Porter as mentor of, 30, 39–40; grandparents of, 32, 32n11, 65, 150–51, 213, 256; teaching positions of, 36–40, 46, 62, 68–71, 109, 128–29, 168–69, 174, 216, 266–67, 276–77, 279, 315–16, 316n17, 325, 371; marriage of, 37, 65; honors and awards for, 64, 108–9, 126, 175–76, 186–87, 217–18, 270, 277n28, 368, 368n40, 369; in Europe, 110–22, 125–28, 132, 165–67, 169, 176–78, 203–5, 216–17, 221–23, 266, 277–78, 341–42; lectures and speeches by, 116, 128–29, 165, 269, 311, 311n9, 315–16, 336; depression and anxiety of, 120–21, 122, 132, 216, 219–20, 259, 261, 268, 270, 274, 307, 331, 337, 341, 368–69; and Dorothy's illnesses, 120, 270; and Volkswagen, 127; and fishing, 128, 165, 170, 173, 219, 221, 222, 267, 271, 275, 277–78, 279, 283,

289, 359, 372; strained relationship between Knopf and, 129–30, 134, 171–73; photographs of, *following p.* 156; and social gatherings, 165, 169–70, 174–75, 176, 276; in Cape Cod, 167, 221, 271; job offers refused by, 167, 168, 308–9; as Porter's literary executor, 169; clothing and high-quality possessions of, 170; conversational style of, 173–75; and Porter's collected edition of essays, 178–79, 262–63; readings of works by, 179, 276, 277, 311n; Indian heritage of, 193, 312, 314; alcohol use by, 216, 219–22, 266, 282, 283, 336, 352, 366–67, 370, 371; visits of, to Clarksville as adult, 218, 277, 311; endings of friendships of, 259–60, 262–63, 353–54; and cross-country skiing, 264; end of publishing relationship between Knopf and, 270–74; literary agent for, 271; and sailing, 279; daily routines of, 282–83; and dressing up in vintage clothing, 283, 366; and Dick Bard's funeral, 309; relationship of, with mother, 311; cleaning woman and handyman for, 337–38, 340; and aging, 341–42, 364, 366–71; hearing loss of, 341–42; garden and apple orchard of, 345, 361–62; and Dorothy's interest in photography, 359; and Dorothy in nursing home, 360, 369; papers of, 367, 367n36; dying and death of, 369–72

—writings: themes in, 1, 4–8, 64–66, 362, 366; literary influences on, 2–3, 8–9, 32, 75–76, 77, 133; Red River County as setting of, 2, 52, 57, 58, 64, 81–82, 179; sentence structure in, 2, 52, 54, 286; in-print status of, 3, 76, 304; reviews of, 3, 66–67, 75–76, 131–34, 181–82, 215, 258–61, 264, 331–34; scholarly criticism of, 3–5, 76–77, 80, 135–36, 150, 155, 190; compared with other southern authors' works, 4–6; present versus past in, 5–7; characters in, generally, 7–8, 282, 336, 336n1; destruction of myths in, 7, 59–60, 335; Northeast as setting of, 7, 179, 215, 278–79; literary allusions in, 8–9, 79–80, 185–86, 225–26, 346–48, 363; figures of speech in, 9, 151–52, 223–25, 242, 282, 324, 327–28, 357–58, 366; early writings, 21, 23, 25, 362; submission of short stories through Grabstald, 28, 52; revision of, 31, 35, 39–40, 63, 70, 103, 105–7, 122–28, 311–12, 323, 345, 351, 355, 367; point of view in, 33, 77–